THE HISTORY OF
Musical Instruments

THE HISTORY OF
Musical Instruments

CURT SACHS

New York

W · W · NORTON & COMPANY · Inc ·

Publishers

PRINTED IN THE UNITED STATES OF AMERICA
FOR THE PUBLISHERS BY THE VAIL-BALLOU PRESS

IN MEMORY
OF
GEORGE E. SACHS
1909–1939

EMILY FLOYD GARDINER

gave generously of her time and interest to help me with this book, the first that I have written in English. Polishing my style, discussing my problems, insisting on the reader's right to understand things without too much effort, she played a vital role in the preparation of this book. I am deeply indebted to her.

Contents

FIRST PART: *The Primitive and Prehistoric Epoch*

CHAPTER I: Early Instruments   25

    MOTOR IMPULSES   25
The "invention of instruments" — rhythm — slapping the body — rattles — sounding amulets — shamanic rites — stampers — rice ceremonials — slit-drums — the teetering tree — the sand drum — drums — wood-cutters' and clay modelers' forms.

    RITUAL FUNCTIONS   34
Drums (continued) — shaman's drumming — construction rites — the sacred drum-yard — symbolism of the drum — symbolism of the drum stick — slit-drum (continued) — drum language — the earliest wind instruments — the ribbon reed — weather charm — friction instruments — girls' initiations — the bull-roarer — woman's taboo — the scraper — love charm — flutes — phallic rites — nose flutes — nostril and astrology — trumpets — solar rites — shell trumpets — sex connotations.

    MELODIC IMPULSES   52
Reduplication in language and music — 'Father and mother' — stamping tubes — xylophone — marimba music — ground harp — ground-zither — musical bow — intimacy and meditation — the jaws' harp.

9

CHAPTER 2: The Chronology of Early Instruments   60

Simplicity and complication — cultural level and form of civilization — prehistory and anthropology — geographic method — relation or parallelism — the three main strata.

SECOND PART: *Antiquity*

CHAPTER 3: Sumer and Babylonia   67

History — languages — script — idiophonic instruments — toys — pipes — horns and trumpets — King Tushratta's gift — drums — "the great bull's hide" — Sumer and Japan — divination — feeding the drum — moon rites — sacrifices — Sumer and East Africa — lyres — lyre playing — harps — harp playing — orchestration — harmony — lutes — King Nebuchadrezzar's orchestra.

CHAPTER 4: Egypt   86

FROM PREHISTORY TO THE END OF THE MIDDLE KINGDOM   86

Prehistoric contact with Sumer — history — script — clappers and concussion-sticks — Arbeit und Rhythmus — sistrum — Hathor and Isis — flutes and clarinets — glass blowers' technique — harps — drawing and photography — drums — Egypt and India.

FROM THE NEW KINGDOM TO THE GREEK EPOCH   98

The Empire — new style in music — oboes — in search of the scale — trumpets, stringed instruments and idiophones — foreign instruments in high civilizations.

CHAPTER 5: Israel   105

THE NOMADIC EPOCH   105

Primitive character — ugab — King David's kinnor — the women's timbrel — the high priest's bell — the magic shofar — the two silver trumpets.

THE TIME OF THE KINGS 114

The academy of religious music — music in the Temple — stringed and wind instruments — sistrum and cymbals — the controversy of the organ — the headings of the Psalms.

CHAPTER 6: Greece, Rome and Etruria 128

Fine art and music — lyres and the musical system of antiquity — the harp and Anacreon — lutes and zithers — pipes — succinere and incinere — the Pythian games — bagpipes — Emperor Nero — cross flute — discovery in an Etruscan tomb — pan-pipes — virginity test — the water organ — trumpets — Roman military music — the question of the Nordic lurer — drums — Dionysian cults — clappers — Mediterranean heritage.

CHAPTER 7: India 151

The Indus civilization — drum and harp — the hieroglyphic script — the Vedas — Rigveda and Atharvaveda — The Dravida — the double trumpet — the double clarinet of snake charmers — bagpipes — drums — sacrifices to the drum — arched harps — temple reliefs — trumpets — drums — the coiled drum stick — cross flutes — the celestial music — lute — the Gandhara style.

CHAPTER 8: The Far East 162

Confucius and Plato — musical ethics — State and music — cosmos and music — substances and music — importance of idiophones — universe and pitch — playing and singing.

THE SHANG DYNASTY (FOURTEENTH–TWELFTH CENTURIES B.C.) 166

The Book of Poetry — globular flutes — the European ocarina — stones and stone chimes — Kawa pounding — bells and bell chimes — blood sacrifices — seasons and intervals — drums — rice stuffing — nails.

THE CHOU DYNASTY (1122–255 B.C.) 174

Percussion-clapper — a beaten book — the trough — rice pounding — the fish — the eyelids and the carved fruit — the tiger — the path of life — pitch- and pan-pipes — the male and the female scale — flutes — sacred measures — the mouth organ — long zithers — music of the sages.

THE HAN DYNASTY (206 B.C.–220 A.D.)   189
Short lutes — The westeastern path.

CHAPTER 9: America   192

CENTRAL AMERICA   192
The Mexican civilization — flutes and trumpets — idiophones — Música muy triste — drums — level of Mexican music.

SOUTH AMERICA   196
The Peruvian civilization — pan-pipes — the question of an American origin — flutes — the rocking whistle — idiophones — drums — inflation of human skins — trumpets — the "Pacific" culture area.

THIRD PART: *The Middle Ages*

CHAPTER 10: The Far East   207
Western influences — idiophones — Turkish metal workers — trumpets — gigantic lama trumpets — reed pipes — a Tataric pibgorn — flutes — different blowing style — drums — Japanese rhythm — bowed instruments — invention of the fiddle bow — flat lutes — long lute — dulcimer and harp — change of musical style.

CHAPTER 11: India   221
Gamakas — rhythmic patterns

PRE-ISLAMIC TIMES   222
Borobudur — idiophones — cymbals in mythology — acrobacy — drums and drum chimes — stick-zither — vina — fiddles — sympathetic strings — flutes and trumpets — the question of the coil.

ISLAMIC TIMES   229
Drums — kettledrums — technique — oboe — broad-necked lutes — the peacock.

CHAPTER 12: Southeast Asia   233

PRE-INDIAN PERIOD   233
Malayan prehistory — drum-gongs — bronze.

INDIAN PERIOD   235
Indian colonies — Borobudur.

POST-INDIAN PERIOD   236
Dynamic style — the orchestras — scales — the xylophone — Malayan civilization in Africa — metallophones — celesta — gongs — magic — gong chimes — Islamic influence.

CHAPTER 13: The Near East   244
The queen of Sheba — The Arabian Nights — Islamic cosmopolitanism — frame drums — flutes — the oboe — procession music — cylindrical drums — kettledrums — clay and metal — short lutes — the lute with a frontal stringholder — the name 'ūd — symbolism of the strings — the spike-fiddle — the long lute — mathematical basis — the trapezoidal zither — combined instruments — the dulcimer — the angular harp.

CHAPTER 14: Europe   260

INSTRUMENTS INTRODUCED BEFORE THE YEAR 1000   260
A northern and a southern zone — the harp — chrotta and harpa — medieval chord playing — lyres — the monochord — Boetius and the monks — the hurdy-gurdy — lutes — fiddles — idiophones — horns and trumpets — bagpipes — the organ — musica ficta.

INSTRUMENTS INTRODUCED IN THE ELEVENTH AND TWELFTH CENTURIES   286
The portative organ — flutes — military music — reed pipes — drums — the trumscheit — zithers — the cimbalom.

FOURTH PART: *The Modern Occident*

CHAPTER 15: The Renaissance (1400–1600)   297

Development of a self-sufficient instrumental music — increasing interest in color — popular treatises on instruments — Virdung — Luscinius — Schlick — Agricola — Bermudo — Praetorius — Mersenne — beauty of shape — collections — inventories — chest and consort — the organ — two keyboards — stops — the plein jeu — regals — single and double — the pair — recorders — one-handed flute — tabor and pipe — flageolet — transverse flute — shawms — bassoon — rankets — cromorne — schryari — rauschpfeifen — cornet — trombone — trumpets — the "noble guild" — kettledrums — clavichords — equal temperament — short octave — the Empfindsame Zeitalter — spinets and harpsichords — virginals — the chessboard — the dulce melos — the lute — modern lute playing — the vihuela — the cittern — viols — tuning — the lira da gamba.

CHAPTER 16: The Baroque (1600–1750)   351

Musical revolution — emotional style — monody — the first violin sonatas — dismissal of wind instruments — monochrome — rise of the violin — the violin family — the formant — good and poor violins — pizzicato and vibrato — Brescia and Cremona — German, English and French schools — concert halls — overspinning — viola d'amore — viola pomposa — baryton — the bow — drone lutes — citterns — guitar — harpsichord — Ruckers — the second keyboard — ravalement — the 16 foot — the pedal — carillons — water chimes — glockenspiel — celesta — English change-ringing — the flute — readmission of wind instruments — the oboe — slide trumpets — horns — the organ — the Praetorius organ — the pitch.

CHAPTER 17: Romanticism (1750–1900)   388

Increasing number of instruments — blending of timbres — striving for power — the pitch — expressive-

*ness — the piano — the harp — the Aeolian harp —
the supernatural — friction rods — the glass harmonica — the harmonium — the Boehm flute — clarinets
— the saxophone — chromatic horns and trumpets —
serpents and bass horns — key trumpets and key bugles
— stopped French horns — valves — the cornet family — trumpets and trombones — machine drums —
— drums — the Turkish music — Janissaries — the
triangle — the crescent — cymbals — the xylophone —
the organ.*

EPILOGUE: The Twentieth Century 445

*Gigantic orchestras — chamber orchestras — preference
given to wind instruments — the rise of percussion —
the banjo — jazz instruments — electric instruments
— archaism — the resurrection of ancient music —
playing on ancient instruments — ancient forms — the
organ — "The World's Greatest Organ" — "Back
to Silbermann" — the Praetorius organ — the new
style.*

TERMINOLOGY 454

REFERENCES 469

INDEX 489

Illustrations

LIST OF PLATES

Facing Page

PLATE I   32
Prototype of the slit-drum. Gigantic slit-drum in its hut.

PLATE II   48
*Slit-drum. Footed drum. Prehistoric whistle flute. Bucium,
Rumania. Lithuanian bark trumpet. Jaws' harp. Esthonian
jaws' harp.*

PLATE III   64
Sumerian lyres.

PLATE IV   80
*Lyre-player entertaining guests. Gigantic drum. Horizontal
angular harp. Hettite drummer. Hettite lutanist. Lutanist.*

PLATE V   96
Egyptian stringed instruments.

PLATE VI   112
Egyptian lyrist. Semitic lyrist. Egyptian harpist.

PLATE VII   128
Greek lyre-players.

PLATE VIII   144
*Etruscan flutist. Stringed instrument. Syrian with ancestor of
organ.*

PLATE IX   160
Indian instruments.

PLATE X   176
*From a Chinese stela. Japanese biwa. Chinese priests playing
stone chime. Mouth-organ player.*

Facing Page

PLATE XI 192
Reliefs from Borobudur. Javanese metallophone, gong chime. Javanese rejong. Javanese xylophone. Javanese barrel-drums. Burmese xylophone.

PLATE XII 208
Arabian frame drum. From an Arabic manuscript. Turkish drum.

PLATE XIII 224
Russian hurdy-gurdy player. Macedonian lira player. South Italian pifferari.

PLATE XIV 240
From a pulpit in San Leonardo, Arcetri. From cathedral, Chartres. From capital in Museum, Toulouse. From cathedral, Amiens.

PLATE XV 256
Harp, horn, lyre, pan-pipes, fiddle. Bowed lyre. Monochord.

PLATE XVI 272
Flemish master, with portative, lute, harp and fiddle. Van Eyck, altar in Ghent.

PLATE XVII 288
Melozzo da Forlì, angel with fiddle. Ambrogio de' Predis, angel with fiddle. Italian master, youth with lira da braccio.

PLATE XVIII 304
Hans Memling, Altar for Najera.

PLATE XIX 320
Vittore Carpaccio, angels with lira da braccio and cromorne in the Academy, Venice. Hans Baldung, woman with viol.

PLATE XX 336
Christoph Paudiss, lutanist. Frans van Mieris, drummer. Pieter Codde, Music with violin and gamba.

PLATE XXI 352
Clavichord, Gerard Dow. Harpsichord, Van Steen.

PLATE XXII 368
18th century cittern, baryton, guitar.

PLATE XXIII 384
Jacques-Louis David, The composer de Vienne. Marguerite Gérard, Lady with guitar. Frans van Mieris, Lady with theorboed lute.

PLATE XXIV 400
Jacob van Loo, Concert at Spanish Court.

LIST OF FIGURES

Figure		Page
1.	Strung rattle, Tucano Indians.	27
2.	Gourd rattle, Cuna Indians.	27
3.	Basket rattle, Peru.	27
4.	Slit-drum from New Guinea.	30
5.	Portable slit-drum, Celebes.	30
6.	Footed drum, East Africa.	31
7.	Cup-handle drum.	31
8.	Goblet drum.	31
9.	Kettledrum, East Africa.	33
10.	Neolithic vessel, Moravia.	33
11.	Frame drum with handle, Greenland.	33
12.	Ribbon reed, Madagascar.	38
13.	Ribbon reed, S. America.	38
14.	Rubbing tortoise shell, S. America.	39
15.	Rubbed wood, New Ireland.	39
16.	Stamping tube, Brazil.	41
17.	Bull-roarer, Brazil.	41
18.	Scraped bone, Ancient Mexico.	41
19.	'Rattle,' India.	41
20.	Whistle flute, Celebes.	41
21.	Vertical bone flute, S. America.	41
22.	Notched flute, S. America.	49
23.	Trumpet, Brazil.	49
24.	Trumpet, Brazil.	49
25.	Side-blown shell trumpet.	49
26.	Gopi Yantra, Bengal.	49
27.	Braced gourd-bow, Kafir.	49
28.	Sistrum, Caucasus.	70
29.	Harvesters with concussion sticks, Egypt, 5th dynasty.	88
30.	Naos sistrum, Egypt.	90
31.	Egyptian shoulder harp, section.	94
32.	Egyptian lyre, section.	101
33.	Egyptian lute, 18th dynasty.	102
34.	Psalterium decacordum.	118
35.	Trumpet, Madagascar.	146
36.	From an East Turkestanic fresco, 5th–7th century A.D.	160
37.	Pan-pipes, raft form.	177
38.	Pan-pipes, bundle form.	177
39.	Modern Japanese cross flute.	179
40.	Chinese mouth organ.	179
41.	Laotic mouth organ.	179
42.	Ch'in.	185
43.	Shê.	185
44.	Chinese lute p'ip'a.	189
45.	Whistle flute of clay, Mexico.	193
46.	From Codex Becker, Vienna.	194

Figure		Page
47.	From Codex Becker, Vienna.	195
48.	Mexican slit-drum.	195
49.	Pan-pipe of stone, ancient Peru.	197
50, 51.	Whistling pots, Peru.	200
52.	Peruvian drum, skeleton.	201
53.	Chinese gong chime.	209
54.	Chinese hooked trumpet.	211
55.	Chinese straight trumpet.	211
56.	Tibetan drum of two skulls.	216
57.	Chinese flat lute yüeh ch'in.	216
58.	South Indian stick zither kinnari.	225
59.	North Indian vina.	225
60.	South Indian vina.	225
61.	Indian fiddle sarangi.	227
62.	Indian fiddle sarinda.	227
63.	Tibetan triple flute.	227
64.	Indian horn.	228
65.	Indian double oboe.	231
66.	Siamese oboe.	231
67.	Javanese oboe.	231
68.	Javanese angklung and suspended xylophone.	234
69.	Javanese gong-chime.	241
70.	Siamese spike fiddle.	245
71.	Mandola.	245
72.	Rabâb.	245
73.	Two-stringed spike fiddle.	256
74.	Three-stringed spike fiddle.	256
75.	Persian long lute.	256
76.	Gothic harp.	265
77.	Caucasian fiddle.	275
78.	Turkish fiddle.	278
79.	Kit.	278
80.	Rebec.	278
81.	Italian bagpipe.	282
82.	French musette.	282
83.	Trumscheit.	291
84.	Wooden flue-pipe.	307
85.	Reed pipe.	307
86.	Bible regal.	309
87.	Treble recorder.	311
88.	Bass recorder.	311
89.	One-handed flute.	311
90.	Large English flageolet.	313
91.	English double flageolet.	313
92.	Bass shawm.	316
93.	Dulcian.	316
94.	Bassoon (18th century).	316
95.	Bassoon (19th century).	318

Figure   Page
96. *Contrabassophon (double bassoon).*   318
97. *Sordun.*   318
98. *Ranket.*   319
99. *Ranket.*   319
100. *Cromorne.*   321
101. *Curved cornet.*   325
102. *Tenor cornet.*   325
103. *Straight cornet.*   325
104. *Double-bass trombone (16th century).*   327
105. *Trumpet (16th century).*   327
106. *Jack.*   334
107. *Lute.*   346
108. *Cittern.*   346
109. *Violin.*   353
110. *Viola d'amore.*   364
111. *Chitarrone.*   371
112. *Theorboe.*   371
113. *Pandora.*   373
114. *Orpheoreon.*   373
115. *Guitar (c. 1700).*   373
116. *Flute (18th century).*   381
117. *Oboe (c. 1700).*   382
118. *Oboe (c. 1900).*   382
119. *Oboè da caccia.*   382
120. *Cor anglais.*   382
121. *Walkingstick flute.*   390
122. *German Prellmechanik without escapement.*   392
123. *German Stossmechanik without escapement.*   392
124. *German Prellmechanik with escapement.*   392
125. *German Stossmechanik with escapement.*   392
126. *Pedal harp.*   399
127. *The double pedal action.*   400
128. *The double action of the disks.*   401
129. *Nail violin.*   403
130. *Gordon's flute.*   409
131. *Early Boehm flute.*   409
132. *Clarinet.*   413
133. *Double-bass clarinet.*   413
134. *Basset-horn in angular form.*   416
135. *Clarinette d'amour.*   416
136. *Saxophone.*   417
137. *Mouthpieces.*   418
138. *Mouthpieces.*   418
139. *Serpent.*   421
140. *Serpent in tuba form.*   423
141. *Basshorn.*   423
142. *Bugle.*   425
143. *Key bugle.*   425

Figure		Page
144.	Stopped trumpet.	425
145.	Piston and rotary valve, both in rest and action.	427
146.	French horn.	428
147.	Post horn.	429
148.	Cornet.	429
149.	Euphonium in oval form.	430
150.	Bass tuba.	430
151.	Helicon.	431
152.	Saxhorn.	433
153.	Trumpet with rotary valves.	433
154.	Tenor-bass trombone with transposing valves.	433
155.	Kettledrum.	435
156.	Military drum.	436
157.	Crescent (old form).	438
158.	Section of a mechanical organ.	442
159.	Evolution of the action.	443
160.	Nailed skin.	460
161.	Buttoned skin.	461
162.	Braces directly attached.	461
163.	Braces in N, directly attached.	461
164.	Braces in net form, directly attached.	461
165.	Braces in Y with a concealed hoop.	462
166.	Double hoop.	462
167.	Braces in W with double hoops.	462

FIRST PART

The Primitive and Prehistoric Epoch

I. *Early Instruments*

MOTOR IMPULSES

MUSIC histories written before the nineteenth century usually start with an account of the mythological invention of the earliest instruments. Cain's descendant, Jubal, is said to be "the father of all such as handle the harp and the organ," Pan is credited with the invention of the pan-pipes, and Mercury is supposed to have devised the lyre when one day he found a dried-out tortoise on the banks of the Nile.

Myth has since been replaced by history, and the invention of musical instruments is no longer attributed to gods and heroes. But people still clamor to know which instruments were invented first, and they hope for the neat answers with which amateur writers so readily supply them—a drum was the earliest instrument, or a flute, or the plucked string of a hunter's bow.

Scholars, however, must disappoint them, because no early instrument was "invented," if we conceive of invention as the ultimate bringing into being of an idea long contemplated and experimented with. The supposition of such a process commits the current fallacy of superimposing modern reasoning upon early man. Actually he was quite unaware, as he stamped on the ground or slapped his body, that in his actions were the seeds of the earliest instruments.

The question of which instruments probably came into being first cannot be answered until a more basic problem is solved: what impulses in man resulted in the development of musical instruments?

All higher creatures express emotion by motion. But man alone, apparently, is able to regulate and co-ordinate his emotional move-

25

ments; man alone is gifted with conscious rhythm. When he has reached this consciousness, and experienced the stimulation and comfort that rhythm gives, he cannot refrain from rhythmic movement, from dancing, stamping the ground, clapping his hands, slapping his abdomen, his chest, his legs, his buttocks. There are only a few very primitive peoples, such as the Vedda in the interior of Ceylon, or certain Patagonian tribes, that not only do not possess any musical instrument, but do not even clap their hands or stamp the ground.

Most emotional movements are audible. But primitives probably stamped the ground or struck their bodies long before they became aware of the accompanying sound as a separate phenomenon. It must have been a still longer process before they stamped or struck intentionally to obtain a sound and, through it, an augmented stimulus.

They produced various effects from these simple movements: muffled beats with the hollow hands, clear beats with the flat palms, stamping with the heels or the toes, hitting either bony or fleshy parts. All these shades contributed to making an actual preinstrumental music.

Among the earliest instruments we find the *strung rattle*, used by modern primitives of a very low cultural standard as well as by paleolithic hunters, as we know from excavations of prehistoric strata. It was made to stress dancing—that is, a complex activity, in which the movements of the head, the arms and the trunk were not audible without an added device.

A RATTLE, in general, is an instrument made of several sounding pieces, the concussion of which results from a shaking motion of the player.

In the so-called strung rattle small hard objects, such as nutshells, seeds, teeth or hooves (fig. 1), are strung in cords or tied in bunches (*bunch rattles*). Suspended from the ankles, knees, waist or neck of a dancer, they respond to his movements with a sharp noise; but their rhythm seldom is accurate, as they sound slightly after the dancer's movement.

Certainly, the exciting noise is not the only quality inherent in the strung rattle; the shells, nuts or teeth of which this rattle is composed, have magic power. Though we do not know whether the sound or the symbolism of the instrument had the priority, the strung rattle must be considered a sounding amulet. Later, the two qualities were separated from each other; old-fashioned bracelets and watch chains with horn-shaped teeth, crosses and other things

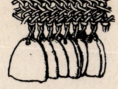

FIGURE 1. Strung rattle, Tucano Indians.

FIGURE 2. Gourd rattle, Cuna Indians.

FIGURE 3. Basket rattle, Peru.

(After Karl Gustav Izikowitz, *Instruments of South America.*)

supposed to bring good luck and to avert evil were a mute survival of chain amulets, while the rattling idea is perpetuated in the disenchanted ankle bells of dancers in modern India and Persia.

Among the numberless later rattles only one will be discussed: the *gourd rattle.* A calabash, held either by its natural neck or a wooden handle, is filled with pebbles or other small, hard objects; these make a rattling sound when the player shakes his gourd. Here the motor impulse is much more direct and conscious. Still, as the shock of the enclosed objects is complex, the sound cannot yet be exactly simultaneous with the motion. (fig. 2)

Gourd rattles are the essential implements of many shamanic rites; their sharp, exciting noise entrances both the shaman and the listeners. An impressive picture of such a rite was given, some sixty years ago, by Stephen Powers, who attended a secret meeting of the Maidu Indians in California:

There was a silence of some minutes in the impenetrable darkness, then the sacred rattle began a low, ominous quivering close to the ground, in which there was sufficient suggestion of a rattle-snake to make one feel chilly about the scalp. . . . At the same time the rattle rose up slowly, gaining a little in force, until finally it shot up all at once, and seemed to dart about the top of the room with amazing rapidity, giving forth terrific rattles and low, buzzing quavers, now and then bringing up against the post with a thud of the holder's fist. . . . When they have sung for about half or three-quarters of an hour without cessation the rattle grows fast and furious, the performer's fist goes tunk, tunk, tunk on the post with great violence . . . the singers' voices sink into a long-drawn, dying wail. . . . The rattle drops to the ground and seems to hover close over it, darting in every direction, and only two of the performers are heard, groveling on the ground and muttering petitions and responses, until finally the rattle dies slowly out, the voices hush, and all is over.

Except in shamanic rituals, the gourd rattle is mostly shaken by women. In some tribes of eastern Africa many hundreds of women stand together and shake gourd rattles as if their life depended on it.

In countries without calabashes, the gourd rattle has been imitated in appropriate materials, such as osier, clay, metal, wood. Basketry and pottery, the products of feminine crafts, have most often been substituted for the natural rattle gourd. As a woman's instrument, the rattling vessel has entered the nursery and lives on as a toy given to babies. (fig. 3)

Rhythmic motor impulse is more accurately reflected if the instrument is a true *extension* of either the leg or the arm, thus intensifying its stamping or striking action without imperiling its precision; or if the leg and the arm act upon an improved device, as, for instance, the *stamped pit*.

STAMPERS. The stamped pit is a hole dug in the ground and covered with a rough lid of bark. When the English traveler, Henry B. Guppy, visited Treasury Island in the Solomon Archipelago, he saw as many as forty women and girls dancing round such a pit, while two women stamped on "a board which was fixed in the pit about halfway down, . . . producing a dull hollow sound, to which the women of the circle timed their dancing."

In some civilizations the pit is replaced by an artificial device; women stamp on a curved board so that there is a resounding cavity beneath, or upon a pot turned upside down on the ground.

Another group of instruments developed when implements were substituted for the stamping feet, such as *stamping sticks, stamping gourds* and, most important, *stamping tubes:* hollow bamboos, or tubes of some suitable wood, closed at one end, were pounded against the ground, producing muffled sounds. (fig. 16)

Stamping tubes are generally played by women, and they are

always connected with fertility rites. Priestesses in Borneo pray every morning and evening at the end of the harvest while two tubes are stamped on a mat in a traditional rhythm. In the Celebes, three, or sometimes five, girls walk home the evening of the harvest sacrifice, stamping seed-filled tubes on the ground and singing: "Stamp, oh friends, for we look down, look down at the imploring, the imploring young rice!"

In connection with the rice ceremonials of the western Malayan Islands and of Siam when the fresh rice is peeled, stamping reaches its highest musical effectiveness in the *stamped mortar*. A series of holes of different shapes are hollowed out of a wooden log lying on the ground, and rice, poured into them as into mortars, is stamped with pestles by a row of women. The sound differs according to the depth of the various holes, and the pounding produces a charming polyrhythmic and polytonic symphony that a native poet describes by the lovely onomatopœia *tingtung tutung-gulan gondang*. This music is also played, even if there is no rice to be ground, when marriageable girls and widows gather on moonlight nights.

In a less complicated ritual, taro roots and dried almonds are pounded at wedding feasts in Melanesia. A wooden mortar is set into a hole in the village square, and two men sing the mournful song of the pounding while eight others dance around, grasping and stamping the two long pestles in turn, which are "eventually broken by being forced with a blow against the inside of the mortar."

In the eastern part of New Guinea there was an even simpler ritual of pounding. The aboriginal tribes had a trough of stone which was pounded with a pestle, and the pestle, the natives explained, was the penis of a spirit and the trough a vulva. This symbolism, familiar to primitive civilizations, is one of the main features of an important instrument, spread over this continent, the Pacific Islands, Africa and, in a degenerated form, also Asia—the slit-drum.

THE SLIT-DRUM, in its earliest form, is a tree trunk, hollowed out like a boat, placed over a pit in the ground and stamped upon.

Its prototype is still found in America. The Uitoto Indians in Colombia fell a large tree, hollow out a long groove in the side and paint the whole implement; at one end they decorate it with a woman's head and at the other end with an alligator as a water symbol. A pit is dug in the ground and covered with planks, some logs are placed at either end of them, and the hollowed tree is laid upon the logs so that it does not rest on the planks. While the women dance around the pit, the men stand in the groove of the tree trunk, stamping and teetering, and the elastic trunk strikes rhythmically against the planks. The natives say the significance of this ceremony is that the New Moon is vanquishing the Old Moon. (pl. I a, fig. 4)

The actual slit-drum is a tree trunk as well, but with a cavity hollowed in it from a narrow longitudinal slit. The earliest specimens

FIGURE 4. Slit-drum from New Guinea. (After Curt Sachs, *Reallexikon*.)

known are some twenty feet long and six or seven feet wide, and are stamped upon by a row of men. Later types were rammed with a stick instead of being stamped upon, and in still more developed slit-drums the edges of the slit were drummed upon with two shorter sticks. (pl. I b)

Nearly always, instruments which originate in a gigantic size grow smaller and smaller as they develop, until finally they become small enough to be portable. This last, and often degenerate, stage of de-

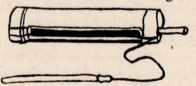

FIGURE 5. Portable slit-drum,
Celebes. (After Kaudern.)

velopment is reached in the case of the slit-drum by the light bamboo instrument carried and struck by Malayan watchmen. (fig. 5)

Many travelers, and even some anthropologists, call the slit-drum a "gong." This is an intolerable abuse; the word "gong" cannot designate anything but the bronze disk with turned-down rim which is made in India and the Far East. The name "tom-tom" is also incorrect.

Most instruments determined by motor impulse depend on the

striking hands. The first step was replacing the natural struck surface—that is, the body or the ground—by an artificial one, and only
the second, replacing the striking hands by some artificial device.

A rare contrivance, related to the stamped pit, is the *sand drum*,
as anthropologists call it. Some have been found among New Guinea
pygmies and in the Ethiopian province, Wollo. The pit is in the
form of a small tunnel with two uncovered openings, and the sand
bridge between them is beaten by the hand.

FIGURE 6. Footed drum,
East Africa.

FIGURE 7.
Cup-handle drum.

FIGURE 8.
Goblet drum.

DRUM in correct terminology, however, means an instrument
in which the sound is produced by a membrane stretched over the
opening of either a frame or a hollow body of any shape. It was
struck upon with the bare hands, until in later times the hands were
replaced by sticks. This important change roughly coincides with
the change from the skins of water animals, such as snakes, lizards
and fish, to the skins of hunted game and big cattle.

Instead of acquainting the reader with the innumerable species
and varieties of drums, this chapter may point at the fundamental
difference between cut wooden drums and modeled clay drums.
Cutting and hollowing wood by tools or by fire is more primitive
than pottery, so wooden drums must be the earlier kind.

Tubular drums, in their most archaic species, betray their descent
from sections of tree trunks. In some places, Nias and Loango for
instance, such drums reach a length of ten feet. They definitely have
preserved the upright tendency of the tree, though they are usually
too large to stand upright on the ground; they are suspended from
the roof or slanted so that they can be played; they have one skin
only, and the opposite end is carved to form a foot.

A great many smaller drums are derived from this early *footed drum*. In some the original upright tendency is given reality; they can be played in vertical position because their smaller size allows the player to reach the skin without inclining the drum. If the ground was sandy, the upright drum had to be sunk in the ground to keep it steady, and this was easier when the base was cut to form three or four large teeth. Drums with teeth can be found in a primitive form on the New Hebrides and all over Africa, and also, more carefully carved, in ancient Mexico. Where the drummer had a hard, even floor, the teeth were replaced by a carved open work (Polynesian type) or a goblet shape with a flat foot, a stem and a cup (Babylonian and East African type), and even a pair of legs in human form on a plinth, both in the eastern Malay Archipelago and in Africa among the Bakundu. (fig. 6, pl. II b)

A second type is due to the tendency to make drums portable. Some drums in Loango, on the Amazon, and in ancient Michoacan, could be ridden by the players like hobby horses, so that the skin, between the thighs, was in a convenient position for the striking hands. Some of the definitely portable drums have cup handles to be carried with the hands (*cup-handle drums*), as the New Guinean drum. Such a handle is generally carved in a central waist, and the two ends of the drum are symmetrical to maintain the equilibrium. In other portable drums the *goblet* form is preserved, which proved to be an excellent shape for a drum held under the arm, the slender stem being easily squeezed between the arm and the chest and the foot preventing the drum from dropping. (figs. 7, 8)

In this stage the forms of pottery drums become confused with wood forms. A small goblet is an earthenware, rather than a wood, form, and all civilizations familiar with pottery, especially with pottery on a wheel, will prefer this easier technique to the laborious shaping with a carver's chisel. The angular profile to which the woodworker hews the drum is then replaced by a softly rounded outline.

There is some connection between drum making and the manufacture of earthenware crocks for keeping food; the evolution from a hard fruit shell to a clay jar through all stages of pottery was similar in both cases. An excellent example of the similarity between drums and household pots is the East African kettledrum. The sides of the upper half of the drum are vertical, but they slant inwards to a small flat base at the ground. This cylindroconical drum corresponds exactly to a certain type of jar excavated from late-neolithic

A. Prototype of the slit-drum. Uitoto (Ph. Tessmann).

B. Gigantic slit-drum in its hut. Ao-Naga, Assam (Ph. Rev. Father Stegmiller).

PLATE I.

strata in Central and East Europe. The African drum is made of wood, not of clay, but that is immaterial; the history of crafts indicates a continual exchange of form and material. (figs. 9, 10)

The same change from clay to wood occurs in the evolution of the *double-headed drum*, which came considerably later than the one-headed drum and became the ancestor of the modern drum. For straight, cylindrical drums, wood certainly was the original material; but bulging cylinders or barrels were first made of clay

FIGURE 9. Kettle-   FIGURE 11. Frame drum with   FIGURE 10. Neolithic
drum, East Africa.   handle, Greenland.   vessel, Moravia.

though most of them, probably for practical reasons, are made of wood today.

In contrast with all these tubular and vessel drums, there are *frame drums*, in which a skin, or two parallel skins, are held taut by some type of hoop or frame. This category comprises two different groups of drums which probably had no connection. One of them, known as the shaman's drum, is spread over India, Central and North Asia and the American continent. It is roughly made and one-headed; the carrying hand grasps either a network of cords stretched over the open side of the drum or a handle attached to the frame; the striking hand uses a stick and sometimes hits the frame, not the skin. The other one, popularly called a tambourine, and spread over the Near East and some parts of Europe, has one or two skins and is struck by the bare hands. (fig. 11)

A summary of the numerous methods of fastening the skin on the shell or the frame will be found in the last chapter.

RITUAL FUNCTIONS

Although the foregoing section of this chapter was only concerned with motor impulse as a shaping force in the province of musical instruments, it could not avoid mentioning the symbolic or magic character of some instruments. Strung rattles are composed of amulets, the gourd rattle is a shaman's instrument, stamped tubes and mortars are used as fertility charms. Still, these may be secondary connotations. Other instruments, and among them drums and slit-drums, are affected by symbolism and magic ideas to such a degree that we discuss them again in a second section.

DRUMS (continued). With the Chukchee in northeastern Siberia,

the shaman sits on the 'master's place' near the back wall; and even in the most limited sleeping-room, some free space must be left around him. The drum is carefully looked over, its head tightened, and, if it is much shrunken, it is moistened with urine and hung up for a short time over the lamp to dry. The shaman sometimes occupies more than an hour in this process, before he is satisfied with the drum. . . . At last the light is put out and the shaman begins to operate. He beats the drum and sings his introductory tunes. . . . Moreover, the shaman uses his drum for modifying his voice, now placing it directly before his mouth, now turning it at an oblique angle, and all the time beating it violently. After a few minutes, all this noise begins to work strangely on the listeners, who are crouching down, squeezed together in a most uncomfortable position. They begin to lose the power to locate the source of the sounds; and, almost without any effort of imagination, the song and the drum seem to shift from corner to corner, or even to move about without having any definite place at all.

The drum is indispensable in primitive life; no instrument has so many ritual tasks, no instrument is held more sacred. Certain rites became important even in its construction. The Lappons chose woods, the fibers of which grew in a certain direction, and in Melanesia the drum maker climbs the tree that is to furnish the wood and remains there until the drum is finished. Fetishes, skulls, shells are often attached or enclosed before the skin is stretched across the opening, and for this reason nobody dares look into an open drum. In East Africa the drum is so holy that criminals and fleeing slaves become inviolable when they reach the drum-yard; even animals that enter the drum-yard become taboo. When the anthropologist John Roscoe came to the Banyankole, he found, at a little distance from the Royal kraal, a

small enclosure in which stood the hut of the royal drums. The hut was always domed and might have no point or pinnacle; inside there was a stand or bed on which lay two drums. At the back of the hut behind the bed lay a quantity of material for repairing these drums, and this had to be carefully guarded for it might not be used for any other purpose. To the left of the hut was a bag, in which were the instruments necessary for taking an augury should it be needed, and beside it lay some whistles and an iron rod upon which the tools for making the drums were sharpened, for this might not be done upon a stone. In front of the bed or stand was a row of milk pots belonging to the drums in which the daily offerings of milk were put. The chief drums were the two which lay upon the bed. These were covered with white skins with a black strip across them, making them look like a pair of great eyes in the gloom of the hut. A sacred herd of cows yielded a supply of milk which was daily offered to these drums in the pots which stood in front of them. It was placed there in the morning and remained until nine or ten o'clock, by which time the drum-spirits had taken the essence and the remainder might be drunk by the guardians. There was also a woman, who was known as the 'wife of the drums,' and whose duty it was to look after the milk, the churning, and the covering of the drums. Another woman looked after the fire in the drum-house, which had always to be kept burning because the drum-spirits required warmth. Offerings of cattle or beer were made to the drums by chiefs when a son had been born to them or when they had received promotion to some office or had been successful in some expedition and earned the commendation of the king. The king also made an annual offering of cows to the drums, so that they possessed a large herd; those offered to the first of them had to be red or white and those for the second black. These cows were sacred and the king alone might order one to be killed; no one but the guardians might eat the meat of an animal thus killed and the skin was kept for repairing the drums. It was from these cows that the milk was taken which was daily offered to the drums, and from the surplus milk butter was made for smearing on them. . . .

The strange beliefs connected with these drums appear also in the saga of the East African Wahinda. To see a drum is fatal; even the sultan must not look at a drum except at the time of the new moon. Men should carry them by night only, but they have the power to move by themselves. Once a drum ran away; a native found it hidden in a swamp, where a bubbling spring of milk had indicated its hiding place.

In these two stories we have a series of characteristic connotations: drum, round, domed enclosure, earth, night, moon and milk, which, in the primitive mind, are connotations of woman and female sex.

But the East African drums of which we spoke have lost the exclusively feminine character, as they are played with sticks instead of the bare hands. Whenever women are the players they use the hands; the stick is a phallic symbol. In 1901, a Reindeer Koryak woman (Kamtchatka) narrated:

It was at the time when Big Raven lived. . . . While still outside, they heard the sound of a drum. They entered the house and found Universe beating the drum and his wife Rain-woman, sitting next to him. In order to produce rain, he cut off his wife's vulva, and hung it on the drum; then he cut off his penis and beat with it, instead of an ordinary drum stick. . . .

In East Africa coronation drums must be struck with sticks made of human tibias, which likewise have a phallic significance. To provide fresh ones after the yearly coronation festival the royal drummers carry away all drums except one; whichever ingenuous onlooker innocently brings this last drum, saying "You have forgotten it," is immediately seized and killed, and his armbones are used as drum sticks.

The masculine idea, though weakened and metaphoric, is expressed in one of the ancient *nô* dramas of Japan. A gardener was in love with a princess. In answer to his pleas she gave him a drum *tsuzumi*; if he were able to play it she would be disposed to accept him. More than happy, he took the drum; but it was wrapped up in silk and he did not see how he could play on it with his stick. So, despairing of his fate, he killed himself.

When the drum was not connected with feminine ideas it often became associated with purely masculine ceremonies, such as circumcisions. In some districts of southeastern Asia drums are beaten at men's funerals, but never when a woman or child dies, and in Oceania a drum is useless if a woman sees it before it is completely made.

Finally, the drum became a warrior's instrument. In monarchies, when the drum was a sacred implement belonging to the king and an insignia of his dignity, this was more than a symbol. It was a talisman for luck and victory.

THE SLIT-DRUM (continued). In some South American and Oceanian belief, the divinity creating the water is also the creator of the slit-drum. In the New Hebrides the slit-drum is struck when the new moon rises; often a pit is dug beneath it; the biggest slit-drum is called the mother and frequently, though not always, the players are women. Oceanians see a female abdomen in its hollow body, a vulva in the slit and cohabitation in the ramming action.

These associations are weakened when, on the Solomon Islands, the upperlip of the slit-drum is called male and the underlip female. Gradually the symbolism of the slit-drum became confused, and perhaps for that reason it lost its well-defined magic power. Finally, it has become a means of sending signals over large distances. In America, Oceania and Africa, the systems of signals developed into whole languages which were based on human speech melody. By strokes of different strength and of different pitch in an appropriate meter, the natives are able to reproduce words and complete sentences of their spoken language. Rare and probably recent are conventional signals. The drum in a guardhouse in western Java that we reproduce (pl. II a) gives special signals for inundation, murder, robbery, theft, meeting and fire.

The drum and the slit-drum bring to their ritual functions a strong rhythm. But a large group of instruments that could not satisfy a motor impulse also became important in tribal ritual. When a primitive man blows into a cane or whirls a bull-roarer about, he does not obey a rhythmic impulse, nor is his vitality stimulated by any rhythmic response. The bare fact is identical; a man's act is answered by a sound. But there is a difference. It is obvious to everyone that stamping, pounding and striking have an audible effect. They are as inextricably connected with sound as men with their shadows. It is not self-evident, on the contrary, that whirling a small slab of wood should produce a stormlike rumbling, or breathing into a bone a shrill whistle. In both cases there is an audible response; but with stamping and striking the sound seems to be produced by the instrument, in the second case by some strange force living inside it. In the former group a motor impulse finds an expected audible result; in the latter an action which is scarcely expected to cause an audible result is unexpectedly followed by a sound, which, consequently, has an unexplained and frightening character that appears to be aggressive and hostile. Something living, a spirit or demon, must have answered.

The fact that certain objects, acted upon in a certain way, produce an ugly, indeed a frightening, noise, leads to using them against hostile beings, animals, enemies, evil spirits. These implements are, in the very dawn of humanity, involved in all beliefs which cause man to protect his existence by magic acts.

The instruments to be mentioned in this connection are the ribbon reed, some friction instruments, the bull-roarer, the scraper, the flute and the trumpet.

THE RIBBON REED. Boys the world over know how to stretch a blade of grass between their two thumbs held side by side, blow into the crack and make the grass-blade vibrate with a shrill squeak.

The Taulipang in Guiana believe that if this blade is taken from a certain kind of reed rain will come, and in Madagascar it is strictly forbidden to make a ribbon reed from a rice stalk before getting in

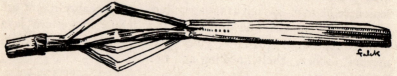

FIGURE 12. Ribbon reed, Madagascar. (After Sachs.)

the harvest lest hail should be attracted. In Melanesia the initiated boys blow the grass-blade to keep away the women. (fig. 12)

More highly developed civilizations use improved types. Of these, the most important one, an ancestor of future instruments, is made of a long, broad blade of grass, rolled up spirally to form a funnel. The thin end of the blade, or else a separate blade, crosses

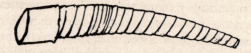

FIGURE 13. Ribbon reed, S. America. (After Izikowitz.)

the upper orifice. The English *with horn* is such an instrument. (fig. 13)

FRICTION INSTRUMENTS. Rubbing produces a great variety of humming and squeaking noises which are easily associated with superhuman sounds. Central and South American Indians take an empty tortoise shell, stop up the tail hole with glue and rub the projecting end of the shell over the sweaty palm of the hand. This is a secret instrument; uninitiated people dare not see it. (fig. 14)

The most highly developed friction instrument is the *rubbed wood* of New Ireland in Melanesia, a rounded piece of hard wood, the upper side of which is cut into four unequal teeth by deep incisions. The player, sitting on the ground, holds it between his

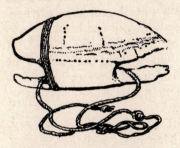

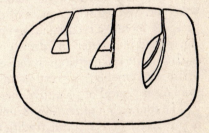

FIGURE 14. Rubbing tortoise shell, S. America. (After Izikowitz.)

FIGURE 15. Rubbed wood, New Ireland. (After Sachs.)

stretched legs, moistens the hands with palm juice and rubs them over the teeth in the direction of his body, thus producing four distinct notes. This instrument also has a secret character and is chiefly used in death rites. (fig. 15)

Much more recent are *friction drums*. In Togoland the Ewhe powder a small rag with ashes and rub it over the drum head. We are reminded of older ceremonies in which manioc, saffron or blood were rubbed into the skin as a sacrifice to the drum. But the hand is rarely rubbed directly upon the skin. Most friction drums have either a friction cord or a friction stick. The cord passes through a center hole in the membrane. Sometimes the stick also passes through a center hole; sometimes it does not pierce the skin, but makes a depression in it and is tied into this position from inside the skin so that it stands upright. In most cases the skin is set into vibration when the stick or the cord is rubbed with resinous fingers. The shape of the drum is not important; all kinds of drums are used; some Bantu Negroes even dig a pit in the ground, cover it with skin and rub the latter like a drum.

We do not know the origin of drums with rubbed cords or sticks; a vibrating cord or rod, however, fastened to the center of a membrane covering a pit in the ground and transferring vibrations to it, is one of the characteristic features of the ground-zither that we shall describe later, and may possibly have been taken from it.

Although the rubbed drum resembles a struck drum, the method in which it is played associates it with other ceremonies. As the rubbing action with its to-and-fro movement symbolizes cohabitation, the friction drum is the characteristic instrument at boys' and girls' initiations in Africa. When the Ba-ila maidens in South Africa were initiated, the maternal aunt "had between her legs a large earthenware pot, covered with a piece of dressed skin; in one hand she was grasping loosely a reed standing upright on the skin; the other hand she dipped into water and drew up and down along the reed." This initiation rite is a preparation for sexual life, and even teaches appropriate movements; instruction mixed in with visible and audible symbols is typical of primitive mentality.

The connection of friction drums with fertility and initiation rites is preserved in European traditions. Martinmas and the days between Christmas and Epiphany—the festivals which the Christians substituted for the rites of winter solstice—are the season in which boys go from house to house to sing old verses and rub the *rommelpot*, as the Dutch say, which often is artlessly made of a kitchen pot or a flowerpot and a bladder. (pl. II f)

The last descendant of the friction drum, the *whirled friction drum*, is merely a toy, and is found in Africa and Asia, in Europe and the United States. Suspended from a small rod by its friction cord, the drum is whirled, and the vibrations of the cord are communicated to the pasteboard membrane. Its Dutch name, *ronker*, or 'snorer,' is descriptive of its sound; the German name, *Waldteufel*, or 'forest devil,' is probably reminiscent of ancient rites in which the friction drum may have produced a demon's voice, like the bull-roarer, of which it may possibly be a descendant on account of its being whirled.

BULL-ROARER is the usual name of this instrument, but not an accurate one. To the most primitive natives its sound is the voice of an ancestor; to us it rather suggests the wind in all its nuances from a light breeze to a gale.

The instrument which is able to produce such an effect is simple enough. It is a thin board that the player holds by a cord tied to one end and whirls over his head. In whirling, the board also spins around its own axis, and by this twofold movement it produces a

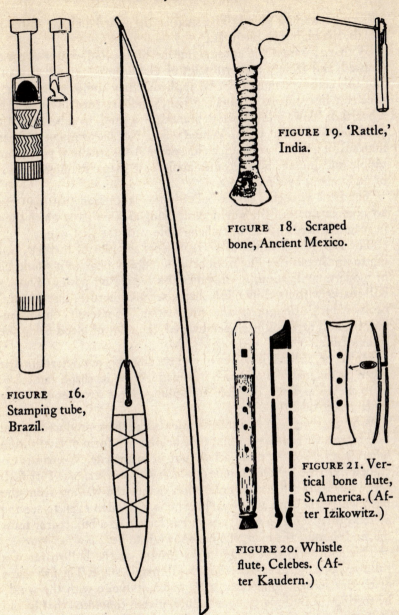

FIGURE 16. Stamping tube, Brazil.

FIGURE 17. Bull-roarer, Brazil.

FIGURE 18. Scraped bone, Ancient Mexico.

FIGURE 19. 'Rattle,' India.

FIGURE 20. Whistle flute, Celebes. (After Kaudern.)

FIGURE 21. Vertical bone flute, S. America. (After Izikowitz.)

roaring or wailing sound. The smaller the board and the faster it whirls, the higher its pitch. (fig. 17)

With this range the musical means of the bull-roarer are exhausted, and from a modern point of view one might call it poor. But this standard should not be applied. Early civilizations do not construct instruments to obtain a rich, attractive tone. Man whirls a board or blows into a hollow branch, or a shell, or a bone, and a voice answers. What voice? Whose voice? Not his own, not another man's. Is it a spirit, a demon, an ancestor? A supernatural power, invisible and impalpable, becomes audible; a magic manifestation is brought about by a man's act.

The basis of such a magic belief is the conception that man can act upon one part of the world by utilizing another part, which then in magic belief becomes interchangeable with the first one.

The fish, for example, often represents the idea of fertility, owing to its copious roe. Far from being a mere symbol, as it would be in modern civilization, it embodies the fertilizing power. Thus, a bull-roarer with its elliptic fish shape, serrated borders like fins and occasional scale design, signifies procreation. To intensify this meaning, the bull-roarer is often painted red, the color of blood being the color of life.

However, the magic power of an instrument is not determined as much by the material of which it is made, or by its shape and color, as by its voice. Tone, invisible and intangible, is stronger than any other magic quality.

Wherever we meet loud, harsh sounds like those produced by the bull-roarer, we can be sure that they belong to a form of civilization where man takes the more active part in magic rite. Woman is excluded from the holy ceremonies; *mulier taceat in ecclesia.* Terrified, she waits apart when the night wind carries the wailing from the bush where the boys are initiated. She is forbidden even to see the sacred instruments; a woman who has looked at a bull-roarer must die, and so must the man who has shown it to her.

This entirely mystic stage in the history of the bull-roarer was followed by a more realistic, though still magic, stage. The fish shape of the instrument connects it with water, its voice with the wind; by forcing the bull-roarer upon nature, man is convinced that he can make her send rain.

Finally, the bull-roarer descends to practical use. Destitute of mysticism and magic, it is used to frighten elephants and keep them off Malay plantations. We do not know of any musical instrument that has been developed primarily to serve practical aims; in all cases, the practical use is secondary and much more recent.

Here and there the bull-roarer has become a child's toy, and modern schoolboys loop a string through the hole of a ruler and whirl the improvised instrument. Even after an instrument has lost its ritual task because religion and belief have changed, and after it can no longer serve practical purposes because better implements have been invented, it sometimes persists as a child's toy. Many toys have had a magic origin.

THE SCRAPER is a notched implement, a stick, a shell, a bone or a gourd, which the player scrapes with a rigid object. Sometimes it is held over a resonating box or a hole in the ground. Its sound is disagreeable and not musical; again the hunters of paleolithic type evidently did not make their instruments for musical purposes, but as life-giving charms.

As bone had a phallic significance, bone scrapers were associated both with erotic rituals and funeral ceremonies, for funeral ceremonies were not an expression of mourning but a magic rite insuring life and rebirth. In ancient Mexico and Michoacan, for example, slaves scraped the bones of men and deer at the funeral of the king before they themselves were put to death. (figs. 18, 19)

These lugubrious bone scrapers also arouse love. The Cheyenne Indians narrate:

Once there was a very beautiful girl in the camp, and all the young men wanted to marry her, but she would have none of them. The Dog Soldiers and the Kit Fox Soldiers had a dance, and each young man tried to do his best, but the girl would look at none of them. Then it came the turn of the Himoweyuhkis, and they felt discouraged, because they thought they could do no better than the other societies had done. But a man who possessed spiritual power spoke to them, saying: "That girl will be here to see you dance, and she will fall in love with one of you, and he will get her. Now go and bring me the horn of an elk—a yearling— one that has no prongs on it, and the shank-bone of an antelope." The young men brought him what he had asked for. He carved the elk-horn in the shape of a snake, and on it cut forty-five notches. Then he made from the shank-bone of the antelope an implement to rub over the horn; and this device was used in the dance. The girl was there to see the dance, and fell in love with and married one of the young men.

We now come to another instrument with which the associations of love and death are inextricably mixed.

A FLUTE, like most other wind instruments, produces its tone by means of an air column within a tube, which is set in longitudinal vibration either by human breath or by artificial wind. The families of wind instruments differ in the special way in which the vibrations are brought about. This is particularly complicated in the flute. It would be going beyond the compass of this book to describe the acoustics of the flute in detail. We refer the reader to the most recent textbooks on musical acoustics and confine ourselves here to stating that the vibrations in a flute are due to little eddies formed at regular intervals when the player blows obliquely across the sharp edge of a mouth-hole. Thus, a sharp-edged mouth-hole is the characteristic quality of any flute.

The mouth-hole of the *vertical flute* is formed by the upper opening of the pipe. In the *cross flute*, or *transverse flute*, the upper end is stopped and the mouth-hole is cut in the side. In the *whistle flute* there is also a hole in the side, but not to be blown into; the upper end is stopped except for a small and narrow channel, called the *flue*, into which the player blows, and which directs his breath to the sharp edge of the side hole. (fig. 20)

The recorderlike whistle flute came before the simple vertical flute and also before the cross flute, though it was more complicated; complication is no criterion of late invention. The earliest whistle flutes were probably made of birds' bones. These produced a sharp, whistling sound, whereas the larger cane flutes made a softer, deeper sound. In all flutes the (fundamental) tone is almost pure; overtones are few and weak. The earliest flutes produced only one note; fingerholes were introduced much later. (figs. 21, 22, pl. II c)

Flutes, like bone scrapers, are phallic. Primitive man cannot overlook the resemblance between a pierced straight instrument and the penis; even in modern occidental slang the penis is designated by flute names. Early civilizations where the masculine impulse predominates connect the ideas flutes—phallos—fertility—life—rebirth, and they associate flute playing with innumerable phallic ceremonies and with fertility in general. Some of these rites have been described in the author's book *Geist und Werden der Musikinstrumente*. In the present book we will confine ourselves to an old, naïve myth of the Sentani in northern New Guinea which shows how primitive man connects the flute with ideas of fertility and rebirth. This is the tale:

One day a man went to the bush with his wife to gather fruit. The man climbed up a high tree and threw the fruit down, and the woman put it into her net. Suddenly a big piece of fruit fell onto a dry bamboo tree and cracked it open with a sharp sound. The frightened woman ran away, for she did not know what had made the noise. Out of the slit bamboo appeared a cassowary [the Melanesian counterpart of the phoenix, symbol of rebirth] making a buzzing sound. The man at once built a fence around the bird, ran into the village and told his friends what had happened. "Now we have a way of frightening the women," they said. They began to cut pieces of bamboo and tried to draw a sound from them and finally discovered that by blowing across a stalk they could make a sound similar to that of the cassowary. This was the first flute.

Thus the flute in Melanesia is clearly a charm for rebirth.

Whatever object brings rebirth is used in funeral rites, either in the burying ceremony or as a gift to the dead. Aztec slaves played bone flutes before being sacrificed to their dead princes, and boys also played the flute as they climbed up the steps of the pyramid, at the top of which the priest cut out their hearts and offered them to the sun. Archaeologists often find a flute at the side of a mummy or skeleton when excavating ancient tombs, and mistakenly believe that they have uncovered the remains of a musician, whereas the flute was probably placed there because it was a life charm. Similarly, one of the southern East Indian tribes, the Toda, who never make or play flutes, have special flutes made by a neighboring people as amulets for their dead tribesmen, to guarantee a fortunate rebirth.

The same life-giving power which connects the flute with death and rebirth connects it with love as well. Young Cheyenne men played the flute in order to help them in their courtship. Some flutes had a special power to influence girls. A young man might go to a medicine man and ask him to exercise his power on a flute, so that the girl he wanted would come out of the lodge when she heard it. The young man began to play the flute when he was at a distance from the lodge, but gradually approached it, and when he had come near to the lodge he found the girl outside waiting for him.

The same charm still exists in Europe. In *A Farewell to Arms* Ernest Hemingway quotes an example from the Abruzzi: "When the young men serenaded only the flute was forbidden. Why, I asked. Because it was bad for the girls to hear the flute at night."

We will speak in a later chapter of a virginity test connected with Greek pan-pipes. A similar ordeal exists with the Cuna Indians in Panama. At a girl's initiation two cane flutes are cut, tied together, wrapped into a leaf and given to a player. If they are still in their original position when he unpacks them, the girl is a virgin; if they have turned, she is not.

Nose flutes, blown through the nostril instead of through the mouth, occur in all five continents and even in Bavaria. Form and type do not matter; there are tubular and globular nose flutes as well as cross and vertical nose flutes.

It would be difficult to fix a date of origin; but distribution goes far to prove that the nose flute was spread over the world by one of the last Malayo-Polynesian migrations. In terms of history this means about the end of the neolithic age and the beginning of the early metal age.

It is more interesting, however, to know how than to know at what time it originated. Several stupid suggestions have been made to explain this strange, and rather incomprehensible, method of blowing. One of them attributes the "invention" of the nose flute to Hindu nose rings which by chance were loosely soldered and accidentally struck by the nose breath. Other authors have claimed that blowing through the nose prevented the mouth from touching a spot which a low-caste's mouth might have defiled. These explanations are so foolish that they are not worth contradicting.

The answer to the origin of the nose flute is found in the association of nose breath with magic and religious rites.

In Melanesia and Polynesia, where the nose flute is chiefly found, the nose breath is supposed to contain the soul and has, therefore, more magic power than mouth breath. Native doctors pinch the nose of moribund patients to keep the soul from escaping, though the victim of this cure may die prematurely by suffocation. When occidental people pinch their nose before sneezing, this in itself meaningless gesture seems to be a remainder of that old idea; and the German *Gesundheit!* called to a sneezer is founded on the same conception that such a violent explosion might force out the soul. The Dogon in the French Sudan have but one word for both the soul and the nose.

The special power of nose breath gives it an importance in an old Brahmanic formula for setting the priest into a semihypnotic state. It prescribes:

> Aspire through the right nostril,
> Aum Am, red of color.

Expire through the left nostril,
Aum Am, black of color.

If the priest turns towards the sunrise, his aspiring right nostril faces the south, his expiring left nostril faces the north. So he receives air from the life-giving south and blows it to the sterile north.

How persistent is the connection between right nostril, red, south, and in general between nose breath and magic power, can be seen when as late as the end of the middle ages European astrologers still grouped together the right nostril, the color red, blood, circumcision, the cardinal point south and the planet Mars.

Considering the belief in the magic power of nose breath from primitive times to the modern occident, it seems more logical to think the nose flute originated on that account than because of some casual and imaginary coincidence.

TRUMPET. We explained on page 44 that in any wind instrument the enclosed air column is set into vibration by some device which transforms the steady breath of the player into a pulsating current. While this transformation in the flute is caused by the sharp edge of the mouth-hole, in a trumpet it is effected by the lips of the player. The lips are held tense and the breath forces them to open as often as their elasticity closes them again, thus allowing the breath to escape in regular pulsations.

The earliest so-called trumpets had no vibrating column of air, no mouthpiece and no expanding end or bell. They were megaphones cut from a hollow branch or a large cane, into which the player spoke, sang or roared. Once more he did not strive for a musical sound; on the contrary, he wanted to distort his natural voice and to produce a harsh sound in order to frighten evil spirits. (fig. 23)

The evolution from a simple megaphone to an actual trumpet was slow, and it is not easy to say when the first real trumpets originated. Even these first trumpets blared only one or two notes.

The terrifying sound of the early trumpets is associated with many magic rites. It is used at circumcisions, at funerals and at sunset rites, when the reappearance of the life-giving star is imperiled; and the Babwende of the Belgian Congo carve their funeral trumpets in the magic shape of a phallos. Even in Europe today trumpets are connected with the same rites. Long wooden trumpets are blown at Rumanian funerals. In some Catholic cantons of Switzerland the kindred *alphorn* sounds at sunset at the same time that the evening

prayer is sung into a megaphone: the early trumpet used as a megaphone, and the later form of a real trumpet, are preserved in the
same rite. (pls. II d, e)

The trumpet is exclusively played by men. Among certain tribes
of the Amazon a woman who has seen a trumpet is killed. Other
Indians destroy it after use and hide the mouth part in a brook. This
same custom is preserved in the south of Holland; wooden trumpets, related to the alphorn, are blown at Advent and hidden in a
well until the following year.

The magic power of the trumpet has often been augmented by the
red color of its painting or drapery; even in European armies of the
present time, trumpets and bugles are wrapped in red woollen material, and red remains the distinctive color of many military bands,
an astonishing example of the tenacity of early traditions.

A later, though still primitive, offshoot of the trumpet is the *side-
blown* or *transverse trumpet* with a mouth-hole on the side. Transverse trumpets are common among the South American Indians
(fig. 24) and the African Negroes, who make them either of antelope
horn or the tusk of an elephant. They also existed far away in Ireland during the bronze age and, as we know of prehistoric relations
between northeastern Africa and Ireland, this otherwise incomprehensible fact is not miraculous.

Primitive men use large *conch shells* as well as their rough tubular
trumpets. The spiral replaces the tube, and the natural opening the
bell. An earlier type of shell trumpet is *end-blown*, the mouth-hole
being cut in the center of the round end, or *apex;* in a later type,
which dates from the end of pre-Christian times, the hole is cut in
the side, thus creating a *side-blown* or *transverse* shell trumpet. In
some countries, ancient Peru for instance, shell trumpets were replaced by clay trumpets in shell form. (fig. 25)

The oldest conch shells were not real trumpets any more than the
earliest wooden or cane trumpets. Gunnar Landtman relates that in
one of the most primitive tribes of New Guinea the king or chieftain
always held "a trumpet shell before his mouth when speaking to his
people, so his voice had a very hollow sound." Once more a musical
instrument was first used for the purpose of masking the voice.

As an actual trumpet, the conch shell has a strong magic power.
This can be increased if a sacred formula is recited into the natural
mouth of the conch.

The magic and nonmagic uses of the shell trumpet are more
varied than those of the tubular trumpet. When the author collected

A   B   C

D   E   F

G

H

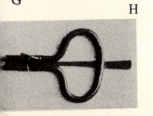

A. slit-drum, W. Java (Ph. D. H. Meijer). *B. Footed drum, Timorlaut. C. Prehistoric whistle flute, found under the Wartburg. D. Bucium, Rumania. E. Lithuanian bark trumpet. F. Rommelpot* (Pinx. Frans Hals). *G. Jaws' harp, Palaung, Burma. H. Esthonian jaws' harp.*

PLATE II.

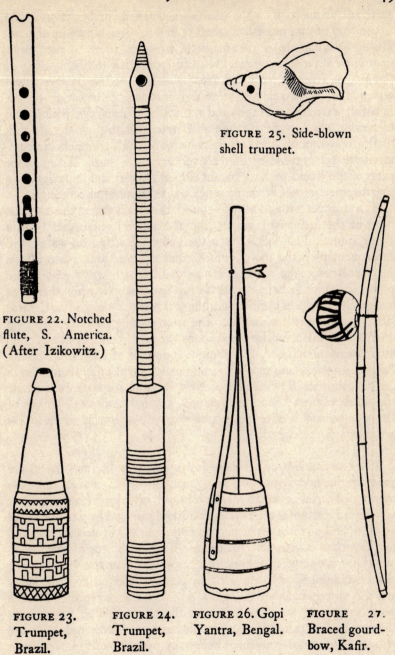

FIGURE 22. Notched flute, S. America. (After Izikowitz.)

FIGURE 25. Side-blown shell trumpet.

FIGURE 23. Trumpet, Brazil.

FIGURE 24. Trumpet, Brazil.

FIGURE 26. Gopi Yantra, Bengal.

FIGURE 27. Braced gourd-bow, Kafir.

material for his book on the musical instruments of Madagascar, he found that on this one island shell trumpets were blown on the following occasions: boys' circumcisions, funerals, ancestral rites, practices in which magicians call the dead from their tombs, healing of the sick, sacrifices after a bad dream, bathing of the fetishes, royal ceremonies, wind charms, wrestling matches, convocation of the faithful, warning of danger and musical performances. Sailors and carters in Madagascar also use shell trumpets to give signals and, finally, a system of long and short blasts on shell trumpets can communicate telegraphic messages over great distances. From other parts of the world we have to add rites at harvest and marriage, rain charms, meetings of secret societies and exhibitions of offerings.

As a trumpet with an horrific sound, the conch shares the connotations of the ordinary trumpet. But the conch itself comes from a water animal. This fact gives it the power of acting on water, and consequently on the moon, which rules the tide and which affects the menstruation of women. Its association with water gave it the power in primitive belief to attract rain, or to stop it when there was too much; instances can be found in so advanced a region as Central Europe, where it is blown into the wind during thunderstorms up to this day. With similar associations the shell trumpet becomes an attribute of moon gods, of Vishnu in India and of Tlaloc in Mexico. Again, as a water and moon instrument, it is kept away from men in certain countries. The natives of New Ireland, for instance, exclude the shell trumpet from men's dances, but it accompanies dances of the women and is even played by women, especially when a first pregnancy is celebrated.

The connotations of all these instruments, in life and myth, are confusing at first sight. One recognizes, however, that in the cases mentioned certain associations are constant, or at least frequent. Four among our examples are almost exclusively played by women, eight by men, and of these eight instruments four are so strictly reserved for men that women who see them are killed. Three of our instruments are supposed to represent a penis, and four the vulva or the female abdomen, while the sticks or pestles which strike these latter are also conceived as virile organs. All instruments representing the penis are played by men only, and the chief occasion for playing them is at funerals; all instruments decorated with red color are reserved for men and must not be seen by women; vulva instruments are frequently connected with water and moon rites.

The most obvious of these contrasts is the attribution to one of the two sexes: gourd rattles are generally played by women, bull-roarers by men; drums are often played by women with the bare hands, but never with a stick. Division of labor according to sex, well known even in modern occidental civilization, is the rule with primitive peoples. Hunting and boat carving are man's work, basketry and pottery, in general, woman's. It may happen that men alter a women's technique; they then keep the altered technique for themselves while the women, far from adopting the improvement, stick to their old method. Such is the case of pottery, for instance. Berthold Laufer, in his essay on "The Potter's Wheel," states that handmade pottery

is as a rule woman's work, the participation of men in this pursuit being always strictly localized and limited. The potter's wheel, on the other hand, is the creation of man. It must therefore be regarded as an entirely distinct invention which entered the field of pottery from the outside, as it were, and when it came, man came with it and took over the pot-making industry. This historic distinctness of the two methods of pottery making is reflected in the customs current in different countries. In India and China the division of ceramic labor sets apart the thrower or wheel potter and separates him from the molder. The potters of India who work on the wheel do not intermarry with those who do not. They form a caste by themselves. There is also a functional distinction between the two kinds of pots. And most important of all, wherever the potter's wheel is in use, it is manipulated by men, never by women.

The example of pottery makes clear why certain forms of drums are exclusively played by women, and other forms by men.

The player's sex and the form of his or her instrument, or at least its interpretation, depend on one another. As the magic task of more or less all primitive instruments is life, procreation, fertility, it is evident that the life-giving roles of either sex are seen or reproduced in their shape or playing motion. A man's instrument assumes the form of a man's organ, a woman's of a woman's organ. And in the latter case the addition of a fertilizing object is not far off.

Early mentality tends toward associating, as equal and interchangeable factors, all kinds of objects and phenomena, provided they have some organic correlation, or at least one common quality. Woman and moon is such a correlation, as the rhythm of woman's life is determined by, or at least synchronized with, the moon's phases. The moon, however, is synchronized with the tides as well. Thus

moon ~ woman
moon ~ water
_____
woman ~ water

The woman conceals her seed in the womb; so does the earth, hiding it beneath its surface. Thus, woman is correlated to the ground and earth pits. Woman's womb is round and hollow; thus, round cavities belong to woman.

Tubular wind instruments, straight and elongated like a man's organ, belong to man, and a mixture of symbols arises when a flute is globular instead of tubular, or when a trumpet is made out of a conch shell which is connected with water. A scraper, played by a man, may lie across an earth pit, and stamping tubes may be pounded by men. This kind of mixture of male and female connotations is sure to occur when an instrument is transferred into a foreign civilization with different social and mental conditions.

Sound, also, is a factor as well as form in these connotations. Most of the instruments reserved for men have a harsh, aggressive, indeed ugly tone; most instruments preferred by women have a muffled timbre. But there are exceptions; flutes of some width have a muffled tone, and the gourd rattle makes a harsh and frightening noise. Musical beauty is not a consideration.

MELODIC IMPULSES

The instruments considered hitherto have grown out of either a strong motor impulse which produced audible rhythm, or out of a man's inclination to give magic interpretation to sound. The conception of, and the need for, instrumental melody, even in the most rudimentary sense of the word, was at first entirely lacking; melody belonged to singing, not to instruments.

In a second stage of evolution another elementary rhythmic impulse began to seize on instrument playing—*repetition*. It resulted first in the pairing of notes, then in the contrasting of their tones, and finally in their arrangement in a series. The same process is found in language as *reduplication*. The speech of children and primitives has a tendency towards combinations such as *papa, mamma, tamtam*. The two syllables of a pair become one strong, one weak; moreover, they often are differentiated by a vowel change: *ding-dong, sing-song, tick-tock*. This is exactly what happens when two stamping tubes of slightly different size are pounded by the same player in a rapid succession, and the beat of one of them is answered by a second, darker beat which contrasts with the clear sound of the first.

The two tubes in the hand of a player were sometimes called "the father" and "the mother." Such associations with the two sexes occur with pairs of bull-roarers, slit-drums, shell trumpets and skin drums. When the sexes are thus attributed to pairs of instruments, the primitives base their decision upon one of two qualities—the size or the sound. If size is the determining factor, the bigger instrument is the man and the smaller the woman; if the sound is considered, the smaller one, having a more active and energetic sound, is masculine, the larger one, having a hollower, duller sound, is female. Sound as the determining factor seems to be much more recent.

The pairlike beating of two notes of contrasted accent and pitch is the first step towards an instrumental melody; this ancient practice is preserved in the two kettledrums of the modern orchestra. Several thousands of years may have elapsed before instrumental music progressed to three-tone patterns.

Though stamping tubes were united to form sets of three and even more, they did not reach the further stage of a strict scalelike accordatura.

This was the destiny of the xylophone.

THE XYLOPHONE, though still in use today, originated among primitive men. It is a set of wooden bars, each supported at two points (the nodes of vibration), and struck with sticks or clubs. As the modern name derived from Greek *xýlon*, 'wood,' it can not accurately be applied to sets of metal bars.

The simplest form of xylophone may be called a *leg xylophone*. The player sits on the ground, lays two or three rough slabs of wood across the legs and strikes them with two clubs. Sometimes a pit is dug between the legs.

The players are generally women. Sitting on the ground with legs stretched out straight is a typical feminine attitude; in many countries, in the Pacific Islands for instance, women are not supposed to sit cross-legged.

The most primitive leg xylophones, consisting of a few bars only, are played in a simple fashion, the bars being struck in turn. But there are also more elaborate types. In Madagascar, for instance, the bars are carefully tuned; one woman holds them on her legs beating the melody, while a second woman, sitting at right angles to the first, plays a drone or ostinato on two bars which are arranged apart, though also resting on the legs of the first woman.

The first step in the evolution of the xylophone leads to the *log xylophone,* in which the bars are loosely laid on two parallel logs. Even in this stage there may be an earth pit under the instrument.

Later, the bars of the xylophone were made fast, either to a stand like a table (*table xylophone*), or to a frame which hung at the player's waist, suspended from his neck and held away from his body by a semicircular hoop (*bail xylophone*).

The xylophones of the Bantu Negroes generally have a gourd resonator under each bar to increase and fill the sound (*gourd xylophones*). Each gourd is carefully chosen and cut according to the size of the bar; the air inside is supposed to vibrate in unison with the wood. A hole is cut in the gourd and covered with the tough membrane taken from the protective covering of spiders' eggs; vibrating sympathetically, this skin makes the timbre sharper.

Though xylophone music is melodic, a strong motor impulse still shapes its melodic style. Obeying the hands rather than the mind, the player indulges in shakes, graces, rolls and flourishes, mostly in a giddy tempo; the music, improvisatory in early stages, has slowly grown to highly accomplished and often intricate structures, which call to mind European toccatas.

But these refined toccatas and the complicated gourd xylophones, or *marimbas,* on which they are played, have carried us far away from the primitive disconnected xylophone and its few indistinct notes on poorly differentiated bars. The advanced xylophone of African primitives, like many of their implements, was not developed by themselves but borrowed from the higher civilizations of the Malays, who had a strong influence on Bantu Africa.

THE GROUND HARP, which exists exclusively in a small central section of Africa, recalls the springing snares of certain African hunters. A pit is covered with bark. Beside the pit a tall flexible rod is stuck into the earth and pulled way over by a string fastened from its end to the bark lid of the pit. The instrument is either struck or plucked, sometimes by several persons simultaneously.

It is particularly interesting to watch the further evolution of the ground harp, which corresponds to that of many other instruments. First step: it is freed from the ground. The Annamese *cai dan bao,* for instance, an instrument played by women and blind people, is supported by the player, but is too heavy to be carried while played. The pit of the ground harp is replaced by a rectangular, wooden soundbox. A flexible rod stands upright near one end of the box, and a wire string is tied from the upper end of the rod to the other end of the box. The string is plucked. When the rod is bent slightly nearer to the box, easing the tension, the plucked string can produce lower notes. The resultant melodic style is characterized by wailing sounds and glissandi.

Second step: the instrument is portable. Many varieties of this kind exist in India. One of them, the *ānanda laharī* of Bengal, has not even a flexible rod, and merely consists of a gut string tied between two small drums, which are held by the player so that the string can be tightened at will as it is plucked. (fig. 26)

THE GROUND-ZITHER, in its Annamese form, has a pit dug in the ground and covered with a piece of bark as a soundboard. A string is stretched horizontally between two posts; another string, tied to the middle of the first and acting as a bridge, runs vertically to the bark lid, severing the string into two acoustical sections. When the horizontal string is struck with sticks, its vibrations are transmitted by the vertical string to the lid, which resounds over the pit. The string has the gigantic length of thirteen or fourteen feet, which is one reason for supposing that the Annamese ground-zither is the oldest one, because experience shows that the evolution of every primitive instrument begins with large sizes and ends with small ones. The string is not made of twisted fiber, nor of gut or horsehair or wire. It is a ribbon or rattan half an inch thick which, owing to its great length, is elastic enough to vibrate when struck with a stick. The rattan is replaced by twisted fiber only in later ground-zithers.

The ground-zither is also interesting from the angle of musical evolution. Two different notes can be produced successively if the central cord severs the string into two vibrating sections of unequal length. On the island of Madura near Java, a very backward country, the natives even make a double-zither with two pits and two bridges. These afford three different vibrating lengths in the same string: from the first peg to the first bridge, between the two bridges, and from the second bridge to the second peg in the earth. Thus, the Madurese play rudimentary melodies of three notes repeated over and over.

A second type of ground-zither is still preserved among Javanese children and by the Bube on Fernando Póo in the African Atlantic. Several strings with a separate pit each are stretched side by side;

this is once more the first principle of uniting instruments of the same kind, but of different length, to form sets.

The only recorded ritual in which the ground-zither is used was found among the Makua in East Africa. There it is struck when, before initiation, girls are taught about sexual intercourse.

The principle of the ground-zither, combined with other principles, is characteristic of the *musical bow*.

THE MUSICAL BOW. The hunter's bow is a familiar object; the two ends of a flexible and curved rod are connected by a string. Since the musical bow is identical in shape, many anthropologists believed it was derived from the hunter's bow; hunters, they said, perceived the humming of the snapped string and began to use their bows as musical instruments. This is plausible but wrong, like many plausible explanations. Those forms of the musical bow which we have good reason to believe are the oldest have nothing to do with a hunter's bow. They are ten feet long and therefore useless for shooting. Some of them are *idiochordic*; that is, the string is formed from a strip split from the same piece of cane of which the instrument is made, but still attached to it at either end. This natural string must be raised off the bow by bridges, and therefore cannot be used for shooting. Furthermore, all of these bows require a resonator; without a sound-amplifying contrivance the instrument is scarcely audible.

Finally, musical bows were not associated with hunters' beliefs and ceremonies. With the Cora in Mexico, the calabash bowl on which the bow rests is a sacred emblem of the goddess of the earth and moon; among many tribes only the women play it; in Rhodesia it is the instrument played at girls' initiations; and the Washambala in eastern Africa believe that a man cannot get a wife if a string of the musical bow breaks while he is making it. In a tale of the East African Wahehe, a man goes on a journey with a girl, has her drink from a brook and breaks her neck when she is bent over the water. At once she is transformed into a musical bow; the back bone becomes the wood, her head the resonator, and her limbs the strings. Similar stories are found in northern mythology.

The musical bow is one of the first instruments used for intimacy and to induce meditation; the Akamba in eastern Africa, as well as the Maidu in middle California, consider it the most effective instrument for getting in contact with spirits. The weak, muffled sound of the musical bow, suited to such a task, is mirrored in the dark vowels and nasal consonants of its native names, such as *nkungu* in Angolese, *vuhudendung* on Pentecost Island in Melanesia, *wurubumba* in Kibunda.

There are three main types of musical bows: bows with a separate resonator, bows with attached resonators, or *gourd bows,* and bows that depend upon the player's mouth for resonance or *mouth bows.*

The bow with a separate resonator is supported on a detached vessel. This may be a calabash bowl, a basket, a pot or a metal vase. The strangest of these bows is the gigantic instrument of some tribes of southern India: a bow, sometimes ten feet long, with jingles suspended from the wood, rests on a large clay pot and is rapidly beaten with two sticks, while a second man strikes the pot with his hands.

Similar instruments, laid on gourds, occur with Mexican Indians. Most anthropologists have tried to attribute them to Negro importation. But this is not likely. No African bow has so large a size, and none is struck in so archaic a way with two sticks.

In the *gourd bow* the bow is attached to a gourd which acts as a resonator. The top of the gourd is cut off and the opening is pressed against the chest or abdomen of the player, increasing its resonance. The gourd can resonate only the open string of the bow to which it has been cut, and when any other tone is played the gourd must be lifted away from the player's body so that its resonance will not interfere with the tone. This shifting of the position of the gourd is *not* a means of altering the tone, as some observers have claimed.

There are other means of altering the fundamental tone. With all kinds of musical bows the vibrating length of the string can be changed, either by bracing, or by stopping, or by both ways. In the *braced bow* the string is divided into two sections by a loop of thread tied round the bow and the string. The two sections produce two different fundamentals with their relative partials. Also, the player can touch the string, as do fiddlers, in order to shorten the vibrating length and raise the pitch. (fig. 27)

In the *mouth bow* the player's mouth serves as a resonator; either the wood is held against the teeth with the string outside, or else the string is allowed to vibrate in the oral cavity with the wood outside. Its musical rendering depends on the reinforcing of partials in the same way as in the jaws' harp.

THE JAWS' HARP, better known under its common misnomer, *jews' harp,* is a quaint instrument, pleasing to the player because of its clear though tiny sound, almost inaudible to a listener.

An elastic lamella is fixed at one end in a frame, while the other end is free. The player's jaws grasp the frame so that the lamella, plucked with a finger or a cord, vibrates between the teeth. The oral cavity, according to its position, amplifies one of the harmonics, just as it does when producing the various vowels of our language. Thus, little melodies can be obtained. Some observers attribute the tone and its pitch to the afflation of the lamella by the player's breath; this, however, is incidental.

All the same, breathing against the lamella may be connected with the origin of the jaws' harp. In Hawaii and the Marquesas Islands a piece of bamboo is deeply notched at one end; a sliver of bamboo held over the notch vibrates when the singing voice is projected against it. Similar contrivances are used in Melanesia and in East Africa. Here is another instrument that starts as a voice mask.

The details of the slow evolution of the jaws' harp are too unimportant for the scope of this book; the author described them at large in an earlier publication. It will suffice to give a short summary. The size decreased gradually; the lamella was at first formed by a strip cut out from the same piece of bamboo as the frame and still attached to one end (*idioglottic jaws' harp*), and was later made from a separate piece of bamboo or metal and bound at one end to the frame (*heteroglottic jaws' harp*); the oldest types had a thin cord at the end opposite the point of the tongue which set the lamella into vibration when it was pulled by jerks, while the most recent had a slender thorn instead. All these jaws' harps apparently originated in Southeast Asia; the most interesting transitional types are still preserved in the islands of Formosa and Engano. There we find intermediate stages between the 'cut out' and the modern 'forged' jaws' harp, which latter consists of a flat steel tongue soldered to the vertex of a bent piece of wire, sometimes the shape of a hairpin, sometimes more resembling a horseshoe. This iron jaws' harp has been made in two forms; in an older form, known throughout Asia and used in the European middle ages, the broad end of the tongue projected behind the frame; in a more recent form it does not. The great elasticity of the steel tongue produces a louder tone; some oriental people therefore consider the iron jaws' harp too loud to foster the meditative state of mind required of so intimate an instrument. (pls. II g, h)

What a contrast between this tiny jaws' harp and the huge slit-drum; between the intimacy and meditation that it arouses and the terrifying sound of bull-roarers and trumpets; between its clear notes and the dull noise of rattles and pounding feet! And all these contrasting, indeed contradictory, impulses and principles have originated in the early stages of human evolution which, antedating town life, the formation of states and the invention of writing, are called primitive. More than ever we feel the necessity of establishing a chronology to bring order into this confusion.

2. *The Chronology of Early Instruments*

COMPARING the gourd or bamboo devices of early civilizations with the involved mechanisms of modern pianos and organs, one might easily come to the conclusion that instruments have developed from simple to complicated patterns and that their origins can therefore be established by tracing the various types back to their simplest forms. Although this is true as a general statement, it is superficial and often misleading as a working hypothesis. What is simple? It is simple to cut down a bamboo stalk and to open it lengthwise in order to make a natural slit-drum. It is much less simple to fell a gigantic tree and to hollow it out by stone axes and fire. And yet we know that hollowed trees were used to make slit-drums long before smaller bamboos were used for the same purpose. Reduction and simplification as results of progressive development outside the instrumental area are well known, for instance, in language: Sanskrit has eight grammatical cases, and English only one or two. This settles the question as far as progress is concerned. But not all evolution is progressive; it is regressive in many cases. The simple pan-pipes of primitive tribes in the Pacific and South America are not prototypes of the refined pan-pipes of China, but imitations in degeneracy. We can compare instruments within a homogeneous group, for instance pan-pipes or slit-drums; but can we decide whether a flute is simpler than a stamping tube or a slit-drum?

Unable to decide chronology on the basis of more complicated or simpler workmanship, one might attempt to arrange peoples and

60

tribes according to their lesser or higher degree of civilization and check their instruments. This, too, is scarcely feasible; a conscientious anthropologist would refrain from establishing such an order. There are, say, three peoples: one poor in material culture, but gifted as artists and socially well organized; the second, rich in material civilization, but poor in artistic imagination and social refinement; a third, well organized, but unskilled in handicraft. Which is the most primitive? And even if such an order could be established, would all peoples of the same cultural standard have the same instruments, notwithstanding their different mentality, social organization and the materials available in their countries? Peoples, like individuals, respond differently to emotion. One reacts as a musician, by singing or playing; another, in a different way. Musical response is weak with the Eskimos and strong with the Negroes, regardless of their cultural standard. But there is not only a difference in musical responsiveness; a similar stimulus might act in one case on the singing throat, in another on the playing hand, again independently from the level of civilization. Ancient Greece sang but neglected her instruments; East Asia excels in playing. Again, the plenty and variety of instruments depends on the habitat of the people; musical culture in the tropics is abetted by the existence of large coconuts and calabashes, and those gigantic bamboos which provide pipes, zithers, xylophones, reeds and strings.

In spite of all these difficulties a rough chronology of primitive civilizations can be made by comparing them with the stages of prehistoric evolution in Europe and other continents. In France or Spain a prehistorian excavates the dwellings and burial grounds of paleolithic hunters with their tools and weapons, and slowly reconstructs the material and even the spiritual culture of these men—an anthropologist will be able to show a similar culture among some aboriginal tribes in Australia or elsewhere. Again, the prehistorian discovers a later, neolithic civilization, in the Danube valley or in Italy, and the anthropologist finds a similar culture existing in some remote district of India, with the same shape of cabins, the same pottery, weapons, tools and instruments. Anthropology and history are drawing together, and by checking their results we can add another clue.

Unfortunately, digging in prehistoric strata yields meager information, as only instruments made of imperishable materials have been preserved. Paleolithic tombs and dwelling places produce the shells of strung rattles, bone scrapers, bone bull-roarers and bone flutes; neolithic excavations produce clay drums and end-blown shell trumpets. Whatever was made of wood or cane or bark has perished by decomposition. The picture of prehistoric music that we owe to the digging spade is not only poor but misleading, if it is not completed by anthropological data.

A second weak point in comparing prehistoric with primitive civilizations still extant is that nearly all existing peoples, notwithstanding their cultural levels, must be supposed to have come in touch with higher civilizations and, though having withstood their influence in their general form of life, to have received instruments from abroad. The Chinese pan-pipe is an example, and this interference is again apparent in the case of the mouth organs sold all over the world by European trade.

When the author, in his book *Geist und Werden der Musikinstrumente,* tried to arrive at a chronology of primitive and oriental instruments, he kept away from all criteria connected with supposed levels of culture and workmanship. Instead, he relied on what appeared to be the safest method—the geographical one. Erich M. von Hornbostel followed the same method when he published his paper on "The Ethnology of African Sound-Instruments" (1933). The chief axioms of this method are:

1) An object or idea found in scattered regions of a certain district is older than an object found everywhere in the same area.

2) Objects preserved only in remote valleys and islands are older than those used in open plains.

3) The more widely an object is spread over the world, the more primitive it is.

How such a distribution originates may be illustrated by a physical phenomenon. When a stone is thrown into a pond it will cause a series of circular waves, which grow larger and larger until they fade away or are stopped by the edge. In this series of concentric circles the first (that is the oldest) is the largest one, while the more recently originated circles have a smaller diameter.

But here a vital question arises: is the world-wide distribution of musical instruments due to migrations from a few centers of inspiration, or rather to the fact that man, at a given stage of development, must invent the same tools and implements? This difficult problem belongs to anthropology rather than to musicology. The author, however, is convinced that each of the oldest ideas and inventions came from one center. We may believe that a tool such as a hammer can be invented everywhere at a certain stage of human evolution; the progression from the use of the bare fist, through the use of a stone in the fist, to a stone on a wooden handle, is quite logical and natural. But a bull-roarer? Is it really acceptable that every human tribe must invent an oval board, held by a cord and whirled around the head, for certain magic purposes? Is it convincing that merely because of natural evolution such a bull-roarer should have been almost universally connected with the fish, and that paleolithic hunters in France as well as modern Eskimos should both have the idea of dentating its rims?

The geographic method, too, may prove fallacious. The commercial dissemination of European goods and, before that, the systematic spreading of Near Eastern instruments following the Islamic conquest, sensibly restrict its worth.

Nevertheless, geographical criteria are safer than any other criteria because they are less exposed to subjective interpretation. It is best to follow them as closely as possible and to check the chronology they provide with prehistoric and historic data, and with the more interpretive answers to the questions of simplicity and cultural level.

This method enables us to outline a chronology of the instruments discussed on the previous pages. Instead of my own twenty-three strata and Hornbostel's eleven strata, three will suffice for the purpose of this book.

The early stratum comprises those instruments which, prehistorically, occur in paleolithic excavations and, geographically, are scattered all over the world. These are:

IDIOPHONES	AEROPHONES	MEMBRANOPHONES	CHORDOPHONES
rattles	bull-roarer		
rubbed shell?	ribbon reed		
scraper	flute without		
stamped pit	holes		

No drums and no stringed instruments appear in this early stratum.

The middle stratum comprises those instruments which, prehistorically, occur in neolithic excavations, and, geographically, in several continents, though they are not universal. These are:

slit-drum	flute with holes	drum	ground-harp
stamping tube	trumpet		ground-zither
	shell trumpet		musical bow

The late stratum comprises those instruments which, prehistorically, occur in more recent neolithic excavations, and, geographically, are confined to certain limited areas. These are:

rubbed wood	nose flute	friction drum
basketry rattle	cross flute	drum stick
xylophone	transverse trumpet	
jaws' harp		

This rough chronology, though established on the objective data of distribution and prehistory, gives satisfaction also to the mind concerned with workmanship and cultural level.

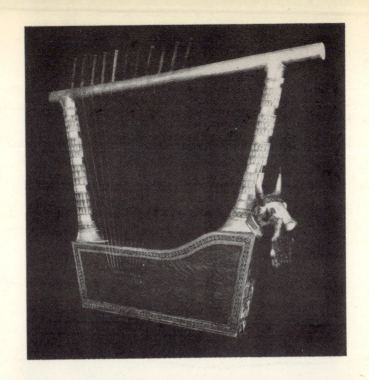

*Sumerian lyres in the University Museum, Philadelphia. The
wooden lyre (above) is greatly restored; the silver lyre
(below) is entirely original.*

PLATE III.

SECOND PART

Antiquity

3. *Sumer and Babylonia*

THE evolution from prehistoric and primitive civilizations to the higher civilizations involves a corresponding evolution from folk and ritual instruments to instruments intended for entertainment and art. Division of labor and class distinctions in an urban culture result in the formation of a professional class of singers and musicians. It is no more the 'people' that play and sing for magic, devotional and social purposes, but a distinct class, or even caste, of musicians. From this moment, instruments can be divided into two kinds—popular instruments and instruments used by professional artists. The latter evolve in the direction of greater musical effectiveness and easier manipulation.

The history of these higher civilizations begins in Mesopotamia, the once fertile plain between the rivers Tigris and Euphrates. Her first rulers were the Sumerians, a people of uncertain race who seem to have come from a neighboring country farther east in the fifth millennium B.C. Contemporaries of the Old Kingdom of Egypt, the Sumerian dynasties were replaced before 2000 B.C. by the Babylonians, a Semitic people who were contemporaneous with the Middle Kingdom in Egypt. At about 1750 B.C., the Kassites, a non-Semitic people, invaded from the east and reigned in Mesopotamia until about 1100 B.C. In the last millennium B.C., Mesopotamia was ruled successively by Assyrians and Babylonians (the Dynasty of King Nebuchadrezzar and the Babylonian Exile of the Jews), by Medes and Persians, and finally by Greeks. The reader may compare the following synopsis.

MESOPOTAMIA	EGYPT	CRETE AND GREECE
Sumerians	Old Kingdom	Early Crete
−2040	−2160	−2100
Babylonians	Middle Kingdom	Middle Crete
2040–1750	2160–1580	2100–1580
Kassites	New Kingdom	Late Crete
1740–1160	1580–1090	1580–1400
Assyrians	Nubians	Dorian migration
1160–625	1090–663	11th century
Babylonians	Saïtes	
625–538	663–382	
Persians		Classic Period
538–331		6–4th century
Greeks	Greeks	Alexander
from 331	from 332	336–323

The two chief languages used in Mesopotamia were Sumerian and Akkadian. Sumerian was a non-Semitic language; Akkadian, comprising Babylonian and Assyrian, was Semitic. As long as Sumerian was generally spoken, the Sumerian names of ritual objects passed from this language into Akkadian and were only slightly transformed according to its phonetic and grammatical rules. Later, when Sumerian was used only as a holy language in the temple, while Akkadian had become the current language, the Akkadian names of newly introduced objects were taken into the Sumerian language. In consequence, most Sumerian names had an Akkadian equivalent, no matter whether the Sumerian or the Akkadian form was the original.

Very few musical instruments have been excavated in Mesopotamia, and most of them were found in the royal cemetery at Ur, Abraham's native town. However, there are many reliefs and plaques, seals and mosaics, from a period extending over three thousand years, that depict players and musical scenes. Cuneiform written texts in Sumerian or Akkadian contain a quantity of names of musical instruments.

The scholar's task of compiling the actual instruments excavated from Mesopotamian soil, as well as the depicted instruments, and matching them to the few names given in contemporaneous texts is particularly difficult. A few ideograms can be traced back to pictures of things: an ear of corn, a bull's head, a hand, a man, a door. In the advanced cuneiform script the original pictures are so schematized that they are unrecognizable, and it is impossible to deduce the form of an instrument from the particular arrangement of the wedges in the cuneiform ideogram of its name. If the ideograms had been recognizable even in their time, the Sumerians would not have helped the reader by occasional *determinatives*, that is, specifying prefixes to make up for the ambiguity of the phonetic symbols. With musical instruments, such determinatives indicate the material of which they are made: *kuš* or *šu*—'skin,' *gi*—'cane,' *giš*—'wood,' *urudu*—'metal.'

Even if a name can be identified, we face a second difficulty: different names do not necessarily designate different instruments, and different instruments do not necessarily have different names. In ancient Egypt both *šr* and *tbn* mean a frame drum, and *ma* is given to flutes, oboes and clarinets.

Thus research must be based on archeological rather than on philological clues.

IDIOPHONIC INSTRUMENTS, vibrating without any special tension, have left few traces in Mesopotamia. It would be wrong, however, to conclude that they were not frequent in ancient Mesopotamia; as the scenes represented by Sumerian and Babylonian artists were in the main ceremonial, they mirror but one side of Mesopotamian life. Altogether we know six types of idiophones employed between the Two Rivers; namely, concussion clubs, clappers, sistra, bells, cymbals and rattles.

Concussion clubs had the bent form of primitive boomerangs of the nontwisted type, such as Australian tribes use for hunting and also to accompany their songs. They are depicted on some of the oldest seals of Sumer, resembling exactly those drawn on prehistoric potteries of Egypt; dancers are holding one in each hand and hitting them together.

On an archaic seal from Ur, which dates from about 2800 B.C. and is owned by the University Museum in Philadelphia, a small animal is playing a pair of short *clappers* of the kind that youths call *bones* in this country. Fourteen or fifteen centuries later similar clappers appear on Egyptian reliefs of the New Kingdom.

More interesting than clubs and clappers are the *sistra*, which will be spoken of more fully in the Egyptian chapter. They had the U form of a spur (the point of the spur forming the handle) with a few loose crossbars, which jingled when the little implement was shaken. Thus, they were similar in shape to those sistra that have been found near Tiflis in Georgia and still exist in the Christian Church of Ethiopia, and also similar, surprisingly enough, to sistra found among the Yaqui in North America and among the Kadiuveo in South America. The clearest reproduction of a Sumerian sistrum is on a seal dating about 2500 B.C. in the Louvre. (fig. 28)

The Sumerian spur sistrum differed from the usual Egyptian sistrum, which had the arch on top opposite the handle. Only one Egyptian specimen, of wood, is carved in the Sumerian shape; it came from a tomb of the Middle Kingdom, about 2000 B.C., and

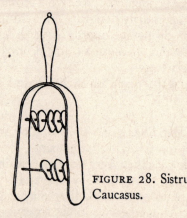

FIGURE 28. Sistrum, Caucasus.

probably was not common at that time. A relationship between the Mesopotamian and the Egyptian sistra cannot be doubted; we know that in prehistoric times the countries were connected by commercial trade. That the sistrum originated in Mesopotamia is not likely, as this country is on the periphery, rather than in the center, of the area of distribution. Also, the earlier spur sistrum was, and is, used on the periphery, except for that one obsolete specimen in Egypt; again, a later type was used in Egypt only. Thus, all the facts indicate that the sistrum came from Egypt rather than from Mesopotamia.

We can trace the sistrum even further back than Egypt. Its ancestors, huge and rough, as might be supposed, are preserved in a peculiar implement of Malayan and Melanesian fishermen. To entice the shark, these men bend a rattan rod, either in the shape of a two-pronged fork or in the shape of the frame of a tennis racket. With the fork shape they squeeze a crossbar between the prongs and string rattling coconut shells on it; with a tennis racket shape, they string the shells on the frame itself. This shark rattle anticipates both forms of the sistrum, the Sumerian and early Egyptian spur sistrum, and also the horseshoe-shaped sistrum of classical Egypt to be described in the following chapter.

Small *bells* were hung around the necks of animals in comparatively recent times. A larger ceremonial bell, with the symbols of the gods Ea, Nergal and Ninurti and a clapper inside, is preserved in the *Vorderasiatische Abteilung* of the Berlin Museum. It dates from the Assyrian epoch, about 600 B.C.

Cymbals appear as late as the seventh century in Assyria. Here they are used in two different forms. In one form they are held in a horizontal position and softly struck in a vertical movement; in the other form they are held in a vertical position and vigorously struck in a horizontal movement. In the former case they are funnel-shaped, the necks of the funnels serving as handles.

Dr. Francis W. Galpin suggests the Akkadian word *katral* as the proper term for Assyrian cymbals, as it is reminiscent of the North Indian word *kartâl*. He is certainly mistaken. The Indian term designates a clapper, not cymbals; but as its component *tāl* is a native Indian word, the Akkadian term ought to be taken from it and transformed by metathesis. This, however, would scarcely fit in the chronology. Dr. Galpin's second argument is that according to a legal code a katral of copper was worn by a mule or a horse, and this could have been cymbals. I doubt whether the ancient Mesopotamians would have designated the small twinkling disks of horses as cymbals (understanding that they existed); moreover, the singular form would not do. But there is a better explanation: in the closely related Hebrew language the verb *kātar* means 'encircle,' *kéter* is 'crown,' and *kotéret*, or *kotārót*, an ornamental crownwork.

Rattles in the form of clumsy clay animals, hollow, with pebbles inside, have been excavated from early layers. They obviously were toys.

PIPES were depicted as rarely as other wind instruments; the Mesopotamian civilization preferred strings. Flutes seem to have been introduced into ritual music as late as about 2600 B.C., as we read on one of the Sumerian priest-king Gudea's seal cylinders, "Enlulim, the shepherd of the lulim-kids, for the Lord Ningirsu, was given a share in his cult to cultivate diligently flute [playing] to fill the forecourt of Eninnu with joy." On an archaic Sumerian seal in the Louvre a sitting shepherd plays the long vertical flute while his dog listens attentively; is it En-lulim?

The Sumerian name of the vertical flute was *ti-gi*, the syllable *gi* meaning 'cane'; the Akkadians transformed the word into *tīgū*. A second name *gi-gid*, 'long cane' (Akkadian *malīlu*), may refer to the same instrument.

The mechanical arrangement of the *whistle flute* may have been used as well, but only in a globular clay flute. Such an instrument, coming from Babylonia, was preserved in the museum of the Royal Asiatic Society in London, but it unfortunately disappeared some years ago.

Some of the pipes depicted in Mesopotamian musical scenes can be ascertained as pipes blown through a reed. Mouthpieces are not distinguishable, and the position of the pipes is misleading. Though the pipes are supposed to project nearly horizontally from the player's mouth, molders of rough, clay figurines model the pipes in the downward position of a flute, close to the body, to avoid the difficulties of a projecting form. They have the typical gemination; all countries of the ancient Mediterranean world and Southwest Asia used two reed pipes blown together by the same player, while the flute was single. Such pipes could have been oboes, with a double reed, or clarinets, with a single reed; both types will be described in detail in the next chapter. Geminated clarinets always were closely tied together without forming an angle; geminated oboes were divergent. This is why we can say that, as far as we can see, Mesopotamian reed pipes belonged in the family of oboes. Actual reed pipes have been preserved; the University Museum in Philadelphia possesses two slender silver tubes with four fingerholes each, which without any doubt have formed a pair similar to the many double oboes found and depicted in ancient Egypt. As they were excavated from the royal cemetery at Ur, their approximate date is 2800 B.C.; that is, thirteen hundred years before oboes first appeared in Egypt.

But it is not likely that they came to Egypt from Babylonia. From their distribution in antiquity, comprising the Mediterranean and the Near East, we conclude that oboes were created in the Semitic world, somewhere between Asia Minor and Arabia. This is confirmed by their Mesopotamian names. Instead of a Sumerian term adapted to Akkadian, the oboe had the Semitic name *ḥalḥallatu*, equivalent to Hebrew *ḥalîl;* written with Babylonian wedges, this word was read *šem* in Sumerian (which possibly has survived in *šemšal*, the name given to the oboe by the Kurds, the nomadic heirs of Mesopotamia). Both the Akkadian and the Sumerian names were written with the metal determinative, indicating that cane had generally been supplanted by some metal, as with the two silver pipes in the University

Museum in Philadelphia. A second name, *imbubu* or *ebubu*, used in a text from Assur written about 800 B.C., is Semitic as well and corresponds to Hebrew and Syriac *abûb*. The names may have been synonyms, as Talmudian tractates asserted that *abûb* and *ḥalîl* in Hebrew designated the same instrument.

HORN AND TRUMPET. Several inscriptions of the Sumerian priest-king Gudea mention an instrument, *si-im*, alongside with the temple drums, a-lal and balag. As *si* (Akkadian *qarnu*) means 'horn,' and *im* 'wind,' there is little doubt that this was a blowing horn. One of the Carchemish reliefs in the British Museum, dating from about 1250 B.C., depicts a rather short and thick horn played together with a large frame drum which, as we shall see, corresponds either to the a-lal or to the balag.

From Gudea's time on, the *si* is occasionally mentioned; some texts add the metal determinative and some refer to horns made of gold. This does not necessarily mean solid gold; an inventory of the presents offered by King Tushratta to King Amenophis IV of Egypt, about 1400 B.C., contains a specified list of forty horns, all covered with gold and some studded with precious stones. Seventeen of them are expressly called ox horns; whether the rest were trumpets of the usual straight shape is uncertain but not probable, as straight trumpets were more often made of gold than covered with it.

Straight trumpets are depicted as late as the Assyrian epoch; soldiers play them.

No straight or curved tubular trumpets have been preserved, but an Assyrian shell, a *tritonium variegatum* in the British Museum, has been identified by Dr. F. W. Galpin as an end-blown shell trumpet.

DRUMS. Literary sources give at least twelve Sumerian words with their Akkadian equivalents which must be supposed to designate drums; some on account of the added determinative *kuš* or *šu*, 'skin,' as *lilis, mesi, su gu galli* and *ub*; some for other reasons, as *a-lal, balag* (formerly misinterpreted as a lyre), *balag-du, balag-lul, dub, ub-tur, ub-zabar* and *a-da-pa*.

Some of these names are more or less anonymous; *ub* equals *lilis*; the term *dub* shares its ideogram with *balag* and therefore seems to be another name of the same object; *mesi* equals *a-da-pa*. Thus the number of terms is reduced to nine. If we take out *balag-di, balag-lul, ub-tur, ub-zabar* as composite terms which probably mean nothing but varieties in shape or size, we arrive at five types. Finally, *su gu galli,* signifying 'the great bull's hide,' is obviously a poetic circumlocution and can be disregarded. This leaves no more than four drums to be identified.

Mesopotamian art works also show four, or perhaps five, types of drums. On an early vase from Bismya in the Istanbul Museum (c. 3000 B.C.), the third man in a procession, marching behind two harpists, seems to strike a rectangular frame drum squeezed under his left arm. But the object is not distinct enough to admit an authoritative interpretation. Apart from this doubtful frame drum, Mesopotamian art works show: 1) shallow or frame drums of all sizes; 2) a small cylindrical drum held in a horizontal position; 3) a large footed drum; and 4) a small drum with one head, carried vertically on a belt and struck with both hands.

Only one of them appears on Sumerian art works of the third millennium B.C.—a gigantic drum which, standing on its side on the ground, reached up to the player's neck or his face; that is, the skin was from five to six feet wide. It was indeed *su gu galli,* 'the great bull's hide.' Big nails projected round about the circular head and the skins were nailed, as they are today in the Far East. In one case, on a green steatite vase in the Louvre, a small figure is set on the top of the drum, a rather unusual detail. (pls. IV b, c)

In all cases two men strike simultaneously; this does not often occur elsewhere. They each strike on both sides; the drums must have had two skins.

The ancient artists did not represent either the second skin or the solid body which held the two skins together, and one is at a loss to know whether these instruments were frame drums, barrel drums or what. This question, however, can be settled. A barrel is usually at least as high as it is wide, which in this case was six feet. No player would be able to strike both skins of such a giant at once. Besides, the sculptors and painters of Sumer and Egypt represented their objects from their most characteristic side, regardless of perspective: a man's head in profile, his trunk in full face, his legs in profile. Thus, a barrel-shaped drum would show its barrel, as it does in archaic Chinese sculpture—not its circular head; a frame drum, on the contrary, would be drawn as a circular head since its profile is a meaningless strip.

Still, frame drums six feet wide are unknown. Two skins as large as that, properly stretched and vigorously struck, would demand a resistance that a simple frame could not afford.

There is a third possibility, besides the barrel and the frame drum.

All features of this drum point to East Asia. The East is the only part of the world in which such gigantic sizes have been made; in some Confucian temples of China drums, apparently barrel-shaped, are six feet wide like the Sumerian drum, and the same is true of the Japanese barrel drum, *da daiko*. Again, nailed heads are specifically East Asiatic. A small figure, set on top of a drum, occurs exclusively in Japan. The Metropolitan Museum of Art in New York displays in its musical gallery a beautiful cloisonné *o daiko* surmounted by a cock. Finally, combined efforts of two players on the same drum have parallels with the Korean *kyo pang ko* and *mu ko*, and with the ancient Chinese war drum, *kao*. Such analogies are not mere coincidences. The Sumerians had come from the east, and the Japanese from the west; it is not surprising that they should have shared certain cultural features.

Thus, we feel entitled to conclude that the unknown profile of the Sumerian drum resembled that of the ancient Far Eastern drums. In Japan, which in general has preserved more archaic forms than China, barrel drums are practically nonexistent, while they are usual in China. Instead, the Japanese have an intermediate type between the barrel and the frame drum that we call a *shallow drum*. It has a broad frame bulging like a barrel and it is much shorter than it is wide. The oldest Sumerian drum may have been a shallow drum.

What was the name of this drum? Contemporaneous Sumerian texts mention the terms *a-lal*, *balag* and *balag-di*. Which is the right one?

The literary sources do not describe the shape of any of these drums. To begin with the best-known name, *balag*, we learn that it came from a verb *bal*, 'to beat,' and that its Akkadian equivalent was *balaggu*. A second significance of *balag* is variously translated as 'gladness, joyful noise,' or as 'cry, howl.' This drum was used in the temple of the god Ea, or En-Ki, who ruled water, exorcism and divination, and a special officer had to guard the sacred instrument, as is the custom in several East African tribes (cf. page 35). Its sound, compared with "a bull's voice" in contemporaneous sources, accompanied ritual songs, summoned the sleeping god and was connected with divination, like the Lapponic drum.

On one of Gudea's statues we read: "The balag (called) *nin-an-da-gal-ki* he prepared, and in its great forecourt set it up." An inscription on one of Gudea's cylinders relates that he "put in readiness . . . his beloved balag, *ushumgal-kalam-ma*, an instrument making soothing music, (contributing) something to his counsels," and another: "In the holy place was its balag which sounded (like) a bellowing bull." Two individual balags are mentioned: *nin-an-da-gal-ki* and *ushumgal-kalam-ma*. Every balag had a proper name, and so important was the individual instrument that the Sumerians, who instead of counting the years named them by their chief event, called a certain year in Gudea's time "the year in which the balag *ushumgal-kalam-ma* was erected."

A second drum, formerly interpreted as a cymbal, was the *a-lal* (Akkadian *alû*). The etymology of this name may be 'hand-stretch.' In some respects the a-lal was related with the balag; its place was likewise in the forecourt of the temple and in one text, dating about 2200 B.C., one reads that ten measures of meal were allotted to it (the same supposed necessity for food that is connected with the rites of drum worship in East Africa). Gudea made it "roar like a storm" when it played with the flute; but it was also the companion of the horn.

A drum accompanying a short horn is depicted on a relief from Carchemish (c. 1250) in the British Museum. Like the drums described above, it is represented as a circle with nails around it, and two men strike it with bare hands. But it is smaller, approximately a yard or a meter wide, and certainly lighter; instead of standing on the ground, it is carried by a third man. No conclusion is admissible, as the Gudea texts in which the word *a-lal* is mentioned and the Carchemish relief are about twelve hundred years apart.

Statuettes of women playing smaller frame drums with their bare hands are roughly dated 2000 B.C. by archaeologists. It is not hazardous to give the third term *balag-di* to these drums. Its Akkadian equivalent, *ṭimbūtu*, or *ṭibbū*, has 'ring' as first significance. One Sumerian text related that a king's granddaughter was appointed player of the drum balag-di in the temple of the Moon in Ur about 2400 B.C. Women in the Near East used frame drums in rites connected with the worship of the moon. Moreover, the radicals of the Akkadian name occur again in the Tamil name of frame drums, *tambaṭṭam*.

While the Sumerian drum obviously belonged in the East and Central Asiatic culture area, the small, probably double-headed, frame drum of the Babylonian era was of Semitic origin. This would be confirmed by the names. There was not a Sumerian word adapted to Semitic phonetics, as with *balag* and *a-lal*; it was, with a new instrument, a new Semitic name, for which the priests modeled a Sumerian equivalent after an older Sumerian word. (pl. IV e)

A clay statuette in the British Museum, also dated about 2000 B.C., represents the player of a small, elongated drum, horizontally suspended from the belt and struck with the bare hands on either side. The Assyrians had small cylindrical or thimble-shaped drums about a foot high, vertically suspended from the players' belts, with single-nailed heads that the men struck with their bare hands. We dare not attribute Sumerian or Akkadian names to these drums.

At last, after so much induction, not to say guesswork, we come to one drum that is labeled with its proper name. On a late Babylonian seal the term *lilis,* frequently mentioned in literary sources, is carved above the figure of a drum. The same type of drum is once more represented on an earlier Babylonian plaque dating about 1100 B.C. Standing on the ground, it reaches up to the belt of the player and may be a yard high. It has the shape of a stout goblet, with a flat foot, a short stem and a large cup. The wide opening is covered with a skin, the fastening of which is not distinctly depicted; the player apparently strikes it with the bare hands. Such foot drums are used in East Africa to this day; but unlike the wooden drums of Africa, the Sumerian drum was made of metal, as its metal determinative indicated.

The instrument was used to raise lamentations of grief and weeping for the darkened moon, and it was worshiped, like the a-lal and the balag. One of its rituals is described in detail in an Akkadian text which has been translated into French by François Thureau-Dangin. From this translation Dr. Galpin has made an English abstract:

A bull without defect, black in color and untouched by stick or whip was selected; if spotted with seven groups of white spots in star-form, it was unsuitable. The animal was brought to the 'House of Knowledge' (the temple) on a propitious day and offerings were made to the great Gods and especially to Lumḫa (Ea), God of Music and Wisdom. A reed mat was placed on the ground and covered with sand: on it the animal was held. More offerings were made and perfumes burnt. A torch was then lighted and the bull was singed. Twelve linen cloths were laid on the ground and twelve bronze images of the Gods of Heaven, Earth and the Underworld placed upon them. Sacrifices were made and the body or bowl of the drum was set in its place. The animal's mouth was washed and, by means of a tube of aromatic reed, incantations were whispered into its ears explaining, in dialectical Sumerian, the honor which was about to be done to the bull by its divine use. A hymn was next chanted to the accompaniment of the double reed-pipe. The bull was then slain, its heart burnt, and the body, after it had been skinned, wrapped in a red cloth. The skin was treated with fine flour, beer, wine, grease, Hittite alum and gall-nut.

We must add that the twelve bronze images of gods were laid inside the drum before it was covered.

All at once we are carried back to the sphere of the East African rites connected with drums, which are described in the first chapter of this book. When modern anthropologists weigh the possibility of the descent of the present East African monarchies from ancient Mesopotamia, they must not forget the drum rituals and the goblet shape of the lilis.

To sum up, we hope that we are closer to truth than our predecessors in matching the Sumerian and Akkadian terms with the drums represented on art works. But we are by no means certain of all of these conclusions. Moreover, there is the likelihood of a variation in the terms over a period of three thousand years. Perhaps we are in the position of a scholar five thousand years from today endeavoring to find out the difference between the French terms *tambour* and *caisse*.

LYRES. While most stringed instruments have a body and a neck, lyres have, instead of a neck, a yoke-shaped frame consisting of two arms and a crossbar that projects from the upper side of the body. The strings are stretched over the frontal soundboard and are fastened to the crossbar.

Experience shows that in a primitive stage portable instruments are generally preceded by larger and heavier types. This is also true of the lyre. This instrument is first depicted on Sumerian art works about 3000 B.C., as resting on the ground and standing higher than a seated man. The three precious lyres in the British Museum and the museums in Philadelphia and Baghdad, all of them excavated from the royal cemetery at Ur, measure a hundred and six, a hundred and sixteen and a hundred and twenty centimeters. As a consequence, Sumerian lyres preserved a strictly vertical position, even when they were carried in the players' arms. (pls. III, IV a)

All Sumerian lyres were asymmetrical, with the shorter arm of the yoke held next to the player and the longer arm away from the player. One has the feeling that the direction of the lyre is outwards, projecting away from the player, and this feeling is accentuated by the fact that frequently a carved bull's head, or a stag, juts out from the outer end of the body. The outer arm of the yoke often looks out of place, as if it were added merely to keep the crossbar from collapsing, instead of being an organic part of the structure. It sometimes even interferes with the carved figure. One of the lyres from Ur, in the University Museum in Philadelphia, could easily be an arched harp; neither the crossbar nor the second arm appear to be essential parts of the structure. (pl. III b)

The strings, eight or eleven in number, were tightened in the same way in which modern Ethiopians secure their lyre strings; they were twisted round about the crossbar and knotted, and could be tightened by means of small pieces of wood wedged into the twisted strings.

The strings were plucked with both hands, without a plectron, similar to the way in which a harp was played.

This archaic lyre did not survive the Sumerian epoch. Later lyres in Mesopotamia, apparently coming from Syria, were smaller and light. The players carried them aslant, the upper end pointing away, and plucked the strings with a plectron, scratching over all strings at once while the fingers of the left hand plucked, or deadened, those which should not be heard in the manner that will be discussed in the Greek chapter.

HARPS have the plane of the strings vertical, not parallel, to the soundboard. As to the outer form, there are two main types: the *arched harp*, in which the body is elongated at one end into a curved neck, together forming an arch; and an *angular harp*, in which the body and the neck form an angle.

Mesopotamian harps are so many and so varied that it is difficult to classify them. We find arched and angular harps, with the strings either in vertical or in horizontal position, plucked either with or without a plectron. How can one put order in this multiformity?

The horizontal harp always seems to have been plucked with a plectron, while the stretched fingers of the left hand deadened those strings which were not to sound. This manner of playing will be described in the Greek chapter. The vertical harp, on the contrary, was plucked by the bare fingers of both hands.

Do the horizontal and the vertical positions depend upon the manner of plucking? Drawing the plectron roughly over all strings is easier in a horizontal position with the strings above each other. This is the argument used by Dr. Marcelle Duchesne-Guillemin in trying to establish a classification and genealogy of the Mesopotamian harps on the basis of their playing style. Her article is an excellent piece of work, in spite of several weak points in her argument, and the author feels particularly indebted to her for having suggested a new working basis.

The first fact to be noted is that Sumer had only arched harps, and that no arched harp has been found in Mesopotamia after the Sumerian epoch. It was superseded by the angular harp at about 2000 B.C.

Since there is no doubt that the arched harp had come from the musical bow, the *vertical arched harp,* which in shape and playing position most nearly resembles the musical bow, must necessarily be the earliest. The arch that it forms is rather shallow and evenly curved; the body can scarcely be distinguished from the stick that forms the neck; and the position in which it is held, vertical with the strings facing outward, is exactly the position in which a musical bow is held. Such harps are depicted on two remarkable pieces in American museums, a stone slab from Khafage (c. 3000 B.C.) in the Oriental Institute of the University of Chicago, and an archaic seal from Ur (c. 2800 B.C.) in the University Museum, Philadelphia.

Of the *horizontal arched harp* we know only four, provided that the beautifully inlaid harp from Ur in the British Museum belongs in this type. Unfortunately, its incorrect restoration does not allow visitors to see its proper form. So we are certain only of three—the two instruments figured on the noted vase from Bismya in South Babylonia (c. 3000 B.C.) in the Museum at Istanbul, and a third one on a clay plaque from Ashnunaq in the Louvre (c. 2000 B.C.). The Bismya harps differ greatly from the musical bow. The harp is more curved than any bow; the body is wide at the base and tapers to a point at the top, thus forming a triangle; and the position in which it is held is entirely different from that of the musical bow, as the strings face the player and the arched stick is held away from him.

We do not offer any explanation for the transformation that had taken place in the harp by the time of the Ashnunaq plaque. The sculptor depicts a late form of the old horizontal arched harp. Its general arrangement does not differ from the structure of the Bismya harp, except that its neck, instead of being curved, is nearly straight. A second clay plaque in the Louvre, from the same place and period, depicts a harp with an improved arrangement. The body is elongated, and at its end a vertical stick is erected at right angles so that there is space for a greater number of strings, and the body is more efficient. This is a true *horizontal angular harp.* A con-

A. Lyre-player entertaining the guests. From a Sumerian mosaic in the University Museum, Philadelphia.

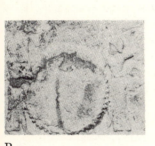

B

C

D

B. C. Gigantic drum; the arm with the stick (right) is not original. Sumer.

D. Horizontal· angular harp, c. 2000 B.C., Nippur.

UNIVERSITY MUSEUM, PHILADELPHIA

E

F

G

E. Hettite drummer, Berlin Museum.

F. Hettite lutanist (no bagpipe), from Eyuk.

G. Lutanist, Mitanni, Berlin Museum.

PLATE IV.

temporaneous clay plaque from Nippur, in the University Museum in Philadelphia, indicates that this second harp was not a single instance. (pl. IV d)

Although a conscientious observer would hesitate to assume the presence of a plectron similar to that used with a lyre on the vase depicting the two Bismya harps, there is scarcely any doubt, despite the rude work in terra cotta, that the three latter harps are being played this way.

Thirteen or fourteen hundred years later, the slender long plectron and the deadening left hand are clearly pictured on Assyrian stone reliefs in the British Museum. The sculptor represents angular harps held in horizontal position with the same body that the earlier harps had, though in a greatly improved arrangement. The stick holding the strings, instead of being erected vertically at the end of the body of the harp, has been shifted inwards and stands a span away from the end. Thus, it has become a bridge that communicates its vibrations to the soundboard.

This final stage persisted until the beginning of our era; an identical specimen, in the Antiquarium of the Berlin Staatsmuseum, was excavated from a Sarmatian tomb in the Crimea. The Sarmates were Iranians, and this fact is worth mentioning for the following reason. Exactly the same instrument is depicted on an Assyrian relief in the British Museum that represents the Elamic, that is, the Iranian court orchestra welcoming the Assyrian conqueror in 650 B.C. Thus, this final stage was possibly reached in Iran rather than in Assyria.

The vertical angular harp has no direct relation to this final stage of the horizontal angular harp, since its neck does not form a bridge. The body of the harp rises close to the player's chest; the stringholder pierces the lower end of the body of the harp and sticks not quite at right angles from it, so that the strings face away from the player.

Differently held, with the body of the harp at the bottom and the strings facing upwards, it would be an angular horizontal harp.

The question is, then, whether the vertical angular harp came from the horizontal angular harp or vice versa. The following fact might help to answer it. On one of the Ashnunaq plaques the strings are concentrated near the body to a surprising degree, while half of the stick is empty and useless. This squandering would have been unexplainable unless the horizontal harp was an overturned vertical harp in which the normally distant strings had to be crowded together in order to facilitate drawing the plectron roughly over the strings. In consequence, it seems that, contrary to Dr. Duchesne-Guillemin's opinion, the vertical angular harp was earlier than the horizontal harp.

How were these harps tuned and how were they played?

An important relief already mentioned, in the British Museum, represents the Elamic court orchestra welcoming the Assyrian conqueror in 650 B.C. Its seven harpists are identically depicted, except that they are plucking different strings. As the style is realistic, indeed almost photographic, this cannot be accidental; the variety in that one point cannot be explained by any consideration for design. Each harpist plucks two strings, but the only strings plucked are the fifth, eighth, tenth, fifteenth and eighteenth of the set. If the instruments, as it is likely to suppose, were tuned to a pentatonic scale —say on *C*, without half-tones—the plucked notes were *A e a e' a' e''*, that is, a fifth chord orchestrated in the modern way, the two notes being distributed among the seven players in different combinations, as double octave, octave, unison and fifth:

first	harpist:	*A-e''*
second	harpist:	*e-e'*
third	harpist:	*e'-e''*
fourth	harpist:	*e'-e'*
fifth	harpist:	*a'-e''*
sixth	harpist:	*a'-e''*
seventh	harpist:	*(a)-e'*

This interpretation seems to indicate three conclusions: that the pentatonic scale, which is the only one to give the picture such musical sense, was used in tuning Iranian harps; that the various instruments of an orchestra played different parts; and that musicians knew the use of chords. These chords corresponded to the two kinds of accompaniment of a melody that Greek authors such as Longinus or Thrasyllus later on specified as *sýmphona kat'antíphonon* or octave and double octave, and *sýmphona katà paráphonon* or fifth and fourth.

LUTES, the ancestors of most modern stringed instruments, including our violin, first appear on Mesopotamian figurines, plaques and seals from about 2000 B.C. They had very small bodies, long necks with many frets, two strings attached without pegs and were played with a plectron. The Greeks called a similar lute *pandura*, and this word was almost surely derived from Sumerian *pan-tur*, 'bow-small,' thus indicating an origin in the musical bow which can be shown to be very probable. The honor of having invented the lute was awarded to the Assyrians by Pollux; but others attributed it to the Cappadocians, or even to the Egyptians. The hypothesis of an Egyptian origin can be eliminated; it is due to a temporary fashion in Greece of attributing all imaginable things, and music itself, to the romantic land of Pharaoh. Assyria and Cappadocia do not exclude each other; about 2000 B.C., Cappadocia was influenced and controlled by Assyria. It seems likely that the Assyrians adopted the lute from the Cappadocians, because the lute is entirely lacking in Assyrian temple ceremonies and was, therefore, probably a popular instrument; it is depicted several times with a shepherd. If the lute came to Cappadocia from Assyria, then the Greeks probably took the name *pandura* rather from Cappadocia or some neighboring country than from the Sumerian language, which was already extinct. The old Sumerian name of the lute still exists in Georgian as *panturi;* in other words, this term, like so many Sumerian words, was exported at a time when Sumerian was still spoken, and the Greeks did not obtain it directly from the Sumerians, but from some people in or near the Caucasus. (pl. IV f, g)

KING NEBUCHADREZZAR'S ORCHESTRA. The music of the last Babylonian empire is referred to in a single sentence in the Bible, and a very unusual one. The sentence occurs four times, in the verses five, seven, ten and fifteen of the third chapter of the Book of Daniel. This book is not written in Hebrew, but in Aramaic, and was certainly penned four hundred years later than the events it records; Daniel and the Babylonian King Nebuchadrezzar lived in the first half of the sixth century B.C., and the Aramaic text dates from about 165 B.C. As this was an epoch of Hellenistic culture, some terms are influenced by Greek words. The sentence reads:

"As soon as you hear the sound of the *qarnā,* the *mašroqītâ,* the *qatros,* the *sabka,* the *psantrîn,* the *sūmponiâh,* and all kinds of *zmārâ,* you shall prostrate yourselves. . . ."

It is not difficult to interpret the first five terms: *qarnâ,* the emphatic form of qeren, means a trumpet or a horn; *mašroqītâ,* from a verb *šriqá,* 'whistling,' designates any form of pipe, probably a double oboe; *qatros* corresponds to Greek *kithara;* and *psantrîn* to Greek *psaltêrion,* the name of the vertical angular harp.

Sabka is the Greek *sambýkē,* Latin *sambuca.* Both terms have an identical second significance; they designate a machine of siege used in war, which was said to share its form with the musical instrument of the same name. This machine is described as a boat with an upright ladder. The only instrument which perfectly corresponds to this form is the horizontal angular harp that has been described in the present chapter. It has the narrow, boat-shaped body in a horizontal position, and an upright stringholder upon it, the lateral knobs of which give it a ladderlike appearance. As this instrument is genuinely Mesopotamian or Iranian, it can very probably be identified with the sabka.

Finally, there is the term *sūmponiāh*. Though there is no doubt that it is derived from Greek *symphōneia*, its meaning has been much contested. It is not worth while repeating once more all the erroneous and arbitrary translations given to this word in nearly two thousand years. The most stubborn of them, 'bagpipe,' was particularly inadequate since no bagpipe existed in those times.

The question is difficult because the Greek word never designated an instrument at all; it signified 'simultaneous sound,' 'playing together,' 'orchestra,' 'band.' The Authorized Version, therefore, is correct when, in the parable of the lost son, fifteenth chapter of Luke, verse twenty-five, it renders the word by *musick:* "Now his elder son was in the field: and as he came and drew nigh to the house, he heard musick and dancing." Even the four passages in the *Deipnosophistae*, in which the Greek Athenaeus quotes the historian Polybius (c. 210–c. 127 B.C.) on the life of King Antiochus Epiphanes of Syria, are inconclusive and do not prove that *symphonia* was an instrument.

About 600 A.D. a learned Spaniard, St. Isidore of Seville, connected it for the first time with a special instrument. In his *Originum seu etymologiarum libri XX*, he defined *symphonia* as a hollow wood covered at either end with a stretched skin, which musicians struck on both sides with sticks. And a sweet sound is brought forth by the concord of a low and a high note: *Symphonia vulgo appellatur lignum cavum ex utraque parte pelle extenta quam virgulis hinc et inde musici feriunt. Fitque in ea ex concordia gravis et acuti suavissimus cantus.*

Thus, the *sūmponiāh* might be interpreted as a drum with two skins of different diameter and pitch, if one insisted that the Aramaic word meant a single instrument. But it would be hazardous to follow a single source written about seven hundred and fifty years later in a foreign country, and to neglect the other sources of earlier, contemporaneous and later times, which agree in calling symphonia a band, not an instrument.

It was a real progress when a commentator on Daniel, Dr. E. B. Pusey, doubted whether the word referred to an instrument at all, and Dr. Francis W. Galpin, coming to the same conclusion, explained it as an ensemble, a "full consort." The passage in Daniel then would mean: "As soon as you hear the sound of the horn, the pipes, the lyre, the horizontal and the vertical harp, the full consort and all kinds of instruments . . ."

But it would be unusual to enumerate separately the instruments of an orchestra and then add the orchestra itself; we would not describe a military band, for example, as flutes, saxophones, trombones, tubas, drums and their ensemble.

Though meaningless from an occidental point of view, such a description is significant when we know the practice of oriental music. If we accept the Aramaic text word for word, the king's subjects heard the various instruments first singly and then all together. And this is exactly the manner of orchestra playing in the Near East. A flourish on a horn or trumpet may attract attention. Then the performance begins. Several leading instruments out of the band display, in an improvised solo performance called *taqsîm* in Arabic, the *maqâm* or melodic pattern of the piece, each one according to the nature and technique of his instrument. After them the full ensemble joins in with either a short ritornello or a longer symphony. In addition to the melodic solo instruments which are admitted to a *taqsîm*, this ensemble comprises drums and other instruments of a merely rhythmical character. It would be appropriate to call them "all kinds of *zmârâ*" or instruments, in the words of the Book of Daniel.

Thus, a literal translation of the Aramaic text suggests the picture of a horn signal, followed by solos of oboe, lyre and harp, and a full ensemble of these and some rhythmical instruments. It does not describe an orchestra, but an orchestral performance in the ancient Near East.

4. *Egypt*

RECENT excavations from Sumerian cemeteries and temples have disclosed so many objects similar to those found in Egypt that the hypothesis that there was a prehistoric contact between the two great civilizations is unavoidable. Their relation is particularly noticeable in music; the so-called Old Kingdom (2900–2475 B.C.) had not one instrument that did not exist in Sumer simultaneously, or even earlier.

The contact between the two nations must, however, have come to an end before 2700 B.C., as the lyre had an outstanding role in Sumerian ceremonies about that time, although it was still unknown in Egypt. Nearly eight hundred years elapsed before an Egyptian painter depicted a passage of Semitic nomads coming down to Egypt with their families and belongings, and among them a man playing the lyre—the first lyre recorded in the vicinity of the Nile. (pl. VI b)

We do not know whether this was a single importation. Presently the curtain fell over the Egyptian, as well as over the Babylonian, stage. There was a violent invasion of peoples from Central Asia, probably caused by a sudden change of climate; the Kassites conquered Mesopotamia and put an end to the Babylonian empire; Abraham, the patriarch of Israel, migrated from Ur in Babylonia to Canaan; the nomadic Hyksos entered Egypt and destroyed the civilization of the Middle Kingdom. During this long intermission we lose sight of the great monarchies; literary and pictorial evidences are scarce. When the curtain rises again, it unveils a vigorous invasion of the Egyptian armies eastward which renews the contact between Egypt and Mesopotamia. One would expect, as a consequence, an Egyptian influence on Asia; but the contrary is true. Once more the Asiatic civilization proved to have the dominant character, and Egypt underwent a strong influence from the east.

The influence, as far as music is concerned, is evident from the sudden appearance of many Asiatic instruments: vertical angular harps, lyres, lutes, oboes and trumpets, while the Egyptian flute and double clarinet disappear. Instruments rarely migrate without their players, and this fact is nowhere more clearly illustrated than in ancient Egypt. When Southwest Asia had been conquered by the pharaohs of the eighteenth dynasty (about 1500 B.C.), the subjugated kings sent singing- and dancing-girls with their instruments as a part of their tribute; in one painting we can see them busy practicing in a special harem in King Amenophis the IV's residence at Tell El-Amarna that the painter has left unroofed like a doll's house.

During the last fifteen hundred years B.C., the migration of instruments from western Asia to Egypt persisted. New types of harps and lyres enriched the musical stock of Egypt, and finally, in the Greek epoch, cymbals and castanets were introduced there. In those centuries the Near East came under the domination successively of the Persians, the Greeks and the Romans. As a consequence of the change of rulers and the cultural unification in various empires, the ancient world underwent a cosmopolitanism that destroyed the exclusively national character of musical instruments.

Research in Egyptian musical instruments is facilitated by two factors: the extreme aridity of the desert soil and the Egyptian belief in the magic power of painting and sculpture. Aridity has preserved hundreds of instruments from decomposition, and many musical scenes are depicted on tomb walls because Egyptians believed that pictorial reproductions of domestic life, of cooking, baking, harvesting, storing, eating, dancing, singing and playing, secured a similarly prosperous and pleasurable existence in the other life.

The philological sources are as rich as the archaeological ones. Egyptian art works are explained by short, naïve texts written between the human figures wherever an empty spot is left. "He is playing the harp," they read, or, "He is playing the flute." Thus, we know the authentic names of practically all Egyptian instruments.

CLAPPERS AND CONCUSSION-STICKS. The clapper is the first instrument that Egyptian sources record. Prehistoric vases made before 3000 B.C. figure female dancers playing or accompanied by clappers, both held in one hand (*one-handed clappers*). The instrument is carefully drawn; it consists of two sticks, bent like boomerangs, both held in one hand and clapped against one another. Sticks similar in shape are well known to anthropologists as missiles used in hunting. The Egyptian missile must have had the same form, since its hieroglyphic ideogram corresponded exactly to that of the prehistoric dance clapper. It is easy to find the link between them; Egyptian hunters approached the papyrus thickets on the Nile banks, clapped their missiles together to scare up the water birds and then hurled them after the soaring game.

This is one of the rare cases in which an implement with a prac-

FIGURE 29. Harvesters with concussion sticks, Egypt, 5th dynasty.

tical use is transformed into a musical instrument. We know a similar instance among the Cágaba in the Sierra Nevada of Colombia, who use the same sticks, made to chase birds from the crops, to accompany a magic dance against these birds. The author saw modern Egyptian farmers in 1930 chasing locusts from the fields in the same way.

Another magic dance insuring a good harvest is represented in an ancient Egyptian tomb of about 2700 B.C.: a file of rural workmen clap together short sticks held in both hands as they advance in those long, easy strides typical of fertility rites. (fig. 29)

A practical use for the rhythm made by percussion sticks is shown on reliefs made soon after 3000 B.C.: while the vintagers press the grapes with their feet, two other men are clapping the rhythm with their sticks, one held in each hand, to facilitate the tiring labor. This is an archaic example of work rhythm as a source of musical activity, the musical importance of which the sociologist Karl Bücher has so much exaggerated in his well-known book, *Arbeit und Rhythmus.*

Two-handed clappers were only depicted in these two instances. *One-handed clappers*, on the contrary, appeared constantly. They were made of wood, bone or ivory, and their heads were carved in the shape of human hands or heads of animals or men. Many are decorated with the head of Hathor, goddess of heaven, joy and death, and on a painting of about 1500 B.C. two women playing these clappers are described as "Glorifyers of the goddess Hathor, mistress of Déndera." The clapper seems to have been an instrument frequently used in the worship of Hathor, and probably every woman had her clapper to worship the goddess, as today every Catholic woman owns a rosary.

SISTRUM is the term generally adopted to designate a certain shaken instrument of Egypt; the Greek word *seîstron* means 'thing shaken.' The sistrum consisted of a handle and a frame with jingling crossbars. The *sistrata turba*, 'the sistrum-shaking crowd' of women, shook it when they worshiped the bovine goddess Hathor. Hathor later on metamorphosed into the maternal goddess Isis, the wife of Osiris, and as the peoples of the Roman Empire gradually lost their faith in the old gods, the joyful cult of Isis became popular in all parts of the Empire; thus, sistra were found as far away as France.

The sistrum was made in two different forms. One of them, called *sešĕšet*, was confined to Egypt; no specimen was found abroad. It is known to Egyptologists as *naos sistrum*, sistrum in the shape of a small temple or *naos*. The upper end is carved in the form of Hathor's head and supports the heavy frame, which looks like the front view of a small temple with a door. Holes on either side of the frame have jingling cross wires strung through them. Originally this implement did not have these wires and was a mute emblem; only later on was the jingling contrivance taken over from the other type of sistrum that the Egyptians called *iba* or *sehem*. (fig. 30)

This sistrum, generally made of metal, also had a handle, but instead of the massive naos a horseshoe-shaped frame with the closed end at the top. Through opposite holes in the sides of the horseshoe frame, two, three or four wires slipped back and forth in the loose holes and jingled when their bent ends touched the frame. During the Old and Middle Kingdoms small jingling disks were strung upon the wires to increase the noise; they were given up in the New Kingdom. Finer specimens had a rich, symbolic decoration which alluded to the ritual purposes of the instruments. The cross rods were given the head and the tail of a sacred snake; Isis with the horn of plenty and her son Horos might stand within the frame;

FIGURE 30.   Naos sistrum, Egypt.

a suckling cat with the moon disk on its head could be carved at the top; or a figure of Bes, the healing god, would serve as a handle.

VERTICAL FLUTES are first recorded on a prehistoric slate from Hieraconpolis (fourth millennium B.C.) on which a disguised hunter plays a flute to allure the game.

The Egyptian flute was a so-called vertical flute (*not* a transverse flute); the player held it slanting obliquely downwards and blew across the open upper end against the opposite, sharp edge. It shared the name *maˑt* or *māˑt* with both clarinets and oboes, the ending *t* indicating the feminine gender. Any other names given by previous writers to the Egyptian flute are erroneous.

Egyptian flutes are smaller than many primitive ceremonial flutes. Cut from a simple cane generally a yard long and half an inch wide, the Egyptian flute had from two to six fingerholes near the lower end; one excavated specimen was even provided with a thumb hole in the back.

This simple cane flute without a whistle head might be supposed to be older than whistle flutes, but it is not. Its comparatively small size enables the player to blow it without the aid of a mouthpiece. In primitive civilizations we find much larger flutes, whose size necessitates the use of a whistle head because the breath of the player is too weak to blow across so wide an opening.

Vertical flutes, such as the Egyptian flutes, had greater musical possibilities than the whistle flutes. Being able to vary the angle of blowing against the edge, the player could give more expression to the tone; no instrument had a more incorporeal sound, a sweeter *sostenuto*, a more heartfelt *vibrato*.

The flute, with its characteristic quality, still exists today all over the Islamic world. It is best known under its Persian name *nāy*, which has replaced the arabic name *qaṣaba* or *quṣṣāba*, except in the western part of North Africa.

DOUBLE CLARINETS. Clarinets are tubes closed at the upper end. Near this end there is a small lateral opening or breath hole, which is covered by a tongue. When the breath sets this tongue in vibration, it opens and closes the passage in a rapid alternation and divides the air current into pulsations. The tongue is so devised that it overlaps the opening and thus never passes through the opening when it vibrates. Acoustically, this style of tongue is known as a *single beating reed*.

Primitive Egyptian clarinets were made of cane. The breath hole was made by a three-sided slit cut into the cane forming a rectangular tongue, the fourth uncut side allowing the tongue to vibrate because of the elasticity of the material. Thus the simple device of slitting the cane formed both the mouth-hole and the tongue, which in later clarinets were much more elaborately devised. Since the slit is cut obliquely, instead of squarely, through the side of the cane, the sharp edge of the tongue overlaps the opening.

The upper end with the vibrating reed is held entirely within the player's mouth. As in glass blowing, breathing is exclusively through the nose, while the mouth emits a constant blast of air. Modification of timbre and force is not possible with this kind of blowing; the sound is emitted with unaltering strength and shrillness. Players of the modern Sardinian triple clarinet, *launedda*, train their pupils in this difficult technique by means of a straw and a vessel filled with water; dipping the straw and blowing, the boy has to keep blowing while he is breathing in and out; if the water stops gurgling, the teacher gives him a box on the ear. The author was told at Cairo that Egyptian oboe players are trained in the same way.

The origin of the clarinet is unknown. It has been found in primitive civilizations, but only in recent layers, and the question of whether it migrated from lower to higher civilizations, or from higher to lower ones, is not yet decided. When the clarinet first appeared in the higher civilizations, it was in the form of the *double clarinet*.

More complicated than the vertical flute, the double clarinet is an even more exciting proof of the incredible perseverance of musical instruments. All over the Islamic Orient, from Egypt to the Celebes, low-caste musicians play a double clarinet made of two canes a foot long, glued and tied alongside one another and provided with equidistant, and symmetrically arranged, fingerholes, either four or five or six in each cane; in the upper ends smaller canes are inserted, out of which the beating tongue is cut by a three-sided slit described above. These double clarinets are best known under their Arabic name *zummâra*. The player stops the corresponding holes of both tubes simultaneously with one finger, and as the holes, roughly cut into an uneven cane, produce slightly different pitches, the effect is a pulsating sound such as in the modern occidental organ stop, *unda maris*.

Double clarinets of exactly the same shape have been excavated from Egyptian tombs of the first century B.C. Moreover, the author recognized this instrument on a relief known to be as early as 2700 B.C. in the Egyptian Museum in Cairo. Above the sitting player the sculptor has carved the text, "Is playing the mat," and added the unmistakable design of a double clarinet as a hieroglyphic determinative. This indicates that the instrument has existed for five thousand years without the slightest change.

THE ARCHED HARP was not quite as long-lived. The more highly an instrument is developed the more apt it is to be even more improved. The harp, depicted on many reliefs for a period of three thousand years and preserved in some excavated specimens, was indeed the most highly prized instrument of Egypt (in this resembling the Indian vina and the Chinese ch'in).

It was closely related to the Sumerian harp. But the question of whether it came from Sumer to Egypt, or from Egypt to Sumer, is not conclusively settled. The most reliable criterion in such a case is supplied by a geographical rule: if one meets identical phenomena on the outskirts of a country, or of a continent, but different phenomena in the center, the phenomena of the border are usually earlier. Now the area of distribution of the arched harp comprises the countries between Africa and Java, Sumer being in the center of that district. The harps on the border are differentiated from those in the center by an important characteristic. While in the central district, from Sumer to India, the strings are wound around the neck without any special fastening device, they were secured by knobs glued into the back of the stick in Egypt and Java. Strings fastened by knobs must be earlier than plain strings; therefore, the Egyptian harp probably came from Sumer, rather than the Sumerian harp from Egypt.

This seems hard to believe. We are far too accustomed to supposing that evolution goes from simple to complicated contrivances. Yet, the omission of knobs in the later harps can easily be explained. A string fastened around the wood without a knob is adjustable because the string can be pushed to a tighter or a looser position without being untied, whereas if the string is fastened to a stationary knob it has to be untied and retied in order to change the tension. With knobs, tuning is difficult; without knobs, it is simple. A harp with unturnable knobs is musically inferior to knobless harps.

Other features also of the earliest Egyptian harp were archaic. During the Old Kingdom the stick comprised the entire length of the instrument, as in the harp's ancestor, the musical bow; it even penetrated the body. This latter was circular and very small, resembling the gourd-resonator attached to the musical bow; the soundboard was a piece of skin.

Harps were 'vertical' in Egypt; the strings faced outward and the stick was next to the player. They generally stood on the ground and were played by a kneeling man. When in the New Kingdom they had grown higher and were provided with as many as nineteen strings, the player stood erect. The harp had long before left the primitive stage in which instruments generally developed from big sizes to smaller forms, and had entered a more civilized stage in which the need for augmenting its musical means involved a reverse process of development from small to large. The highest development of this instrument is exemplified by two gigantic harps which are depicted in the tomb of Rameses III (about 1200 B.C.). They are about two meters or nearly seven feet high and decorated with paintings and mosaics in many colors. It was these impressive harps that first gave musicologists an idea of the outstanding role of music in Egypt. An English traveler of the eighteenth century, James Bruce, saw them and had a drawing made of them, which he later handed over to historians of music. Eventually a copy of his picture was used to illustrate Johann Nicolaus Forkel's *Geschichte der Musik,* first volume, Leipzig, 1788. The eighteenth century draftsman transformed the large crowned head of a sphinx upon the resonance box into the small statue of an entire sphinx; he gave the neck the S shape of modern harps and decorated it with scrolls in a late rococo style; he omitted the pegs and misrepresented the construction as a whole. Such an experience should put scholars on their guard against illustrations in prephotographic publications. (pl. VI c)

As well as the large erect harp, the Egyptians of the New Kingdom had a smaller *footed harp* that rested partly on a slanting leg,
partly on the knees of the seated harpist. A crossbar connecting the
leg with the body of the harp frequently was carved in the shape of
a symbol of Isis or Osiris.

A third form, found in the Middle and the New Kingdoms, was
the small *shoulder harp* in the shape of a shallow arch; it had from
three to five strings only and was borne on the left shoulder and
played with the arms gracefully lifted. As its neck projected, not
from the front, but from the back of the body, it may have been

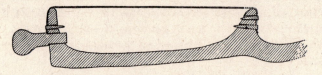

FIGURE 31. Egyptian shoulder harp, section.

related to the strange *bow-lute* of West African Negroes, in which
each string was stretched by a separate flexible rod projecting from
the back of the body. (pl. V a, fig. 31')

The harp was exclusively played by men during the Old Kingdom; later on women were harpists as well, but they played most
the footed harp and the shoulder harp, and rarely the traditional,
older harp that stood on the ground.

The Egyptian name of the harp was *bīn·t*, the letter *t* being the
feminine ending. Probably an *i*, which, as a short vowel, was not
written, followed the *n* in pronunciation; for Flavius Josephus calls
the Egyptian harp by the name *tò buní*. A mistake has caused later
writers to attach the Greek article *to* to the noun; this was the origin
of the erroneous term *tebuni* given to the Egyptian harp by so many
music historians of the nineteenth century. In an earlier book the
author has shown that the Egyptian name *bīn·t* was probably identical with the well-known name *bīn* in Hindustani, and *vīṇā* in
Sanscrit, given to several stringed instruments of India.

We showed in another publication that out of seventeen harpists
represented on Egyptian art works with sufficient realism and distinctness to be reliable records, seven are striking a fourth chord,
five a fifth chord, and five an octave chord; that is, taking for granted
that the accordatura was pentatonic without semitones, because the
assumption of a heptatonic tuning does not make any sense.

Both the pentatonic accordatura and the frequent use of simultaneous consonances are indicated by similar evidences in Iran and
Assyria.

Moreover, the pentatonic tuning is corroborated by the passage
from Flavius Josephus quoted above. There, the Egyptian harp is
called "an enharmonic triangular instrument," *órganon trigōnon
enarmónion,* used by "temple musicians," *hieropsáltai.* The Greek
term 'enharmonic' had two different, indeed opposite, meanings.
The so-called later enharmony consisted in dividing the fourth or
tetrachord into a major third and two quarter-tones; this strange
scale is out of the question in tuning a harp. But another, earlier
scale, also called enharmonic and attributed to the piper Olympus
(about 700 B.C.), was made by omitting the notes F and C in the
Dorian and Phrygian modes. It was a pentatonic scale without half-
tones.

THE ANGULAR HARP. A vertical angular harp of Assyrian
type is accompanied by the harp name *bint* in an Egyptian inscription of the Greek epoch. Thus, it is certain that this name was given
to the angular harp as well.

The angular harp in Egypt came from Asia; it first appears on
art works representing Asiatic musicians. Three nearly identical
specimens from a more recent epoch have been preserved. One is
displayed in the Egyptian department of the Metropolitan Museum
of Art in New York; a second one can be seen in the Louvre, though
displayed upside down; a third one was bought in Cairo by the
author of this book for the Museum of Musical Instruments in
Berlin. A famous relief in the museum in Alexandria, made in
Heliopolis about 500 B.C., shows a similar harp in use and affords
the only possibility of dating the three preserved specimens.

All of them have an upright, narrow body in one piece, with the
front open. It is slightly deeper at the upper than at the lower end.
This body is entirely sewn into a piece of leather, and the part of the
leather which covers the open front serves as a soundboard. Just
under the soundboard, forming its axis, there is a thin bar of wood
held in position by crosspieces and used as a stringholder. The outer
ends of the strings are fastened to a round stick, projecting at an
acute angle from the lower end of the body. This stick, piercing the
body, rests on the lap of the seated player while the body is held up
against his chest, the strings facing outwards. Sometimes the player
stands, supporting the stick between her legs. The strings, number-

ing twenty-one, twenty-two or twenty-three, are tied to cords, which in turn are tied around the stick and kept in position by unturnable knobs of alternately clear and dark color. The strings end in ornamental tassels hanging down from the stick.

DRUMS. One of the most surprising facts in the history of Egyptian music is the complete absence of drums until about 2000 B.C. Drums might have existed before then without being depicted on art works. But even if we admit this vague possibility, the lack of any archaeological reference in a country so rich in realistic art documents would seem to prove that they did not exist. One can only suppose that Egyptian music was inspired by melodic impulses rather than by rhythm, just as it is nowadays.

Yet, there is one exception to prove the rule. A fragment from Ne-user-re's temple of the Sun (about 2700 B.C.) near Abusir, now in the Munich museum, shows the top of a large drum like the big temple drum mentioned in the Sumerian chapter and supposed to be identical with the instrument *a-lal*. As this instrument is unique in the Old Kingdom of Egypt, we suppose its existence is due to an importation from Sumer.

Nearly two thousand years later another drum scene appears on a relief from Osorkon II's festival hall in the great Bubastis temple; a frame drum, three or four feet in diameter, is carried on the shoulders of a porter and beaten by the bare hands of a second man. From the position of the player's right arm and the disappearance of his right hand behind the drum, one infers that the drum had two skins.

Cylindrical and barrel drums occur during the Middle and New Kingdoms. The Cairo museum owns a cylindrical drum which probably was made during the twelfth dynasty, 2000–1788 B.C.; it is sixty-five centimeters long and twenty-nine centimeters wide, and has a network of thongs with a tightening tourniquet to stretch the leather skins. A similar drum is still in use on the Congo.

Two later drums, in the Egyptian departments of the Metropolitan Museum of Art in New York and of the Louvre, are a foot long, stout and barrel-shaped. They are braced by a system of thongs looped through the skins, running parallel and very close together, and caught through two thongs which run around the body of the drum near each end. So many thongs were not necessary merely to tighten the skins, and probably served to protect the body of the drum as well. The necessity for protection seems to indicate that the drums originally were made of earthenware. Another circumstance

A

B

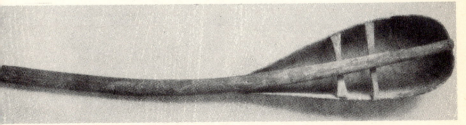

C

Egyptian stringed instruments, New Kingdom, in the Berlin Museum.
A. Shoulder harp. B. Lyre. C. Lute.

PLATE V.

which indicates that they were earthenware is that more recent Hindu drums, *khol* and *mādalā*, with similar thongs, are also made of earthenware. The drum in New York is composed of wooden staves cemented together, and this form may have been derived from an original clay drum strengthened by staves.

The New Kingdom also had barrel-shaped drums, but they were more elongated. All representations of barrel drums agree in two points: they were carried horizontally and struck on both skins with the bare hands.

Once more we are reminded of Indian drums by a relief of the late epoch, about 500 B.C., that depicts a woman playing a barrel drum of a double-conical shape tapering from a ridge in the middle to the smaller ends. This is the characteristic form of ancient Hindu drums, *khol, ḍholaka, mṛdaṅga* and *pakhavāja*. A trade route connected Egypt and India from early times.

The name, or one name, of the drum is ascertained by an inscription in the Great Temple at Karnak, in which the picture of a barrel drum is inscribed with the name *tbn* (vowels were not written in Egyptian). But this inscription belongs in the Greek epoch, and the word *tbn* is so closely related to Greek *týpanon* that the Karnak version is probably a hieroglyphic transcription of the Greek word rather than a genuine Egyptian name.

Small frame drums were more usual in the New Kingdom than either large frame drums or barrel drums. Most of them were circular, but some had four concave sides. Only women played them, but sometimes the god Bes is represented with the frame drum. This divinity was strongly associated with feminine activities in spite of his male sex; he was even supposed to attend at childbirth.

Some specimens of circular frame drums can be seen in more than one museum; the only known specimen of a rectangular frame drum has recently been excavated at Thebes by an expedition of the Metropolitan Museum headed by Mr. Ambrose Lansing, and preserved in the Cairo museum.

The frame drum, too, was given the Greek name *tbn*, while earlier inscriptions designated the frame drum as *śr*.

Harps and drums have already led us into the second epoch of Egyptian history, beginning with the New Kingdom and lasting until the Hellenistic Age.

FROM THE NEW KINGDOM TO THE GREEK EPOCH

In the fifteenth century B.C. the bellicose Pharaohs, Thutmosis and Amenophis, conquered the highly civilized Southwest of Asia. Manners and ideas were influenced, and music underwent a decisive change. Nearly all of the ancient instruments were discarded. The standing harp became larger and abounded in strings; several new types of harps were introduced; shrill oboes replaced the softer flutes; lyres, lutes and crackling drums were introduced from Asia. A new kind of noisy, stimulating music seems to have taken possession of the Egyptians, while the ancient music, nearly always composed of flutes and harps without drums and clappers, must have had a rather quiet character.

The completeness of this change is obvious when, in a museum of Egyptian art, one passes to the section of the New Kingdom. A relief, such as the funeral dance from Sakkara in the Cairo museum, with its crowd of whirling, straining women who strike their drums and crack the clappers in a frantic orgy, shows what music could be in the eighteenth dynasty. Even in chamber music, singers and players betray the tension which emphatic music induces in its performers. And the performers have greatly changed as well. Except for some blind harpists and playing priests who carry on the old tradition, they have lost the reserve and dignity which had been indicated in the reliefs and paintings between 3000 and 1500 B.C. Men are superseded by professional women, and one supposes that they have been professional prostitutes as well.

The most stirring among their new instruments was the oboe.

THE OBOE (*ma·t*) has a *double reed* to interrupt the player's breath. A double reed is made of two blades of cane, or tough grass, laid one on top of another. The lower ends bound together form a tube which is inserted into the upper end of the oboe. The upper ends are not bound together and, when looked at from the top, form a narrow oval opening. When the player takes the double reed into his mouth and blows, the opening is alternately closed and opened.

Oboes in Egypt were cut from a slender cane about two feet long and less than half an inch in diameter. They always were used in pairs, two of them being loosely held together in the mouth and blown simultaneously. The left one sounded a lower drone accompanying the melody produced by the right one. This drone playing can be inferred from three facts: the peculiar arrangement of the players' fingers on Egyptian art works; the present practice in other countries, India for example; the excavation of a pipe with all except one fingerhole stopped with wax.

The fingerholes of the Egyptian oboes, frequently four on the right and three on the left pipe, were the subject of some important research. Several scholars, François-Joseph Fétis, T. L. Southgate, Victor Loret, Victor-Charles Mahillon, tried to find out what kind of scale the Egyptians had by playing these oboes, or reproductions made of them. Their attempts were complete failures because they did not take into account some essential considerations. Pipes made of such delicate material, having been laid in the ground for thousands of years, and then stored in museums of a different climate, could not avoid shrinking. Even microscopic changes suffice to alter pitch and intervals. Moreover, all players sharp or flatten the notes unconsciously in order to correct the scale according to their own musical habit, and corrections of this kind are particularly easy with an instrument so roughly made that it sometimes allows a latitude of more than a half-tone for each hole. Further, we do not know whether, and to what extent, the ancient players used half-stopping and cross-fingering. Finally, these experiments were made with modern mouthpieces, though it is well known that the nature, shape and size of the mouthpiece affect, indeed determine, the scale. The reader may imagine how unreliable the conclusions were, and one will not blame Giuseppe Verdi for having written to Count Arrivebene about the attempts of Fétis to play on an Egyptian pipe:

Do not think that I abhor this charlatan because he has run me down, but because one day he rushed me head over heels to the Egyptian Museum in Florence, to inspect a pipe on which he pretends to have discovered the system of the ancient Egyptian music, as he asserts in his *History of Music.* . . . The arch-rogue!!!. Thus history is falsified, and fools grow without watering!

The author, in his book *Die Musikinstrumente des alten Aegyptens* and a paper *Die Tonkunst der alten Aegypter*, tried to replace this kind of experiment by using the measurements between the fingerholes as a basis for determining the scale, which is the function of the geometrical progression of the fingerholes.

In the meantime, the American Charles Kasson Wead had shown that, in general, at any time and in any country the disposition of the fingerholes was not based on musical principles until, as late as

1832, the flutist Theobald Boehm made his reform in flute construction. In search of a nonmusical standard, both Victor Loret and the author of this book tried to identify the distances between the holes of Egyptian oboes, clarinets and flutes with Egyptian measures of length. This means of solving the problem was pursued by the late Dr. Erich M. von Hornbostel. His general results, however, will not be presented until the eighth chapter of this book, since their appropriate place is in a discussion of Chinese music.

TRUMPETS in Egypt were made of a yellow metal and had a conical form with a distinct mouthpiece and a rather wide bell. As it was only about two feet long, this trumpet must have been tuned more or less to the upper octave of our modern cornet; the ground-tone may have been approximately *c'*, and it is not likely that it could produce more than this note, its higher octave and its twelfth. Such small instruments have not an agreeable sound, and we can appreciate the Greek historian Plutarch's disdainful remark that the blare of an Egyptian trumpet was like an ass's bray.

The instrument is pictured for the first time about 1415 B.C. as used by soldiers. But it did not serve military purposes only. It was used as a sacred instrument in the worship of Osiris, and its invention was attributed to the god himself.

Homer's commentator, Eustathios, who relates this myth, says the name of the trumpet was *chnouē*, but no word of the kind can be found in Egyptian dictionaries. Hieroglyphic inscriptions call the trumpet *šnb*.

This contradiction might possibly be explained in the following way. Let us suppose that the vocalized form of *šnb* was *šnobē*. A Greek, transcribing this word into his alphabet, would have been forced to replace *š* (English *sh*) by the letter *chi*, which was pronounced like German *ch* in *ich*. This would give *chnobē*. Moreover, Greeks were inclined to transform a foreign *b* combined with a vowel into a diphthong, as they did, for example, when they changed the Phoenician name of the angular harp, *nabla*, into *naula*. This would give *chnouē*. Thus, Eustathios's word might have been a transcription of the Egyptian term *šnb* or *šnobē*.

The word may have been derived from the same root as German *schnauben*, in Middle High German *snûben*, 'to blow.'

THE LYRE of the New Kingdom had a shallow, square sound-box, two divergent and asymmetric arms, and an oblique crossbar. The strings were fastened to a holder on the front of the box; the

upper ends of the strings were wound around the crossbar and could
be shifted until the strings had the desired pitch. From the classic
Greek and the modern Nubian and Abyssinian lyres, we can conclude that the tuning was pentatonic, even when the number of
strings was greater than five. In this case, the additional strings
probably continued the pentatonic scale up and downwards. Higher
numbers, such as ten and fourteen, are to be understood as dupli-

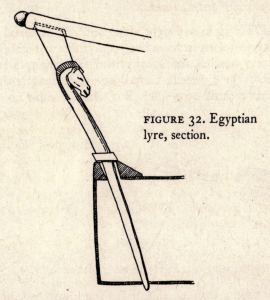

FIGURE 32. Egyptian
lyre, section.

cating the individual strings, as for instance in the modern Abyssinian
lyre. The manner of playing, too, corresponded to the Greek and
Nubian fashion. The right hand scratched with a plectron over all
strings at once, while the fingers of the left hand, stretched against
the strings, deadened those which were not wanted. Therefore, the
lyre was held in the most convenient position for this kind of playing, that is, with the strings inclined away from the player. One
example only of a lyre held upright is known from the New Kingdom, and in this case both hands are plucking the strings without a
plectron in the same manner as the *psilê kithárisis* described in the
Greek chapter. (pls. V b, VI a, fig. 32)

After 1000 B.C., a new type of lyre came from Asia. It was small
and symmetrically rectangular with parallel arms and a crossbar
running at right angles to them; the player held the instrument
upright in his arm.

The lyre was never common in Egypt. The Egyptian language had no proper name for it, but called it by its Semitic name *k·nn·r*, a word which appears on a papyrus of about 1300 B.C. As stated before, the hieroglyphic script omitted the vowels and wrote only the skeleton of a word in consonants. In this case, we assume that the first vowel was *i*; not only the Semitic forms of the word had it, as kinnor in Hebrew and kinnâra in Arabic, but also the late Egyptian or Coptic form, *ginêra*.

THE LUTE came to Egypt along with the lyre and the small frame drum; it seems to have been played by women exclusively. The body was wooden and usually oval; a covering skin acted as soundboard. A long handle pierced the body lengthways (like a piece of meat pierced by a spit). But while in most non-Egyptian

FIGURE 33. Egyptian lute, 18th dynasty.

lutes the handle protruded slightly at the lower end, in Egyptian lutes the handle ended within the body. Lacking the support it would have had if it protruded, it was held in place by wooden crosspieces inside the body; sometimes, to make it even firmer, it was stuck in and out through the skin once or twice. A round or triangular opening was cut into the skin to let through the strings fastened to the lower end of the handle. The opposite ends of the strings were wound around the top of the handle and held in place by thongs ending in tassels. Their average number was two; in rare instances there were three or even four. The right hand plucked them with a plectron, while the left hand stopped them by pressing them onto one of the many frets tied around the stick. (pl. V c, fig. 33)

The Egyptian lute, with the handle ending inside the body, has survived in the Northwest of Africa. It first degenerated to a clumsy Negro instrument, used in Morocco and Senegambia and called *gunbrī* in Sudanese. When the Arabs conquered Morocco in the latter part of the seventh century, they reduced the size of the instrument and adapted the name correspondingly; a smaller, pear-shaped or ovoid or hemispherical body replaced the heavy, oblong, troughlike body, and the strings were attached to lateral pegs. The Negro instrument has preserved the name *gunbrī;* the Arabian instrument evolved from it is designated by the diminutive form *gunibrī.*

CASTANETS AND CYMBALS. The term *castanets* is here used in the narrower sense of clappers, the striking faces of which are hollowed out to give a fuller resonance. Egyptian castanets existed in two forms. The first one was shaped something like a very small wooden boot, cut in half lengthwise and grooved in the leg part, while the tapering foot part served as a handle. The second form was nearly the shape of modern Spanish *castañuelas;* but it was less flat and looked like the chestnut, *castaña,* for which it was named.

Neither form was properly Egyptian. No art work figures them, and the specimens preserved came from Christian tombs. The best castanets were Greek; many Hellenic vases depict them in the hands of Dyonisian dancers. The chestnut castanet may have been Phoenician, since it was, and still is, used by dancers of Andalusia, the Balearic Islands and southern Italy, all of which were formerly Phoenician colonies.

Cymbals must also have been imported from Greece, as the Coptic translation of the Bible had no native word to designate them and was forced to adopt the Greek word *kýmbala.*

Egyptian cymbals had a wide, flat brim and a large, flat boss in the middle which served as a resonance-chamber. They were probably held upright and struck violently together by a horizontal movement of the player's hands. So they may have corresponded to the Hebrew *şelşlê trūâʿ.*

The specimens preserved in museums, in the Metropolitan Museum of Art in New York for instance, are of two different sizes: a larger one, from five to seven inches in diameter, and a smaller one, from two to three inches in diameter. The small cymbals may have been played like those antique cymbal-castanets which dancers play, castanetlike, between thumb and middlefinger up to this day.

But it is also possible that they are remnants of *cymbals on clappers.* These strange implements, which are depicted on art works and several specimens of which have been preserved, are a combination of cymbals and a bamboo clapper. In Burma simple clappers still exist along with the improved cymbals on clappers. A piece of bamboo is slit down the middle except for a short section serving as a handle; when shaken, the two halves slap against each other with a sharp click. The click is replaced by a tinkle, if a small cymbal is fastened inside of each half. The Egyptian instruments of the late Coptic epoch were identical with these Burmese cymbals on clappers.

This picture of the instrumental development in one country during three thousand years is typical enough. A native origin can be attributed at most to two instruments out of twenty-six—the sistrum and the clarinet. And of these two the sistrum can be traced back to primitive prototypes. The rest have been adopted as the result of various Asiatic influences. About the year 1000 B.C. not one of the instruments of the Old and Middle Kingdoms has survived in the scenes of musical life that painters and sculptors depict. Again the established tradition has been lost in the press of foreign influences, the same tradition whose inspiration two thousand years before had come from foreign importation. The Greek and Roman, Indian and Chinese chapters will reveal the same process; the majority of the instruments have been borrowed from abroad. It is a feature of a high civilization that it is receptive to foreign ideas and implements of all kinds, and vital enough to assimilate them.

5. *Israel*

THE Pentateuch makes little mention of music. This, how-ever, does not mean that music was unusual or that it was disdained. On the contrary, musical expression was universal and consequently taken for granted. But, unlike Babylonia and Egypt, Israel did not know professional musicians or professional dancers. Everyone practiced music; singing, playing and dancing were common achievements. After the exodus from Egypt and the crossing of the Red Sea, Moses himself struck up the holy tune to glorify the Lord, all his people joined the Leader's voice, and Miriam, his sister, led the women in response. When Saul and David returned from the victorious battle against the Philistines, the women welcomed them with singing, dancing and playing. They still expressed joy and sorrow impulsively with all the means at the body's command; their music still exulted and wailed; coming from inspired hearts, it inspired the hearts of others. Music chased the demons from Saul's soul when David played for him, and musical ecstasy took possession of the seers so that the spirit of God came upon them and made them prophesy.

Artistic representations gave us a basis for investigating Mesopotamian and Egyptian instruments; assistance from philological sources was secondary. Our position is reversed when we study Hebrew instruments. As the Bible was opposed to depicting men and objects of any kind, we have no reliefs or paintings to consult concerning the nature of the few instruments named in the Holy Script.

105

Some lyres and oboes, represented on coins from the time of Bar Kokba's revolt against Emperor Hadrian (132–135 A.D.), are too late to give any information about Biblical instruments. Etymology, and the few epithets given to the names of instruments in the Bible and the Talmud, are almost our only sources.

THE UGAB is one of the two first instruments mentioned in the Bible. Jubal, Lamech's son, so says Genesis 4: 21, was "the father of all such as handle the harp and organ." The Hebrew text has the words *kinnor* and *'ugâb*. This latter term is extremely rare; it occurs in two other books only, Job 21: 12 and 30: 31, and the 150th Psalm. These belong in the most recent sections of the Old Testament, while the first one is among the earliest.

In all these passages the word refers to an instrument contrasting with stringed instruments, but no detailed information is given. Etymology is not helpful either; at best, *'ugâb* may be related to *'agâb*, 'was in love.' If this is true, the interpretation 'flute' is indicated, as among wind instruments flutes were the most closely connected with love charm.

Several translators have interpreted *'ugâb* as pan-pipes. This is certainly incorrect; the first evidences of pan-pipes in the Near East are almost two thousand years later than the epoch described in the Genesis. A further reason is linguistic. The Hebrew language had a more suitable word to express the clear sound of so small an instrument—the verb *šriqá*, 'he whistled.' The dark color of the word *'ugâb* more probably reflects the hollow, *oo*-like timbre of a long, wide, vertical flute. This instrument, usually played by shepherds, must be supposed to have existed in Palestine, as it existed in Mesopotamia, Egypt and ancient Arabia. If originally *'ugâb* was a vertical flute, the term might have become a general one later on, just as the term *ma't* in Egyptian signified a vertical flute at first, and later all pipes, including oboes and clarinets.

THE KINNOR was the other instrument connected with Jubal. The word had two plural forms: one masculine, *kinnorîm*, and one feminine, *kinnorót*. Its etymology is unknown.

The kinnor was the famous instrument on which, later on, King David excelled, and which for a thousand years has erroneously been called "King David's harp." The first translators were more careful. The word was interpreted as *kithara* on twenty out of forty-two references in the *Septuaginta*, the oldest Greek translation of the Bible, which was made by seventy-two scholars in Alexandria from the third to the first centuries B.C.; in seventeen more references it was interpreted by the kindred word *kinyra*. The *Vulgate*, St Jerome's Latin version of about 400 A.D., has *cithara* in all thirty-seven cases. Thus, we conclude that the kinnor was a lyre of the kind that the Greeks called *kithara*. The last doubt is silenced by the fact that *k·nn·r* designated the same lyre in Egypt.

The Bible gives few details. It indicates that the material was wood, probably the ordinary cypress, though in the time of the kings exotic woods and precious metals were used as well as decorations of electron—that is, either a composition of gold and silver, or yellow amber. As to the shape, a quantity of coins, struck in Palestine between 132 and 135 A.D., shows various forms of kitharas with curved outlines and horizontal crossbars; but, considering that they were made two thousand years after the times of the Genesis and twelve to thirteen hundred years after King David, we must beware of so late a source. A second reference, Abraham ben Meir ibn Ezra's commentary on the Book of Daniel, is even more recent (twelfth century A.D.). Yet, his assertion that the kinnor had the shape of a candelabrum sounds particularly reliable. The old Jewish candelabrum, with its parallel branches arranged in a semicircle, can easily be compared with Cretan, Mycenian, Cyprian, Phoenician and early Greek kitharas—that is, those lyres which chronologically and geographically come near to the Hebrew lyre. No doubt this small, rounded lyre was held in a slanting position, the upper end away from the player as all Syrian lyres of that time.

The strings, *minnîm*, singular *mēn*, were made of sheep gut; more exactly, they were made, according to a passage in the Talmudian tractate *Qinnim*, of the "sons" of sheep gut. The expression *bnē*, 'sons,' is used as a diminutive. It probably refers to those parts of the small intestine directly under the stomach, called chitterlings, which are particularly thin in sheep.

Broken strings on lyres used in the Temple were not supposed to be knotted in the sanctuary; when possible, they had to be loosened and shifted so that the longer end could be reattached either to the yoke or to the stringholder. According to Flavius Josephus, the Jewish historian and a general in the Roman Army (born in 37 A.D. at Jerusalem), they were plucked with a plectron, and their number was ten, as with the Ethiopian lyre *bagannâ* which will be discussed in the Greek chapter. They probably were tuned pentatonically without semitones through two octaves, like the strings of this instrument.

The plectron indicates that the kinnor was an accompanying instrument. This will be explained in detail in the next chapter. The fact is confirmed by I Chronicles 16:42, where kinnor and nevel as *klê šîr*, or 'tools of singing,' are contrasted to trumpets and cymbals. This could also mean 'melody instruments'; but as II Chronicles 9:11, and I Kings 12 call the kinnor and the nevel instruments *lšarîm*, 'belonging to the singers,' the significance, 'instruments of accompaniment,' cannot be doubted.

Is it a contradiction when I Samuel 16:23 relates that young David reached for his kinnor to play before Saul "and played with his hand" (*wniggên vyādó*)? Mentioning the playing hand would be superfluous unless the fact had to be emphasized as something unusual, contrasting with the normal manner. The interpretation 'without a plectron' is corroborated because, according to the passage quoted, David did not sing. Such cases of harplike plucking without a plectron occurred in Egypt as well as in Greece, where this practice was called *psilê kithárisis*, as opposed to the *kitharōdia*, or plectron playing to accompany a song.

The melodies that the kinnor played or accompanied were gay, and unsuited to sorrow; the Jews refused to play that instrument during the Babylonian Exile. They suspended their kinnorîm on the willows; how should they "sing the Lord's song in a strange land"? The kinnor was gay, and when the prophets admonished the people they threatened that the kinnor, symbol of joy and happiness, would be silenced unless the people desisted from sin. Instruments still were bound to well-defined occasions and moods.

THE TOF. In Genesis 31:27, the Aramaean Laban reproaches his son-in-law, Jacob, for his flight with Rachel and Leah; had he known his intention to leave, he would have escorted him "away with mirth, and with songs," with *tupîm* and *kinnorot*. The form *tupîm* is the plural of a Hebrew word *tof* that corresponds to Arabic *duff*, and to Greek *týpanon*. All these names belong to the old Semitic frame drum that we found in ancient Mesopotamia and Egypt, and that we shall find again in Greece and Rome. This drum was made of a wooden hoop and very probably two skins, without any jingling contrivance or sticks. In Palestine the heads were taken from the hides of horned animals, either rams or wild goats, according to a passage in the Talmudian tractate *Qinnim* III 6. The frame drum was almost exclusively played by women, among the Jews as well as in the other countries where it was found. "And Miriam the prophetess, the sister of Aaron, took a timbrel in her hand; and all the women went out after her, with timbrels and with dances"; Jephthah's unfortunate daughter "came out to meet him with timbrels and with dances," and the Jewesses welcomed the conquerors after the victory over the Philistines "with tabrets." Though drums were not mentioned by the Bible in wedding ceremonies, we can be sure that they were used at Jewish weddings, as they are today all over the Orient. "Publish the marriage and beat the drum," Muhammad has said. It seems that a passage in the Talmud refers to such a use of the drum when it calls it, not *tof*, but *ērús* (from *ārás*, 'to betroth'). If the lexicographers are right in identifying *ērús* with *tof*, the drum referred to must have been rather large, as the women sometimes sat upon it when wailing.

The same Talmudian tractate that speaks of the *ērús* also mentions an object called *nīqaṭmón*. This term has likewise been considered a musical instrument, although it was not translated by any of the Talmudian translators. Its etymology is *ānqiṭmîn*, a word which designates an artificial arm or leg. If this term does mean an instrument, it might refer to those typical Egyptian clappers of wood or ivory which were carved to form a human arm with the hand and which were exclusively played by women; or to the boot-shaped clappers of the Greeks. But this is nothing more than a suggestion.

THE PA'AMON was either a small bell or a jingle. The etymon obviously was the verb *pā'ám*, 'struck.' When God prescribed the garments which the high priest should wear, he ordered:

And beneath upon the hem of it thou shalt make pomegranates of blue, and of purple, and of scarlet, round about the hem thereof; and bells of gold between them round about: A golden bell and a pomegranate, upon the hem of the robe round about. And it shall be upon Aaron to minister: and his sound shall be heard when he goeth in unto the holy place before the Lord, and when he cometh out, that he die not.

The meaning is obvious. Here, as everywhere, the bell is used as a defense against evil spirits. The demons like to frequent sanctuaries and thresholds. Therefore, the high priest does not have to be protected when he is *in* the holy place, but when he *goeth in* and *cometh out*.

Bells and jingles *upon the hem* were not found only in Israel. South American Indians, as well as Siberian shamans, wear them;

in the middle ages they adorned the fop; in Wolfram von Eschen-
bach's *Parzival*, Segramors decked himself out with jingles, and in
the fourteenth and fifteenth centuries they were an almost indispensable accessory for elegant people. Finally, they are sewn on the
fool's motley at carnivals and in the morris dance.

THE SHOFAR or *keren,* 'horn,' is a plain goat's or ram's horn
without a mouthpiece. It is steamed until soft and then flattened
and sharply bent (though neither the Bible nor the Talmud mention these details) and produces only two harmonics (the second
and the third). It is the only ancient instrument preserved in the
Jewish cult today. In orthodox communities it is blown at New
Moon services, and in eastern Europe even in exorcising ceremonies, as many spectators have seen in Anski's famous play
Dybbuk; and in all synagogues, liberal and orthodox, New Year's
and the Day of Atonement end with the violent, awe-inspiring
blasts of the traditional shofar.

There are four blasts:

tqîâ ('blast'), an apoggiatura on the tonic prefixed to a long blow
   on the fifth;
švarîm ('breaks'), a rapid alternation between tonic and fifth;
trûâ ('din'), a quavering blow on the tonic, ending on the fifth;
tqîâ gdolâ ('great blast'), with a longer sostenuto on the fifth, always
   played at the end.

As for the relative metric lengths of these fanfares, the Talmudian tractate *Rosh-hashana* IV: 9 prescribes this proportion:

$$1\ tqîâ = 3\ trûâ = 9\ švarîm$$

This rule, formulated at the latest in the Talmudian epoch—that is,
in the first or second century B.C., but probably much earlier—has
a striking resemblance to the so-called *modus perfectus* of medieval
musical theory, which arranged metric values in threes:

$$1\ (nota)\ maxima = 3\ longae = 9\ breves$$

In consequence, the scholastic theory interpreting this trisection as
a Christian symbol of Trinity is incorrect.

The same tractate, *Rosh-hashana* III: 2–6, gives a detailed description of the shofar:

All shofars are valid save that of a cow. . . .
The shofar [blown in the Temple] at the New Year was [made
from the horn] of the wild goat, straight, with its mouthpiece overlaid

with gold. And at the sides [of them that blew the shofar] were two [that blew upon] trumpets. The shofar blew a long note and the trumpets a short note since the duty of the day fell on the shofar. [The shofars] on days of fasting were rams' horns, rounded with their mouthpiece overlaid with silver. And between them were two [that blew upon] trumpets. The shofar blew a short note and the trumpets a long note, since the duty of the day fell on the trumpets. The Year of Jubilee is like to the New Year in the blowing of the shofar and in the Benedictions. Rabbi Judah says: "At the New Year they use rams' horns and at the Years of Jubilee wild goats' horns." A shofar that has been split and stuck together again is not valid. If the broken pieces of a shofar have been stuck together again it is not valid. If a hole had been made in it and it was stopped up again, if it hinders the blowing it is not valid, but if it does not, it is valid.

The old ritual distinguished between two kinds of shofarim, one being made from the horn of the ibex, or wild goat, for New Moon ceremonies, and one from the horn of the ram for Fastdays, which never coincided with New Moon days. It was certainly more than a coincidence that the ibex horn was used for New Moon rites; zoologists describe it as "crescent-shaped." It is interesting in this connection to cite a Burmese people, the Karên, who attribute eclipses of the moon to "the facts that wild goats are eating the luminary."

Thus, we find the shofar involved in magic beliefs and tasks. The origin of the ideas connected with this horn is very old. One of these ideas is its secret character; in the synagogues the shofar is covered and must not be seen by the worshipers. No satisfactory reason for this has been given by liturgists; they do not know that this is a remnant of the old taboo forbidding the sight of sacred implements, preserved among many primitive peoples. The Colombian Tuyucá, for example, hide the mouth parts of their ritual wooden trumpets in a brook, and Dutch peasants conceal the bark trumpets they use at winter solstice in a well from Christmas until the following Advent. A religious law in Israel says that, while men are obliged to listen to the voice of the shofar, women and children are exempted from this duty. Whoever is familiar with the rites connected with primitive trumpets cannot refrain from seeing in this indulgence a last remnant of the old taboo forbidding women and children all contact with the holy instruments.

One single magic deed of the shofar is referred to in the Bible, and a very strong one. When Joshua, the Judge, besieged Jericho, seven priests with shofarim strode round the town for six days, followed by the Ark of the Covenant; on the seventh day they did so seven times, and as they blew and all the people joined in with shouts, "the wall fell down flat, so that the people went up into the city, every man straight before him, and they took the city." Here, Hebrew legend meets with Greek mythology. Amphion, Niobe's husband, son of Zeus and Antiope, reached for his lyre when he was about to found Thebes, and as he played the scattered stones gathered and built the wall by themselves. This is a fundamental idea behind all primitive and oriental music: sound governs matter.

In connection with the shofar, the Talmudian tractate *Roshhashana* discusses the orthodoxy of blowing the trumpet in a pit, cistern or barrel. Even the nearly contemporary Talmudian comment *Gmara* was no longer able to understand this passage; the players, it supposed, stood in a pit or cistern. What the Talmud actually means cannot be understood without a knowledge of primitive rituals. Negroes of Loango, for example, dip their trumpets into a barrel, New Hebridians into a hollow tree trunk or half a coconut shell filled with water, and Northwest Brazilians, as well as Singhalese, into pots. One idea may be to obtain the unnatural, terrifying sound which is an important requirement in magic rituals. But this is not all. As the Singhalese compare the pot in question to the earth, the hollow objects blown into must be regarded as magic cavities, such as were discussed in our first chapter. The trumpet dipped into a cavity is the combination of the male and the female principle; it is a forgotten fertilization charm.

THE HASOSRA. "And the Lord spoke unto Moses, saying, Make thee two trumpets of silver; of a whole piece shalt thou make them; that thou mayest use them for the calling of the assembly, and for the journeying of the camps. . . . And if ye go to war in your land against the enemy that oppresseth you, then ye shall blow an alarm with the trumpets; and ye shall be remembered before the Lord your God, and ye shall be saved from your enemies. Also in the day of your gladness, and in your solemn days, and in the beginnings of your months, ye shall blow with the trumpets over your burnt offerings, and over the sacrifices of peace offerings; that they may be to you for a memorial before your God: I am the Lord your God" (Numbers 10: 1–2, 9–10).

This idea of drawing God's attention towards his worshipers by a strong sound is primitive, and not in keeping with the uplifted

C. Egyptian harpist, *18th Dynasty.*

B. Semitic lyrist, c. *1900 B.C.*

A. Egyptian lyrist, *18th Dynasty.*

PLATE VI.

Judaism of the Prophets as Elijah preached it. When on Mount Carmel the heathen priests cried to Baal, Elijah scoffed and shouted to them: "Cry aloud: for he is a god; either he is talking, or he is pursuing, or he is in a journey, or per adventure he sleepeth, and must be awaked" (I Kings 18: 27).

Yet, popular thought clung to this naïve conception. As late as the middle as the second century B.C., when Judas Maccabaeus revolted against the Syrian kings, the Israelites prayed to the Lord: "How shall we be able to stand against them, except thou, O God, be our help? Then sounded they with trumpets, and cried with a loud voice." And again, after the first victory, they came to Jerusalem, and finding the Temple deserted, they "fell down flat to the ground upon their faces, and blew an alarm with the trumpets, and cried towards heaven."

This strange habit had a striking parallel in Egyptian rites. On a painted coffin from the last Roman epoch of Egyptian antiquity, a worshiper is depicted blowing a trumpet before, one rather should say up to, Osiris, and this is done with the same purpose.

The outer shape of the Hebrew trumpet also corresponded to the Egyptian trumpet. Flavius Josephus has described the hasosra as a straight tube, "a little less than a cubit long" and ending in a bell. And when, in 70 A.D., the Romans erected an arch for Emperor Titus after his conquest of Jerusalem, they depicted on it his triumphal return to Rome with the holy objects robbed from the Temple, and among them a trumpet which corresponded exactly to the description of Josephus and also to the many trumpets on Egyptian reliefs and paintings.

The gemination of the Jewish trumpets, on the other hand, was probably non-Egyptian. God's commandment was: "Make thee *two* trumpets." Though non-Egyptian, this duality was by no means confined to Palestine. Curved, metal trumpets of the Nordic bronze ages, the so-called *lurer*, were almost always found in pairs; twin metal trumpets in ancient Afghanistan were played simultaneously, as they are still in modern India and Tibet; and the same is true with the wooden trumpets of Lithuania, Rumania and Chile. Musicological dilettanti dream that the two Nordic lurer played two parts. This is nonsense; twin trumpets are deeply rooted in old ideas of symmetry and pair formation. The two trumpets must have been played either simultaneously or alternately, and, in this latter case, either on the same or on a different note. Both these customs are preserved in modern India.

THE TIME OF THE KINGS
(FIRST MILLENNIUM B.C.)

The critical years for the cultural life of Israel came in the eleventh century B.C., when the old patriarchal system was replaced by a kingdom after the model of the surrounding countries. Israel wanted the monarchical government of her neighbors, and when she was established as a kingdom with a court she was even more open to their influences. The influx of foreign ideas came to its peak under Solomon who "loved many strange women, together with the daughter of Pharaoh, women of the Moabites, Ammonites, Edomites, Zidonians, and Hittites."

The musical scene was completely altered. Israel developed a musical organization and professional musicians. Both David and Solomon supported court musicians, and David, a musician himself, founded the first official body of musicians for the temple that he was to build. The head of the Levites was bidden to send musicians to sing and play before the Ark of the Covenant when it was carried up to Jerusalem, and he chose Asaph, Heman and Ethan as cymbalists, eight other Levites to play the nevel, and six the lyre; seven priests were to trumpet before the altar. The head himself, Chenaniah, trained them in singing, as playing and singing always accompanied each other.

The great days of ritual music came when David had surrendered the royal dignity to his son Solomon. No less than four thousand out of thirty-eight thousand Levites were selected students of an actual academy of religious music. They were divided into twenty-four groups, each group being taught by twelve masters. On the day of consecration

the singers, all of them of Asaph, of Heman, of Jeduthun, with their sons and their brethren, being arrayed in white linen, having cymbals and psalteries and harps, stood at the east end of the altar, and with them a hundred and twenty priests sounding with trumpets: It came even to pass, as the trumpeters and singers were as one, to make one sound to be heard in praising the Lord; and when they lifted up their voice with the trumpets, and cymbals, and instruments of musick, and praised the Lord, saying: For he is good; for his mercy endureth for ever: that then the house was filled with a cloud, even the house of the Lord; So that the priests could not stand to minister by reason of the cloud: for the glory of the Lord had filled the house of God" (II Chronicles 5:12–14).

Nevel and cymbals, mentioned in the description of the Temple, were entirely new; like some other instruments, they had not been mentioned in the holy books before the days of the kings, and may belong to those "pagan" objects imported when the first kings established their courts. To what a large measure music was exposed to influences from abroad appears in a passage from the Talmudian tractate *Shabbat* 56 b, which says that the Pharaoh's daughter, whom King Solomon took for wife, carried with her *élef minê*, 'a thousand kinds,' of Egyptian musical instruments.

After the Egyptian, the Phoenician civilization probably contributed more than any other. For, when the First Temple was to be built, King Solomon made a contract with the king of Tyre in Phoenicia for Phoenician woodworking craftsmen, and he sent for a noted master in that town, Hiram, to make all the metal work for the sanctuary. Two instruments at least were probably imported from there: the double oboes, which later on were called 'Phoenician pipes' by the Romans, and the *nēvel*, which certainly was identical with the instrument that the Greeks called the "Phoenician" *nabla*.

THE NEVEL, plural *nvālîm*, was a stringed instrument; but of what kind? A harp, a zither, a lyre, a lute? The lute, two- or three-stringed in all the ancient civilizations, must be excluded. For the historian Flavius Josephus (born 37 A.D. in Jerusalem) relates that it had twelve strings plucked with the bare fingers. That it was plucked is confirmed by the prophet Amos (6:5) who, with *nēvel*, uses the verb *pārát*, 'to pluck fruit.' Thus, the possible alternatives are a zither, a lyre and a harp.

Etymology does not help much; *nēvel* designates an inflated and somewhat shapeless object such as a leather bag, and is related to English *nebulous*.

We then consult the Septuaginta to see how the seventy-two Greek interpreters have expounded the enigmatic word. Instead of one Greek equivalent the Septuaginta present three different terms in the various passages in which *nēvel* occurs: fourteen times *nabla*, eight times *psalterion*, once *kithara*. The Vulgate, on the other hand, has *psalterium* seventeen times. The word *nabla* does not tell us anything as it is a Greek form of *nēvel*, or its Phoenician equivalent (for, according to Athenaeus, the nabla had come from Phoenicia); therefore, the terms *psalterion* and *psalterium* are in the majority, and they point to the harp. Moreover, the identity of the terms is confirmed by two later authorities. The Byzantine Suidas stated in the ninth century A.D. that *psalterion* and *nabla* were one and the same instrument, and the Jew Saadia said in his commentary on the Book of Daniel, in the twelfth century A.D., that the Aramaean *psantrîn* was a *nēvel*.

Both the Greek word *psalterion* and its Latin equivalent designate the vertical angular harp (cf. page 81), and the Church Fathers, among them St. Jerome who is responsible for the Vulgate and consequently for the translation *psalterium,* define the instrument called by this name as having "the body above": *psalterium lignum illud concavum unde sonus redditur superius habet*—that is, the instrument was held so that the body was above the horizontal stick. This is indeed the specific feature of a vertical angular harp. This body, rising above the stringholder, is rounded and completely covered with a skin. So it is reminiscent of an oriental skin bottle like the one called *nēvel* in Hebrew. And Rabbi Joseph was right when he associated the name of the harp with the shape of the skin bottle.

A further detail can be drawn from a passage in the Talmudian tractate *Qinnim* III: 6. The strings of the nevel, so it reads, were made of the [thicker] intestines of a sheep, while the kinnor was provided by the chitterlings. Moreover, the tractate *Arachin* II: 6 says that the nevel was louder than the kinnor. Thus, it must have been larger and lower in pitch.

If so, then a strange passage in I Chronicles 15: 20 f. has certainly been misunderstood. It runs:

And Zechariah, and Aziel, and Shemiramoth, and Jehiel and Unni, and Eliab, and Maaseiah, and Benaiah, with psalteries on alamoth; And Mattithiah, and Eliphaleh, and Mikneiah, and Obededom, and Jeiel, and Azzaziah, with harps on the sheminith to excel.

In this passage 'psalteries' should have been translated as 'harps,' and 'harps' as 'lyres,' the original Hebrew words having been *nvālîm 'al-'alāmót* and *kinnorîm 'al-hašmīnît.* The usual interpretation is guided by the verbal meaning of the two epithets, *'almâ* being 'maiden,' and *hašmīnît* 'the eighth.' The maidenlike nevel has been interpreted as a treble instrument, and the 'eighth' kinnor as a lyre that was pitched eight notes or an octave lower than the nevel. This translation is arbitrary and erroneous. The two epithets do not belong in the same category and cannot be interpreted as comparing the pitch of the two instruments. If the higher octave was expressed by the idea 'maidens,' one should expect, for the lower octave, 'men' or 'youths' in the same way that the Greeks distinguished between *auloì parthenikoí, paidikoí* and *andreioí.* If the word *'almâ* is really concerned, it would be wiser to think of the significance that the same word, in the form *'alma,* has in Arabic: an educated, singing- and playing-girl.

The second epithet implies that the ancient Jews had the concep- tion of octaves, and particularly of octaves consisting of eight dia- tonic notes. But this is by no means proved, and quite improbable. Finally, if the nevel was a harp and had longer strings than the lyre kinnor, the pitch relation between them ought to have been the reverse, with the kinnor higher and the nevel lower.

On the other hand, both epithets, without being connected with the name of an instrument, occur, one at a time, in the headlines of the Psalms, which will be discussed in a special section of this chapter.

Dr. Erich Werner suggested, in a letter to the author, the As- syrian *ḥalimū,* 'wooden,' as a possible etymology of *'alāmot,* and re- ferred to the Greek name of a small pipe *elymos,* which is phoneti- cally related. The epithet *ḥašminît* remains a mystery.

ASOR. The word means ten; no translator, from the earliest to the most recent times, has doubted that in the three Psalms 33: 2, 92: 3, 144: 9, it designates some instrument with ten strings. A more detailed interpretation is rendered difficult by the uncertain position and connection of the word in the three passages. In the first and the third it follows the term *nēvel* without any conjunction: "Sing unto him with the nevel asor." Most translators consequently have taken asor for an adjective accompanying nevel and read the two words as 'ten-stringed nevel.' But this interpretation is contradicted by the second passage, in the 92nd Psalm, which runs *'alê-'asor wa'alê-nēvel.* This is unmistakably 'on the asor *and* on the nevel.' Thus asor and nevel were different instruments, and the Authorized Version is correct in interpolating an *and* in the 33rd and 144th Psalms: "Sing unto him with the psaltery and an instrument of ten strings."

The asor was a separate instrument and probably neither a lyre nor a harp, as its name is mentioned with the nevel in the 33rd and 144th Psalms, and with both nevel and kinnor, in the 92nd Psalm. There is but one possible family of stringed instrument left that could be furnished with ten strings: zithers.

Zithers did not exist either in Egypt or in Assyria, the two great monarchies of the Near East. But Israel's most civilized neighbors, the Phoenicians, used a strange type of zither. Two specimens of this instrument are carved on a beautiful ivory pyxis of the eighth century B.C. in the British Museum, no. 118179, which came from the Southeast Palace at Nimrud in Assyria, and was taken for Assyrian until recently when its Phoenician origin was recognized. On this relief the backs of the two zithers cannot be seen, and it is impossible to determine whether they are flat or bulgy. The front, on the contrary, is distinct; it consists of a small rectangular frame with strings across and running parallel to the smaller sides. The position is upright in the player's hand, and the female musicians

FIGURE 34. Psalterium decacordum. (After Jerome's letter to Dardanus, reprod. 1511 by Virdung.)

play with the bare fingers. The main point is the number of strings: probably ten on one zither, and clearly ten on the other one.

The asor might have been such a Phoenician zither.

This interpretation is confirmed by the strange, illustrated letter, attributed to St. Jerome and addressed to Dardanus. Under the title *psalterium decachordum*, the artist depicts a rectangular zither, exactly the shape of the Phoenician zither, and the writer explains: "It has ten strings, as it is written: I shall praise you on the ten-stringed psaltery," and he adds: "*forma quadrata*," expounding, in the kind of symbolism so dear to the Church Fathers, that the ten strings meant the ten commandments, and the four sides the Gospels. (fig. 34)

HALIL AND ABUB. Though the Bible does not mention these names before the time of the kings, a rabbinic tradition traces them back to Moses (about 1250 B.C.). The story reads:

There was a pipe of cane in the Temple, well made and polished, and it came from the days of Moses. The king ordered it to be covered with gold, but it lost its soft timbre. The cover then was removed, and the sound was soft again.

Covering or lining with metal foil was not unusual in antiquity. The Talmudian tractate *Kelim* XI: 6 mentions *ḥalilîm* both of solid metal and covered with metal. Such pipes existed in other civilizations as well. About twenty years ago the author was given a very old and rare Peruvian flute by the collector, Dr. Gaffron; it was made of cane and had a silver lining.

Other passages in the Talmud confirm the preference given to pipes of cane. The tractate *Arachin* says expressly that one did not play on metal pipes; cane pipes were favored because their sound was more pleasant (*'arêv*). And the *Gmara* adds: "the pipe is called *ḥalîl* because its sound is sweet (*ḥala*)."

This supposed etymology was incorrect; *ḥalîl* came from a verb *ḥalál*, 'pierced,' and is identical with Akkadian *ḥalilu*. The Talmudian tractates use *ḥalîl* as well as a second term which never occurs in the Bible, *abûb* or *m'abuba*, and Rabbi Papa emphasizes in the *Gmara* of *Arachin* that both names mean exactly the same instrument. The term *abûb*, likewise derived from a verb 'pierced,' that is bored, and related to Akkadian *imbubu*, was a Syriac word which later on was latinized; the *ambubaiae*, mentioned by Horace and Suetonius, were Syrian girls of ill fame who resided in the basement of the Roman circus and earned their living by pipe playing and a less honorable trade. Thus, it is more than probable that the Jews got their pipes from Syria.

These pipes are called 'flutes' by the modern translators of the Bible. But in 1000 B.C. no artist, whether Babylonian, Assyrian, Iranian, Phoenician, Hittite, Egyptian, Greek or Etruscan, ever depicted a flute. All over the ancient world pipers used the double oboe. Jewish pipes must also have been oboes, particularly as *ḥalîl* is translated by the Septuaginta exclusively as *aulós*, and by the Vulgate as *tibia* (terms associated with the oboe).

Their use, too, corresponded to that of double oboes in other countries of the ancient world. They were played at joyous festivities as well as mourning ceremonies. When Christ entered Jairus's home to restore to life his apparently dead daughter, he found the funeral pipers in action, and the Talmudian tractate *Ktubot* IV: 4 asserts that in Israel even the poorest men hired at least two *ḥalilîm* for the funerals of their wives.

No pipes were used in the First Temple, which was destroyed in

586 B.C. The Second Temple, on the contrary, which was established after the Babylonian Exile at the end of the sixth century B.C., used no less than two and no more than twelve of them. They were heard twelve times a year: at the first and second Passover sacrifice, on the first Passover day, at Shvuot and in the eight days of the Tabernacles. The Talmudian tractate *Arachin* II: 3 adds that the final cadence came from one pipe only, "to make it more agreeable." This passage definitely proves that the instrument was a double oboe, as it speaks clearly of "the pipe" played before the altar, while the cadence was blown by "one pipe only"—that is, by one cane of a double oboe. It is difficult to decide for which of several reasons the two canes played together were less agreeable. Perhaps they were played *unisono*, thus causing unpleasant pulsations when not tuned or blown with perfect exactness; or they might have played separate parts, possibly and even probably in the manner of a drone, as was customary in ancient civilizations.

The description of Jewish pipe blowing would not be complete without mentioning its power to induce a state of trance. The apocryphal acts of the apostles relate that one day a Jewess played the pipes behind St. Thomas for an hour before he got into an ecstasy, and none could understand the words he then spoke except the piper.

In these later times, the cylindrical, cane form of the oboe, which we have to picture as resembling the oboes of Mesopotamia and Egypt, must have been replaced by a conical model. Among the Jewish coins stamped during Bar Kokba's revolt against Emperor Hadrian (132–135 A.D.), some show pairs of wind instruments. Numismaticians call them trumpets, or even trombones; but this is incorrect. The stout shape, the reedlike top, the disk that supports the lips, and the bell are all features of the modern Arabian oboe *zamr* and its relatives. Consequently, this oboe existed in Jewish Palestine at the beginning of the second century A.D. This statement is confirmed by an Arabian book of the seventh century A.D., the *Kitâb alḡānī*, which refers to the *mizmâr* or zamr and the *duff* as the martial instruments of the Jewish tribes of Al-Hijaz.

The tractate *Kelim* XI: 6 mentions an instrument *simpuniâ* in the same sentence as *ḥalîl*. Some of the translators interpret it as a double flute, and some as a bagpipe. Nothing is certain about the name except its origin from Greek *symphoneia*. This etymology, however, does not advance our knowledge. For the Greek word did not mean an instrument, as we explained on page 84. The Talmudian *simpuniâ* is characterized as eventually having *knafayîm*.

The term *kānâf* means a wing or a similar appendage, as a leg or an arm; the ending indicates duality. This is an obscure epithet, and we have to postpone its discussion for the time being.

As to the interpretation as *bagpipes*, such an instrument never existed in Israel. The term *śimpuniâ* or *śumponiâ* in the tractate *Kelim* XI: 6 owes this translation to a commentator on the Book of Daniel, Saadia, who lived in the twelfth century A.D. and therefore cannot be quoted as a reliable authority. If *śumponiâ* was a bagpipe, why does the same tractate mention the same instrument under a different name a few chapters later? For, the term *ḥēmát ḥalilîm* in *Kelim* XX: 2 is likewise interpreted as bagpipe, and even with a better reason, as the two words mean 'bag of pipes.' Yet, it is hard to believe that the author of this tractate, which lists all kinds of objects as being either pure or impure, would have listed the bagpipe or, rather, one sort of bagpipe, not with other musical instruments, but with mortars and troughs. Moreover, should not a bagpipe rather have been called *ḥālîl ḥêmet*, that is 'bagpipe,' not 'pipebag'? If *ḥālîl* means a musical pipe in that passage, it would be more correct to think of a bag to keep and carry the pipes in, such as is often depicted on Greek vases.

THE MNAANIM are mentioned in one passage only; the Second Book of Samuel describes how the Ark of the Covenant was carried up to Jerusalem, and David, with all the house of Israel, played before it on stringed instruments, drums, cymbals and *mna-ʿanʿîm*. Since this term came from the verb *nūaʿ*, 'shook,' the name might have applied to a rattling vessel. Such a rattle, dating from about 1000 B.C., was excavated at Tell bêt-Mirsun near Hebron, and later rattles of clay were found in various places of Palestine. But these rattles were children's toys rather than ceremonial implements.

Some scholars have interpreted *mnaʿanʿîm* as 'sistra,' since this word likewise means a 'shaken' instrument. The author disagreed with them in an earlier publication, alleging that the sistrum was too closely related with the worship of Hathor and Isis to find a place in the Jewish ritual. This objection can no longer be maintained. In the last years excavations from Sumerian cemeteries have proved that sistra existed entirely unconnected with cults of Isis. Thus, the mnaʿanʿîm might have been sistra.

SELSLIM AND MSILTAYIM. The interpretation of the two terms *mṣiltâyîm* and *ṣelṣlîm* (Talmudian *ṣlāṣál*) is not difficult.

Both go back to a verb *ṣalâl,* 'clash'; the dual ending of one of them, *-âyim,* hints of a two-parted object; kindred terms in other oriental languages, as *zīl* in Arabic and Turkish, *ṣalāṣil* in Arabic and *sil-sil* in Tibetan, signify 'cymbals'; finally, the seventy-two Septuaginta translated both Hebrew terms by the Greek *kýmbala.* Thus the interpretation 'cymbals' can be considered correct.

The Bible mentions two different kinds of *ṣelṣlîm: ṣelṣlê šāmaʿ* and *ṣelṣlê trūāʿ* (the Hebrew plural ending *-im* changing into *ê* when the word is followed by an attribute). The adjective *šāmaʿ* means 'clear,' and *trūāʿ,* as with the shofar, 'harsh,' 'noisy.' The distinction indicated by these attributes is by no means restricted to Jewish cymbals. The Tibetans, for example, use two kinds of cymbals; one kind, broad-rimmed with small central bosses, are held in a horizontal position and softly struck in a vertical movement to worship the divinities of heaven; the other kind, narrow-rimmed with large bosses, are held in a vertical position and vigorously struck in a horizontal movement to worship the divinities of earth. This distinction seems general throughout Asia in both past and present times. The reliefs on the Hindu-Javanese temple at Borobudur in Java, carved about 800 A.D., make a clear difference between the same two forms of cymbals and manners of playing. Both types are found even in medieval Europe. The vigorously struck vertical cymbals are represented in a Spanish apocalypse from 1085 A.D. in the Biblioteca Nacional in Madrid and in a Mantuan manuscript of the eleventh century, while the Florentine sculptor, Luca della Robbia (about 1430), figured a whole group of angels with horizontal, softly played cymbals on the singers' estrade of the cathedral in Florence. Was it accidental that he gave the cymbals of 'heaven' to angels?

The Bible furnishes no further details on cymbals. They are referred to in the Talmudian tractate *Arachin:* "In the Temple there was a cymbal of metal having a soft sound. As it was damaged, the sages sent for craftsmen in Alexandria; but after the repair the soft timbre had gone. They restored the previous state, and the sound was soft again."

To conclude from this passage that the Jews had got their cymbals from Egypt would be erroneous; while cymbals were used in Israel as early as about 1100 B.C., the first evidence of cymbals in Egypt dates only from the beginning of our era—that is, more than a thousand years later.

The name *mṣiltayîm* probably does not mean two-handed cymbals.

As has been described in the foregoing chapter, small cymbals in one hand occurred in two forms: either attached to the thumb and middlefinger of dancers and played in the manner of castanets, or fastened inside the prongs of a flexible split cane, as *cymbals on clappers*. The tiny castanet-cymbals, known as *ṣanûǵ* in modern Egypt, can easily be eliminated because *mṣiltayîm* are nowhere mentioned as an instrument of dancers, but always connected with ritual. To be sure, the Arabic version of the Bible has the word *ṣanûǵ*, but not as a translation of *mṣiltayîm*. In spite of its Arabic meaning, it stands for *ṣelṣelîm*—that is, for cymbals which, according to the historian Flavius Josephus, were *mégala*, 'wide.'

The interpretation 'cymbals on clappers,' on the contrary, is backed by the fact that the word *mṣiltayîm* appears in the dual form while *selṣlîm* is written in the simple plural form. It would be logical, then, to suppose a stronger gemination of the two parts in the *mṣiltayîm*.

Nevertheless, as the two terms are etymologically similar and never occur together in the same text, it is possible that they designate the very same instrument.

SHALISHIM are mentioned in only one verse of the Bible, I Samuel 18: 6, when the women of Israel welcome King Saul after the glorious battle against the Philistines. This word has been the most disputed musical term of the Hebrew language; as *šālišîm* is clearly connected with *šlošâ*, 'three,' and *šalóš*, 'thrice,' translators of the Bible suggested now triangles, now triangular harps, three-stringed lutes and even fiddles. None of these translations can be accepted.

The verse reads: "And it came to pass as they came, when David was returned from the slaughter of the Philistine, that the women came out of all the cities of Israel, singing and dancing, to meet king Saul, with tabrets, with joy, and with instruments of musick [*uvšālišîm*]." The reader will realize that the Holy Script separates the precarious word from the one musical instrument mentioned in the same verse, *vtupîm*, "with tabrets." Poets and chroniclers never separate coherent notions; so the term cannot mean an instrument. Also the Talmud does not mention it.

Possibly the word indicates some form of dance, as dance names composed with 'three' are not unusual, such as the Roman *tripudium* of the priests of Mars, the old German *Treialtrei* and the Austrian *Dreysteyrer*.

MAGREPHA was the Hebrew name given to the Greco-Egyptian water organ, *hydraulos*. This earliest organ will be discussed in full in the Greek chapter; the Hebrew chapter is only concerned with its problematical existence in Israel.

Using adaptations of the Greek term *hardūlîs*, or *ardablîs*, the Talmudian tractates *Arachin* and *Tamid* describe it as having ten holes (probably what we call grooves), each producing ten (according to the tractate *Sukka*, one hundred) notes so that the organ was capable of producing one hundred or, according to *Sukka*, one thousand notes. Its height and its width were an *amma* each, that is, an ell of twenty inches. The tractates say nothing about the pipes, the slider action or the hydraulic pressure.

Modern writers have doubted this description and even the existence of the organ itself in Israel. The theologian, Johann Weiss, for example, calls the number of notes "ridiculous" and says, this information is a "Talmudian childishness." Still, other organs of antiquity had as many as eighteen keys or sliders and *tot acies tibiarum*, 'as many rows of pipes' belonging to each, as the Church Father Tertullianus says in *De anima*, chapter 14; the medieval author called Bern Anonymus, who drew his statements from antique sources, replaced *tot* by *aut V aut X*, 'either five or ten'; and again, Wolstan in his *Vita S. Swithuni* indicated ten rows or stops.

The only question is whether the Temple had an organ or not. The old comment on the Talmud relates: Rabbi Shimon ben Gamliel said that no *hirdōlîs* was in the Temple; on the contrary, Rabbi Rabba ben Shila said, in the names of Rabbi Mathna and Rabbi Shmuel, there was a *magrepha* in the Temple. Who was right? Rabbi Shimon lived in the second century A.D., while Rabbi Rabba was two centuries later, though this authority, Rabbi Shmuel, had lived about the year 200 A.D. Rabbi Shimon, as the oldest of them, is perhaps the most reliable. On the other hand his information is meager, and it may be that the foreign term confused him. Thus, it would be risky to make a decision. Besides, the question has but little importance, as so recent an instrument as the organ cannot have been used except for the last period of the Third Temple at the end of Israel's national existence.

THE HEADINGS OF THE PSALMS. We have purposely omitted several terms which frequently have been claimed to be names of musical instruments, such as *ngînót, gittit, šošanîm*. These terms, among others, occur in the headings of a great number of

Psalms. A frequent example of such a heading is *lamnaṣêaḥ bingīnót mizmór ldawíd.*

There can be no doubt of the meaning of *mizmór ldawíd;* the latter word means 'belonging to David,' while *mizmór* is a kind of poem. The word *lamnaṣêaḥ,* used in as many as fifty-four Psalm headings, has often been translated "to the chief musician" or "to the conductor"; the correct meaning is 'to be performed.' It is more difficult to understand those words which explain the manner of performing. To begin with, *ngínâ* was, and is, generally conceived as a 'stringed instrument'; so, *lamnaṣêaḥ bingīnót* would mean 'to be performed on stringed instruments,' and *bingīnót al-hašmīnít,* 'on the eight-stringed instruments.' Consequently, some scholars took the headings of the Psalms for indications concerning the instruments on which the various Psalms were to be accompanied. Even as late as 1921, an English author, Dr. Langdon, emphasized that the Hebrews "classified their psalms and liturgical services chiefly by the names of the instruments employed in accompaniments."

This is an error. Certainly, allotting well-determined tasks to musical instruments is very frequent in oriental civilizations. But it would be unparalleled to assign different instruments to the various poems of a homogeneous collection of religious poetry. Besides, were the Psalms accompanied at all, or at least intended to be accompanied? If so, why not by a kinnor or a nevel, a ḥālîl or a tof? Though some of these instruments are referred to in the text of the psalms, not one is mentioned in a heading; the so-called "classification by the names of the instruments employed" actually omits all known names of instruments!

In their place, the headings name a series of the strangest terms: *ngīnót* (Psalms 4, 54, 55, 61, 67, 76), *nhīlót* (5), *ngīnót ha-šmīnît* (6, 12), *gittít* (8, 81, 84), *mût-lēbên* (9), *šošanîm* (45, 69), *ʿalamot* (46), *ayelit-hašaḥar* (22), *idûtûn* (39, 62, 77), *maḥalat* (53, 88), *yonât illêm rḥaqîm* (56), *šošan-ʿēdût* (60, 80).

Except for the term *ngīnot,* which will be discussed afterwards, these words mean: heritages, eighth, wine press or from the town Gat, die-white, lilies, maidens, hind of the dawn, confessors, diseases, mute dove far off, lily-testimony. This series is unintelligible at first sight; but at any rate it is not a "classification by instruments."

Is not even *ngínâ* a 'stringed instrument'? The word belongs to the verb *nāgaʿ,* 'strike.' An intermediate verb, *nāgan,* a form used in connection with strings, reminds us of the old German expression *die Laute* (*Harfe, Zither*) *schlagen,* 'to strike the lute (harp, zither).' It is the connection with strings that caused philologists to translate *ngînâ* by 'stringed instrument.' Yet, this was not correct, as no passage in which the word occurs supports this interpretation. In some passages, Psalm 69: 13, Job 39: 9, Lamentations 3: 14, the word is apparently used as meaning a satirical song, and some dictionaries have gone to the trouble of discovering that by the process of "synecdotic specialization" this meaning could be a derivation of the original meaning 'stringed instrument'!

It would be more sensible to compare the Hebrew group of words with a corresponding group in Greek. There, *krûô* means 'strike' and especially 'strike strings,' just as *nāgaʿ* and *nāgan* in Hebrew; however, its noun, *krûma,* does not signify any instrument, but a certain melody—that is, 'a thing struck.' And this is exactly the significance of the post-Biblical noun related to *nāgaʿ,* the well-known *nigûn* or 'melodic pattern.' *Ngînâ* may be the older form of *nigûn.*

Oriental music has always been, and still is, composed in well-defined designs or melodic patterns. These melodic patterns might be compared to the three Greek orders or styles in architecture, the composition of which had detailed rules with which the artist was compelled to comply, and only within these specifications could he follow his personal interpretation. In music, melodies using the same scale, and related to each other by their general mood, belong to one melodic pattern. Such patterns are familiar in Arabian and in Hindu music, where in later times they were called *maqamât* and *râgas.*

The list of Arabian maqamât has a striking resemblance to the Hebrew headings in the Psalms printed above. If *gittít* is a *ngînâ* described by the geographical epithet 'from Gat,' the Arabs also have geographical maqamât, such as *isfahan, nahawand, rehaw,* which are the names of places. Ordinal numbers, like 'the eighth' of the Hebrew series, occur in the Arabian maqamât as well: *siga,* 'the third,' *ʿašîrân,* 'the tenth.' For general terms, such as the Hebrew 'heritages,' or 'wine press,' the maqamât have titles such as *mahur,* 'jumping,' or *ʿušaq,* 'passion'; and for the 'hind of the dawn,' they have 'the chaste love of the doe.' Curious, and apparently meaningless, combinations, such as 'die-white,' are matched by similar hyphenations in Arabic, as *higâz-kar, bayat-šuri, rast-šanbar,* which signify a combination of two maqamât.

Since maqamât and râgas belong to certain moods, we can test our interpretation by seeing if those Psalms which have similar headings have the same mood as well. The material is rather limited for such an investigation, but encouraging as far as it goes. If we confine ourselves to examining those groups which consist of at least three Psalms, we find that the eight nginot Psalms are prayers for escape, based on confidence in God and his power and magnificence: "Answer me when I call, O God of my righteousness" . . . "O Jehovah, rebuke me not in thine anger" . . . "Help, Jehovah" . . . "Save me, O God" . . . "Give ear to my prayer" . . . "Hear my cry" . . . "God be merciful unto us" . . . The three gittit Psalms, on the contrary, are gay and filled with thankful joy: "O Jehovah, our Lord, How excellent is thy name in all the earth" . . . "Sing aloud unto God our strength" . . . "How amiable are thy tabernacles" . . . Two of the three idutun Psalms are in a mood of resignation: "I said, I will take heed to my ways" . . . "My soul waiteth in silence for God only" . . .

The problem of the words 'to be performed . . .' seems to be solved except for the term *ngīnót*. If *nginâ* is the Hebrew name for *maqama* or any similar idea, not for one particular maqama, then the expression 'to be performed in *ngīnót*' needs some further explanation that we are not able to give. It is mere guesswork to suggest that the word in question might have meant both 'maqama' in general as well as a certain kind of maqama.

6. *Greece, Rome and Etruria*

ARCHITECTURE and sculpture were native arts of the Greeks. To be sure, early Greek artists borrowed technique, style and ideas from the older Mediterranean nations. But out of this heritage they made the classical canon which determined the destiny of occidental art for more than two thousand years, and which even influenced the art of the Buddhist Orient.

In sharp contrast to the fine arts, Greek music was almost entirely imported. The Phrygian and Lydian tonalities were reminiscent of Asia Minor; Olympus, the patriarch of Greek music, was said to have been a son of the Phrygian Marsyas; and his disciple, Thaletas, was a Cretan. No instrument originated in Greece. The geographer Strabo writes: "One writer says 'striking the Asiatic cithara'; another calls auloi 'Berecyntian' and 'Phrygian'; and some of the instruments have been called by barbarian names, nablas, sambyke, barbitos, magadis, and several others."

Most instruments were surprisingly simple, indeed primitive, and it is not easy to connect them with the maturity of contemporaneous architecture and sculpture. Down to the Hellenistic period pipes remained in a rough state without any contrivance to improve or facilitate playing; even the kithara of the virtuosi had its strings distastefully glued on with thongs of greasy napeskin; additional strings were forbidden; the importation of better instruments from abroad was severely criticized. All these facts testify that instrumental music in Greece did not become a self-sufficient art. The terms

A. Kithara.

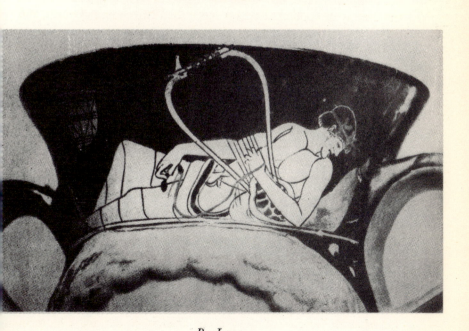

B. Lyra.

Greek lyre-players, Classical Epoch.

PLATE VII.

kithárisis and *aúlēsis,* expressing two types of independent instrumental music, occur much less frequently in Greek texts than the words 'kitharody' and 'aulody,' which mean the accompaniment, on a kithara or an aulos, of song (*ōdê*). And how extremely seldom do pictures show soloists on the kithara using both hands in plucking, instead of employing the plectron to contribute a few accompanying notes! Plato went to the length of condemning purely instrumental music.

Our poets [he says in the second book of the *Laws* §669] divorce melody and rhythm from words, by their employment of kithara and aulos without vocal accompaniment, though it is the hardest of tasks to discover what such wordless rhythm and tune signify. . . . Nay, we are driven to the conclusion that all this so popular employment of kithara and aulos, not subordinated to the control of dance or song for the display of speed and virtuosity, and the reproduction of the cries of animals, is in the worst of bad taste.

Plato may have represented the most conservative point of view, but he clearly delineates a general Greek view; music, in Hellas, was so closely connected with poetry that its creative impulse came from the spoken word. This meant subordination of instrumental music to singing.

Still, the Greeks, as other peoples, were indebted to instruments for having given them a well-organized musical system with scales and notation. All their musical terminology was reminiscent of the instrumental origin of their notations. A 'note' was called *chordê,* after the string; a certain note, *lichanós,* or forefinger, took its name from the string plucked or deadened by this finger; *kroûma* or 'percussion' (with the plectron) signified melody; even the system itself was called *lyra* by the theorists.

LYRES were indeed the chief, the divine instrument. When "the blest gods the genial day prolong, Apollon tun'd the lyre," and in the famous contest between Apollon and Marsyas, the national divinity opposed the kithara to the aulos of the foreign silenus. Being Apollon's attribute, the lyre expressed the so-called Apollonian side of Greek soul and life, wise moderation, harmonious control and mental equilibrium, while the pipes stood for the Dionysian side, for inebriation and ecstasy.

Lyres are mentioned in the *Iliad,* that is, in the ninth century B.C. "The youthful dancers in a circle bound" moved to its tunes, the professional epic singers accompanied themselves on the lyre, and so did the heroes. When the Greek kings went to reconcile Achilles, "amus'd at ease, the godlike man they found, Pleas'd with the solemn harp's [i. e., lyre's] harmonious sound." The adjectives to characterize this sound are not very enlightening; like French *haut*, they signify both 'loud' and 'high.'

Homer calls the lyre now *phorminx*, now *kítharis*. Most writers interpret these names as equivalent to the later word *lyra*, which meant, as we shall see at once, a loosely connected, light and simple lyre. This is certainly erroneous. There is little evidence of such a lyre in the ninth century. Homer, on the contrary, mentions the bulging form of his lyre (*glaphyrós*) and emphasizes its costly decoration. *Kalós*, 'beautiful,' *daidaléos*, 'skillful,' *perikalléos*, 'marvellous,' are the epithets he gives it. "The well-wrought harp [i. e., lyre] from conquer'd Thebae came, Of polish'd silver was its costly frame." Homer's lyre was unmistakably a kithara, such as depicted on several so-called geometric vases: small, rounded and held in a slanting position. It was a Syrian lyre, familiar on Aramaean, Hittite and Phoenician reliefs.

In the following centuries, the names *phorminx* and *kítharis* were replaced by new terms, *kithara* and *lyra*, which corresponded to new types of lyres.

The kithara had a heavy, solidly joined body, a wooden soundboard and strong arms. In most cases the strings were wound around the crossbar and held fast by greasy rolls of oxskin. By turning or shifting the sticky rolls on the crossbar, the player was able to tune his instrument. Only in a more recent epoch the kithara adopted elaborate contrivances that seem to have supplanted the old napeskin rolls. Among them was an ingeniously made, and artistically carved, lever which lifted the crossbar, thus tightening all the strings at once. This invention had a forerunner, however; as early as the fifteenth century B.C., Egyptian lyres had movable arms which, piercing the body, could be pushed upward at will by the player's knee or chest. (pl. VII b, fig. 32)

The kithara was held vertical, or even leaning towards the player. It would have been too heavy to be inclined forward.

The kithara was used by the early bards to accompany their epic songs inspired by the deeds of gods and heroes. It was still the instrument of professional musicians a thousand years later when they had degenerated into capricious and intriguing virtuosi who, at exorbitant fees, performed in public theaters where adoring ladies would snatch away their plectra as highly prized souvenirs.

The lyra belonged to beginners and amateurs. It was more primitive than the kithara, although more recent. It was doubtless a retrogressive form of the rounded Syrian lyre, though the Greeks attributed it to the Thracians.

Lyras were loosely constructed. The body was either a tortoise shell or a shallow wooden bowl placed on edge and covered by a piece of skin as a soundboard. Two horns of an animal, or wooden arms, projected from the bowl and supported the horizontal crossbar. The strings, fastened on the underside of the bowl and held away from the soundboard by a bridge, were attached in the same way as those of the kithara. In playing, the lyra was held aslant, or even horizontal, away from the player. (pl. VII a)

There seems to have been no difference in the strings of the lyra and the kithara. The earliest strings were probably made of hemp. An old Greek legend relates that Apollon killed the singer Linos for having replaced the "usual" hemp strings by gut strings. But this legend is not convincing; the Greek word for hemp being *linon* (English *linen*), it would be more logical to credit Linos with the introduction of hemp strings than with having done away with them.

The number of strings varied from three to twelve, four and seven being the most usual. Lyres with three and four strings were described and depicted from the ninth century B.C. on; with five strings from the eighth century, with six and seven from the seventh century, with eight from the sixth century, and with nine, ten, eleven and twelve strings from the fifth century.

The author, in a previous paper, was able to prove that the customary tuning was pentatonic without half-tones in *E G A B D* (but not necessarily in this order). Additional strings duplicated these notes in the higher or lower octave instead of filling in the missing diatonic notes, *F* and *C*. It seems, however, that the *E* and *B* strings were tuned to *F* and *C* when certain tonalities required them.

This throws light upon the strange story of Timotheus, the Milesian, who lived from about 450 to about 360 B.C. This famous revolutionary poet, composer and player, with the proud motto "I do not sing tradition," is said to have been condemned by a Spartan court for having added some strings to his kithara, and the ephors decided that they had to be cut off. It was probably not the increased number for which he was reproached, but for having added special strings which altered the pentatonic character of the instrument and facilitated the modulation from one tonality into another.

Transcribing the Greek accordatura as *E G A B D* conforms to our conventional transcription of Greek notes, which translates arbitrarily by our white key notes, *A-a'*, the two standard octaves that the Greek called the *sýstēma téleion,* or 'perfect system.' But, as the *sýstēma* was supposed to coincide with the natural range of untrained men's voices, tenors and basses, it would probably be more correct to transpose the conventional notes by a major or minor third lower.

The two diatonic notes, *F* and *C*, which were lacking in the lyre as well as the semitones and quarter-tones, were produced, in the rare cases in which they might have been needed, by pressing and thus tightening the next lower string with one of the fingers. One used the forefinger when the next note lower could be produced on the open string, *b-c* for example. One used the middlefinger when the next note lower had already occupied the shortening forefinger, *c-c♯* for example, or when the next note lower was two semitones distant, *b-c♯* for instance. This explains the three positions of most signs in Greek notation: erect, flattened and reversed; the normal, erect sign indicated 'open string,' the flattened position 'forefinger,' and the reversed position 'middlefinger.'

In postclassical times the touching fingers were frequently replaced by complicated devices to tighten the strings, similar to the double action of a modern harp. One sees them more or less distinctly on many reliefs and vases of the later centuries. A passage in Ptolemaeus indicates how complicated they must have been; for the kithara he enumerates six tone systems, which differ in the width of their whole tones and semitones. Examining the pitches required, we find that the player needed four artificial notes from the *B* string and three from the *E* string. These demanded not a double action, as our harp, but a quadruple action. The lyra, on the contrary, had only two tuning systems, and not more than one artificial note was required of any string.

The manner of plucking was almost similar with the lyra and the kithara. Three sources of information have contributed to our knowledge: detailed representations on art works; a few poetic descriptions; actual practice, preserved in Nubia and watched by the author himself. In Nubia the right hand scratches all strings at once with a big plectron, while the stretched fingers of the left hand, opened like a fan, deaden those strings which must not sound. The technical and musical possibilities are rather limited; the Nubians continually repeat a small ostinato motif of five notes throughout the song. Doubtless, most art works depicting lyre players in

Greece, Etruria and Rome represent a technique similar to the Nubian manner of playing: the right hand is scratching over the strings in a violent dash, and the fingers of the left hand are stretched along the strings.

This, however, was certainly not the only way to play. On some vases we see the left fingers plucking, not deadening, and this is confirmed by Pseudo-Asconius, who says that while the right hand uses the plectron the fingers of the left hand pluck the strings (*chordas carpunt*). We can form an idea of this technique from the playing of the Japanese long zither, *koto:* "In the right hand a small slip of ox-horn, or other hard material, is held, with which all the six strings are scratched rapidly, from the first to the sixth, close to the long bridge at the right of the instrument. The strings are then at once damped with the left hand, and a little melody accompanying the voice is tinkled out with the left little finger, the 'scratch' coming to mark the pauses in the rhythm" (Piggott). Essential features of this description recur in the poetical record of the statue of a musician, written by Lucius Apuleius in the second century A.D.; the player's left hand, he says, "moves (*molitur*) the strings with fingers held apart, while the right hand is getting the plectron ready to play just as the singing pauses (*pulsabulum admovet ceu parata percutere cum vox in cantico interquiescerit*). Both Piggott for Japan and Apuleius for classical antiquity mention a singing voice, the left hand plucking the strings, and a plectron in the right hand marking the pauses in the rhythm. Both describe the same technique. So it is possible, indeed probable, that they share a fifth point that only the Japanese description adds: dampening the strings after having scratched them with the plectron. This seems obligatory, if the strings are scratched with normal force.

With the help of the Japanese parallel the usual attitude of players on Greek art works is sufficiently explained; the right hand has just scratched, being drawn beyond the last string, while the left hand is busy dampening in preparation for plucking. The Greek sculptor and painter prefers the final to a transitory movement in a gesture.

It would be unnecessary, then, to mention the Nubian technique, except that such a technique must have come to Africa with the instrument and, if so, it must have existed either in old West Asia or in Greece, or perhaps in both places. Possibly the Greeks were familiar with both manners of playing.

While the Nubian technique suggests a Nubian—that is, an ostinato accompaniment of the voice—the Japanese technique points to a more elaborate form of accompaniment. Plato gives an idea of the complication of the latter form of accompaniment when, in the *Laws* 7: 812, he warns teacher and pupil to "make their tones accord with those of the voice. As for diversification and complication of the instrumental part—the strings giving out one tone and the composer of the melody another—and, in fact, for correspondence of lesser interval with greater, quicker note with longer, lower tones with higher, and equally for all sorts of complication of the rhythm by instrumental accompaniment, no such devices are to be employed with pupils."

Besides the one or two forms of playing with a plectron, the Greeks used, under the name *psilê* ('empty') *kithárisis*, a solo playing without singing, both in natural notes and in octave harmonics; either hand plucked with the bare fingers. Similar methods were mentioned in the Sumerian, Egyptian and Hebrew chapters. It seems that in Greece this technique was almost exclusively confined to the kithara.

This restriction, however, does not suffice to explain why, according to ancient writers, it was more difficult to play the kithara than the lyra. It would be more likely to suppose a different disposition of the strings on the two instruments. Indeed, modern Ethiopia, the only country with two lyres besides ancient Greece, tunes them in a different arrangement, though to the same pentatonic scale:

Kerâr   d'' g' d' b' e''
Bagannâ   d' b' e'' d'' g' d' e' g a b.

Although a relationship drawn over two thousand years and two thousand miles is rather farfetched, it may be of more value than none at all. Let us then go a step farther and suppose, as a working hypothesis, that the Ethiopian lyre *kerâr* has preserved the ancient Greek, or even Mediterranean, accordatura. The author feels easier in using this hypothesis because he saw exactly the same arrangement with the Nubian lyre in Upper Egypt.

If we assume that the Greek lyres, which were tuned to the same notes as the kerâr, also had the same peculiar arrangement with a high string close to the lowest one of an ascending scale (like the modern banjo), this accordatura would read in Greek terminology:

paranêtē (d')   first string
lichanós (g)   second string

mésē	(*a*)	third string
paramésē	(*b*)	fourth string
nêtē	(*e'*)	fifth string

This is particularly significant. The *mésē* or 'middle' (note and string) holds the center. The *nêtē* or 'low' string surprisingly designates the highest note in Greek music, not because it is the lowest when the lyre is held in its normal, inclined position, but because the Semitic Orient calls high sounds low, and low sounds high. *Paramésē* and *paranêtē* are clear, as *pará*, in Greek, means both 'opposite' and 'beside.' There is only one name left—*lichanós*. When, in the usual way, the player deadens the five strings with the five fingers of the left hand, the thumb touches the first, the middle-finger the third, the fourth finger the fourth, and the fifth finger the fifth string; the string (and note) *lichanós* is left to the forefinger. And the Greek word for 'forefinger' is *lichanós*!

This seems so conclusive that our hypothesis, taking the Ethiopian and Nubian lyre accordatura as the key to the ancient Greek tuning, is apparently more than a mere supposition.

Among the four terms for strings and notes, derived from their position in space, *lichanós*, as the name of a finger, is surprising and very probably more recent than the others. The four remaining notes, *d' a b e'*, must, therefore, be supposed to represent the tuning of the earlier four-stringed kithara; Otto Johannes Gombosi, in his latest book on Greek tonalities, comes to the same conclusion from a different approach.

In conclusion, we are still unable to see the musical difference between lyras and kitharas. The puzzle becomes more intricate when we learn that the Greeks had a third kind of lyre, *bárbiton* or *bárbitos*. From all the passages dealing with this instrument we obtain no further information than that it was played with a plectron and tuned to the lower octave of the *pektis*, which, however, was a harp, not a lyre. There was a kindred word, *barbat*, in Persian; but the relation is not helpful, as we know only that it designated a stringed instrument used about 600 A.D. by Byzantine singing-girls.

THE HARP was angular and 'vertical'; arched harps occur only in an archaic statuette from the Cyclades in the Athens National Museum, and, much later, in a painting from Herculaneum (first century A.D.) in the National Museum at Naples.

In continental Hellas no harp is represented earlier than about 450 B.C., although it was probably known before that.

The harp was always considered an alien instrument in Greece and Rome, coming from the Orient. Plato condemned it because its greater number of strings and notes facilitated modulation, instability and, therewith, *hēdonê*—that is, sensory pleasure. Being an instrument of intimacy and dreamy absorption, its players were almost exclusively women, hetaerae as well as ladies of correct society.

Among the terms for 'harp' in Greek literature, the most important were *psaltêrion, mágadis* and *pēktis*. The magadis was called "ancient" and of Lydian origin. The Spartan poet Alkman, a Lydian himself, was the first to mention it, in the seventh century B.C. It was played with the bare fingers without a plectron and had twenty strings, that is, ten double strings tuned in octaves.

A hundred years after Alkman, Anacreon in one of his love lyrics sang:

> O Leucastis, I play
> Upon a Lydian harp,
> A magade of twenty strings,
> And thou art in thy youthful prime!

The pektis, too, was immortalized by Anacreon:

> I have eaten the mid-day meal of honey-cakes broken fine;
> And now on the graceful harp I daintily thrum the strings,
> Making merry with song for thee,
> O dainty maiden mine!

The epithet *eróessa* that the poet gives this harp can be literally translated by 'lovely.'

The pektis was sometimes said to be identical with the magadis; but in some passages the two names are mentioned beside each other.

Later on, says Euphorios, the magadis was altered and was called *sambýke*, while Apollodoros relates the magadis to the more recent *psaltêrion*. On the other hand, the sambyke had very short strings and, consequently, according to Aristides Quintilianus (c. 100 A.D.), an effeminate timbre. The reader may compare what has been said on the sambyke on pages 83–84.

The *trígōnon*, or 'triangle,' called either a Phrygian, or a Syrian, or even an Egyptian instrument, may have been a variation of the psalterion.

THE LUTE of the Greeks and the Romans corresponded exactly to that existing in western Asia and Egypt, so that the ancient authors could call it alternately an Assyrian, a Cappadocian and an

Egyptian instrument. It had a long neck without pegs, a small body, frets and three strings. The Hellenes, therefore, called it by the Greek name *tríchordon*, 'three-stringed,' as well as by its foreign name, *pandûra*, which seems to have been derived from Sumerian *pan-tur*, 'bow-small.' If this etymology is correct, the term is a strong evidence that the pierced lute was derived from the musical bow.

Lutes, however, were extremely rare both in Greece and in Rome.

ZITHERS. Had the Greeks zithers? A few passages in Aristotle, Julius Pollux and Juba (d. 24 A.D.), possibly suggest the existence of such an instrument. These authors speak of a *simíkion* with thirty-five, and an *epigóneion* with forty strings, as old and foreign instruments. So great a number of strings excludes both a lute and a lyre. The harp was a real polychord; but even the largest antique harps had no more than twenty-three strings at most. There is no possibility left, then, except the board-zither. The Chinese *shê*, which belongs in this category, had fifty strings in antiquity. A board-zither can be placed either on the ground, or on a table or on the player's knees; the choice depends upon the customary position of rest. The Greeks did not squat on the floor and they were not accustomed to tables; but they had seats. Thus, the normal playing position of a Greek zither would have been that of lying across the knees of a sitting musician. The literal translation of the name *epigóneion* is indeed 'a thing on the knees,' as *epi* means 'upon' and *góny* 'knee.' This etymology is far more convincing than the ancient anecdote that a certain Epigonos had brought the instrument from Alexandria or Ambracia in Epirus. Etymologies dependent upon an inventor's name are apt to be false. Julius Pollux's information that the *simíkion* was invented by a man named Simos must be rejected as well. A connection with the Persian word *sīm*, which means 'string,' would be more likely.

Neither an epigoneion nor a simikion has been depicted by sculptors or painters. There is, however, another strange stringed instrument depicted on three later Roman sarcophagi, two in the Louvre and a third one in the cathedral at Agrigenti. The outer appearance resembles a lute; one distinguishes a small, round, bulging body and an unusually wide neck. The strings are numerous, eight to ten, and they are *open* and played like zither strings. Vertically held with the left hand, the instrument is leaned against the left shoulder. One of the three specimens, on a sarcophagus in the Louvre, is particularly fascinating, as the strings do not reach the top of the neck but end near the middle at different heights, their ends thus forming a diagonal line that descends towards the treble side. (pl. VIII b)

Looking for parallels, we find in a Persian manuscript written in 1345 A.D. an instrument called *muḡnī*. It is described as "a combination of the *rubâb*, a *qānūn*, and a *nuzha*," that is, of a lute and two zithers; an accompanying drawing shows a remarkable resemblance to the Roman instrument. The *muḡnī* is composed of a small, circular body and a long, wide neck without frets. Nine strings are indicated by their lateral tuning pegs, and their upper ends form a diagonal line across the neck. The similarity is so striking that some connection must be supposed. Besides, the muḡnī was said to have been invented in Magnesia in Asia Minor, a town formerly belonging to the Roman Empire.

PIPE would be the best translation of the Greek term *aulós* (plural *auloí*, in modern pronunciation *avlí*) and its Latin equivalent *tibia*, exactly as we have used the word "pipe" to translate Akkadian *ḫalilu*, Egyptian *ma·t* and Hebrew *ḥālîl*. The usual rendering of *aulós* as 'flute' is wrong and misleading. The author cannot forget his old teacher in Greek, who was a victim of this false interpretation. Whenever *aulós* occurred in a text that we read in class, he did not fail to point out the sensitive ears of his beloved heroes, so obviously superior to the Wagner-glutted ears of modern college boys; a flute, the weakest of instruments, sufficed to inflame their ecstasy and desire for combat!

The pipes on vases and reliefs, Greek and Roman, are not flutes, but double oboes of oriental shape, the sound of which could be as shrill and exciting as the sound of their relatives, the bagpipes of modern Scotch regiments.

So strong was the power required to blow such pipes that a great many contemporaneous paintings and reliefs show the player wearing a leather band which passes over the mouth and ties at the back of his head, and which is held in place by a thong running over the top of the head. At the mouth it had two holes just large enough to allow the pipes to pass through. This contrivance gave a regular pressure to the cheeks, which acted as bellows, as they do with a glass blower (see also on p. 91). The Greeks called it *phorbeiá*, and the Romans *capistrum*. It is a freak of history that this mouth-band has been preserved in one remote country only—in Java, with her neighboring island Madoera, where the ancient double oboe was used and pictured in the first millennium A.D.

Yet, there are many pictures of pipers without such a mouth-band, and poets occasionally praise the "sweet" tone of pipes (*gly-kýs*), just as the Hebrews called their pipes a *ḥāla* instrument, and as later on in Europe certain oboes had a name derived from *dulcis*. We do not know whether such a difference of tone was caused by the size of the reed, the shape of the instrument or the mouth-band.

But we do know that Greeks and Romans possessed many kinds of double oboes. The most important of them were the *Phrygian pipes*, in which the two tubes differed in length, the longer one being curved and ending in a wide, trumpetlike bell; the fingerholes were placed at different heights on either tube and, according to Prophyrios, the bore was narrow. A Greek name for these pipes was *auloì élymoi*. The *Lydian pipes*, on the contrary, called *tibiae serranae* or 'Phoenician pipes' by the Romans, had tubes of equal length with identical fingerholes.

The pipes were made in several sizes and pitches. The Greeks distinguished *parthénioi* or 'girls'' pipes as sopranos; *paidikoí* or 'boys'' pipes as altos; *téleioi* or 'perfect' pipes as tenors; *hypertéleioi* or 'superperfect' as basses. There are many other names which are not yet understood.

According to ancient writers, the earlier pipes had only four, or even three, fingerholes. The bore was narrow enough to exclude the production of fundamentals, so that overblowing meant a jump of only a fifth instead of the usual octave. Even with more than four holes, the pipe was restricted to melodies in one of the three types of tonalities on which Greek music was based—that is, diatonically filled fourths with the semitone respectively placed at the bottom (Dorian), in the middle (Phrygian), or at the top (Lydian). Only since the fifth century B.C. has the number and arrangement of the fingerholes permitted playing in all three of these tonalities. Later, the number was increased to fifteen, and the makers were forced to invent special contrivances that stopped or half-stopped those holes which were not needed and could not be reached by the stretched fingers. They provided the pipes with collars that had corresponding holes and could be turned to cover or uncover the pipe holes, and sometimes the wind outlets of these collars had cup-shaped extensions to lower the pitch. Such perfected pipes have been found in Pompei and Herculaneum.

It is a difficult problem to find out for what musical purpose twin oboes were used. Only one contemporaneous author, the Roman Marcus Terentius Varro (first century B.C.), gives a hint when he calls one of the tubes of a pair *tibia incentiva,* and the other *tibia succentiva,* but he does not explain why. It might be possible to interpret this enigmatic passage by referring to the use of the same word *succinere* in the early Christian Church. There it designated the interjection of an Amen or Hallelujah, with which the congregation responded to the psalmody of the soloist. *Incinere,* on the contrary, doubtlessly meant 'intone'; the Roman poet Propertius, who lived at the same time and in the same country as Varro, used it in connection with the words *varios ore modos,* to intone 'various melodies with the mouth.' Thus, one pipe gave the intonation, and the other the response. But this still would be unintelligible. If the intoning pipe had played with the singer, both pipes would have played alternately, and it would be hard to understand why the player needed two pipes. It would be logical, on the contrary, to suppose an intonation in the narrower sense—that is, giving the tone and sustaining it throughout the verse. The second pipe, perhaps, played the refrain, while possibly the drone went on and supported it, as in ancient Egypt and in the modern Orient.

But all generalizations should be avoided. Within an era of nearly two thousand years and within a gigantic empire, the style of playing probably changed no less than the styles of architecture and fine art. The single Phrygian oboist who accompanied the Greek drama and whom one poet wished to silence because of his "loquacity," certainly obscured the melodic idea with cascades of tumbling passages and roulades in the manner of modern oriental pipers. His style might have been very different from the art of that oboe-girl who in the early morning came with the drunken Alkibiades to knock and shout at the door to attend Plato's symposium with Agathon.

And both styles might have been entirely different from that of the pipers in the musical competitions at the Pythian games in Delphi. The 'Pythian Nome' performed by the competitors consisted of five parts or movements, such as the movements of a modern sonata, having different, indeed contrasting, characters. The most famous of these performances occurred in 586 B.C., when Sakadas, a celebrated piper, represented on his instrument the contest between Apollon and the dragon in five movements: the prelude, the first onset, the contest itself, the triumph following the victory and the expiration of the dragon hissing out its last breath in a sharp harmonic.

BAGPIPE. In a bagpipe, the mouth, in so far as it serves as a windchest, is replaced by the hide or bladder of an animal. A short tube, conducting the wind from the mouth, is inserted in one of the natural openings of this bag, and a clarinet in the other. This arrangement has two advantages: the wind chamber is larger, and the air can be compressed by a simple movement of the elbow instead of requiring constant pressure from the mouth.

The origin of the bagpipe is unknown. On a relief from the thirteenth century B.C., belonging to the Hittite palace at Eyuk, all too eager students have imagined they detected the earliest bagpipe; in reality, the bag is an animal offering, and the two "pipes" are ribbons hanging down from the two strings of a lute carried before it. It was also an error to see a bagpipe in the Aramaic word *šumponiāh* of the Book of Daniel, as we have shown on page 84. Again, we have explained on page 121 that such an instrument did not exist either in Israel or in classic Greece. (pl. IV f)

The first bagpipe of which one can be sure existed in the first century A.D. Suetonius, the historian of the Roman Caesars, relates of Nero that "towards the end of his life he had publicly vowed that if he retained his power he would at the games in celebration of his victory give a performance on the water-organ, the *choraulam et utricularium.*" This latter name, meaning a leather bag, can hardly be explained otherwise than as a bagpipe. All doubts are silenced by the following passage, in Suetonius's Greek contemporary, Dio Chrysostom, narrating that Nero "knew how to play the pipe with his mouth and the bag thrust under his arms." And still a third author of the same time, Martial, speaks of an *ascaules*, or 'bagpiper,' using the Greek word in a Latin epigram. The instrument, then, must have been recently imported from Asia and, like modern South Asiatic bagpipes, was probably provided either with a single or a double clarinet.

The further development of the bagpipe belongs to the history of medieval and modern Europe.

CROSS FLUTE. While in pre-Christian times Greek and Roman artists have depicted many oboes, they have left no trace of a flute. The reader must be on his guard against statues in museums because the hands holding the instruments, being the frailest parts of the sculptural work, are nearly always broken off and restored by recent artists in an unauthentic form. The first and only flute depicted in Greco-Roman antiquity, as far as we knew a few years ago, was a cross flute stamped on a coin of the Syrian town Panias, or Caesarea, from as late as 169 A.D.

This flute has now been antedated by an Etruscan flute.

The Etruscans have not yet been touched upon in this chapter. On the whole, the music of this people remained on a rather primitive level. Their paintings and reliefs almost invariably show reed pipes and plain lyres of the lyra shape; no kithara, no improved aulos occurs. The wall paintings in tombs such as the *tombe delle Leonesse, del Triclinio, della Pulcella, dei Leopardi,* are distinct enough to remove all doubt.

However, a recent excavation of an Etruscan tomb of the second century B.C., the *Sepolcro dei Volumni* near Perugia, has revealed an urn, the so-called *urna del flautista,* on which the sculptor had carved the head of a musician playing a cross flute, the earliest ever depicted. The instrument is rather short; if it were life-size it would measure less than two feet. It has the mouth-hole about a quarter of the way down its length and is held to the player's right side. Both hands are stopping the fingerholes. (pl. VIII a)

PAN-PIPES will be discussed in the chapter on Chinese antiquity. In Greece they were only shepherds' instruments. "Behind the sheep, piping on their reeds, they go," sings Homer. They had no place in art music.

Pan-pipes were a set of graduated tubes, generally seven in number, each resembling a simple vertical flute, stopped at the lower end and without fingerholes, giving one note of the scale; they were all joined together to form a raft. The upper ends formed a horizontal line, and the player could shift his mouth along them according to the note required. The line formed by the lower ends of the tubes varied in shape. The earlier Greek pan-pipes, up to about 400 B.C., resembled the Chinese pan-pipes of the Han Dynasty at the end of the pre-Christian era: the raft was rectangular, the tubes being graduated in length internally. Later forms had one lower end cut off the rectangle; or a larger corner, leaving a wing shape, which followed the real length of the tubes; or the diagonal line of the tubes sometimes descended in steps.

Their name was *syrinx* or, more exactly, *syrinx polykalamós,* 'the syrinx with many canes,' while *syrinx monokalamós* designated a single vertical flute in learned texts. Philologists disagree on the etymology. The most likely root is Semitic *šrq,* as in Hebrew *šaráq* and Syriac *šraq,* 'he hissed,' and Hebrew *šriqâ,* 'whistling.'

The few excavated specimens are made of wood, bronze, clay or of a kind of resin; cane may also have been used but it is too perishable to have been preserved. One of them, a Roman instrument, consists of whistle pipes formed by channels in a solid piece of earthenware.

Wherever there are pan-pipes, in Greece or in primitive countries, they are connected with love charm. Legend relates that Pan was in love with a beautiful Arcadian nymph and pursued her until her flight was stopped by the river Ladon; she would have been caught had not a protecting divinity changed her into a cane. It was from this cane that Pan cut his syrinx to play upon when passion and longing possessed him. Preserved in Diana's cavern near Ephesus after his death, it could test a maiden's virginity by its sound.

THE ORGAN, in Greek *hydraulis*, was the last step in the mechanization of human blowing. It excluded the mouth and replaced its action by pistons and hydraulic compressors. The pipes were played by means of the most elementary type of keyboard.

Looking for the origin of the organ, the author found an Alexandrian terra-cotta figurine, from the last century B.C., of a seated Syrian piper, singing and playing. In the manner of itinerant minstrels this man combines several activities. An inch under his singing mouth he is holding a pan-pipe; its long, bass canes are connected with a bag that communicates by a flexible tube with a bellows worked by the man's right foot and compressed by his arm. The singer obviously plays his pan-pipes only between the verses, as singing excludes blowing. While singing, he seems to work the bellows and produce a drone on one of the bass canes. (pl. VIII c)

The combination of a set of pan-pipes and an artificial wind action must have been a slow evolution, and the famous invention of *the* organ, attributed to the engineer KTESIBIOS in Alexandria in the second half of the third century B.C., consisted in a special technical solution of the problem rather than in the principle of the organ itself. From the ancient descriptions in Heron's *Pneumatiká*, written about 120 B.C., and Vitruvius Pollio's *De architectura* (first century A.D.) one knows that the wind pressure of the hydraulis was not supplied by bellows, but by a water compressor and pistons. Hence the name *hýdraulis*, or 'water organ.'

We do not know exactly to what extent this instrument was used in antiquity, but we know that it had a vogue in post-Christian times, especially in the Roman circus. Its loud, penetrating tone, so entirely

rent from the reserved sonority of most Greek and Roman in-
~~~ents, was particularly appropriate to robust entertainment.

At first sight, the organ seems to be inconsistent with the simplicity of Greek and Roman instruments. The contrast is explained
by the triumph of mechanics and machines, indeed of the engineer,
in the last two centuries of the pre-Christian era. The center of
technical art was Alexandria, the native town of the organ.

A quantity of pictures on reliefs, clay figures, carved gems, vases,
etc., and especially a clay model made in the beginning of the second
century A.D. and preserved in the Musée Lavigérie de Saint-Louis
at Carthage, show the general outline of such an organ. The pneumatic action is concealed in a narrow, columnlike box reaching up to
the player's waist. The box is flanked on either side by hydraulic
pumps worked by two additional men. The pipes stand vertically in
rows similar to ours on the cover of the box. The player standing in
front of the box between the two pumps pushes and pulls the sliders
connecting the individual pipes.

The Carthage model clearly shows stops, that is, sets of pipes one
behind another; and stops are mentioned by Vitruvius. The Roman
architect explains that the windchest had longitudinal grooves, which
could be opened by turning gears. The question is whether this contrivance was a stop arrangement in the modern sense.

The first idea would be to suppose that the ancient organ had
stops differing either in pitch (such as our sixteen foot, eight foot,
four foot), or in the type of pipe, such as open and stopped, narrow
and wide, wood and metal, flutes and reeds. The organs depicted on
art works, and even the Carthage model, do not indicate different
types of pipes, nor do the literary sources. On the contrary, the Roman poet, Claudianus Mamertus, who lived in the fifth century
A.D., says in one of his poems, speaking of the water organ: "Let
there be also one who by his light touch forcing out deep reverbera-
tions, and managing the numberless slides (*linguas*) in the soundboard of metal pipes, can with nimble fingers cause a powerful
sound." There is no mention whatsoever of a contrast between soft
and loud.

Differences in size, however, are indicated on the Carthage
model, where the third row is nearly twice as tall as the front row,
while the middle row has an intermediate height.

Nevertheless, it would be overhasty to interpret the three rows as
unison, fifth and octave stops, as in modern organs. A musical tractate
of the first century A.D., the so-called Anonymus Bellermann, hints

A. Etruscan flutist (after Albini).

Stringed instrument, Rome. Louvre.

C. Syrian with the ancestor of the organ.

PLATE VIII.

at another answer. The hydraulis, it says, can only be played in six *tropoi* or tonalities: Hyperlydian, Hyperiastian, Lydian, Phrygian, Hypolydian and Hypophrygian. Consequently, Dorian melodies were excluded.

This selection is incomprehensible as long as the modern reader thinks of his chromatic keyboard running through seven octaves. This is a recent abstraction of all existing tonalities that we must not expect in antiquity; the Greek organist probably united in rows, in a musical way, the pipes necessary for a certain tonality, and not, in a logical way, all pipes belonging in all tonalities. Of the six tonalities that the Anonymus Bellermann indicates, Hyperlydian has, in our modern notation, two flats, Hyperiastian one sharp, Lydian one flat, Phrygian three flats, Hypolydian no sign, Hypophrygian two flats. The three Dorian tonalities, on the other hand, would require four, five and six flats. So the exclusion of Dorian from the organ is easily intelligible: the organ of that time had no flat beyond $A\flat$.

TRUMPETS, the Greeks and the Romans said, were invented by the Etruscans, who were the leading bronze founders of the Mediterranean world before the Celts came.

The Greeks had only a *straight trumpet* that they called *sálpinx*, while the Roman name was *tuba*. It was closely connected with the trumpets of the ancient Assyrians, Egyptians and Jews, and the initial s+vowel indicates a pre-Hellenic origin of the name too. Generally, however, it was longer than those ancient ones. The only Greek trumpet preserved was recently acquired by the Museum of Fine Art in Boston. Its tube is made in thirteen sections of ivory neatly fitting into one another, and strengthened at the joints by bronze rings; a long funnel-shaped bell is made of bronze; the mouthpiece is only slightly enlarged without being cup-shaped. As the trumpet is one and fifty-seven centimeters long it must be an alto with a note between *f* and *g* as the lowest available tone. The curator, Mr. L. D. Caskey, assigns it to the second half of the fifth century B.C.

Roman tubas, chiefly used to give trumpet calls in the army, were simpler, made entirely of bronze with an evenly conical bore, a slightly expanding bell and a mouthpiece of either horn or bronze. Their average length was about four feet. A few specimens have been preserved, and most of them seem to have been military instruments. The pressure in blowing must have been considerable. On some representations of trumpeters the free hand is on the back of the head; a chain, attached to the bell, might have been pulled to allow the player to brace his lips more firmly against the mouth-piece, and we even find the mouth-band of oboists used with the trumpet. The sound is said to have been harsh: "The loud trumpet's brazen mouth from far With shrilling clangor sounds th' alarm of war" (*Iliad*, 18). Aeschylos, in the *Eumenides*, calls the salpinx *diátoros*, 'yelling,' and Roman authors designate the sound of the tuba as *horribilis, raucus, rudis* or *terribilis.*

Besides the straight trumpet the Roman army had a *hooked trumpet* that they called *lituus*, a long, slender, bronze tube curving upward at the end to form the bell. Its prototype was obviously a cane or tube of wood stuck into a cowhorn which then formed the bell. In bronze civilizations the combined form of two natural objects was replaced by a homogeneous bronze trumpet in one piece, which at first showed its composite origin but in its later form had lost all vestiges of the original components. The original form still exists in Ethiopia and the Burmese hinterland; some of the oldest Irish *kárnykes*, kept in the British Museum and in the Irish Academy at Dublin, show the earlier stage of the hooked bronze trumpet. A similar development in the east is marked by the hooked trumpet carved on the temple at Angkor Vat in Cambodia (c. 1100 A.D.), and the modern Chinese trumpet, *cha chiao*. Later on, the former combination of a tube and a horn became less obvious, and the tectonic shape was replaced by a fantastic design; the bell had the form of a dragon's head with open mouth and a crest reaching to the middle of the tube. This was the typical Celtic karnyx described by the ancient writers and also carved on the triumphal arch for Emperor Hadrian (113 A.D.) and on Roman, Gallic and Britannic coins. Some Roman litui had a bell that recalled the Celtic dragon head, but the usual and final form of the lituus was undecorated. (fig. 35)

FIGURE 35. Trumpet, Madagascar. (After Sachs.)

Preserved specimens are conical and short (seventy-eight and seventy-nine and five-tenths centimeters long); their pitch must have been a seventh above that of our bugles. The lituus is consequently designated as *acutus* or *oxýphōnos* by Roman and Greek authors, its sound as *stridor*, 'shriek,' and *strepens*, 'bray.'

Curved trumpets. Too long a tube cannot be carried; the long trumpets of the Mongols and Tibetans rest on the ground, but skillful bronze-founding civilizations make the trumpet in a curved shape. Ancient Europeans, Swedes, Gauls and Iberians preferred curves shaped like the figures 6 or 9. The best solutions, however, were the Roman *cornu* and the ancient Nordic *lurer*.

The *cornu* was used in infantry bands, at funerals and other solemn ceremonies as well as at bacchanals and circus plays. It had a narrow, evenly conical bore in the shape of a round letter G with a slender bell; a wooden crossbar, forming the diameter, rested upon the player's left shoulder and was grasped by his left hand, while the right one pressed the mouthpiece against the lips; the tube curved over the level of his head, and the bell turned to face forward. Specimens in a good state of preservation were found at Pompei and have been kept in the National Museum at Naples. Their tubes measure eleven feet long and closely resemble those of French horns in G. While modern experiments with a facsimile produced "a soft and yet voluminous sound, recalling that of our French horn," and "already rather wide melodies in a range of seventeen harmonics," Horace speaks only of the *minax murmur*, the 'threatening rumble' of the cornu; modern experiments usually show what one could do on an ancient instrument, but not what ancient players really did.

The Roman army had also a variety of the circular cornu in the shape of a short trumpet. But its only evidence is on the monument of a Roman horse-soldier in the *Städtische Altertümer-Sammlung* in Mainz.

A thousand or more years earlier a Baltic people had already solved the problem of making curved trumpets. Although the cornu has some features in common with these earlier trumpets, we have no evidence of any relation between them.

Lur, plural *lurer*, is the Danish name applied to these trumpets of the Nordic bronze age. If we say 'trumpets,' we are not strictly consistent with modern terminology in which trumpet means an instrument with a bore, the greater part of which is cylindrical; they actually are tenor or alto horns, their second harmonic being situated between *c* and *g*. The three dozen examples of excavated lurer are entirely conical. They have a flat disk attached at the end of the tube, instead of a bell, and their mouthpieces resemble those of modern tenor trombones. All of them have a common characteristic: the second curve of the S-shaped tube is twisted in a plane at right angles to the plane of the first curve, and the two trumpets that form a pair are twisted in opposite directions. This is exactly the form of a pair of mammoth's tusks, and these may have furnished the material for lurer, until the extinction of the mammoth necessitated finding some other material.

The undeniable importance of the lurer has been foolishly exaggerated by modern Germanic enthusiasts. We already have shown that the use of twin trumpets was frequent, and that they were not played in parts (cf. page 113). Here we may add that the possibility of producing twelve notes on this instrument, as asserted by *modern* trombonists with *modern* mouthpieces, is a scientific falsification. Modern violinists would be able to play medieval fiddles in as many positions as desired, and yet we know that in their time they were played in the first position only. It is a grave error to confuse the potentiality of an instrument with the music it actually performed.

On the other hand, it is edifying to compare the supposed nobility of Nordic trumpet playing with the few violent notes that are roughly blown on a contemporaneous descendant of the S-shaped trumpet family, the *raṇa śṛinga* or *kombu* of modern India, or with the sound of the Tibetan ceremonial trumpets which is called "hippopotamus-like" by one witness, and compared with the roar of factory sirens in an industrial town by another. Remembering that a Greek author compared the sound of Egyptian trumpets with the bray of an ass, and that Roman writers spoke of the "horrible," "rauque" and "shrieking" tone of their trumpets, it must be admitted that not one evidence of ancient and oriental trumpet sounds points to anything related to the noble tones of modern trumpets.

THE DRUM (*týmpanon*) of the ancient Greeks and Romans was the usual hand-beaten frame drum of the eastern Mediterranean; it had no jingles and was generally painted. As a rule it had two skins. The handles attached to some drums of the fourth century B.C. would have been unnecessary with single skins, and the Byzantine lexicographer of the ninth century A.D., Suidas, clearly said that the ancient Greek tympanon was made of skins, *ek dermátōn*, in the plural. When played, the drum was held upright from underneath.

Besides the ordinary frame drum, Apulian vases of the last centuries B.C. show a strange variety of drum: instead of being flat, it looks like the shallow segment of a sphere, or a reversed bowl with the bottom cut off; the skin, though strikable only where it covers this small opening, yet is drawn all over the top and slanting sides; along its rim there are fastening nails, while the center is generally marked by a dark circle surrounded by small dots.

There are only two parallels among all known types of drums: the Chinese *pang ku* and the South Indian *daṣari tappaṭṭai*. The Chinese drum is made of six wedges of wood, kept together by a metal hoop and forming a sort of cake with a hole in the middle; the skin, fixed with many iron nails, covers this hemisphere entirely, so that only its center, above the hole, can be struck as a drum head. The Indian drum has a metal frame and a calf's skin and is played by the bare hand.

The players of both Greek and Roman drums were almost exclusively women in the cults of Dionysos and Cybele. The drum had no place in any other form of music, including military music.

CLAPPERS were also played almost exclusively by women. The *krótala*, Dionysian dance clappers, were made in various forms of all kinds of materials, mostly of wood in boot shape, similar to those described in the Egyptian chapter (cf. page 89).

Another clapper, called *kroúpalon* by the Greeks and *scabellum* by the Romans, belonged to the paraphernalia of the chorus leader and served to beat time. It was a kind of thick sandal, tied to the right foot and consisting of a block of wood cut out to form an upper and an under board, fastened together at the heel. Each board had a kind of castanet inside. In stamping, the boards with their castanets were clapped together with a sharp cracking sound.

Cymbals came from western Asia to Greece at a relatively recent time with the orgiastic rites of oriental goddesses such as Cybele. They then were taken over into the service of Dionysos and into the theater. They were considered effeminate. Passages in contemporaneous writers and representations on art works indicate that both the harsh and tinkling cymbals were used, as in Mesopotamia and Israel.

Struck disks of metal with a large central hole for a suspending cord were used as signal instruments. Their name was *discus*. In Rome, drivers struck them at the street corner before entering a narrow lane. Their origin was certainly Asiatic; in the temples of India metal disks with a clear, bright tone are used up to this day.

One of the older Pythagoreans, HIPPASOS from Metapontos, devised four disks of bronze, so that they had the same diameters, but the thickness of the first was 4/3 of the thickness of the second, 3/2 of the third, 2/1 of the fourth (e. g., c' g f c), "and by striking all of them he achieved a certain symphony."

In all sections of this chapter, Greece and Rome, and sometimes Etruria, were treated without much distinction. South Europe was a coherent musical district with a common heritage, in which the terms differed more than the instruments themselves. Greece, including the Greek colony, Magna Graecia, which covered southern Italy and Sicily, was dominant in art and science. Even in the times of the Roman Empire, Rome was ready to accept the cultural superiority of Greece. In the musical field she did not develop any musical instruments independent of the Grecian ones, except for some military trumpets.

7 . *India*

ALL India was settled by the dark peoples speaking Munda and Dravidian languages before the pre-Aryan and Aryan civilizations in the northwest pushed them southwards. Still, it is hardly possible to begin a history of Indian instruments with the Dravidian civilization because prehistoric evidences are almost lacking and historic evidences are comparatively recent.

Instead, we begin with the pre-Aryan, so-called Indus civilization in the third millennium B.C., about which we know from the recent excavations at Harappa in the Punjab and Mohenjo-Daro in Sind.

This civilization was remarkably advanced, resembling the cultures of Sumer and of Elam, and certainly related to them. The excavations have been fruitful enough to give an idea of how the Indus peoples lived, what they grew and ate, what their tools and weapons were and what kind of religious belief they had. Unfortunately, the excavated material is extremely poor from a musical point of view. Some children's *rattles* and *whistles* have survived, but those are all that can be claimed as instruments. A vertical conch shell found in the Indus valley may or may not have been a *shell trumpet,* and some round bronze objects resembling *cymbals* were more probably lids from vessels. Their form, however, with a central boss and a softly sloping and slightly turned up brim, is so closely related to actual cymbals that we may consider them precursors of the musical instrument.

The only object that with certainty can be accepted as an instrument is depicted on an excavated clay statuette. The small figurine, though roughly made, distinctly shows a woman playing a small drum held under her left upper arm. The faithfulness of this statuette can be assumed, as such *axillary drums* struck by women are represented on the oldest Indian temple reliefs, at Bharahat (second century B.C.). (pl. IX a)

Further information must be sought in the still undeciphered, ideographic script of the Indus Valley civilization. One of its signs, and a very frequent one, seems to have been used as a suffix and vaguely resembles a lyre. But a careful comparison of all its variants was not able to convince the author that this sign portrayed any musical instrument.

There is no doubt, on the contrary, that a second sign represents the Sumerian *vertical arched harp* with its nearly angular curve, resembling the one which is depicted on a Sumerian seal from about 2800 B.C. in the University Museum in Philadelphia. This identification is not without foundation; pottery, art and script of the two civilizations are closely related and indicate an early intercourse between the two countries.

The vertical harp and the axillary drum are the only musical instruments that we are entitled to ascribe to the earliest known civilization in India.

Subsequent information from the north of India comes more than a thousand years later with the Rigveda, the religious hymns of Aryan invaders, the date of which is supposed to be between 1500 and 1000 B.C.

The Rigveda mentions four instruments: *āghāṭi, bakura, gargara* and *vāṇa*. The first term is obscure, and its translations as 'clappers' or 'drum' are merely a guess.

We know more about the *bakura*; it is characterized as a loud instrument used in battle to terrify the enemy. The name itself, like several other Sanskrit words, was traced by the author to modern Madagascar: in the northern district of this large island, *bakora* is the name of the shell trumpet. We may accept this interpretation for the Sanskrit word, as many ancient Indian poems give the shell trumpet (afterward called *śankha*) the frightening and vindictive character that the Veda attributes to the bakura.

The *gargara* is described as a stringed instrument; therefore, it probably was the horizontal arched harp, the only stringed instrument depicted on Indian reliefs before the Christian era. The instrument *vāṇa* was probably a flute, since it was played by the Maruts, who were spirits of storm. A simple vertical flute, *veṇu* or 'cane,' is still used by aboriginal tribes of India.

New names are mentioned in the more recent Vedas. The Atharva Veda, the last of them, describes the *dundubhiḥ* as a wooden drum with cow skins, used as a thundering war instrument, which before battle was smeared with an offering-mixture, possibly of blood. Modern Hindu mistakenly make the word synonymous with *nāgarā*, a modern kettledrum; no kettledrum existed either in Vedic times or in post-Vedic antiquity, and the *dundubhiḥ* was certainly a different kind of drum. The word *karkarī*, in the same Veda, may be a more recent form of *gargara*. For *tūṇava* the usual translation 'flute' may be correct, but this interpretation is by no means certain. We also find, in the Yajur Veda V S 30, the classical terms *śankha*, which must have replaced *bakura*, and *vīṇā*, which has supplanted *gargara*.

Before the Aryan invasions, there was in India "a Dravidian civilization of a more elaborate and developed character than the civilization, if civilization it can be called, of the Aryans." (Slater) The Dravida later were pushed south and still occupy the southern part of India. "In so far as this Dravidian civilization was derived from outside sources its origin is to be traced to Egypt and Mesopotamia, linked up with India by sea commerce" in the third millennium B.C., or perhaps later.

Are there marks of Mesopotamian or Egyptian influences on Indian instruments?

The most striking evidence of an Egyptian influence is the word *vīṇā*. As this term, according to its spelling (*n* without a preceding *r*), must be a foreign word, there is little doubt of its identity with the Egyptian name of the harp. The term will be discussed again later.

The typical South Indian *trumpet*, called *tirućinnam* in Tamil, the main Dravidian language, is quite different from the more recent Indian trumpets. Like the Assyrian and Egyptian trumpets, it is about two and a half feet in length and consists of a rather large cylinder and a comparatively slim conical bell. Two of these trumpets are blown simultaneously by the same player, though it is hard to understand how this is possible. A letter from the Government Museum at Madras, replying to an inquiry from the author, says: "The tiruchinnam have no special mouthpieces. In blowing them the upper ends are pressed against the lips. I am afraid the author of the Catalogue has used the expression 'in the mouth' incorrectly. The two trumpets of a pair are blown simultaneously or very nearly so, and as there is little difference in the sound, only the volume is increased. We shall watch the professionals and let you know whether any other results are observable." Such a pair of twin trumpets is depicted in use on one of the reliefs of the Tjandi Djawi in Java, which were carved at about 1300 A.D.

The Indian *double clarinet* (Tamil *magudi*, Hindustani *pūngī*) is made of two parallel canes glued together, exactly like the Egyptian double clarinet. Still, it has undergone an important change that the tropical flora made possible: the mouthpieces are concealed in a large calabash, the slender neck of which is held in the player's mouth while its cavity serves as a wind chamber. The left pipe sustains a lower octave drone while the right pipe produces the melody. This is invariably played in the mode *hanumatodi*, which resembles the European Phrygian mode with minor second, third, sixth and seventh, or $e'\ f'\ g'\ a'\ b'\ c''\ d''\ e''$. It would seem logical to attribute Indian double clarinets to influences from the west, as the single reed is rare eastwards from India. They are played by Indian snake charmers to allure serpents out of their baskets or earth holes and to make them dance; and the traditions and the implements of such jugglers are usually very old.

Replacing the rigid calabash by a flexible bag, the Hindu and Dravida, as well as the Burmese, make single *bagpipes* which produce either a melody or a drone. Sometimes the bagpipe has a double clarinet so that it can play a melody and a drone at the same time. The chief names are Tamil *śruti* and Hindustani *mašak*.

The Singhalese preserve a particularly large and archaic *frame drum*, the *tẹmmẹṭṭama*, which has a nailed skin and reaches a diameter of nearly four feet. It is not improbable that this Ceylonese drum, forced away to the extreme south of the continent, is a remnant of the old Babylonian temple drum. When, in the Babylonian chapter, we mentioned a frame drum *ṭimbūtu*, we stated that the radicals of the Akkadian name occurred again in the Tamil name of frame drums, *tambaṭṭam*.

The barrel drum is the last of these instruments similar to Egyptian instruments. It is first mentioned in the *purânas*, collections of myths and legends written in early Christian times, and its Egyptian counterpart is late as well. Both have the same peculiar shape: instead of being evenly curved, the outline is broken; the body has the form of two truncated cones united at their larger bases. This is a characteristic potter's shape; clay is turned on a potter's wheel and made to taper towards both ends, a straight board serving as a pattern. Clay is still used today as a material for these drums, and their Indian names, *khol* and *mṛdanga*, signify 'clayey.' When made of wood, a single block of the same shape is hollowed out; jack- and red-wood are preferred.

The composite skins have always been made in a peculiar way, as they still are today, by gluing one or two overlapping circles of different hides on top of the original layer of sheepskin. The center of the right head is covered by a hard, black paste of boiled rice, tamarind juice and Manganese dust or iron filings. The left center has a paste as well, made of boiled rice, ashes and water, or of soojee and water; but it is applied at the beginning of the performance and scraped off at the end.

The ring and the paste give the drum 'harmonic overtones'; while drums as a rule have irregular partials, a khol produces a fundamental with its octave, twelfth, double octave and the major third above. Besides, the pastes enable the heads to be turned an octave or fifth or fourth apart, and even the rim and the center of the same head can be tuned to different notes. The intervals are varied according to the mode of the piece, the left hand producing the lower note. But the original significance of the tuning pastes was quite different. The code of sacrifices, the Atharva Veda, said that blood or red color could be painted on the skin as a sacrifice. Later, these sacrifices were replaced by agricultural offerings. The Chamar women in southern India, for instance, mix a paste of rice and saffron with a betel leaf, a betel nut and two pices, and also paint the skin with five spots of cinnabar before they use the drum to worship *Dhartī mātā*, Mother Earth. The origin of the tuning paste, however, is unknown to modern Hindu musicians.

The two skins are fastened by hoops made of twisted thongs which run around the body at a slight distance from the heads. The two thong hoops are laced together by thongs which describe narrow W's and which are tightened by small wooden dowels wedged between them and the body.

The skins are struck either with the whole hands, the finger tips or the base of the thumb. The players are noted for their technique; no musicians perform the thirty-five *jātis* or rhythmic schemes better than these drummers. "It takes a life time to acquire full proficiency in the art, as the performer must not only possess musical skill, but must be of good physique and have an accurate memory and supple hands" (Fredilis).

Although these drums may have been influenced by Egypt, it

would be hazardous to claim an Egyptian origin for them. This intricate style of drumming and the dominance of rhythm is characteristic of Indian music; it has no place in the very different art of Egypt.

Information becomes more exact and safer when, under the influence of Greek sculptors, Indian artists in northern and central India begin to carve reliefs on the walls of temples and of burial mounds. The oldest reliefs, on the stupa or mound at Bharahat in Central India dating from the second century B.C., include musical scenes with single musicians and bands, with trumpets, drums and harps.

The arched harp is figured over a period of a thousand years, from the Bharahat reliefs to temples erected about 800 A.D. The small, narrow body extends into the long neck to form a semicircle, and the upper end of the neck is bent outward to form a beak or a scroll. The strings are crowded close together leaving the two ends of the instrument free, and are attached to the neck by simple loops without pegs. The player sits on the ground; she holds the harp in a horizontal position under the left arm and plucks the strings with a short plectron. (pl. IX a)

In its shape, position and manner of playing, this instrument corresponds exactly to the horizontal arched harp of Sumer depicted on the noted vase from Bismya. It cannot have been influenced by Egyptian harps because the latter were never of the horizontal type played with a plectron. The name of this instrument was probably *vīṇā*. The gigantic poem Mahabharata, which was composed between the fourth century B.C. and the seventh century A.D., mentions in 19:35 that the girls playing the vina had their thighs skinned by the lower part of the instrument as if they were scratches of fingernails. This was perfectly possible with an arched harp, which rested on the lap, but not with a vina in the later sense, which rested on the ground and on the shoulder. The great theoretician Bharata, who lived in the first half of the first millennium A.D., made his experiments with two "vinas," either having twenty-two strings. This number, again, is consistent with a harp, not with a stick zither.

Trumpets. An end-blown shell trumpet, with a mouthpiece, is played by an ape on one of the reliefs at the temple of Bharahat (second century B.C.). The shell trumpet of modern India is a slim, white, polished *turbinella rapa*, pierced at the top to form a mouth-hole. Occasionally a mouthpiece and gold or silver decorations are added. Its name is *sankha* in Sanskrit, Bengali and Cannarese.

The śankha is an exclusively religious instrument, used in divine worship and connected with legend and myth. As a trumpet, or simply as a sacrificial vessel, it is an attribute of Vishnu and other gods; worshipers of Vishnu paint it on their arms, and Lakshmi, his wife, has Sankha as a second name. A shell sucks away the blood of the giants that Parvati combats, just as in Greece Triton conquers the giants with a shell trumpet, and on the Last Day, when the world is in flames, Siva will sound the shell trumpet, as Heimdal blows the giallar horn at the Twilight of the Gods and the angel sounds the last trumpet on the Day of Judgment.

On a relief of the first century A.D. at the temple of Sanchi in Central India, two (once more two!) non-Indian men, probably Afghans, play long trumpets which bend upward just beyond the mouthpiece for four or five feet and then jut forward to form a bell shaped like the gaping mouth of an animal. Exactly the same trumpets are depicted at about the same time on a silver kettle from Gundestrup, Denmark.

DRUMS, in their most usual form carved on ancient reliefs, have a slightly bulging barrel with two heads; the thongs are directly fastened to the skins without a hoop and laced crosswise in X form; a central belt to which they are tied increases their firmness. This drum is struck either with the hand or with one or two sticks. The position in which it is held varies. Sometimes it is horizontally suspended from the neck. On the same relief referred to in the preceding paragraph, members of the band carry the drums from the shoulder so that they hang diagonally across the man's chest and are struck on the same head with two sticks. A third position, in a women's dance, may be axillary; but as the player is carved in profile, the shape and the position of the drum are not distinct enough to be conclusive. (pl. IX a)

On some reliefs at Bharahat, the drum stick is hooked or coiled in the form of a bishop's crosier instead of being straight. Such sticks, possibly connected with forerunners of a Chinese symbol, the mace of fortune, still exist in Tibet, South India, Sumatra and Borneo, while they have disappeared from Europe, northern India and Persia.

It probably was Persia that gave India the hooked stick and the cylindrical drum with X-laces as well; drums of this kind with crosier sticks are not found anywhere except on medieval Persian miniatures. In the third century B.C. the provinces of the northwest were under Persian rule and accepted a quantity of Persian words and Persian customs.

Two such drums are sometimes placed together, one standing and one lying, to form a pair, at Bharahat as well as on later reliefs up to the fourth century A.D. One of the drums is horizontally laid on the thighs of a sitting woman, and the other drum stands erect before her; both are played with bare hands. Twin drums of a similar shape, but separately played by two standing men, appear on a relief of the temple at Sanchi in Central India (first century A.D.).

Twin combinations of this kind exist far beyond the boundaries of India. Children in modern Bali have preserved exactly the same custom, and the Koreans suspend two cylindrical nailed drums from an upright frame so that they hang horizontally at right angles one above the other; as small clapper drums placed crisscross on a handle, they still are used in Japan.

A different kind of drum is played in a martial scene at Bharahat, where apes are the performers. One sees a large drum supported against the player's chest, his left arm is bent around the trunk of the drum and his right hand is striking with a stick. The author is inclined to conclude from this position and the analogy with ancient Peruvian representations that this drum is 'shallow'—that is, an intermediate form between a barrel and a frame drum. Small dots around the skin are probably not nails as one might suppose; the sculptor's style is too realistic to admit such a misplacement. They are more likely to be dabs of sacrificial paste, mixed from pills and vegetables. Later on, such pastes used on the skins of drums lost their symbolic character and became a device for tuning the skin by increasing the weight.

One of the Bharahat reliefs shows an ape playing the oldest *hourglass* drum—a waisted drum narrower in the middle than at the ends. It is not much longer than it is wide, and the skins are laced with nearly parallel thongs or cords and a central belt around the narrow waist. Suspended from the ape's shoulder, the drum is played with two sticks, each striking one skin.

Modern Indian hourglass drums are generally shorter and smaller. They have the central belt but the thongs are laced in W form. When played, they are held in the hand so that by pressing the lacing cords the man is able to alter the pitch. An apparently older type, called *davaṇḍai* in Tamil, is bigger, made of wood and struck with a stick; the usual smaller type is made of metal and struck with the bare fingers (Tamil *uḍukkai*).

A typically Indian variety, *ḍāmaru*, is constructed as a *clapper drum;* one or two cords, tied to the side of the drum and ending in a knot or ball, strike the skins when the drum is rapidly moved to and fro by a twisting movement of the forearm. It is the sacred attribute of several divinities: Siva above all; then, Brahma's learned wife, Sarasvati; the goddess of death, Bhadra-Kali; the fourteen-handed god of anger, Aghora.

The reliefs of Amaravati also depict a drum that seems to be related to certain types of the Far East. It is represented as a circular disk, some two feet wide and suspended by a handle from a horizontal pole that two men carry on their shoulders while one of them, or perhaps both, beat it with violent strokes of a hooked stick. It closely resembles the Japanese *ni-daiko*, a laced drum some two feet wide which is carried in exactly the same way.

All instruments discussed so far can be traced back to pre-Christian times; the following instruments belong in the last, post-Christian centuries of antiquity.

CROSS FLUTES. While *notched flutes* and *pan-pipes* had no importance in India and *beak flutes* were mere shepherds' instruments, the *cross flute* (Sanskrit *vāṃśī*) was the outstanding wind instrument of ancient India. It first appears on the reliefs of the temple at Sanchi in Central India in the first century A.D. On the reliefs of Amaravati, carved within the following three centuries, this flute forms a part of the so-called *celestial music*—that is, instruments of an aristocratic character which are depicted by the artists as being suspended in heaven to be touched by superhuman and invisible hands as an entertainment for the gods. One of the divinities, Krishna, played it himself as, saved from death by being hidden in a shepherd's house, he became a cowherder. When his flute sounded, "the spirits were enchanted; the rivers paused and stopped flowing; the birds, halting in their flight, flew down and listened jealously; all the inanimate things under the sun grew brighter."

SHORT LUTE. In the first centuries A.D., Northwest Indian art was under a strong Greek influence and developed into a mixed style which generally is called Gandhara, after the name of a small country in Kashmir. Several statuettes and reliefs carved in this style represent players of a short lute, the venerable ancestor of the Islamic, the Sino-Japanese and the European lute families.

The 'short lute' has a neck shorter than the body. Its origin is a wooden body tapering upward to form a neck and a fingerboard, not, as with the long lute, a stick with a small resonance shell at its under end. The musical difference is that in short lutes the melodic scale, in principle, is formed by all strings consecutively, whereas in

FIGURE 36. From an East Turkestanic fresco, 5th-7th century A.D. (After Grünwedel.)

long lutes it is obtained from one string only by stopping while the others accompany.

The oldest short lutes are depicted on Persian figurines of the eighth century B.C., excavated from the Tell at Suza. The body is rather small and narrow, about two feet long and eight inches wide; details cannot be distinguished.

No trace of short lutes has been found between this earliest evidence and the Gandhara statuettes some eight hundred years later. But, again, the Gandhara style points toward an Iranian country.

The Gandhara lute has a pear-shaped body tapering towards the short neck, a frontal stringholder, lateral pegs and either four or five strings. These are the well-known features of Far Eastern, Near Eastern and European lutes.

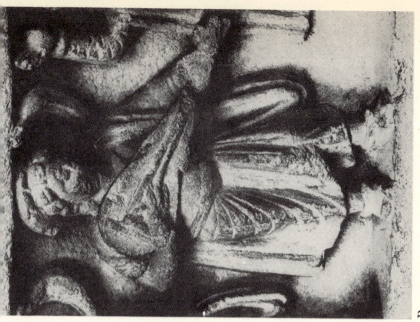

B

A

*Indian instruments. A. Relief from Sharahat (2nd cent. B.C.)
with arched harp and drums. B. Relief from Gandhara (c. 100
A.D.) with lute (after Marcel Dubois).*

PLATE IX.

Still, the Gandhara lute forms a strange variety within this large family: instead of a continuously tapering outline, the face has a contour broken on either side by a kind of barb. No Chinese, Arabian or European lute has a barb. It therefore must be supposed that the spreading of the lute from Iran east and southward had begun before this local variety developed. (pl. IX b)

The barb has survived in many forms in India, Afghanistan and the Pamirs. In a modern lute called *rabôb* or *sarôd*, the hollow under the barb is so exaggerated that it forms a deep channel and makes a kind of waist in the outline of the front, which forms a groove in the side of the body. All these *waisted lutes* (and some Indo-Persian long-necked lutes) are abnormally deep; instead of being softly rounded at the rear, they have a ridge so that they look "chicken-breasted." In stating this, we remember a passage in the *Mafātīḥ al-ʿulūm*, the Arabian encyclopedia of the tenth century A.D., according to which a certain Persian lute was called *barbaṭ* for its resemblance to the breast of the duck. Was this the same instrument?

In ancient India, as in Egypt, there is no instrument for which we can trace a native origin. All of them seem to have come from the west and the north. Strangely enough, we will have to wait for the middle ages to find a native stock in Indian music. (fig. 36)

8. *The Far East*

THE relationship between the Chinese and the Greek mentality is most striking in their similar attitude towards music. Plato, in the fourth century B.C., had suggested that music should be one of the basic influences in Greek education. Music shapes soul and character; good music guarantees a well-ordered community, whereas bad music brings the State into danger; national control of music and obligatory education would be essential to the community.

These ideas were familiar to the Chinese mind before they came to Greece. More than a hundred years earlier than the Greek philosopher, the wise Confucius (551–478 B.C.) had preached exactly the same doctrine.

In John Steele's translation of the *I-li*, or *Book of Etiquette and Ceremonial*, written in the time of the Chou, we read: "Of the six arts which covered the attainments expected of a gentleman in Old China . . . the knowledge of ceremonial practices which guided a man in daily life, at his audiences with his ruler, and in his approaches to the ancestral spirit came first. . . . The practice of music and the knowledge of the significance of tunes, comes next."

Such a requirement is reminiscent of the musical equipment that the Italian Renaissance expected of a *corteggiano*. But the musical achievement of Chinese noblemen was less a social distinction than a necessity for a well-balanced personality. Confucius said, "It is by the odes that the mind is aroused. It is by the Rules of Propriety that the character is established. It is from music that the finish is received." And the philosopher Mencius (372–289 B.C.) followed him: "By hearing the music of a prince, we know the character of his virtue."

162

The music of a prince includes not only the music that he performs personally, but also the music in his service. The State needs equilibrium as the individual does, and the emperor personifies the State. According to Confucius, "When good government prevails in the empire, ceremonies, music and punitive military expeditions proceed from the emperor. When bad government prevails in the empire, ceremonies, music, and punitive military expeditions proceed from the princes." So one understands a story told in the works of Mencius: "Chwang Paou, seeing Mencius, said to him, 'I had an audience with the king. His Majesty told me that he loved music, and I was not prepared with anything to reply to him. What do you pronounce about that love of music?' Mencius replied, 'If the king's love of music were very great, the kingdom of Ts'e would approach a state of good government.' "

Once "the people of Ts'e sent Loo a present of female musicians, which Ke Hwan received, and for three days no court was held. Confucius took his departure." His leave was probably an act of protest because the text goes on to say that he "returned from Wei to Loo, and the music was reformed, and the pieces in the Imperial songs and praise songs each found their proper place."

As the State, the organized frame of the nation's life, was considered a microcosmos, an inseparable part and effigy of the macrocosmos, it could be good only if in harmony with the universe. Music, securing the welfare of the State, had to take its law from the cosmos.

The cosmos embodied eternal time; it then was the integration of the alternating seasons, of spring and summer, fall and winter. It embodied eternal space; it then integrated whatever was in the east and west, in the north and south. It was matter, integrating wood and metal, skin and stone; it was force, embodying wind and thunder, water and fire. Lastly, the cosmos was sound, in both conceptions, as pitch and as timbres. The universe is one; so time and space, matter and music, are congruent, as they are but various manifestations of the same One. Their differentials, then, must be congruent as well: a certain season corresponds to a certain cardinal point, a certain matter, and a certain musical instrument; and the four seasons are separated from each other, not only by definite amounts of time but also by musical intervals. A false combination would endanger the world's harmony.

In consequence of this conception, ancient Chinese wisdom indulged in all sorts of co-ordinations. Lao-Tsze, in condemning sensual pleasure, compares the five notes of the pentatonic scale with the colors black, red, green, white, yellow, and with the tastes salt, bitter, sour, acrid and sweet.

> Color's five hues from th' eyes their sight will take;
> Music's five notes the ears as deaf can make;
> The flavors five deprive the mouth of taste.

The most important co-ordination in conditioning music is the one called *pa yin*, of which we present the following abstract:

CARDINAL POINTS	YEAR'S SEASONS	PHE-NOMENA	SUB-STANCES	MUSICAL INSTRUMENTS
northeast	winter to spring	thunder	gourd	mouth organ
east	spring	mountain	bamboo	pan-pipes
southeast	spring to summer	wind	wood	trough
south	summer	fire	silk	zither
southwest	summer to autumn	earth	clay	globular flute
west	autumn	dampness	metal	bell
northwest	autumn to winter	heaven	stone	sonorous stone
north	winter	water	skin	drum

Following this co-ordination, the Chinese have adopted a classification of instruments unique in the world. They distinguish eight classes according to the material used: gourd, bamboo, wood, silk, clay, metal, stone, skin instruments.

Matter, in Chinese music, is far more than a means of bringing forth a sound. Like body and soul, a material and its sound are manifestations of the same phenomenon. Sound is almost tangible, and a sonorous stone, in Chinese terminology, would "receive the tone" at the end of each verse of the hymn to Confucius in order to transmit it to the following verse. A tone, in Far Eastern conception, does not need any definite length or rhythm; it should not be cut off or superseded by other sounds; the longer it lasts, and the more it is isolated, the more a listener perceives the life of the substance that has produced it. Occidentals might experience a similar sensation in the slowly fading pulsations of a church bell.

From this ideology one can understand the relative importance of idiophones in Chinese music. Only one of the eight Chinese substances provides a stringed instrument, and one a drum. Three substances, on the other hand, furnish wind instruments, and three idiophones. Idiophones are more essential in the Far East than in other civilizations.

Being more important, **many East Asiatic idiophones developed** into instruments capable of melody, although in western civilizations they were almost entirely restricted to percussion. An idiophone, however, could not be stretched or stopped in order to supply a series of notes; playing melodies required a set of them, similar in shape but of different size and pitch, and united in some frame to form a well-tuned chime. Such sets of stones or bells or gongs or metal slabs are the outstanding feature in East Asiatic music; no other civilization has created chimes of any kind.

Exactness of pitch was harder to achieve in making chimes than in making stringed instruments or the majority of wind instruments. No stretching or relaxing, no artificial fingering, no correction by breath or lips could influence their scales; they had to be correct from the beginning, and pitch and scale became more important than anywhere else in the world.

Pitch and scale, too, were controlled by the laws of cosmology. Their accordance with the universe was achieved by taking musical measures from nonmusical categories, just as nonmusical categories were measured by musical proportions. For example, the distance between the seasons could be measured by octaves, fifths and fourths while the pitch tone was provided by a tube exactly one (Chinese) foot long, and the distances between the fingerholes of a flute were ruled neither by musical nor by technical reasons, but by inches. Myth relates that a new emperor, as one of his first acts, sent his minister to the western mountains in order to get the correct pitch from the bird Phoenix. In historical times the Minister of Measurements was in charge of the music; when invading barbarians had destroyed the standard instruments, subsequent dynasties tried hard to re-establish pitch and scale to save the nation. So Mencius could say that "in the matter of sounds, the whole empire models itself after the music-master K'wang."

Men who conceived of music as sounding matter, and who exacted chromatic scales from the brittlest substances, of course stressed instrumental rather than vocal music. In Marie Du Bois-Reymond's musical diary, written in Shanghai in 1908–09 and given to the author, we read that a certain Chinese gentleman and player consented to sing into Mrs. Du Bois's phonograph on the condition that the record would not be heard in China, as singing "did not suit a decent Chinese." While in the Near East singing was much more essential, and instruments were rarely given independence, the Far East tended towards a self-sufficient instrumental music which culminated in the exuberant plenty of its orchestras.

THE SHANG DYNASTY
(FOURTEENTH–TWELFTH CENTURIES B.C.)

Chinese history began in the fourteenth century B.C. with the Shang people who lived at Anyang in Northeast China, at the same time that the Kassites were ruling in the Near East and the eighteenth dynasty was ruling in Egypt.

Some parts of the vast anthology of ancient Chinese poems called *Shih ching*, the *Book of Poetry*, go back to the time of the Shang. In one of its odes, which can be dated 1135 B.C., we read:

> In what unison sounded the drums and bells!
> What joy was there in the hall with its circlet of water!
> The lizard-skin drums rolled harmonious,
> As the blind musicians performed their parts.

The Chinese names used are *chung* for the bell, and *ku* for the drum. Although bells and drums are mentioned, no specimens have been preserved.

The only instruments of the Shang which have been excavated and preserved are sonorous stones, said to be like those of later periods, and something quite extraordinary—a globular flute carved from bone.

GLOBULAR FLUTES (*hsüan*) have a small and bulging receptacle instead of the usual tube; their tone, extremely poor in harmonics, resembles the vowel sound *oo*.

Tracing back this instrument, we meet an early type in South Africa, where Caffre children sing into a hollow fruit instead of blowing. The globular flute may have been a mere voice mask, like early tubular and shell trumpets. As it developed from a voice mask to an actual flute, it was provided with a number of fingerholes. The original shell, usually a coconut, was replaced by earthenware in those countries where appropriate shells were lacking, in Central and East Asia for example. In this case the sharp-edged mouth-hole, cut somewhere in the side, was superseded by an upper orifice. Ancient Chinese authors said that such an instrument was molded on two eggs, a fowl's egg for the outer, and a chicken's egg for the inner surface. The number of fingerholes was five, and is now six.

Though the globular flute of the Shang evidently has the shape of the modern hsüan, it is the only one made of bone. As we have not seen it, we describe it in Herrlee Glessner Creel's words:

The Shang example is about two and a half inches high and more or less barrel-shaped. It is decorated with two so-called *t'ao-t'ieh*, or 'ogre masks,' such as are found on bronzes. There is a hole at the top to blow into, and five holes on the sides which may be stopped with the fingers to vary the pitch. Mr. Liang, who kindly demonstrated it to me, blew 'do, re, mi, fa,' and said that by blowing harder on one note it was possible to produce 'sol.' There are two remarkable things about this. In the first place, it shows that the Shang people must have known quite a little about music. Not all of the intervals were exact, though this might have been because the instrument was not completely clean. But the interval from 'do' to 'fa' was a perfect 'perfect fourth,' accurately tuned. The most interesting thing about this instrument is that the notes mentioned are the first five notes of the major scale, involving a half-step which is not present at all in the modern Chinese five tone scale. They would seem, in fact, to indicate that an entirely different tonal system was in use at that time.

We quote the last sentences not because we share the view they express, but, on the contrary, because they give the cue to combat a common but erroneous conclusion. The series of notes available on an instrument does not necessarily represent its scale; the keyboard of an occidental piano with its twelve semitones within an octave gives the *possibility* of playing scales in twenty-four tonalities, but the scales themselves comprise only seven notes. Likewise, the notes *mi* and *fa* on the old globular flute *can* have been used alternately, to play either in the anhemitonic scale *do re mi sol*, or in the scale *do re fa sol*, anhemitonic as well.

The clay flute has given birth to a strange offshoot: the egg shape has been abandoned for the form of any animal, usually a bird. The sound is not produced by the simple mouth-hole but by a whistle head, similar to that of the recorder family, inside of the head of the bird, which is at the outer end of the instrument. The mouth of the player is applied to the tubular tail which serves as a breath conductor; the hollow body is a windchest. Thus, the whistle is at the end of the wind system instead of at the beginning. If the player pours some water into the flute, it bubbles and interferes with the air current; the tone then becomes quavering, as with the tremolo stop of an organ.

In this form the globular flute is spread over the ancient and modern world as a cheap child's toy. But there is no doubt that it once had a charm power emanating from its zoomorphic shape.

It was one of the curiosities of history when, about 1860, a certain Donati at Budrio in southern Italy "invented" a globular beaked flute of clay or porcelain in the shape of a turnip with a whistle head and eight fingerholes in a convenient arrangement. This unpretentious instrument, called *ocarina*, 'anserine,' or 'of the nature of geese,' became very popular with modest amateurs. Since the ocarina was made in complete sets from trebles to basses, ocarina societies, and even orchestras, using only this instrument were founded. Unconsciously Donati reunited the two separated branches of the globular clay whistle: the cavity sound and fingerholes of one with the cross arrangement and the whistle system of the other.

STONES AND STONE CHIMES (*ch'ing*) are much valued as musical instruments by the Chinese. Certain calcareous stones struck with a sufficiently heavy stick produce an excellent sound; when they have been long exposed to the sun and are perfectly dry, their timbre is less brilliant than that of metal and clearer than that of wood.

While today the use of stones is confined to Confucian temples, they were indispensable in antiquity on all formal occasions, official as well as private, at banquets and receptions, and they were even played in intimacy. The philosopher Mencius (372–289 B.C.), comparing Confucius with a musical performance, said: "A concert is complete when the large bell proclaims the commencement of the music, and the ringing stone proclaims its close." Performing on a stone did not mean a plain and rough hammering. Confucius's pupils relate that "the master was playing, one day, on a musical stone in Wei, when a man, carrying a straw basket, passed the door of the house where Confucius was, and said, 'this heart is full that so beats the musical stone.'" The word reveals a delicacy in playing that we can hardly understand.

The biggest sonorous stone occurs in Annamese temples; there, enormous slabs, many feet in width and about four inches in depth, are struck with small, though heavy, wooden clubs. The Chinese slabs are only from one to two feet in the largest dimension and cut in the shape of an L, except that the angle is obtuse. They are suspended. In this form they were probably used as money in remote times, just as today actual gongs circulate as money in southeastern Asia; some of the earliest coins of China had the same L form, though reduced in size.

Sonorous stones are known far beyond the boundaries of China. Some have been found in Venezuela, and some replace the bells in Christian churches of Ethiopia and on the Mediterranean island of

Chios. Still, there is no reason for connecting these with the Far Eastern stones.

A relation with a certain West Polynesian rite, on the contrary, is possible, indeed probable, for reasons of cultural geography. To prepare the intoxicating drink *kawa* for religious purposes, maidens perform the solemn ceremony of sitting on the ground and pulverizing the roots of the pepper plant, piper methysticum, on flat, sonorous stones which are insulated with small pieces of coconut and tuned to definite pitches. In a former book the author has transcribed a piece of Samoan stone music.

This may be an older stage that has been preserved, or a degenerated one, or even an independent development. It shows, at all events, that sets of tuned stones can exist without the use of single stones; single stones did not necessarily precede combined stones. Moreover, the discovery that different stones produced different tones can be supposed to have led to musical utilization rather than to the much less impressive discovery that a beaten single stone could sound.

The Far-Eastern *stone chime* or *lithophone*, called *pien ch'ing* in Chinese, consists of sixteen slabs, L-shaped, about one foot on the longer side, all identical in size but differing in thickness. The slabs are suspended in two horizontal rows above each other from a rectangular stand; the upper row is tuned to the male, the lower row to the female semitones, which will be explained later. Each verse of the hymn to Confucius is ended by a single blow with a disconnected hammer in order "to receive the tone" and transmit it to the following word. (pl. X c)

BELLS AND BELL CHIMES are the bronze age counterparts of the neolithic stones and stone chimes.

A bell is a vessel, the edge or *sound bow* of which produces the strongest vibrations while the top is mute.

Chinese bells were either struck by a clapper hung inside the bell (Chinese *ling*), or struck from the outside with disconnected hammers (*chung*). Both types are usually suspended, the former from the necks of animals, the latter from an upright stand. Besides, military bands of the Chou dynasty comprised at least two *hand bells*. In this section we will speak of the empty bell only.

We do not know how the bell originated. Primitive peoples possess rough bells made of natural material, such as crab pincers, shells and wood. But it is not sure that nonmetallic bells preceded the metal bell; most of them are clumsy imitations probably due to the lack of metal and foundries. It is not even certain that the riveted iron bells of African Negroes came earlier than the Chinese bells.

Bells are amulets, in the Far East as everywhere else. They are hung around the necks of bulls and cows—not to control the animals, but to protect them against evil spirits. Bells are suspended at the door to be rung by entering persons, not to warn the owner as today in some old-fashioned stores; the house and the caller must be protected against the demons who lurk under the threshold. Bells originally were not intended to call the churchgoers but to purify the holy place.

In planter civilizations bells assume the special function of a fertility charm. In the modern Tyrol, farmer boys, each with a small bell in his hand, march round the fields to secure a good harvest. The Bari, a Nilotic Negro people, try to attract rain by filling a bell with water and sprinkling the soil.

Bell ringing as a fertility and rain charm is a Chinese practice as well. The largest bell of China, in Peking—a gigantic instrument about fourteen feet in height, cast in the fifteenth century A.D.—was only struck when the emperor prayed for rain. The usual decoration of Confucian bells is associated with ideas of fertility. The exterior is divided into two zones: one of them is left undecorated and represents the field concealing the seeds; the other one generally has four squares of nine bosses each—nine being a sacred number that symbolizes renewal—and the bosses, according to Chinese sources, indicating female breasts, or rather nipples.

In contradiction to these feminine connotations, blood was sometimes mixed with the alloy. Legend relates that one emperor witnessed the trembling ox dragged to the slaughter as a sacrifice to the bell, and, pitiful, spared him; but a sheep had to be offered in his place.

The memory of human sacrifices has survived in the legend of the casting of the Great Bell. Yung-lo, the third emperor of the Ming dynasty, ordered a mandarin to cast a bell which should be heard in every part of Peking. The mandarin obeyed, but the bell was honeycombed when the mold was detached from it. He made a second attempt and failed again. When, urged by the emperor, he tried a third casting, his lovely young daughter learned from an astrologer that success could only be secured if a maiden's blood were mixed with the ingredients. So when the melted metal rushed into the mold, she threw herself into the boiling fluid. While the unfortunate father, insane with sorrow, was taken home, the bell was found to be perfect.

In the Far East bells were originally quadrangular in cross section, as they were also in ancient Egypt and Ireland and still are in the Shan States of the Burmese hinterland. The dynasty of the Chou is said to have replaced the rectangular shape of the cross section by an elliptic one. From elliptic, it became circular in the sixteenth century, and in the eighteenth, oval. The characteristic beehive shape of Chinese bells, so different from the tulip shape of modern European bells, is also attributed to the Chou.

The size must have been rather impressive as early as the Han dynasty. Chang Heng (78–139 A.D.), the author of satires against the luxury of the imperial residences, speaks of gigantic bells in the palaces weighing three hundred thousand pounds. This, however, is certainly exaggerated. The world's largest bell, the Tsar's bell in Moscow, weighs 443,772 pounds and the Great Bell mentioned above, which is rammed with a heavy beam hung horizontally, is estimated at fifty-three tons, or 118,720 pounds.

Single bells in the palaces and the Confucian temples are called *po chung*. Suspended in a large ornamental frame with tigers and a hawk carved on it, the temple bell was placed on the moon terrace and struck with a beater between the verses of the Confucian hymn. As Chinese cosmology associated notes and seasons, the pitch of the bells, like that of sonorous stones, changed with the season of the year; the spring required a bell tuned to $f\sharp$, while the autumn needed a bell in b.

This association must have originated farther west. The Greek author Plutarch (c. 40–c. 120 A.D.), who, of course, did not know anything about Chinese cosmology, related that the Babylonians considered the proportion spring-autumn equivalent to a fourth in music, while spring and winter formed a fifth, and spring and summer an octave. These are the two systems:

Interval	Babylonia	China
octave	summer	
fifth	winter	winter
fourth	autumn	autumn
second		summer
ground-tone	spring	spring

The two systems are identical except for the position of summer.

It seems that *bell chimes* were older than single (empty) bells.

Our earliest sources always speak of bells in the plural form, and when we read in the *Shih Ching* that to entertain the guests at banquets "the bells and drums are properly arranged," it is hard to think of anything but tuned sets of bells.

The bell chime, called *pien chung* in Chinese, corresponds exactly to the stone chime. Sixteen bells, identical in shape and size but different in thickness (the thicker the higher), are suspended in two horizontal rows, one above the other, from a rectangular stand; the upper row is tuned to the male, and the lower row to the female semitones (to be discussed later on).

The history of Chinese bell chimes reflects a continued frustration. We read, as in an exciting novel, how the alien Emperor Tsin-hwang-ti had his men destroy all Chinese books and musical instruments in order to strike at the spiritual roots of the nation. We then read how some faithful court and temple musicians secretly buried a few of the venerable old bell chimes in their gardens to preserve them; how, later on, national emperors tried to re-establish the ancient music, but on the basis of doubtful tradition and erroneous calculation; how these same emperors destroyed the old and authentic relics in order to dispose of unwelcome witnesses to the inaccuracy of their own attempts; how for many centuries musicians and mathematicians tried to correct the false restoration; and how, also, these men failed.

THE DRUMS. The earliest sources closely connect "the large bells and drums." But it seems that a drum *po fu* or 'right-left' is even older than the drum *ku* mentioned in the *Shih Ching*. Unlike the modern *po fu* it was filled with rice hull. A temple musician held it horizontally on his knees and, at the end of each verse of the hymn to Confucius, beat it three times with the bare hands—once with the right hand on the right skin, *po*, once with the left hand on the left skin, *fu*, and a third time with both hands on both skins, *po fu*.

Drums filled with grain were, and still are, found over large districts of Asia, and were known by North American Indians, such as the Ojibwa and the Cree. These American frame drums are similar to the oldest two-skinned frame drums represented on statuettes from ancient Mesopotamia. The purpose of the second skin could not have been for tuning as the oldest drums were not tuned. These widespread examples of two-skinned drums filled with grain indicate that the second skin may have been originally necessitated by the filling.

Besides the grain drum, China had a clapper drum, *t'ao ku*, as early as the Shang dynasty. A stick passes diametrically through the body and projects on one side to form a handle. Two beads suspended on the outside of the drum strike the skins when the drum is rapidly twirled to and fro. Today this small drum is a toy; in the times of the Shang and the Chou it seems to have been larger.

Much more important than the grain drum and the clapper drum is a family of big barrel drums, made of wood, with thick cow skins nailed over both ends, and played with two heavy sticks. The difference between the numerous members of this family consists in their varying sizes and playing positions. It is nearly impossible to put order in the chaos of names given to these drums at various times in China, Korea and Japan. The survey is facilitated if we keep in mind two chief shapes and two playing positions:

Shapes:
long drums, in which the length of the barrel is larger than the diameters of the heads
short drums, in which the length of the barrel is smaller than the diameters of the heads
Positions:
heads horizontal
heads vertical

Drums with the heads vertical are usually more archaic.

In the Mesopotamian chapter we pointed out that the large Sumerian drums and the large barrel drums of the Far East were closely related and probably had a common origin somewhere between Mesopotamia and China. If so, then the use of two sticks striking the same skin can be interpreted as derived from the two drummers striking the same skin on Sumerian reliefs. It should be emphasized that striking with a pair of sticks does not achieve the same rhythmic refinement as beating with the hands.

The characteristic nailing of these Far Eastern barrel drums, excluding definite pitch and tuning, might have been practical as well as magic. All we know is that in Asia, Africa and Europe nails have a magic significance and are connected with certain rites; nails are laid in tombs and driven into doors and trees, and up to this day Italians put nails in their pockets to protect themselves against the evil eye.

Mrs. Marie Du Bois-Reymond relates in her diary that before being nailed the skins were tightly stretched with cords. This vaguely shows a connection between the nailed and the laced drum and draws our special attention towards certain African drums which are both laced and nailed, wooden pegs being driven through the same holes in the skin which allow the cords to pass.

The magic character of the nails enhances the magic character of the drum itself. As a talisman for luck and victory, the drum embodied the fate of the army. According to the book *Tso Chuan* (c. 600 B.C.), it was consecrated by smearing the skins with the blood of sacrificed men, usually war captives. In battle, the commanding chariot carrying the drum and the flag was the palladium on which defeat or victory depended: "The eyes and ears of the army are on the flag and drum. It will advance or retire as this chariot does."

THE CHOU DYNASTY (1122–255 B.C.)

Of the instruments of the following dynasty, the Chou, we have a more complete knowledge. Poetical sources are more frequent, and an exhaustive contemporary list of the instruments that the Chinese used at that time has been preserved.

The idiophones among the instruments enumerated in the list are the percussion clapper, the trough, the tiger, the lithophone, the stone and the stone chime, the bell and the bell chime.

THE PERCUSSION CLAPPER. This term seems to be somewhat paradoxical; clappers are concussion, not percussion instruments. Here, however, the term is exact. Twelve narrow, flat bamboo strips, each twelve inches long and one inch wide, are tied together by a leather thong like a bunch of keys. When struck against the palm of the left hand, the percussion of the whole implement against the hand combines with the concussion of the individual strips. These clappers were used by temple singers; the sacred poem that should be sung, was engraved on the strips. A bunch of engraved bamboo strips was the ordinary form of a written book and the earliest pictographic sign for 'book,' in the Shang script, reproduced it distinctly. Thus, the clapper was said to commemorate the invention of writing, especially at the sacrifice to heaven, when thanks were given for the gift of writing as well as for all other cultural benefits. This may be true; but we rather believe that, to a more primitive mentality, the power of the holy words was strengthened when they were sung, moved and written at once.

The name of this clapper, *ch'ung tu*, meant originally a different instrument, a piece of bamboo split several times, about seven Chinese feet high and five to six inches thick, which was struck upon the ground. It still exists in Korea under the name *tok*.

THE TROUGH, *chu*, first mentioned, as far as we know, in a poem written about 1100 B.C., is a wooden percussion instrument. A board, a foot or two square, forms the bottom; the four side walls slope outwards. A hammer, linked to a pivot inside on the bottom, is reached through a large hole in one of the sides and strikes the bottom at the beginning of the Confucian service. In the hymn to Confucius it gives three blows before each verse—that is, before each group of the four syllables which are sung in four prolonged musical notes.

As the trough had the form of an ancient grain measure, the instrument must have originated in a farming civilization. It obviously was connected with the music of certain agricultural rites similar to the Malayan rice pounding in tuned mortars. Its use for pounding grain would explain why the Chinese strike the inside of the bottom of their trough instead of the outside of the walls, which would be more natural. A forerunner to the trough still exists in the Korean *chuk*, a large trough some thirty inches high and pounded with a pestle in phallic shape.

THE WOODEN FISH (Chinese *mu yü*, 'wood fish,' Japanese *mo kugyo*). The Taoistic and Buddhistic cults of the Far East employ a strange offshoot of the slit-drum, which belongs here, though it is not mentioned in the list of Chou instruments. A fish, in an increasingly stylized and unrecognizable shape, is carved from a piece of camphor wood, hollowed out through a small ventral slit and lacquered gold and red. The craftsmen skillfully carve a small ball, imprisoned, but free to move inside the cavity. Suspended or placed on a cushion or stand, the fish is struck with a heavy pointed stick.

The animal has no eyelids; it symbolizes wakeful attention. When beaten, it attracts the notice of the divinity, exactly as Hebrew and Egyptian trumpets. Being a water animal, it is particularly efficacious with prayers for rain. But as explained in the section on the bull-roarer, fish are closely connected with rites of death and resurrection. From this point of view, the ball moving inside may recall resurrection myths much as the Biblical tale of Jonah in the whale. Another detail connects the wooden fish with another familiar myth. The oldest specimens have a piece of fruit carved in the mouth; this is the noted penny for the journey of the dead that we have preserved in a denegerated custom of our kitchen when we dish up a fish with a lemon placed in its mouth.

THE TIGER, *yü*, scraped three times, marks the end of the Confucian service. It is carved out of a piece of wood to represent a crouching tiger on a socle. Along the back a dentated strip, suggesting the animal's spine, is scraped with a wand of bamboo, one end of which is split down to the middle into twelve switches.

To the Chinese the tiger is the animal belonging to west and harvest, to sunset and death. The late sinologist, Richard Wilhelm, once said that in the dying sound of the tiger an initiated person experienced the mystery of the Tao, the spiritual path of life. This may be true. But the association with death seems to be counteracted by both the rod and the scraping action. The life-giving significance of scraping has been mentioned (cf. page 43), and the split rod is a well-known symbol of life in Asia, America and even Europe.

PITCH- AND PAN-PIPES. The earliest Far Eastern wind instrument, mentioned in a Chinese poem written about 1100 B.C., has been interpreted as 'double flute' by the translator of the *Book of Poetry*. The Chinese term, however, is unmistakably *kuan*. This word means a short cylindrical oboe in modern language. But we know from Tsai Yü, in the sixteenth century A.D., that in ancient Chinese the name was given to a vertical pitch-pipe without fingerholes, which was tuned to one of the twelve *lü* or 'standards.'

The *lü*, carefully fixed in ancient times by the Music Office of the Ministry of Norms, were the basis of the musical system of the Chinese. They were determined by a cycle of either ascending fifths or descending fourths which started from the central note or *huang chung: F* sharp, *C* sharp, *G* sharp, *D* sharp, *A* sharp, *E* sharp or *F, C, G, D, A, E* and *B*. As the Chinese conceive the cosmos as the harmony of *yang* and *yin*—the male and the female force—and as they understand music as a substitute and representative of the universe, they attribute six out of the twelve lü to the male, and six to the female principle. Numbers are also either male or female, odd numbers being considered male, and even numbers female.

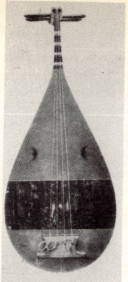

B. *Japanese biwa (8th century A.D.) in the Imperial Treasury at Shosoin.*

*. Chinese priests playing the
one chime (Ph. Du Bois
eymond).*

D. *Mouth-organ player, Black Karên (Ph. Scherman).*

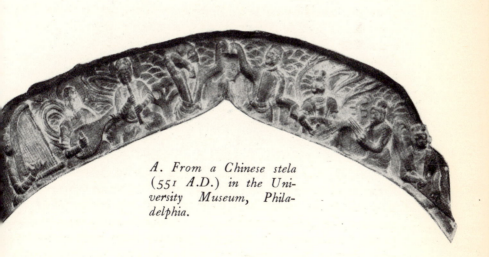

A. *From a Chinese stela (551 A.D.) in the University Museum, Philadelphia.*

PLATE X.

Thus the first, third, fifth, etc., lü are male, the second, fourth, sixth, etc., female:

> Male *F♯—G♯—A♯—C—D—E*
> Female *G—A—B—C♯—D♯—F*

The scale of lü does not exactly correspond to our tempered chromatic scale. For they are not brought forth by an actual cycle of fifths under the control of a musician's ear, but by pitch-pipes, the lengths of which are in the ratio 2:3 or 3:4. But these proportions, though consistent with theory, are inaccurate with stopped pipes; musical intervals thus obtained are too small. So the Chinese at last introduced fourteen lü instead of twelve in order to fill in the octave.

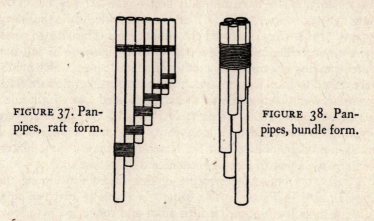

FIGURE 37. Pan-pipes, raft form.

FIGURE 38. Pan-pipes, bundle form.

The junction of a whole set of these twelve pitch-pipes resulted in the *p'ai hsiao* that we blunderingly call *pan-pipes* in honor of the Greek god Pan, though it was an unimportant instrument in Hellas.

Generally speaking, pan-pipes are sets of canes, usually stopped at their lower ends, which are tied together either in the fashion of a raft (*raft-pipes*) or of a round bundle (*bundle-pipes*) and blown across the upper ends in the manner of vertical flutes. (figs. 37, 38)

Pan-pipes of the Far East have notched canes (see next section) and raft form. The classical number of twelve canes has been increased to sixteen by adding four shorter canes, just as in stone and bell chimes the original number, twelve, has been increased to sixteen. The modern flat case, from which the upper and lower ends of the canes project, is said to have been added only under the Mongol Yüan dynasty, about 1300 A.D.

Even in the joined form of pan-pipes the set of twelve lü pipes must have preserved its character as a standard instrument for determining pitch long before it became a musical instrument. Otherwise it is not intelligible that, disregarding melody, it would be arranged in male and female groups up to this day. At present, its disposition resembles the symmetric fronts of occidental organs; it has the male canes on one side and the female canes on the other side, the canes being arranged in such a way that the longest are in the center with the shortest at the sides, or else the longest at the sides and the shortest in the center.

This symmetrical arrangement, however, must be a later disposition. In earlier times the scale ran straight from side to side; the lowest note is said to have originally been on the left side, but in the Sung dynasty (960–1278 A.D.), on the right side, while the Ming dynasty (1368–1644) restored the ancient plan. This change possibly was not a difference of age, but rather a difference of sex, one source speaking of a male and another of a female pipe, which finally were united to form a composite instrument. An intermediate stage was preserved in ancient Peru; there, a left-sided and a right-sided raft of pan-pipes, though separately blown by two players, were nevertheless connected by a loose cord. The same arrangement is found in modern Bolivia, and the Karen-ni in the Burmese hinterland also use a pair of pan-pipes connected by a loose cord.

A still more important evidence of this stage exists among the Cuna Indians in Panama. The same player blows two pan-pipes called man and wife, tuned a fifth apart and connected by a loose cord. (A brief look at the scheme on page 177 will show that of two lü a fifth apart one is necessarily male and one female.) When played, the two instruments are joined face to face and blown simultaneously, a male cane always accompanied by the corresponding female cane a fifth above.

FLUTES. The oldest sources mention four flutes: the *kuan* and the *hsiao* in the twelfth or eleventh century B.C., the *ch'ih* in the ninth, and the *yüeh* in the eighth century B.C. Later sources speak of the *yo* and the *ti*. These names must be interpreted with the greatest care; in three thousand years they have changed their meaning more than any other musical instrument of China.

The *ch'ih* was a bamboo flute played in unison with the globular flute:

Heaven enlightens the people,
When the bamboo flute responds to the porcelain whistle;
As two half maces form a whole one,

says an ode of the ninth century B.C. In medieval sources it is said
to have had 5 + 1 fingerholes and to have been a stopped *ti*, with a
blow-hole "like a sour jujube." The word "stopped" can only apply
to the upper end and not, as we would use the term, to the lower one.

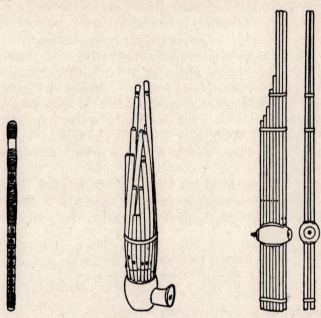

FIGURE 39. Modern
Japanese cross flute.

FIGURE 40. Chinese
mouth organ.

FIGURE 41. Laotic
mouth organ.

Since it had a blow-hole, the *ch'ih* must have been a cross flute—indeed, the oldest cross flute in history. (fig. 39)

To anticipate the result of the following paragraphs: all the other
terms designate a *notched flute*, that is, a vertical flute with a small
notch cut in the edge of the upper orifice; the notch, being beveled,
facilitates blowing.

The *kuan* has already been discussed; it was a notched pipe without fingerholes. The *ti* was said to have been similar to the kuan,
except for having three fingerholes. Prince Tsai Yü said that he had
heard that the ti came from the Ch'iang people. This was the name

given to the Chou by the Shang; it hints of a western origin of the instrument.

The *hsiao* is mentioned in the same verse as the kuan. James Legge, the translator of the *Book of Poetry*, renders it by 'pan-pipes.' This translation is certainly not correct. The pan-pipes, called *p'ai hsiao*, were composed of twelve pipes, *kuan*. Would it not be meaningless to mention in the same verse, as being played together, both the single and the united pipes of exactly the same kind? The flute *hsiao* must have been something different. No medieval Chinese writer, indeed, thought of the pan-pipes. Among them, Prince Tsai Yü seems to be particularly trustworthy when he says that *hsiao* is the ancient name of the *yo*. Asserting this, he does not contradict the "common opinion," as A. C. Moule says, but, on the contrary, he confirms it in its statement that the hsiao was a *ti*.

For the *yo*, in spite of the six fingerholes that it has in modern China, had only three holes in ancient times, as in Korea today, and since it was a notched flute it must have been identical with the ti and the hsiao.

And finally the hsiao was identical with the *yüeh*. Moule says that "the yo is now obsolete except as a wand used by the mimes in ritual dances." Indeed, the *yüeh* is referred to when, about 700 B.C., the dancer sings:

> I dance in the ducal courtyard . . .
> In my left hand I grasp a flute;
> In my right I hold a pheasant's feather.

And again, in the eighth century:

The dancers move with their flutes to the notes of the organ and drum
While all the instruments perform in harmony.

We cannot end this section on the ancient flute without mentioning that the modern *hsiao* or *tung hsiao*, to use A. C. Moule's words, is "a bamboo pipe made in the same way as the yo, except that the top is closed by a knot of the bamboo. In this knot a notch is cut joining that in the side." This instrument is intermediate between the whistle flute and the simple vertical flute and certainly more archaic than the latter. We may be sure that the hsiao of the Chou had this form; but it must be an unsettled question whether the other flutes mentioned in this section had the knot as well.

The standard flute was tuned to the note *huang chung* (the 'yellow bell') or *f♯*, which probably was identical with the Greek 'middle tone' or *mésē*. To produce this note the tube must be cut exactly the length of an old Chinese foot, that is, 229.9 millimeters or nine and one-sixteenth inches. Therefore, the flute is called *yo* in Chinese and *yak* in Korean; both terms designate 'stalk, foot, measure.' If we add that the center of the lowest fingerhole was at a distance of three (Chinese) inches from the end of the flute, and that the centers of the three fingerholes were each two inches apart, we face one of the most arresting problems in the history of musical instruments: what was the principle that guided primitive man when he got his knife or burning iron ready to cut fingerholes in a pipe? Did he pierce them at random? Or was he led by any special idea? The reader must not forget that these men had no pitch, no fixed intervals, no scale, no system.

The question touched upon in the Egyptian chapter was finally answered by our late friend Dr. Erich M. von Hornbostel. The following were his principal points:

1) The series of fingerholes on pipes are not determined by any musical conception.

2) They are, on the contrary, determined by measures of length, that is by feet and inches.

3) Certain measures and certain musical notes were, to the ancient civilizations, akin, indeed identical, being different manifestations of the same idea; for both of them were equally expressions of the cosmos.

4) Measures have migrated with the instruments over wide continents and epochs.

Let us try to explain these four statements.

Concerning 1: most pipes, both primitive and highly developed, have equidistant fingerholes. But this equidistance absolutely precludes the production of any musical scale unless the notes are corrected by the size of the holes, the breath, the fingering, or some special device. Scales require a geometrical progression of the spaces between the holes, not equidistance; the distances must increase towards the lower end.

Concerning 2: inches are not the same as the American and English measures of this name, which are equivalent to 2.54 centimeters. The inches spread over the world by pipe making are measures of the early civilizations, the Sumerian and the Chinese. Among the most common we quote:

the inch of 16.53 millimeters,
the inch of 19.84 millimeters,
the inch of 20.04 millimeters.

The first one is recorded on a statue of the Sumerian king, Gudea (about 2400 B.C.). The other two cannot be dated.

Concerning 3: these inches, and the feet made up in groups of fifteen, sixteen or twenty, are sacred measures. Using them in a musical instrument was equivalent to giving it the sacred character necessary for the magic and religious purpose it served.

Concerning 4: measures were not invented by primitive men who had no use for them. They came, on the contrary, from the highly developed cultures of ancient Asia, which had to survey areas in order to distribute land for cultivation and to erect temples and palaces. With the world-wide migrations of tribes, ideas and objects, these measurements were spread over the five continents. They persisted even in European instruments as long as the nineteenth century; the flutist and flute maker, Theobald Boehm, was practically the first, in 1832, to abandon the equidistant holes which always had to be corrected.

If we are called upon to measure a pipe, we lay a ruler alongside the instrument so that zero is at the upper end (the end near the player's mouth). Then we measure from the upper end to the *center* of each side-hole. The entire length is seldom important.

The kind of inch that we find as the standard used for determining the distances between the holes is a valuable clue in seeking the provenance of a type of pipe. The author's latest experience in using this method was in investigating the flutes of Madagascar. Their simple shape gave no hint. The native name *sódina* (pronounced *súdina*) was certainly derived from Malayan *suling*, as *d* and *l* are interchangeable in some idioms of Madagascar, and it pointed to a Malayan origin of the flute. However, as the kind of inch utilized never occurs with Malayan instruments, but is a frequent standard of measurement of Arabian flutes, it can be taken for granted that the flutes came to Madagascar with one of the Arabian migrations across the sea.

THE MOUTH ORGAN (Chinese *shêng*, Japanese *shô*) was originally made with a gourd. Today the gourd is replaced by a piece of wood cut in the same shape. The neck serves as a mouthpiece and air conduct, while the body forms a windchest to feed the pipes. Thirteen or more slender canes of different length (the highest measuring sixteen to twenty inches) project upwards out of the windchest in a circular arrangement; inside the windchest each pipe has a side-hole which is covered by a thin metal tongue. This tongue interrupts the air current in the manner of a clarinet's reed. But instead of being a 'beating reed,' the tongue of mouth organs is a 'free reed'; that is, it is made precisely the same width as the hole, so that it is free to move to and fro through the hole without being stopped by its edges. Outside the windchest each pipe has a fingerhole which, if the pipe is expected to sound, must be closed for the following reason. As the tongue is less elastic than in occidental organs and harmoniums, it is permanently held open because of the air pressure in the windchest. But if this outer hole is stopped, the pressure inside the pipe equalizes the pressure in the windchest and the tongue is again able to close, so that the pipe is able to sound. (fig. 40)

The player holds the pipes nearly horizontal. He 'blows' mainly during aspiration, probably to prevent the metal tongues from growing damp and oxidized. The sound is extremely delicate and sweet.

Mouth organs are tuned by semitones or *lü;* the melodies, however, are pentatonic without semitones. These melodies are accompanied by chords. In the court music of Japan old harmonies are preserved which were brought to the country a thousand years ago from China; some comprise three notes, some five, some six notes. Only two of the eleven usual chords correspond to occidental minor triads; the others consist of the notes of pentatonic scales sounding simultaneously (for instance: $A\ B\ D\ E\ F\sharp$), or in other combinations (for instance: $G\sharp\ A\ B\ C\ D\ F\sharp$). In modern China these complicated harmonies are replaced by simple parallels of fifths and fourths. In both cases the melody is below, as in ancient Greece and the earlier part of the European middle ages.

Prototypes of the mouth organ are still found in the south and the east of Asia. The Hei Miao in western China use shêngs with bamboo pipes fourteen feet high with brass reeds. The Mro and the Kumi in the district of Chittagong in Bengal have huge single pipes which are as long as a man is tall. A bottle-shaped calabash, pierced by the pipe, is situated somewhere near the middle of the pipe's length and serves as a windchest. Inside the calabash the pipe has a hole covered by a free reed. The player's mouth is applied to its neck.

The circular arrangement of a set of smaller pipes in one calabash, that we find in China, Korea and Japan, has its primitive counterpart in Borneo, while the district between them—Upper Burma and Laos—has a mouth organ in raft form; in Upper Burma and the northern part of Laos two rafts of pipes cross inside the gourd, and either project beneath it (X-shaped), or else are cut off at the bottom of the gourd (V-shaped). In the most highly developed form of the raft-shaped mouth organ, in Middle and South Laos, the two rafts, sometimes as tall as twelve feet, are laid on top of each other and this double raft pierces through an elongated, wooden windchest, which is situated near the lower ends of the rafts. Even these tall mouth organs are light enough to be carried, as are all mouth organs. Several of these instruments played together, particularly by young fellows in wooing games, combine rich harmonies in four parts. This is one of the most attractive musical styles in the Orient, pure, serene and transparent. (fig. 41, pl. X d)

In China the mouth organ is said to have been invented by Emperor Nyu-kwa in the third millennium B.C. as an imitation of the bird Phoenix with its body, head and wings. This tradition might have caused the use of mouth organs in Chinese funeral processions up to the present day, though today they are carried without being played; funeral music can be a resurrection charm as well as a protection against evil spirits.

In spite of tradition, the mouth organ is not mentioned before about 1100 B.C., and no earlier picture of it could be found than on a votive stele dated 551 A.D., now in the University Museum, Philadelphia. (pl. X a)

By that time the instrument had its widest range of distribution; the Persians then knew and used it as the *muštaq sini*, or 'Chinese mushtak,' and depicted it on reliefs at Taq-i Bustan and elsewhere.

Once more in the eighteenth century the mouth organ was carried westward. A certain musician, JOHANN WILDE, known as the inventor of the nail violin, purchased or was given a shêng in St. Petersburg and learned to play *die liebliche Chineser Orgel* ("the charming organ of the Chinese"). The physicist Kratzenstein from Copenhagen heard him, examined the free reed and suggested to the organ builder KIRSCHNIK in St. Petersburg that he introduce the free reed into the organ. Kirschnik, however, made no organ with free reeds, but only organ pianos. The first organ with free reeds was built by the famous Abbé GEORG JOSEPH VOGLER in Darmstadt. A large family of reed instruments, such as mouth harmonicas, accordions, harmoniums, was created from 1800 on.

THE LONG ZITHER is the oldest stringed instrument of China, and up to the end of the Chou dynasty the only one. Zithers, erroneously called lutes by the translator, are first mentioned in an ode written about 1100 B.C.:

> The modest, retiring, virtuous young lady:—
> With lutes, small and large, let us give her friendly welcome.
> The modest, retiring, virtuous young lady:—
> With bells and drums let us show our delight in her.

The terms 'small' and 'large' lutes are supposed to correspond to the two words *ch'in* and *shê* in the Chinese original. These two types are nearly always associated in the sources of the Chou time:

> Loving union with wife and children
> Is like the music of shê and ch'in.

Both exist to this day. (pl. X a, fig. 42, 43)

There are many varieties of both the ch'in and the shê, but they

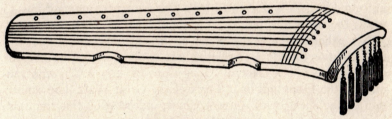

FIGURE 42. Ch'in.

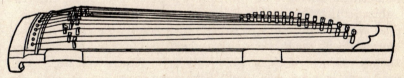

FIGURE 43. Shê.

all have certain features in common. The strings are longitudinally stretched over a narrow, slightly convex board, the concave under side of which is closed by a flat bottom. When played, it is horizontally laid either on the ground, or on the knees, or on a table. The strings, made of silken threads, sound clearer than gut strings and less sharp than wires.

First we will speak of the *shê*, one of the instruments played by Confucius. This is an *unfretted long zither* with twenty-five open strings in pentatonic tuning (in earlier times there are said to have been fifty). A smaller form, called *cheng* in Chinese and *sō-no-koto* in Japanese (*sō* corresponding to Chinese *shê*), has only fourteen strings in China. On unfretted long zithers the vibrating length of each string is determined by a shiftable triangular bridge wedged between it and the soundboard.

Both the cheng and the shê are composed of three parts, a main section that supports the strings, and two end pieces which are bent back. This triple arrangement recalls the *tube-zither* and the *half-tube-zither* of the Malayan Archipelago and a few African countries including Madagascar, all of which have a piece of bamboo as a body, either an entire tube or half of a bamboo split lengthways; the strings run parallel to each other the length of one internode in the bamboo and are formed by strips cut off the bamboo itself. Parts of the adjacent internodes (we call these parts *transnodes*) are left to form a head and a tail piece. The head and the tail piece are often of different lengths, and their lengths vary in different instruments. That these bamboo zithers were the prototypes of the Far Eastern unfretted zithers is confirmed by a Chinese tradition, according to which the cheng was originally made of bamboo.

Nevertheless, the cheng is not earlier than the shê. Even Chinese tradition considers it a relatively recent instrument; its inventor is said to have been General Mong t'yen (d. 209 B.C.), who vanquished the Huns and built a part of the Great Wall. The connection of the cheng with western China, indicated by this tradition, is corroborated by several other facts. At the Chinese court the instrument belonged to the two Mongolian orchestras; the Kirghizes still have it as *jataga* in a comparatively recent form with a flat board and seven wire strings; and, finally, the name *cheng* is identical with the Persian name of the harp. However, bamboo large enough to make a cheng grew only in a southern climate, so that the early bamboo cheng must have come from farther south. An unexpected picture of the cheng was discovered by the author on the plafond of the Kolberg cathedral in Pomerania, painted in the fourteenth century A.D.

Japan and Korea have preserved chengs with a smaller number of strings; Japan, especially, has kept all varieties, from the *ichi-gen-kin* or 'one-string-zither,' the *ni-gen-kin* or 'two-string-zither,' and the *san-gen-kin* or 'three-string-zither,' up to the nine-stringed *sage-koto*. The most important of these varieties is the six-stringed *ya-mato-koto*, or *wagon*, which is said to have existed in Japan before the times of Chinese influence.

The fretted long zither is called *ch'in* in Chinese, *koto* or *kin* in Japanese, and *kum* or *komunko* in Korean. Its body tapers slightly towards the rounded lower end; the strings held by two knobs at the back of the instrument run around the lower end and, diverging over the soundboard, are fastened by a row of pegs at the top. To-day the classical number of strings is seven, as it probably was also in antiquity. Some authors have concluded from ancient sources that the original number was only five, but they have mistaken the number of notes for the number of strings. The scale was pentatonic without semitones, and the sixth and seventh string continued the five-tone scale without adding new notes. There was a similar con-fusion in interpreting authorities on the Greek lyre; here, as well, the sixth and seventh strings continued a pentatonic scale without adding new notes and it was uncertain whether the word *chordê* meant string or note. Japan, however, has preserved to this day a fretted long zither with only five strings, the *go kin*, and as Japan still retains many objects forgotten in China, it is likely that once a five-stringed *ch'in* existed.

The seven strings of the modern *ch'in* are made from a varying number of silk threads twisted together, and this quantity is in accordance with the so-called 'Pythagorean' relation between the tones to which they are tuned.

Downwards, the succession of thread numbers runs: 48, 54, 64, 72, 81, 96, 108, thus reproducing, in the number of threads, the tonal proportions $\frac{9}{8}$, $\frac{32}{27}$, $\frac{9}{8}$, $\frac{9}{8}$, $\frac{32}{27}$, $\frac{9}{8}$, or a half-toneless, penta-tonic scale of whole tones and minor thirds. But the tone of the strings depends on other factors as well, and the effectiveness of this traditional proportion is consequently imaginary. A similar calcula-tion occurs once more, in another instance: Arabian theorists of the tenth century A.D. report that the four strings of the lute, *'ūd*, tuned by fourths, were composed by 27, 36, 48 and 64 threads—that is, not only the principle but the numbers as well were similar, 48 and 64 identical, and 27 and 36, as halves of the Chinese numbers 54 and 72.

Instead of frets, there are thirteen nacre studs inlaid in the sound-board under the outer (lowest) string. Their arrangement is en-tirely different from the usual manner of fretting stringed instru-ments. Instead of being unilaterally arranged from one end of the string and giving a consecutive scale of half-tones, the studs are symmetrically disposed from the center towards the two ends, in $\frac{1}{2}$, $\frac{1}{3}$ and $\frac{2}{3}$, $\frac{1}{4}$ and $\frac{3}{4}$, $\frac{1}{5}$ and $\frac{4}{5}$, $\frac{1}{6}$ and $\frac{5}{6}$, $\frac{1}{8}$ and $\frac{7}{8}$ of the total length. The musical result would be this curious scale: *c d e♭ e f g a c′ e′ g′ c″ e″ g″ c″′*. This would be absurd, unless the studs were intended to serve the only form of playing in which it does not make any difference whether the string is touched either in one third or in two thirds of the string, in one eighth or in seven eighths —that is, when harmonics are used.

A harmonic is produced when, instead of pressing the string against the fingerboard, the player lightly touches it in, say, a half, a third or a quarter of its length. He then does not shorten the string, but creates a node of vibration which hinders the string from sounding in its entire length and producing the fundamental; instead, he forces it to produce a partial or harmonic, the octave in the case of the node being in the middle, the twelfth, when the node is made in one third or two thirds—the double octave plus a major third, when the node is made in one fifth or four fifths (or two or three fifths), and so on. Notes produced in this way are somewhat frail as a consequence of lacking the fundamental vibration and several partials.

Players of the ch'in do not use harmonics exclusively. For, the manner of sound production is much more variable than with any occidental instrument. The right hand plucks while the left hand taps the string at a certain spot and glides to the following position without leaving the string and without lessening the pressure. If both hands play on the same string, the left hand action stops the plucked string but is separately audible as a series of vibratos, glissandi and dull beats; if the left hand plays on a different string, it forms a second part, which can be a counterpoint or a simple drone; chords are rarely heard. A special notation has symbols not only for pitch and time, but also for playing with one, two or three fingers, for pulling the string towards oneself or away, for plucking, rubbing, tapping. In China plectra and finger rings have been abandoned in order to obtain an even more refined style of playing.

Occidental listeners have great difficulty in perceiving the delicate shades of ch'in playing and in appreciating its spirituality. But the average Oriental cannot appreciate it either. The ch'in does not court popularity, nor does it suit dilettantism. It is the instrument of philosophers and sages. In the privacy of a closed room, alone or before a few selected friends who listen respectfully and silently, the immaterial notes of the ch'in reveal to the listeners the ultimate truths of life and religion.

THE HAN DYNASTY (206 B.C.—220 A.D.)

THE SHORT LUTE. Under the Han, the Chinese Empire reached the peak of its power; the Caspian Sea became its western boundary. As a consequence, western instruments were brought to the east, and from that time on stringed instruments had a more

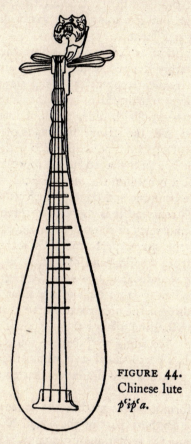

FIGURE 44.
Chinese lute
p'ip'a.

important role in the music of China. It will suffice to discuss only the most important one, the short lute, which is called *p'i p'a* in China and *biwa* in Japan. It has already been mentioned in the Indian chapter. (fig. 44)

The Far Eastern offshoot of the West Asiatic lute has a graceful, pear-shaped body. Its back is rounded, though shallow, and its front is covered with a wooden soundboard. The silken strings are attached to a cross ledge on the soundboard near the lower end and do not run beyond it. Their upper ends are tied to lateral pegs, which have the specifically eastern form of slim reversed cones. The usual number of strings is four; five strings are rare and so are six (two of these duplicating the two lower strings in a set of four). Their order, from the base to the treble string, follows the occidental arrangement, but the accordatura varies greatly, in China as well as in Korea and Japan.

The melody is almost exclusively played on the highest string; the next string is rarely stopped, and the lower ones are generally left open. Players frequently pluck two notes simultaneously, producing seconds, thirds, fourths, fifths and other intervals, especially when the singer is silent. With older types of lutes a large heavy plectron is dragged over the strings and lands on the soundboard with a knock; lutes of a recent type are plucked with the bare fingers.

The classic form of a pear-shaped lute is represented by the lute of the Japanese court orchestra, the *bugaku biwa*—that is, the biwa for the classic style in music and dance, which was brought to perfection in the tenth century. It is more than three feet high, very broad and heavy, and rests in slanting position on the ground between the legs of the sitting performer. To withstand the strong blows of the plectron, a solid band of leather is glued across the central part of the soundboard; two small, crescent-shaped soundholes, above it, face away from each other. Four ledges glued on the edge at intervals upon the fingerboard serve as frets; the delicate trill of the strings vibrating against them is a characteristic quality of the biwa sound. According to Japanese sources, this biwa was originally played in a percussional style rather than in a melodious one, and perhaps played a role similar to that of the banjo in our jazz bands.

A more recent form is represented by the Japanese *satsuma biwa*, so called after the southern part of the island Kyushu. This lute, serving to accompany the recitation of old epics, is laid on the knees of the sitting performer. It is shorter, only about three feet long, and appreciably narrower and lighter. The band of leather is replaced by a band of lacquer; instead of crescent-shaped soundholes, two ivory crescents are inlaid and a small slit is cut in each of them.

The *chicuzen biwa*, a variety of the satsuma biwa, derived its name from the northern part of the island Kyushu. It is still shorter, two feet seven inches long, and the two sides are more straight than pear-shaped. It sometimes has five strings.

The Chinese *p'i p'a* represents the most recent stage of the lute. It has four strings tuned to 1–4–5–8. The fingerboard is reeded with four adjacent convex frets, and six to thirteen more regular frets follow on the soundboard; this latter has no soundholes. Held upright on the thighs, it is played with the bare fingers which, in a rapid repetition, produce a kind of roll, while the left hand stops with much *vibrato* and *Bebung* (cf. clavichord). Usually several strings are played together in order to create either drones or chords. But most of these chords give the effect of drumlike percussion rather than of harmonies in an occidental sense.

The earliest archaeological evidences of this lute family are on Chinese sculptures of the sixth century A.D., and from the year 623 A.D. they are found on Japanese sculptures as well. The oldest specimens preserved were made in the eighth century A.D.; the Imperial Treasury, Shôsô-in, at Nara near Osaka, Japan, still owns the marvellous Chinese lutes of sandal wood with tortoise shell and mother-of-pearl marquetry which Emperor Shomu of Japan offered to a new Buddha statue in 749 A.D. Consequently, the date 935 A.D., generally indicated as the year in which the lute was introduced in Japan, is certainly erroneous. (pl. X a, b)

The old path from West and Central Asia to the Far East, that is more clearly traced by the lute than by any other object, seems to have been extended, as early as the neolithic age, to a further westeastern path leading from the Pacific coast of China to the Pacific coast of America. There has been much discussion about whether, how and where the American civilization was influenced by ancient China. The following chapter will show to what extent the instruments of America resemble those of ancient China.

9. *America*

IN TWO regions of the American continent the Indians attained a relatively high level of civilization—in Central America, particularly in Mexico, and in the northwest of South America, particularly in Peru.

The Mexican civilization originated in the conflux of peoples descending from the arid mesas in the north and south to the fertile plains and valleys. Such peoples were the Nahua (including the Aztecs), the Maya, the Chorotega and the Chibcha. As they were arrested in their evolution at a transitory stage between a neolithic and a copper age, their cultural development was uneven. Apparently in the eleventh century A.D., they reached a level far above primitivism in their hieroglyphic script, in a complicated calendar, and in magnificent works of architecture, sculpture and miniature painting. In comparison, they remained astonishingly behind in music, at least in instrumental music.

FLUTES AND TRUMPETS. Central America had not one stringed instrument, and among all her idiophones, drums and wind instruments there was only one instrument capable of playing a simple melody. This was a small flute, called *çoçoloctli*, *huilacapitztli* or *tlapitzalli* in Mexican, and *cuiraxezaqua* in Tarascan. It was a *whistle flute*, in which the upper end was stopped except for a small channel into which the player blew, and which directed his breath to the sharp edge of a side-hole. The upper end was sharpened to form a beak (*beaked flute*), which allowed the player to grasp it with his lips. Mexican flutes usually had four, occa-

192

A. & B. Reliefs from Borobudur (c. 800 A.D.).

Javanese metallophone and gong chime (Ph. Bandara).

D. Javanese rejong (Ph. Bandara).

Javanese xylophone (Ph. Bandara).

F. Javanese barrel-drums (Ph. Bandara).

G. Burmese xylophone (Ph. Scherman).

PLATE XI.

sionally three or five, fingerholes near the lower end, the distances between which did not follow any metrical rule; sometimes two such flutes, with two fingerholes each, were tightly fastened together to form a double flute. Flutes were made either of bone or of baked clay. In the latter case they usually ended in a false bell, the tube itself ending without expansion. As this form was neither technically nor musically justified, we can assume that it was imi-

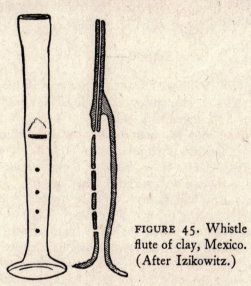

FIGURE 45. Whistle flute of clay, Mexico. (After Izikowitz.)

tated from the shape of Spanish oboes (*chirimías*), unless at some future date native specimens are excavated from pre-Cortesian tombs. (fig. 45)

Older than the usual whistle flute was a whistle pipe without fingerholes, in which both the block and the side-hole were shifted down to the middle of the flute. This archaic type is still in use in British Columbia, Central California and, in South America, with the Tucáno and the Cayapó.

The miniatures in the Mayan codices show a second form of whistle pipe without fingerholes, which still exists among North American Indians. Instead of streaming directly into the flute, the wind is forced to leave the flute and to re-enter it by the following contrivance. Near the upper end the flute is stopped; the wall has an outlet just above the stopper and a sharp-edged side-hole just beneath; a grooved piece of wood is tied over the two holes forming

FIGURE 46. From Codex Becker, Vienna. (After Seler.)

a detour and directs the wind from the first against the edge of the second hole. This curious variety of a whistle (*outside flue*) is distinctly drawn in the miniatures. (fig. 46)

As far as these flutes had fingerholes, they were the only melodic instruments of Central America. Even the bone flutes blown by human victims about to be sacrificed as they climbed the steps of the pyramid, or by the doomed men accompanying the hearse of a prince, seem to have had no holes, as today the bone flutes of North American Indians rarely have fingerholes. They did not serve melodic purposes any more than the clay whistles, known as *cohuilotl* or *chilitli,* which were sometimes molded in the shape of flowers, fish, snakes or birds, or any of the following instruments.

Trumpets were made in two forms. The priests of the rain gods used end-blown shell trumpets, called *tecciztli, tepuzquiquiztli* and *quiquiztli* in Mexican. Besides, there were tubular trumpets, called *pungacuqua* in Tarascan, which were made of wood, cane or clay and sometimes provided with a gourd that served as a bell.

Most of the other instruments were idiophones.

IDIOPHONES. Central America had two rattling instruments —*rattling vessels,* made either of gourds (*ayacachtli*) or of unglazed terra cotta, and *rattling sticks* (*ayon chicuaztli*). These latter were used in the worship of water, rain and mountain divinities, in the same way that Malayan planters' sticks, which contained a cavity filled with seeds, were rattled when the stick was pounded on the ground.

More important was a *scraped bone* with a series of notches cut in one of its sides; the Mexicans gave it the name *omichicahuaztli.* It played, as the first Spanish observer said, *música muy triste,*

FIGURE 47. From Codex Becker, Vienna. (After Seler.)

"very sad music," at memorial ceremonies for those who had died in battle or as prisoners on the sacrificial stone.

Its ordinary companion was the turtle shell, *ayotl*, played with a stag's antler. It certainly was erroneous to interpret this playing as a gonglike striking; on miniatures as well as on clay figures the antler is represented as being so close to the shell that it must have been used to scrape the uneven surface rather than to strike it.

The slit-drum called *teponaztli* was relatively short and often carefully carved. Occasionally, it was made in the form of some animal, such as an alligator, ocelot or puma. Its narrow slit had the shape of the letter H, thus detaching two tongues which faced each other. Chiseled off on the inside to different thicknesses, these tongues produced different notes when they were struck with two

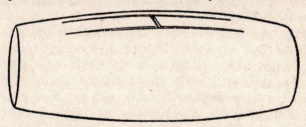

FIGURE 48. Mexican slit-drum.

sticks, *olmaitl*. The slit-drums were placed on tripods to avoid the deadening contact of the ground. (figs. 47, 48)

DRUMS (*huehuetl* or 'old-old' in Mexico) were known in various forms. Two features seem to have been common to all of them: the lack of braces and of sticks. Probably all Central American drums were struck with the bare hands. Clavijero, one of the earliest authors on Mexico, writes: "They struck them only with their fingers, but it required infinite dexterity in the striker." The skin seems to have been attached either by gluing or by a nailed ribbon.

The actual shape of the smaller drums cannot be seen in the miniatures, which are our only source. A larger drum was held in a hobbyhorse position, as are certain drums of the Serpa on the Amazon as well as of some West and East African Negroes.

The largest drums, called *tlalpa huehuetl*, were either cylindrical or barrel-shaped, but played in a vertical position. Though a clay statuette from Michoacan in the Berlin Museum shows such a drum resting directly on the ground and played by a sitting man, the classical large drum of Mexico stood on a stand which, either separate or cut from the same piece, stood on three wide legs or rather triangular lobes, each of which tapered to the ground in steps. Some of these drums were finely carved. Similar drums on three legs occur in Polynesia, Melanesia, East and South Africa, and the African forms also have the skins nailed on. (fig. 47)

A last drum is unique. Pictured in one of the Mexican codices it looks like a calabash in the form of a wide low U; one end is open, and the other is covered with a drum skin. The instrument stands on the ground before a squatting player.

Earthenware objects have been excavated in Costa Rica which obviously were drums, though quite different from these Mexican drums. Their shape varies between the goblet and the hourglass drum, and their plastic decoration, fluted grooves and a belt, suggests earlier bracing.

All these instruments—rattles, scrapers, tubular and shell trumpets, whistle flutes, slit-drums, hobbyhorse drums and footed drums played without sticks—belong to a very early stage of development; all of them are included in the strata numbered three to six in the list of twenty-three pre-European strata in the author's book *Geist und Werden der Musikinstrumente*. If China had any influence on the evolution of ancient Central America, it must have been in early prehistoric times.

SOUTH AMERICA

South American antiquity refers to the pre-Colombian epoch of Peru and her neighboring countries in the north and west of the continent, Colombia, Ecuador, Bolivia and Chile. In historical times, up to about 700 A.D., the Aimará people ruled Peru; the

Inca probably did not dominate the vast territory of northwestern South America earlier than 1200 A.D.

The cultural standard of these countries, and even of Peru, was certainly lower than that of Central America in spite of their advanced social organization, architecture and pottery; they had neither a calendar nor a script. Music, on the contrary, must have reached a higher level, as far as we can judge from excavated instruments and scenes represented on vases. Flutes with numerous fingerholes and pan-pipes of many canes are evidence of elaborate melodies. The pan-pipes seem to have been brought to this continent by some contact with the Far East. The ocean current that streams southward from Melanesia to encircle New Zealand, and then east- and northwards to Peru may have brought over occasional ships and men.

PAN-PIPES (*huayra-puhura*) were made of canes, but also of solid pieces of wood, clay, stone or metal with channels hollowed

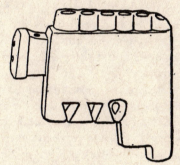

FIGURE 49. Pan-pipe of stone, ancient Peru.

out inside them. Some had the lower end open, some stopped; occasionally an open and a stopped set, an octave apart, were joined to form double pan-pipes played in a way that is not familiar to us. (fig. 49)

Several features in South American pan-pipes point to the west: the instrument itself, well known and much used in East and Southeast Asia and the Pacific Islands; the arrangement in double pipes, occurring in certain islands of Melanesia and Polynesia; the peculiar Melanesian and Polynesian ligature, the tubes being held in place against a cane splint by a laced cord. Moreover, the late Erich M. von Hornbostel found a striking conformity between the absolute pitches and the scales of American, Melanesian and East Asiatic pan-pipes. Hornbostel's results were not fully accepted by Americanists who, more than other anthropologists, are inclined to deny foreign influences on their special protégés. It is true that musical measurements on museum pieces are not always convincing, and that most similarities are counterbalanced by appreciable differences. If we discount this evidence, another fact is so striking that it can hardly be overlooked. In our first Far Eastern chapter, we explained that the pan-pipe of East Asia was tuned to the twelve *lü*. These are the standard semitones, derived from a series of consecutive fifths and transposed into the same octave; six of them, the odd numbered ones in the series, are considered male, and the six even numbered, female. The two resulting whole tone scales fit into one another, but the sets are divided, either into two separate instruments or into two wings of the same instrument. And this has happened also in America. Several potteries of ancient Peru depict twin pan-pipes exactly in the modern form that the American archaeologist, Charles W. Mead (who does not know the Chinese parallel), describes in the following words: "Two pan-pipes fastened together by a long cord and played by two performers are very common in Bolivia today. Each instrument has but half the notes of the scale, every other one being absent, and these must be given by the man playing the complementary pipe." The Cuna Indians in Panama (who have a script related to the most ancient Chinese script) unite 'male' and 'female' pan-pipes in order to blow fifths parallels. To complete the picture, we recall that also the Karenni in the Burmese hinterland use their pan-pipes in pairs connected by a loose cord. No skepticism can deny the western origin of the American pan-pipes. A scale, alternately distributed between two pan-pipes which are connected by a loose cord, can hardly be supposed to have originated spontaneously in several parts of the world. Whoever believes in such a possibility would have to prove that male and female semitones are native to Indian music and cosmology.

FLUTES were vertical, with or without a notch. Cane and the bones of pelicans, llamas or deer provided the material. A cane flute from Peru with a silver lining was given to the author by its collector, the late Dr. Gaffron.

There were from three to seven fingerholes; the holes of cane flutes were always frontal; some bone flutes had also a rear hole for the thumb. The scales printed in some catalogues of old Peruvian instruments, which were obtained by blowing and fingering these flutes without knowing whether or not cross-fingering and other correcting devices were originally used, are entirely meaningless and certainly false, particularly as "the written note is in many cases not the one given out by the instrument, but the one nearest to it in our diatonic scale." It would be more important to find a non-musical measurement between the fingerholes as we have seen used in other flutes. Following this idea, the author found, on a well-preserved cane flute of the Gaffron collection, that the distances from the upper end to the centers of the seven front holes were in accordance with the oldest Chinese foot of 229.9 millimeters; the maximum deviation was 1.1 millimeters, and the minimum 0.1 millimeter; the average deviation was only 0.6 millimeter. This is one more proof of a connection with the Far East.

Another resemblance may be noted. The ancient Peruvians had a peculiar notched flute with five fingerholes made of black pottery. The outer end tapered and turned sideways, like a sausage. This apparently unique shape is also found in a flute of the Maori in New Zealand.

Globular flutes, generally of earthenware, existed both in a plain form and in the shape of men and animals. They had only a few fingerholes, or sometimes none at all. Beside these more or less universal types of globular flutes, there was a native Peruvian form in the shape of various species of conch shells.

The *whistling pot,* best known by its modern Spanish name, *silbador*—'whistler'—was also indigenous. It consisted of two communicating earthenware vessels, both of which were half-filled with water. When the player blew into one of them, the water was driven into the second one where the increased volume of water compressed the air and sent it through a whistle head. (fig. 50, 51)

A strange variety has been found as far north as San Salvador. A pottery figure representing a man sitting by a barrel contains two connecting cavities filled with water. When it is rocked from side to side in the player's hands the air is forced through the whistle head.

Except for pan-pipes and flutes, ancient South American instruments are quite similar to Mexican instruments. Here as well, stringed instruments are entirely lacking.

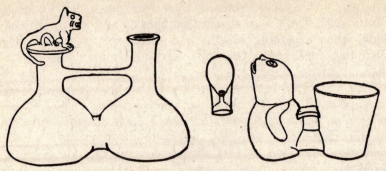

FIGURES 50, 51. Whistling pots, Peru.

IDIOPHONES. The Peruvians inherited from prehistoric times *gourd rattles* and primitive *strung rattles*, usually made of shells or deer hooves, as in North America. They had metal *jingles* filled with pebbles as well, and small metal *bells* without clappers, either founded or made of thin metal bent into a conical shape. They were sounded before certain idols. The Peruvians also had strange wooden bells in rectangular form provided with several clappers which are also used in Esthonia, Burma and the western part of the Malayan Archipelago.

On some statuettes players with *spondylus pictorum* shells in the position of cymbals are represented. Were they cymbals? It is not probable that a civilization familiar with metal work should have used shell for cymbals, and also that the two shells were held near together instead of being separated. Shells in an analogous position are used in Torres Strait between Australia and New Guinea—but not to be clashed together. The natives scrape them against each other. This may also have been the case with the Peruvian shells.

Slabs of *sonorous stones* have been found in Venezuela and Ecuador, though not in Peru; and circular, and slightly concave-convex, metal disks have been discovered in Peruvian tombs which, on account of their clear and resonant sound, are claimed to be *gongs*.

DRUMS (*huancar*) were shallow and cylindrical. One of the three excavated specimens, in the Munich museum, is well preserved; it consists of two wooden hoops held apart by a few cross-pieces of wood. The two skins of these drums are sewn or nailed together in such a way that they completely cover the cylinder. One of the three drums is covered with painted designs. (fig. 52)

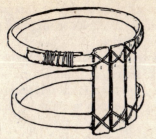

FIGURE 52. Peruvian drum, skeleton. (After Izikowitz.)

Held in one hand, the drums were struck by one beater only, as some statuettes from the central part of Peru indicate. But it is not clear whether the beater was a tiny stick tied to a cord, or the knotted end of the cord itself. The material for the skin came from the llama or the deer, and also sometimes from the human hide of slain enemies. Making use of a foe in this way was a method of acquiring his vigor and of terrifying the enemy, and was a well-known magic rite among American Indians. One ancient writer tells in detail how an Inca king, entering his capital after a rebellion, had the complete skins stripped from the live bodies of six subjugated chiefs; he then had them inflated in human shape, and ordered his soldiers to drum upon the stomachs.

TRUMPETS were made either of conch shells or of wood or of clay. The *shell trumpet* was an end-blown *strombus* with or without a metal mouthpiece, as in East Asia. Sometimes the shell shape was imitated in clay. One single, side-blown *triton tritonis* has been excavated in Peru, which is the more remarkable because this sea shell is said never to be found on the west coast of South America.

Tubular trumpets occur as straight tubes of wood without any mouthpiece or bell, and as coiled trumpets made of clay, sometimes with only a slight expansion at the end, sometimes with a bell representing a jaguar head or even a human shape. It has been suggested that this astonishing coiled form was inspired by European models. The author is inclined to deny such a relation, since in this case the coil would have imitated the elongated shape of the European trumpet instead of being small and circular. Inorganic imitations usually are recognizable from their lack of appropriateness; here, on the contrary, the coiled tube is better suited to clay technique and to the fragility of the material than a long straight tube.

Very short, straight, clay trumpets have been preserved in the old cemeteries of Nasca, that is, in the earliest stratum of Peruvian civilization. As there is no mouthpiece and the upper orifice is rather large, they may have been voice masks or megaphones.

Metal trumpets, too, were played in ancient Peru. The Chronicle of the First Augustine Friars tells us that worship of the god Tantazoro included the use of fourteen trumpets of silver and copper. A silver trumpet in the Ethnographical Museum in Berlin is seventy-seven centimeters long and ends in a funnel-shaped bell.

We must now try to answer the question asked at the end of the preceding chapter: whether, in neolithic times, these instruments are likely to have been brought to America from China.

It would be hard to deny a connection between both the Chinese and the South American notched flutes, and the Chinese and the South American pan-pipes. We have presented our arguments in the sections dealing with the two instruments. Here, it will only be emphasized that the notched flute, outside of America, is confined to the Far East, including Mongolia. In this case, as in those following, we neglect Africa as a continent acculturated by the various Asiatic countries. Some other common features are also striking: the lack of stringed instruments, the occurrence of nailed drums, the use of sonorous stones.

But instead of confining ourselves to these particular instruments, we must examine the field as a whole and find the area of distribution of all ancient American instruments in order to come to a scientific conclusion as to their provenance.

Ancient American instruments include a first group, existing all over the world: jingles, bells, shell trumpets, whistle, vertical and globular flutes. But the remainder of the instruments offers a significant picture. The curious 'outside flue' of the whistle flutes is known in Bhutan, Borneo and the Philippines; the central flue occurs in eastern Bengal, in Burma and on the Nicobar Islands; sausage flutes are made in New Zealand; trumpets of wood and cane, with or without gourd bells, in Burma, Australia and the Pacific Islands; gourd rattles in Hawaii; stick rattles in the Malay Archipelago; scrapers in India, the Far East, Java, Torres Strait; slit-drums in Burma, Malakka, the Archipelago and the Pacific Islands; wooden bells in Burma; elongated tree drums in Nias; drums on legs in the Pacific Islands.

This implies that, except for a few universal instruments, all relatives of American instruments are exclusively found in a territory comprising China, the area between China and India, the

Malay Archipelago and the Pacific Islands. More than fifty per-cent can be located in the Burmese hinterland and the adjacent countries—that is, among peoples supposed to have been the abo-riginals of what is called China today, who were driven southward by the invading Chinese in neolithic times. Ancient American in-struments can be classified as 'Pacific.'

THIRD PART
The Middle Ages

10. *The Far East*

IN THE middle ages, China was more than ever exposed to western influences. Frequently being conquered by foreign rulers, or conquering foreign countries herself, she was in continuous contact with neighboring civilizations. These influences were particularly strong in music. The court established orchestras from India, Samarkand, Kashgar, Bukhara as well as Tibet, Mongolia and other countries, and Chinese tradition, usually well informed and reliable, traces most Chinese instruments back to Indian, Mongolian, Turkestanic and "barbarian" origins. (pl. X a)

It would be tempting to bring order into the confusing mass of Far Eastern instruments by basing a classification on their provenance. But this cannot yet be done. We know too little of medieval Central Asia and the migrations and trade routes from or across Mongolia and Turkestan. Thus, we prefer a systematic arrangement.

IDIOPHONES. In the middle ages bronze cymbals and gongs were added to the bells and bell chimes of antiquity.

Cymbals (Chinese *po*) were said to have been brought from India; another Chinese source enumerates them among the instruments of an East Turkestanic orchestra which was established at the imperial court after the conquest of the Kingdom of Kutcha in 384 A.D. This statement is corroborated by the important fact that the Korean name of the cymbals, *tjapara,* is obviously derived from a Turkish word; in modern Turkish cymbals are called *čălpăra.* Moreover, Central Europe first acquired cymbals when Avars and Huns—that is, Turkish peoples—invaded the Continent in the middle ages. Turks were expert metal workers.

Most Far Eastern cymbals have a large boss, and the rim is either flat or curving slightly upwards. Their size varies greatly; beside small specimens one finds very large ones in lama temples; the Crosby Brown Collection in the Metropolitan Museum in New York owns a pair twenty-two to twenty-three inches wide. But these Chinese lama cymbals are not as large as some gigantic cymbals in Mongolian temples which measure one meter.

About three hundred years after the first mention of cymbals, a *metallophone* (Chinese *fang hiang*) is said to have been introduced. It was an imitation in iron or steel of the old Chinese stone chime, a set of sixteen slabs about eight inches long suspended in an upright frame. The new instrument was first brought to China by the orchestra of a "barbarian" people—that is, either Turkish or Tungus —in the seventh century A.D. As there were probably no Tungus orchestras, the reference apparently indicates a Turkish origin, and this is the more likely because some of the Turkish tribes, the Tu-kiu for instance, were skillful workers in iron at the time of this orchestra.

A *gong* (differing from a bell in that the vibrations issue from the center, while the rim is dead) is first mentioned in the time of Emperor Hsüan Wu (500–516 A.D.), and the Chinese attribute its origin to the country, Hsi Yü, between Tibet and Burma. It seems, however, that this ancient instrument was not the small, bossless gong, *lo*, that the Chinese use today; its name *sha lo* meant also a basin; it was larger than the present gong and had a powerful sound. It was possibly similar to two instruments existing to this day: the Korean *tjing*, from fifteen to sixteen inches wide and rather deep, and the *rang* of the Garo (an aboriginal tribe in Assam, which has preserved many implements of ancient China).

There is also a *gong chime*, called *yün lo* and attributed to Mongolian influences by the Chinese. It has no relation with either the usual gong or the splendid chimes of the Malayan Islands, and is musically of little interest. Ten small, bronze disks shaped like small soup plates, about four inches in diameter, are suspended in a wooden stand to form three vertical rows. The arrangement within these rows is either

$$
\begin{array}{ccc}
 & 10 & \text{or} & 10 \\
9 & 8 & 7 & \quad 9 & 8 & 7 \\
4 & 5 & 6 & \quad 6 & 5 & 4 \\
3 & 2 & 1 & \quad 3 & 2 & 1
\end{array}
$$

A

A. Arabian frame drum (12th century), from a relief in the Museo Nazionale in Florence.

B

B. From an Arabic manuscript (early 13th century), Museum of Fine Arts, Boston.

C. Turkish drum. From a painting by Vittore Carpaccio (early 16th century) in the Academy in Venice.

PLATE XII.

1, indicating the lowest, and 10, the highest note of a more or less diatonic scale; number ten, added at a later time, is never played. (fig. 53)

A new type of instrument may be called a *resting bell*, Chinese *ch'ing*. It is a heavy basin of bronze, placed on a cushion with the open side up and struck on its thick edge with a plain wooden stick. Most resting bells are small; the largest, in the Chao Ch'ing

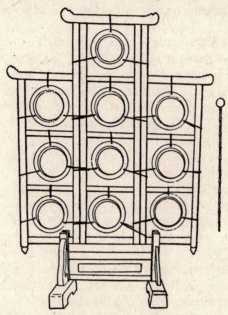

FIGURE 53. Chinese gong chime.

Monastery at Hangchow, is two and a half feet wide. The sound of these bells is remarkably full and clear, much better than the tone of Chinese suspended bells. Their prototype is possibly preserved in a Korean earthenware pot (*tjangkun*) that the player strikes with a split bamboo wand.

We could pass over a small rectangular block in the form of a brick, made of redwood and called *pang* in Chinese, had it not a certain interest as having recently been introduced in occidental dance bands. It is nearly ten inches long and slit both next to the upper and the lower surface, as if one had started to cut a piece from the top and the bottom of a loaf without detaching the slices. Struck with a stick, the two slices or, acoustically speaking, tongues, produce a dry but definite tone.

This section cannot be concluded without mentioning the *jaws'* *harp* (Chinese *ku ch'in*), the first evidence of which is said to be in a book of the twelfth century. In its North Chinese form it seems to be the oldest iron jaws' harp. Instead of being made in two separate parts welded together, like the European jaws' harp, it is cut out of one flat piece of iron in a horseshoe shape. A tongue, wide at the root and pointed at the end, is cut loose from the frame by two slits, thus being reminiscent of the earlier bamboo instrument.

TRUMPETS are made in several forms. The oldest one is an end-blown *shell trumpet* (Chinese *hai lo*, Japanese *hora*) held by inserting the hand into the natural opening of the conch. The instrument is used by boatmen and also by Buddhist priests.

Among tubular metal trumpets, one type (Chinese *hao t'ung*, Japanese *dokaku*), too large to be played without being rested on the ground, is particularly remarkable because, instead of a bell, it has a long wide cylinder, made either of wood, iron or brass. The tube itself is sliding—that is, when not in use it can be pushed into the bell in the manner of a telescope. The mouthpiece, as in all trumpets of the Far East, is shallow and broad-rimmed. A pair of these clumsy trumpets, employed in funeral processions, are played only when the men stand still and can rest the bell on the ground.

This curious instrument has a parallel in a region of South America centering in Brazil. The bell, in this Indian trumpet, is made of a wider section of bamboo than the tube. (fig. 24)

A trumpet with a hook-shaped end, *cha chiao* in Chinese, has been mentioned in the Greek and Roman chapter. (fig. 54)

The usual brass trumpet (Chinese *la pa*, Japanese *rapa*, both from the same Mongolian term, *rapal*) is reminiscent of the straight trumpets depicted on medieval European art works. It has a thin, conical tube, made of two or three sections fitting and telescoping into each other, a rather large bell, and bulging rings that mark the beginning of each section. (fig. 55)

This trumpet, as its name indicates, came from Mongolia and Tibet. However, the most characteristic trumpets of these countries, the Mongolian *buri* and the Tibetan *dung*, were never introduced in China. They are made of red copper in straight form, occasionally with gold and silver decorations added. Since they reach the gigantic length of sixteen feet they have to be rested on

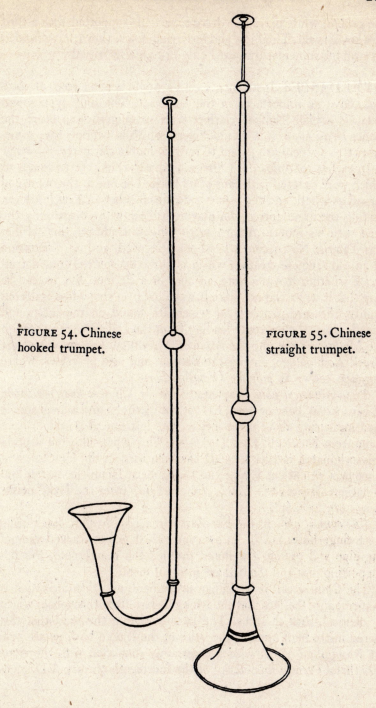

FIGURE 54. Chinese
hooked trumpet.

FIGURE 55. Chinese
straight trumpet.

the ground while played, or have their bells supported with a cord by a boy servant. Their low and terrifying notes, alternately sounded on twin instruments, are heard only in Lamaistic rituals.

REED PIPES. Instruments with a single beating reed, or *clarinets*, have no importance in the Far East. The only type found today is a plain bamboo clarinet with six fingerholes, under the names *ch'un kuan* or *la pa* in Chinese, which is a child's toy; sometimes two of them are joined to form a double clarinet, *tui hsiao*.

In earlier centuries the Chinese used a clarinet, the two ends of which were covered with caps of ox-horn. The one at the outer end served as a bell, and the other as an air chamber that enclosed the beating reed and forced the player to blow without grasping the reed with his mouth. According to Chinese tradition, this clarinet was Tataric. No specimen has been preserved, and an illustration in an old Chinese treatise, which is our only source, does not indicate whether it was a flute, an oboe or a clarinet. But we can be sure that it was a clarinet since it was similar in shape to a scattered family, the rare members of which are found on the coasts and islands along the sea route leading from the Indian Ocean through the Mediterranean into the Atlantic. They occur in Ceylon and the Greek Archipelago, among the Basques and also in Wales, where they are known as *pibgorn* (English *hornpipe*).

The cylindrical oboe (Japanese *hichiriki*, Chinese *kuan*) is made of hard wood, bone or horn, has 7 + b fingerholes and a long double reed measuring about three inches. The instrument is said to have come from Kutcha in East Turkestan. This is possible; but it probably originated farther west. It has been used in the Caucasus and Phoenicia, in ancient Egypt and the modern Islamic countries and in ancient Greece; the Arabic name *'irâqīa*, 'from the Irak,' points to western Asia. (pl. X a)

The conical oboe of the Far East is remarkably slim. Each of its 7 + b fingerholes lies in its own individual groove carved around the pipe and giving it a fluted profile; the mouthpiece, the lip-supporting disk and the bell are made of metal.

The Chinese call it an Indian instrument, and this derivation is confirmed by the fact that the Mongols also trace their oboe, which is identical, back to India. The lamas, relating this, add that this sacred instrument imitates the voice of the Indian bird, *galatingga*. Its Mongolian name, *bišur*, is certainly connected with the word *bīša* that a Persian manuscript of the fourteenth century A.D. mentions as the name of one pipe (the modern spelling is *pīša*). The Chinese name *sona*, on the other hand, is identical with Turkish, Persian and Hindustani names of the same instrument, *surnā* and *surnāy*; an older Mongolian form is *suru-nai*. The strange Japanese name *charumela* or *charumera* (*r* and *l* are not differentiated in Japanese) is obviously the old Spanish term for oboe, *charamela*. Portuguese traders and Spanish Jesuits went to Japan in the six-teenth century, and being the first Europeans who had come there, they had an influence on terminology.

FLUTES in the Far East are usually made of bamboo, except for the globular clap pipes spoken of in Chapter 8.

The only *whistle flute* is the Chinese *t'ai p'ing hsiao*, with six front holes and, above them, a hole covered with a delicate mem-brane which, vibrating with the flute, makes the timbre somewhat nasal.

The notched flutes of the ancient Far East have already been dis-cussed. Here we add a vertical flute (Japanese *shaku hachi*), unique because of its thickness, which is made of bamboo and provided with 4 + h fingerholes, yielding a chromatic scale by half-stopping. There is no notch; but the fact that the underlip of the player al-most completely covers the open end shows the relationship with the old notched flute, *tung hsiao*, the upper end of which is blocked except for a narrow flue. "Well played, it is one of the mellowest of wind instruments; but the exceeding difficulty of playing it at all justifies the tradition of secrets which have been handed down from Omori Toku, a hermit of Yedo, from generation to genera-tion of patient teachers and patient pupils" (Piggott).

Of *cross flutes* the Far East knows four main types. The first one (Chinese *ch'ih*) has 5 + 1 holes; the second one (*ti tse* in Chinese, *sei teki* in Japanese) has six fingerholes in front and an additional, nonstopped hole covered with a delicate membrane, usually onion-skin, to give the tone a nasalizing timbre by its vibration; the third one (Japanese *yamato fuye*), of the same kind, is delicately wrapped in silk threads and lacquered; the fourth one (*yoko fuye*) has seven front holes. The Japanese term *fuye* derives from *fuku*, 'to blow'; *yamato* means 'mountain-pass' and probably designates the ancient pass taken by the immigrants from Korea. (fig. 39)

The art of playing these flutes differs essentially from the oc-cidental styles; sustained notes are considered lifeless and dry, un-less the player slightly sharpens or flattens their beginning and their end, and his skill and taste in producing these deviations is one of his greatest achievements.

DRUMS. In the medieval and modern Far East there are two main types of drums always distinguishable from each other by the manner of fastening the skins—that is, either nailed or braced.

In the chapter on the ancient Far East we discussed nail drums in barrel shape with the length about the same size as the diameter. Another type of nailed drum, so shallow that its diameter was much greater than its length, was certainly used in medieval times, and probably also in antiquity, although there is no direct evidence of it. Today it is found in Japan, but no longer exists in China or Korea; its principal species is the large, picturesque 'hanging drum,' *tsuri daiko*. The wooden body is lacquered, and the skins are covered with colorful paintings of the Phoenix or the Dragon surrounded by jagged clouds. The drum is suspended in the middle of a circular stand, which is richly carved and lacquered and terminates in a golden flame with three balls of fire. The player, sitting in front, strikes the center with two leather-knobbed sticks, the right one of which is called the male, and the left one the female stick.

Braced drums in spool shape probably existed in medieval times in China and Korea though today they are found only in Japan, where their origin is attributed to Turkestan and Tibet.

The shape of these drums is similar to that of a spool; two projecting disks are connected by a cylinder, either straight or slightly bulging, of smaller diameter. The disks are formed by skins stretched over wide, flat rings; hemp or silken cords are laced in W form between them and are encircled by a central belt.

The most important is the 'large drum,' *da daiko*, the skins of which are more than six feet wide while the cylinder has a length of five feet. Piggott states that it is used

only on the great occasions in the Bugaku orchestra instead of the tsuri-daiko. It is erected on a special platform, draped and tasseled, with a gold railing and steps. The drummer, who is specially selected for his skill, stands in front of the drum, the directions being that he should, for greater vigor in striking, place his left foot on the platform, and his right on the upper step. It is surrounded with a broad rim ornamented with phoenix and dragon, and edged with red *kwayen,* or 'flames.' This frame is fixed into a socket in the platform.

Of the small varieties, the *kakko,* lying on a low stand, is the most important as counterpart of the tsuri daiko in the bugaku orchestra.

Their rhythmic style is interesting as the accents differ from ours; indeed, they are the reverse:

occidental accents ↓↓		↑		
beats	1	2	3	4
Japanese accents	'	↑	↓↓	

Outside the Far East, drums with protruding rings occur only in South India and Ceylon. *Tavil* is their native name. These also have the W-laces and the central belt of the da daiko.

In the area between these two districts, Ceylon and Japan, the W-laces plus the belt are found on a special form known as the *hourglass drum*—that is, a drum consisting of two cups united by their small ends. Their structure is reminiscent of the spool drums, and there is probably an intimate connection between the two drums. Both have protruding rings, W-laces and central belts. The only question is which came first. According to the historical sources, the hourglass drum was imported from East Turkestan in the fourth century A.D.; the provenance of the kakko and its relatives is not indicated. The geographical criterion suggests that the hourglass drum is newer, as it occupies a vast central territory between the two small districts of the barrel drum. Technical criteria back this conclusion: all hourglass drums are small and portable, while the Japanese barrel drums can be traced back to gigantic specimens more than six feet wide and include an archaic type filled with rice. The development from barrel-shaped spool drums to hourglass drums is easy to understand. The purpose of a central belt is to gather in and thus tighten the laces. But a bulging body would prevent the laces from being gathered by a central belt, whereas the addition of broad, protruding rings holds the cords away from the body so that they can be drawn in at the middle. Such rings, then, are justifiable only with cylindrical and barrel-shaped bodies. In hourglass drums they are not necessary and must be vestiges of an earlier form. The latter must be more recent.

Again, the older hourglass drums are preserved in the Far East. Their Korean name, *kal ko*, similar to Japanese *kakko*, emphasizes the connection with the barrel drums of the head-ring type. Moreover, the Korean is the largest of all hourglass drums; some specimens are three feet long. The ordinary Far Eastern hourglass drum, best known by its Japanese name *tsuzumi*, is much smaller. The body is lacquered black with gold decoration in all cases; but the colors differ according to the player's rank: lilac for the highest,

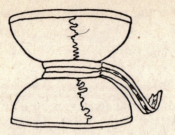

FIGURE 56. Tibetan drum of two skulls.

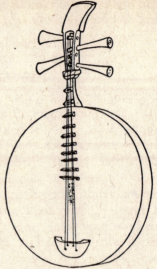

FIGURE 57. Chinese flat lute *yüeh ch'in*.

light blue for the next rank, orange for the ordinary rank. The drummer grasps the cords tightly in his left hand so that he can alter the pitch, and strikes with a stick one foot long. (cp. fig. 56)

BOWED INSTRUMENTS. Who were the inventors of the fiddle bow? In the last century, some scholars have ascribed it to Scandinavia, some to India. Both were wrong.

Looking for the earliest evidences of the bow, we find the first mention in Persia in the ninth century; in China, a bowed zither is spoken of in the ninth or tenth century; in Europe, fiddles are depicted in the tenth century. No fiddle bow is represented on the detailed reliefs of the Hindu-Javanese temple at Borobudur (c. 800 A.D.). Apparently, the fiddle bow came to be known in the civilized world between 800 and 900 A.D.

The Chinese bowed zither is attributed to the Mongols, and the usual fiddles of the Far East are said to have come from "the barbarians in the west." A tradition in the Islamic world indicates Kurdistan as the homeland of certain Persian fiddles; the oldest European fiddles are closely related to modern Turkestanic instruments, and so are the fiddles of India. Thus all evidences point to Inner Asia.

The bowed zither just mentioned is said by the Chinese, Lyeu Hyu, in about 900 A.D., to have been related to the zither *chêng* (cf. page 186) and to have been played at the Chinese court in a Mongolian orchestra. Such an instrument still exists in modern North China as *ya chêng* or *la ch'in*. Its hollow wooden body is shaped like one half of a truncated cone (i. e. bisected longitudinally). Ten pairs of silken strings, tuned to a pentatonic scale without semitones, are stretched lengthwise over the rounded front and regulated by iron pegs.

Later, at a time that we cannot as yet ascertain, another instrument, the *fiddle* (that is, a bowed lute), became popular all over the east, the usual name of which, *hu ch'in*, hints to a Central Asiatic origin, as *hu* is one of the names that the Chinese gave to the Turkish Uighurs. The body is formed by a tiny cylinder, a few inches long, one end of which, covered by a lizard- or snakeskin, serves as a soundboard, the other end being left open. The body, usually made of bamboo, or sometimes of a hexagonal piece of wood or of a coconut, the top of which has been removed, is diametrically pierced by the handle in the manner of a spit. The two strings are generally tuned to a fifth, and there is no fingerboard. The player, holding the fiddle down in a vertical position, stops the strings with the fleshy part of the fingers. The bow cannot be removed from the instrument, as its hair passes between the strings; it rubs the underside of one string and the upperside of the other. The bow is grasped with the palm facing upward so that the thumb is above the bow and the fingers below. Because of the constant vibrato and glissando of the left hand, the sound is rather whimpering.

The Chinese distinguish a quantity of types and varieties that we enumerate here in the interest of museum curators.

I. With rear pegs, soundboard of snakeskin, strings looped to the handle by a cord
   A. Cylindrical body of bamboo and two strings
      a. diameter of the body 2 inches: *tan ch'in*
      b. diameter of the body 1 inch: *hui hu*
   B. Hexagonal wooden body
      a. two strings: *êrh hu*
      b. four strings: *su hu*
II. With lateral pegs, soundboard of wood, strings passing over a ledge at the upper end of the stick which terminates its vibrating length
   A. Body made of coconut
      a. soundboard fitting over opening without projecting, like a lid: *hu hu*
      b. soundboard fitted into the opening: *t'i ch'in*
   B. Pear-shaped body of wood: *ta hu ch'in*.

Archaic forms of these fiddles, with only one string and without pegs, still exist on the northern and the southern periphery, among the Gilyak on the Amur and the Assamese between Tibet and Burma (and occasionally in East Africa), although they have entirely disappeared in the Far East. A step farther back leads to one of the oldest stringed instruments, the musical bow (cf. Chapter 1). Like this primitive instrument, the oldest Far Eastern fiddle consists of a body pierced by a wooden handle, a string stretched between the two ends of this stick, and a small cord looping the string to the handle near its upper end, often with no apparent purpose since the tension is controlled by a peg.

FLAT LUTES. About 500 A.D. the family of lutes was enriched by a new branch, confined to Central and East Asia, in which the bulging shell was replaced by two flat surfaces connected by a shallow wall in the manner of the guitar. Its modern representative, because of its circular form, is called *yüeh ch'in* in Chinese, and *gekkin* in Japanese, *yüeh* and *getsu* meaning 'moon.' It has a short but distinct neck, a pegbox with lateral pegs, ten frets, a stringholder on the wooden soundboard, two silken, double strings a fifth apart, and is played with a plectron. (fig. 57)

The present short neck replaced an earlier longer one which appears on East Turkestanic frescoes of about 500 A.D., and still exists in Mongolia, China, Japan, Annam, Cambodia. Chinese tradition attributes the invention of the instrument to the Tsin Dynasty (265-419 A.D.). A specimen of the eighth century is preserved in the famous treasury, Shô-sô-in, at Nara near Osaka in Japan; it is a marvelous inlaid piece with ten frets on the neck and four on the soundboard.

A general survey of the lute shows two stages of development, the earlier one being characterized by a medium length neck, and the later one by a short neck. We distinguish:

Medium length neck
  Octagonal body, in Mongolia, Japan (*genkwan*) and China (*shuang ch'in*)
  Circular body, in Annam (*cai dan nguyet*), Japan (*ku*) and Korea (*wol kum*)
Short neck and circular body,
  in Japan (*gekkin*) and China (*yüeh ch'in*).

LONG LUTE. A small, heavy, redwood frame, sometimes square, sometimes rounded, is covered with skin on both faces. It is pierced by a plano-convex stick of redwood about a yard long; three silken strings, tuned by long lateral pegs, are plucked with a large heavy plectron. The older, Japanese accordatura is ground-tone, fourth, seventh (1–4–7); a more recent tuning is 1–5–8. This is a popular instrument, which is said to have been brought to Japan as late as about 1560 A.D.

It is easy to see that this instrument has come to the Far East from western Asia; with its long pierced stick, its small body and its three strings on lateral pegs, it is the counterpart of the Persian tanbur or sitar. Even the names correspond; both Persian *si tār* and Chinese *san hsien* mean 'three strings.' It is tempting to try to explain the Japanese name, *shamisen*, in the same way. This is not possible: 'three strings' would be *san gen* in Japanese; moreover, the original form of the Japanese term is *jamisen*, or 'snakeskin-line,' which only later was changed to resemble the Chinese word.

THE DULCIMER AND THE HARP. The section on Far Eastern stringed instruments is not complete without mention of two foreign instruments, the more recent one of which has proved popular, while the other one, although of a venerable age, has never gained a footing.

The dulcimer, called *yang ch'in* or 'foreign zither' in Chinese, will be mentioned later on among the Persian instruments. It has been generally accepted in the Far East.

The harp was imported from East Turkestan with several kinds of drums and cymbals, after the Chinese had destroyed the kingdom of Kutcha in 384 A.D. Its shape, preserved in some native illustrations, corresponded to that of the vertical angular harp with twenty-five strings as used in Persia, and so did its Chinese name *k'ung hu*, derived from *čank*, the Persian name of the harp. (pl. X a)

The harp was never really accepted in the Far East; it was played only by foreigners from the west, and was soon given up. Obviously, it could not compete with the highly developed native zithers which had been adapted to the new flexible style of postclassical times.

In the B.C. centuries, Chinese music must have been very precise, being based on the regulated distinctions between the notes of the scale. It had only two stringed instruments and depended on a great quantity of idiophones and chimes with unalterable pitches. Medieval and modern Chinese music, under the influence of Central Asiatic taste, abandoned rigid pitches. Preferring gliding scales and the delicate shadings of sustained notes, it did not favor idiophones and chimes and adopted instruments, particularly stringed instruments, that were capable of a flexible style.

II. *India*

THE passage from antiquity to the middle ages in India was marked by a process similar to that in the Far East. The only stringed instrument of Indian antiquity—the harp, with its open strings—was abandoned in the middle ages in favor of a quantity of instruments with stopped strings, zithers, lutes and fiddles. The new style that resulted, however, differed from that in Far Eastern music. There, instruments with flexible intonation were introduced to compensate for the rigid and unyielding pitches of chimes. In India the rigidity of melody was eased by the *gamakas*. These constitute a style that is characterized by numberless shadings, graces, slides, tremolos, rising and falling, which soften the melodic line of Hindu music. They are the "life and soul" of Indian melody; in Somanatha's words, "music without gamaka is like a moonless night, a river without water and a creeper without flowers."

Melodic disintegration is counterbalanced by submission to a strict rhythm. Rhythm to the Hindu is far from being mere time beating; it is the regular repetition of a complicated pattern of beats, which is indispensable as an accompaniment to every kind of music. As a result, there is a disproportionate percentage of drums in Indian music.

It would be tempting to attribute both the shaded melody and the rhythmic patterns to the strong penetration of Islamic culture between 1000 and 1600 A.D., as they are the typical features of Persian and Arabian music as well. But the importance of rhythmic patterns is native to India; the reliefs of Indian antiquity almost always depict one or more drums in any musical scene.

In the following sections of this chapter we will usually indicate the Sanskrit names of the instruments, although this classic language is no longer spoken. This seems to be the best expedient, as otherwise each instrument has numberless names, varieties and spellings in the hundreds of Indian dialects.

PRE-ISLAMIC TIMES

The most important source of information about Indian musical instruments and their chronology is found outside India, at Borobudur in Java, where, about 800 A.D., Indian settlers erected a gigantic temple, the outer walls of which were covered with several hundreds of reliefs depicting Hindu life before Islam. Some twenty among them represent musical scenes with aristocratic, military and popular instruments, probably a complete anthology of the instruments used in India in the second half of the first millennium A.D. Some other sources confirm the evidence of Borobudur.

IDIOPHONES. The first iconographic record of the *hand bell* or *ghaṇṭā* is not conclusive. As late as the seventh century, it is depicted in one of the caves at Aurangabad; yet five hundred years earlier the Greco-Syrian philosopher, Bardesanes, had related that while the Hindu priest prayed, he sounded the bell. It was small and tulip-shaped, with a thick clapper. As it was exclusively used by priests in the worship of Hindu divinities, the handle was finely decorated with religious symbols, such as Siva's trident, Vishnu's eagle or Hanuman, the king of the apes.

Hindu-Javanese reliefs depict several other kinds of bells: twin bells held in either hand, bells hanging from the necks of elephants and larger bells suspended in an upright stand, in the fashion of the Far East. Frequently, two small empty bells are clashed together like cymbals, a manner of playing that probably had come from East Turkestan. They are not always easy to distinguish from cup-shaped cymbals.

Cymbals might have been introduced by the invading Huns; they are first represented on a relief of the temple at Garwha, which dates from the fifth century A.D. In Hindu mythology they are attributes of Ravana, head of the night spirits, and of the Kinnari, the sirens of the Hindu pantheon; Vishnu himself strikes them when the Destroyer Isvara and Bhadrakali, the goddess of death, dance at Chidambaram.

Hindu cymbals are either 'clashing' or 'tinkling.' The tinkling cymbals (*mandirā* or *tālā*) are small, heavy and unconnected; they have a sloping rim and a broad central boss, or no rim at all, and may be related with the cymbal bells just mentioned. They are used in chamber music; all rhythmic patterns can be performed on them. The clashing cymbals (*jhānjha*), connected by a loose cord, are made of thin bronze with a wide, flat rim and a central boss.

Gongs (*kāṃsya*) are small and flat without a boss; they are not frequent in India. The first evidence of them is on a relief of the temple at Aihole in the seventh century; no specimen is depicted on the Borobudur reliefs.

Instead of gongs, all temples of India have a thick circular *disk* of bronze (*ghaṛī*) suspended on a cord. Struck with a wooden hammer at a particular moment in the Hindu service, during the *pūjā* (adoration), it produces a clear and brilliant tone. On the eastern peninsula and in Tibet, the disk has a fanciful, triangular outline that the natives interpret as a crescent or a mountain.

The Borobudur reliefs depict a specifically Indian instrument that up to this day has played a certain role in ordinary street music —the big pottery jar, called *ghāṭa* in Sanskrit. Its mouth is generally pressed against the player's stomach to fill and deepen the sound; but sometimes the man holds it away to make the timbre higher and drier. Both hands alternately play, hitting with wrists, fingers and nails, continually varying the timbre and the pitch and performing the rhythmic patterns with an astonishing technique. Moreover, it seems that many players have preserved the old association of instrument playing and acrobacy; they like to toss up the pot between two strokes and let it fall down at the end of a piece so that it is dashed to pieces with the final note.

DRUMS. The pot is sometimes depicted with a skin covering the mouth, and used as a hand drum. But the pot drum seems to have disappeared since the days of Borobudur and to have been replaced in Islamic times by the *ṭablā* and the *bāṃyā*.

Of tubular drums Borobudur depicts three kinds: one, cylindrical with W-laces, played with a stick; a second, barrel-shaped, with Y-laces that is handbeaten; a third, elongated, conical and bulging, handbeaten at the smaller end. The latter drum is represented in a set of three, two standing upright and the third one lying on the ground before the sitting player. This set-playing doubtless goes back to the drum pairs described in the first Indian chapter.

And probably it was these sets which finally developed into the unparalleled *drum chime* of Burma (*tshaing vaing*). A quantity of carefully tuned drums, normally twenty-four, are suspended inside the walls of a circular pen; the player squats in the center and with his bare hands strikes the drums in a swift, toccatalike melody. The drums themselves, ranging from about five to sixteen inches in height, are wooden, conical and slightly bulging; leather thongs laced in narrow W's are stretched between the two twisted thong hoops. The drum chime is an interesting fusion of Indian and East Asiatic elements: India has adapted the East Asiatic idea of a chime to her drums, the least appropriate of instruments.

STICK-ZITHER. It is a common error to suppose that a name has always been applied to the object that now bears it, whereas their union is often rather loose. The noted *viṇā* is a good example. Usually it is referred to as one "of the earliest instruments of India." But the name alone is old, and is very probably derived from Egyptian *vīn*, as explained on page 94; the instrument to which it belonged in antiquity, the harp, disappeared from India more than one thousand years ago. After its extinction, the name passed to the stick-zither. (fig. 58)

Not earlier than the seventh century A.D. the temple at Mavalipuram depicts the first stick-zither. There, as well as on reliefs in Ceylon, Cambodia and Java, it has a primitive form which still exists in Siam and Cambodia as *p'in* and *sadiu;* it consists of a stick with a half calabash attached near one end to serve as a resonator. It usually has two strings. The calabash is rested against the player's chest, with the stick pointing toward the ground; the left hand stops the strings while the right hand plucks them. About 1000 A.D. the half calabash was rested a little higher against the man's shoulder; soon after 1000 A.D. the opposite end of the stick was provided with half a calabash as well; the modern form with a whole calabash at each end was created about 1400 A.D., and since that time the upper calabash has rested upon the left shoulder.

The vina, or *mahatī viṇā* ('large vina,' Hindustani *bīn*), in its classical and present form is a zither with a round stick and two big gourds suspended near the ends. One of the gourds rests on the player's left shoulder, the other one under his right arm, the stick being held obliquely across his chest. Four or five wire strings, plucked with a wire plectron worn on the finger, produce a clear delicate melody and occasional chords; one of two additional thin

South Italian pifferari with piffero and zam-pogna.

Macedonian lira player.

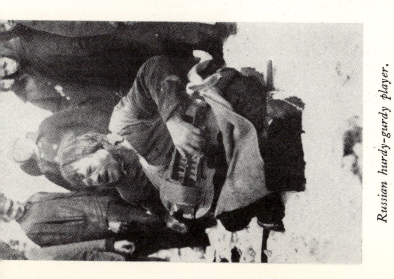

Russian hurdy-gurdy player.

PLATE XIII.

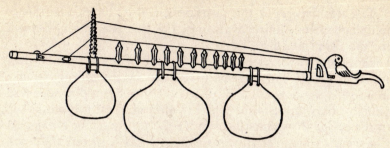

FIGURE 58. South Indian stick zither *kinnari*.

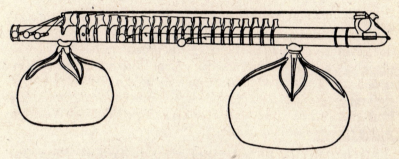

FIGURE 59. North Indian vina.

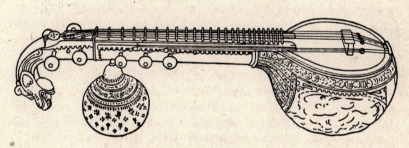

FIGURE 60. South Indian vina.

steel strings placed outside the melody strings and played with the small fingers of either hand, or with the right thumb, contribute a jingling and sparkling treble in the higher octave; and all this silvery tone secures volume by the resonance of the big gourds. The melodies themselves are free and expansive, and some twenty, large, moveable frets, projecting from the stick like vertebrae in a backbone, are shifted so easily that the different intervals of the innumerable Indian scales can be observed. (fig. 59)

The sensitiveness of this instrument and its complicated finger technique exclude amateur playing; the vina is a solo instrument for the finest musicians only.

This older vina is rather rare today. All over the south, including Bombay, the lower gourd is replaced by the solid body of a lute with a wooden soundboard, and the upper gourd is preserved only in a diminutive form. A narrow strip of metal laid on the top of the bridge is supposed to improve the timbre of the strings. At Channapatna and Bareilly in southern India a special caste possesses the secret process for manufacturing the wire strings and sells them at a high price. (fig. 60)

Before discussing the instruments introduced under Islamic influence, we must describe some fiddles and wind instruments which do not belong either to the older Hindu group represented on temple reliefs, or to the Muhammedan group. With one exception they came from the north at a time remote enough to be spread all over the vast country but also recent enough to prevent them from being handed eastwards to the Malays, or even to the Burmese. We begin with a curious species of fiddle.

SHORT FIDDLES in India have a really fantastic shape. One of them, the *sārindā*, played by lower castes, has a body which, though made of wood, is a shape more typical of leather or some pliable material. The box is a thin shell, the edges of which are drawn together like a bag at the lower end. In their upper part the edges are pulled out to form curved barbs on either side, and this part of the body remains entirely open so that one can look into it. Only the narrow space between the lower edges is covered by a small piece of skin which forms the soundboard. Altogether the outline of the opening resembles the longitudinal section of a mushroom. The instrument has a short neck without frets, lateral pegs inserted in a cubic block of wood serving as a pegbox, and three horsehair or gut strings in g' f' c'. (fig. 61)

A specifically North Indian variety is the *sārangī*. It is a clumsy instrument, hollowed out of a single block of heavy wood, with a waisted front which is entirely covered with skin. As with the sarinda, the short, broad neck has no frets, and the button-headed pegs are laterally inserted in a cubic block of wood which forms the pegbox. Three gut strings in c' g c are the regular equipment; but usually a fourth wire string in d is added. The finger tips do not stop the strings by touching them on the front; instead, the fingernails are used to stop them on the side, as with certain bowed instruments of eastern Europe. Behind the three or four *bowed* strings, a quantity of thin wire strings, eleven to fifteen, are attached to smaller pegs in the neck. These wires resound sympathetically, as in the

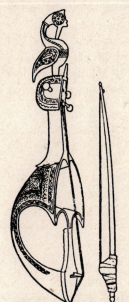 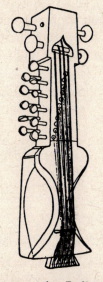 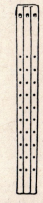

FIGURE 61. Indian fiddle sarangi.

FIGURE 62. Indian fiddle sarinda.

FIGURE 63. Tibetan triple flute.

European *viola d'amore*. The bowing hand is held with the palm upwards. (fig. 62)

There is little doubt that these fiddles came from a horse-breeding country in western Central Asia; primitive forms are still in use in Turkestan (as *kobyz*) among the Kirghizes and the Tatars.

FLUTES AND TRUMPETS. Besides the vertical and the crossflutes mentioned in the first Indian chapter, India has various whistle flutes both with and without a beaklike, chamfered upper end. Possibly they appear on one of the Borobudur reliefs, but we are not sure that our interpretation is correct. A native authority, Mr. P. Sambamoorthy, tells us that their tone is low and sweet and charms "the sheep when played by the shepherds in the valleys by the side of the hills. This is the common pastoral instrument of the shepherds and cowherds."

In the north, two flutes, tightly bound together, are used as *double flutes,* and the Tibetans have even *triple flutes* of the same kind (*gLingbu*). (fig. 63)

As to *trumpets,* Borobudur depicts only single and double specimens of the short and clumsy instrument that we discussed in the first Indian chapter. The modern trumpet of the north is entirely different, resembling the Chinese trumpet. It is slender and conical and consists of four sections fitting into each other like those of a telescope; the end of each section is marked by a bulging hollow ring. Telescoping construction and bulbs are not functional parts

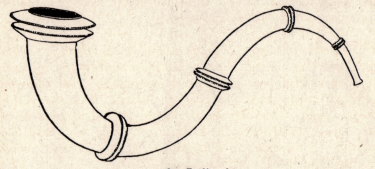

FIGURE 64. Indian horn.

of the instrument. A close relation to trumpets of Central Asia and the Far East therefore seems probable. Many Indian trumpets borrow even the peculiar embossed leaf decoration of the bell characteristic of Mongolian trumpets, as well as their Mongolian name, *buri.*

The coiled trumpet (Sanskrit *tūrya*) is also related to Central Asian trumpets. The tube is bent in the shape of the European trumpet. It has been questioned whether it came from Asia to the Occident, or vice versa. The Mongolian name seems to indicate an Asiatic origin.

The large curved *horn* of India (*raṇaśṛnga*) has certainly not come from Mongolia; nor do we find horns of this kind anywhere else in Asia. It probably is a native form. Two curved sections of brass or bronze fit into each other so that they can be turned to form either a crescent or an S. The sections form a continuously conical bore and are demarcated by bulging rings. The vehement sound of such horns is heard on various occasions, among which is a sunset ceremonial, a custom reminiscent of the old solar charm connected with trumpets. (fig. 64)

ISLAMIC TIMES

The continual cultural influences felt from the northwest and north culminated in a strong penetration of Islamic faith and Arabo-Persian influence. It is not difficult to distinguish the Arabo-Persian part in Hindu music, and especially in Hindu instrument making. Not only were the outer shapes of most of the foreign instruments preserved, but the foreign names also were kept intact or else superficially adapted to native idioms. Terms such as *sitâr* and *rabâb* were not changed, and others, as Sanskrit *sānāyī* and *tamburī*, or Marathi *sarôd*, can easily be traced back to the Persian words *surnāya, ṭanbūr* and *šarûd*.

DRUMS. The group of frame drums includes both pre-Islamic and Arabo-Persian types. The pre-Islamic drums have a large frame of wood or iron, usually not a perfect circle, and one thick skin with tightening thongs which converge radially to form a star on the open back. Two small sticks strike the head. This drum is only used by aboriginal tribes, the Khota for example, who call it *tambaṭṭam*, and the Khondo. It is probably related to the drums of Central and North Asiatic shamans.

A second group belongs in the Semitic type and is frequently designated by Arabic and Persian names such as *daf* and *dāera*. These instruments are strictly circular or octagonal; the single skin is glued or nailed on the frame and struck with the bare hand.

Kettledrums will be discussed in detail in the Near Eastern chapter. In India they are chiefly used in the *nahabat*, the noisy band officiating in state ceremonies and processions, which, beside the kettledrums, includes cymbals, trumpets and oboes. Emperor Akbar, in the sixteenth century, had a band of forty-two drums, a pair of large cymbals, eleven shrill oboes, ten trumpets and two horns. These bands are much smaller today.

The most impressive instrument of such a band is the *sahib-nahabat*, or 'master drum,' a pair of silver kettles, having the gigantic diameter of five feet and weighing about four hundred and fifty pounds. They are mounted on an elephant and draped with a hanging cloth ten feet long; each drum has its own player sitting on its rim and striking with a silver stick.

The *sutri-nahabat* brings up the rear of the procession. It is a pair of smaller copper kettles, draped and mounted on a camel, and both struck by the same drummer.

Smaller kettledrums, placed on the ground, are made of clay in an oval form; all of them have Y-shaped thongs attached to a twisted thong hoop, and interlaced with a central belt also of thongs. Pairs of shallow drums of this kind are usually called *nāgarā;* the deeper drums are called *ṭikārā* and *dāmāmā.*

Unlike other countries, India uses kettledrums also in chamber music. The most important chamber drum is the *bāṃyā.* This is a small kettledrum of clay, wood or copper. A hoop is rolled up in the edge of the skin; it is stretched by means of leather thongs laced in W or Y formation. The usual partner of the bāṃyā, the *ṭablā,* has the shape of two truncated cones, the lower one being much smaller than the upper one, and is made of wood painted in various colored stripes—red, yellow, black, green. The skin has a circular, black paste and an outer hoop made of twisted thongs, from which other thongs run down in W's and are tightened by shiftable wooden dowels. The manner in which the bottom is carved shows clearly that this instrument originally had a second skin, such as with the *pakhavāja,* which was given up when the drum came to be used in a vertical position. Both drums are played with the bare hands. When played by the same man, the bāṃyā is at his left, the ṭablā is at his right and produces the higher note.

Great technique is required in playing the bāṃyā, for it is the left drum that mars or makes the performers' efforts. When a new singer appears, the town-people of the musical circle always produce their most trusted Tabalchi [ṭablā player] to try the new comer's capacity . . . and every possible cross rhythm is put forth to lure the Gavaya (singer) into the many pit-falls prepared for him.

THE OBOE, imported from Persia, preserved its Persian name *surnā* in North India, though Sanskrit changed both the spelling and pronunciation to *sānāyī.* Sometimes two of these oboes are connected at an acute angle to form a double oboe; but usually a second man accompanies the sānāyī on a separate drone oboe of the same kind called *śruti* (the term for 'quarter-tone'), in which all the finger-holes, or all but one, are closed with wax. The same custom is found in South India; there the large *nâgaśuram* plays with the drone oboe *ottu.* Mr. P. Sambamoorthy relates that oboe "music is in great demand at weddings, ceremonials, processions and festivals. Expert performers are paid fabulous sums for their performances." Playing "is the monopoly of certain castes in southern India and elsewhere." Having "a continuous tradition behind them," they

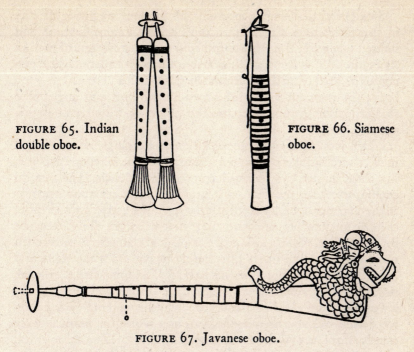

FIGURE 65. Indian double oboe.

FIGURE 66. Siamese oboe.

FIGURE 67. Javanese oboe.

often "hold hereditary appointments and in most cases they are given inams of land" in return for their services. (figs. 65, 66, 67)

BROAD-NECKED LUTES are a distinct and exclusively Indian variety of the Southwest Asiatic tanbur-sitar family. With the tanbur, they share the small and pear-shaped body covered by a perforated wooden soundboard, the long straight neck with a flat, fretted fingerboard, the wire strings and the mixed frontal and lateral position of the button-headed pegs. Contrary to the tanbur, they have a disproportionately wide neck and shiftable wire frets which, before each piece, are placed in the position necessary to produce the tonality required.

Lutes of this kind are called *sitâr*. But the name is misleading, as this Persian word means three-stringed. Three-stringed sitars are rare in India, most of them having from four to seven strings. The melody, however, is played on the last string only (with a few exceptions), while the others serve as a drone accompaniment, sounding beneath or tinkling on the highest string opposite the melody string. To pluck them, the player puts a tiny wire plectron on his right thumb.

The exuberant imagination of India has created more varieties of this instrument than can be conveniently enumerated. It will suffice to mention the large *kaččapī viṇā*, with a big gourd and six strings in *c''' c'' g c' c' f'*; the *śauktikā viṇā*, with a nacre body tapering to the head of an ibis; the *kinnarī viṇā*, with an ostrich egg for a body; the *prasāriṇī viṇā*, with an additional neck and fingerboard alongside with the first one; and the *kāča viṇā*, with a glass fingerboard.

Much more usual than these species is a strange form which is used to accompany singers with a drone without playing a melody. *Tamburi*, its name, is derived from Persian *ṭanbūr*. The general outline resembles the sitar—a long, broad neck, cut away squarely at the upper end, and a relatively large round body of wood or, in cheaper instruments, of gourd. But there are some differences: the soundboard is slightly convex; the pegs are attached in different positions, two being inserted in the front, one from the right, and one from the left side; frets are lacking. The four wire strings are tuned to *g c' c' c*. The three first are made of steel, and the fourth of brass. They are invariably plucked one after another in the indicated order without using a plectron; as a result, the harmonics are clearly heard, above all *e''*, the fifth partial of *c*. The timbre is full and delicate and provides an ideal background to the voice.

The family of broad-necked lutes has a branch of bowed lutes or fiddles. The main instrument is the *esrār*, a strange mixture of the sitar and the sarangi. From the latter the esrar has taken the waisted body, skin-covered front and sympathetic strings which echo the metallic, but delicate, sound of the bowed strings; the sitar has contributed the long broad neck, the shiftable frets and the wire strings. The accordatura is not uniform.

Even more elaborate than this hybrid instrument is a variety called *mayurī* in Sanskrit, and *tāyuś* in Hindustani, both names meaning 'peacock.' It is picturesquely shaped and colored like a peacock, the bird consecrated to the queen of the gods. A mayuri is mentioned in the Hindu orchestra at the imperial court of China as early as 500 A.D. But it is not likely that this was the same instrument that bears the name today.

This plenitude of Islamic instruments shows the importance of Islamic influence on Indian music. With Indian culture, Islamic influence spread eastward to the island settlements of India, affecting their religion and their social habits. The musical influence, however, was slight.

I2. *Southeast Asia*

EVEN in prehistoric time the vast peninsulas and islands to the east and southeast of India were particularly devoted to instrumental music and created numberless instruments of an original character, which were carried both eastwards to the Pacific Islands and westwards to Africa in early migrations. The xylophone was among them, and the *tube-zither*—a piece of bamboo with strings slit from the rind itself and held away by tiny bridges. A few later instruments, originating in an epoch between middle and high culture, must be mentioned separately. There is the strange rattle *angklung,* the two or three vertical bamboo tubes of which, carefully tuned in octaves, slide to and fro in grooves of the rectangular frame and strike against the rim. (fig. 68) A mouth organ of the type found between Burma and Borneo, and a large bell in an upright stand are both carved, with other Hindu instruments, on the Borobudur reliefs of which we will speak in one of the next paragraphs. The most characteristic of the bronze instruments of that late prehistoric epoch is the drum-gong.

DRUM-GONGS, made of an alloy which contains a certain admixture of lead, are cut in two pieces; a rather short, hollow cylinder, one to two feet high with gracefully curving sides, is covered at one end by a flat circular plate, the other end remaining open. This plate in early specimens is larger than the opening and is soldered to the end of the cylinder, with its edges projecting slightly. The gong is suspended from the ceiling so that the head hangs vertically; a squatting player beats the center of the plate with a big stick, and the side wall with a light bamboo; the plate produces a lower sound.

Among tribes of a middle standard of civilization, in a vast area between southern China and the islands of Leti at the east end of the Archipelago, these archaic instruments, rare today, are precious

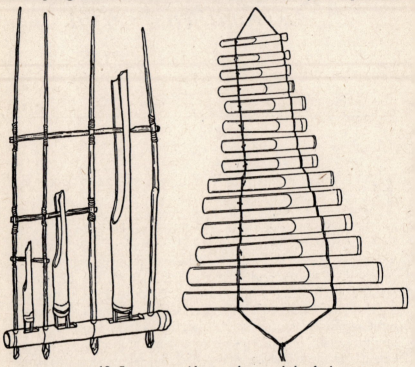

FIGURE 68. Javanese angklung and suspended xylophone.

pieces of property, highly valued in financial transactions of all kinds.

Their musical quality and role are insignificant. Archaeologists, on the contrary, have been much attracted by their plastic decoration. The head plate is divided into a number of concentric circles and has, at the center, an engraved star with either eight or twelve rays; little frogs cast in bronze, single or two or three sitting on one another, are soldered along the rim, and ear-shaped handles for the suspending cords are soldered to the cylinder. Older instruments are large and have single frogs on a projecting head; more recent specimens are smaller and have double or triple frogs; the latest, Chinese, type is small and has a head plate fitting into the opening without frogs.

The relation of the drum-gong to the ordinary gong is uncertain.

On the other hand, there is little doubt that it came from, or at least was inspired by, a skin drum. Most drums are similarly divided into a resonating cylinder and a flat circular head that is meant to be struck; several drums have ear-shaped handles as well, and the decoration of the head is paralleled by the frequent painting of drum skins; the star with eight rays, in particular, occurs in Muhammedan North Africa.

Though the transformation of bamboo, wood and skin into bronze with musical instruments probably began before, and was continued during, the time of Hindu influence, the bulk of bronze instruments did not appear till much later when the Indian period in Southeast Asia had come to an end.

INDIAN PERIOD

History in the southeast began in the first centuries A.D. when it became an immense, though loosely knit, Indian colony. Nearly the entire coast from Burma to the boundaries of China, some districts in the interior, and the large Malayan islands, Sumatra and Java, formed numerous states under the predominance of Indian civilization.

One state, the Sumatran empire of the Salendra dynasty, became particularly important, in the eighth century, extending its hegemony as far as western and Central Java. The outstanding monument that it left in Central Java, the gigantic stupa at Borobudur, is a fertile source of information not only about Indian religion, architecture and sculpture in the Archipelago, but also about Hindu-Malayan music. Many musical scenes are depicted on the two thousand reliefs which adorn its walls.

There we find several kinds of bells and cymbals; conical, cylindrical, hourglass and pot drums; cross flutes, single and double trumpets and shell trumpets; arched harps, stick-zithers and lutes. All instruments of ancient India are represented. At the same time their Sanskrit names appear in the older Javanese literature as well as in a quantity of inscriptions on stone and bronze: *ghaṇṭā, mṛdanga, śankha, tāla, vīṇā* and many others. (pl. XI a, b)

All these Indian instruments have already been discussed; the pear-shaped *short lutes* only deserve special consideration because they resemble not only the lutes represented on Indian art works about 500 A.D., but also the Sino-Japanese lutes of the biwa family.

The West Asiatic lute may have come to the southeast through China as well as through India, though a single instance of Chinese influence in the Indian period is not probable. (pl. XI a)

Far Eastern influence had full scope only in the next period when Hindu influence had declined.

POST-INDIAN PERIOD

This period begins with the end of Sumatran supremacy in Java in the ninth century. A short time afterwards, about 920, Central Java was deserted, we do not know why, and East Java became the political and cultural center. The Indian character was rapidly lost. René Grousset's words in regard to sculpture can also be applied to Malayan music of this later period: it had less serenity, but was "more living and dramatic in its inspiration and more impetuous in its movement."

Balinese music (which has preserved this earlier post-Indian character better than Javanese music) is certainly dramatic and impetuous. All instruments sound together in a noisy introduction that culminates in an overpowering crash followed by a sudden silence full of tension; a flute, soft and dreamy, emerges from the void and soars high above the dumb rhythm of a drum, until it fades away in a glitter of the orchestra hurrying on to another stretta and another crash.

Even the briefest allusion to Southeast Asiatic music cannot avoid the word 'orchestra.' Everywhere else music of the highest rank is performed by soloists or small chamber groups; in the southeast, between Burma and Bali, it is played by orchestras, or *gámelans* in Malayan. Some are small. The one which accompanies the Burmese marionette play (*pwe*) consists of a clapper, two different pairs of cymbals, a gong chime, a drum chime, one or several barrel drums and a loud oboe; it is very picturesque, with the two chimes in red and golden lacquered circular pens, and the biggest drum suspended from a snake-shaped beam.

In Bali, on the contrary, some bands are as large as our symphonic orchestras. The largest type of orchestra, called *gamelan gong*, is composed of a large quantity of metallophones in various sizes and forms, several gong chimes, two gigantic gongs suspended from an upright stand, half a dozen or more single gongs and two conical drums which guide the changing tempo. In the glittering peal of this strange orchestra one can distinguish the plain and solemn melody of the bases, its paraphrase and loquacious figuration in the smaller chimes, and the punctuation of the gongs, of which the smaller ones mark the end of shorter sections while the powerful basses of the large gongs conclude the main parts. (pl. XI c, f)

While these gamelans, with the one exception of the drums, are entirely composed of bronze instruments, other orchestras consist exclusively of bamboo and wood. The Balinese *gamelan djogèr,* which accompanies performances of public dancing-girls, has three instruments closely resembling metallophones with suspended slabs, but made of bamboo instead of bronze; three instruments of a gong-like sound, each made of a bamboo strip suspended over a resonance box; and a drum. Some authors have taken this gamelan for an older type preserved from premetallic times. The opposite is true. It is hardly necessary to prove that single strips over resonance boxes are substitutes for gongs, and actual bamboo xylophones would have been made, as other bamboo sets of the Malayan Archipelago, of round bamboo—not of strips that exactly imitate the shape of bronze slabs. The bamboo gamelan must be postmetallic.

No doubt these orchestras, sometimes made of bamboo, sometimes of metal, do not represent consecutive stages of evolution. They embody the same idea, found previously in ancient China, that the elements themselves are to take life and to sound; the mystic gongs, which at regular intervals divide the symphony and then fade away, belong to the same conception of "matter called to life" of which the introduction to our first Far Eastern chapter has spoken.

The scales of the southeastern orchestras are five-toned, though differing from the pentatonic scales of China and Japan. Three main systems are used: one Siamese, and the two Javano-Balinese systems, *S(a)lendro* and *Pelog.*

In Siam the octave is divided into seven equal parts each of which measures $\frac{1200}{7}$ or between 171 and 172 Cents, that is, hundredths of an equally tempered semitone. Since two hundred Cents correspond to a whole tone, the Siamese tone is approximately ⅞ of an occidental tone.

In *Slendro* the octave is divided into five equal parts. Expressed by the same musicological measure of a Cent, this division is $\frac{1200}{5}$ or 240 Cents to each degree. Compared to the two hundred Cents of an occidental tone, 240 Cents are ⅚ of a tone.

Pelog is more complicated. The octave is divided into five unequal parts, and their size varies considerably in different instruments. On an average the scale is composed of two major thirds, one whole tone and two semitones (e. g., *e f g b c′ e′*).

The Siamese scale and (sometimes) Pelog are heptatonic or seven-parted, but only as far as the system is concerned; the melodies composed in these systems omit two notes; they select only five of the seven available notes and thus are pentatonic or five-parted, like slendro.

Occidental musicians have great difficulty in conceiving of the equidistance of these unfamiliar $\frac{6}{5}$ and $\frac{7}{8}$ tones; they are always tempted to relate them to western distances and to think of them as alternating minor thirds and major or minor seconds.

Since slendro and pelog are used in the same orchestras, Javanese and Balinese instruments with fixed pitches—xylophones, metallophones and gong chimes—are made in both systems.

THE XYLOPHONE, discussed in the first chapter, reached the high point of its development in the *trough xylophone* (Javanese *gambang*) in Southeast Asia. The light, supporting frame is replaced by a rectangular wooden resonator in the form of a trough or a cradle; the wooden slabs, carefully cut and tuned, lie crosswise on its upper edges and are generally secured by small pins which pierce the slabs at one end and lie between them at the other end. (pl. XI e, g)

On reliefs at the temple of Panataran in Java, carved in the fourteenth century, such xylophones figure in a little story which, though not conforming to morals, is unfortunately true to man's habits. In a landscape two xylophones are placed alongside one another. A girl is playing on one of them while, in front of her, an older man, possibly her teacher, is playing the other. On the next relief practicing is brusquely interrupted; the two instruments are leaned against a tree and the professor withdraws with the girl in a somewhat impetuous manner. The third relief can be passed over, since it omits the xylophones as irrelevant to the situation.

These distinct reliefs show some interesting details. Three points are noteworthy: a duet is being played; two longer slabs are added at the right side of each instrument; and, finally, the sticks are in an unusual form. They are not simple sticks with a striking knob; each player holds a pair of sticks at a uniform angle in each hand. It is not clear whether the sticks are separate or attached in a Y-shaped fork, but in either case the player beats two slabs simultaneously, thus doubling his melody in parallels.

The same method of playing is current among African Negro tribes, for instance the Azandeh in East Africa; and here, as elsewhere in Africa, two or more xylophones are played at once.

This similarity is probably not a coincidence. Many implements, tools, weapons and instruments in a well-defined area of African Bantu districts are so closely connected with the corresponding objects of southeastern Asia that an early communication across the Indian Ocean through the Zambezi valley can be assumed. Certain accordances in the tuning of xylophones in Asia and Africa confirm this statement.

METALLOPHONES are bronze adaptations of the xylophone. No primitive types existed; the bronze slab came late enough to profit from the highly developed trough xylophones; the Javanese *saron* cannot have been constructed much earlier than 900 A.D.

The modern saron has a wooden resonance box which frequently is carved in the shape of a crouching dragon. Resting crosswise on its upper edges, the slabs are secured by small pins; these pierce the slabs at one end and are inserted between the slabs at the other end, thus isolating them. The slabs are tuned with a file—filing the ends of a slab raises the pitch, filing the central part lowers it.

Sarons are constructed in four main sizes an octave apart, each one comprising one octave. They play different parts in the orchestra, the lower ones in heavy notes, the higher ones in tinkling semiquavers.

The saron is not the only metallophone of the Archipelago. A second type, the *gendèr*, said to have existed as early as 1157 A.D., is a further departure from the xylophone and is better equipped to resonate metal sound. Its slabs are strung on two cords stretched over the edges of the trough at a distance of less than an inch. Under each slab is an open, resonating bamboo tube, placed vertically inside the trough and tuned in unison with its corresponding slab. As the resonator reinforces the fundamental, the tone is fuller and softer, persistent and mysterious. In rapid passages the left hand acts as a damper as the right hand strikes the following slab.

This instrument, too, is constructed in four sizes an octave apart with distinctive roles in the gamelan like the metallophones with resting slabs. (pl. XI c)

Readers familiar with modern instruments will have realized that the gendèr is similar to the French *celesta*. Possibly its inventor had seen a Javanese gamelan in Paris; but this is not certain.

GONGS are the most important metal instruments in the southeast. There are many types and sizes. Still, all of them are covered by the same short definition: a gong is made of bronze in the form of a flat or bulging surface in circular shape with the rim bent down; it is hit in the center by a stick, the rim being dead (unlike a bell, in which the center is dead).

The provenance of the gong is not certain. But Chinese tradition seems to be right in ascribing it to a country between Tibet and Burma. The earliest mention of a gong is in a Chinese source in the first years of the sixth century; in the ninth century the gong is reported in Java, and in the following centuries it is found in nearly all the islands of the Malay Archipelago, and finally even in some parts of New Guinea. With this expansion the center of gravity was shifted to the western islands; the making of the best gongs today is the specialty and privilege of a few old foundries at Semarang in Java, in which the skill has been handed down from generation to generation.

The gong is involved in every kind of human activity. It accompanies dances, songs, religious and secular ceremonies, and is even used to transmit messages by a sort of drum language. It also has a strong magic power attributed to it, especially in lower civilizations. It chases evil spirits, heals sickness and attracts the wind; drinking from a gong enforces an oath, and bathing in a gong gives health. This power, added to the price of a gong, makes it an object of the highest value, a badge of rank and property and even a form of currency. The esteem in which it is held is indicated by the fact that certain individual gongs have proper names, such as Sir Tiger or Sir Earthquake.

The oldest gongs were apparently *flat gongs* with a flat or slightly bulging surface and a shallow rim. They are more widely distributed than any other gongs, extending from India to Japan and Borneo.

This kind of drum probably came from the shamanic frame drum used all over North and Central Asia and India. It has its outer shape, and in some cases the rim slanting inward as in certain Ceylonese frame drums; like the shamanic drum, it is held in a vertical position and struck with one stick. Frequent decorations in form of concentric circles engraved around the center are reminiscent of similar paintings on ancient Greek frame drums.

A second form is the *gong with a boss* in the center of the face, which is struck by a stick. It does not exist in India, but is found in the eastern part of the Archipelago. Possibly the boss has developed

rom a pulpit in San Leonardo in Arcetri, Florence (10th century).

From the cathedral in Chartres (12th century).

om a capital in the Museum at Tou-louse (12th century).

From the cathedral in Amiens (14th century).

PLATE XIV.

from the circular, slightly convex lump of tuning paste that we frequently meet in the center of the head of Hindu and Malayan drums.

The most recent type is the *deep gong* which is used only in the area between Burma and the eastern Archipelago. Its walls are thick, and the rim is deep; a boss makes it look like the cap (biretta) of Catholic priests. Gongs with deep bosses are called male, those with shallower bosses female. Both forms are made in all sizes; some are just a few inches wide, some reach a diameter of more than three feet and a weight of one hundred and eighty pounds. (pl. XI c, d)

Of all types the deep gongs have the greatest musical value; their tone is pure, distinct and full without clinking harmonics. Their notes act as punctuation points in the gamelan. Smaller gongs, resting on low, four-legged stands, mark the end of smaller periods, while the largest gongs, suspended from upright frames, accentuate the main divisions with the solemn pulsations of their majestic basses.

The deep gong alone, owing to its pure and distinct tone, could be used in a gong chime.

GONG CHIMES (Javanese *bonnang*), the outstanding instruments of Southeast Asia, have been built in various arrangements. The fundamental arrangement, however, was not changed. There is a low horizontal frame or bed; each gong rests on crossed cords

FIGURE 69. Javanese gong-chime.

in a separate partition of the frame, and is easily reached by a squatting player. A relief on the temple at Angkor Vat in Cambodia (eleventh century A.D.) shows nine gongs in a quadrant-shaped bed, and in Java we have evidence of a previous semicircular arrangement. The full circle is the characteristic shape of Burmese, Siamese and modern Cambodian chimes.

The Archipelago in Malacca have straight, not circular, beds, with a row of gongs tuned either to a slendro or to a pelog octave. Only Java has an enlarged gong chime comprising two octaves arranged in two rows resting on the same bed. The row next to the player consists of female gongs and produces the lower octave; the farther row consisting of male gongs is tuned to the higher octave. As the melody is usually struck in parallel octaves, the arrangement of the gongs does not follow the scale, in order that gongs tuned an octave apart will not lie directly behind one another, thus inconveniencing their simultaneous playing. But there is no definite rule. (fig. 69, pl. XI c)

All kinds of gong chimes are built in several sizes an octave apart. As in the case of the metallophone, the higher chimes dissolve the plain melody played by the lowest chime into a rapid tinkling figuration.

Bali and Java have one more gong chime, the curious *rejong*. This is a dumbbell-shaped piece of wood, with a deep gong nailed at either end. The sitting player holds the instrument across his lap and strikes the two differently tuned gongs, each with one stick. Rejongs are always played in pairs, so that four different notes are available. "The larger rejong voices one rhythm, arising from the syncopated alternation of the two lowest notes of the scale, while the smaller one sounds an opposite rhythm with the two highest notes. The two opposing rhythms interlock in such a way that an even and rapid stream of notes may be kept up indefinitely" (McPhee).

ISLAMIC INFLUENCE has left a quantity of traces in Southeast Asia, but most Islamic instruments have been absorbed by primitive tribes and have no place in art music, with the exception of the Persian *spike fiddle* (called *rabâb* or *kamânga a'gûz* in the Near East). It has a small coconut shell covered with skin and pierced by a long stick with lateral pegs. The three gut strings are replaced by silk threads, and the spherical body is transformed into a shallow heart shape. The Siamese and Cambodian varieties (*sâ tai* and *tro khmer*) are carefully made and tastefully turned out of ivory and nacre, while Malayan fiddles, which have preserved the old Persian name in the form *rebab*, are much simpler. Though quite foreign to the nature of the Javanese gamelan, the flexibility of tone of this fiddle is often used by orchestra leaders to counterbalance the rigidity of the fixed scales of xylophones, metallophones and gong chimes. (fig. 70)

And now we turn to the Arabo-Persian instruments in their native area.

13. *The Near East*

THE Arabian civilization is older than is generally supposed. Arabian kingdoms can be traced back to the third millennium B.C. One of them was Sheba, whose queen visited King Solomon. When the old trade routes between the Mediterranean and the Orient, on which these civilizations depended, were gradually abandoned at the rise of the Roman Empire, their wealth, power and culture decayed. New centers, however, deriving their trade chiefly from the west, grew up in the first centuries A.D.; Al-Hijaz on the west coast of Arabia, for example; and outside the Arabian territory, Al-Hira close by ancient Babylon, and Palmyra in Syria. A quantity of large towns in the Near East still preserved the traditions of an old Semitic civilization, notwithstanding foreign domination.

In these towns migrating Arabs mingled with all the nationalities of the Near East, and their musical life had an international, interoriental character which, much too carelessly, we call Arabian. The young Persian king, Bahram Ghur (430–438), was sent to the Mesopotamian town, Al-Hira, to study Arabian music. In about 600 A.D., Hassan ibn Thabit saw at the Syrian court of the Ghassanids "ten singing-girls, five of them Byzantines, singing the songs of their country to the accompaniment of the lute *barbaṭ*, and five others from Al-Hira, who had been given to King Jabala by Iyas ibn Qabisa, singing the songs of their country. Arab singers also came from Mecca and elsewhere for his pleasure." Everywhere slaves, sold from country to country, spread the styles and instruments of their homelands; in the tale of King Omar bin al-Nu'uman in *The Arabian Nights* the princess has her slave girl bring some

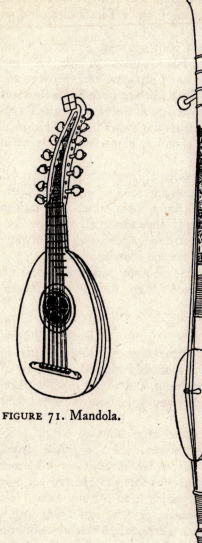

FIGURE 71. Mandola.

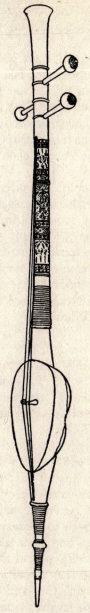

FIGURE 70. Siamese
spike fiddle.

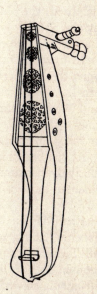

FIGURE 72. Rabâb.

instruments of music, and the maid "returned in the twinkling of an eye with a Damascus lute, a Persian harp, a Tartar pipe, and an Egyptian dulcimer."

Gradually the instruments lost their regional character when, beginning in the seventh century, Islam unified the Near East and extended a homogeneous culture to an immense zone between the Malayan Archipelago and Spain. The Kurdish spike fiddle then was found in the Balinese gamelan as well as in the hands of the Egyptian bard; the old Semitic frame drum was struck by the Arabian as by the Spanish girl; the Persian oboe was blown by the Dayak in Borneo as in Morocco.

In Europe, more than in Asia, oriental instruments went far beyond the frontiers of Islamic empires and settlements. From southern Italy and Sicily and, above all, from Spain, which had Arabian and Moorish rulers from 711 to 1492, they spread all over the Continent. Only a few of the earlier instruments remained hidden away as folk instruments in remote valleys and islands.

At the beginning of modern times Europe possessed almost exclusively instruments of Near Eastern descent, some of them Byzantine, but most of them Islamic.

FRAME DRUMS were the first instruments mentioned in pre-Islamic Arabia, where they played the same role that they did in all Semitic countries, as the indispensable musical attributes of women both in mirth and in mourning, and as the rhythmical instruments on which the professional singing-girls accompanied their songs and dances. (pl. XII a)

One of their names must have been *mizhar*, which probably is preserved in one modern name of the frame drum, *mazhar*, and did not designate a lute, as Dr. Henry George Farmer believes. A better-known name, closely related to Hebrew *tof*, was *duff*. This term has the general meaning 'frame drum' today; in a narrower sense, it is given to a square or octagonal drum with a shallow frame, two skins and inner snares, which resembles certain frame drums in ancient Egypt and Sumer. Round drums, on the contrary, have the general name *dā'ira* or 'circular.' The *ǧirbāl* is mentioned in Muhammad's time and later on in the Arabo-Spanish middle ages; as its name means a riddle or sieve, it probably had a rather large frame.

The four kinds of modern round drums can be divided into two main groups. The first sometimes has no jingling contrivance, or sometimes has jingling disks in its frame. In this group the (Berber?) *bandaïr* is large (diameter of sixteen inches) with snares, the *ṭar* middle-sized (diameter of twelve inches) with no snares, the *req* small (diameter of ten inches) with no snares. The second group has jingling rings, and the only example is the *mazhar*, which is large (diameter of sixteen to nineteen inches). All these round drums have one skin only. With a few exceptions there are five groups of jingling contrivances, in medieval miniatures as well as in modern specimens. Since to Arabian mathematicians five is the first so-called circle number, the five groups of jingling disks or rings in the frame were very probably the numerical expression of the circular form of the drum.

The fingers strike either the middle, the border or an intermediate place, according to the three dynamic intensities of Arabian music, *tum, kā* and *tak*, or forte, piano and mezzoforte. The method of holding the instrument varies; the Egyptians, for instance, grasp the drum with both hands, the Tunisians with the left hand only.

These modern drums, the names of which do not appear earlier than the Abbassidic epoch (from 750 A.D. on), brought their names with them when they came to Spain.

FLUTES. Only one wind instrument is used in Arabian art music, the simple vertical flute, which in Egypt can be traced as far back as the centuries before 3000 B.C. The Algerians still use its oldest Arabic name, *qaṣaba* or *quṣṣāba* (not 'gesba'), the plurals of which are *qaṣabat* and *qiṣab*; the Persian name *nāy* is used between Egypt and Persia. The instrument is a cane, some sixty or seventy centimeters long and provided with five or six fingerholes arranged in two groups. Its scale starts on the octave harmonics, the fundamentals being too weak to use. In some specimens overblowing is facilitated by a rear hole which divides the air column exactly in the middle. The musical qualities of the vertical flute have been described on page 90.

A smaller variety, half the length, with 6 + b fingerholes, is called *šabbāba* or 'young.' This name has migrated as far southwards as Madagascar, where it still exists as *sobaba*, and in medieval Spain it reappears with the assimilated article *aš*, as *axabeba* or, in a more modern spelling, *ajabeba*.

Pan-pipes—mūsīqār or *mūsīqāl*—are no more indigenous than their names imply. All the pan-pipes that the author saw in Egypt were very small and made of pasteboard. They obviously were imported from Europe.

A *beaked flute*, roughly made of cane and very short, is known in the western half of the North African coast and called *gawâq*. It has no place in art music.

THE OBOE of the Near East is conical, except for a few varieties. It is made of wood and turned on a lathe so that it is smooth and perfectly round, and it expands at the end to form the bell. Occasionally the bell is of metal. Out of 6 or 7 or 8 + b fingerholes, the three uppermost can be closed at will by a turning device inside, which has the effect of an occidental guitar *capotasto*, that is, cutting off a part of the range. The player holds the double reed entirely inside his mouth, and his stretched lips rest against a circular disk that surrounds the reed at the point where it enters the tube. He is trained to blow without pausing for respiration, like other oriental pipers, and the author was told in Egypt that the apprentices practice this technique with a bamboo dipped into water. We have already spoken of this manner of playing on page 91.

The earliest evidence of a conical oboe is on Jewish coins of the second century A.D. (cf. page 120). With the Muhammedan conquest, this kind of oboe spread over the world of Islam, from Turkey to Madagascar, from Morocco to the Malayan Archipelago, and even beyond, over Tibet and the Far East. (pl. XII c)

The classical names are *ṣūrnāya* in Persian, and *mizmār* in Arabic. Still, various countries use their own idiomatic terms; in Algeria and Morocco it is called *ḡaiṭa* (spelled *rheita* in the bands of French colonial regiments as the Arabic sound is intermediate between *gh* and *r*); in Tripolis and Tunisia the oboe is called *zūqra*. The author has found, in Egypt, the modern names *sibs* for the smaller variety and *aba* (from French *hautbois*) for a larger variety.

Both sizes of oboes belong to an ensemble called *ṭabl baladî* which plays at wedding and circumcision processions. It consists of three extremely shrill oboes, two large ones and a small one in the hands of the leader, a pair of kettledrums, *naqrazān*, and a cylindrical drum, *ṭabl baladî*, after which the ensemble has been named. In the *taqsîm*, or prelude, the drums are silent; the sibs plays the melody while the larger oboes play a drone. In the second part, when the drums join in, the two larger oboes accompany the sibs in the lower octave. This must be an old custom, for the same is true for the Turkish oboes *surle* played by Croatian gypsies.

CYLINDRICAL DRUMS like the *ṭabl baladī* are made of wood in a shallow form, the height of the cylinder being smaller than the diameter. The two skins are stretched by two hoops at either end, one concealed 'flesh hoop,' as American drummers say, and an outer 'rope hoop,' the rope hoops being connected by Y cords. The player hangs the drum from the shoulder so that the heads face sidewards. He strikes both skins with flexible beaters which are either two sticks or, as in Egypt, a stick (right) and a bundle of thongs (left); dull sounds (*dum*) are produced by hitting the center, clear sounds (*tak*) by striking the border.

Shallow drums are typically Near Eastern. They are unknown even in Islamic India, while, on the other hand, no barrel drum exists in the Arabian area. The shallow drum certainly originated either in Turkey or in Arabia, but it is not clear which. The Arabs give the name *ṭabl turkī* only to a large variety carried on the back of a donkey, which became the ancestor of our occidental bass drum; they call the smaller type, from which our side and tenor drums originated, *ṭabl baladī*—that is, domestic drum. (pl. XII c)

It is also doubtful at what time these drums originated. As late as about 1200, Mesopotamian miniatures still depict a 'long' drum, not a shallow one. Its length is twice the size of the diameter; it is made of a yellow wood and laced by cords in X; decorations in triangles and lozenges are indicated between the laces. The player stands erect in the middle of the sultan's band; he carries the instrument on a shoulder belt and plays with a hooked stick (right) and the bare hand (left). Some relation between this drum and the drums of early India is obvious.

On the other hand, Dr. Jeffrey, head of the Oriental Department, Columbia University, kindly writes me that *ṭabul* "is not an Arabic word in origin, but was borrowed from the Latin *tabula*."

KETTLEDRUMS are open receptacles which, in the majority of cases, are egg-shaped or hemispherical with a skin stretched over the opening. Clay was the original material which afterwards was replaced by metal.

The first evidence of Arabian kettledrums is in the tenth century encyclopedia of the *Iḫwān al-Ṣafāʿ*. The book enumerates the bowl drum, *qasaʿ* (a name which it shared with the bulging body of the lute, ʿūd), and the deeper kettledrums, ṭabl al-markab (the *naq-qāra*) and *kūs*.

Dr. Henry George Farmer believes that the kūs was an earlier drum. He writes that an Indian "is credited with having played the kettledrum kūs in the Prophet's military expeditions." This would hint of an Indian origin. Farmer's source, however, is neither contemporary nor Arabian; the statement is taken from the narrative of a Turkish traveler who wrote in the seventeenth century, a thousand years after the Prophet's expeditions. It is likely that the Turk called the drum by the name which was familiar to him.

As far as we can tell, the kettledrum originated in two forms. The older one can be seen on a relief at Taq-i Bustan in Persia, carved about 600 A.D. and representing a drummer with a small shallow bowl drum which stands on the ground and is struck with one, or perhaps two, sticks. It may have been the *tās* mentioned in Persian texts of that time, as such a drum still exists in northern India under the name *tāsā*.

The first evidence of a larger kettledrum is found on Mesopotamian miniatures of the twelfth century A.D. The very first of them gives an invaluable clue to their origin; instead of being rounded, the instrument has the flat bottom of a pot drum. Thus, it seems probable that the larger kettledrums were derived from the pot drums of primitive men, which on a higher level are depicted on the Hindu-Javanese temple at Borobudur (c. 800 A.D.). Through many centuries the Persian miniatures depict them as preserving the same form. Later on, the kettledrum was rounded like an egg; this may have been an adaptation to facilitate carrying the drums on the back of a horse or a camel. In all the miniatures two drums of different size are used simultaneously; they are placed on the ground and inclined not towards the player, as in occidental orchestras, but away from him, this being a better position when the player stands erect. An interesting detail is the hook form of the oldest kettledrum sticks, which has been referred to in Chapter 7. In a miniature of the Loutrell Psalter (early fourteenth century), in the British Museum, a player is represented in the same fashion, with two kettledrums inclined away from him and played with hooked sticks.

On the later oriental miniatures the sticks are only slightly bent, or sometimes straight, with either pointed or knobbed ends; on some paintings the drums are struck with the fists. A final detail which these miniatures present is the change from the egg shape to a more or less hemispheric shape—that is, with the largest diameter at the head. This change accompanies the transition from clay to metal, the bulging egg shape being typical of pottery, the hemisphere, on the contrary, of metal work. The earlier, oval form using clay as material persists to this day in Indian kettledrums of Persian origin, *khorāḍhāk, dāmāmā, ṭikārā, nāgarā,* and, with them, a shallow bowl drum *tāsā* or *qaṣaʿa.*

In modern times one can distinguish the following kinds of kettledrums.

Naqqārya: two large flat kettles played on the back of a camel, the lower in pitch at the player's right, the higher at his left, and struck with two sticks

Naqrazān: two smaller kettles played on the back of a donkey, shallow, but nearly hemispherical, struck with two sticks

Naqqāra: two small kettles, played with two sticks

Ṭabl šāmī: one kettle of a very shallow shape, carried by the player and struck with two sticks

Ṭabl al-ġāwiġ or *šāwiš:* one shallow kettle played on horseback, struck with one stick

Ṭabl migrī: one shallow kettle, struck with thongs.

All these kettles are made of metal and tightened with cords.

The naqqāra and its Arabic name came to Europe chiefly as a result of the crusades. As early as about 1300, the French were using the Arabic term *nacaires,* the Italians *naccheroni,* and the English *nakers.* The instrument is depicted in the Loutrell Psalter that we quoted, and, for example, on Lippo Memmi's painting, "The Coronation of the Virgin," in Munich (first half of the fourteenth century).

SHORT LUTES, carved out of a single piece of wood with no distinct neck and tapering towards the pegbox, are found first in Iran, the same country which afterwards became their center; Elamic clay figures attributed to the eighth century B.C. show them in rough outlines; the strings and their attachment are not distinguishable.

There is no further evidence of the short lute until, many centuries later, it reappeared in the Islamic Near East; its pegbox was bent backwards in a sickle shape and contained lateral pegs; the stringholder was not frontal but on the lower end of the body, and a skin served as the soundboard.

Islamic migrations and conquests carried this lute eastwards from

Persia as far as the Celebes, and southwards to Madagascar. In all these countries it has been called by a name probably of Turkish origin, and variously spelled as *gambus, kabosa* or *qūpūz*. Arabic literature adopted this name at the end of the Abbassidic Dynasty, in the beginning of the eleventh century A.D.; in Egypt it was introduced at about 1200 A.D. Today this lute is extinct in the Near East.

The short lute with an inferior stringholder traveled westwards into southern Europe. In the tenth century such an instrument was carved on a wooden pulpit in the small church of San Leonardo in Arcetri at Florence. Pegs are not indicated, but the pegbox, bent back, suggests lateral pegs. The soundboard is divided by a cross line into two halves, probably of wood and of skin. The three strings are plucked with a big plectron probably made of wood, similar to that used on Indian lutes of the short type. (pl. XIV a, c)

The short lute is frequently pictured on Spanish miniatures of the thirteenth century, and it found its way into Europe through Spain rather than through Italy.

Nevertheless, the Turkish name *qūpūz* seems to have been unknown in South and West Europe, though it was used in the central and eastern parts of the continent. In a poem written in the early fourteenth century, *Gottes Zukunft* by Heinrich von der Neuen Stadt, verse 4672 mentions *die kobus mit der luten*. This word had probably entered through Hungary, where it can be traced back to the middle ages as *koboz;* and it certainly had come to Hungary from Byzantium, since a Greek tractate on alchemy, written about 800, mentions a *kobuz* or *pandurion* with seven frets and three, four or five strings.

The Christian Spaniards, on the contrary, seem to have called the same instrument a Moorish guitar; in his poem, *El libro de buen amor* (fourteenth century), Juan Ruiz, archpriest of Hita, mentions it immediately before the lute:

> *Ally sale gritando la guitara morisca*
> *de las bozes aguda e de los puntos arisca. . . .*

"There the Moorish guitar emerges with its shrill and harsh notes."

The Moorish guitar was more and more influenced by the instrument which we call a lute today. In the sixteenth century it was given a new name, *mandola* or *mandora*, a thin pear-shaped body composed of slender staves or 'ribs,' a frontal stringholder, a sound-hole with a carved rose, a short neck and double strings; only the sickle-shaped pegbox of the older instrument was preserved. (fig. 71)

The lute in question was given a bow before the year 1000, and as a bowed instrument was called *rabâb;* it existed beside the plucked lute. It kept the pear-shaped body tapering towards the pegbox, the front covered with skin and the lateral pegs. But the number of strings was reduced to one or two, and the sickle-shaped pegbox was cut off so that only its stub was left. (fig. 72)

THE LUTE WITH A FRONTAL STRINGHOLDER corresponds in the Near East to the vina in India, and the koto or ch'in in the Far East. It is the noblest instrument of art music, made according to mathematical principles and the object of cosmological speculation. It is characteristic that in an area in which singing is more important than playing the chief instrument is one which serves to accompany the voice.

The Asiatic countries and Egypt designate it by its classical, Arabic name *'ūd.* The principal meaning of this noun is not 'wood,' as generally supposed, but 'flexible stick.' This corroborates our assertion that the earliest lute came from the musical bow; but, obviously, the name must have belonged to a long lute whose handle was derived from a 'flexible stick,' before it was given to the short lute, which probably was not, or at least not directly, connected with the musical bow.

The North African countries west of Egypt prefer the Greek word *qīṭārā*, which was taken over into Arabic before 1000 A.D. with many other musical terms of the ancient Greeks. The philosopher Ibn Sina (Avicenna), who was born in Persia in 980 A.D., was the only writer who used the Persian term *barbaṭ*.

According to a writer of the fourteenth century A.D., the 'ūd was "invented" in the third century A.D. in the days of Shapur I, who was king of Persia from 241 to 273 A.D. This is not true, as we have seen on page 160. Not only do we possess art works in the so-called Gandhara style of about 100 A.D. with representations of this lute, but the instrument had also existed in the orchestra of the Chinese Han Dynasty (206 B. C.–220 A.D.).

These earlier lutes, as well as the ones that Persian painters later depicted in their miniatures, had the main features of modern oriental lutes: the bulging wooden body with a thin wooden soundboard, the frontal stringholder, the lateral pegs and the double gut (or silk) strings. Still, they resembled the modern Japanese and Chinese lute rather than the modern Arabian lute. The wide, pear-shaped body tapered towards the pegbox, not forming a distinct neck, and two crescent-shaped soundholes were cut on either side of the soundboard instead of the large central soundhole.

The classic number of strings was four pairs. They were called, from the lowest to the highest, *bamm, maṭlaṭ, maṭnā, zīr*, the lowest of which, *bamm*, means 'high,' just as the Greek *hypátē*.

The four strings symbolized the elements, the phases of the moon, the directions, the seasons, the weeks of a month, the divisions of a day, of the body, of human life, and the four humors—that is, in descending order, the yellow bile, the blood, the phlegm, and the black bile. They were tuned a fourth apart and, according to the theorists of the tenth century, they were twisted from threads, the number of which decreased in the proportion 3:4; from bamm to zīr they consisted of 64, 48, 36 and 27 threads respectively.

A fifth pair of strings, above zīr, seems to have been introduced as early as the ninth century to make the range of two octaves complete. The present five pairs of strings are tuned to *d e a d' g'*, that is, the fifth pair is added below.

Lutes seem to have had no frets, either in old times or today, in spite of the constant use by the theorists of the word *dāsatīn*, plural of Persian *dast* or 'hand,' which is used to indicate frets. And it would have been difficult to string them securely around the sloping end of a pear-shaped lute. Very probably, the frets existed only theoretically to symbolize the positions of the stopping fingers.

The strings are plucked with a quill plectron, *zaḥma*. The tone, therefore, is more energetic than that of a European guitar. Skillful players produce a surprisingly multiform timbre and a delicate *cantabile*, which is far superior to the dry and boring tone of modern occidental players who try to reproduce the lute music of the sixteenth and seventeenth centuries.

All strings are used to play the melody. Chords are unknown; occasionally drones are played to accompany a melody. The effect of a sustained note is achieved by repetition or by a swift alternation between the note and its octave.

In its modern form, the oriental lute has a distinct neck, an almond-shaped body and a central soundhole with a rose. These transformations seem to have taken place in Andalusia, where oriental and occidental tendencies mingled. From Andalusia the improved instrument was carried back to Egypt, and forward to Europe. There it became the instrument known as *lute* in the modern sense of the word, an instrument which achieved and sustained an important position for more than three centuries.

THE SPIKE-FIDDLE, found all over the Islamic world, including Siam and Cambodia, is a 'pierced fiddle'; the round handle projects through the body and protrudes at the lower end, forming a foot similar to the spike of a cello, on which the instrument is rested. The pegs are lateral, and a piece of skin forms the soundboard. While east of India the spike is of wood or ivory, it is made of iron in the west.

At the western and the eastern extremities of its area of distribution the spike-fiddle is rather primitive; the Malayan as well as the Egyptian fiddles have only one or two strings. Egypt has several species, the *kamānġa a'ġūz* or 'old fiddle,' tuned to *a* and *e;* and the *kamānġa farḫ* or *soġaīr* or 'part of a fiddle,' tuned to *e'* and *b,* both having a small coconut body and two hair strings. Besides the two kamānġa, there is a related fiddle, *rabâb,* with a quadrilateral frame, the upper and lower sides of which are parallel, and two skins closing it from the front and the back, forming a kind of frame drum which replaces the coconut body. With one string this instrument is called *rabâb aššā'ir* or poet's fiddle. As such, it accompanies the endless recitations of public narrators. With two strings it is called *rabâb al-moġanni,* or 'singer's fiddle', and accompanies songs.

In southwestern Asia the *kamānġa a'ġūz* has sometimes three or even four strings, and in some countries—Turkestan and Kashmir, for instance—a set of sympathetic wire strings is stretched behind the bowed strings. The accordatura for three (bowed) wire strings is usually the ground tone, its fifth and its octave or ninth.

The spike-fiddle is mentioned as early as the tenth century A.D. by the great theorist Al-Farabi who, although he wrote in Arabic, was a Turk. Tradition assigns its origin to the North Iranian district, Kurdistan.

THE LONG LUTE, in Arabic *ṭanbūr,* has a full metallic timbre, but can also be played very delicately. The player can shake the lute at the end of a melodic period and make the sound fade away with a vibrato that resembles the *Bebung* of a clavichord.

The long lute has a small, pear-shaped body and a long neck without a pegbox, many gut frets, a few thin wire strings and a plectron made of tortoise shell. It has faithfully preserved the outer appearance of the ancient lutes of Babylonia and Egypt; its pegs, however, are curious in form and position. Shaped like the letter T, they are inserted, some from the front, some from the side; their position is *mixed*, as we shall call it, thus possibly testifying to

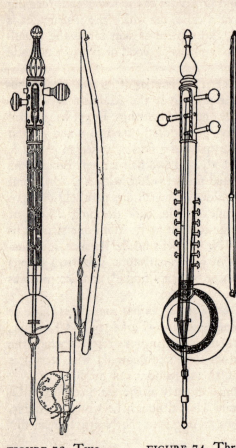

FIGURE 73. Two-stringed spike fiddle.

FIGURE 74. Three-stringed spike fiddle.

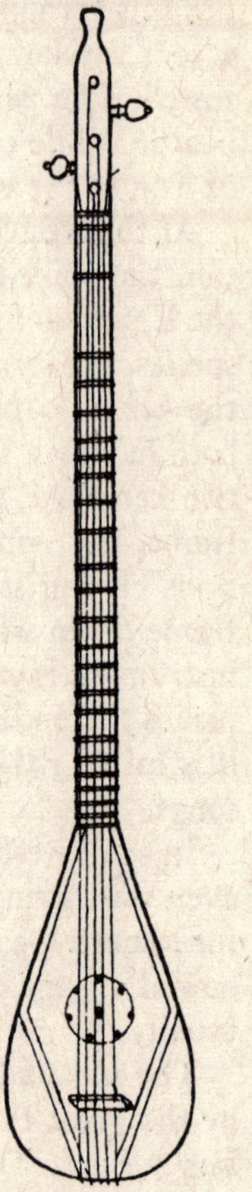

FIGURE 75. Persian long lute.

a mixed origin of this recent form of the long lute, from the Arabo-Persian area of lateral pegs as well as from the Turkish area of rear pegs. The Arabs, indeed, call its largest variety *ṭanbūr kabīr turkī* or 'large Turkish lute.' The Persians, however, do not use the word *ṭanbūr;* they designate the instrument by the word *tār*

harp horn   lyre   pan-pipes fiddle

From Bibliothèque Nationale, Paris, ms. lat. 11550 (11th century).

Monochord. From Preus-
sische Staatsbibliothek, Berlin, ms. theol. lat. fol. 358.

Bowed lyre. From Bibliothèque
Nationale, Paris, ms. lat. 1118
(11th century).

PLATE XV.

or 'string,' combined with a numerical prefix indicating the number of strings—the *dutār* has two strings, the *setār* three, the *čartār* four, the *pančtār* five strings. (fig. 75)

The long lute is interesting because of its scale. The positions of the stopping fingers, like the positions of fingerholes in a pipe, were determined according to a metrical, not a musical, rule. Henry George Farmer quotes a manuscript in his possession according to which the tanbur came "from the Sabaeans who measured the earth, and so it was called the 'measured' " lute or *ṭanbūr al-mīzānī*. This instrument was probably identical with the lute that afterwards was called 'tanbur from Baghdad.' The length of its two strings was divided theoretically into forty equal parts, which may have corresponded to an ancient Mesopotamian standard measure. The first five divisions only were used in playing and were indicated by gut frets, so that the scale was a small series of (unequal) quartertones. The second string, instead of being lower, was tuned to the second fret of the first string—that is, less than a semitone higher. The range of the whole instrument did not exceed a minor third. But this "pagan," that is, pre-Islamic, tuning was given up as early as Al-Farabi's time (c. 900 A.D.).

More recent was the 'tanbur from Chorassan,' the northeastern province of Persia and seat of the Abbassids. Its frets were musically arranged in order to produce an enharmonic seventeen-tone scale.

A European offshoot of the sitar-tanbur, the *colascione*, was particularly played in Italy in the sixteenth and seventeenth centuries. In this instrument a long neck was combined with the body and the lateral pegs of the usual European lute; most colascioni had gut frets and two or three gut or wire strings in (E) A d.

THE TRAPEZOIDAL ZITHER was first depicted by the Syrian lexicographer, Bar Bahlul, at about 963 A.D.; it then had ten strings. He called it *qithoro*, from Greek *kithara*. But about the same time, its classical name *qānūn*, from Greek *kanôn*, appears in one of the oldest stories of *The Arabian Nights*, the tale of Ali ibn Bakkar and Shams al-Nahar (hundred and sixty-ninth night), which is ascribed to the tenth century. An epithet to its name, *miṣrī*, indicates *Maṣr* or Egypt as its home. According to a Persian treatise of the fourteenth century, the qanun then had sixty-four strings arranged in sets of three.

In its present form, the qanun is a flat box the shape of whose face is a trapezoid. The twenty-six triple gut strings, fastened at the lower rectangular end of the box, run parallel to the parallel sides of the box and over the end of the opposite, oblique end, where they are tuned by wooden pegs inserted in the side; the soundboard is half of wood, half of skin. Within the range *c'-g'''*, the tuning, though diatonic, changes according to the tonality of the piece. The strings are plucked with wire plectra; the right hand plays the melody and the left hand doubles it in the lower octave, except for those passages in which it stops a string to raise its pitch by a minor or major second.

Through Spain the qanun came early to Europe, and up to the fifteenth century it preserved its form, its oriental decoration and its name; the Spaniards called it *caño*, the Germans *kanôn*. A smaller variety was called a 'half qanun,' *meo canno* in Spanish, *micanon* in French, and, with a curious popular etymology, *medicinale* in late Latin.

We add here an instrument *muğnī*. A Persian treatise on music, the *Kanz al-tuḥaf*, dating from the middle of the fourteenth century, attributes its invention to Safi al-Din (d. 1294) and describes it as a zither in lute form: a large bulging body with a wide, flat neck and thirty-nine open strings arranged as in the qanun and passing over a diagonally placed bridge. The name is preserved as *mughni* in Georgia. A similar instrument still exists in Ukraine as *torban*, a lute with two pegboxes one above the other in the manner of a theorboe (see Chapter 16) with thirty or thirty-one open gut strings.

THE DULCIMER is a Persian and Iraqian instrument, the name of which, *santir*, is derived from Greek *psalterion*. It usually has a shallow chestnut box in the form of a symmetrical trapezoid, and eighteen quadruple brass strings tuned by pegs inserted in the side of the box. The player strikes them with two very light sticks which end in a broad blade.

The migration of the dulcimer was strange enough. The Arabs carried it through North Africa, where it still is played by Jews, and from North Africa to Spain. There, its earliest evidence is a relief from 1184 on the porch of the cathedral Santiago de Compostela. Later on it passed through the continent and became a popular instrument of the southeast of Europe. In about 1850 this "Frankish dulcimer" was found side by side in Turkey with the genuine Turkish dulcimer of a similar construction which had come directly from Persia. The most important remainder of this group is the *cimbalom* of the Hungarian gypsies.

Eastward the dulcimer migrated in about 1800 to China, where it still is called the foreign zither (*yang ch'in*), and thence to the Japanese, Mongols and Buriats. In Korea a native tradition asserts, however, that the instrument was introduced as early as about 1725.

THE ANGULAR HARP had come from Iran to the Near East at a remote time and was still specifically Persian in the middle ages. Three types are depicted on Sasanian reliefs at Taq-i Bustan (c. 600 A.D.). One type is the final evidence of the horizontal harp that we have followed from Babylonian reliefs to the *sabka* of the Book of Daniel, and then to a specimen excavated from a Sarmatian tomb in Crimea. Its body is comparatively wide in the form of a modern violin case, and the string-fastening stick erected at its outer end is as long as the body.

The second type depicted in Taq-i Bustan is the vertical angular harp with the body growing larger at the top that was used in Assyria and Egypt. This, too, is the last form of an archaic instrument.

The third type, also vertical, is the first evidence of the modern Persian harp, depicted on innumerable medieval miniatures, and used until recently. The body, often gilded and inlaid, tapered and curved forward at the upper end to form a hook or a scroll. The strings were attached at the lower end to a horizontal bar without pegs, and beyond this bar the body projected downward to form a curled tail upon which the instrument rested while the player knelt on the floor. The number of strings varied from thirteen to forty. They occasionally were arranged in pairs or even in groups of three. The fingers of both hands plucked, and on one miniature we distinguish a plucking device on the thumbs.

The Arabian colony at Al-Hira, near Babylon, obtained this harp from the Persians and in the last centuries before Islam introduced it to Arabia. The Arabs kept it for many centuries under its Persian name *čank*, which in Arabic was spelled either *ǧank* or *ṣanǧ*, as the sound and letter *č* (English *ch*) does not exist in this language. The instrument was still used in 1554 in Arabic-speaking countries, when a French traveler, Pierre Belon, saw it in the hands of Egyptian women and emphasized the beauty of its sound, "which was scarcely less harmonious" than the tone of a European harp.

Still, the harp was nearly the only instrument of the Near East that did not enter Europe during the middle ages.

I4. *Europe*

INVESTIGATION of medieval instruments is dependent principally on the interpretation of contemporary art works. The contribution of literary sources is comparatively small. Except for the fragment of an ivory harp in the Louvre and a few ivory horns, no instrument has been preserved.

Nearly all the musical instruments of medieval Europe came from Asia, either from the southeast through Byzantium, or from the Islamic empire through North Africa or from the northeast along the Baltic coast. The direct heritage from Greece and Rome seems to have been rather insignificant, and the lyre is the only instrument that might possibly be considered European in origin.

Before discussing the instruments of medieval Europe, two general statements can be made. First, all European stringed instruments up to about 1000 A.D. had rear pegs. This kind of peg is found not only in medieval Europe including Spain, but also in southwestern Asia among the Byzantines, Caucasians, Turks and Kirghizes. These instruments on which rear pegs are found are sharply distinct from the instruments with lateral pegs of the Arabo-Persian district.

Second, within Europe we distinguish between a southern zone, in which the stringed instruments (other than the harp) took the form of 'lutes,' that is, with necks, and a central and northern zone, in which they took the form of 'lyres,' that is, of a two-armed body with a crossbar at the top. These two zones point to a twofold origin of early medieval instruments, the first from an uncertain source and feeding the north of Europe, the second feeding southern Europe and probably coming from that area of southwestern Asia in which we find rear pegs. In a central zone of Europe, such as France, both lutes and lyres are found side by side.

THE HARP. The question, often asked and never satisfactorily answered, of what kinds of stringed instruments Central and North Europe had in antiquity and in the early middle ages, depends on the interpretation of a few philological and pictorial sources.

The philological sources begin with Diodorus Siculus, a Roman historian of the first century B.C., who described the instrument used by Celtic bards as similar to, though not identical with, the Roman lyre. Five hundred years later, another Roman historian, Ammianus Marcellinus, who lived approximately between 330 and 400 A.D., again stated that the Celtic bards sang to "the sweet notes of the lyre." While Ammianus did not differentiate between the Celtic and the Roman instrument, the older writer expressly emphasized that they were not identical. Unfortunately, he failed to specify the difference.

Two hundred years after Ammianus, the bishop of Poitiers, Venantius Fortunatus, wrote, in a poem,

> *Romanusque lyra plaudat tibi, Barbarus harpa,*
> *Graecus achilliaca, chrotta Britanna canat.*

Of these four instruments, the Roman lyre is the only one that can be identified with certainty. All music historians have supposed that *achilliaca* referred to Achilles's lyre mentioned by Homer in the tenth book of the *Iliad*. But why should Venantius have called the instrument after a hero who had had no more in common with the lyre than any other Greek in one or two millenniums? It would be more convincing to think of *ē chelys*, a Greek name of the lyre, which the bishop, not knowing Greek, changed into something vaguely familiar. Whatever the correct etymology, achilliaca probably meant lyre.

Two terms are left to be identified, *chrotta* and *harpa*. As the word *harpa* suggested a harp in our sense, the term *chrotta*, obviously designating some other instrument, was identified with some kind of lyre. Both suppositions were incorrect. The term *harpa* did not designate a harp in our sense; it will be discussed below. And *chrotta* did not indicate a lyre.

Chrotta, the Latin equivalent of Irish *crot* or *cruit* and a continental *rotta*, can only be identified by examining the qualities attributed to it by medieval authors from the eighth to the fourteenth centuries in England, France, Germany and Spain. An abbot, Cuthbert (eighth century), speaks of the *cithara* that "we" call *rotta;* Notker Labeo in St. Gall (tenth century) has seven strings on his *rotte;* the Bavarian poem *Ruodlieb* (eleventh century) credits King David with the invention of the *psalterium triangulum, i.e., rotta;* a copyist of Notker Balbulus (twelfth century) complains that the jugglers had taken possession of the ancient ten-stringed *psalterium*, changed its mystic triangular shape, increased the number of strings and called it by the barbarian name *rotta;* the same writer says that the *saltirsanch* is now called *rotta* in German; the troubadour Girauz de Calanson (twelfth century) considers seventeen strings an appropriate number for the rotta; the poet Gottfried von Strassburg, in his *Tristan* (thirteenth century), describes both a "small" rotta suspended from the player's neck, and another one large enough to conceal a little dog in its body; finally, Juan Ruiz, in his poem *El libro de buen amor* (fourteenth century), describes a *rota* towering over the orchestra "higher than a rock."

To sum up, the rotta was now small, now very large; it had seven, sometimes more than ten, and even as many as seventeen strings; the rotta originated from a triangular *psalterium*. These qualities point to the harp; not one indicates a lyre. The *harpa* of the Barbarians, in Venantius's poem, must have been something different. The term will be discussed in the next section.

The oldest pictorial evidences of Irish instruments are some reliefs on stone crosses of the eighth and ninth centuries. It has been questioned whether these archaic implements were lyres or harps. After careful examination, the author is inclined to think they were harps. The rude and eroded reliefs are not clear, but a few significant facts are evident; all these instruments have distinct frames, such as harps with bodies, necks and pillars; all of them are asymmetric in the manner of harps; one, on the Castledermot North Cross, has exactly the form of an instrument depicted in the twelfth century on a miniature of a psalter in St. John's College, Cambridge, which is clearly a harp; some are larger than the usual lyres. The structural criteria are backed by the manner of holding and plucking the instruments.

The conclusion from pictorial and literary sources that the crot of ancient Britain and Ireland was a harp, not a lyre, is confirmed by a famous manuscript of the twelfth century, which juxtaposes the pictures of a harp and a lyre, calling the harp *cythara anglica,* and the lyre *cythara teutonica.* Ever since, the harp has been considered the national instrument of both Britain and Ireland. The *Leges Wallicae,* or *Laws of Wales,* said three things were necessary to a man in his home: a virtuous wife, a cushion on his chair and a well-tuned harp. In the thirteenth century, *harpeors* in France had come from *Ingleterre,* and in the fourteenth century, Dante traced the harp to the Irish in his *Divina Commedia.*

It is with good reason that the harp is the heraldic symbol of Ireland.

Nevertheless, it was known on the continent as early as the ninth century. The Utrecht Psalter, painted at about 832 in France, depicts it several times.

The ancient European instrument was what we call a vertical angular harp, which was like the eastern harps of this type except that it was held upside down, so that the stick (or neck) was on the top and tuning pegs were inserted in it. It also had a *front pillar,* that is, a stick squeezed between the end of the body and the end of the neck, forming the third side of the triangle, to counteract the tension of the strings. (pl. XIV c)

The European harp was not without precedents. Both the tuning pegs and the inverted position of the stringholder existed in the Syrian harp of the early middle ages, and we know that at that time an active Syrian trade carried oriental goods to West and Northwest Europe. Thus, the harp was probably not indigenous in the Occident, though it is not yet possible to say from what country the Europeans obtained it. If Ireland was one of the first countries of Europe to adopt it, it is easily conceivable that from there it spread over the continent; Irish minstrels swarmed over Europe in the early middle ages.

The older harp had wire strings tuned by means of a key like that of modern pianos. The Middle High German name of this key, *plectrûn,* must not induce readers of ancient texts to believe that the harp was plucked with a plectron. In size harps differed greatly. Some were small enough to be carried suspended on a thong; others were too large to be portable. Some had as few as seven strings, as testified by an old poem that compares them with the seven planets. The harp that the composer Guillaume de Machault describes in the fourteenth century had twenty-five strings. Such a wide range tempts one to connect with this statement a verse of Guillaume de

Machault's contemporary, the poet Eustache Deschamps: *La harpe tout bassement va*, and to translate it by "the harp goes down very low." But this interpretation would be open to question. In the last centuries of the middle ages the French distinguished between instruments *bas et hauls*, which however did not mean 'low and high' instruments; the meaning was *instruments coys ou qui font grant noise*, 'soft instruments and those which make great noise,' that is, instruments intended to be played indoors and outdoors.

Of all indoor instruments, the harp had the highest rank; members of royal families and the aristocracy played it. When it was played skillfully, it would *destroy the fendes myght*; the evil spirits fled, the rivers stopped flowing and the cattle forgot to eat. How familiar this picture is (cf. page 159).

The two hands played two parts on the harp. There is a Spanish poem of the fourteenth century, by King Alfonso XI, with the verse *La Farpa de Don Tristan que da los puntos doblados*, 'Don Tristan's harp which plays double notes,' and this is confirmed in a French poem in which the poet, speaking of the strings, says: *as quantes feiz chanter, as quantes organer*, 'he had several [strings] play the melody, and several the accompaniment.'

The later medieval development of the European harp form had two main stages, the first of which we shall call the *romanesque harp* and the second the *gothic harp*. The stout romanesque harp had a curving pillar, and the distinction between the three parts, body, neck and pillar, was emphasized by ornamental decoration. The slender gothic harp had an almost straight pillar, and the construction tended to unify rather than to separate the three parts, so they seemed to be made of one piece of wood. The transition from the first type to the second took place as late as about 1430. (fig. 76, pls. XVI b, XVIII b)

The English name *harp* and its Germanic and Romanic relatives probably go back to an Indo-European root meaning 'to pluck or pick.' The Latin equivalent is *carpere*, from which 'harvest,' the picking season, is also derived.

LYRES in northern and central Europe have for years constituted a puzzle that has been even further confused by speculative theories. If a solution is possible, it must be based upon sober facts rather than on preconceived ideas.

The district of the lyre reached northward to England, southward to what was later called France and Germany, and eastward to

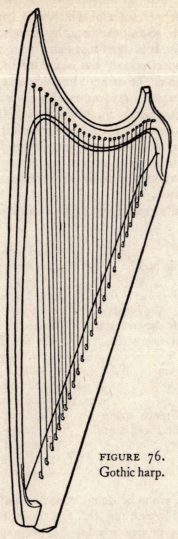

FIGURE 76.
Gothic harp.

Scandinavia, Finland and Esthonia. The southern boundary is marked by a lyre excavated from the tomb of an Alemannic warrior, which may belong in the middle of the first millennium A.D.; in Wales, lyres were played up until the eighteenth century, and in Finland and Esthonia they are still in popular use.

Lyres, like other medieval stringed instruments, varied in different parts of Europe and in different centuries. Moreover, the almost exclusive sources of information are art works, and especially illuminated manuscripts, some of which were copied and recopied from earlier models, so that the data they furnish are often impossible to place exactly. It is significant that among the many students of musical instruments nobody has succeeded in publishing an exhaustive monograph on the stringed instruments of the middle ages.

In order to attempt a classification of lyres we have to look for the following characteristics. First, whether the right hand plucks or bows the strings; second, the action of the left hand, which may be either deadening (or plucking) the strings from the back, or grasping the lyre over the top, or reaching through the strings from the back to stop them; and third, whether the sides of the instrument are parallel or waisted.

According to these characteristics, we can divide lyres into four main types:

1. Plucked strings
   deadened from the back
   parallel sides
   5–6 strings
     Recorded in Anglo-Saxon manuscripts of the seventh and eighth centuries
2. Plucked strings
   grasped over the top
   waisted outline
   4–6 strings
     Recorded in French manuscripts of the ninth and tenth centuries

3. Bowed strings
   stopped by reaching through the strings
   parallel sides
   3–6 strings
     Recorded in manuscripts of the twelfth century and still used today in Esthonia and Finland
4. Bowed strings
   grasped over the top
   waisted outline
   3–6 strings
     Recorded on art works from the eleventh to the thirteenth century

An intermediate group between the second and third type, which are bowed, stopped by reaching through the strings, and waisted in outline, with three to five strings, are pictured in some French manuscripts of the twelfth and thirteenth centuries.

Hence we obtain the following historical aspect:

Lyres were plucked before 1000 A.D.; after that they were bowed. (pl. XV a, b)

The strings were deadened or plucked from the back by the outspread left hand, in the antique manner, up to the eighth century. The instrument was grasped over the top until the thirteenth century; beginning in the twelfth century and continuing up to this day the left hand has stopped the strings by reaching through them.

The first group, plucked, deadened and polychordic, may have been related to the Greek and Roman lyre. This would be easy to explain, since the minstrels who, in the early centuries A.D., wandered from the shores of the Mediterranean to the northern parts of Europe must have kept the two places in frequent communication. In one miniature, in an Anglo-Saxon manuscript of the early eighth century (British Museum Vesp. A i), the player even uses a broad plectron as did the Greeks and Romans.

Yet, most northern lyres differ in one important point from the ancient lyre: arms, and usually the crossbar, are not added, but are cut from the same piece of wood as the body so that the instrument is all of one piece. Besides, the antique devices for securing tension are replaced by frontal or rear pegs.

The separate crossbar, made from a different piece of wood, is sometimes pictured in the early middle ages; some of the lyres, represented, for example, in the famous psalter of the ninth century in the library of the university at Utrecht, have the curved outline of the antique lyre and a separate crossbar. But this psalter can be traced back to fifth century sources, and it probably mingles antique and contemporary features. The Alemannic lyre from the middle of the first millennium that we referred to, has a crossbar braced between the tops of the two arms. But we do not know the origin of the early northern lyres and cannot determine whether their relation to the Greek and Roman lyres was direct or indirect.

It is tempting to compare the European lyres with the only type of lyre still known in Asia today, particularly as its players, Ostyaks and Voguls on the West Siberian river Ob, are Finnish peoples related to the European Finns who use a bowed lyre. The instrument has five strings and is diatonically tuned, generally in a major, occasionally in a minor, pentachord. Both hands play on the front of the instrument; the melody is plucked by the left hand while the right hand plays an accompaniment on two high strings. No plectron is used; but sometimes the nails of the right hand scratch across the strings as did the Greek plectron.

So the Siberian lyre is a vestigial instrument rather than a prototype. While the scratching nails are remainders of a lost plectron technique, the two hands playing on the front side of the lying instrument indicate complete departure from the lyre. The accompaniment on two high strings is characteristic of the classical manner of playing the Indian vina, and the modern names of the Siberian lyre go back to Sumerian and Babylonian words; Ostyakish *nares-yuh*, or 'musical wood,' has come from Sumerian *nar*, 'musician,' and Vogulish *sangkultap*, or 'playing,' from Babylonian *zaqqal*, or 'stringed instrument.' Both these indications point to a southerly direction.

The lyre referred to above, which is preserved in the Berlin Ethnographical Museum, excavated from the tomb of an Aleman-nic warrior who probably lived about 500 A.D., is difficult to classify. This instrument has a slender form resembling a bootjack, although tapering toward a rounded point at the lower end, a shallow resona-tor, a separate crossbar, a bridge and a stringholding cord that en-circles the lower end. These features are West Asiatic rather than North European; but, as we do not know how the Alemannic lyre was held and played, we cannot determine the origin of this single piece.

Two types of bowed lyres have survived the middle ages. The first one is the *crwth* of Wales, the name of which corresponded to Irish *crot* or *cruit*. In its last, eighteenth century form, it was in-fluenced by the violin. Body, arms and crossbar were one piece; the outline was nearly rectangular, but tapered slightly toward the top; the back was bulging. A narrow fingerboard was wedged longitudi-nally between the crossbar and the body, partitioning this space into two parts. Four strings were stretched over it and two drones were added on one side. They were tuned in octave pairs, *g-g′*, *c″-c′*, *d′-d″*, or in a similar way. The most peculiar, indeed unique, feature in this lyre was the bridge: it had two feet, a short one that rested on the soundboard and a longer one that passed through one of the small circular soundholes and rested on the back of the body, thus serving also as a soundpost transmitting the vibrations to the back.

The second type, still in existence today, is the bowed lyre of Finland and Esthonia, a roughly carved instrument with three or four horsehair strings stopped by the fingernails, on which Otto Andersson has written a copious monograph.

This archaic lyre is called *harpa* in Swedish, just as the instru-ment of the "Barbarians" in Venantius Fortunatus's poem. The identity of name corroborates our conclusion that in the early mid-dle ages the leading instrument in the northwest was the harp, and in Germanic countries the lyre.

THE MONOCHORD. The three centuries from 800 to 1100, from Charlemagne to the first crusades, developed an ever-growing tendency towards polyphony, which finally gave European music its distinctive feature. *Concentus concorditer dissonans,* as the Irishman Johannes Scotus Erigena called it about 867, or concordance and dissonance, demanded exactitude of pitch and intervals. Gregorian plain chant, folksong, jugglers' melodies—homophonic as they were—had not required any mathematically regulated scale. It did not matter whether their tones and semitones varied a little in size. But when two or three parts were combined in polyphonic harmony, music could not exist without rule and system. Consequently, the essential problem of medieval music became the standardization of a scale of tones and semitones. Medieval men felt no confidence in their senses; the musical ear proved to be unsufficiently reliable. Scholarly procedure did not involve investigation and experiment, but consisted in finding a classical authority and adopting his conclusions to contemporary problems. Certainly, from the Greek Aristoxenos the medieval musicians should have learned to respect a musical ear, but on account of his reliance on sensory impressions he was rejected by the monks; an anonymous writer, probably of the eleventh century, naïvely said: Boetius never would have agreed with Aristoxenos. . . .

Boetius, King Theodoric's unfortunate chancellor, was inevitably referred to in musical matters. Indeed, his five books, *De Musica,* written about 500 A.D., in which he undertook to make a summary and condensation of the intricate Greek and Roman theory, were the supreme authority to medieval musicians.

In this classic work the monks found the description of an implement consisting of a string running over a long and narrow, calibrated soundbox, which gave the various intervals based on mathematical calculation. Medieval treatises on this *monochord,* or 'one-string,' explaining the method of basing the scale upon mathematical divisions, do not occur earlier than the tenth century. The instrument, at that time, was a long box with a calibrated ruler and a string stretched above; a shiftable bridge shortened the string at the points indicated by letters of the alphabet. One of the tractates, Odo's *Dialogue* (tenth century), adds: "Since our singers did not know the right way, they were troubled all their lives. Man sings to the best of his ability; but the string is divided by scholars with such skill that it cannot lie."

The scholars, however, though agreeing with each other as to octaves, fifths and fourths, could not decide on a standard for thirds and seconds. Greek mathematical intricacy did not concern medieval

musicians, who were entirely indifferent to the Hellenic tonal gen-
ders or *géné* with the subtleties of their tiny intervals, while the
ancients had been interested in a multitude of melodic thirds rather
than in a standard third for harmonic consonance. As the monks
could not find a standard for the minor intervals in Greek theory,
they were forced to determine them by the ear rather than by calculation. This fact is clearly represented on an interesting miniature
in Codex latinus 2599 in the Munich State Library, which was made
in the thirteenth century in a German monastery, depicting a man
with a monochord and a harpist with his instrument. It would seem
probable that the harpist, having no fixed accordatura, would tune
the harp to the monochord. But he does not. As the left hand holds
the crossbar, he is neither playing nor tuning; the key is hanging
down. Instead, he is plucking a string in order that the monochordist
may calibrate his instrument accordingly. The monochordist shortens his string till the testing finger finds the desired spot; there the
knife, held in readiness, scratches a mark in the wood. This place is
at one sixteenth of the entire length; the demanded interval, therefore, must be the minor second of the ground-tone, the most uncertain of medieval intervals.

When did the testing instrument turn into a playing one? We do
not know exactly; but we know that the actual monochord with only
one string and without keys was used as a musical instrument before
1100. On a miniature in a codex of about 1100, at St. John's College
in Cambridge, the monochord is played among the instruments
accompanying King David, and in a psalter from the monastery at
Werden on Ruhr the monochord is played together with a bowed
lyre and a zither. One might think that in these illustrations the
musicians were tuning their instruments according to the standard
pitch of the monochord. But on the second of the above-mentioned
miniatures two dancing jugglers indicate that the scene represents
an actual performance. (pl. XV c)

The musical effectiveness of the monochord was certainly improved and facilitated by using more than one string. The history
of the polychordic monochord needs some correction. No evidence
of it can be found before the fourteenth century. The well-known
passage in the treatise of Theoger of Metz, in the eleventh century,
indicated that the monochord *antiquitus constabat octo chordis*,
that is, consisted of eight strings in antiquity; it does not refer to an
instrument of Theoger's time. In the fourteenth century the Englishman Simon Tunstede (d. 1369) proposed two strings, and Jo-

hannes de Muris four strings. Another monochord also mentioned by de Muris, with nineteen or more strings, cannot have been a monochord as described above; it must already have been a clavichord, which at first was also called a monochord.

THE HURDY-GURDY was a kind of mechanical fiddle in which, instead of a bow, a revolving wheel, concealed inside and turning by a handle, rubbed the strings, and a set of stopping rods were substituted for the touching fingers. We do not know its exact age. But the Abbot Odo de Cluny, who died in 942, devoted a study to this instrument entitled *Quomodo organistrum construatur*, 'How the hurdy-gurdy should be made'—in other words, how the rods were to be placed correctly in relation to the string to produce the eight notes *C D E F G A B♭ B♮*. Thus, we have evidence of the scholastic name and of the monastic use of this instrument in the beginning of the tenth century. It certainly was used to guide and support the conventuals.

Pictures of hurdy-gurdies do not occur earlier than the twelfth century. At that time the instrument was fiddle-shaped and about five or six feet long, and was held and played by two sitting men; one stopped the rods and one turned the crank. It had three strings, probably in unison, which were stopped and sounded simultaneously. The device that we call stopping rods were small pieces of wood which projected at one side of the instrument like keys. At the other end each rod had a small 'bit,' which, when the key was turned like a latch key, touched the strings, thus stopping them. This detail clearly shows the influence of the monochord.

This instrument, five to six feet in length, with three strings which had to be played all together, producing one open and eight stopped notes, would have been impossible to hold and play with the hands like a fiddle. For many centuries the method of playing the fiddle was in the first position only—that is, the fingers were pressed down to produce the first four diatonic notes next to the scroll and then passed over to the neighboring string to produce the following notes without shifting the hand along the fingerboard. Since the hurdy-gurdy had only one (double or triple) string for the melody, its player would have been forced to stop it beyond the reach of his hand in the second, third and fourth positions. Besides, the stopping positions were even wider apart in such a bass instrument than those to which players were accustomed. Therefore, the fingers were replaced by the artificial contrivance of rods. Bowing, too, would have been extremely difficult. The hurdy-gurdy lay horizontally across the players' laps; otherwise, it would have been impossible to handle the stopping rods. But in this position the bow could not conveniently be moved to and fro.

The fiddle-shaped body and the rear or frontal pegs on the earliest pictures of hurdy-gurdies seem to testify that the instrument was derived from the fiddle. On the other hand, there is no evidence that the fiddle or any other bowed instrument came to western Europe before the first hurdy-gurdy was constructed. The riddle is unanswered.

During the thirteenth century the hurdy-gurdy changed completely. Possibly it was the victorious career of the organ which expelled the clumsy hurdy-gurdy from church and school. Being then an ordinary instrument among other instruments, it became popular because it was so easy to work. It was made small enough to be portable and no longer required the second player. At the same time it had to get rid of the unwieldy rotating rods. They were replaced by devices with a tooth for each string that could be pushed in so that the teeth stopped the strings laterally, just as the early fiddles were stopped laterally. When the finger was removed, the stop fell back both by its own weight and by the elasticity of the string.

The hurdy-gurdy then was no longer called *organistrum*, but *symphonia* in Latin (or rather Greek), *chifonie* in French and *cinfonia* in Spanish.

In the fifteenth century the hurdy-gurdy lost its position in regular music. But as paintings of the early sixteenth century depict it in the hands of angels, it cannot have passed entirely into disrepute; it rather was considered archaic. By the seventeenth century it had become exclusively a folk instrument, called *leier* in German and *vièle* (*à roue*) in French.

As a folk instrument, the hurdy-gurdy began to resemble the bagpipe; besides the two unison strings for the melody enclosed in a box, it adopted two, three or four drones outside the box, all of which strings were reached by the wheel. Their classic tuning was *g'* for the melody strings and, for the drones, either *c g c'*, or *G g d'*. Sometimes sympathetic strings in *c' e' g'* or *a c' e' g'* were added. (pl. XIII a)

In modern times the name hurdy-gurdy has been given to the street organ, on account of the fact that this instrument, too, is played by turning a crank. The Germans also have given to the

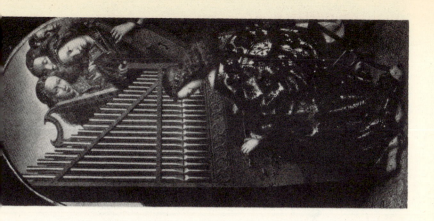

Van Eyck, altar in Ghent (c. 1425), with organ, harp and fiddle.

PLATE XVI.

street organ their name for hurdy-gurdy: they call it *Leierkasten* after *Drehleier*. Schubert's famous lied, *Der Leiermann*, refers to a stringed hurdy-gurdy, not to a modern street organ.

LUTES, in the early middle ages, were of two kinds. The first one was a *long lute*. It is chiefly depicted in the famous psalter in the library of the University at Utrecht in Holland, which was written and painted about 832 in Champagne, but which represents an earlier stage. Its painter gives the lute a slender neck two or three times as long as the body, a pegdisk with two or three rear pegs and six frets. The body, looked at from the front, has shoulders which are either straight as in a spade, or concave, or curving over in the shape of tulip petals.

The closest relative of this lute is the oval *dombrá* of the modern Kirghizes, which again is a close relative of the Russian triangular *balalaika*. The dombra has the long neck with six frets, the pegdisk with two rear pegs, and it also is played with the bare fingers.

Another manuscript of the ninth century, the Golden Psalter of St. Gall, depicts King David with a very similar instrument. The broad neck is three times as long as the body, the pegdisk (depicted without pegs) is circular, and there are three strings. Although on the famous picture of King David with his musicians the instrument is almost hidden behind the king's left thigh, its nearly circular body is clearly shown on another miniature of the same codex representing the setting down of the Ark of the Covenant. Both paintings depict a long, hooked plectron.

Instead of the long lute, the tenth century had an unusual *short lute*. A German psalter of that time, the Biblia folio 23 of the Stuttgart State Library, which Princeton University has published in a marvellous facsimile, has ten different pictures of the same curious stringed instrument. It is a heavy lute, obviously carved out of one piece of wood; the narrow body is rectilinear with parallel sides and sloping shoulders, a pear-shaped pegbox, rear pegs in a semicircular arrangement, a stringholder projecting from the lower end and an open bridge (i. e., a frame only). Generally, there are five pegs and five strings; once, five strings and seven pegs; once, five pegs and four strings; once, four pegs and four strings; and twice, six pegs and six strings. The entire length is approximately five feet. The player holds the instrument on edge in a horizontal position, leaning the lower end on his right forearm; sometimes a supporting stick bears the weight. The left hand shortens the string in the modern fashion with the finger tips; the right hand plucks them with a big, hooked plectron. In one case, the instrument is still larger and has six strings and pegs; the sitting player holds it upright. In all ten miniatures the Latin text calls this instrument by the (Biblical) term *cythara*.

The Dashkov Museum in Moscow displays a similar, though much smaller, Turkestanic instrument probably still in use today, with the same narrow body, the sloping shoulders, a circular pegbox and rear pegs; but it only has two strings.

The best source on early medieval lutes are miniatures in Spanish manuscripts of the tenth and eleventh centuries. There we distinguish two kinds of lutes, one of which is definitely a short lute while the other cannot yet be classified. The latter has a narrow, elliptic body and a distinct neck of equal length. The short lute is narrow, pear-shaped and tapers to the upper end without a distinct neck. Both are given the same unusual head, a short slender crosspiece, forming a T or an L with the neck, with three or four pegs sticking out of it. Such a contrivance does not, and cannot, exist in reality; it must be the embarrassed expedient of artists incapable of drawing in perspective a bent-back pegbox, or else the result of a painter copying paintings instead of the object itself. This is quite obvious in one of the miniatures, fol. 87ʳ of the *Beatus Commentarius in Apocalypsim*, Ashburnham Yates-Thompson Morgan 644.

Thus Spain, under south oriental influence, had a lute with lateral pegs, as we would expect, instead of the lute with rear pegs influenced by the northern Orient.

FIDDLES. The word *fiddle* is closely related to the Italian word *viola*. The derivation usually given by lexicographers to either word is from *vitulari*, a vulgar Latin word meaning 'to skip as a calf does,' the to-and-fro motion of the bow supposedly resembling the skipping of a calf. It is a foolish comparison. Moreover, the old Nordic word *fiðlu* did not at first designate a bowed instrument; the epics before 1200 call the player *fiðlu-slætti*, 'fiddle striker.' The accompanying verb *draga*, 'to draw,' [the bow] was not used earlier than 1200. And in the south of Europe the old meaning of a nonbowed instrument has been preserved; *viola* in Italian and the corresponding Spanish form, *vihuela*, have designated guitarlike instruments as well as fiddles.

The author has suggested a western Asiatic origin of the word: Ossetic *fandir* (related with *pandur*), Tawgy *féandir*, Jenissei dia-

lect of Samojedic, *fedilo*, Old Nordic *fiðlu*, Anglo-Saxon *fidele*.
Later on, the word lost its dental between the two vowels and became *fele* in Norwegian, *vièle* in Old French and *viola* in Italian.

The first evidence of a bowed instrument is found in Spanish
manuscripts of the tenth and eleventh centuries. In the tenth century
the instrument was tall, about a man's height, and the outline resembled a bottle with a cork; the lower end was cut square and the
head was a round disk which probably contained three rear pegs.
The bow was semicircular. Once more we find that similar instruments exist in the northern Near East; bottle-shaped fiddles are
still used in Georgia, Caucasus and the neighboring districts, as
panduri or *fandur*.

A second form of bowed instrument came from the Byzantine

FIGURE 77. Caucasian
fiddle.

Empire and is still known as *kamānġa rūmī*, or 'Byzantine fiddle,'
in the Near East, and as *lira* in Greece, Bulgaria and Jugoslavia. It
is pear-shaped with a shallow, slightly bulging body, without a distinct neck, ending in a disk or box with three rear pegs. The gut
strings are tuned to 4–1–5, the longer, middle one producing a permanent drone, while the outer strings are generally touched with
the fingernails instead of the finger tips, and are played in harmonics
only. Therefore, the instrument does not need a nut between the
neck and the pegdisk, as do modern instruments with a fingerboard.
(fig. 77, pl. XIII b)

The first evidence of the Byzantine lira is in a Persian literary
source of the ninth century. Byzantium may have exported it to
western Europe at that time, along with many other kinds of goods.

It appeared again in Spanish manuscripts of the tenth or eleventh century. The name itself was preserved a long time; in two German manuscripts of the twelfth century the instrument was entitled *lyra;* in Italy fiddles were called *lira da braccio* and *lira da gamba* as late as the seventeenth century, and in the same epoch England had a *lyro-viol;* the German derivative, *leier,* is still the name of the hurdy-gurdy.

The Byzantine lira, under the names of *fiddle, vièle, viola,* became the principal bowed instrument of Europe in the middle ages, and long after historical evidences of the origin of the European viola had been lost, the Flemish musician, Johannes Tinctoris, had a vague idea of the truth when he wrote in 1484: "The viol, as they say, was invented by the Greeks."

The first illustrations of European fiddles, dating from the tenth and eleventh centuries, show the number of strings varying between one, three, four and five. One string may have been an artist's abbreviation; three is still the number of the oriental lira. Five strings became the classic number of the medieval fiddle, and it is important to know that the Persian source of the ninth century mentioned above already had given five strings to the oriental lira.

The tuning of these five strings in the Occident is mentioned by only one author, Hieronymus de Moravia, a Dominican who lived at Paris about 1250 A.D. According to his statement, there were three different accordaturas by octaves, fifths and fourths:

$$d \; G \; g \; d' \; d'$$
$$d \; G \; g \; d' \; g'$$
$$G \; c \; g \; d'$$

The first *d* in the first accordatura, on one side of the fingerboard, was a drone which was plucked with the thumb, as shown on several paintings of the epoch. This accordatura is nothing else than the original three strings, two of which are duplicated, one in the octave, and one in unison. The oriental drone is kept but taken from the middle in order to make a droneless playing possible. In the following accordatura the fifth string is separated from the fourth. In the last one the drone is dropped and all four strings are on the way to a modern tuning; if either the lowest string were tuned to *F,* or the three upper strings raised by a tone each, this would be the exact tuning of a tenor violin in the seventeenth and eighteenth centuries.

Still, drones were preserved on many fiddles. Some art works of the fourteenth century clearly show a drone string stretched beside the fingerboard and plucked with the finger, and the next chapter will speak of the two plucked drones on the *lira da braccio* in the sixteenth and seventeenth centuries. (pls. XVII c, XIX a)

The shape of the fiddle underwent decisive alterations in the middle ages. The small bulging body, tapering to the pegbox, became larger; later, it was replaced by a flat oval box with side walls which at first were one piece with the back, but which were made separate by about 1300. The neck became distinct from the body to facilitate fingering. As early as the twelfth century fiddles were waisted to allow more freedom of bowing; still, we find unwaisted specimens up to the fifteenth century. There was no direct line of evolution; all forms were intermingled. (pls. XIV b, XVI a, XVII a, b, XVIII b)

At the beginning, the oriental fiddles certainly were played in oriental position with the fiddle pointing down like a cello and the bow held with the palm upward in 'supination,' as physiologists would say, the thumb being above and the fingers beneath. But in Europe, almost from the beginning, the position was changed; the fiddle was shouldered like a modern violin, and the bow was held in 'pronation' with the palm downward, the fingers above and the thumb below. If the fiddle was too large to allow shouldering, it was held across the chest. Only in a few instances was the oriental fashion preserved.

I think it is not possible to explain this rather sudden change by a different way of fingering. I rather believe that it was connected with a general contrast between doing work in the two civilizations. In a (German) paper on "Rotary Motion" H. T. Horwitz makes the following important statement: "In certain actions, as sawing, planing, filing, the power stroke, in Europe, is pushing, that is, away from the body, while the return stroke is pulling. The reverse is true in most regions of Asia; the power stroke is pulling, toward the body, and the returning stroke is pushing, away from the body." At first sight, the words "pushing" and "pulling" seem to contradict the experience found with bowing in Europe and Asia. But the essential point is: towards and away from the body, which, in the case of a working line parallel to the body, inversely involves pulling for the inward and pushing for the outward movement. So far, nothing certain can be said on the connection between bowing and general working motion, but the question is worth investigating.

Besides the fiddle, the middle ages had a second bowed instrument, the *rubebe* or *rebec*, derived from the Arabian *rabâb* and traceable to the eleventh century. The old oriental form was preserved till the fourteenth century. But a European variety was made at that time, as Juan de Ruiz, in his poem *El libro de buen amor*, mentions a second *rabé* beside the *rabé morisco* or Moorish rebec. The European rebec had the sickle-shaped pegbox of the mandola and a soundboard made either of wood, or of wood and metal. The

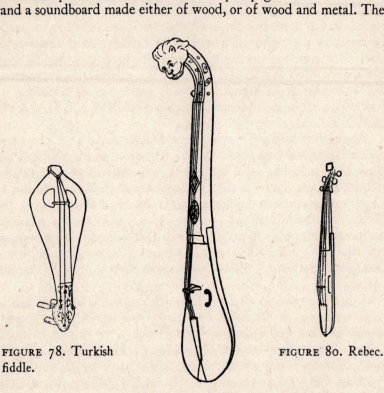

FIGURE 78. Turkish fiddle.

FIGURE 80. Rebec.

FIGURE 79. Kit.

upper part of the soundboard, with the fingerboard, was raised above the level of the lower part. (fig. 79)

The rebec gradually deteriorated until, in the seventeenth century, it was reduced to a small narrow *kit* or *pochette* to be carried in the flap pockets of dancing masters. (fig. 80)

IDIOPHONES. Except for the chime, medieval idiophones served practical purposes rather than musical ones. *Clappers* or 'bones' were carried by lepers as a warning; a wooden board, like the one used as *sēmantêrion* or 'sign giver' in oriental churches, was suspended on two chains from the castle gate to be struck with a hammer when a stranger wished to enter.

Jingles attached to the closing have already been mentioned. The epics of the later middle ages cannot describe often enough the *schellen* jingling on the hems or belts of their heroes. These jingles were seriously worn as amulets, not simply as the latest whim of fashion as has sometimes been asserted. Because they had the magic power of amulets, their use was customary in battle, tournament and duel. The delicate, tinkling sound of the jingle is admirably expressed by its names; Italian *bubbolo*, French *grelot* and German *schlotter* are derived from verbs which mean 'tremble.'

Bells were of two kinds—cup-shaped and shallow, struck from the outside with a hammer, and more or less conical and deep with a clapper.

The bell with a clapper was shaped like a beehive, similar to Chinese bells; it was small and thin with a weak, whimpering tone. The modern tulip form was introduced about 1200. A certain quantity of the early bells are preserved; the oldest dates seem to be 1098 from Drohndorf in Germany, 1106 from Pisa, 1202 from Fontenailles in Normandy. From that time on, the size increased continuously up to the fifteenth century.

The shallow, cup-shaped bell without a clapper, called *cymbalum* in medieval Latin, and *zimbel* in Middle High German, had a much thicker wall, like its Asiatic relatives; it consequently had a more musical tone; it could be played both loudly and softly and was able to be tuned to a definite pitch.

Differently tuned *cymbala*, therefore, were often united to form sets, as they were in East Asia and in India in two different forms— the suspended and the standing bell chime. The Chinese suspended chime has been discussed in the first Chinese chapter; the Malay Archipelago and India have sets of open porcelain or metal cups arranged on the floor. This kind of chime was also known in Greek antiquity. Suidas, a well-informed Byzantine lexicographer of the ninth century A.D., relates that a certain DIOCLES (but probably not, as Suidas thinks, the poet) was said to have invented a chime of metallic and earthenware bowls which were struck with a wooden stick. A Greek alchemistic tractate of that time (c. 800 A.D.) mentions a metal chime as well. Such an instrument is already depicted in a Greek manuscript of the fourth century A.D.

The most important illustrated book of that time, the so-called *Viennese Genesis*, shows the picture of Pharaoh's meal to the accompaniment of an oboe player and a woman beating with two slender sticks on four gray metal cups arranged in a row on a stand.

As early as the ninth century, perhaps earlier, western monks cast bell chimes tuned to the major key, composed of bronze calottes, which were suspended from a stand and struck with mallets. Such chimes were relatively often depicted in medieval miniatures; but most of the pictures mistakenly illustrate the words from Psalm 150, *Laudate eum cum cymbalis*, with chimes because of the identity of the names, which gives a false importance to chimes in the middle ages. That it had a sufficiently important place, however, is indicated by several medieval treatises relating the great difficulties of the monks in finding the necessary proportions appropriate to the various notes.

HORNS AND TRUMPETS. Deerhorns of warriors, hunters and watchmen, and even their bronze copies of all sizes, may have been made without foreign influence. The straight and hooked trumpets pictured in contemporaneous miniatures, on the contrary, must be considered a heritage from classic antiquity. Roman garrisons were spread over Europe for many centuries; they must have influenced the design of military instruments. So it is not surprising to meet the Roman lituus in the Bible of Charles the Bald, Codex latinus 1, of the Bibliothèque Nationale, Paris. (pl. XIV a)

A new form of horn traveled westward from Byzantium in the tenth century and was in use for about two hundred years; it was short and thick, carved from the tusk of an elephant and, therefore, called *oliphant*. It has close parallels in modern Africa, and, as Byzantium had no elephants, Africa may have been the home of these beautiful instruments. But, unlike the cross-blown horns in Africa, European oliphants were end-blown. Ivory horns were royal instruments in both places; they were the insignia of kings and chieftains in Africa and the exclusive and precious possession of princes and knights in Europe.

A straight metal trumpet without a bell, obviously a degenerated Roman tuba, is depicted as early as the eighth century in Irish miniatures. It became slimmer and longer, and acquired a rather large bell soon after 1000. This improvement was due to the influence of Arabian trumpets which the Christian armies met in Spain, in southern Italy and in the Holy Land. Not only the shape was influenced; poets of that time spoke of trumpets "blown in the manner of the heathens" or even of *cors sarrazinois*. While the Spaniards adopted the Arabic name *al nafîr* (pronounced *annafîr*), transforming it into *añafil*, the French called the new trumpet by a name of their own, *buisine*, which was derived from the Latin *buccĭna*.

In Europe the trumpets preserved the old social privileges they had had in the Orient. The right of maintaining trumpeters was restricted to the high nobility and, in later times, also to the cavalry (originally formed of noblemen), and to the Free Cities of the German Empire. Therefore, a standard with the seignorial arms was nearly always suspended from the trumpet.

The trumpet evolved in two sizes. In 1240, Emperor Frederick II, residing at Arezzo in Italy, had four silver *tubae* and one *tubecta* made to order. This diminutive word was probably a formal version of a vernacular term *trombetta*, which some decades later occurred in Dante's poem. While the smaller size became a *trumpet*, the larger size kept the old name *buisine* in French, or *busîne* in Middle High German. But the names of musical instruments are generally selected and transformed according to the sound of the instrument; those with a light sound will be given a name with a light, rather than a dark, vowel. The word *busîne*, applied to the large size only, was subjected to what philologists call an assimilation of the second vowel by the first one; the result was the term *busûne* at the end of the middle ages and its modern German form, *posaune*, after the sixteenth century.

BAGPIPES, a combination of a skin bag as a flexible windchest, supplied either by human breath or by bellows, and one or more reed pipes, were discussed in the Greek and Roman chapter and touched upon in the second Indian chapter. Their further history belongs in the medieval Occident, as bagpipes then were spread all over Europe, sometimes as folk instruments, sometimes as military instruments. As folk instruments, they still are used in all parts of Europe; as military instruments, they have survived in Scotland and Ireland.

The first medieval mention of bagpipes is in a spurious letter of St. Jerome to Dardanus, which can be traced back to the ninth century: "The *chorus* is a simple skin with two brazen pipes, and one [the player] inspires through the first one, and it emits the sound through the second." Is not the much contested name *chorus* simply derived from *chorion*, 'hide'?

Up to the fourteenth century bagpipes had no additional drone; but it was certainly overhasty to assert that the earlier bagpipes had no drone at all. A great number of types have preserved the oriental form of a double pipe, one serving as a melody pipe, and the other, lying directly alongside the first, as a drone. On some miniatures

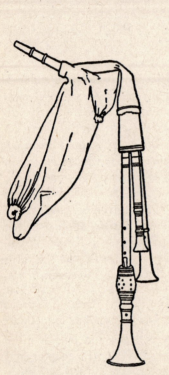

FIGURE 81. Italian bagpipe.

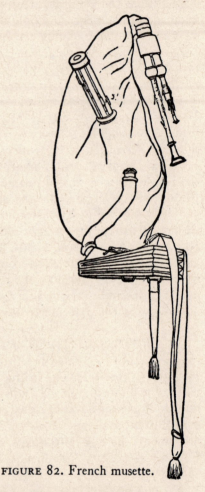

FIGURE 82. French musette.

the playing pipe is so wide that it probably represents a double pipe. This double pipe is carved on English reliefs of the fifteenth century and still exists in the Balkans and in France. In the Balkans this arrangement coexists with single reeds; both pipes are cylindrical clarinets. Nowhere else in western or Central Europe (as far as we know) are clarinets used without oboes in bagpipes. In Scotland,

Ireland, Brittany and some other parts of France, the drones are clarinets, but the melody pipes, or chanters, are oboes. In Italy and parts of France both chanters and drones are oboes. In East Europe bagpipes are entirely oriental; in Italy and in some parts of France they adopted the oboe principle of European shawms. So one distinguishes six stages of development:

1. clarinets only; two pipes, one chanter and one drone lying directly alongside one another.
2. oboes and clarinets; the same arrangement.
3. oboes and clarinets; the chanter separate from the drones.
4. oboes only; one drone lying alongside the chanter, the others being separate.
5. oboes only; the drones separate from the chanter.
6. oboes only; three drones separate from the chanter.

With a few exceptions, cataloguers in museums of instruments have confined themselves to describing the external qualities of bagpipes, as the number of drones and whether there is mouth action or a bellows to supply the wind; but they have not examined the most important feature, the nature of the reeds. Thus, it is not possible, with the present data, to present a complete typology of bagpipes. (fig. 81)

Separate drones first appear on miniatures of the thirteenth century. A possible reason was that occidental music required a drone an octave below the tonic, so that the bass pipe, twice as long as the melody pipe, for convenience was taken away and set in another opening of the bag. (pl. XIII c)

In the fifteenth century bagpipes were used in the service of courts and free cities; but they never lost their character as folk instruments, not even when the bucolic fashion at the French court had brought forth an aristocratic variety in the seventeenth century. This *musette* was composed of a bag wrapped in silk or velvet, a bellows, two slim cylindrical oboes lying close together and an oboe drone only six inches high, in which the bore ran up and down like that in a ranket, which could be shortened by small sliders. (fig. 82)

A smaller medieval variety of the bagpipes was the *bladder pipe,* a single or double clarinet with a bladder instead of a bag. It is mentioned and depicted from the thirteenth to the beginning of the seventeenth century and apparently came from the east; the earliest poetic source speaks of it in connection with the land Krain in the eastern Alps; a woodcut of 1529 represents a Turk with a bladder pipe; and the Chuvash in Russia have played the instrument up to modern times.

THE ORGAN. It is uncertain whether in antiquity all organs were hydraulic, as no general conclusion can be drawn from the etymology of the word *hydraulos*. How unreliable terms of this kind are, how seldom a change in the mechanism implied a change in the name, may be seen again and again. Johannes de Muris, a musician of the fourteenth century, owned a *mono*chord with *nineteen* strings, and in 1400, when there were surely no more water organs, the accounts of one of the German municipalities refer to the town organist as the *hydraulier*.

The first incontestable evidence of a purely pneumatic organ is on an obelisk erected in Byzantium before the death of Emperor Theodorus the Great (393); the small organ which it shows has its bellows compressed by the weight of two youths standing on the top. Byzantium was, in fact, the earliest center of organ building in the middle ages. From here organs and treatises on organ building were exported to western Europe, to Spain, France, Germany, England, and eastward to the Near East and even to China.

Organs were made in Spain as early as the middle of the fifth century; they are said to have been in common use in Spanish churches by that time. In England organs began to be built about 700. In 757, Emperor Constantine Copronymus the Sixth sent an organ with pipes of lead to King Pippin the Short who had it erected at St. Cornelius's in Compiègne; in 812, Byzantine envoys presented an organ to Charlemagne at Aix-la-Chapelle. The monk Notker, who wrote the life of Charlemagne, related that, when the Greek craftsmen arrived to assemble the organ, the Frankish workmen stood about and watched so carefully that afterwards they were able to build organs themselves. A few years after 870, when Pope John VIII wanted an organ and an accomplished organist, he did not send to Byzantium, but to the Bishopric Freising in Bavaria.

The early history of the organ culminated in the large organ erected in 980 in the monastery at Winchester in England; it had twenty-six bellows and two keyboards (probably on opposite sides and requiring two players as in the organ pictured in the Utrecht Psalter); each of them consisted of twenty sliders, and each slider when it was pulled out connected ten pipes at once. Its noise, a contemporary poem asserts, was so great that everyone stopped with "his hand his gaping ears, being in no wise able to draw near and bear the sound."

The powerful sound of the organ was emphasized by many chroniclers. In the twelfth century Ælred, abbot of Rievaulx, declaims against the organ: "Why are there so many organs and chimes in church? To what purpose, pray, that awful roar of the bellows, which is more like the rumble of a thunderstorm than the sweetness of the voice?" And he describes the poor "crowd inside which trembling and thunderstruck wonders" at the overwhelming noise. The sound must indeed have been powerful in a time used to the meager music of a tabor and pipe or some few stringed instruments. The action of the primitive bellows, without any contrivances for stabilizing the pressure, doubtless resulted in sudden starts and fadings. Moreover, larger organs as in Winchester, had several pipes on the same key, either in unison or in fifths, octaves, twelfths and double octaves, which sounded at once; no stop existed to disconnect some of them and to change volume or timbre.

Still, contemporary authors claimed that the organ could equal (*coaequabat*) the roar of thunder, the loquacity of the lyre and the sweetness of the cymbala. But it is a mistake to suppose that the player relied on stops to produce such differences; playing alternately the lower, the middle and the higher register of the keyboard would have sufficed to suggest such a figure of speech, exaggerated in the style of medieval poetry. Still, there was a factor likely to increase the different, indeed contrasting, effect of high and low; in medieval organs the width of the pipes did not change in proportion with their length, as in modern organs. Therefore the higher pipes, relatively too thick, had a comparatively soft timbre.

Instead of pressure keys, the early organ had sliders, *linguae*—that is, horizontal strips of wood, the front part of which projected, while their rear parts interrupted the passage of the wind. When a strip was pulled out, the wind was free to enter the corresponding pipes. This arrangement is described as late as the twelfth century in Theophilus's tractate on mechanics, called *Schedula diversarum artium*. The musical means were consequently limited; only a few organs had sliders with an automatic return to the original position to simplify manipulation.

The modern arrangement dates from the thirteenth century. Levers supplanted the sliders; pressed down, they opened the valves or *pallets* controlling the pipes. At first, the levers themselves were inside; they were worked by buttons pushed down on them from on top, resembling the keyboard of a typewriter. But as early as the thirteenth century some organs were already given the present arrangement with the levers projecting and directly worked by the fingers. Organs then had a range of three octaves. Though they did not at first have all semitones, the organ was the first instrument to become entirely chromatic. A contemporaneous source expressly said the *musica ficta*—that is, melodies using semitones other than the two natural half-tones of the diatonic scale—was specially appropriate to the organ. At the beginning, diatonic and chromatic keys were arranged in one or two rows without any distinguishing color of the keys; but paintings of the fourteenth century already show white and black keys in the modern arrangement. The medieval history of the instrument had come to an end, and already Guillaume de Machault could call the organ *de tous les instruments le roi.* (pl. XVI b)

INSTRUMENTS INTRODUCED IN THE ELEVENTH AND TWELFTH CENTURIES

THE PORTATIVE ORGAN. Besides the large church organs, the middle ages had a small organ for secular purposes, which generally was suspended from the player's neck with the keyboard running outwards and easily available to the right hand, while the left hand worked the triangular feeder bellows on the back of the organ. This position of the keyboard at right angles to the player involved running up and down the scale with two fingers only, as the use of the whole hand would have necessitated a nearly impossible position of the arm. Dr. Hans Hickmann, author of a monograph on the portative organ, was the first to see that this custom was the explanation for the otherwise incomprehensible fact that up to the eighteenth century players of keyboard instruments still performed their scales with two fingers only, although the position of the keyboard no longer required it.

Another important conclusion of Hickmann is that the scales of earlier portatives were not regularly diatonic or chromatic, but selective, omitting those notes which were unusual in the kind of music played on the instrument.

Although in a portative organ the pipes are generally arranged in rows resembling what in larger organs are the stops—that is, sets of pipes differing in octave or timbre—Hickmann discovered that no portative had stops, all the pipes belonging in one set, and that the arrangement in rows was merely a space-saving device. There were as many keys as pipes, and each key played only one pipe. This is confirmed by a ground plan in Henry Arnault's manuscript; there the following notes are in the circles marking the diameters of the pipes:

$$c\ d\ e\ f\sharp\ g\sharp\ a\sharp\ \dots$$
$$b\ c\sharp\ d\sharp\ f\ g\ a\ \dots$$

Even if the portative had some control near the keyboard, a lever or a slide, it served to prolong certain notes as drones and not to work stops.

The first portative organs are recorded in the twelfth century; the instrument reached its greatest use in the fifteenth, and disappeared in the sixteenth century. (pls. XVI a, XVIII b)

FLUTES. The middle ages had two kinds of flutes; a French poet of the fourteenth century, Guillaume de Machault, called them *flaustes traversaines* and *flaustes dont droit joues quand tu flaustes*, "cross flutes and flutes that you play straight when you pipe." The straight flute, usually called *flageol* in Old French, was certainly a beaked flute or recorder. Sometimes they were used in pairs; a text of the thirteenth century, *Li contes des hiraus*, mentions *flajos doubliers*, and in the fourteenth century they are depicted on Italian paintings in the divergent position of the ancient aulos.

Transverse flutes came from Asia through Byzantium, rather than from Etruria or Rome. They were mentioned in a Greek treatise as *plágioi* about 800 A.D. and depicted in Greek miniatures of the tenth and eleventh centuries. Their first occidental evidence is a miniature in the *Hortus Deliciarum*, the famous encyclopedia that the Alsatian abbess Herrad von Landsberg wrote at the end of the twelfth century. In this miniature the instrument is given the Middle High German name *swegel*. In the thirteenth century a *flauste traversaine* is mentioned in France.

The path of the cross flute westward from the Byzantine Empire is marked by a cross flute player on a Hungarian aquamanile of about 1100 in the National Museum at Budapest; moreover, it is marked up to this day by a particular predilection for this instrument in the folk music of Rumania, Jugoslavia, Hungary, Bohemia, Austria and Switzerland.

In the later middle ages Germany became a new center, from which it spread over the world. All European countries associated it with Germany: it was called *German flute* in English, and *flauta alemana* in Spanish. Nevertheless, in the sixteenth century the Frenchman Vincent Carloix wrote that it was a mistake to call the transverse flute a *flauste d'Allemand;* for, the French played it better and in a more musical way than any other nation, and flute quartets, which were customary in France, were unknown in Germany.

Indeed, the cross flute was mainly a military instrument in Germany. It had already been coupled with the cylindrical drum in the century after the Hortus Deliciarum, and more and more it had become a martial instrument. From the end of the crusades to the twentieth century, *fife and drum* were the leading infantry instruments.

REED PIPES are first recorded in the French literature of the twelfth century. But the terms used for them are confused. Both French *chalemele* and German *rôrphîfe* are derived from words meaning 'reed' (Latin *calamus* and German *rôr*). Consequently, these terms might be used not only to designate instruments having a reed as a mouthpiece, such as clarinets and oboes, but also flutes made of reed, and particularly pan-pipes; several medieval French poets speak of *chalemeles* with seven pipes (*tuyaux*).

Reed pipes in the strict sense of the word seem to have been oboes; no source, pictorial or literary, refers to a clarinet. Comparing the pictorial sources, we are aware of two different types of oboes. One of them is rather wide and must have had a loud, broad tone similar to that of certain folk oboes of southern Italy (*piffero*) and Spain (*caramillo*). The other oboe, represented on art works of the Mediterranean border in the twelfth and thirteenth centuries, is slim and has a pear-shaped bell; its tone must have been more delicate. The contrast between the two kinds of oboes is mirrored in the poetry of that time. Gui de Bourgogne's verse: "*Olifans, grelles et chalemiaux et busines bruiants*" couples the oboes with "noisy" horns and trumpets, and certainly refers to the loud oboe. Albrecht von Halberstadt (c. 1200) speaks of the soft oboe when he calls it "sweet" (*sûze*). It seems that the latter names, *bombarde* and *doucine* (Italian *dulzaina*), express the same contrast of timbres and instruments. (pl. XIII c)

DRUMS were not used in the earlier middle ages, strange as it may seem. About 600 A.D., St. Isidorus of Sevilla had described, in his encyclopedic *Etymologiae*, a drum called *symphonia*, "a hol-

Italian master, youth with lira da braccio in the Kunsthistorische Museum, Vienna (early 16th century).

Ambrogio de' Predis, angel with fiddle in the National Gallery, London (late 15th century).

Melozzo da Forlì, angel with fiddle in St. Peter's in Rome (c. 1480).

PLATE XVII.

low wood, covered with skin on either end, that the musicians strike with sticks from both sides. And there is a *suavissimus cantus* produced by the *concordia gravis et acuti.*" But such an oriental instrument is nowhere else described or depicted.

There is a single evidence of a barrel drum in Europe. An English miniature of the twelfth century depicts a juggler disguised as a bear and striking with his two hands the two skins of a bulging barrel drum which is horizontally suspended from his neck. No such drum was familiar at that time in Europe; it certainly was meant to increase the strange, exotic effect of the scene.

But there are evidences of drums in regular use from the twelfth century on. The usual drum was beaten by a man who played a horn or a flute simultaneously—*tabor and pipe.* It was light and small and buckled on the chest or the left arm. The painters generally represented the circular skin only, often with a snare, but unfortunately they did not indicate the body of the drum. At least we can see that it was rather shallow; its Middle High German name *sumber* meant a grain measure. Still, there is also evidence of deep cylindrical drums with two skins, in which the height nearly equaled the diameter. The skin was struck with a stick, the form of which sometimes was rather curious. In the English St. Alban's Psalter of the twelfth century, in Hildesheim, it was depicted as an ordinary stick from the end of which a needle, ending in a small bulb, projected at right angles so that a twisting motion of the wrist sufficed to strike the drum. Since such drums were used merely as a time-beating accompaniment they required no power. About the fourteenth century they became independent and larger, and were struck with heavier sticks.

At the beginning of the thirteenth century we first hear of oriental, jingling, frame drums, which were chiefly used by girls, as in the Near East. Their most frequent names were *temple* in Provençal, *timbre* in French, and *timbrel* in English; the Germans called it *rotumbes.* In modern times it is known as *cembalo* in Italian, and *tambourin* or *tambour de basque* in French. These three latter terms are incorrect or misleading and should be avoided. The instrument is not Basquish, a *tambourin* is correctly a long Provençal cylinder drum with one stick, and the word *cembalo* connotes a nonexistent relation to *clavicembalo.*

Altogether the role of drums was insignificant in the middle ages. Later, however, it succeeded in securing a place as a soldier's instrument. The crusades had altered the military organization of European countries; the knight with his train was replaced by armies of mercenaries. The new infantry, like oriental soldiers, needed inspiring music and took possession of the cross fife and the drum. Here, time beating was more important than melody, and loudness was an urgent need. German epics of the fourteenth century speak of the *grosse hersumper*—that is, large army drums. This evolution finally led to the enormous drums of the Swiss lansquenets of the fifteenth and sixteenth centuries who, according to the Italian Paulus Jovius (1483-1553), kept pace with the beating of the drums (*justis passibus ad tympanorum pulsum*).

Those interested in the beats and rolls of the large soldiers' drums may consult Thoinot Arbeau's *Orchésographie*, printed in Paris in 1588, and available both in a French and an English modern edition.

THE TRUMSCHEIT was a curious stringed instrument, the origin and history of which are quite obscure. A French sculpture of the twelfth century shows it for the first time. There, the three-sided body is approximately four feet long; it is composed of three slender boards which taper toward the rhombic pegdisk. The single string runs the whole length of the instrument and is tightened by a rear peg; it is stopped near the upper end with the fingers of the left hand, while the right hand is placed on the string and is not holding a bow. A French painting of the fourteenth century offers the same picture but does not clearly show whether there are one or two strings.

The instrument preserved its outer appearance in the fifteenth century, but the manner of playing changed. It was held in an oblique position, either with the lower end resting on the ground or else turned up the other way with the lower end in the air. A second string was added, either the same length or only half the length. The strings were not stopped, but lightly touched to produce harmonic notes; a short bow played *above* the touching fingers near the upper end. (pl. XVIII a, fig. 83)

The sixteenth century replaced the disk with rear pegs by a box with lateral pegs.

The instrument had by that time acquired its most peculiar feature, an unsymmetrical bridge with two dissimilar legs. One was a short, vertical supporting leg, leading the vibrations to the soundboard in the usual way, and the other was a free leg which ran diagonally sideways to the soundboard, drumming on it and producing an actual wood-on-wood sound. The only name the instru-

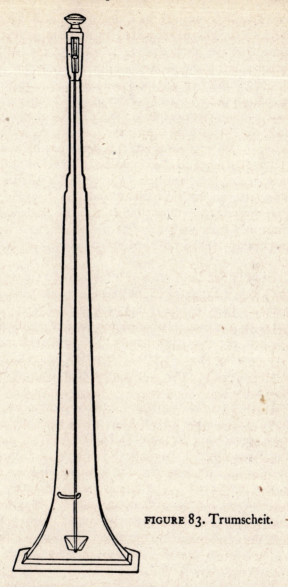

FIGURE 83. Trumscheit.

ment had before 1600, German *trumscheit*, or 'drum log,' was due
to this drumming effect.

The drumming bridge also gave the strings a penetrating, almost
brassy timbre, which made the instrument all the more reminiscent
of a trumpet, as the scale of the trumscheit was composed of the same

harmonics that formed the scale of a trumpet. Hence, a new group of names began to be applied to it after 1600, such as *trumpet marine*, comparing the instrument to a trumpet. The attribute, *marine*, is responsible for the most whimsical suggestions. One of them says that the trumscheit was used as a signal instrument at sea; it would be difficult to find a less appropriate object for this purpose. Another explanation makes *mariana*, 'Mary's,' out of *marina* and hints that nuns used the trumscheit in the convents to replace the masculine trumpet. No convincing interpretation has been suggested.

The instrument had no importance for art music in modern times; as early as 1511, Sebastian Virdung, in his *Musica getutscht*, called it *onnütz*, 'useless.' We should mention, however, a kind of after-growth in France during the eighteenth century. At that time the trumpet marine was given a set of sympathetic strings inside the box, and in this case was called *trompette marine organisée*.

ZITHERS. Both types of Near Eastern zithers came to Europe, the plucked Egyptian *qānūn* and the struck Asiatic dulcimer *santir*. This word was derived from Greek *psalterion*, as was also the medieval term *psaltery*; but the term 'psaltery' was usually given to the plucked, not the struck, zither. The first evidence of a psaltery is on a relief of the church, Santiago de Compostela, in northwestern Spain, carved in 1184; but representations are rare before the fourteenth century.

It is not easy to distinguish between plucked psalteries and struck dulcimers on early reliefs. After 1300, however, dulcimers seem to have prevailed in the north, and psalteries in the south. The German Praetorius defined the psaltery as a kind of dulcimer plucked with the fingers, indicating that the dulcimer, but not the psaltery, was known in Germany. The Italians, on the contrary, called the dulcimer *salterio tedesco*, a 'German psaltery'; they were familiar with the psaltery, but not with the dulcimer. Probably the plucked psaltery was introduced through South Europe, and the struck dulcimer via Byzantium through East Europe, which would account for their distribution. (pl. XVIII a)

Usually these instruments had the general shape of a symmetric trapezoid, with the nonparallel sides either straight or curved inward. But in many cases they were *half-zithers* (Spanish *medio caño*, French *micanon*, etc.), so called because their shape was one half a symmetric trapezoid, thus forming a rectangular trapezoid. If the slanting side was curved, the half-zither had the wing form that the harpsichord and the grand piano have preserved. Sometimes the wing form was indicated by the French word *ele:* the much-discussed term, in its latinized form *ala*, is unequivocally defined by Paulirinus (c. 1460) as either a triangular instrument (*ala integra*) or a semitriangular instrument (*media ala*) with upward running wire strings that are plucked with a plectron (*penna*). Not many players, he says, know how to play the entire ala; more musicians play the media. As half a triangle is a triangle as well, the triangular shape that Paulirinus attributes to the ala must not be taken too literally.

The stringing of these instruments never had fixed rules. One modern method for the dulcimer indicates wire strings stretched over two bridges, from two to four in unison for each of the thirty-two notes. These sets are arranged in three rows, the first comprising the notes from g to b' diatonically, the second from g' to c^3 diatonically, the third from d^2 to g^3, this latter series being diatonic as well, but having $f\sharp'$ and $f\sharp''$ instead of the natural notes.

The most evolved form, sometimes provided with a damper pedal, is the Hungarian *cimbalom*. Some of its strings are divided into three parts by two bridges, some into two parts by one bridge, some are undivided. The lower register, chromatic from D or E to B, has three strings to each note; the middle register, from c to f, has four strings to each note; the high register, from f to e^3, has five strings to each note.

The oriental lute, *'ūd*, was brought to Europe at about the same time as the zithers. But we postpone its discussion till the next chapter, as it reached the climax of its development only between 1400 and 1600.

FOURTH PART

The Modern Occident

15. *The Renaissance*
(*1400-1600*)

THE most outstanding development in the history of music between 1400 and 1600 is the emancipation of instrumental from vocal music. Before 1400, players generally accompanied singing; after that time they slowly began to make themselves independent, at first by taking over dancing songs and adapting them to the particular technique of their instruments. Gradually, instruments took possession of all kinds of vocal forms, not restricting themselves to dance music; motets and madrigals were performed on instruments, and as late as the seventeenth century printed collections of pieces bore the subtitle, "to be sung or played." Along with the vocal style of these amphibious compositions, however, styles characteristic of certain instruments began to be developed. Keyboard instruments had evolved into polyphonic and chord instruments as early as the fourteenth century, and the lutes may have followed in the fifteenth century. Organists and lutanists using music written in several parts, each intended to be performed by an individual musician, adapted it to the special conditions of their hands and instruments and developed a style of their own; indeed, they invented particular *tablatures* to replace the common notation. Finally, composers created exclusively instrumental forms of composition entirely different from those used for voices. In the sixteenth century melodic instruments followed in the path of the polyphonic instruments. In 1532 the German Hans Gerle wrote a method for the fiddles, in 1535 the Italian Sylvestro di

Ganassi published a method for the flute, and in 1553 the Spaniard Diego Ortiz for the gamba, each of them with the aim of fostering a true instrumental style.

The final stage in the emancipation of instrumental music began in the second half of the sixteenth century when orchestration was first considered. Chroniclers began to enumerate in detail which instruments were used in playing certain compositions at certain occasions. The most minute indications are given in Massimo Trojano's account of the wedding ceremonies when Duke William V of Bavaria married Princess Renate of Lorraine in 1568. There we learn that, at table, the court orchestra performed a six part motet of Orlando di Lasso with five cornets and two trombones; that, during the seventh course, twelve musicians formed three groups—one of four gamba players, the second of four recorders, the third of a bassoon, a cross flute, a pipe and a cornet; and many other combinations. This testifies to an increasing interest in color, that is, the contrast and blend of timbres, as a vital part of music. Orchestration, which at first was at the discretion of the performers, at last became important enough to be indicated by the composer; about 1600, Giovanni Gabrieli in Venice first fixed the instrument required for each part in writing his scores.

The new delight in timbre acted as a strong stimulus in making instruments. Never before and never since has the palette of musical hues been as rich as in the sixteenth century; no potentiality was neglected. To confine ourselves to one example: double reed instruments, today represented by the two families of oboes and bassoons, existed in ten complete families essentially differentiated by the diameters and forms of their bores.

The new wealth of musical instruments and their increasing importance, which began to be obvious about 1400, resulted in the sudden emergence of popular treatises on the subject at the beginning of the sixteenth century.

In 1511 a German priest, Sebastian Virdung, published a small book entitled *Mvsica getutscht vnd außgezogē*, or 'Music Germanized and Abstracted.' It is written as a dialogue, the didactic form that the Renaissance had taken over from antiquity. A fictitious friend, Andreas Silvanus, is the pupil; ignorant but eager, he supplies the cues for Virdung's lecture with his questions. The cold and arid tone of medieval treatises is avoided, and also Latin is replaced by the native idiom. Besides, the book speaks to the eyes; it is illustrated by numerous woodcuts. Many of them show instruments which do not belong to 'regular music,' but rather to the so-called *musica irregularis,* such as carnival implements, children's toys, hunters' horns, jaws' harp, cow bell and scraped pot. Although Virdung protests against being expected to speak of so inartistic a branch of his subject, he mentions all these popular and folkloristic instruments. His book is popular in form though scientific in approach. He begins by a classification, and in this point he is remarkably modern. His system comprises three classes: instruments blown by human or artificial wind; stringed instruments; and instead of the incorrect and unsatisfactory term "percussion" instruments, those *die vō de metallē oder ander clingendē materien werden gemacht.* Four hundred years later, English musicologists introduced the term *sonorous substances,* a translation of Victor-Charles Mahillon's *instruments autophones* and my own *idiophones,* unconsciously adopting Virdung's *clingende materien.*

The reader may be surprised to find that Virdung still refers to Boethius. Had not the time gone by when the last musicologist of antiquity was still the incontestable authority on music? Virdung speaks of Boethius, indeed, and he speaks of Guido of Arezzo, of *genus diatonicum* and *genus chromaticum,* of *diatessaron* and *quadrilatera;* but this is just a bow to classic erudition. On Virdung's pages the various *genera,* the *semitonia,* the *gsolreut* are illustrated by clear woodcuts of keyboards with white and black keys or of the fretted fingerboards of lutes. And Virdung does not forget that the strings of a lute must be carefully chosen before they produce the required *tonos* and *semitonia.* So he proposes the test well known by all violinists: stretch the string in your hand and pluck it with the thumb; the more you see the vibration of the string, the less good it is. A charming little woodcut illustrates his words. A new epoch begins with the matter-of-fact spirit of Virdung's practicality, a departure that cannot be too much admired.

It was significant of the uncertainty of those times that, in 1536, Othmar Nachtigall, who called himself Luscinius, took a step backward and translated Virdung's German book into Latin as *Musurgia, seu praxis musicae.*

In the same year, 1511, in which Virdung had printed his work, Arnold Schlick, the court organist at Heidelberg, published a small *Spiegel der Orgelmacher uñ Organisten,* or 'Mirror of Organ Makers and Players,' the first printed monograph on the construction of a special instrument.

Seventeen years after Virdung's and Schlick's treatises, another book on musical instruments was published by the famous Georg Rhaw, printer at Wittenberg. Its author was Martin Sore (1486–1556), a cantor at Magdeburg in Saxony, who, in the scholarly style of the time, called himself *Martin Agricola*. The book came out as *Musica instrumentalis deudsch*; the full title, translated into English, is: "*Musica instrumentalis* in German, which comprises a method of learning to play on various wind instruments based on the art of singing, and how to play organs, harps, lutes, viols, and all instruments and strings according to the correct tablature." The first edition was dated 1528, the fifth and last one came out in 1545.

Agricola's book is based on Virdung's treatise, but it is written in doggerel verse in order to be more easily memorized. For Agricola's purpose is by no means scientific research; his object is merely educational. He says in the preface: "It must be, and in fact it is, highly necessary that the youths who begin to learn, be not overwhelmed and deterred with many superfluous words and rules, but rather taught by short and plain information and enticed and allured to study."

A few years after Agricola's last edition, a Franciscan friar from Andalusia, Juan Bermudo, published several editions of a book entitled *La declaración de instrumentos* (Ossuna 1549, Ossuna 1555, Granada 1555). But in spite of so promising a title, this 'explanation' is a general theory of music rather than a treatise on instruments.

Agricola had no successor before 1618, when Praetorius published his fundamental work. At first sight we have the impression of a step backward, away from educational purposes, when we see the frontispiece of the new book and read the scholarly title, *Syntagmatis Musici Michaelis Praetorii C. Tomus Secundus de Organographia*. But this, too, was nothing more than a bow to humanistic education. The few Latin words precede a long subtitle in German which promises the nomenclature, intonation and quality of all ancient, modern, barbarian, foreign, rustic, domestic, unknown and known instruments including their correct pictures, and so on. The last sentence of the elaborate title asserts that the book will be useful and necessary to organists, musicians and instrument makers, as well as to all those loving the Muses, and also entertaining, and pleasing to philosophers, philologists and historians. Though it is not certain whether this second promise has been fulfilled, the scientific and artistic part of the book is indeed more useful than any former book written on musical instruments.

Its author was Michel Schulz or, in scholarly Latin, Michael

Praetorius (1571–1621) from Creuzburg (hence *C.*), who had studied in Venice with Giovanni Gabrieli. He was *Kapellmeister* to the Brunswick court at Wolfenbüttel and one of the most fertile German composers at the beginning of the seventeenth century. The Organographia is the second of three volumes that treat exhaustively of all branches of music: volume I, the theory; volume II, the instruments; volume III, the practice.

The attitude of Praetorius is entirely different from that of Virdung and Agricola. In the preface he apologizes for having written this book in popularized form: please, do not believe that I wish to make music too vulgar and to put it at the disposal of bunglers and duffers by employing our German mother tongue. After all, music is no Rosicrucian mystery; most organ and instrument makers and players do not understand Latin, and it would be difficult to translate the innumerable technical terms into Latin. Praetorius wrote for musicians and makers, not for beginners.

Two parts, therefore, are particularly new and interesting. The first is a *tabella universalis,* a table showing the compass of all wind and stringed instruments. The second is a *Theatrum Instrumentorum seu Sciagraphia,* a woodcut supplement published two years later in 1620. In this the instruments in all their sizes and kinds are depicted on an exact scale; each page has a reduced scale in Brunswick feet, which can be compared with a foot in actual size cut on the first page.

Comprehensive and reliable, the Syntagma is the standard reference book on sixteenth century instruments.

The last treatise to be mentioned is the section on instruments in the gigantic *Harmonie Universelle* published in 1636 and 1637 by Father Marin Mersenne, a friend of the philosopher Descartes. The title is French and so is the text. But this does not mean vulgarization. "I know," he writes in his preface, "that you do not follow the opinion of some ancient who said that science is profaned when reduced to practice and use. . . ." *Harmonie Universelle* is the work of a scientist, a mathematician, a physicist. There are no chapters, but *propositions* and *corollaires,* just as in mathematical treatises. The chief concern is the construction of instruments rather than their outer shape. Detailed tables indicate the gauges of wire and gut strings; the exact thickness of a good soundboard and the best position of its ribs are discussed; and all items are thoroughly illustrated by excellent engravings and woodcuts. But this book, as well as its Latin counterpart, *Harmonicorum libri* (1635 and 1636), correctly belongs in a later chapter, both in its date and in its attitude.

From these books one gathers an idea of the quantity and importance of musical instruments in the sixteenth century. Still, this picture is incomplete. The Renaissance, in its natural disposition to visual enjoyment, took a fancy to instruments as objects in themselves. A viol was more than an acoustical machine to the men of that epoch. Without hearing its sound they were delighted by the elegance of its curves, by the harmony of its proportions, by the bright transparence of its varnish; they would have been disgusted to listen to a voice of perfect beauty produced by an ugly piece of wood. Sabba da Castiglione was a true man of his time when, writing on instruments that "much delight the ears and animate the spirits," he added, "They also greatly please the eye." This idea is crystallized in a motto painted on one of the oldest preserved harpsichords, made in 1560 by Vitus de Trasuntinis: *Rendo lieti in vn tempo gli occhi el core*, "I give pleasure at once to the eyes and to the heart."

At that time the violin and most other instruments were given their classical shapes. Moreover, many instruments of that time were carefully joined, turned, carved and inlaid; precious material was used—exotic woods, ivory, tortoise shell, nacre, gems; harpsichords and spinets were decorated by first-rate painters. Marvelous specimens are preserved in the Victoria and Albert Museum in London and in the Kunsthistorische Museum, Vienna.

Instruments were again and again depicted in art works by painters and sculptors, and when Albrecht Dürer wrote his treatise on perspective, he chose a lute as the object of his demonstration. The beauty of musical instruments has never been so much appreciated before or since.

For the same reason instruments were collected by art lovers and preserved in special museums. Count Raymond Fugger in Augsburg, for example, had, in 1566, a *musiccammer* with about four hundred costly instruments, among which there were more than a hundred and forty lutes and a hundred and eleven flutes.

Inventories of such collections, or of the instruments owned for practical purposes by court orchestras, are highly significant. Dead and dusty as such enumerations might appear, they give us more information than any treatise.

King Henry VIII of England left, in 1547, a collection of three hundred and eighty-one instruments:

78 cross flutes	5 bagpipes
77 recorders	32 virginals
30 shawms	26 lutes
28 organs	25 viols
25 cromornes	21 guitars
21 horns	2 clavichords
5 cornets	

3 combinations of organ and virginal.

This makes a total of 272 wind instruments (72%) and 109 stringed instruments (28%).

In 1582 the orchestra of the Berlin court possessed:

24 flutes	3 trombones
17 reed pipes	7 viols
9 cornets	4 virginals
7 organs	1 harp

or sixty wind instruments (85%) and twelve stringed instruments (15%).

The famous collection of the Dukes of Tyrol at the castle of Ambras near Innsbruck, preserved to this day and recently taken to Vienna to form the nucleus of the musical gallery in the Kunsthistorische Museum, comprised more than one hundred and eighty-six wind instruments (79%) and only fifty stringed instruments (21%).

We see that, in contrast to the following centuries, there was a strong prevalence of wind instruments. We also see that there was a surprising number of seemingly identical instruments. Musical instruments between 1400 and 1600 were made in families or *consorts*. They were often played in homogeneous groups, all parts of a composition being performed by instruments of the same family, gambas or trombones or recorders. This involved making all instruments in several sizes, which, when not used, were kept together in one case and therefore formed a *chest*.

In the fifteenth century three sizes sufficed, as most compositions had three parts only. The number of parts was greatly increased during the sixteenth century. In consequence, the lower limit of medieval music, *G*, did not allow a sufficient range, and the makers faced the difficult problem of constructing basses and contrabasses. Consorts became so large that Praetorius could record *ein Accort oder Stimmwerk* of eight recorders, from a *gar klein exilent* to a *Groß Bass*.

THE ORGAN, the truest mirror of the new attitude towards musical instruments, may suitably be the first to be described in this chapter. The slow pace at which it had evolved in the earlier middle ages became tremendously accelerated between the years 1400 and 1600, possibly owing to the polyphonic playing on keyboard instruments that we can trace back to the fourteenth century. In 1441, the largest pipe at Salem in Southwest Germany was four spans wide (or ten inches in diameter), and twenty-eight feet high; its tone must have been underneath the lowest string of the modern piano. Ten years later the organ of the chapel in the castle at Blois in France had pipes wide enough to let a man crawl through. This organ, as well as the organ in the cathedral at Barcelona which was made at the same time, had no less than fourteen hundred pipes; even earlier, in 1429, the cathedral at Amiens in France had twenty-five hundred pipes.

An organ with *two* manuals (or hand keyboards) existed already in 1386 at Rouen in Normandy. The rule was from thirty-five to forty-seven keys in one manual, starting on f, B, F, or B_1. From the fifteenth century on both manuals could be coupled to be played together. The coupling device connected the two manuals so that pressure on a key in one board acted upon the corresponding key in the other board as well.

The *pedal* keyboard, too, seems to have been invented in the fourteenth century, either in Flanders or in Germany. At the same time, the *pipe work* underwent a decisive change.

In the middle ages large organs had had several pipes on each key in order to enrich the timbre. Sometimes as many as twenty pipes answered the pressure of a key; these were tuned in unison (8 foot), in the octave (4 foot), twelfth ($2\frac{2}{3}$ foot), double octave (2 foot) and so on. The pipes were arranged in cross-rows, one row comprising all octave, all twelfth, or all double octave pipes. (Organ builders designate the pitch of a set of pipes by the length in feet of the pipe answering the great C key; 8′ is normal, that means, the answering note is C; 4′ is an octave higher, the answering note being small $c′$; 16′ an octave lower, the answering note being C_1.) The medieval organ was, in modern terminology, a *mixture* or *furniture*. Like the mixtures in our organs, the medieval organ invariably sounded as a compound which, when several chords were played,

*ns Memling, Altar for Najera, Museum in Antwerp (late 15th century), with
zither, trumscheit, lute, trumpets, oboe, portative, harp and fiddle.*

PLATE XVIII.

formed dissonances and frictions and gave the organ a jangling sound.

Apparently at the end of the fourteenth century, solo stops began to be added—that is, rows of pipes, each row imitating the timbre of a certain wind instrument and contrasting with the neutral color of the *principals* or *diapasons* which composed the mixture. The original compound part of the organ was then called by the names that we often find in ancient organ music, *plein jeu* in French, and *órgano lleno* in Spanish. It became necessary, with the addition of solo stops, to devise a contrivance connecting or disconnecting at will now one of the solo stops, now the old compound. It consisted in a slider projecting from the case which, when pulled out, admitted the wind to one complete row of pipes. Such a contrivance was called a *stop* in English, and the same name was also given to the row of pipes that it connected.

The first solo stop was the *flute*, which is wider or, as organ builders say, has a larger *scale* (diameter in relation to height) than the principals. As late as 1513 the organ of Saint-Sauveur at Aix-en-Provence, a very old-fashioned organ for its time, had only a single flute stop contrasted to a plein jeu of principal, octave, double octave, nineteenth and triple octave.

The great change in organ building at the time of the introduction of solo stops was due to a change in the style of music and in the role that the organ played in it. The new polyphony introduced by Okeghem and culminating in Palestrina needed more transparence. Solo stops had to be inserted to counterbalance the compound stops with their antipolyphonic fifths and even thirds. It was these new stops that gave the organ the quality which today seems to be its distinctive feature: the contrast and mixture of different timbres. As late as 1511, Arnold Schlick writes: "It is good to have the stops isolated, so that the organist may use them one after another, as he likes." (*Auch ist gut die register all ab zü ziehen, das der organist gleich register allein eins nach dem andern hörn mag lassen, wie ym oder andern geliept.*) "Besides it is rather pleasant to hear two stops together, as cymbals with diapasons." (*Dan fast lustig zü hörn etwan zwey register zü sammen, als die zymmeln zü den principaln.*) This combination and contrast of timbres which today we take for granted was a new discovery of the sixteenth century.

Two years before, in 1511, Arnold Schlick had published a plan of *viij. oder ix gut register,* "of eight or nine good stops which would delight the ear, if well combined and alternated":

Manual	Pedal
Diapason 8′	Diapason
Octave 4′	Octave
Gemshorn 4′	Trumpet or Trombone
Cymbal	Hintersatz
Hintersatz	
Reed stop	
Xylophone	
(Flute)	

Hintersatz or 'rear set,' as opposed to *prestant* or 'front set,' was a furniture with sixteen or eighteen pipes on each key, which was penetrating but not too strident.

While, as late as 1475, the organ of the *Dom* at Bamberg had been given a compass from *A* to *f″* only, Schlick's organ had twenty-four keys from *F* to *a″* in the manual, and twelve keys from *F* to *c′* in the pedal, plus the semitonia. This must not be taken too literally, however. The organists distinguished between large and small organs. 'Large' organs were tuned a fifth lower. As Schlick says that the *F* pipe was six and a half Rhenish feet long (or 2041 millimeters), the corresponding *a′* pipe must have produced either 337 vibrations in a large organ, or 504 vibrations in a small organ. In the Halberstadt *Dom* organ, built in 1361, *a′* had 506 vibrations. Compared with modern pitch, *a′* corresponded to a note between *e′* and *f′* in a large organ, and between *b′* and *c″*, in a small organ. As organs were not equal-tempered (although Schlick attempted to make them so), the organists could not transpose at will according to the individual voices they had to accompany; 'large' and 'small' keyboards allowed them at least to transpose according to the general ranges of the singers' voices.

Flemish and German organ builders were the first to pass from the simple liturgical mixture organ to the new organ with solo stops. At the end of the fifteenth century they introduced *stopped diapasons* (the pipes having the upper ends closed by caps so that their timbre was soft and hollow), tapering pipes such as *Gemshorn*, reed stops (the French *trompes* of that time were flue pipes in spite of their name), the pulsating *Tremulant* (Hagenau 1491) and the pedal keyboard with stops of its own (1390–1400). The rich and sonorous pedal and the penetrating furnitures and cymbals constituted the main departures from the French organ of that time. (figs. 84, 85)

Spanish organs also had only flue stops; the pedal, which in most cases had no more than seven or eight keys in diatonic succession, was

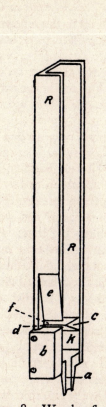

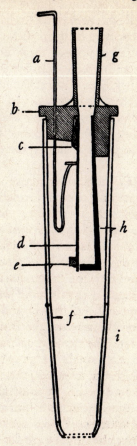

FIGURE 84. Wooden flue-pipe.

R body, *a* foot, *b* cap, *c* block,
d flue, *e* toplip, *f* mouth, *k* wind
way.

FIGURE 85. Reed pipe.

a tuning spring, *b* block, *c* wedge,
d vibrating tongue, *e* weight, *f* boot
or socket, *g* shank, *h* shalet, *i* section of a reed.

generally neglected. English and Italian organs remained in a fifteenth century style. They usually had no solo stop except for a
flute and were entirely built on the basis of principal and mixture.
Italians did not even care for inventing special names; they used
principals—wider in size and softer in tone than the German ones—
and above them, octave and fifth stops that they called 8a, 12a, 15a,
19a, 22a, 26a, 29a, 33a and 36a—that is, in our terminology, 8′,
5⅓′, 4′, 2⅔′, 2′, 1⅓′, 1′, ⅔′, ½′. Registers with stopped pipes were
not used, and reeds only rarely.

All countries liked foolish contrivances, though serious organists disapproved of them. Bells and jingles on rotating wheels were the most acceptable of these humorous stops. As *Zymbelstern* in German and *cascabeles* in Spanish, they were used up to the nineteenth century. The organ at the *Dom* in Magdeburg, built in 1604, had no less than forty-two carvèd *Figuren,* such as a crowing cock, twelve of which moved by machines. In an organ erected at about 1500, so Schlick tells us, there was the figure of a monk in the lower part of the organ case, falling out of a window and jumping back again.

REGALS were small reed organs. Their pipes were shaped like cylindrical beaks of clarinets; the beating reeds were made of metal. In the inventories of the sixteenth century they were mentioned as *One paire of single Regalles* or as *A paire of double Regalles.* The word *paire* is misleading since it meant simply a whole set, in this case a set of individual pipes forming one organ. *Single* and *double* referred to the contemporaneous use of doubling the letter which indicated a certain note when the lower limit in medieval music, *gamma-ut* or *G,* was exceeded. Thus, a Single Regal did not descend beyond *G,* whereas the Double Regal ended in the octave of double letters. The name *regal* can be traced back through English *rigol* to French *rigole,* or 'trough,' on account of the shape of the pipe.

It seems, however, that *regal* was not yet applied exclusively to the reed organ. It must also have meant what later was called a *positive organ.* In a source like Henry VIII's inventory of 1547, this latter word does not occur; except for *one paire of portatives,* all chamber organs are designated as regals. On the other hand, one item of this inventory runs: *One paire of single Regalles with iiii Stoppes of pipes, of woode vernisshed yellowe and painted with blacke anticke woorke standinge uppon a foote of wainscott the Bellowes lieing in the same: it hathe but one Stoppe of pipes of woode a Cimball of Tinne and a Regall.*

In modern words this regal had a stop of wooden flue pipes, a cymbal stop of tin, which according to Praetorius was a furniture with two pipes on each key, and a 'regal.' This arrangement is corroborated by the preceding item: *One paire of single Regalles with two Stoppes of pipes of timbre and one Stoppe of pipes of Tinne . . . the same hathe but one Stoppe of pipes of woode the Regall of papire and hathe a Cimball.* Here again a regal is a stop within a regal; the word meant a reed stop, as well as a chamber organ with different stops.

The origin of the regal, or reed organ, is obscure. We know it existed in the time of the German Emperor Maximilian I, who died in 1519. The engraver Conrad Weiditz has depicted the famous composer Paulus Hoffhaimer accompanying the Emperor's choir on a special kind of regal, the pipes of which had globular resonating caps. A hundred years later, Michael Praetorius pictured the same instrument on one of the woodcuts in his Syntagma musicum and calls it *Köpfflin-Regal;* according to his words, the tone was *gut und lieblich,* 'good and lovable.'

Generally, however, the sound of a regal was rather reedy and

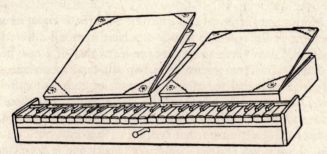

FIGURE 86. Bible regal.

harsh, so that musicians in Bach's time abandoned it because of its *eckelhafften,* 'loathsome,' tone as Bach's friend, Johann Mattheson, said.

The prevalent kind of regal was the Bavarian *bible-regal* which, when it was folded up and packed into the book-shaped bellows, looked like a large bible. (fig. 86)

THE RECORDERS formed the leading group among the flutes. The German name *Blockflöte* expressed its nature as a beaked whistle flute, the upper end of which was stopped by a block or plug that left only a narrow flue to lead the breath towards the sharp edge of a mouth-hole in the side. The bore tapered toward the lower end, the diameters at the upper and lower end being in the ratio 5: 3. Because of this shape, as well as because of the absence of a bell, the recorder had a pale tone which is reflected in its names, Italian *flauto dolce,* French *flûte douce;* the English term *recorder,* from the obsolete *record,* 'warble,' compares it to a singing bird. An ensemble of recorders was unsurpassed in dignity and reserve.

We do not know where the recorder originated. Its first evidence is in a French miniature of the eleventh century. Up to the seventeenth century it was made in one piece and turned in a very simple profile; it had one high dorsal fingerhole and seven front holes, the lowest of which was duplicated to accommodate either right- or left-handed players; the unused hole was kept stopped with wax.

As early as the beginning of the sixteenth century the recorder was made in whole consorts; in King Henry's inventory of 1547, one item among others quotes *viii Recorders greate and smale in a Case couered with blacke Leather and lined with clothe.* That the family comprised already bass, if not double bass, recorders, is confirmed by the following item: *One greate base Recorder of woode in a case of woode.* (fig. 87)

It is, however, erroneous to conclude that those eight recorders, or even the *ix Recorders of woode* in a later item, all differed from each other. From Virdung (1511) we learn that, if a case held six recorders, two of them were trebles, two alto-tenors, two basses; and we are informed that the two instruments of each pair differed in pitch by one note as do our C and B♭ clarinets and, like these, were alternately used according to the tonality of the composition. The ideal consort of recorders that Michael Praetorius outlines in his *Syntagma musicum* (1618), comprises twenty-one instruments, but only seven sizes, each of which has two different pitches. These seven sizes are:

Size	Length	Lowest note
Exilent	c. 9 in.	*g″*
Treble	c. 12 in.	*c″*
Alto	c. 17 in.	*f′*
Tenor	c. 24 in.	*c′*
Basset	c. 38 in.	*f*
Bass	c. 60 in.	*B♭*
Double bass	c. 80 in.	*F*

Bass and double bass were blown through a brass crook like that used on a bassoon. Basset, bass and double bass had an open key for the lowest hole. (fig. 88)

The *open key*, first recorded in a Netherlandish source in 1413, was for the purpose of closing a fingerhole too distant from the others. In larger instruments it was impossible to reach the lowest fingerhole, as the little finger was too short. Therefore, a longitudinal brass lever with a padded cap at its lower end was so arranged that the upper end of the lever was within the reach of the little finger, and the cap stood above the hole without covering it. When the

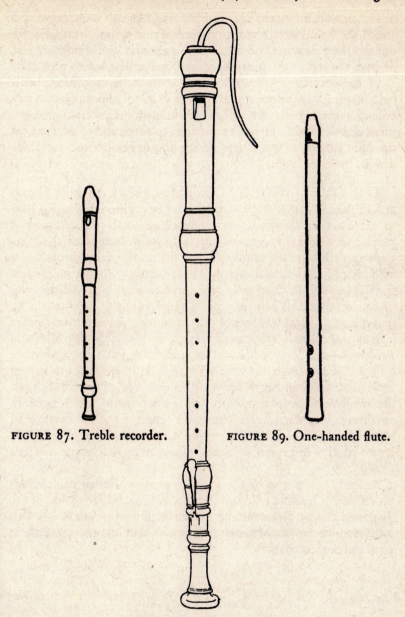

FIGURE 87. Treble recorder.

FIGURE 89. One-handed flute.

FIGURE 88. Bass recorder.

finger pressed the upper end of the lever, the cap went down and closed the hole; when the finger was lifted, a spring drew back the cap and the hole was again open. A bulging wooden cylinder slipped on over the top of the instrument, fitting over the key to protect it.

In the seventeenth century *closed keys* were used along with open keys, for a different purpose—that is, to add supplementary holes for chromatic notes without disordering the normal arrangement of holes and fingers. The padded cap at the end of a lever kept the hole closed; it was opened when the finger pressed the lever down.

THE ONE-HANDED FLUTE, best known under its French and Provençal names *flûtet* and *galoubet*, was a recorder with a bore so narrow that no fundamentals could be obtained; normal soft playing produced the higher octave, and overblowing the fifth above. Consequently, the fingerholes had to fill up the distance of only a fifth instead of the usual octave. Three holes sufficed—two in front and one behind—with cross-fingering and an occasional half-stopping of the open end. These few holes required only one hand. The player's other hand was free to play some second instrument: either a drum—the small *tabor* in England, or the large *tambourin* in Provence—or a longitudinal zither with thick gut strings tuned to tonic and dominant, such as the *tambourin du Béarn* in South France and the *altobasso* in North Italy. *Tabor and pipe*, as the English call the one-handed drum combined with a small drum, are depicted in miniatures beginning in the thirteenth century; the combination of a one-handed flute and a drone zither is figured on Filippino Lippi's fresco of the Ascension in Santa Maria sopra Minerva in Rome (1489).

As early as the end of the fifteenth century Italian painters depicted two different sizes of one-handed flutes, and at the end of the sixteenth century Germans and Italians also used larger basses with a bassoonlike crook. Michael Praetorius mentions the same three sizes and depicts them:

Treble	20 in.	*d″*
Tenor	26 in.	*g′*
Bass	30 in.	*c′*

The one-handed flute still exists in southern France and among the Basques of both Spain and France. It has been revived in England with the renascence of the old folk dances. (fig. 89)

FLAGEOLET, a term derived from a late Latin word, was, in the middle ages, a French name for certain flutes; the poet Eustache Deschamps, in the fourteenth century, praised *les doulx flajolez ressonans*. The old name was revived when, about 1581, JUVIGNY in Paris constructed a small, narrow recorder with six holes—four in front, and two in the back for the two thumbs. The instrument is seldom mentioned; yet, the great number of specimens preserved in museums proves its popularity. In the eighteenth century, at least,

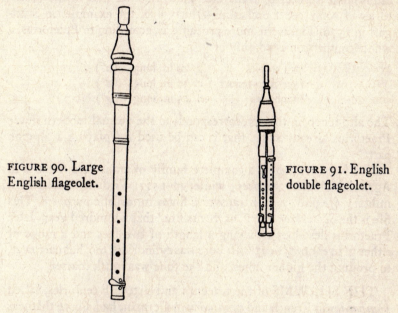

FIGURE 90. Large English flageolet.

FIGURE 91. English double flageolet.

it was important even in art music; called *flautino* or *flauto piccolo,* it performed the highest part in the orcnestra which later was given to the octave cross flute.

After about 1750, the recorderlike beak was replaced by a nozzle of bone as a mouthpiece leading into a bulging chamber which enclosed a sponge to absorb the saliva.

One must be careful to distinguish between this *French flageolet* and the so-called *English flageolet.* The latter, an amateur instrument of the first quarter of the nineteenth century, was likewise constructed with a nozzle and a sponge, but had the hole arrangement of the recorder. (fig. 90)

Both the French and the English flageolet were made either as single or as double instruments—that is, one mouthpiece leading to two tubes to play chords. The English double flageolet had a shutter in order to deaden one of the tubes when required. (fig. 91)

THE TRANSVERSE FLUTE was one of the few cylindrical instruments, as it is today, although for two hundred years beginning in the seventeenth century its bore was conical. Since it was made in one piece, it could not be tuned by being pulled out like later flutes. Therefore it was made in different pitches, and this may explain the astonishing number of transverse flutes that we find in the inventories of some court orchestras—thirty-five, for example, in Stuttgart in 1576. This is the more probable as, according to Praetorius, a whole consort consisted only of:

two trebles	c. 20 in. long	(d')
four alto-tenors	c. 30 in. long	(d'')
two basses	c. 45 in. long	(g)

The alto-tenor, in this set, corresponds to the normal modern flute; Praetorius already states that it can be used for playing a soprano part.

The first mention of a complete family of transverse flutes is in Agricola's *Musica deudsch*, while, in 1511, Virdung speaks of a military *fife* only, not of transverse flutes for artistic purposes. This fife is the *Schweizer Pfeiff*, or 'Swiss fife,' that a hundred years later Praetorius describes as having a length of two feet and a range of either g' to c^3 or $c\sharp'$ to $a\sharp''$. Its bore was cylindrical, too, but narrower, to produce the higher notes, and the tone was much coarser.

THE SHAWMS of the fifteenth and sixteenth centuries, called *bombardes* in French and *pommern* in German, had a bore that was narrow and very slightly conical and, like all reed pipes of that time, a double (oboe) reed. Six fingerholes formed two groups of three; a seventh one was provided with an open key which lay inside a protective cylinder. The family comprised:

Small discant	c. 21 in. long	(b')
Discant	c. 24 in. long	(d')
Small alto	c. 30 in. long	(g)
Big alto (*nicolo*)	c. 36 in. long	(c)
Tenor	c. 52 in. long	(G)
Bass	c. 75 in. long	(C)
Double Bass	c. 100 in. long	(F_1)

In 1376, Jean Lefevre de Ressons designated the *grosses bombardes* as *nouvelles*. (pl. XVIII a, fig. 92)

The bassanello was a shawm with an even narrower, slightly conical bore. The instrument appeared to have a bell, but it was a false one as the small bore continued to the end of it. There were six front holes and an open key for the small finger under a protective cylinder; a brass crook held the reed. The timbre was a little softer than that of ordinary shawms. Bassanelli were built in three sizes:

Treble	c. 32 in. long	(*d*)
Alto-tenor	c. 45 in. long	(*G*)
Bass	c. 64 in. long	(*C*)

No specimen has been preserved.

The instrument is mentioned for the first time in 1577, when the estate of the deceased Archduke Karl of Austria was inventoried; the last evidence is in Michael Praetorius's *Syntagma* of 1618–1620. In speaking of the instrument, Praetorius affirms that its name is derived from the Venetian composer, Bassano. This is not likely. The first-known date in Bassano's life is only 1585—that is, eight years after the earliest mention of bassanelli outside Italy. Moreover, inventors' names were rarely given to instruments before the nineteenth century.

THE BASSOON is a slightly conical double-reed instrument, the tube of which is bent back on itself like a hairpin, first descending and then ascending. A brass crook containing the reed projects at right angles from the upper end of the tube.

In the sixteenth century both channels were bored out of the same long block of wood; only a brass crook containing the reed for one channel, and a narrow bell for the other channel, projected at the top. In the seventeenth century the long, thick piece shrank to what is called the *butt*, in which the U-shaped knee is bored; inserted into the butt, two separate tubes—the *wing* and the *long joint*—comprised the descending and the ascending channel, exactly as in the modern form of the bassoon. (figs. 93, 94, 95)

The compressed, narrow tone of the bassoon is derived from the prevalence of the third partial.

The earliest reliable reference to this instrument is in an English private inventory from 1574, where it is called *curtal*. But it was older; for, a famous bassoon maker, SIEGMUND SCHNITZER, died at Nürnberg in 1578, and in the same year Philip van Ranst, musician to the court of Brussels, was appointed player of the new instru-

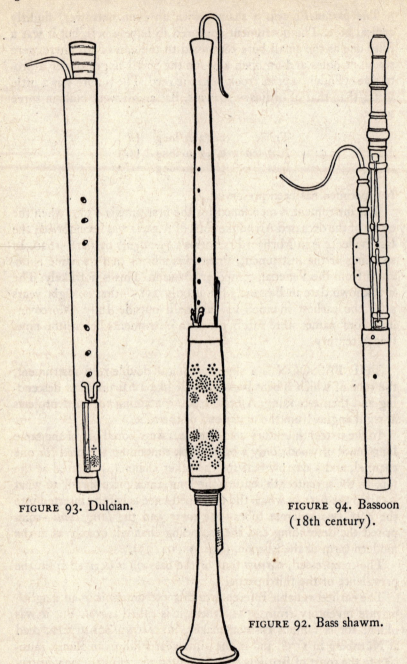

FIGURE 93. Dulcian.

FIGURE 94. Bassoon
(18th century).

FIGURE 92. Bass shawm.

ment. Thus, it may have originated about the middle of the sixteenth century.

At about 1600 the family consisted of the following five sizes:

Treble	c. 1'3" high	
Alto	c. 1'6" high	
Tenor	c. 2'3" high	(G)
Rechter or *Choristfagott*	c. 3'3" high	(C)
Bass	c. 4'9" high	(F_1)

Both tenor and chorist fagott were made either open or *gedackt*. But though this latter word meant 'stopped,' they were only covered with a kind of sieve, which was supposed to muffle the tone without lowering it.

According to Michael Praetorius, HANS SCHREIBER, musician to the electoral court in Berlin, was constructing a *fagotcontra* with C_1 as lowest note in 1618. "If he is successful, it will be a marvellous instrument never seen before." This was the earliest *double bassoon*. (fig. 96)

The bassoon had a different name in every language. The Italian *fagotto* or 'fagot' was translated into German as *fagott;* the Italian *bassone* or 'big bass' led to English *bassoon* and Spanish *bajón*. Praetorius mentions that the English call the tenor bassoon a *singel corthol*, and the ordinary bassoon a *doppel corthol*. In usual spelling this is the British word *curtall*, which derives from Low German *kortholt* or 'short wood' and signifies an instrument shortened because of its folded tube. A last family of names comprises such terms as *dolcian, doucine, dulzian*. This word occurs as early as the middle ages; apparently every soft-voiced instrument with a double reed could be given this name.

Smaller bassoons were built as late as the early nineteenth century. The older scores of Joseph Haydn's *Stabat Mater* (1771) demand (tenor) *fagotti* in $E\flat$ with $B\flat$ as the lowest note; HEINRICH GRENSER in Dresden made bassoons in the upper octave of the ordinary bassoon about 1810; and, by 1820, LAZARUS in London had constructed a similar model under the name *tenoroon*.

An *A* bassoon, a minor third under the normal bassoon, is included in Johann Sebastian Bach's cantata no. 150 (*Nach dir, Herr, verlanget mich*).

The sordone was a cylindrical bassoon, the channel of which ran down and up two or three times within the same piece of wood and ended in a lateral hole. The sound was soft and muffled; hence came

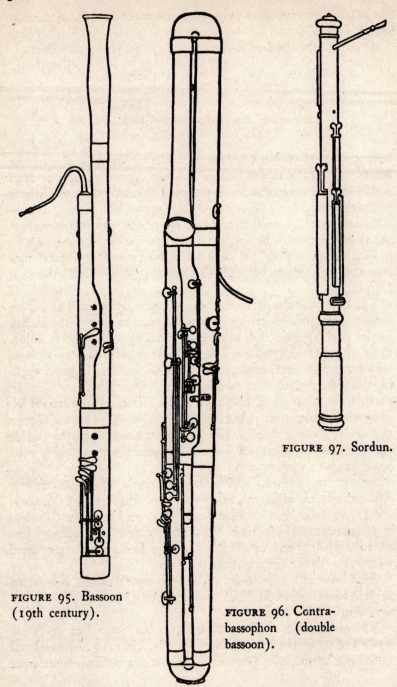

FIGURE 95. Bassoon
(19th century).

FIGURE 96. Contra-
bassophon (double
bassoon).

FIGURE 97. Sordun.

the names (mostly used in the plural forms): Italian *sordoni,* from *sordo* 'deaf,' German *sordune* (incorrectly *sordunen*), French *sourdines.* They were built in five sizes:

Treble		$(Bb$)
Alto		$(Eb$)
Tenor		$(C$)
Bass	87 cm high	$(Bb_1$)
Double bass	90 cm high	$(F_1$)

The instrument must have been extremely rare; the only four preserved specimens, two basses and two double basses, the same which were mentioned in an inventory of the Archdukes of Tyrol in 1596, belong to the Kunsthistorische Museum in Vienna (no. 226–229). (fig. 97)

RANKETS or *rackets,* from Upper German *rank,* 'to and fro,' in French *cervelas,* 'sausages,' were short, thick cylinders of solid

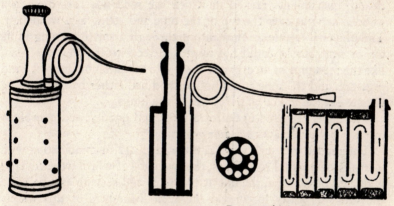

FIGURE 98. Ranket.   FIGURE 99. Ranket (del. C. Manger).

wood or ivory pierced lengthwise by many cylindrical channels all of the same size. The channels were arranged in a circle with one in the center, and each was connected with one neighbor at the top and another one at the bottom, so that they formed a continuous cylindrical tube. A cup called *pirouette* in French was inserted in the central channel, concealing the lower part of the reed and supporting the player's lips. Holes involving a complicated fingering were cut in the walls of the cylinder. The sound was muffled and reedy. Five sizes were built:

Treble	½′ high	(c)
Alto	¾′ high	(G)
Tenor	1′ high	(C)
Bass	1¼′ high	(F_1)
Double bass	1¾′ high	(C_1)

Rankets first were mentioned in Austria in the beginning of the sixteenth century, and the last evidence of this kind of rankets may be found in Mersenne's *Harmonie Universelle*, 1636.

A slightly different form was made in the seventeenth and in the first years of the eighteenth century. The diameters of the channels were unequal; the tube as a whole became conical. The narrowest channel formed the mouth end of the tube and was provided with a bassoon crook. The widest channel, which was in the center, wore the bell of a bassoon. Thus the term *ranket-bassoon* would be appropriate for this instrument. (figs. 98, 99)

CROMORNE. Besides the double-reed instruments already discussed, instruments existed in which the reed was concealed in a wooden cap put over the top of the pipe and acting as a windchest. The player was able to blow into it through a small opening in its top or side, but he could not touch the reed itself. Thus the reed, like the reed pipe of an organ, was set into vibration by indirect wind pressure, and the tone could not be modified either by the varying pressure of the lips or by the power of the lungs.

The notes persisted in uniform force and quality, and overblowing into higher octaves was not possible.

The reader met such wind caps on page 212 in combination with a family of oriental reed pipes, the two ends of which were covered with caps of ox horn, the one at the outer end serving as a bell and the other as a cap to conceal the reed. Members of this widely scattered family were found along the sea route from the Indian Ocean to the Atlantic.

There were similar folk instruments in southern and western Europe, the history of which is not clear. Apparently wind-cap instruments were first introduced to art music in the fifteenth century.

The cromorne was the oldest European instrument with a wind cap. It was a slender cylindrical oboe ending in a curve that was reminiscent of the folk instrument with an ox horn. This explains the original German name *krummhorn*, or 'curved horn,' which was adapted to English and French as *cromorne*. Since the bore was

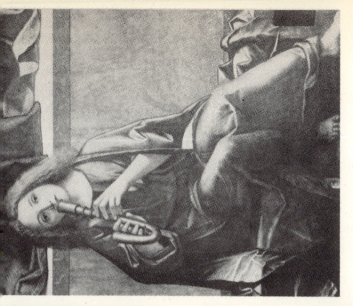

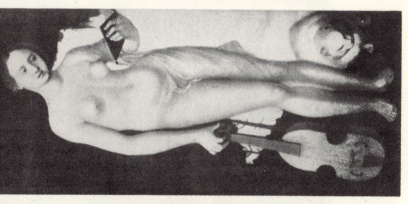

cromorne in the Academy, Venice (1510).

Hans Baldung, woman with viol, in the Pinakothek, München.

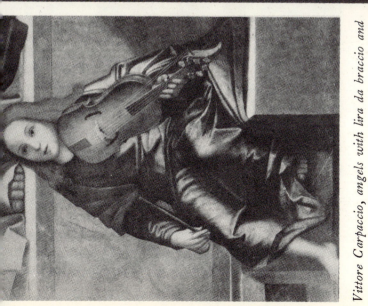

Vittore Carpaccio, angels with lira da braccio and

PLATE XIX.

almost entirely cylindrical, the timbre was softer and darker than the tone of the oboe, and this was probably why the French were inclined to transform the name *cromorne* into *cor morne*, or 'mournful horn.' As no overblowing was possible, the range was limited by

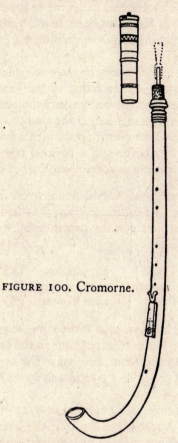

FIGURE 100. Cromorne.

the number of fingerholes, seven in front and one at the back. (fig. 100)

Five sizes were made:

Exilent	c. 13 inches long	(*c'*)
Treble	c. 16 inches long	(*g*)
Alto	c. 23 inches long	(*c*)
Tenor	c. 32 inches long	(*G*)
Bass	c. 39 inches long	(*C*)
Double bass	c. 48 inches long	(F_1)

The term 'krummhorn' is first mentioned in Dresden in 1489 as an organ stop, indicating the prior existence of the instrument. In 1510 the Venetian painter Carpaccio depicted an angel with a cromorne in his "Presentation in the Temple" (now in the Academy in Venice). The instrument had a lifetime of about one hundred and fifty years only; it is last mentioned in 1617, when Johann Hermann Schein, the Saxon composer, published a pavan for four cromornes. (pl. XIX c)

Curiously enough, the history of the cromorne had a postlude in France. About 1650 it was included in the band of the *Grandes Ecuries* at Versailles, and the best makers competed in manufacturing it. This, however, was no longer the slim cromorne with its soft sound, but a heavy outdoor instrument with a bore as much as two inches wide, a leather cover and a bassoon crook without a reed-concealing cap. Its name was *tournebout* 'turned end.'

SCHRYARI were loud, shrill, double-reed instruments with a tapering bore and a reed-concealing cap; they had seven fingerholes in front and two in back for the two thumbs. Praetorius describes and depicts three sizes:

Treble	c. 9 in. long	(*g*)
Alto-tenor	c. 17 in. long	(*c*)
Bass	c. 26 in. long	(*F*)

Bass and alto-tenor had two keys at the same height above the regular fingerholes, one in the front and one in the back, to enlarge the range upward. Alto and tenor differed in the upper limits of their compasses: the first ended on *f'*, the second on *d'*. No specimens have been preserved.

The oldest evidence of schryari is in a 1540 inventory of the municipal band of Augsburg in Bavaria; the last reference to them is made in 1686 in an inventory of the court orchestra of Brandenburg-Ansbach. All mention of them is in German sources.

There is evidence, however, that the instrument came to Germany from the Mediterranean. The two upper keys of the schryari were the characteristic feature of the Italian folk oboe *calandrone*. Also in 1541 the trumpet maker JÖRG NEUSCHEL in Nürnberg wrote to Duke Albrecht of Prussia to offer him some *schreyende pfeiffen* that he had received from Lyons and Venice with other instruments. These two ports point to an oriental provenance. Following this indication we find that there was an oboe with a tapering bore and seven front-holes in Turkey in the ninth century; also there is a modern Japanese oboe *hichiriki* which, like the treble schryari, is nine inches long, has a tapering bore and seven front-holes.

The etymology of the name seems to confirm the oriental origin of the instrument. Praetorius lists it as *schryari* (*auf deutsch Schreier-pfeiffen*). Obviously schryari was not a German word, and probably it is not even an Italian word adapted into German. If this had been the case, Praetorius, who was familiar with Italian, would have written it in a correct Italian spelling and form. It is more likely to think of an originally oriental name based on the same root, *šr*, that we have found in other names for wind instruments, *mašrokīta* and *syrinx*.

RAUSCHPFEIFEN were a German family of oboes with a narrow bore, a hole in the back, seven front-holes with the lowest duplicated for the right or the left little finger, a small bell and a cap concealing the reed. The only six specimens preserved, made in the second half of the sixteenth century, are in the Berlin Museum of Musical Instruments. They form a consort of

two trebles	42 cm long	(*e′*)
two tenors	54 cm long	(*c′*)
two basses	86 cm long	(*g*).

Players of rauschpfeifen were depicted in Hans Burgkmair's engraving, *Triumphzug Kaiser Maximilian's* (1518).

The German name was a High German transformation of Middle Low German *rus*, 'reed.' It has survived in an organ stop *rausch-quinte*, producing the twelfth and the double octave of the pressed key. A treble rauschpfeife was known in France in the seventeenth century and called *hautbois du Poitou*.

THE CORNET OR ZINK. A short animal horn with a few fingerholes occurs in medieval Persia at a time directly after the dynasty of the Sassanids—that is, about 700 A.D.; it is represented on a silver dish of that period. Even today shepherds use a similar primitive horn in Finland, Esthonia, Sweden, Norway and Jugoslavia and also among the Bongo in the eastern Sudan.

Later, in European art music, the rough horn of an animal was replaced by a wooden or ivory tube. This became the *curved cornet*, in French *cornet à bouquin*, in German *Krummer Zink*. Miniatures depict it as early as the tenth century; did it come from Byzantium? In the twelfth century the outside of the tube was already octagonal in cross section as in its classical form. A smaller cornet was called *cornettino* or *Kleinzink*. On the other hand, the sixteenth century had a large cornet, *cornon* or *corno torto*, in German *Grosszink*, in the shape of a stretched out S:

cornettino	(*e'*)
cornetto	(*a*)
cornone	(*d*)

The curved piece of wood of which the cornet was made was slit lengthwise; the two halves were hollowed and then again glued together and held in position with a leather coat, which often was nicely engraved. (figs. 101, 102)

A less frequent type of cornet was the *cornetto diritto* or *Gerader Zink*, 'straight cornet,' whose cup-shaped mouthpiece instead of being inserted in the upper end was hollowed out of it. This cornet had a softer sound; Italians, therefore, called it the *cornetto muto*, and Germans *Stiller Zink*. Since it was harder to blow, it did not survive the beginning of the seventeenth century and was not even mentioned by Mersenne in his *Harmonie Universelle* (1636). (fig. 103)

The sound of both cornets was less brilliant than the tone of the trumpet, as the tube was short, conical, relatively wide and more rigid than the thin metal of brass instruments. This lack of brassy brilliancy or, acoustically speaking, of high harmonics, gave the cornet a distinctness and precision which enabled it to support the human voice or to supplant it better than any other instrument. Mersenne tells us that good cornettists could blow eighty measures in one breath and adorned their melodies with all the graces in which singers excelled. A hornlike tone was despised.

Nevertheless "the labor of the lips is too great," as Roger North (1653–1734) says. The golden age of cornet playing came to an end when, after 1600, the thorough-bass style disposed of the old polyphony in which the cornet had often played the treble, and gave the first role to the violin. For some decades, German pieces were printed with the indication, "for violin or cornet," *ad libitum*. But in Johann Gottfried Walther's *Musicalisches Lexicon*, published in 1732, the instrument was nearly forgotten; an article *Cornetto* is entirely copied from Praetorius who had written more than one hundred years before, and there is no heading *Zink*. Still some German town bands kept it during the eighteenth century, and Johann Sebastian Bach had the municipal cornettists accompany the choral of

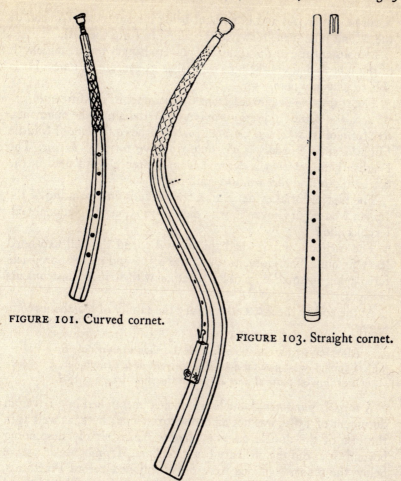

FIGURE 101. Curved cornet.

FIGURE 103. Straight cornet.

FIGURE 102. Tenor cornet.

the boys in several of his cantatas. A few old-fashioned town musicians played the zink as late as the first years of the nineteenth century.

An offshoot of the cornet, the *serpent*, will be discussed in a later chapter.

THE TROMBONE is narrower and generally longer than the trumpet. Two parallel tubes are held several inches apart by a bridge. A third, U-shaped tube—the *slide*—connects the lower ends of the two parallel pieces, fitting over them for several feet, so that

it can be pulled out and in without being disconnected. The end of
the second tube turns forward, spreading to form the bell.

By constant use of the slide, the player changes the actual length
of the tube and alters the note as well as its overblown tones. He is
able to play any note.

The trombone originated from the trumpet in the fifteenth century, as the names indicate; *trombone,* in Italian, is the augmentative form of *tromba,* and German *posaune,* the equivalent of Middle
High German *busûne,* is the augmentative form of *busîne.* The
English name *sackbut* is derived from a French word used in the
fifteenth century: *sacqueboute,* 'pull-push.'

The first pictorial evidence of a trombone is on a painting of the
Italian Matteo di Giovanni, who died in 1495, in the National Gallery, London.

The earlier trombone had thicker walls, and the bell expanded
less than ours. Therefore, its sound was softer and more appropriate
for playing in small ensembles together with stringed instruments
or pipes.

At the end of the sixteenth century the family of trombones comprised:

> Alto: lowest natural note *f*, with the slide drawn out, *B*
> Tenor: lowest natural note *B♭*, with the slide drawn out, *E*
> Bass: lowest natural note *E♭*, with the slide drawn out, *A*

A *toppelt pusaunen,* 'double trombone,' mentioned in a Bavarian
document of 1581, was not an octave trombone; here, as well as in
the case of the double bassoon, *double* means simply descending
beyond *G*, as did the ordinary bass trombone. Trombones an octave
below the tenor trombone were not mentioned before Praetorius,
1618. He speaks of a 'false' one, being merely a bass with additional
crooks, and a real one, made "four years ago" by HANS SCHREIBER,
the inventor of the contrafagotto, with a tube twice as long as the
tube of the tenor trombone. (fig. 104)

A *treble trombone,* an octave above the tenor trombone, was only
added in the latter part of the seventeenth century, but it was as rare
as the octave trombone.

In the second half of the nineteenth century the alto also became
rare and was given up, except in a few bands. On the other hand,
new attempts towards a contrabass trombone were made in England,
France and Germany. The successful model, proposed in 1816 by
Gottfried Weber, was a double slide trombone. The tube was folded

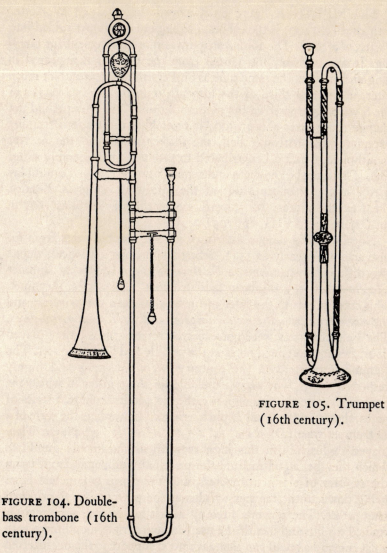

FIGURE 105. Trumpet
(16th century).

FIGURE 104. Double-
bass trombone (16th
century).

to present a double tubing exactly the shape and size of the tenor trombone; pulling the slide to a normal position, the player extended four branches instead of two and lowered the tone twice as much.

Again, the true bass trombone, needing a rather long arm, is replaced by a *tenor-bass* in many bands—that is, by a tenor trombone with a valve to throw the instrument a fourth lower.

TRUMPETS. A figure on a carved choir seat in Worcester cathedral (c. 1400) is the earliest evidence of a trumpet folded into a narrow S form. The folded shape was more convenient for carrying. It was probably introduced from the Orient; it appeared in England at about the same time as on Persian miniatures. Not much later, in the first third of the fifteenth century, the two curves of the S were superposed in the modern fashion. The trumpet did not change much after about 1500; it resembled the modern trumpet except for the narrower bell, the thicker metal and the heavier mouthpiece, which all contributed to produce a considerably softer tone. This must be known to understand how the trumpet could play a role in the chamber music of the following centuries. Besides, there existed mutes; Monteverdi scored them as early as 1607 in his *Orfeo*. (pl. XVIII, fig. 105)

No player was supposed to draw all the possible notes from his instrument. As early as 1511, Sebastian Virdung's woodcuts depict two different instruments, a *Felttrumet* and a somewhat slimmer *Clareta*—that is, a military 'field trumpet' and a 'clear' trumpet. This corresponds to the later distinction between the *principal* and the *clarin* trumpets, the *Feldtrompeter* and the *Kammertrompeter*. The Feldtrompeter were not expected to read music; they played flourishes and sustained notes in the middle and lower register. The Kammertrompeter, on the contrary, were musicians and highly respected artists, who played melodies in the register in which the harmonics were close enough together to admit a coherent series of notes, that is, in the usual D pitch, from d'' upward, as the scale of a D trumpet was: (D) d a d' $f\sharp'$ a' (c'') d'' e'' $f\sharp''$ g'' a'', etc. They played exclusively in this high register, as the "noble guild" to which they belonged forbade the principal trumpeters from using the register of clarin trumpeters, and the clarin trumpeters from going down to the register which was the prerogative of principal trumpeters. The player's lifelong restriction to the high register trained his lips and breath; he used an appropriate mouthpiece with a flat cup and a broad rim that gave good support to the overexerted lips. This is the "secret" that enabled the trumpeters of the Bach epoch to play such surprisingly high parts, up to d^3, e^3 and even g^3, in spite of the low pitch of their instruments (D alto, a minor third below our F trumpets, a minor sixth below our $B\flat$ trumpets). But we should not forget that in those times solo parts were written expressly for one artist and his special skill. Modern artists, required to play the complete range, are not able to perform these parts in a satisfactory style. Makers in the nineteenth and twentieth centuries have tried to facilitate blowing by constructing so-called *Bach trumpets* a third, a fifth or an octave above our B♭ trumpets—that is, an octave, a tenth or a thirteenth above the trumpets of Bach's time. Such trumpets have a poor tone without being much easier to play. Some outstanding swing trumpeters, however, are able to give us an idea of the brilliancy and ease of the high register.

KETTLEDRUMS. The history of the modern kettledrum began when large specimens were imported from West Asia, although the small kettledrums had been known in Europe since the thirteenth century. In 1457, King Ladislas Posthumus of Hungary sent envoys to France to solicit the hand of Princess Madeleine, daughter of King Charles VII, and they were accompanied by kettledrums. Father Benoît, describing this event, added: *On n'avoit ni mi oncques veu des tabourins comme de gros chaudrons qu'ils faisoient porter sur des chevaux.* "One had never before seen drums like big kettles, carried on horseback." From this we know that the large modern kettledrums were unknown in western Europe, though they existed in the east of the continent. About 1500 they were introduced in Germany. In his *Mvsica getutscht* (1511), Virdung writes that "now with us" the name *tympana* is given to the big army kettledrums of copper, which the princes have at court. "These are enormous rumbling barrels. They trouble honest old people, the ill and the sick, the devotees in monasteries who study, read and pray, and I think and believe that the devil has invented and made them. . . ."

Kettledrums had come to East Europe in the ancient Asiatic form, having laces to tighten the skin. As late as 1636, Mersenne depicts a Polish kettledrum of this kind. In Germany the kettledrums had already undergone an essential change in Virdung's time; instead of laces, such as were used in Asia and eastern Europe, some screws round about the head raised or lowered an iron hoop stretching the skin.

Germany had become a center of kettledrum playing even before the importation of the large instrument. As early as 1384, Duke Philip of Burgundy had sent one of his drummers to Germany to learn the art of playing. Later, the kettledrum was considered a specifically German instrument.

It was a symbol of aristocracy as well. The kettledrum was the inseparable companion of the trumpet, and kettledrummers were included in the same "noble guild" and invested with the same rights as trumpeters. As late as 1683, the Scotch officer, Sir James Turner, states that "the Germans, Danes and Swedes permit none under the rank of baron to have them unless they are taken in battle from an enemy."

As symbols of wealth and nobility, kettledrummers were expected to show a certain extravagance. The classic monographer of the "Heroic and musical art of the trumpet and the kettledrum," Johann Ernst Altenburg, emphasizes in 1795 "the affected figures, turns and movements of the body" of German kettledrummers, and Zedler's gigantic *Universallexikon* (1735) calls a kettledrummer the one "who knows how to strike the drum elegantly. This is done with certain movements of the body which elsewhere would be ridiculous." Sometimes, to make the appearance more spectacular, Negroes were employed as kettledrummers. Cavalry regiments delighted in the same extravagant parading of their kettledrums, which they used more and more as a special privilege. As late as the twentieth century such a cavalry drummer would wear a full beard, ride on a black horse and throw up and catch the sticks while playing. When, about the middle of the sixteenth century, a German, Baron von Dohna, came to France, his ostentatious entrance annoyed the French so much that the Duke de Guise ordered his kettledrums to be dashed to pieces "to his great abashment."

CLAVICHORDS were stringed keyboard instruments of a simple construction. In a small, shallow box without a stand or legs, the strings were stretched from the tuning pegs at the right end around the hitch pins inserted in the left end. A plank of hard wood (*wrest plank*) into which the tuning pegs were screwed, was squeezed into the right end of the box; a small soundboard made of tender fir wood was supported by the wrest plank at the right end, but extended leftward beyond it to the position of the highest key. There were one or more bridges on the soundboard. A vertical metal *tangent* on the rear end of each key gently touched the corresponding string and produced a remarkably soft, indeed meager, tone. While in the modern piano, the hammer, falling back after the strike, releases the string and causes a vibration belly at the point of contact, the tangent of the clavichord did not fall back and set the string free unless the key was released and therefore caused a vibration node at the point of contact. The superfluous section of the string, at the left of the point of contact, was deadened by a strip of felt woven between the strings; the vibrating section was bounded by the bridge on the soundboard at the right, and the point of contact of the tangent at the left. As the length of the vibrating section did not depend on the whole length of the string, but on the distance between the bridge and the stopping tangent, several neighboring tangents could use the same string to produce different notes. Thus, the clavichord had fewer strings than keys. One of the oldest sources, Henry Arnault's treatise, gives the clavichord nine double strings and thirty-five keys—that is, with an average of four notes to each string. (pl. XXI a)

The clavichord evolved from the polychordic monochord (cf. page 271). The link between them is missing. But we can easily reconstruct it. Such a polychord needed the strings tuned a third apart, as the third was the smallest consonance of that time. The intermediate notes could be produced in the usual manner by shifting the stopping bridge. It would have been difficult, however, to shift bridges to and fro under so many strings without endangering the accuracy of the intervals. When the right places were found and fixed, musicians gave individual bridges to each note, which could stop or release the string without difficulty or loss of time. The required contrivance already existed in other instruments; the hurdy-gurdy had the shortening bridges or tangents, and the organ provided both levers and keys.

The date of this transformation is not certain; but the keyboard doubtless existed in 1323 when the Frenchman Johannes de Muris, in his *Musica speculativa,* mentioned a monochord with nineteen (diatonic) strings, covering two octaves and a fifth, besides the real monochord with from one to four strings.

Following the principle of polychordic monochords, an older type of keyboard instrument, still existing at the beginning of the sixteenth century, had strings of equal length, thickness and tension. A more recent type, already made in the fifteenth century, had strings of different length, thickness and tension. According to a passage in Ramis de Pareja's *Musica pratica,* in 1482, the first one continued to bear the old name 'monochord' while the second one was called clavichord. Eberhard Cersne's poem *Der Minne Regel* (1404), the earliest source that mentions the name 'clavichord,' includes the term 'monochord' as well. Still the name 'monochord' was less and less used; in 1511, Virdung depicts a *clavicordium* as an instrument with strings of equal length.

Clavichords were first depicted more than a hundred years after

Johannes de Muris: in a woodcut of the *Weimarer Wunderbuch,* in a design in Henry Arnault's treatise and in a wood carving in St. Mary's Church, Shrewsbury, all of them dating about 1440. A few years later a clavichord was carved on a Dutch wood sculpture now in the Rijksmuseum at Amsterdam. These early evidences came from England, France and Holland, indicating that the clavichord probably originated in the northwestern section of Europe.

One of the most striking features of all older clavichords was the shortness of the keys. They projected only three centimeters beyond the semitones, while the keys of modern pianos project five centimeters. This seems to have been due to the mechanical action required, the weight of the front of the key needing to balance exactly the weight of the rear. A player using modern fingering would stumble against the semitones on such a keyboard. The shortness of the keys necessitated the awkward fingering of the sixteenth and seventeenth centuries; the players used the second and third fingers when they ascended, and the first and second fingers when they went down, while the thumb and the fourth finger were seldom engaged. This fingering was already familiar to players of the portative organ, in which the keyboard was situated at right angles to the player.

Keyboards depicted by German artists between 1440 and 1462 have only three semitones in the octave instead of the five that the organ had acquired long before: *B* flat as the Dorian changing note, *C* sharp as the Dorian leading note, *F* sharp as the Mixolydian leading note.

Though the Italo-Spanish theoretician, Bartolommeo Ramis de Pareja, had outlined the idea of an equal temperament in his *Musica pratica* (1482), all instruments were tuned to an unequal temperament. The notes *E* and *B* were slightly lower than in the modern scale, and all tuning rules of the sixteenth century agreed in prescribing that the fifths producing the accidentals should be either a bit too low or a bit too high, but never exact. An accurate standard did not exist.

Up to the first third of the sixteenth century the lower limit of the keyboard was *F*, while the highest note was *g″*, *a″* or *c‴*. After the musical range in the fifteenth century had been extended below *G*, keyboards had to be enlarged as well. But only the diatonic notes were important; composers and players did not think it necessary to have the lowest octave chromatic, as no leading or changing note was required in the bass. Still, virginal and clavichord makers probably would have added chromatic strings and keys in spite of their uselessness. But to organ makers and consigners four superfluous keys meant a hundred or more superfluous pipes of the largest size, the omission of which made an organ considerably cheaper. Instead of leaving out the black keys from the octave *C* to *c*, they arranged a *short octave* which looked like *E* to *c*, in which the apparent *E* was a *C*, while the *F♯* key produced a *D* and the *G♯* key an *E*:

As organs, clavichords and virginals were built by the same makers and played by the same artists, this arrangement was adapted to the stringed keyboard instruments as well. Our graphic symbol for this short octave is *C/E*.

Players became so used to the short octave that, when the semi-tones *F♯* and *G♯* could no longer be dispensed with, the previous arrangement was not given up. The expedient was to add the required strings without adding special keys; both the *F♯* and *G♯* keys were cut into two sections, an anterior and a posterior part; the anterior parts played *F♯* and *G♯*, and the posterior parts *D* and *E*.

This division of some semitone keys must not be confused with another short octave which enabled the player to distinguish between *F♯* and *G♭*, between *G♯* and *A♭*. In about the middle of the seventeenth century, a new short octave was introduced. An apparent B_1 was added which produced a G_1. It may be designated by the symbol G_1/B_1.

Short octaves were not completely abandoned by makers until the middle of the eighteenth century. It was the new 'long' octave that, in one of his sonatas, Scarlatti designated as *ottava stesa*, or 'stretched octave.'

In about 1720, the clavichord had been perfected in another way. Certain neighboring notes had to be played on the same string, and when they formed a chord the lower of them did not sound. According to tradition, a certain TOBIAS FABER at Crailsheim in Württemberg constructed the first *bundfrei* or 'unfretted' clavichord with as many strings as keys. Dr. Francis W. Galpin, however, saw such an instrument dated 1700 in Dr. Henry Watson's collection at Manchester. But in spite of this improvement the unfretted clavichord was not able to oust the earlier model. Having more strings, it was larger, heavier, more expensive, and it took longer to tune.

The clavichord revived with a redoubled vigor in the eighteenth century as the leading house instrument of the German *Empfindsame Zeitalter*. To the generations between 1720 and 1780 its small tone reflected the current aversion to grossness and ostentation, and its meagerness stood for noble simplicity. The finger was not supposed to *strike* the key, but to touch it "caressingly," as Karl Philipp Emanuel Bach said. As only one mechanical link acted between the finger and the string, the slightest feeling of the finger communicated itself to the vibrating string. Consequently, we owe the delicacy in modern piano playing to the clavichord. The *manieren* or graces could be played with greater transparence, stress and tenderness than on any other keyboard instrument. The strings *sang* the melody, and even a single tone was animated. In the same manner that the violinist removes the rigidity of his tone by a *vibrato*, the clavichordist gave warmth and passion to the note by the *Bebung*, the trembling pressure given to the key without letting it go. "Who dislikes noise, raging and fuming, whose heart bursts in sweet feelings, neglects both the harpsichord and the piano and chooses the clavichord," said Christian Friedrich Daniel Schubart (1739–1791).

SPINETS AND HARPSICHORDS were keyboard instruments in which the strings were plucked by quills instead of touched by tangents as in clavichords. On the rear end of each key stood a *jack*, that is, a small upright piece of wood, from which projected a small quill or a leather tongue. These jacks were not fastened to the keys, but stood free, and were held in an upright position by a kind of *rack* inserted in the soundboard (which in these instruments ran the entire length of the box). When the key was pressed the jack jumped up, making the quill pluck the string, and then, owing to a springing device, fell back without plucking the string again. (fig. 106)

Quill instruments were made in three principal shapes; namely, winglike *grand, upright grand* and *square*. In the upright grand the strings were stretched vertically, in the two other forms horizontally. In the grand form they ran from front to back, and both the wrest plank with the tuning pegs and the set of jacks were in the front, taking up the width of the instrument. In the square form, on the contrary, the strings ran from the right to the left at right angles to the keys, the lowest string being in

FIGURE 106.
Jack.

the front. The wrest plank was at the right end, while the rack that supported the set of jacks pierced the soundboard, describing a diagonal line from the left anterior to the right posterior corner.

Whatever the particular form, the case was loosely set on a stand —that is, a horizontal frame with legs; legs fastened to the instrument itself did not appear earlier than 1750.

The whole structure was much lighter than that of modern pianos. No metal was used, and soundboards were not thicker than four millimeters (in modern pianos they are from eight to ten millimeters). The gauge of the strings was considerably inferior to that of modern strings (.325 millimeters for *c′* as against one millimeter of modern), and overspun strings did not exist. Consequently, the tone was much more delicate.

The names varied according to the epoch and the country. The most important were:

GRAND FORM	SQUARE FORM
English: *harpsichord*	*virginal* or *spinet*
French: *clavecin*	*épinette*
Italian: *clavicembalo*	*spinetta*

Up to the seventeenth century, the term "virginal" in English designated both the grand and the square form; the Inventory of the Guarderobes of King Henry VIII, for example, lists in 1547 *Twoo faire paire of newe longe Virginalles made harpe fasshion.* In the same way the famous collection of pieces for a keyboard instrument in the Fitzwilliam Museum at Cambridge, the *Fitzwilliam Virginal Book*, was not exclusively intended for square instruments. And even within the square type, the term 'virginal' was not reserved to a special form; the use of the words *spinet* and *virginal* was not only vague but contradictory. In this book all plucked grand forms with quills will be called harpsichords; and all square forms spinets.

The name *virginal* has mistakenly been connected with virginity and, as a result, with the maiden queen, Elizabeth; this princess was born in 1533, twenty-two years after Virdung's mention and description of a virginal. The term goes back to the fifteenth century. It occurs in a poem of the epoch of Henry VII (1485–1509), and even in a manuscript in the university at Cracow written between 1459 and 1463, the *Liber viginti artium* of the Bohemian Paulus Paulirinus. The word probably is related to medieval Latin *virga*, 'rod, jack.'

The history of plucked keyboard instruments seems to begin in the second half of the fourteenth century. At that time English, French and Spanish sources mention an instrument variously spelled as *chekker, eschequier* and *exaquier*, all meaning chessboard. The first specimen of which we hear was made by a Frenchman, JEHAN PERROT, and given in 1360 by King Edward III of England to his prisoner, King John of France. Between 1370 and 1380 two French poets mentioned it—Eustache Deschamps and Guillaume de Machault—and the latter, in his poem *Li temps pastour,* called it the *eschaqueil d'Angleterre,* 'the chekker from England.' In 1385 such an instrument was made in Tournay and bought by the Burgundian court, and a few years later King John I of Aragon tried to obtain from Duke Philip the Bold of Burgundy an *exaquier,* being an *isturment semblant d'orguens, qui sona ab cordes,* and an organist *abte de tocar exaquier* [e] *los petits orguens.*

Twice in the Aragonese letters the exaquier is expected to be played by an organist able to handle the *petits orguens,* that is, the portative organ. Consequently, Dr. Hans Hickmann, in his book on the portative, suggested that the exaquier might have been a stringed instrument closely related to the portative in size, construction, playing position and musical means. The only stringed instrument sufficiently like a portative organ would be a small upright harpsichord, of which we have two representations. Edmond Vander Straeten depicts a small upright harpsichord (that he mistakenly calls a clavichord) from a manuscript of about 1450. It has a socle, white and black keys and eight strings; the upper side is broken to form a step. A more reliable evidence is on a sculpture of about 1480 on the altar at Kefermarkt in Upper Austria; it represents an upright harpsichord, shaped and carried like a portative organ, with eleven double strings.

Instruments of this kind should be mentioned in a Burgundian source of the first half of the fifteenth century; in other words, the tractate written by Henry Arnault of Zwolle, quoted several times in this chapter, ought to describe them. Unfortunately, the descriptions in this and other medieval treatises do not tell us what we most need to know; the shapes of instruments are left unmentioned. But there is at least one kind of stringed instrument which may have been related to the portative; its action contains little chains and "the keys must be long and bitumed as they are in portatives, for their length." Again there is a connection, indeed a combination of

*ristoph Paudiss, lutanist, Pinako-
thek München (17 century).*

*Frans van Mieris, drummer, Pinako-
thek München (17th century).*

*ter Codde, Music with violin and gamba, in the Liechtenstein Gallery, Vienna
(c. 1625)*

PLATE XX.

the portative and an upright harpsichord described about 1460 in Paulirinus's tractate (cp. page 293).

These evidences corroborate the hypothesis that the exaquier or échiquier was a portative upright harpsichord. Besides, it is probable that in plucked keyboard instruments the vertical portative form preceded the horizontal one laid on the lap, a table or a stand. The keyboard, taken from the portative, must have been given first to that form of psaltery which had its strings in a similar position to that of the pipes of a portative.

Etymology is not helpful in this problem. An old suggestion, based on one specimen two hundred years more recent than the first evidence of the name 'échiquier,' that it might have been the combination of a spinet and a chessboard, is farfetched. The author of this book pointed out many years ago that a musical instrument *schachtbret*, in a German poem of the time, literally signified 'quillboard,' not 'chessboard'; but the earlier evidences of the Romance forms weaken this argument. Some portative organs had keyboards in two rows of alternating black and white square keys. But if this arrangement accounted for the term, one would hardly understand why the name was given only to the stringed instrument and not to the portative organ as well. Another possibility is suggested by Low Latin *scacherium*, similar to *scacharium*, 'chess board,' and equivalent to *abacus*, a term which was used by some theorists of the Renaissance to designate the keyboard. But this etymology is not convincing either. Recently Dr. Henry George Farmer has proposed an Arabic etymology, *al-šaqira*—this name, allegedly a musical instrument, being mentioned by an Arabian writer who died in 1231. This derivation, too, is weak. The Arabian writer does not describe the instrument; the mention is too early to be connected with exaquier; keyboards are not in the Arabian line; an Arabian origin would suggest that the instrument came to Europe through Spain, not from northwestern Europe to Spain; other Arabists deny the existence of such a word as the name of a musical instrument in Arabic literature.

Thus, the name remains unexplained.

The oldest pictorial evidences of the grand form were a miniature in the *Très belles heures* of the Duke of Berry, 1409, which depicts a harpsichord in a celestial concert; the woodcut of a harpsichord in the *Weimarer Wunderbuch*, about 1440; and, at about the same date, a drawing in Henry Arnault's treatise.

A reference to the grand form occurred much earlier, in 1323, in Johannes de Muris's *Musica speculativa*. The passage indicates that the 'monochord' with nineteen strings (and keys) could be made in various shapes; one of them, a rectangular triangle with one concave side, seems to be the wing form of the harpsichord. At first sight, this is a confusing contradiction between the term 'monochord,' which suggests a (square) clavichord, and the wing form of a harpsichord. The explanation is that the term 'monochord' indicated a keyboard instrument in any form and type. This is confirmed by a further statement of de Muris that the monochord combines practically (*in virtute*) all instruments. The word 'monochord' occurring in the Munich manuscript of this tractate is changed to *instrument* in the eighteenth century Gerbert edition which was probably based on another manuscript. 'Monochord' as well as 'instrument' apparently meant keyboard instrument in general. Similarly, Henry Arnault's treatise states: "It can be made that the clavichord sounds like a harpsichord" (*potest fieri quod clavicordium sonaret ut clavicembalum*); further, "With a certain action one can make both a clavisimbalum or a clavicordium or a dulce melos." What were these actions?

Previously it has been taken for granted that the early instruments had the jack action of later harpsichords. This now appears more than doubtful. Henry Arnault's treatise on instruments gives the descriptions and diagrams of four kinds of *forpices* or 'tongs' which serve to stir the strings of keyboard instruments; stirring is called *percutere* and *ictus*. The descriptions are poor and the diagrams almost undecipherable; we cannot even be sure that they mean plucking devices. The words *ictus* and *percutere* designate 'striking'; they do not seem to indicate plucking. Only the fourth kind of forpex is a jack, but it is unmistakably described as a striking contrivance.

Yet, on a fragmentary page, Arnault refers to a monochord with quills, obviously a plucked instrument in the shape of a clavichord. This passage throws light on a sentence written about one hundred years later by the Italian doctor Julius Caesar Scaliger, who lived from 1484 to 1558: "This was the origin of those that people call monochords today, in which slim *plectra*, arranged in orderly fashion, produce sounds. Points of raven quills, afterwards (*deinde*) added to the plectra, elicit a more expressive harmony out of the wires. [The instrument called] clavicymbalum and harpichordum when I was a boy, is now called *spineta* after these points." It was incorrect to conclude from Scaliger's statement that the use of quills was started during his boyhood. Not only Arnault's statement contradicts such interpretation; also Paulirinus, whom we mentioned above, defines, about 1460, the *clavicimbalum* as an instrument played *per pennam introrsus coannexam.* It was also a mistake to deduce from Scaliger that the quills replaced plucking points of metal, as he speaks of quills added to the plectra of monochords.

The change of name that Scaliger indicates adds to the confusion in the vocabulary of early keyboard instruments. In Arnault's treatise, *clavicymbalum* designates the grand harpsichord, as in later times. But Scaliger identifies it with *spineta* and *arpicordo,* which were both square instruments. The same is true of Virdung (1511); he depicts the same square instrument twice with two different titles, *Virginal* and *Clauicimbalum,* and describes the latter as follows: "This is like the virginal, but it has other strings of sheep gut and nails which make it harp; it also has quills like the virginal; it was recently invented, and I have seen only one." All previous writers have associated this definition with the *Clauiciterium,* because of the peculiar arrangement of the page in Virdung's book. But this was a mistake, as an upright harpsichord is not "like the virginal."

To sum up, the grand harpsichord can be traced back to 1409, and the square spinet to about 1440. The latter was a clavichord onto which the quill mechanism was grafted, a *clavicordo da spinetta* or 'thorn' clavichord.

It seems, though it cannot be proved, that the customary form in the fifteenth century was the grand, whereas in the sixteenth century the square form prevailed. The grand form not only developed sooner, but also survived the square form.

Two main square types existed: the Italian and the Flemish spinet.

The Italian spinet had a pentagonal case varying in length from four to six feet, and a soundboard of the same shape, both made of cypress or cedarwood; the characteristic smell of cedar is a charm of these tasteful instruments up to this day. The walls were extremely thin in order to vibrate with the strings. Therefore, the instrument was inserted into a strong outer case from which it had to be removed for playing. The keyboard generally projected like a balcony; it had the compass E/C to c^3 or f^3; the keys were boxwood or ivory, the semitones darker box or ebony.

The Flemish spinet, on the contrary, was made of a cheap pine-wood in a large, and rather clumsy, rectangular form. Scattered flowers were painted on the soundboard in water colors, and instead of the intricate rose generally carved in the soundboard of Italian spinets the Flemish rose was made of unchased pewterware. The keyboard was recessive and placed at the right or left, not in the center; its keys were usually made of bone, seldom of ivory, never of box; the semitones were of ebony or stained black. A further difference was in the interior arrangement; the tuning pegs were no longer arranged in a straight but in a broken line, and the bridge was also angular instead of being curved, as in Italian spinets.

Spinets were made in two sizes: the normal 8′ instruments (*double virginals* or, in Italian, *spinette*), and small 4′ instruments (*single virginals* or *spinettini*). In about 1600, the masters of Antwerp made a few combined virginals; the case of such an instrument was wide enough to house a smaller octave instrument as a kind of drawer beside the keyboard of the larger one. When used, the small instrument was pulled out and set upon the large virginal so that the player was able to play both of them either together or alternately. Two fine specimens are in the Metropolitan Museum of Art in New York and one is in the Belle Skinner Collection at Holyoke, Massachusetts.

To save space, certain octave spinets were built in a different model. The wrest plank with the tuning pegs, instead of being at the right end, were arranged in front like those of the harpsichord, and the strings were stretched diagonally across the box.

English makers at the end of the seventeenth century enlarged this small spinet with its wrest plank in front and its diagonal strings to form a normal 8′ instrument, and it was in this form, an intermediate one between the spinet and the harpsichord, that the spinet, at least in England, survived the seventeenth century. Everywhere else its existence came to an end before 1700.

Harpsichords, that is, plucked instruments in grand form, in the sixteenth century were almost exclusively made in Italy; Venice was the center. All preserved specimens are made in splendid style; precious materials, inlaid work, careful carving and an excellent painting of the outer case.

At the beginning of the sixteenth century some harpsichords still had single strings; an example is the beautiful instrument of Do-MINICUS PISAURIENSIS (1533) in the Leipzig Museum. Double-stringed harpsichords already existed when Henry Arnault wrote his treatise, but then the two strings of a set were arranged above one another so that one jack sufficed to make them both vibrate. A harpsichord made by HIERONYMUS PISAURIENSIS in 1521, now in the Victoria and Albert Museum in London, already has strings stretched in pairs and played in unison by two jacks each. Since the jacks necessarily plucked the unison strings in slightly different places, the second set of jacks being inserted behind the first one, the two notes had a different timbre due to the favoring of different partials.

The idea of making use of these contrasting timbres by a device like a stop, allowing one set of jacks to function while the other was disconnected, was brought forth in the sixteenth century. Extensions of the racks pierced the right side wall of the harpsichord and could be shifted like the stops of an older organ.

It is not possible to give an exact date to this improvement. In 1514, a Venetian organ builder made a *clavicembalo grande con do registri* for Pope Leo V; but we are not certain whether *registri* meant stops or only a double set of strings.

The stops could provide the player either with different timbres or else with different degrees of loudness. The alternation of a meager and a full tone obtained in this way is probably the meaning of the mysterious *Instromento Piano e forte*, listed in an undated Este inventory of the sixteenth century.

As early as 1538, we have evidence of the combination of an 8' and a 4' stop; the hitch pins of the 4' strings, which were about half as long as the strings of the 8', were inserted in the soundboard. Italian sources call this 8' 4' arrangement *instrumento in ottava*.

The earliest evidence of three stops is in the inventory of the Fugger collection in Augsburg, dated 1576: "A beautiful long instrument of fine black ebony with ivory busts in relief inside a skillfully painted case, and three stops, ivory keys and gilt nails, and a powerful tone. Has been made by Franco Ungaro in Venice." Very probably these stops were 8' 8' 4'. Six years later, the inventory of the instruments at the Brandenburg court records *eine Symphonei* with four stops, probably 8' 8' 8' 4'.

A Dresden inventory of 1593 lists three harpsichords, with two keyboards each. But also the undated Este inventory includes a *clavicembalo cromatico con due tastadure*. The two keyboards were a step forward in facilitating the use of different timbres and dynamic degrees.

The upright grand harpsichord had the usual horizontal keyboard; but the wing-shaped body stood vertical.

Early portable uprights and their possible connection with the échiquier have already been discussed. The first evidence of a non-portable upright is a woodcut in Virdung's *Musica getutscht* (1511) with the caption *clavicyterium*. We find this name up to the seventeenth century, but as it was rather rare, and not generally used, we had better avoid it.

In an upright harpsichord the jacks jut horizontally forward instead of standing perpendicularly on the keys, and they must be pulled back by a special device instead of falling back by their own weight. Owing to this complicated action, upright instruments were not frequent. However, the vertical arrangement saved space and projected the sound directly to the listener. Therefore, it never was entirely given up as long as harpsichords were made. At the end of the eighteenth century, upright harpsichords were replaced by upright pianos.

Claviorgan is the name generally given to a combination in one instrument of a small organ with a stringed keyboard instrument—either a spinet, a harpsichord, a clavichord or, later, a piano. One should be skeptical, however, when this term occurs in old sources. The two *clabiórganos* owned by the Spanish chamberlain, Sancho de Paredes, in 1480 (the earliest known mention of the name) were probably not combinations. In an inventory of the Este collections, dated 1612, we find an item, *Cinque organi grandi, detti claviorgani*, 'five large organs, called claviorgani.' The name obviously was given to larger chamber organs. In another Este inventory, dated 1625, there is an item reading *8 Arpicordi grandi computatovi uno che è sopra un claviorgano*, 'eight large harpsichords including one which is upon a claviorgano.' Consequently, a claviorgan was not a combination, but could be paired with a harpsichord or another stringed keyboard instrument.

Still permanent combinations existed as early as the middle of the fifteenth century. Paulus Paulirinus describes, about 1460, an instrument [?]*nnportile* in the shape of a *media ala* (that later on he defines as semitriangular), being a positive organ on one side and an upright harpsichord with wire strings on the other side. The keyboard of a portative connects both of them so that their sounds mingle with marvelous sweetness.

In the oldest preserved specimen of a horizontal claviorgan, however, made by the Fleming Lodowicus Theewes, dated 1579 and kept in the Victoria and Albert Museum, a harpsichord is simply laid on the organ, and in an instrument in the Viennese Kunsthistorische Museum, made in 1587 at Augsburg, a regal is contained in one half, and a spinet in the other half, of a chess box.

In 1618, when Praetorius was writing his *Syntagma,* pipes were mingled ("*mit eingemenget*") with the strings. He is probably referring to the later type, in which one keyboard ruled both the organ and the stringed instrument with a device that allowed the player to couple or uncouple them.

THE DULCE MELOS. In a Latin manuscript of the fifteenth century at the Bibliothèque Nationale in Paris, a French student, Bottée de Toulmon, found the description, as well as several designs, of a keyboard instrument—dulce melos—and, realizing its importance, he published a short extract of the text in his *Dissertation sur les instruments de musique au moyen-âge,* Paris, 1844. There he called it a piano. A piano, described in a treatise of the fifteenth century and forgotten for three hundred years before the invention was made anew—this was an exciting and almost unbelievable discovery.

The manuscript has since been published in an excellent facsimile, and the dulce melos can be studied as far as the obscurity of the text and the designs admit. This is what we find.

The dulce melos, according to the manuscript, was derived from the zither struck with two sticks that the English call *dulcimer.* It was a stringed keyboard instrument in square form with a range from B to a''. The arrangement was peculiar, indeed unique. There were four bridges extending from the front to the back of the box, one at either end and the other two dividing the strings in the proportion, 4: 2: 1. The three sections acted like three separate strings, producing a ground tone, its octave and its double octave. In other words, the same string provided c in its first section, c' in its second section, and c'' in its third section; the instrument had twelve strings only for a range of thirty-five chromatic notes. The keyboard extended from the middle of the first section beyond the last section; while the anterior parts of the keys were of equal size, the rear parts had to diverge in the first section and converge in the third to meet the three sections of the strings.

The action consisted of jacks loaded with lead standing upright on the rear ends of the keys. A U-shaped, brass staple projected sideways from the upper end of each jack. When a key was pressed, and its action checked (*obviat obstaculo superius prope cordas*), the jack jumped up vertically to touch the string.

To this passage the editors of the facsimile add a footnote in bold type saying that one could not better describe the action of a piano, thus following Bottée de Toulmon's suggestion.

This is a mistake. The action of a piano is also checked (and that of a harpsichord as well!), but it consists of a hammer performing a rotary movement. In the dulce melos, on the contrary, the jack made a plain vertical movement; it was a kind of struck spinet and closely related to the Bavarian *Tangentenflügel* of the late eighteenth century, in which the jacks struck the strings instead of plucking them.

THE LUTE. The harmonic and polyphonic style of the fifteenth and sixteenth centuries assigned a privileged role to all instruments capable of playing several notes at once. This explains the increase of keyboard instruments after 1400. There was another instrument that successfully competed with keyboard instruments—the lute. Handier, and with the advantage of being traditional, it became the universal instrument. It could replace in an ensemble any other instrument, high or low; it accompanied singers, indeed it could reproduce all parts of an instrumental or choral composition at once; lute arrangements of all kinds of instrumental and vocal ensemble music were published in the sixteenth century as piano scores are published in our time. The importance given to the lute is indicated by the fact that violin makers are called *luthiers* in France to this day.

The lute of the fifteenth century still had many specific features of the Arabian lute *al'ūd*, the name of which it carried. In many cases the neck was not distinct from the body; it was unfretted and relatively narrow. Certain players still used the oriental plectron as late as the seventeenth century. Plucking with the bare fingers, however, was more and more necessary as the lutanists developed a technique for playing chords. (pls. XVIII a, XX a)

The new tasks necessitated a further development of the musical means of the lute. Between 1400 and 1520 the neck was fretted, first with four, gradually increasing to eight frets. The number of strings was six, seven or eight in 1400, and reached the classic number of eleven at about 1450. Eleven did not mean eleven single strings. Ten of them formed five double strings, only the highest string being single to facilitate producing delicate grace notes. Occasionally the number of frets and strings was increased.

The usual accordatura was, in the sixteenth century, A/a d/d' g/g' b/b e'/e' a'. The pitch, however, was relative.

The outer shape acquired its definitive outline at about 1500;

since then it has had the elegant almond form and the shallower shell. The slender staves, from nine to thirty-three, which composed the shell were sometimes made of exotic woods, ebony, brazil, sandal, cypress or of ivory and even of whalebone, and often separated from each other by delicate purflings.

The lutanists of the seventeenth century scorned the inaccuracy of this kind of lute. Thomas Mace is typical of that generation when he writes, in 1676, in his *Musick's Monument*, p. 41:

> There is found by Experience a Better manner of Laying our Lutes, (as we term it) which is done, by causing the Fingerboard, 1. to lye a little Round, or Up in the middle; as also that the Bridge (answerably) rise a little Round to it. Then 2dly. to lay the strings so close to the Finger-board, that the Strings may almost seem to touch the first Fret. This is call'd Laying of a Lute Fine, when all the Strings lye near the Frets. 3dly. Laying the Ranks of Strings so carefully, that the Pairs may be conveniently Near, and the Ranks pritty wide. By which means we have a more ready and certain Command over them, for neat and clean Play.

Modern lutanists are anxious to revive that ancient art, but with a few exceptions their style is stiff and wooden; it does not resemble the delicate sound of "the warbling lute," to use Dryden's word. One cannot understand the dominant position of the lute between 1500 and 1700 without knowing from the style of oriental lutanists, and even outstanding Spanish guitarists, how expressive and varied the plucking can be.

Though a favorite instrument all over Europe, the lute was never popular in Spain, in spite of its having come through that country. Spanish folk music was played on the guitar, and aristocratic music was performed on a compromise instrument, the *vihuela* or, more exactly, the *vihuela de mano*, in contrast with the *vihuela de arco* or fiddle. It had the flat and waisted body of the guitar, but the size and accordatura resembled those of the lute. Six or seven double strings were tuned to $G c f a d' g'$, or $G c f g c' f' g'$. Some different accordaturas are indicated in the fourth book of Fray Juan Bermudo's *Declaración de instrumentos* (1555). The outstanding music for the instrument is to be found in Luys Milan's *Libro de Mvsica de vihuela de mano, intitulado El Maestro*, 1535–36.

CITTERNS in their classical form had shallow bodies, flat on the front and back surfaces, and fretted necks; wire strings were stretched between inferior stringholders and lateral pegs and were plucked with the bare fingers.

The origin of this instrument is obscure. It probably originated in southern Europe as a plucked fiddle; the Mediterranean peoples have always preferred plucking to bowing, as testified by many medieval sculptures of plucked fiddles in Spain and Italy. The rear

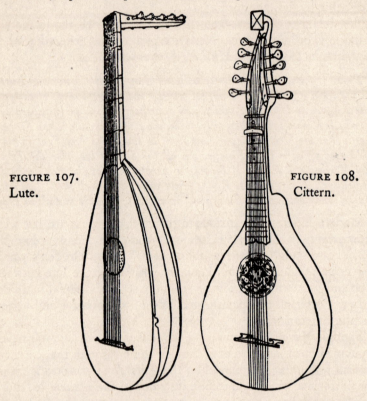

FIGURE 107.
Lute.

FIGURE 108.
Cittern.

pegs of the fiddle existed with citterns as late as the fifteenth century. In the sixteenth, citterns sometimes had a combination of front and lateral pegs; in their later form they had lateral pegs exclusively.

The usual cittern, between 1500 and 1750, had an elegant, pear-shaped body shallower at the lower end, and a characteristic neck in which the bass side was thinner than the treble side so that the thumb could easily reach around. Nine strings in four groups were the standard, though the number varied. They were tuned in different ways; the most common accordaturas were *d b g d' e'* and *F e c g a*. In several specimens the outer string on the bass side was a high treble.

The later cittern, after 1750, had a less elegant form; the body was the same depth throughout, or else was slightly deeper at the lower end, and the neck was equally thick on the bass and the treble sides. (fig. 108)

Finally, a certain CHRISTIAN CLAUSS obtained a British patent on October 2, 1783, for giving the cittern a piano action to replace the plucking right hand, though it left stopping on the fingerboard to the fingers. One piano key for each set of strings was arranged on the soundboard; these keys acted on piano hammers striking from inside. The instrument was misnamed *keyed guitar*.

VIOLS, in the sixteenth century, belonged to two distinct families: 'leg viols' or *viole da gamba*, and 'arm viols' or *viole da braccio*. The first of them comprised those obsolete instruments that the modern musician calls *viols* or *gambas;* the second family corresponded to the bowed instruments of our days, violin, viola, cello and double bass. This seems surprising, as cellos and double basses are not held in the arm. The family names refer to the playing position of the oldest members of both families, and the names were retained for all the members regardless of their sizes and playing positions.

A comparison of their distinctive characteristics follows:

Viole da gamba	*Viole da braccio*
flat back	bulging back
back sloped off at the upper end	back not sloped off
deep ribs	shallow ribs
sloping shoulders	round shoulders
edges of soundboard and back not projecting	projecting edges
reinforcing crossbars inside	a reinforcing longitudinal bassbar inside
C or flame holes	*f* holes
broad neck	narrow neck
gut frets	no frets
six or seven thin strings	four thick strings
sound pale and flat	sound round and full

The viola da gamba became a distinct type in the fifteenth century, earlier than the viola da braccio, when musical evolution made large fiddles necessary. In large fiddles the stops on the fingerboard were much farther apart than those to which the artists were accustomed. The natural expedient was to simplify the action of the fingers by shortening the tonal distances between the strings—that is, by tuning them, lutelike, in fourths with a major third in the middle, instead of in fifths. To avoid reducing of the range, the players increased the number of strings to six and, in the seventeenth century, to seven.

In a few decades we find a whole family modeled after the original bass viol. Even double basses were constructed; for, in 1493, Spanish musicians came from Rome to Mantua with viols tall "like myself," as one chronicler said. But they did not belong in the family in a narrower sense. According to Thomas Mace's *Musick's Monument* (1676), *a Good Chest of Viols* consisted of six instruments, viz. 2 *Basses* 2 *Tenors and* 2 *Trebles: All Truly, and Proportionabley Suited*. The bass was from sixty-one to seventy-six centimeters high and was tuned to *D G c e a d'*; the tenor, from fifty to fifty-eight centimeters high, to *A d g b e' a'*; the treble, from thirty-two to forty-five centimeters high, to *d g c' e' a' d''*.

The differences in sizes within the same category are remarkable. They are explained in John Playford's *Introduction to the Skill of Musick*, which was printed in nineteen editions from 1658 to 1730: *A Bass Viol for Consort must be one of the largest size, and the Strings proportionable. A Bass-Viol for Divisions must be of less size, and the strings according. A Bass-Viol to Play Lyraway, that is, by Tablature, must be somewhat less than the two former, and strung proportionably.* In other words, the large bass viols were made for ensembles, the medium size served for ordinary solo music, and the small bass viols were supposed to be played "lyra-way."

This term needs explanation. At the end of the sixteenth century, the English favored full chords on the bass viol. This was facilitated by tuning it "lyra-way," that is, following the principle of the lira da gamba and superposing fifths and fourths—accordaturas like the three following:

$$A_1 \quad E \quad A \quad e \quad a \quad d'$$
$$A_1 \quad D \quad A \quad d \quad a \quad d'$$
$$A_1 \quad D \quad G \quad d \quad g \quad d'$$

As more stretching of the fingers was required on bass viols in which the open strings were tuned a fifth apart, playing was easier on a smaller instrument. Such an instrument, therefore, was called a *lyro-viol* or, as it was small enough to be confused with a tenor viol, a *viola bastarda*.

Playford, in his *Musick's Recreation on the Lyra Viol*, London

1661, relates that DANIEL FARRANT, who was a violist in the king's band between 1606 or 1607 and 1625, *invented a Lyra Viol, to be strung with Lute Strings and Wire Strings, the one above the other; the Wire Strings were conveyed through a hollow passage made in the Neck of the Viol, and so brought to the Tail thereof, and raised a little above the Belly of the Viol, by a Bridge of about ½ an inch: These were so laid that they were Equivalent to those above, and were Tun'd Unisons to those above, so that by the striking of those Strings above with the Bow, a Sound was drawn from those of Wire underneath, which made it very Harmonious. Of this sort of Viols, I have seen many, but Time and Disuse has set them aside.*

The discussion of the strings and their accordatura should not be concluded without a general remark on what we call absolute pitch. In earlier times no such thing existed, and uniformity of pitch was a consideration only in ensemble music. As late an author as Jean Rousseau, in his *Traité de la viole* (1687), tells the player to begin with tuning the middle string *c* and to stretch it to a *raisonable* note!

All gambas, even the treble, were played in a vertical position on, or between, the legs. The bow, which Rousseau calls the "soul" of the viol, was slightly shorter than ours and held palm upward with the thumb above and the middlefinger on the hair, about two inches from the nut; its position on the strings was three or four fingers from the bridge. In playing, the accents were given by pushing the bow forward, beginning with the outermost point—not, as with the violin, by pulling it back. The delicate, fine-pointed sound resulting from this peculiar manner of bowing is the most characteristic feature in viol music, and modern gambists who handle the bow in cello fashion produce entirely the wrong effect. It is also incorrect to undo the frets, to lengthen and round the fingerboard and to raise the bridge.

The outer shape of the viol has undergone many changes. Throughout the fifteenth and sixteenth centuries the outline varied. Sometimes the waist was almost indistinguishable and sometimes so deep that it touched the fingerboard; the soundholes were cut, now above, now beneath, now beside the bridge. Every maker had his own shapes, and artists unaccustomed to instrument making tried to design the forms. A well-known case is Leonardo da Vinci's "invention" of a bowed instrument in the form of a horse's head, mentioned by his biographer, Giorgio Vasari. Many a writer has racked his brains over the existence of such an awkward instrument. The author believes this must have been a form of fiddle, occurring at the beginning of the sixteenth century, the elongated body of which was wide at the top and narrower below, like a horse's head seen from the front. (pls. XIX b, XX c, XXI a)

The viol did not adopt a definite form earlier than the seventeenth century. The soundholes were placed a little below the middle of the soundboard. As to the position of the bridge, Thomas Mace asserts in his *Musick's Monument*, London 1676, that it *is to stand just in 3 quarter dividing of the Open Cuts Below; though Most, most Erroneously suffer them much to stand too High, which is a Fault*. In other words, the bridge should be placed at one quarter of the height of the soundholes.

With the holes and the bridge correctly placed, the viol achieved a perfection of appearance that could even surpass the pattern of the violin. Though less 'classic,' according to the standards of a violin enthusiast, its curves have a more appealing diversity.

THE LIRA DA GAMBA, or *lirone*, was a late bass modeled on the lira da braccio—in other words, a hybrid of various instruments. The body was copied from the viola da braccio, the rear pegs and two drone strings from the medieval fiddle (called lira da braccio at that time), a small rose above the two ordinary holes from the lute. Besides the drones, the instrument had from nine to fourteen gut strings, tuned in fourths and fifths as well as in octaves. Cerreto, Praetorius and Mersenne indicated various accordaturas; only that given by Scipione Cerreto in his book *Della prattica musica* (1601) will be reproduced: $G\ g\ c\ c'\ g\ d'\ a\ e'\ b\ f\sharp'\ c\sharp'$. With a rather flat bridge, such an accordatura allowed the lirist to play full chords, and only chords. Their effect was increased by sympathetic vibrations, as all notes played had partials coinciding with some open strings. Unknown in modern instruments, sympathetic vibrations were possible because the strings were extremely thin, so thin that the highest of them could be tuned an octave above the highest string of the modern violoncello in spite of its equal length.

The lira was too unemotional to be successful. As a mixture of several kinds of stringed instruments, it was the typical product of an epoch in which every possibility was explored. But it came too late. Between 1584 when its name first appeared, and the middle of the seventeenth century when it dropped out of use, the reserved style of the Italian Renaissance already had begun to change.

16. *The Baroque*

(*1600-1750*)

A RADICAL revolution in music broke out at the opening of the seventeenth century. Never before had composers emphasized the contrast to the old style with the same decisiveness, indeed arrogance; never before had they laid stress on the novelty of their style with similar determination.

The new generation strove for strong emotion; it tried to appeal to the listeners' hearts. "What passion cannot Music raise and quell," sings Dryden. Composers represented human feelings with a fervor resulting in the complete illusion of the hearer. Father Mersenne relates that Italian singers of his time expressed passions so violently that the audience would think they themselves were involved; and when, in an opera by Monteverdi performed in 1608 at the Mantuan court, Arianna, forsaken by Theseus, sang her heart-rending lament, the listeners burst into tears.

With such tendencies, the lyric madrigal of the sixteenth century was necessarily superseded by the musical drama. This change involved another contrast. The Renaissance, aiming at equilibrium, had given equal weight to all parts, from the treble to the bass. At about 1600, composers re-established the prevalence of one of the parts. The polyphonic style was replaced by a monodic style, which was better able to express man's mind and emotion. The polyphonic style had utilized instruments and voices within the compass of a tenth only, to avoid the interference of neighboring parts; the new monody, on the contrary, required a wide range to express passion

351

and the sudden changes from joy to grief, from melancholy to exultation.

The new style necessarily started in the vocal field; singing was the natural medium of an expressive style. The instruments soon followed the lead of the voice. Salomone Rossi Ebreo wrote the first sonata for two violins in 1613, and Biagio Marini the first sonata for one violin in 1617, both in *stile rappresentativo*, in a highly emotional style.

Instruments had to undergo a severe process of selection. Only those could be kept which had a sufficiently wide range and enough flexibility to afford all dynamic shades from pianissimo to fortissimo; instruments were expected to sing like human beings.

The first symptom was the dismissal of the majority of those oboelike instruments, the reed of which, being concealed within a wind cap, could not be grasped by the player's lips. As they had no 'expression,' no dynamic elasticity, and were not able to 'overblow' into a higher octave, they were not appropriate to the new style. All at once rankets, cromornes, schryari, rauschpfeifen, bagpipes were put aside. Only bassoons and, especially in France, the smaller shawms or oboes were preserved, and with them the flutes.

There was a coloristic reason as well. The taste of the Renaissance, in painting as in music, had favored the alternation of contrasting colors. The seventeenth century, again in painting as in music, preferred dominating color, indeed monochromes. In music, this dominating color was the timbre of bowed instruments.

To illustrate the change it would suffice to compare an inventory of the Berlin court orchestra from 1667 with the 1582 inventory listed on page 303. While in 1582 wind instruments comprised eighty-five percent of the total, the inventory of the seventeenth century lists

17 viols	2 pandores
1 violin	1 harp
1 dulcian	

or twenty-one stringed instruments (including eighteen bowed instruments) to one wind instrument. And this one wind instrument had been bought only recently.

Still, this inventory illustrates the English and German taste of the seventeenth century but does not indicate the advanced tendency in Italy and France. In Italian and French orchestras the proportion of seventeen viols to one violin would have been impossible; the

Clavichord
Gerard Dow, in the Dulwich Gallery.

Harpsichord
Van Steen, in the National Gallery, London.

17th century

PLATE XXI.

reserved sound of the viols had been replaced by the powerful and flexible tone of the "sharp violins," which, again in Dryden's contemporary words, "proclaim Their jealous pangs, and desperation, Fury, frantic indignation, Depth of pains, and height of passion."

THE VIOLIN FAMILY shares the same general construction with the viols. In spite of some differences in detail, the curving outline of the body is marked off into the same carefully propor-

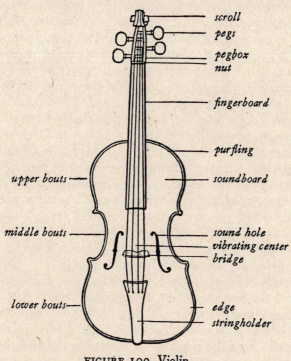

scroll
pegs
pegbox
nut

fingerboard

purfling
soundboard

sound hole
vibrating center
bridge

edge
stringholder

upper bouts

middle bouts

lower bouts

FIGURE 109. Violin.

tioned sections—the *lower bouts* separated from the smaller *upper bouts* by the waisted *middle bouts*. The bulging *back* of the body is made of one or two maple boards and slightly depressed near the outline. The sidewalls or *ribs* are also made of maple but are extremely thin so that they need to be reinforced by narrow ribbons of pinewood called *linings* that follow the outline inside the body. Further reinforcement is secured by six *blocks*, four of which fit into the corners between the bouts, the other two at the upper and lower ends of the body. The front of the body, or *soundboard*, which is made of pine, bulges like the back and has the same depression near the edge. It is inlaid with *purflings* that follow the outline and are said to increase its elasticity. The edges of both the back and the soundboard project lightly over the ribs. Two soundholes in *ff* are cut half in the middle, half in the lower bouts. On the inner side of the soundboard there is a tiny ledge or *bassbar*, which is carved or glued on, placed longitudinally underneath the position of the lowest string, serving to strengthen the tension of the bulging board. A *soundpost* is wedged upright between the front and the back near the treble foot of the bridge to transmit the vibrations to the back. The *neck* is inserted in the upper block. It is covered by a slightly bulging *fingerboard* of ebony which projects at the lower end over the soundboard. It ends at the top in a tiny cross ledge, the *nut*, which terminates the vibrating section of the strings and holds them away from the fingerboard at the upper end. The *pegbox* is crowned by a *scroll*. Four strings run from a *stringholder*, loosely attached to a *button* in the middle of the lower rib, to a *bridge*, and from the bridge over the nut to lateral pegs. (fig. 109, pl. XXIV)

A *mute*, that is, a comb-shaped rider placed on the bridge, suffocates some of the vibrations of the bridge and, consequently, of the body; the resulting timbre is thinner and less material than that of unmuted violins. The first evidence of such a device is in Renaud's air in the second act of Lully's opera *Armide* (1686), *Plus j'observe ces lieux;* there, all parts of the string orchestra bear the direction: *"Il faut jouer cecy avec des sourdines."*

The special features of the violin family, which distinguish it from the viols, have been shown in a juxtaposition on page 347.

The construction of the violin depends upon an important acoustical phenomenon. The function of its body in forming the characteristic timbre is not confined to picking up the vibrations of the bowed strings and to radiating them from a broader surface. To use the words of Sir James Jeans, it is expected "to add something of its own." This is the *formant*.

In the old theory,

the timbre of an instrument was uniquely determined by the number and proportions of the harmonics relative to the fundamental. If the same instrument played another note, the timbre would be unchanged, but all the harmonics would be shifted so as to retain the same relation to the fundamental. But according to the new formant theory, all harmonics lying within a certain range of pitch would be prominent in the note of the instrument, no matter what the fundamental, and it is the predominant range which characterizes the timbre of the instrument (Richardson).

Generally speaking, a formant is "an emphasis of certain harmonics lying in a particular region of the musical scale. . . . It is pointed out that not merely the *range of the formant*, but also the *intensity within that range* relative to the fundamental, together determine the timbre" (Richardson).

Most violins have the formant between three thousand and six thousand frequencies;

and it is through the reinforcement of harmonics having these frequencies that the violin gains its distinctive rich tone. The free vibrations of the viola are of lower frequency because of its larger dimensions, and this explains why a low note on the violin sounds quite different from the same note on the viola—the body of the violin reinforces a group of quite high harmonics, while the body of the viola reinforces a group of much lower harmonics (Jeans).

The formant does not only cause the tonal difference between the violin and other kinds of instruments, but also between good and poor violins. The frequencies of the body vibrations are high and evenly distributed in good violins; they are lower and less well distributed in mediocre instruments. The varnish does not seem to have any importance.

The origin of the violin is hard to trace. It underwent an extremely slow process of crystallization. Several instruments contributed to its formation. The fiddle in Europe was always held on the shoulder and bowed palm-downward as it is today. Other characteristic features of the violin appeared occasionally in the fiddles from the thirteenth century on: the bulging soundboard with a depression near the outline, the projecting edges, the lateral pegs and even the four strings. At the end of the fifteenth century several of these features were combined. For instance, an instrument pictured on a French tapestry of that time has three distinct bouts, lateral pegs and four strings; it is leaned against the left shoulder and bowed palm-downward.

It is not difficult to guess the accordatura of the four strings. Fiddles, according to Lanfranco's *Scintille di musica* (1533), were tuned in g g′ d′ a′ e″; if the strings were reduced to four, it would be natural to omit the doubling g′ and keep g d′ a′ e″, that is, the accordatura of the violin.

The fiddle was not the only instrument to contribute to the violin.

The medieval rebec also became an important factor in its evolution. At the beginning of the sixteenth century that old oriental instrument had no place in serious music. Though Virdung depicts a rebec or *clein geigen* in his *Musica getutscht* (1511), he does not describe it in the text, since he ranks it with the *onnütze instrumenta* or useless instruments.

Seventeen years later the situation has changed. The rebecs or *kleine geigen* that Agricola depicts in his *Musica deudsch* (1528) are given equal importance with the *grosse geigen* or viols. Their tuning is identical with the three lower strings of the violin, the viola and the tenor violin:

Treble:		g	d′ a′
Alto-Tenor:	c	g	d′
Bass:	F	c	g

Agricola is not the only authority; in 1543 the same tunings are indicated in Ganassi's *Regola Rubertina*.

Two details are particularly remarkable in Agricola's explanation. First, the viols are called *wälsche*, which, in older German, means Italian. Second, the *kleine geigen* are closely related to a third kind mentioned by him—the *Polische geigen*—except that in the latter the strings are touched with the nails instead of the fleshy finger tips, in consequence of which the strings are more widely separated. A direct confirmation of a contact between the Polish instrument and the violin is given by Michael Praetorius, who in 1618 writes that musicians call the *Violen de gamba mit dem Namen Violen, die Violen de bracio aber, Geigen oder Polnische Geigeln*. He adds: "Maybe this kind of instrument came from Poland, or there are, in that country, prominent artists who play it."

As early as 1528 some rebecs had begun to abandon their oriental shape, while retaining other of their characteristic features. Agricola gave two sets of woodcuts illustrating the *kleinen geigen*, one depicting the usual rebec shape, the other one the shape of the *grosse geigen* or viols. This seems to be the first evidence of blending the two types.

Five years later an Italian writer, Giovanni Maria Lanfranco, mentioned in his *Scintille di musica* (1533) a similar family of three sizes and called its members either *violette da arco senza tasti* ('small bowed viols without frets') or *violette da braccio* ('arm viols'). Except for the four-stringed bass, these violette had three strings tuned in fifths.

About two years later the Italian painter Gaudenzio Ferrari decorated the cupola of the Saronno cathedral with a large fresco representing a celestial concert. Among the crowd of playing and singing angels, three are playing a consort of *violette da braccio senza tasti* with three strings in the true shape of the present violin family, with shallow ribs, pointed corners, round shoulders, a depression running near the edge, *ff* and a scroll. Moreover, the alto-tenor is played in the third or fourth position, that *rechte kunstliche applikatz* which Hans Judenkunig had taught in his *Utilis et compendiaria introductio* (1523).

Thus, the violin with its alto-tenor and bass (later on called respectively *viola* and *tenor violin*) existed at the end of the first third of the sixteenth century, though with three strings only. The family that the Hispano-Italian Pedro Cerone described in his *Melopeo y Maestro* (1613) was still three-stringed.

The uppermost string began to be added in the second half of the sixteenth century.

In Sylvestro di Ganassi's *Lettione Seconda* (1543), which again refers to the three sizes of *violette senza tasti* with the same pitches mentioned in Agricola, we have the first reference to playing *pizzicato* and *vibrato*. The vibrato may have been taken from the Polish fiddlers; Agricola said that they caused "by a trembling play the melody to become sweeter than on any other instrument." The pizzicato was probably an old Italian technique, as on many Mediterranean sculptures of the middle ages players are represented plucking, not bowing, their viols.

In its classical, though not final, form the new family is mentioned and pictured in Praetorius's *Syntagma musicum* (1618–20) and is called *viole da braccio* or 'arm viols,' including in this term not only the smaller sizes but also the basses and double basses which could not possibly be held by the arm. The terminology, however, varies greatly at that period. For instance, Giovanni Gabrieli, who seems to have been the first composer to prescribe definite instruments for his scores, writes, in his *Sacrae Symphoniae* (1597), a part for a *violino;* but having an alto clef and descending beyond g, this is clearly a viola part. Correspondingly, Lodovico Zacconi, in his *Prattica di musica* (first published in 1592), includes in the term *violino* both the violin and the viola. In the same way, writers of the earlier part of the century had given diminutives, *violette* and *kleine geigen*, to all three members of the family.

This indefiniteness must be taken into consideration in interpreting the strange term *violini piccoli alla francese* in the score of Monteverdi's opera *Orfeo* (1607). Previous authors have concluded that they were small violins a fourth higher than the usual violin. But the family of violins in this score consists of the two *piccoli,* two *violini ordinarj da braccio* and one *basso de viola da braccio;* if they were, in our terminology, two small and two usual violins and a bass, the quintet would not have had any alto or tenor. But there are no inconsistencies when we interpret the *violino ordinario* as a viola, following Gabrieli and Zacconi, and the *violino piccolo* as a violin in the modern sense.

The strange epithet *alla francese* is repeated in a Florentine text of 1612, which says that French musicians in that year played the *violini alla francese.* Although *violino* is an Italian term, and although all preserved specimens are Italian, it seems that even before the Italians recognized the violin as the leading instrument it had an outstanding place, not in French music in general, but in French ballet music. A violin orchestra, indeed the classic violin orchestra, had first been formed to accompany the *ballets de cour* in the middle of the sixteenth century, though by an Italian player, Baldassare de Belgiojoso, whom the French called Balthasar de Beaujoyeux.

The first great makers of violins lived in Brescia in Lombardy: the masters GASPARO BERTOLOTTI, called DA SALÒ (c. 1542–1609), and GIOVANNI PAOLO MAGGINI (c. 1580–1632). They favored a small pattern, less deeply waisted middle bouts, corners with shorter points, deeply bulging bodies, shallow ribs and long, steep, angular holes.

Almost at the same time the neighboring town, Cremona, had begun to become the world center in violin manufacture. ANDREA AMATI (c. 1535–after 1611) was the founder of this new center and of a large dynasty of leading violin makers. His sons ANTONIO (c. 1555–after 1640) and HIERONYMOUS (c. 1556–1630) made and signed their instruments jointly; his grandson NICOLA (1596–1684), Hieronymus's son, became the greatest artist of the family. For a period of more than a hundred years these men determined the forms of violins. They flattened the body, deepened the middle bouts, sharpened the corners, rounded the holes and improved the varnish; they created the classical shape of the violin. It was Nicola Amati's greatest disciple who became the grand-master of all epochs and countries—ANTONIO STRADIVARI (c. 1640–1737). His violins can easily be recognized, but it would be difficult to describe them, since during the almost one hundred years of his life he was continually altering his pattern. Violins are like human beings; no two are identical. Their differences and similarities cannot be classified by any systematization, nor do they lend themselves to scientific description. The historically trained scholar has to give up his place to the sensitive eye of the connoisseur.

Around Stradivari arose an innumerable quantity of masters. The most outstanding of them were CARLO BERGONZI (c. 1675–1747) and JOSEPH GUARNERI 'del Gesù' (1687–after 1742). By about 1750 the peak of Italian violin making was already over. One hundred and fifty years of producing first-rate instruments, which improved instead of deteriorated with use and age, provided enough violins for a long time. With necessity lacking for great makers, inspiration and skill passed rapidly away.

The German school started at Absam near Innsbruck with JACOB STAINER (1621–1683), who was the first to introduce refined Italian workmanship into his country. His influence was strong enough to act on the violin industry of Mittenwald and to make this small Bavarian town a center in which the dynasty of the KLOTZ had a leading position. The most important members of this family were MATHIAS (1653–1735), his sons GEORG (1687–1734) and SEBASTIAN (1696–after 1743), and this latter's son, AEGIDIUS SEBASTIAN (1733–1815).

In England a native production of some importance began with THOMAS URQUHART (born 1625), and was continued principally by EDWARD PAMPHILON (c. 1680) and BARAK NORMAN (died 1740).

France, on the contrary, had no great name before FRANÇOIS TOURTE (1747–1835), who was the great-master of bow makers, and FRANÇOIS LUPOT (1774–1837).

The brief survey shows that England and France were behind Italy in violin making. The chief reason was that, unlike Italy, these countries did not consider the violin the queen of instruments. They used it as a dance instrument but were less ready to accept it in chamber music. The heavier strings and the stronger resonance of the bulging back, probably also its different bowing, made it more vigorous than the treble viol. Playford calls it "cheerful and spritely," and Jean Rousseau (1687) expects the *dessus de viole* to caress (*flater*), and the violin to enliven (*animer*). But it should be confined to this, Thomas Mace (1676) thinks: *You may add to your Press, a Pair of Violins, to be in Readiness for any Extraordinary Jolly, or Jocund Consort-Occasion; But never use Them, but with This Proviso, viz.*

In France the resistance persisted to the eighteenth century. Father Ménestrier, who in 1682 published a book *Des Ballets anciens et modernes*, calls the violin somewhat noisy (*quelque peu tapageur*), and in 1705, Jean-Laurent Lecerf de la Viéville, making a *Comparaison de la Musique italienne et de la Musique françoise*, states: "The violin is not noble, everyone agrees on this." It was the violinist and composer Jean-Marie Leclair (1697–1764) to whom the violin finally owed its social rank in France, and due to his efforts "decent folk," to quote the *Mercure de France*, were not ashamed of cultivating this instrument. The struggle of the viol to keep out the violin was paralleled by the struggle of the gamba against the violoncello. The competition between the two families was so animated that in 1740 a French Doctor of Law, Hubert le Blanc, felt compelled to publish a *Défense de la Basse de Viole contre les Entreprises du Violon et les Prétensions du Violoncel*. There we read: "The violoncello, that until now has been looked upon as a miserable hated and pitiful wretch, whose lot was to starve to death for lack of a free meal, now flatters itself that it will receive many caresses in the place of the bass viol; it already conjures up a bliss that will make it weep with tenderness." How dreadful are "the thick strings demanding an exaggerated pressure of the bow and a tension that makes them shrill!" After all, the new instruments, the violin and the cello, "not being able to dispute the delicate touch of the viol, its euphonious resonance in a suitable place where its attractions may be closely scrutinized and intimately impressive, falls back on the expedience of setting itself up in an immense hall capable of producing effects as harmful to the viol as they are favorable to the violin."

The "immense hall" of the eighteenth century, as opposed to the chamber of the sixteenth, is one of the essential factors which explain the change in musical instruments and style. The new tendency towards dramatic, overpowering music favored the strong accents and the dynamic contrast of the violin. As soon as the first operas were performed, the violin dislodged the viols and became the leading instrument in the orchestra and the chamber. It was characteristic that England and France, the two countries most opposed to a general introduction of the violin, were the last to accept the opera.

The classical shape of the violin was not its final form. At the end of the eighteenth century, when music strove for more brilliancy and power, the bridge was raised and more highly arched. Consequently, the strings had to run downhill from the bridge to the pegs, and the neck and fingerboard were slanted back to follow the angle of the strings; thinner strings were used, and the bassbar became heavier to counterbalance the stronger pressure. Not only were new violins made after this pattern; old instruments that were still in use were transformed, so that it is extremely rare to find a violin in its original condition.

More radical innovations, such as FRANÇOIS CHANOT's edgeless and cornerless violin (Paris 1817), FRANÇOIS SAVART's straight-sided model (Paris 1817), as well as many others, have been failures.

One recent improvement, on the contrary, has been successful: the G string *overspun* with silver. When Jean Rousseau published his *Traité de la Viole* in 1687, overspun strings already existed; but there is no evidence of their being used on violins. In the same year Daniel Speer, in his *Grund-richtiger Unterricht*, related that some violas had strings overspun with silver or copper. There is no mention of them in the most detailed method of violin playing in the eighteenth century, Leopold Mozart's *Versuch einer Violinschule*, first published in 1756. The first mention of overspun strings in violins seems to be in a British patent dated January 31, 1772, which protects William Lovelace's special "manner of wiring fiddle strings so as not to injure the gut, and to wire them more compactly and firmly." Some eighty years later, however, such strings were not yet universally accepted. In 1855 an instrument maker, Heinrich Welcker von Gontershausen, wrote that some violinists imitated the example of the three lower strings of the guitar by overspinning the G string with silver, but that most players preferred gut strings.

Small violins existed as early as the end of the sixteenth century. Some puzzling items in German inventories of that time must have been similar to the small treble tuned to *c' g' d'' a''* mentioned by Praetorius in 1618. Several German composers, Philipp Heinrich Erlebach, for instance, and Johann Sebastian Bach, used this sharp-sounding instrument in their scores. Strung and tuned to the pitch of normal violins, they are still employed to teach children.

Quinton was the French name of a violin with five strings in *g d' a' d'' g''*. It is a mistake to apply this name to five-stringed treble viols.

The viola is the alto of the family and has its strings tuned to *c g d' a'*. It ought to be larger than it usually is to have enough resonance. Its insufficient size is a consequence of the subordinate position of violas in the eighteenth century. Sandwiched between the melody of the violins and the accompaniment of the basses, they had an unimportant role. Consequently, they were played by superannuated violinists who, unwilling to adjust themselves to the larger size, had them reduced. Even precious old specimens were clipped. The instrument is not always clearly designated by composers; in German scores one finds the term *violetta,* and in French scores *quinte, cinquiesme, hautecontre,* or *taille,* which are names of a part rather than of a definite instrument.

The tenor-violin in *F c g d',* the strings of which had a vibrating length of less than twenty inches, was constructed between the end of the sixteenth and the middle of the eighteenth centuries. It had a deep body and must have been held like a cello. It was rare, however, and was finally given up; all modern attempts to revive it have been failures.

The violoncello began its career as *bass viola da braccio.* It was tuned either to *C G d a* or a tone lower. As a bass, it was not expected to play solo parts; its role was to provide music with a solid foundation. Specimens up to the middle of the seventeenth century, and even beyond, were larger and broader than the later cello, and they must have had thicker strings. Like gambas, they were bowed in palm-upward position.

The modern pattern of the violoncello must have originated in the middle of the seventeenth century. The Bolognese composer, Domenico Gabrielli (1659-1690), wrote the first solo pieces for this instrument, two sonatas for cello and basso continuo, ricercari for cello without accompaniment, a canon for two celli and several ricercari for cello and basso continuo, all of which bear the date 1689. We do not know whether the Italian cellists of that time played palm up- or downward; at any rate, Frederick the Great's teacher, Johann Joachim Quantz, in his *Versuch* (1752), ascribed the palm-downward position of the cello bow to the Italian. (pl. XXIV)

The usual violoncello in Germany was probably not as advanced as the Italian type. It must have been too clumsy for a brilliant technique. Johann Sebastian Bach preferred, in solo pieces, a so-called *violoncello piccolo,* a hundred to a hundred and ten centimeters high and some thirty centimeters wide. It was tuned like the usual cello and not a fifth higher, as some writers have claimed; the parts written for it in Bach's scores require low *C.*

The violoncello a cinque corde, on the contrary, that Bach prescribed at about 1720 in the sixth of his suites for cello solo, was not necessarily a violoncello piccolo. But the fact that it would be hard to keep an *e'* string from breaking on a large instrument suggests a small cello with five strings rather than the usual cello.

An eighteenth century variety of the cello, suspended from the shoulders of ambulant musicians, was, in a scholarly terminology, called *viola da spalla* or 'shoulder viol.' Contemporaneous pictures seem to indicate that this portable cello was shallower than the ordinary one.

The violone, pictured by Praetorius under the name *große baß-geige*, was intermediate between the violoncello and the double bass. It was, according to Praetorius's woodcut, four and a half Brunswick feet or one hundred and twenty-five centimeters tall and had five strings in $F_1 C G d a$. Under various names (*Kammerbass, Halbbass*) and in various accordaturas it has persisted to this day, though it is officially replaced by the double bass.

The double bass existed in Germany as early as the sixteenth century. Praetorius pictures such a gigantic *groß-contra-baßgeig*, two hundred and twenty-five centimeters or ninety inches high, with five strings, the accordatura of which he does not indicate. Striving for a strong foundation of the orchestra, makers in three centuries pursued the phantom of "giants." The Victoria and Albert Museum, London, owns a double bass of the seventeenth century which is over eight feet high. But JEAN-BAPTISTE VUILLAUME's *octobasse* (Paris 1849) is four meters high, has the strings stopped by seven pedals and is played by a bow that is supported by blocks shaped like oarlocks. An American model (1889) by JOHN GEYER is even taller. The most practical types, however, do not exceed one hundred and eighty centimeters or seventy-two inches.

As to the form, one can distinguish the German and the Italian model. The double bass of German makers approached the form of the viola da gamba; it had sloping shoulders, a flat back with a slanting upper part, deep ribs and sometimes even frets. It usually had five strings tuned by fourths, and even when it dropped the fifth string, it kept the tuning $E_1 A_1 D G$, which was generally accepted. The Italians, on the contrary, preferred a true violin form and even reduced the number of strings to three. Most players use the palm-upward position (*Dragonetti bow*), some prefer the palm-downward position (*Bottesini bow*).

In the nineteenth century the fifth string was restored in order to extend the range of the double bass to C_1, in accordance with the cello, which the double bass was expected to accompany in the lower octave. As the fifth string increases the pressure on the bridge and the soundboard interferes with bowing, some players prefer the mechanical contrivances created at the end of the nineteenth century in order to change the pitch of the fourth string. This is lengthened on a narrow extension of the fingerboard running parallel to the scroll. It produces E_1 in its usual length, and C_1 in its total length. Four keys for the left hand, arranged at the upper end of the fingerboard, work metal stoppers that can lengthen the vibrating section of the string from E_1 to $E\flat_1$, D_1, $D\flat_1$ or C.

THE VIOLA D'AMORE as we usually think of it, is a bowed instrument the shape of a treble viol, with a set of thin wire strings

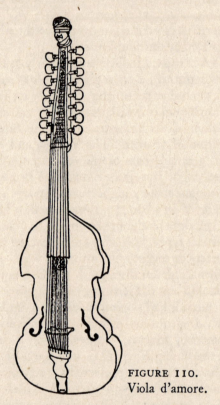

FIGURE 110.
Viola d'amore.

stretched behind the bowed gut strings which vibrate sympathetically without being bowed themselves, thus producing a silvery echo; the instrument has no frets and is held and bowed like a violin. The sympathetic strings are the principal trait in this picture. It happens, however, that they were a late acquisition and not at all characteristic of the instrument called viola d'amore by the generation before Bach and Handel. (fig. 110)

At first the name was given to a violin with *bowed* metal strings. Praetorius (1618) had already stated that violins produced a soft and charming sound when strung with brass and steel strings, but he had no special name for such a violin. Sixty years later the name 'viola d'amore' is first mentioned in Evelyn's *Diary* (1679); he had much enjoyed *for its sweetnesse and novelty, the viol d'amore of 5 wyre-strings plaid with a bow, being but an ordinary violin, play'd on lyre way by a German*. In 1687 two excellent authorities, one French, one German, gave the same definition as Evelyn. Jean Rousseau in his *Traité de la Viole* described the *viole d'amour* as a kind of *dessus de viole* with wire strings which, when bowed, made a bad effect and sounded too sharp (*aigre*); this is why the French never used such strings. According to Daniel Speer's *Grund-richtiger Unterricht*, the *viol de l'amor* had double steel or gut strings.

Even in the first decades of the eighteenth century the literary sources do not mention any sympathetic strings. Sébastien Brossard's *Dictionnaire de Musique*, first published in 1703, defines in its last (English) edition of 1740 the viole d'amour as "a kind of triple viol or violin, having six brass or steel strings, like those of the Harpsicord, ordinarily played with a bow." Both Johann Mattheson, in *Das neu-eröffnete Orchestre* (1713), and, referring to him, Johann Gottfried Walther in his *Musicalisches Lexicon* (1732) give it the accordatura $g\ c'\ e'(\flat)\ g'\ c''$, while Johann Philipp Eisel's *Musicus autodidactus* (1738) indicates $F\ B\flat\ c\ g\ c'\ f'\ b\flat'$. Not one of them speaks of sympathetic strings, and it is hard to believe that specialists on the viol, such as Rousseau, or on the orchestra and timbre, as Mattheson, would have failed to mention them if they existed. The question then arises whether such noted pieces as Heinrich Biber's partita for two violes d'amour and bass, written at the end of the seventeenth century, Attilio Ariosti's sonatas of about 1720 for a viola d'amore with only four strings in the range of the violin (tuned between a and c''), or those in four works of Johann Sebastian Bach, were actually intended for, and played with, sympathetic strings.

Sympathetic strings had come to England from the Near East, apparently in the sixteenth century. Praetorius related that the English used sympathetic viol strings to sound *per consensum* with the bowed gut strings. Details about the arrangement of sympathetic strings can be deduced from English sources of the middle of the seventeenth century. Chancellor Francis Bacon of Verulam (d. in 1626), in his natural history, *Sylva Sylvarum*, published after his death in 1648, writes:

It was devised, that a Viall should have a Lay of Wire Strings below, as close to the Belly as a Lute: And then the Strings of Guts mounted upon a Bridge, as in Ordinary Vialls: To the end that, by this means, the upper Strings strucken, should make the lower resound by Sympathy, and so make the Musick the better; Which, if it be to purpose, then Sympathy worketh as well by Report of Sound, as by Motion.

And four years later, in 1652, John Playford speaks of sympathetic strings on the lyra viol (cp. page 348). *Of this sort of Viols, I have seen many, but Time and Disuse has set them aside.*

Not until 1741 was there any mention of sympathetic strings on the viola d'amore. In that year Joseph Friedrich Bernhard Caspar Majer published a book *Neu-eröffneter Theoretisch- und Pracktischer Music-Saal*. Its § 13 distinguishes between two kinds of viole d'amore, a smaller one like a violin, and a larger one slightly bigger than a viola. Both have six strings. After having indicated as many as seventeen different accordaturas, Majer adds in a footnote that there are six sympathetic strings which can be tuned to the upper octave of the bowed strings. Even here, where there are sympathetic strings, almost all the bowed strings are of metal: the first two are overspun with silver wire, three middle strings are steel or brass and only the highest one is gut.

Actual specimens, too, give no evidence of early sympathetic strings. Some authors have cited a viola d'amore in the Musikhistorisk Museum at Copenhagen (no. 376), which bears a label of the famous viol maker, Joachim Tielke, in Hamburg, and a date, the three first figures of which can be deciphered as 168. Unfortunately, this instrument belongs in the eighteenth century and has nothing whatsoever to do with Tielke. The label, as so often happens, must have been taken from quite a different instrument. But there are in existence viole d'amore with sympathetic strings, the authenticity of which cannot be doubted, made in Bavaria about 1720. Consequently, the first literary evidence in 1741 does not give the earliest date of viole d'amore with sympathetic strings.

Antonio Vivaldi's concerto in D minor, written about 1740 for lute, muted strings, a keyboard instrument and a viola d'amore with seven strings in $A\ d\ a\ d'\ f'\ a'\ d''$, is then doubtless intended for an instrument with sympathetic strings.

In spite of the great number of specimens preserved in museums, the actual significance of the viola d'amore was small. The compositions mentioned, by Biber, Ariosti, Bach and Vivaldi, represent the bulk of good music written for the instrument. Soon after the publication of Vivaldi's concerto, it fell into almost complete oblivion. There is almost no music for it dating from the second half of the eighteenth century, with the exception of a weak sonata by Karl Stamitz (1746–1801).

Though apparently forgotten, the instrument was recently resurrected in the air "Doux comme Hermine" in Meyerbeer's opera *Les Huguenots* (1836), with the accordatura $d f a d' f\sharp' a' d''$. A new fashion for it started in about 1900. Charles Martin Loeffler in America had used it in his *Death of Tintagiles* (1897). It was given parts in Gustave Charpentier's opera *Louise* (1900), in Massenet's *Le jongleur de Notre Dame* (1902), in Puccini's *Madame Butterfly* (1904) and in Wilhelm Kienzl's *Der Kuhreigen* (1911).

We do not know why this instrument was called a viola d'amore. Its tone was not loving but metallic. The name is probably not connected with love. As the majority of these viols have a blindfold boy's head instead of a scroll, it seems more logical to interpret the name as 'Amor's fiddle' without any reference to the emotion that the little god symbolizes. Moreover the blindfold head is not confined to the viola d'amore and, therefore, is not indicative of its characteristic sound.

Musicians often speak of the "viola d'amour," thus carelessly combining an Italian with a French word. The term is either Italian, *viola d'amore*, or French, *viole d'amour*.

THE VIOLA POMPOSA. Johann Sebastian Bach is credited with the 'invention' of a bowed instrument of this name. But no contemporaneous source has mentioned or described it, nor did Bach write any part for it in his scores. The sources which mention it, dating 1782 to 1792, are unreliable, not only because of their dates but because they confuse the pomposa with the violoncello piccolo. Fortunately, a few pieces written for the instrument have been preserved, though not compositions of Bach: two in Georg Philipp Telemann's *Der getreue Music-Meister*, Hamburg, 1728, a concerto by Karl Heinrich Graun (1701–1759) and a sonata *per la Pomposa col Basso* by the Viennese Cristian Giuseppe Lidarti about 1760. The information drawn from these pieces is first, the highest note is e^3, the lowest note f; second, two of the open strings were doubtless d' and g, as in the violin and the viola; third, a transposition into a lower octave would be musically impossible. Thus, the pomposa must have had the range of the violin with an additional note below.

These conclusions call to mind a strange passage in Heinrich Christoph Koch's *Musikalisches Lexikon* (1802): "Once in a while one uses a viola in the usual shape and accordatura with the addition of the *e* string of the violin, which by some is also called *violino pomposo*."

This violino pomposo must have been identical with the viola pomposa, as its accordatura fits in with the compositions; its lower limit even exceeds the lowest note in Telemann's and Lidarti's pieces. The fact that in one passage Lidarti breaks the melodic line in order to avoid the notes below *g* is no reason to suppose there was no *c* string. The lowest string was weak on all instruments before over-spinning came into general use; and that melodic line of Lidarti's demanded a particularly full tone up to the end. Besides, the lowest string must have been unusually weak on the viola pomposa; five strings tuned in fifths required a compromise in the size of the body which could not be large enough to give sufficient resonance to the lowest string. The change of name is easily explained. Being a combination of violin and viola, the instrument could be called by either name. This is confirmed by Graun's concerto. There are two manuscripts of it; they are identical, except that the instrument in question is called *violino pomposo* in one of them, and in the other, *viola pomposa*.

Such a combination of violin and viola could certainly not be larger than a viola, and according to Koch, the violino pomposo was *eine Viole in gewöhnlicher Form*, 'a viola in usual form.' Thus, one should not classify as viola pomposa certain five-stringed instruments of the early eighteenth century which were thirty inches long and had ribs as deep as three or three and a half inches. These instruments were tenor violins, intermediate between the viola and the violoncello and tuned to *F c g d' a'*. This has been confirmed by experiments made by Ernest Closson in Brussels, and by the author, together with Paul Hindemith, in Berlin.

THE BARYTON was a bass gamba with six bowed strings in *A d f a d' f'* and sometimes as many as forty wire strings. These latter were stretched inside the neck as usual, but the neck was open from the rear side so that, as well as vibrating sympathetically, the strings could be plucked by the left thumb. (pl. XXII b)

Barytons were almost exclusively built and played in South Germany. The first evidence of them is in a collection of nine *Partien auf die Viola Paredon*, composed by a certain Johann Georg Krause

Cittern

Baryton

Guitar

18th century

PLATE XXII.

and dedicated to Duke Christian Ulrich of Württemberg. As this prince died in 1704, the instrument must have existed before that date. Among the outstanding amateurs of the baryton was the Prince Nicolaus Esterházy; it was for him that Joseph Haydn, the conductor of his orchestra, wrote a hundred and seventy-five pieces for the instrument. The baryton stood on the periphery of musical life rather than at its center, even at the peak of its existence at about 1750. There was one single player of the instrument in the nineteenth century—Sebastian Ludwig Friedel, member of the royal orchestra in Berlin (d. 1842). Playing was particularly difficult and tuning laborious; considering the effort necessary to overcome these impediments, the musical result was poor.

THE BOW has always been neglected in the history of musical instruments; dated specimens have not been preserved, literary sources are lacking, and on art works the decisive part of the bow is generally hidden under the player's hand.

The essential step in its early development was the passage in Asia from rattan to wood. European bows were exclusively made of wood. Wooden bows are not as elastic as rattan and are less easily curved, and therefore need a device to keep the hair away from the stick. The most primitive expedient is the choice of a stick with the stump of a branch, to which the hair can be tied; this is what players of the Jugoslavian fiddle *gusla* do, and such bows can be seen on Italian paintings representing violists as late as the sixteenth century. A less primitive expedient was used for instance in India, a small piece of wood wedged between the stick and the hair at the lower end and held in place by a wrapping band of cloth. In later specimens the wedge was fastened to the stick and was called the nut. Such a device seems to have been known in Europe as early as the twelfth century. For many centuries the nut was reminiscent of the loosely wedged piece of wood. Its shape was improved by being rounded and slightly grooved, and it was held fast on the stick by slipping into a small track. The hair was still wrapped around it and was caught in place by being squeezed between the nut and the stick.

In the sixteenth and seventeenth centuries the bow had generally a *horn-shaped nut,* the base of the horn being attached to the stick and the tip curving toward the head of the bow.

At the end of the seventeenth century a special device allowed the player to alter the tension of the hair; the nut ran in a slide in the stick and could be adjusted at will by a wire loop that could hook onto any one of a series of teeth in a piece of iron inlaid in the outer side of the stick. This *dentated bow* had only a temporary importance, but it has survived in Swedish folk instruments.

At the beginning of the eighteenth century the dentation was replaced by an inner screw, the head of which, forming a turnable end of the stick, shifted the nut and regulated the tension at will. This is the modern device.

Up to about 1650 the head of the bow was sometimes distinct from the stick; it was a kind of tooth made of bone curving toward the hair with the tip pointing upward. After 1650 the head was always one piece with the stick and in most cases elegantly curved in the form of a pike's head. In the eighteenth century the head became curved more and more steeply, until it was at right angles to the stick. Finally, François Tourte in Paris (1747–1835) gave it its modern form.

At the same time its curve was changed. The older bow curved very slightly outward (but certainly not as much as some violinists imagine if they consider the difficulties in playing Bach's polyphonic sonatas). The modern bow was curved inward to increase the elasticity and response of the stick and to enable the player to give the expression required in modern music by a minimum of pressure. Half a century earlier the stick had been lengthened and fluted or cut in an octagonal form.

ARCHLUTES (Italian *arciliuti*). In the second half of the sixteenth century, when basses became more important than they were before, the lutanists tried to add lower strings to their instruments. But the reach of the stopping left hand was limited; a certain width of the fingerboard could not be exceeded. So they no longer tried to stop the required bass strings. Instead, they arranged them as open drones outside the fingerboard and tuned them beforehand in accordance with the bass notes demanded in the piece that they were going to play. To maintain a safe tensile strain, the drones had to have a separate pegbox. Three different arrangements were devised.

The chitarrone seems to have been the oldest among them. The first clear evidence of it is on a portrait of Lady Mary Sydney (d. 1586) in Penshurst Place, Kent, that Dr. Francis W. Galpin has discovered. This new Italian instrument was man size. It had the body of a large lute, but the peg arrangement was different. The pegbox was straight instead of being bent back. Above, the neck was

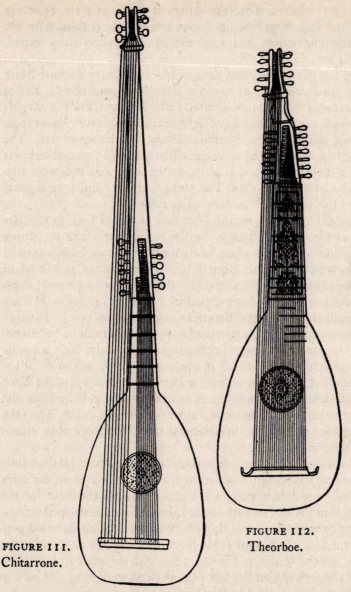

FIGURE 111.
Chitarrone.

FIGURE 112.
Theorboe.

considerably lengthened and bore a second pegbox for the drones. Praetorius distinguishes two main kinds: the Paduan chitarrone, nearly seven feet high, with eight pairs of strings on the fingerboard, and the Roman chitarrone, six feet high, with only six pairs of strings on the board. The two strings of each pair were an octave apart. Both chitarroni had eight open bass strings. A third type, the Bolognese chitarrone, had wire strings. The accordatura varied. (fig. 111)

After the chitarrone came the *theorboe*. It is, says Thomas Mace in 1676, *an Instrument of so much Excellency, and Worth, and of so Great Good Vse, That in dispite of all Fickleness, and Novelty, It is still made use of, in the Best Performances in Musick.* Its arrangement was similar to the chitarrone except for the upper part. The first pegbox was straight as in the chitarrone. The second one was placed a little higher and slightly to the side. The two were connected by an S-shaped neck. The strings, at first single, were geminated in the eighteenth century. (fig. 112)

What did the name mean? It cannot be traced back to any Romance or Germanic language, but the root *trb*, meaning something bulging like a belly or a bag, is frequent in Slavonic languages. A relation with a Slavonic word is the more possible as a kind of theorboe exists in the Ukraine under the name *torban*. Nevertheless the torban cannot have been copied from the Italian tiorbo. It is not only much clumsier, but different in one important point—fourteen or fifteen open strings are stretched over the treble side of the soundboard and fastened to pegs in the edge of the body. Such a combination of a lute and a zither in one instrument is unknown in the Occident, but not in the Orient; a Persian book of 1345, the *Kanz al-tuhaf*, describes an instrument *muġnī*, which had the neck and the body of a lute and the string arrangement of a zither. The relation between the Italian theorboe and the Ukrainian torban cannot yet be determined.

A third kind of drone lute was the theorboed lute (Italian *liuto* [*at*]*tiorbato*). Though Praetorius gives this name to an ordinary theorboe with double strings, we should reserve the term for the usual lute of the seventeenth century. In this lute the stopped strings, running over the fingerboard, were tuned by pegs in the usual pegbox turned back at a right angle from the neck; the pegbox for the drones, on the contrary, formed a straight elongation of the bass side of the neck so that the first pegbox stood at right angles both to the neck and the second pegbox. (pl. XXIII c)

CITTERNS. The general tendency towards increasing the bass range led, in northern Europe, to the construction of several larger citterns which still had the essential features of the family—that is,

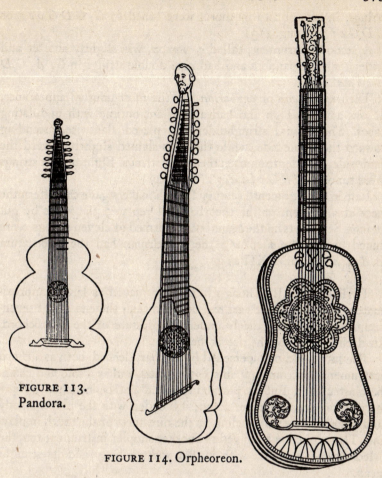

FIGURE 113.
Pandora.

FIGURE 114. Orpheoreon.

FIGURE 115. Guitar (c. 1700).

the flat front and back, lateral pegs and wire strings—but which differed in some details.

Pandora was the name of one of them, which was said to have been invented by a certain JOHN ROSE in London in 1562. The name first appears in 1566 in the scenario of Gascoigne's tragedy *Jocasta* and, for the last time, one hundred years later, in an inventory of the Berlin court orchestra dated 1667. It must, however, be noted that this name was given to entirely different instruments. Rose's pandora was four feet high; its outline was doubly scalloped, thus forming three lobes; the stringholder was frontal and lutelike. The strings, in sets of two or more, were tuned to $G_1 C D G c e a$ or $C D G c f a d'$. (fig. 113)

A second instrument, called *penorcon*, was slightly shorter and wider than the pandora and had nine double strings in $G_1 A_1 C D G c e a d'$.

The *orpheoreon* or *orpharion* had the most unusual appearance. It was a meter high and had an elegant outline with undulating lobes. The frontal stringholder was placed slantwise, ascending toward the treble side, while the frets slanted slightly toward the same side, in order to shorten the upper strings. Eight double strings were tuned to $C F G c f a d' g'$. (fig. 114)

Late in the eighteenth century French makers gave the cittern the neck arrangement of the theorboe and replaced the wires by gut strings. Seven sets on the fingerboard, formed of eleven strings, were tuned to $e a c\sharp' e' a' c\sharp'' e''$; the five drones had the accordatura $A B c\sharp d d\sharp$. (pl. XXII a)

THE GUITAR. Though lutes were played as late as approximately 1750, the lutist's art had declined after the end of the seventeenth century, particularly under the pressure of the harpsichord. Its decline involved the rise of the guitar.

The lute could be superseded by the harpsichord, both as a chord instrument to accompany on a figured bass, and as a solo and chamber instrument. But its portability could not be matched by any harpsichord, clavichord or piano; it blended with the player's body and reflected his every feeling by the directness of the touch in playing. This attraction belonged to another simpler instrument too, the Mediterranean guitar, with its flat waisted body and its straight head.

At the beginning of the seventeenth century the guitar still had only four double strings in either $c f a d'$ or $f b d g'$, though VINCENTE ESPINEL, a guitarist in Madrid in the second half of the sixteenth century, is credited with having added a fifth pair below. Compared with a modern guitar, the body was narrower and deeper and the waist was less emphasized and higher in the body; the soundhole was covered with a rose and the head had a quadrangular outline. The strings in these earlier guitars were knotted through holes in the crossledge which served as a stringholder. (pls. XXII c, XXIII a, fig. 115)

In the seventeenth century the Hispano-Italian guitar began to overrun the aristocratic world of France; it seems that *les Italiens,* the Italian actors in Paris, brought it into fashion. Painters à la mode, like Watteau and Boucher, depicted it in the hands of both comedians and ladies of high society.

When it became an amateur instrument it was simplified. Six single strings in *E A d g b e'* (written one octave higher) replaced the five double strings; to counteract the loss of sound volume, the body was made larger, relatively broader and shallower, and the soundhole lost its rose. The new form was easier to handle and musically more robust; it was to the old form what the cello was to the gamba.

Handling was still more facilitated in the nineteenth century by metal screws replacing the wooden pegs.

THE HARPSICHORD. In the sixteenth century the best harpsichords were made in Italy. But in the seventeenth century the Italian harpsichord began to lose its former supremacy. The makers, persisting in the old tradition, were reluctant to adopt foreign improvements. The first evidence of two keyboards on an Italian instrument is an Innsbruck inventory of 1665—that is, eighty or ninety years after the first mention of *zweyen clavieren* in the north. The reason for adopting a second keyboard so late was a prejudice against the use of stops; they finally went as far as to increase the number of keyboards to three for only three stops in order to avoid pulling out the stops. A harpsichord by Vincenzo Sodi in the Crosby Brown Collection in New York, dating from 1779, has three stops, 4' 8' 8'; the upper manual worked the 4' stop, the middle manual worked one 8' and the 4', and the lower manual both 8'.

In about 1600, when most of the Italian centers of harpsichord making had lost their importance, Antwerp with the Ruckers dynasty became the uncontested center. (pl. XXI b)

The Ruckers were the first of those famous families in which genius and skill for a certain branch of instrument making was kept alive and fertile for generations. To own a harpsichord or spinet of one of the Ruckers was the pride of musicians and music lovers in all countries of Europe for two centuries; when, in 1792, under the Terror, a special commission inventoried the estates of the émigrés, an astonishing number of Ruckers instruments were found in the forsaken homes of French aristocrats.

Until recently, the eldest, Hans Ruckers, was credited with all imaginable improvements of the harpsichord. Today we know that stops and double keyboards existed long before him; the merit of the Ruckers consisted in the rare quality of their instruments rather than in the invention of special contrivances. The very quality of the instruments has made them difficult to study, because they were not put aside or chopped up for fuel when superseded by improved, 'modern' harpsichords, but transformed according to the latest fashion. Our museums possess more than a hundred Ruckers instruments; scarcely one of them is in its original condition, without additional or altered keyboards or keys or stops. Investigators cannot be too skeptical of such museum pieces.

The second keyboard, that we now suppose to be a means of rapidly changing force and timbre, seems to have originally had an entirely different purpose. A Dutch organist, Quirijn van Blankenburgh (1654–c. 1739), who knew many harpsichords in original condition and witnessed their transformation, described the old arrangement and its significance in his book *Elementa musica of nieuw licht tot het welverstaan van de musiec* (1739): transposition was difficult on a keyboard instrument (and certainly unsatisfactory because the temperament was unequal). A satisfactory transposition was brought about without any mental effort on the part of the player by adding a second keyboard under the first that was shifted five semitones to the left. A *C* on the lower keyboard coincided with a *G* on the higher one, and the harpsichordist could seemingly play *C* major from his book and yet produce the required *G* major. One specimen of a harpsichord with two transposing keyboards is preserved in the Morris Steinert Collection of Keyboard Instruments at Yale University, New Haven, Connecticut. When musicians after 1700 had no more use for this obsolete transposition, the two keyboards were shifted and completed to coincide. The instrument became what the French called *à ravalement* or 'let down.' Instead of ending on the apparent *E* (which actually was a *C*), the five additional keys made it end on an apparent B_1, which was actually a G_1, forming a kind of short octave already explained on page 333. (pl. XXIV)

The seventeenth century transformers of old harpsichords had to make use of four stops, each keyboard having two. As then the two keyboards were used to enrich the timbre instead of transposing music into another key, the four stops were embarrassing. Three of them could be used as 8' 8' 4', and all combinations of them were made possible if the keyboards could be coupled by pushing in or pulling out one of them. The fourth was useless; it was either disconnected or changed into a clipped and dry sounding *lute-stop*. This could be arranged by plucking the strings near the bridge or by muting with a felted ledge the strings plucked by the jacks of one of the three first stops.

Harpsichord players of today may wonder why the fourth stop was not used for a 16′. This was not done for two reasons. First, the instrument was not long enough. Second, there was no need, indeed there was a dislike, for a 16′. No English, Flemish, French, Italian or Spanish harpsichord ever had one; it occurs exclusively in a few German harpsichords of the eighteenth century. This should be learned by modern harpsichordists who are continually pressing the 16′ pedal in Couperin's *Pièces de Clavecin* as well as in rounds of the *Fitzwilliam Virginal Book*.

Moreover, it cannot be too often repeated that the harpsichord, generally speaking, had no pedal to facilitate the change of timbre and power. In the sixteenth and seventeenth centuries it had *lateral stops*, piercing the right wall of the case almost beyond the reach of the player's hand and eluding any change in the middle of a piece. They were replaced by *frontal stops* in the eighteenth century, which to a certain extent allowed the player to connect or disconnect them even during a piece, but not without taking the hand off the keys.

It is true that a *pedal* was invented in the seventeenth century. In Thomas Mace's *Musick's Monument* (1676) we read an astonishing report on a new harpsichord called *pedal*. This was

an Instrument of a Late Invention, contriv'd by one Mr John Hayward of London, a most excellent Kind of Instrument for a Consort, and far beyond all Harpsions or Organs. The player had several Various Stops at Pleasure; and all Quick and Nimble, by the Ready Turn of the Foot. . . . There being right underneath his Toes four little Pummels of Wood, under each Foot two, any one of those four he may Tread upon at his Pleasure; which by the Weight of his Foot drives a Spring, and so Causeth the whole Instrument to Sound, either Soft or Loud, accompanying as he shall chuse to Tread any of them down.

In spite of this marvelous quality, the pedal had no success; not one source besides Mace mentions it. If the failure had been in the mechanical field, then cleverer hands would have improved the contrivance. It rather must be looked for in the musical field. "Several various stops at pleasure, and all quick and nimble"—this was certainly not to the taste of the seventeenth century. Music in that time was much less motley and variegated than we like to imagine, and we had better modify our ideas than force an inappropriate style upon ancient music.

When finally the harpsichord was given a pedal, it was in England and only in the last two decades of its existence, when the competition of the piano caused the harpsichord makers to think of all possible accommodations in order to keep up with the newcomer. As far as the author knows, one wooden pedal was sometimes attached near the left leg of the instrument after 1760. One must not confuse this kind of harpsichord with the German *Pedal-Klavizimbel* (e.g. in Bach's possession) which had a pedal keyboard like an organ and was a practicing instrument for organists.

CARILLONS. On page 279 we spoke of sets of bells used in monasteries, suspended from horizontal bars and struck by hand with hammers. They were made mechanical in the thirteenth century by being connected with tower clocks; a cogwheel in the works caused the hammers to strike the tuned bells in a prescribed melodic sequence. Flanders and northern France, later also Holland, made this contrivance more and more elaborate. Little iron nails, inserted in a rotating cylinder in an appropriate arrangement, released the hammers so that finally a complete tune, indeed a series of tunes, was played without a man's interference (as in our musical boxes). After about 1500, if not earlier, these carillons could be disconnected from the clock and the rotating cylinder and played by hand from a keyboard, and, after 1600, even by foot. When John Evelyn came to Amsterdam in 1641, he went up to the carillon in the tower of St. Nicholas and found, according to his *Diary*,

one who played all sorts of compositions from the tablature before him, as if he had fingered an organ; for so were the hammers fastened with wires to several keys put into a frame twenty feet below the bells, upon which (by help of a wooden instrument, not much unlike a weaver's shuttle, that guarded his hand) he struck on the keys and played to admiration: all this while, through the clattering of the wires, din of the too nearly sounding bells, and noise that his wooden gloves made the confusion was so great, that it was impossible for the musician, or any that stood near him, to hear any thing himself; yet, to those at a distance, and especially in the streets, the harmony and the time were the most exact and agreeable.

These carillons became the pride of Netherlandish towns and objects of their competition. To outdo rivals, carillons were made with more than fifty bells and ten thousand nails in the rotating cylinder. Other countries also have adopted the carillon and its cheerful music. But their manufacture has almost exclusively been confined to the Netherlands, and nowhere else did they enter so intimately into the daily life as in their native land.

Park and chamber chimes were an offshoot of carillons. In seignorial parks the Netherlands had a predilection for all kinds of automatons released by water works, and especially for hydraulic chimes. When John Evelyn visited such a park in Amsterdam in 1641, "there was likewise a cylinder that entertained the company with a variety of chimes, the hammers striking upon the brims of porcelain dishes, suited to the tones and notes, without cracking any of them."

Chimes in chamber size encased in a piece of furniture with a keyboard served for the entertainment of amateurs, or even practicing purposes of those in charge of the large town chimes. But as the needs of professional players required the full range of tower chimes, including even the big bass bells, Dutch bell founders devised the system of replacing the bells by space-saving slabs of bronze, which may have been suggested by native metallophones in the recently conquered Dutch colonies in East India. From that time, sets of metal slabs, generally called *glockenspiel* both with or without a keyboard, were used at home, in orchestral performances (from Handel's *Saul*, 1738, and Mozart's *Zauberflöte*, 1791, to Gustav Mahler's Seventh Symphony, 1908), in musical bands and even in the organ. It probably was an organ glockenspiel on which J. S. Bach played the *campanella* in *b* and *e* of his cantata no. 53, *Schlage doch gewünschte Stunde*.

Sometimes the higher harmonics of a struck metal slab are stronger than the fundamental, or even drown the fundamental entirely so that the musical effect is uneven. To prevent this drawback, a Frenchman, AUGUSTE MUSTEL in Paris (1886), perhaps inspired by the resonance bamboos of the Javanese metallophone *gendèr*, made a piano out of the old glockenspiel, with tuned steel slabs instead of strings, which singly or in pairs were placed on tuned resonance boxes. The vibrations in these boxes reinforced the fundamentals of the slabs and, consequently, muffled the penetrating tinkle of the harmonics. This instrument, known as *celesta*, is much used in the modern orchestra.

Flemish carillons must not be confused with English *change-ringing*. Here, the bells of a chime are rung with ropes by individual men, and the purpose is not to play tunes but to change the order of the bells; starting from a scale arrangement, the players pass through a number of permutations until the scale is finally re-established; in these permutations each bell either keeps its position or else is rung in the position adjacent to that in which it was struck before; for instance:

$$
\begin{array}{ccccc}
1 & 2 & 3 & 4 & 5 \\
2 & 1 & 3 & 5 & 4 \\
2 & 3 & 1 & 4 & 5 \\
3 & 2 & 4 & 1 & 5 \\
3 & 4 & 2 & 5 & 1
\end{array}
$$

and so on. Practiced for three hundred years, this kind of ringing has become a traditional sport of enthusiastic amateurs.

THE FLUTE. The introduction to this chapter has said that the passage from the sixteenth to the seventeenth century involved a particularly decisive change in the importance of wind instruments. For two reasons their former prevalence declined. The first reason was that most of the older wind instruments were inadequate for the expressive style of the new epoch; the second reason was the strong tendency away from the variegated colors of the past to the monochrome style in which one color, that of stringed instruments, dominated almost exclusively. This process was completed at different times in different places. The string orchestra, which is still the nucleus of our modern orchestra, was established at that time. But no sooner had this restriction taken place than wind instruments came back, only in a less important position. They were needed both as a spice to enliven the monotony of the strings and, in the opera, as a means of characterizing typical scenes and personages.

Flutes, oboes and bassoons were the first to be readmitted to the orchestra. But they had to undergo some changes in order to compete with the violins and the singers in 'cantability' and agility. The first improvement was to make the instruments out of two or more pieces tightly fitting into each other instead of making one clumsy tube. This allowed the player to regulate the pitch by adjusting the length in the manner of a telescope.

The second improvement, in oboes and bassoons, consisted in adapting the cut of the reed to the new conditions, although we do not know exactly how this change took place.

The third improvement was in the bore, which procured a

smoother tone. Here again, a careful investigation has not yet been made.

The *transverse flute*, even more than other instruments, was greatly enhanced. As a shrill military instrument it had had a cylindrical bore. French makers in the second half of the seventeenth century made it conical, decreasing from nineteen millimeters at the mouth-hole to fourteen millimeters at the lower end. Six open

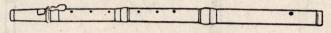

FIGURE 116. Flute (18th century).

front holes were arranged in two groups; a key covered a seventh hole producing $d\sharp'$ when opened, as this lowest semitone could not be produced by cross-fingering. The axis of this key was fixed in a bulbiform swelling of the tube which did not affect the bore.

An earlier type, in the seventeenth and the beginning of the eighteenth century, sometimes made of ivory instead of wood, had a rich profile, and its six fingerholes were united in an undivided section of the tube. JACQUES HOTTETERRE LE ROMAIN was its outstanding maker, player and theoretician (*Principes de la flûte traversière*, Paris, 1707). The later flute, after about 1710, had the two groups of holes in different sections of the instrument and a simpler profile. This was the flute on which King Frederick the Great of Prussia excelled, for which Michel Blavet wrote his sonatas, and Johann Joachim Quantz his fundamental treatise, *Versuch einer Anweisung die Flöte traversière zu spielen* (Berlin, 1752). (fig. 116, pl. XXIII b)

It must, however, be emphasized that this flute was expressly designated as *traversa* or *traversière* in the compositions of the first half of the eighteenth century; *flauto*, for instance in Johann Sebastian Bach's scores, meant the recorder, which had the privilege of seniority. Accordingly, *flauto piccolo*, for instance the one prescribed in Handel's opera *Rinaldo* (1711), where it accompanies Almirena's song, *Augeletti*, with the warble of birds, was a French flageolet, not a transverse piccolo.

Earlier authors sometimes call the flute a *D* flute, because its natural scale, when finger after finger is lifted, is *D* major. This is a mistake. An instrument should be called in *D* only if it transposes into *D*, that is, if a note written and played as if it were *C* sounds a note higher (cf. the section on the clarinet in the next chapter). In spite of its *D* scale the flute is a *C* instrument.

THE OBOE. The French term *hautbois* has generally been translated by 'high wood' (as opposed to *grosbois*, 'low wood'), but doubtless meant 'loud wood' originally, according to the old French contrast between *instruments hauts et bas*. The Italian term *oboè*,

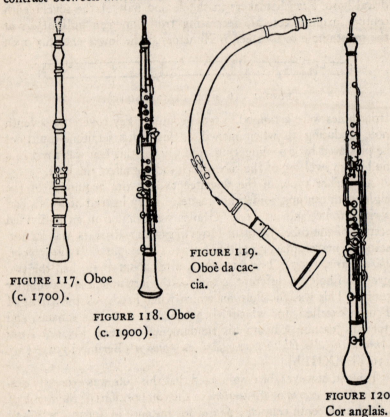

FIGURE 117. Oboe (c. 1700).

FIGURE 118. Oboe (c. 1900).

FIGURE 119. Oboè da caccia.

FIGURE 120. Cor anglais.

derived from *hautbois*, is a correct transcription of the French word as it was pronounced in the eighteenth century.

Though the French had formed, and occasionally employed, this word for shawms as early as the late fifteenth century, the history of musical instruments applies the term 'oboe' only to the modern instruments that the French developed in the later seventeenth century out of the older shawms.

The earliest form of this modern oboe, such as we find in specimens made between about 1660 and 1760, had a slim conical bore, the diameter at the lower end being twice the size of the diameter at the upper end. The head was cup-shaped, probably a last vestige of the oriental lip-supporting disk. As a distinguishing characteristic, this form of oboe had two pairs of smaller holes pierced side by side instead of the two middle fingerholes, which allowed the player to produce f', $f\sharp'$, g' and $g\sharp'$ by stopping either one or both holes of a pair. Moreover, the oboist had three keys at his disposal—one open to add a c', and two more, on the right and the left side, to produce $d\sharp'$ either with the right or with the left little finger. (fig. 117)

The tone of modern oboes has twelve or more partials. Their formant is very high and loud, so that the partials lying in the formant region are even stronger than the fundamentals and give the sound its piercing quality. (fig. 118)

The *oboè d'amore*, in French *hautbois d'amour*, was a larger oboe in A, a minor third below the usual oboe, sixty-one to sixty-two centimeters long, with a pear-shaped bell to soften the timbre. Thus, it was a link between the pitches of the ordinary oboe and the cor anglais.

The oboe d'amore was created about the year 1720, very probably in Germany. The first records of its use were in Georg Philipp Telemann's opera *Der Sieg der Schönheit*, Hamburg, 1722; in Johann Sebastian Bach's cantata no. 37, *Wer da glaubet* (1725); and in Georg K. Schürmann's opera *Ludwig der Fromme* (Wolffenbüttel 1726). This instrument with its beautiful warm tone fell into oblivion in the middle of the eighteenth century, but has recently been recalled. The Belgian CHARLES MAHILLON was the first, in 1874, to reconstruct it in a modern form for authentic performances of the forty-nine cantatas and two passions in which Bach had prescribed it; and, in 1904, Richard Strauss introduced it into the orchestra of his *Sinfonia Domestica* to characterize the "dreaming child." Some French composers followed his example.

Parallel to the development from the shawm to the oboe was the development from the alto pommer to the *alto oboe* in F, a fifth below the ordinary oboe. The oldest form of alto oboe was straight with an expanding bell. The expanding bell which continued to exist in some specimens down to the second half of the eighteenth century, was usually replaced by a pear-shaped bell that was designed to soften the rather rough timbre of the larger oboes. The straight-shaped alto oboes with such bells were called *oboi da caccia* or 'oboes of the hunt'; there are evidences of oboes used in hunting at the beginning of the eighteenth century. The oboi da caccia were called, we do not know why, *cors anglais* or 'English horns,' when they had a curved or angular form; in the nineteenth century, however, the cors anglais were again given a straight form. (figs. 119, 120)

Oboes with pear-shaped bells, as the oboè d'amore and the cor anglais, were not a new invention. Instruments of this kind occur as early as the thirteenth century in the miniatures of King Alfonso el Sabio's *Cantigas en loor de Santa Maria* at the Escorial, and certain provinces of France have preserved the form in instruments called *musettes*, which must not be confused with the bagpipes of the same name.

HORNS. In the second half of the seventeenth century the hunter's horn was transformed into an art instrument. But the details of the transformation are not indicated anywhere, and the confusion grows when from one source we hear that in England the instrument, because it was transformed in France, was called *French horn*, and from another source that it was rare in France, having been admitted there only at a late date and called *cor allemand*. We are certain only of two phases—its undeveloped form, used by hunters and depicted by Mersenne in 1636, and the definitive horn a hundred years later. During this hundred years the horn developed from a short to a long tube; from a wide to a narrow bore; from a purely conical to a partly conical, partly cylindrical bore; from a narrow bell to a widely expanding bell; from a cup-shaped trumpet mouthpiece to a funnel-shaped French horn mouthpiece; from a limited range up to the eighth partial, to a wide range at least to the sixteenth partial; from the timbre of a bugle to the bright tone of a trumpet; and, finally, to the mellow timbre of the French horn. The various stages cannot yet be traced. It seems, however, that in Bach's time, about 1725, the horn was in the trumpet stage of its evolution. In many German scores of that epoch the composer prescribes *tromba ò corno* or *corni ò clarini*, and in an edict of 1736 the Elector of Saxony bars interfering with the rights of privileged trumpeters.

SLIDE TRUMPETS. On a painting by Antonio Vivarini of the three magi (fifteenth century), now in the Berlin Kaiser Friedrich Museum, appears a trumpeter carrying his trumpet and, separately, its mouthpiece. The 'throat' of the mouthpiece, destined to be inserted in the tube, is not the usual length of one inch, but approximately ten inches long. So abnormal a throat may have served to

Jacques-Louis David, The composer François de Vienne, Museum, Brussels (late 18th century).

Marguerite Gérard, Lady with a guitar, Eremitage, Leningrad (early 19th century).

Frans van Mieris, Lady with a theorboed lute, in the Gallery, Dresden (17th century).

PLATE XXIII.

adjust the tone of the instrument, but it is no less possible that it served to complete the natural scale of harmonics by being pulled in and out while played. This is the more probable as pictures of the fifteenth century often show the trumpet forming a trio with two shawms, so that it must have been capable of producing a diatonic scale.

An unmistakable slide trumpet, made at Naumburg in Saxony in 1651, is preserved in the Berlin Instrumental Museum. It is a trumpet in the usual coiled form; it cannot be distinguished from other trumpets except that the throat of its mouthpiece is so long that by pulling it out gradually all gaps in the scale can be filled up. The trumpeter had to press the mouthpiece against his lips with two fingers of the left hand and draw the trumpet out and in like the slide of a trombone. This was doubtless the *tromba da tirarsi*, or 'trumpet to be pulled out,' that Bach has prescribed in the cantatas 5, 20, 46 and 77.

In cantata 46, however, Bach writes *tromba ò corno da tirarsi*, and in two other cantatas, 67 and 162, he indicates *corno da tirarsi*. As a horn cannot be shifted, Charles Sanford Terry interprets the latter term as a tromba da tirarsi with the funnel-shaped mouthpiece of a French horn. Such a combination is unprecedented and hardly possible, as the bore of a horn's mouthpiece is much too narrow for a trumpet. It would be more probable to suppose that the two terms both referred to the same instrument. The real trumpets in Bach's time were in the hands of privileged "knightly" members of a guild, who jealously guarded their rights. Though the tromba da tirarsi was free to all, players probably felt safer in calling it a horn so that they could not be troubled by the guild.

The small success of this instrument can easily be explained. The steadiness required of the playing lips was not easily achieved; and, although the instrument was coiled, the slide was single, so that it necessitated twice the length of traction that a trombone with its U-shaped slide would demand. An English slide trumpet, constructed at the beginning of the nineteenth century by WOODHAM in London, was much superior, as the U in the coil of an ordinary trumpet was transformed into a springing, trombonelike slide. English trumpeters have used this instrument to perform the high parts in Handel's and Bach's scores by playing the horns (*Waldhörner*) in trumpet fashion. This is important for those who interpret Bach's orchestra works: his *corni* were not yet the romantic French horns with the bell held downward.

THE ORGAN of the seventeenth century is particularly interesting to us because it was the model for a certain type of modern
organ generally called the *Baroque* or *Praetorius organ,* which will
be discussed in the chapter on the twentieth century.

On the whole the organ in about 1600 had a light, transparent
color. The timbres of the various stops were sharp and contrasting,
so that the effect was penetrant although not harsh because the wind
pressure was low. The majority of the stops were 4'; in one of the
ideal plans in Praetorius's book the proportion of 4' to 8' stops is two
to one. Moreover, some vigorous compound stops gave the organ
a metallic glitter. Although the various stops of one keyboard had
different timbres, they nevertheless were enough alike in character
to form a homogeneous group. The stops of the first keyboard or
Great organ were grave and solemn; those of the second or *Choir
organ* were keen and penetrant; the third manual keyboard was
delicate and sweet, and the pedal powerful.

A hundred years later the colors had been softened, though the
timbre was still transparent and silvery. The plans of GOTTFRIED
SILBERMANN, for instance, mirror the contrast between the sixteenth
and the seventeenth centuries. Unyielding stops such as *nachthorn*
and *ranket* have disappeared; instead we find pungent *bowed stops*
like the *viola da gamba.* The epoch also favored vibrato effects,
achieved either by the *tremulant* or by the pulsating *vox humana*
tuned a vibration higher or lower than the other stops.

In 1712, the London organ maker, ABRAHAM JORDAN, even invented a crescendo pedal called *nag's head swell,* which opened at
will the door of the Echo, that is, a case including a series of soft
stops. It was the same tendency towards an expressive style that was
typical of contemporary music in general, and came to its climax
in the period between 1750 and 1900.

From the viewpoint of a pure organ, however, these expressive
devices inaugurated an era of degeneration. In the latest phase of
modern organ building, builders are trying to recapture an un-
spoiled organ, inspired by the plans of Praetorius and Silbermann.

THE PITCH. It is a common belief that "the old pitch" was
lower than ours. It is further a misinterpretation that in earlier days
there was a higher 'organ pitch' or *Chorton,* and a lower 'chamber
pitch' or *Kammerton.* Organs of those times varied between 347
vibrations and 567 vibrations, that is, their *a'* varied as much as a
fifth, from *f'* sharp to *c''* sharp according to modern pitch; the

chamber pitch varied between 403 and 563 vibrations, or *g'* and *c''* sharp. In 1714, the same year that GOTTFRIED SILBERMANN gave 420 vibrations (or modern *g'* sharp) to an organ in Freiberg, his brother, ANDREAS SILBERMANN, gave 337 vibrations (or *f'* sharp) to an organ in Strasbourg. Mersenne indicates as a chamber pitch first 403, then 563 vibrations. Johann Sebastian Bach's pitch is indicated by two organs of Gottfried Silbermann's, the above mentioned Freiberg organ of 1714 with 420 vibrations, and the *Hof-kirchenorgel* at Dresden (1722) with 415 vibrations, a half-tone below our standard. Handel has left us his tuning fork of 1751 with 423 vibrations. Italy, in the time of Scarlatti, seems to have preferred a still lower pitch; some Roman pitch pipes of 1720 produce 395 vibrations or *g'*, and a Roman tuning fork of 1730 has 404 vibrations. There was no accepted standard of pitch until the nineteenth century.

17 . *Romanticism*

(*1750-1900*)

THE epoch 1750–1900 follows the trends of both the seventeenth and the sixteenth centuries. Its instrumental style was reminiscent of the sixteenth century. The quantity of timbres increased astonishingly; clarinets, cors anglais, cornets, tubas, saxophones and numberless others were added. Moreover, all instruments following the example of strings were established in families, the clarinets, for instance, being built in eight sizes—octavines, small clarinets, normal clarinets, alto clarinets, basset horns, bass clarinets, contrabasset horns and double bass clarinets.

Notwithstanding this interest in timbre, which was reminiscent of the sixteenth century, the eighteenth century carried on the tendency begun in the seventeenth century towards an expressive emotional music. Feeling which had been confined to a few general moods, majesty, liveliness, joy, affliction, now spread into new romantic fields. Striving for emotional atmosphere, romantic musicians made use of all possible timbres, but not for the purpose, as in the sixteenth century, of polyphonic distinctness and contrast.

Instead, they tried to express all the shadings of human feeling. They discovered the effectiveness of mixing colors and of modulating from timbre to timbre in the same way that they modulated from chord to chord. No detail could be left to the performer; the composer, in his score, was minute. Orchestration became a self-sufficient branch of musical composition.

In order to have the musical palette of the orchestra as complete as possible, practically all instruments were drawn into it, and for this many of them had to be basically improved. Centuries, indeed millenniums, had accepted the defective range of trumpets. Now, as a color in the composer's paintbox, the trumpet had to respond to every note required. Kettledrums were freed from the rigid scheme of beating *d* and *A* to the flourishes of trumpets; they had to be made available for any note of the scale. The harp, strictly diatonic for five thousand years, was made chromatic.

Under the influence of modern orchestration all instruments were developed to the greatest possible technical efficiency and musical effectiveness.

The most outstanding requirement was power. Even the softest of them, the flute, was given a stronger sound. In violins, the Stradivari pattern was preferred to the weaker Amati, and the nineteenth century abounded in futile attempts to increase the power of bowed instruments by all kinds of devices, shapes and materials.

Again, striving for power necessitated cumulating all available instruments. In 1784, a Handel Commemoration held at Westminster Abbey in London amassed an orchestra of

48 first violins	6 flutes
47 second violins	26 oboes
26 violas	26 bassoons
21 violoncellos	1 double bassoon
15 double basses	12 trumpets
4 drums	12 horns
2 organs	6 trombones

Dreams are more characteristic than facts, as they do not depend on the impediments which restrict reality. The truest mirror of what the time desired was Hector Berlioz's vision of an ideal orchestra, which included in its 465 instruments a hundred and twenty violins, forty-five cellos, forty violas, thirty-seven double basses (four of them gigantic *octobasses*), thirty harps and thirty pianos!

There were various causes for stressing the power. The passage from an aristocratic to a democratic culture, in the eighteenth century, replaced the small salons by the more and more gigantic concert halls, which demanded greater volume. But this was only one manifestation of the larger tendency. It is more important to realize how, after the French Revolution, the arts evolved from an aristocratic reserve to unfettered passion, from Racine's Alexandrines to Byron's *Manfred*, from Couperin's *Concerts royaux* to Beethoven's *Eroica*, from the Neopolitan opera to Wagner's music dramas.

Overwhelming forcefulness was perhaps the most important, but was only one of the many kinds of expressiveness required. Sentimental reverie, too, had to find its musical outlet. Amateurs needed instruments at hand that allowed them to pour out their emotional effusion in the very midst of the daily round. Pianos were concealed in writing desks and sewing tables, and also in tea tables which could be revolved to face the guest expected to contribute a rondo. Even on a solitary walk one had to be prepared to react to sunsets or ruins,

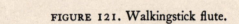

FIGURE 121. Walkingstick flute.

for which occasions there were canes that in a twinkling could be transformed into flutes, clarinets, violins. (fig. 121)

In all cases emotion was the principal requirement, in the performances of gigantic orchestras, in chamber music, and in the sentimental effusions of languid amateurs. Instruments, consequently, were expected to have a maximum of musical flexibility, that is, of span between strong and soft, of crescendo and decrescendo, of almost imperceptible shades. The transformation of the hunter's horn into the versatile French horn is one of the most striking examples. But there are others: the replacement of the recorder by the transverse flute, and of the viols by the violin family and, above all, the successful invention of the piano.

PITCH. Before discussing the instruments typical of that time, it is necessary to remark on the rising pitch which is indicative of the general tendency towards a stimulating tone. Between 1762 and 1789 it varied between 377 and 428 vibrations, that is, from a minor third to a half-tone below the modern standard. The French preferred a low, the Germans a middle, the English a high pitch. The fork used in 1780 by JOHANN ANDREAS STEIN in Augsburg to tune a piano for Mozart had 422 vibrations, a half-tone lower than the modern pitch.

The nineteenth century started with 423 vibrations; the Grand Opéra in Paris had 427 in 1811, 434 in 1829 and 446 in 1856; the Opéra Comique still had 423 in 1820, but 428 in 1823. In Vienna, the pitch reached 456 in 1859, and STEINWAYS tuned their pianos to 457 in 1880, that is, a quarter-tone above the normal pitch.

The constant and increasing elevation of the pitch presents inconveniences by which the musical art, composers, artists, and musical instrument-makers all equally suffer, and the difference existing between the pitches of different countries, of different musical establishments, and of different manufacturing houses, is a source of embarrassment in musical combinations and of difficulties in commercial relations.

A first attempt to fix a standard was made in 1834. A congress of physicists held at Stuttgart proposed the present four hundred and forty vibrations but had no success. In 1858, the French government nominated a committee of six physicists and six musicians (among them Berlioz, Halévy and Meyerbeer) to investigate the question. Their decision to stabilize the pitch at 435 was confirmed in 1889 by a conference held in Vienna. Nevertheless, the pitch has continued to rise and is still doing so today.

THE PIANO was invented "to obviate the bad habit of the harpsichord which could not express coloring at all, or expressed it in exaggerated contrasts by its stops."

The problem was solved by devising a lever that slung a hammer against the string when the finger pressed the key; the force of the pressure was answered by a corresponding force in the resulting tone.

Most writers have taken for granted that the idea of a struck keyboard instrument was due to the activity of a curious artist, PANTALEON HEBENSTREIT, who, improving the despised and primitive dulcimer and playing it throughout Europe as an admired virtuoso, showed how delicate and powerful strings beaten by soft hammers could be. In 1716 and 1717, the Parisian MARIUS and the Saxon GOTTLIEB SCHRÖTER presented models of pianos to the Paris Academy and to the Dresden court respectively; Schröter admitted that Hebenstreit had inspired his invention. However, neither he nor Marius was the first. As early as 1709 the harpsichord maker BARTOLOMMEO CRISTOFORI at Florence had published the diagram and description of an excellent piano, and this was so far ahead of the dulcimer that it cannot be traced directly to it, even less because Hebenstreit never had played in Italy. Cristofori's action even had the upright springing *hopper* or *escapement* which, after slinging the hammer up to the string, set it free immediately, so that it fell back and was ready for repetition even though the finger did not release the key. Two of Cristofori's grand pianos have been preserved; the older one, dated 1720, is in the Crosby Brown Collection in New York. They are entirely reminiscent in form and arrangement of

FIGURE 122. German Prellmechanik without escapement; del. Carmina Manger.

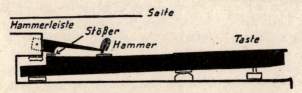

FIGURE 123. German Stossmechanik without escapement; del. Carmina Manger.

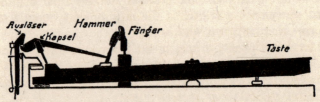

FIGURE 124. German Prellmechanik with escapement; del. Carmina Manger.

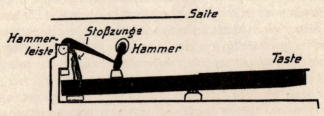

FIGURE 125. German Stossmechanik with escapement; del. Carmina Manger.

the harpsichord. The name that Cristofori gave to these oldest pianos was *gravicembalo col pian e forte,* or harpsichord with [the faculty of producing] piano and forte [by the touch].

Italy invented the piano, but then abandoned it. The Germans adopted the art and evolved and transformed the piano; for the following forty years pianos were made exclusively in Germany.

The first and best early maker of grand pianos in Germany was the famous organ builder GOTTFRIED SILBERMANN, of Freiberg, Saxony. He was well acquainted with Johann Sebastian Bach, who criticized and advised him in his attempts, and Frederick the Great of Prussia bought three of the pianos which are now in Potsdam palaces.

Germany had a decisive influence on the transplanted Italian instrument, not only on its action but also its shape. German homes had been more accustomed to the clavichord with its square form than to the wing-shaped harpsichord, and therefore did not easily accept the grand form of piano. The problem was how to enclose in the square form the complicated new action which had been devised for the grand form. Cristofori's action was too big to be placed in so shallow a case, too heavy to be played by persons accustomed to the clavichord, too expensive for the average music lover. In trying to make an action that was smaller, lighter and cheaper than Silbermann's, the German makers that followed him produced a square piano much rougher in craftsmanship.

The actions of these German square pianos were built according to two principles—action with a hammer connected with the key (*Prellmechanik*), and action with a hammer disconnected from the key (*Stossmechanik*).

In the action with a hammer connected with the key, the rear end of the key bore an upright wooden fork (*Kapsel*) in which the hammer pivoted. In resting position, the hammer butt rested on the key in front of the fork, while the hammer tail projecting behind the fork reached under an overhanging rail that ran the entire width of the piano. When the key was pressed, the tail was checked by the rail and the hammer was jerked up against the string. (fig. 122)

This simple action was given an escapement about the year 1770, probably by JOHANN STEIN in Augsburg. In 1777, Wolfgang Amadeus Mozart wrote to his father that he had called on Stein's workshop. "His instruments distinguish themselves by an escapement; not one in a hundred makers troubles himself about that; but without an escapement a piano clatters and leaves a sound; when one presses the keys, his hammers fall down again in the very moment in which they bounce against the strings, whether one holds the key down or releases it." In place of one continuous rail to check the action of the tails, each key in such an instrument had a separate escaper—that is, an overhanging piece of wood at its rear end—that, after checking the tail momentarily in order to jerk up the hammer butt, slipped back to allow the tail to rise and the butt to fall again, even though the key was not released. This action with an escaping hammer connected with the key was called first the *German action*, and later on, when the STEIN family had moved to Vienna, the *Viennese action*. (fig. 123)

In the action with a hammer disconnected from the key, the rear end of the key bore, not a fork, but an upright wire pusher (*Stößer*). The hammer, instead of being fastened to the key, was fastened at its tail end to a rail running the entire width of the piano. When the key was pressed, the pusher knocked the stem of the hammer so that it pivoted on its fastening and the butt hit the string. (fig. 124)

This action, too, was given an escapement by supplanting the rigid fastening of the pusher on the key by a moveable fastening. This has always been called in Germany the *English action*, since it was devised by German makers working in England, though the true English action at the end of the eighteenth century differed in that the hammer pointed backwards, not forwards. (fig. 125)

The sounds that these various actions provided were all rather rigid and uniform. No wonder that the makers made use in the piano of the old expedient in harpsichord making—stops that by some device gave special timbres to the instrument. Among these stops we find the two modern stops—*forte*, lifting the dampers, and *una corda*, shifting the keyboard so that the hammers strike only one string in each set. They also had many other stops, among them the *piano*, inserting a strip of cloth, felt or leather between the hammers and the strings; the *harp*, inserting such a strip between the hammers and one of the strings of each set; the *swell*, raising a lid above the strings. The stops, modeled after those of the harpsichord, were in the form of handles to be pulled out or to be shifted, until, in the seventeen seventies, knee stops (to be pressed up or to be shifted) were introduced. The first patent for a *pedal* was taken out on July 17, 1783, by JOHN BROADWOOD, though an English piano, dated 1782, already had a pedal.

In 1760 a dozen Saxon piano makers, jobless on account of the Seven Years' War, came to settle in London. After this move Germany was no longer the exclusive piano-making country; England began to compete seriously and soon became the leading center. The most famous among the German makers in London were JACOB KIRCHMANN, who changed his name to KIRCKMAN, and JOHANN CHRISTIAN ZUMPE, a former pupil of Silbermann. Zumpe entered the noted factory which first bore the name of BURKAT SHUDI, and afterwards of JOHN BROADWOOD, which became the leading firm in British piano making. The first pianist, too, was a German on English soil—Johann Christian Bach, Johann Sebastian's youngest son, gave the world's first piano recital in 1768 in London.

The instrument that the German makers had carried to England was the square piano; but there the harpsichord, not the clavichord, was the prevalent keyboard instrument. Therefore, the makers had to turn to the grand piano and abandon the square form. Under the influence of JOHN BROADWOOD the new English grand became essentially different from the older Italian and German models. It abandoned the tradition of the harpsichord; it became much heavier and was given the two modern pedals; its keyboard, instead of being recessed between the walls of the case, projected so that the hands of the virtuoso were visible.

While England prepared the modern form of the piano, Austria created a special type of piano. The outstanding German master in the second half of the eighteenth century, JOHANN ANDREAS STEIN in Augsburg, died in 1792 and left his factory to a son and, more important, to an energetic daughter who afterwards became NANETTE STREICHER. In 1794, Stein's factory was moved to Vienna, at that time the coming center of German music. The Stein-Streicher grand became the typical Viennese instrument imitated by all piano makers of the town. It was charming in its way, depending for its outer appearance on the harpsichord, and preserving the musical qualities and the delicacy of touch of the old clavichord. It was archaic even in the preservation of the many pedals that German makers had created in the eighteenth century. Some Viennese pianos had as many as six pedals, among them two characteristic new ones— the *bassoon* pedal, which pressed a strip of wood lined with tissue paper against the bass strings so that they rattled, and the *Turkish Music*, a pedal operating a triangle, cymbals and a drumstick hitting the soundboard. Johann Nepomuk Hummel, an outstanding Viennese pianist and composer of that time, claimed that "the Vienna grand can easily be played by the most delicate hands. It allows the pianist to produce all kinds of nuances, responds promptly, has a round flutelike tone . . . and does not interfere with fluency by being too stiff."

To the nimble easiness of Hummel's art the Viennese piano could give satisfaction. It was not made for the power and passion of Beethoven, who personally preferred a Broadwood. As we see now, it led to a dead end in the history of piano making.

Finally in Beethoven's time, Paris after long resistance had also become a center of piano making. Though a few stillborn inventions in this field were submitted to the *Académie des Sciences,* no factory was opened until the seventeen eighties. PASCAL TASKIN, a noted harpsichord maker, made at that time a few fine pianos with a peculiar action in which the hammer, disconnected from the key, pointed forward. When he presented his first piano to the court, the organist Jean Balbâtre exclaimed: "Whatever you may do, this newcomer will never oust the majestic harpsichord!" Taskin did not witness the extinction of the harpsichord, but SÉBASTIAN ÉRARD (1752–1831), who had made his first piano in 1777, was so successful with his new instruments that the harpsichord was abandoned.

The modern piano emerges at this time. Érard shares with Broadwood and the Americans the honor of having created it. The strings became much heavier and, consequently, the soundboard thicker. As at the same time the range of the keyboard was greatly increased and the pitch raised, the tension (up to twenty thousand kilograms or the weight of nearly three hundred adults) was much too great for the old wooden frame. After some experiments made by various piano makers in the seventeen nineties, JOHN ISAAC HAWKINS in Philadelphia (1800) inserted metal braces between the wrest plank and the soundboard; in 1821, BROADWOOD extended steel bars longitudinally over the strings; and, in 1825, ALPHAEUS BABCOCK in Boston produced the first full cast-iron frame, which took all the tension off the wooden parts.

About the same time, 1821, SÉBASTIAN ÉRARD in Paris created the definitive form of action, appropriate to the heavier strings of the new type of instrument, while in the older actions the hammer had fallen back to its resting position even though the finger did not release the key (*single escapement*). Érard gave it an intermediate rest, from which it fell back to its original position only after the finger had left the key (*double escapement*). This allowed the player to repeat a note with more promptness as the hammer on its second trip started from a position nearer the string. The action as a whole became stronger and more reliable.

The last step in the evolution of the piano was taken by creating the *overstrung scale*. Overstringing or cross-stringing consisted in a new arrangement of the strings within the case; the treble strings diverged in the form of a fan, thus spreading over the largest part of the soundboard; the bass strings crossed over them at a slightly higher level. There were two main advantages. No strings had to run along the less resonant borders, the arrangement allowing them all to run nearer the middle of the soundboard, and the closeness of the bass and the treble strings favored the formation and intensity of harmonics when the right pedal was pressed. Thus, the over-strung piano is much more powerful than the older piano; but it is lacking in transparence, and certain full chords that composers of the beginning of the nineteenth century have written in the basses cannot be played on a modern piano without causing confusion.

The inventor of cross-stringing was BABCOCK; he took out a patent for it on May 24, 1830. But it was not until STEINWAY AND SONS in New York gave it the definitive form at about 1855 that the over-strung scale was generally introduced.

All these improvements since the days of Broadwood and Érard were created for the grand piano, but were adopted by the nine-teenth century square piano as well. Just as the grand had abandoned the traditional model of the harpsichord to develop an arrangement appropriate to itself, the square shook off the rules of the clavichord. Even the basic structure, with the wrest plank on the right side, was given up in the nineteenth century; in order to accommodate the in-creased number of strings, the wrest plank had to be enlarged and was removed from the side to either the front or the rear. The square piano, then, became just as heavy as, and not much smaller than, the grand. The last square pianos in the United States, made at about 1880, were more than two meters wide and more than one meter deep. All other countries, except South Germany, had aban-doned this type for the upright.

Uprights had been devised at the very outset of piano making by giving a hammer action to the upright harpsichord. Already in 1716, MARIUS in Paris had presented the model of an upright piano, and a German upright, dated 1735, has been preserved in the In-strumental Museum at Leipzig. Ten years later, the organ builder ERNST CHRISTIAN FRIDERICI in Gera, Saxony, replaced the wing form by a symmetric *pyramid*, in which the strings were arranged in a slanting position. However, it was not easy to construct a reliable action in this complicated model, and the piano maker BLEYER in

Vienna was right when he wrote laconically in 1811: "If one looked closely at the engine, one saw the inventor's sweat on it."

Altogether, upright pianos were rare until 1795. On January 12th of that year WILLIAM STODART in London took out a patent for "an upright grand piano in the form of a bookcase," that is, a high, rectangular case in which the extra space beside the winglike piano frame was used for music shelves. For the next forty years upright pianos were common; the old harpsichords and clavichords had to disappear before the new space-saving home instrument could come into favor. Soon after 1800, the Germans reverted to Friderici's *pyramid*, and the Viennese created the asymmetric *giraffe* with a vertical bass side and an oblique treble side meeting in a point at the top and tumbling over in an ornamental scroll. A last form, in favor in the second quarter of the nineteenth century, was the Berlin *lyraflügel*. It had the symmetrically arched sides of an antique lyre and a number of gilded sticks, imitating lyre strings, to enliven the dead front.

All these upright grand forms proved musically unsatisfactory. Therefore, JOHN ISAAC HAWKINS in Philadelphia, and MATTHIAS MÜLLER in Vienna, both in 1800, began to abandon the grand piano scheme in building uprights. The old form had its case with the strings beginning at the level of the keyboard and ending in a point at the top; in the new form (that the French call *piano droit*, and the Germans *pianino*), the case with the strings reaches down to the floor and stands the other way round—that is, the wrest plank forms the horizontal top, and the pointed end of the frame is at the lower end of the case. This new form has become the leading type of home instrument.

THE HARP may owe its advancement at the end of the eighteenth century to the victory of the piano over the harpsichord. As long as the harpsichord existed, between the fifteenth and the eighteenth centuries, the harp, which was also a plucked instrument, was regarded as inferior in chords, polyphony and technique. With the disappearance of the harpsichord, the field was clear for an instrument like the harp, provided that it could be given a chromatic scale.

At the beginning of the eighteenth century, the harp differed from its medieval ancestors only in the greater number of its strings; its accordatura was still diatonic without semitones. A first attempt

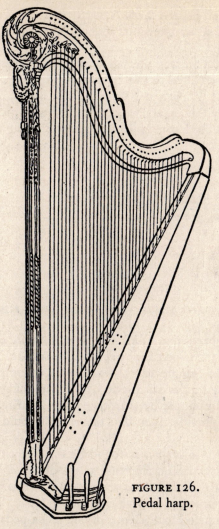

FIGURE 126.
Pedal harp.

towards adapting the harp to the modern evolution of music was
made in the Tyrol in the second half of the seventeenth century.
Some iron hooks were driven in the neck close to the upper ends of
the strings. Such a hook, when turned to touch the corresponding
string, acted as the stopping finger of the violinist; the string was
then higher by a semitone. Thus, it was possible to avoid an eternal
playing on 'white key' strings; the G major scale could be produced

by sharpening all *F*s, and so on. Nevertheless, even a simple modulation could not be accomplished without interrupting the performance.

A better solution was the *pedal harp*, the invention of which, about 1720, is credited to two Bavarians, HOCHRUCKER in Donauwörth and J. P. VETTER at Nürnberg. The hooks, instead of being manipulated by the fingers, were connected with pedals through an action of wires inside the hollowed pillar. Pressing the *F* pedal re-

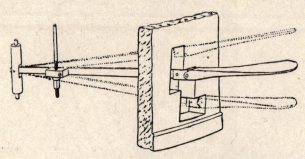

FIGURE 127. The double pedal action.

sulted in the sharpening of all *F* strings, not only one of them; in the same way the *C* pedal moved all *C* hooks, etc. The weak point of this so-called 'simple action' was the impossibility of playing in flat tonalities. As a flat was produced by sharpening the next lower string, *B*♭ for example by sharpening the *A* string, there was no string left to provide *A*, so that the seventh could not be played. (fig. 126)

A satisfactory solution was found by the French in about 1800. P.-J. COUSINEAU was the first to conceive of a *double-pedal harp* in 1782. But a suitable model was not made until 1820 when SÉBASTIAN ÉRARD built the same harp which is in use today. This instrument is diatonically tuned to *C*♭, each of the seven pedals has a double action, and the crooks are replaced by rotating disks with two projecting studs. By pressing the pedals down, the player revolves the disks one complete revolution and shortens the strings by *two* semitones; the *C* pedal changes *C*♭ into *C*♯, and the *D* pedal changes *D*♭ into *D*♯. The pedals, however, can be stopped midway. The disks then make a half-revolution only, and it is the first stud which shortens the string by *one* semitone; *C*♭ becomes *C* and *D*♭ is transposed to *D*. The entire range of the modern harp is $C\flat_2$ to $b\flat^4$. (figs. 127, 128)

Jacob van Loo, concert at the Spanish Court (Eremitage, Leningrad): the king listening, the queen playing the harpsichord, the musicians accompanying on violins and a violoncello.

PLATE XXIV.

Besides this evolution of the diatonic harp, a second evolution concerned the problem of how to arrange a *chromatic harp*, that is, with twelve strings in each octave. It would seem simple to tune the harp strings in semitones instead of arranging them diatonically. The difficulty in a chromatic arrangement was that, if the strings belonging to a chord were near enough to be reached, their distance from the neighboring strings was not sufficient to allow their vibration without hitting one another. Three solutions were tried: the disposition of the strings in two parallel planes in the seventeenth

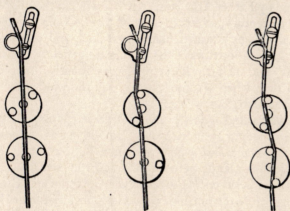

FIGURE 128. The double action of the disks.

century; in one plane in the eighteenth; and in two crossed planes in the nineteenth century. This latter model, having the diatonic strings in one plane and the semitones slanting in the opposite direction, was conceived of by J.-H. PAPE in Paris in 1845 and improved by LYON & HEALY in Chicago and GUSTAVE LYON in Paris. It is still in use, though rare because the strings are so close together at the intersection that they touch each other when vibrating in forte.

Developing at a time when the piano was striving for an ever-increasing power, the harp was particularly assigned to the feminine province of musical expression, where its ornamental shape was an added attraction. It has been a lady's instrument since the days of Marie Antoinette, both at home and in the orchestra, and composers have stressed its aptitude for tenderness and mystery. Thus, the harp expressed one of the most typical moods of romantic feeling.

This responsibility was shared by a large group of new or resurrected instruments that had no function other than to be ethereal and mysterious, such as the aeolian harp and rubbed rods and glasses.

THE AEOLIAN HARP. A Jewish legend relates that King David's lyre, suspended above his bed in the night, sounded in the north wind; and an old Indian poem speaks of the breeze that played the strings of a vina. Archbishop Dunstan of Canterbury, who lived in the tenth century, is said to have been suspected of magic as he experimented with wind-blown strings. In any case, the middle ages were suspicious of this phenomenon, and not until the sixteenth century was such an instrument seriously discussed in Giovanni Battista Della Porta's *Magia naturalis*. The first modern aeolian harp was constructed by Father Athanasius Kircher who, in the middle of the seventeenth century, stretched a set of strings over an oblong box and added screens attached like lids to catch and concentrate the wind. In such an instrument the strings are generally tuned to the same note, but their thickness and, consequently, their elasticity differ, so that, when set into vibration by the wind, they produce various harmonics.

The supernatural, ghostly sound of these chords, changing, increasing and fading away with the wind without any player or any artificial contrivance, was wholly romantic. Between 1780 and 1860, therefore, aeolian harps were much in favor in parks, on roofs and on ruins of medieval castles, especially in Germany and England.

But long before the romantic period its immaterial sound had been appreciated in England. The finest words on the aeolian harp are due to James Thomson (1700–1748) in his poem, *Castle of Indolence:*

> A certain Music, never known before,
> Here sooth'd the pensive melancholy Mind;
>
> .   .   .   .
>
> The God of Winds drew Sounds of deep Delight:
> Whence, with just Cause, The Harp of Æolus it hight.
> Ah me! what Hand can touch the Strings so fine?
> Who up the lofty Diapason roll
> Such sweet, such sad, such solemn Airs divine,
> Then let them down again into the Soul?

The instrument must have been rare at that time; for the editor of the second edition of Thomson's poem (1748) comments in a footnote that such an instrument did exist in reality, not only in the poet's imagination.

FRICTION RODS. In the middle of the eighteenth century there lived in St. Petersburg a certain musician, JOHANN WILDE, who, when he came home in the evening, used to suspend his bow on a nail in the wall. Discovering the peculiar flageoletlike sound of the hair rubbing the nail, he got the idea of a *nail violin*. In spite of the name, this was simply a wooden resonator shaped like a large pill box (or half a pill box) with a set of nails, or of U-shaped iron pins, driven into its edge or side wall; the deeper they were driven, the shorter was their effective length and the higher their pitch. Thus, the nails could be tuned to form a scale. Smaller specimens were held in one hand and rubbed with a bow held in the other hand; larger specimens, such as one in the Crosby Brown Collection in New York with no less than sixty-six pins, were screwed on the table and played with two short bows simultaneously. (fig. 129)

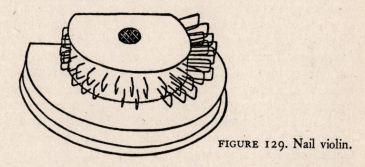

FIGURE 129. Nail violin.

Wilde's nail violin was the earliest and simplest of a long series of instruments based on the friction of rods. In 1788, CHARLES CLAGGET in London obtained a patent for a piano with metal rods or tuning forks instead of strings, with a special *celestina stop* which consisted of "an endless fillet (rub'd with resin dissolved in spirits of wine) producing the sounds on these bars as it does on the strings." Three years later, in 1791, a drawing teacher in Bernburg, Saxony, transformed in a similar way the nail violin with a rubbing wheel into a *nail piano*.

About the same time, the famous physicist ERNST FRIEDRICH CHLADNI in Halle, the father of modern acoustics, constructed instruments of thin glass rods rubbed lengthwise by the fingers and transferring their longitudinal vibrations to iron rods which resounded in a "soft and æthereal" way. The inventor called them *euphones*. In 1799, he replaced the rubbing fingers by piano keys and a rubbing cylinder and called this keyboard instrument *clavicylinder*. It was more practical, but less immaterial than the euphone—"a strong and healthy food, of which one can eat much and frequently," while Chladni compared his euphone with "a dainty that one can eat only in lesser portion as a dessert."

An infinite quantity of instruments was constructed on this principle between 1790 and 1820, but not one had much success. Among all "soft and æthereal" friction instruments, only the glass harmonica, based on bells instead of rods, attained an important place in musical life.

GLASS HARMONICA. As early as 1677 an author describes "a gay wine music," popular in convivial circles, which was made by rubbing the rims of wineglasses with moistened fingers. This kind of music seems to have been formalized in Great Britain and Ireland. In 1743, the Irishman Richard Pockrich caused a sensation with a set of tuned glasses and he continued performing on them in England as well as in Ireland until 1759, when he was consumed by fire with his instrument. Meanwhile, in 1746, Gluck had given at the little Haymarket Theatre in London "a Concert upon Twenty-six Drinking Glasses, tuned with Spring water, accompanied with the whole Band, being a new Instrument of his own Invention, upon which he performs whatever may be done on a violin or harpsichord." In 1749, he gave a similar performance in Denmark. By 1761, the instrument had become so fashionable that English ladies, as Oliver Goldsmith's *Vicar of Wakefield* describes them, "would talk of nothing but high life, and high-lived company; with other fashionable topics, such as pictures, taste, Shakespeare and the musical glasses." Simple instruments of this kind are still existent and are occasionally used in variety entertainment and public gardens.

In about 1761, the American inventor BENJAMIN FRANKLIN made a well-constructed instrument out of the loose set of glasses. Some thirty or forty bowls of decreasing size, each pierced with a hole in the middle, were strung on a horizontal spindle as close together as possible without touching, so that only the rims were visible. The spindle, set into a desklike piece of furniture, could be rotated by a pedal. The player touched the moving rims with his fingers and this arrangement allowed him to play full chords.

The beautiful sound of the *glass harmonica*, as the instrument was called, was indescribably vague and immaterial; it seemed to emerge from infinite space and to fade away into endlessness. Thus, it anticipated one of the romantic ideals. No wonder, then, that Germany became its homestead in spite of its foreign origin. "Of all musical inventions, the one of Mr. Franklin has created perhaps the greatest excitement," says the *Musikalische Almanach für Deutschland auf das Jahr 1782*. It belonged to the indispensable requisites of romantic novels; their heroines, hearing the ghostly chords of a harmonica hidden in a bosket of the countryseat, were expected to faint. Not only amateurs played the harmonica; the instrument was rewarding enough to attract virtuosi and outstanding composers, among them Mozart and Beethoven.

The drawback was that both the irritating permanence of extremely high partials and the continuous contact of the sensitive finger tips with the vibrating glass bowls caused serious nervous disorders. Marianne Davies, the blind Marianne Kirchgessner and other artists were compelled to retire from their profession. To obviate such consequences, PHILIPP JOSEF FRICK at Baden-Baden made experiments with artificial pads in 1769, and ten years later the Italian abbate MAZUCCHI introduced violin bows. In 1784, three men, independently of each other, constructed harmonicas with keyboards: DAVID TRAUGOTT NICOLAI at Görlitz and HESSEL and KARL LEOPOLD RÖLLIG in Berlin. In 1787, the American composer, politician and poet FRANCIS HOPKINSON, followed with a similar construction. But these early attempts had no more success than later ones. The essential quality of the glass harmonica was the sensitive touch of the fingers, and this had gone.

Finally, the glass harmonica in both forms, with and without a keyboard, was driven out by the cheaper, easier and less fragile instruments of the new harmonium family.

THE HARMONIUM is a keyboard instrument with free reeds. To use the words of Sir James Jeans, the reed

consists of a spring of metal which is screwed down tightly at one end and is shaped to fit closely into an aperture in a rigid piece of metal, which lies between a lower wind-chest, and an upper wind-chest. When the appropriate stop of the harmonium is drawn, air under pressure fills the wind-chest and spreads round the reed into the upper wind-chest. In the top of this latter chest is a second opening, which is normally covered by a felted block of wood. When the appropriate key of the harmonium is depressed, the block is raised and air under pressure escapes from [the upper chest]. As the reed now has a greater pressure of air below than above, it is forced upwards, air rushing past it from the lower chest to the upper wind-chest. But before the pressures in the two chests have become fully equalised, the elasticity of the reed carries it back to its original position, so that the flow of air is checked and the pressure in [the lower chest] again increases. By a continued repetition of this process, the reed is set into violent vibration, with a period equal to that of its free vibration.

The eighth chapter has mentioned that the *free reed* of the Chinese mouth organ was brought to Russia in the second half of the eighteenth century. This heretofore unknown kind of tongue spread over Europe with unusual rapidity. Makers of organs and automatic instruments accepted it, and at the beginning of the nineteenth century an entirely new group of instruments was based on the principle of the free reed. The most long-lived among them were two inventions of FRIEDRICH BUSCHMANN in Berlin—the *mouth organ*, German *Mundharmonika*, in 1821, and the *accordion*, German *Ziehharmonika*, in 1822. The mouth organ had the form of a small, flat box with tiny tongues in grooves; the accordion was a bellows itself, with reeds in the two headboards. Both combined aspiration and expiration, pushed-out tongues and drawn-in tongues.

While these handy instruments were popular with everyone, another group of free reed instruments, with a keyboard and a pressure bellows inside, was accepted rather by the bourgeois class. Many such pseudo organs were constructed between 1810 and 1840 and called *aeoline, aeolodicon, mélophone, physharmonica,* or by other scraps of Greek. These attempts culminated in 1840 with ALEXANDRE DEBAIN's *harmonium*. This was almost identical with the modern instrument, especially when three years later the inventor had added to it the *expression*, allowing the player to disconnect the equalizing 'reservoir' so that his action on the treadle was reflected through the feeder bellows directly on the wind channels, and he was able to produce crescendo and diminuendo. At about the same time L. P. A. MARTIN DE PROVINS invented the *prolongement* to sustain notes after the finger had released the key, and the *percussion* in which small piano hammers struck the tongues as if they were strings, giving a quicker and more precise response than the reluctant wind action.

As early as 1836, FRIEDRICH BUSCHMANN, then in Hamburg, had constructed a *physharmonika* with sucker bellows instead of pressure bellows. A French workman was said to have conceived of the same aspirating device and to have brought it to this country. It then became the principle of the so-called *American organ*, the har-

monium with sucker bellows constructed in 1856 by ESTEY in Brat-
tleboro, Vermont, and in 1861 by MASON AND HAMLIN in Boston. Its
tone was softer and more organlike, though slow to act.

Romanticism vibrated between two poles of expression. At one
end of its sphere were mysticism and sentimentality, and at the other
violence and passion. This contrast required the overwhelming
power and the strong accents of wind instruments. The introduction
of new types of this class, and the adaptation of older ones, became
one of the most important features in the musical life between 1750
and 1900.

THE BOEHM FLUTE. The fingerholes of the flute, when
opened successively, produce a diatonic D major scale. Other notes
than these had to be produced either by cross-fingering or by 'half-
stopping.' In cross-fingering, the player, for example, flattened his
normal $F\sharp$ to $F\natural$ by closing the D hole and leaving the intermediate E hole open; in half-stopping, the player could, for instance,
sharpen D to $D\sharp$ by partially closing its hole. Notes produced in
these artificial ways were difficult to play and slightly muffled. Thus,
it was scarcely feasible to play in other tonalities than D, G and A
major and their minor parallels. This difficulty was emphasized
when in the second half of the eighteenth century composers, having
the benefit of an equal-tempered system, did not hesitate to write
even in remote tonalities. In consequence, the flute was given a
quantity of auxiliary keys, for $B\flat$, F, C, $D\sharp$, $G\sharp$.

Nevertheless, the flute was still imperfect; every new hole com-
promised the correct intonation of the already existing holes. A reform was necessary; but it was not made by professional manufac-
turers. In 1808, the Reverend FREDERICK NOLAN in England took a
first step by inventing the *ring-key*, permitting the addition of cor-
rective holes. This was a springing metal ring suspended over the
regular open hole and connected by a lever with another key over an
auxiliary hole somewhere beyond the reach of the finger. As long
as the hole under the ring-key was open, the auxiliary hole was also
open and functioned as a correction. But when the finger closed its
hole it had to press down the ring, thus automatically closing the
auxiliary hole as well so that it did not interfere with the lower holes.
Between 1820 and 1830, the flutist CHARLES NICHOLSON in London tried to improve the quality and correctness by larger holes.

About the same time, WILLIAM GORDON, a former captain in the French king's Swiss Guards, changed the position of the holes and employed Nolan's ring-key. The German flutist THEOBALD BOEHM became acquainted with these attempts in 1831 and based an entirely new system on them. His principles were 1) the holes were to be as large as possible; 2) their position would depend on acoustical correctness only, without considering the player's comfort; 3) this latter would be accommodated by an appropriate arrangement of keys covering all holes; 4) all keys were to be open in their position of rest (except G♯, which only later was transformed into an open key). (figs. 130, 131)

Boehm's first flutes, issued in 1832, were still conical; it was as late as 1846 that he created the modern cylindrical bore with a parabolic head. This made the pitch more accurate and equalized the timbres of the various registers. But the actual flute character was completely altered. A great deal of its sweetness had gone; instead, the timbre was more 'reedy' and powerful and, in the lower register, almost hornlike. These qualities were emphasized when flutes were made more and more of metal. The harder the material, the brighter the timbre; silver flutes are more brilliant than the rare golden ones.

As to the timbre of a modern golden flute, the greatest authority on flutes, Dayton C. Miller, says:

When played pianissimo, the tones are nearly simple, containing about 95 per cent of fundamental, with a very weak octave and just a trace of some of the higher partials. The pianissimo tones of the middle register . . . are simple, without overtones. When the lower register is played forte, it is in effect overblown, and the first overtone becomes the most prominent partial . . . the fundamental is weak, being just loud enough to characterize the pitch. The player is often conscious of the skill required to prevent the total disappearance of the fundamental and the passing of the tone into the octave. The tones of the low register, when played loudly, have as many as six or eight partials, and at times these sounds suggest the string quality of tone. The tones of the middle register played forte consist mainly of fundamental with traces of the second and third partials. In this respect these flute tones are very similar to those of the soprano voice of like pitch. . . . The average of all of the tones of the lower and middle registers of the flute . . . leads to the conclusion that the tone of the flute is characterized by few overtones, with the octave partial predominating. The tones of the highest register have been analyzed and found to be practically simple tones.

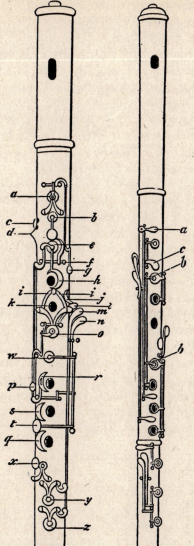

FIGURE 130.
Gordon's flute.

a D shake, *b* C sharp,
c C, *d* keeps the
thumb in its place,
e B, *f* axle, *g* D
shake, *h* E, *i* G
sharp, *j*, G sharp,
k G sharp, *l* G
sharp, *m* C, *n* C
sharp, *o* G sharp,
p G and G sharp
shakes, *q r s w*
F sharp, *t* F sharp,
x E flat, *y* C, *z* C
sharp.

FIGURE 131.
Early
Boehm flute.

a D shake, *b*
arms for clos-
ing the valves,
c C sharp.

Neither Boehm nor the flutists who adopted his flute gave much emphasis to its powerful sound; still, it is hard to believe that such a flute could have been accepted before the 'loud era.'

Its introduction was not easy, however. Flutists opposed the adulteration of the genuine timbre and, though they rarely confessed it, the new fingering. And up to this day attempts have been made to revive the "old" conical flute.

Besides the ordinary flute, the modern orchestra uses a small flute, *flauto piccolo* (or simply *piccolo*), in the upper octave of the former. With its shrill and penetrating tone it dominates the tutti of the orchestra.

Larger flutes are less frequently made and used. Some scores prescribe an *alto flute*, which is either a fourth lower, as in Rimski-Korsakov's opera ballet *Mlada* (1892), or a fifth lower than the ordinary flute, as in Ravel's *Daphnis et Chloé* (1913). In both scores it is called "in sol." But Ravel is wrong; his flute is "in fa." The incorrect terminology is due to the fact that a century ago the ordinary flute, which, being nontransposing, is in *C*, was called a *D* flute because the series of fingerholes produced a *D* major scale. Sometimes these alto flutes have erroneously been called *bass flutes*.

An actual *bass flute*, in the lower octave of the ordinary flute, was constructed by the middle of the eighteenth century. The maker had given it a peculiar shape by folding in both the upper and the lower ends so that the practical length was reduced. At the beginning of this century, in 1911, an Italian, ABELARDO ALBISI, created a new type, the *albisifono*. Its mouth part is bent to form the top of a T, while the rest of the tube is upright so that the latter is held in a vertical position. The original width of the bore was thirty-nine millimeters; as this demanded too much breath, a more recent model has a smaller bore (and slants down from the headpiece in an oblique position). After this model, Albisi also made an alto in *F*.

CLARINETS. The principle of the clarinet has been explained on page 91. In the European clarinet the mouthpiece or *beak*, made of wood or any other hard material, looks as if it were pinched to form a sharp edge at the top; its front is rounded, while the back is flat and smooth. A rectangular orifice cut in the flat back is covered by a thin piece of cane that is screwed or tied on to serve as a *beating reed*. (fig. 132)

Clarinets have a cylindrical bore; the lower end only is conical. The acoustical consequence is a debilitation, or else complete obliteration, of the even-numbered partials, that is, the second, fourth, sixth and so on. It is a mistake to believe that a clarinet has no even-numbered partials at all, although they cannot be obtained by overblowing. When the player increases the pressure, he passes directly from the fundamentals to their twelfths and from the twelfths to the thirds above their double octaves:

$$d \quad (d') \quad d' \quad (d'') \quad f\sharp'' \quad (a'') \quad \dots$$

This involves a certain complication. A flutist needs only six holes and fingers to fill diatonically the gap between the fundamentals and their next harmonics, the octaves. A clarinetist, on the contrary, requires ten holes and ten fingers to fill the longer gap between the fundamentals and their twelfths. Tonalities remote from the natural scale of the instrument had to be avoided more than ever, and clarinets began to be constructed in *C*, *B♭* and *A*. These letters are symbolic; they have nothing to do with the tonalities bearing the same letters. An instrument in *C* is a *nontransposing instrument*, that is, one on which we play the notes as they are written (as we do on a violin); the written *C* corresponds with the heard *C*. A clarinetist used a *C* clarinet when the tonality of the piece did not require too many sharps or flats. The *B♭* and *A* clarinets, on the contrary, are *transposing instruments*. In the key of *B♭* major the fingering would have been difficult on a nontransposing clarinet and the tone rather unsatisfactory. So he played it on a *B♭* clarinet, in which the arrangement of the holes and keys was identical. He pressed what he called the *C* key, and the instrument, being a little longer, produced a *B♭* for a *C*, an *F* for a *G*. Not only *B♭*, but any flat tonality was easier on a *B♭* clarinet. Likewise, all sharp tonalities were easier on an *A* clarinet. *D* major, for example, played on an *A* clarinet would require one flat instead of two sharps, and *D♭* major on a *B♭* clarinet would require three flats instead of five.

When the clarinet was gradually given modern keys so that playing was simplified, it did not need these different tunings. The *C* clarinet disappeared, and the *A* clarinet, though not extinct, has become rarer than the *B♭* clarinets.

But this belongs to the history of the clarinet and we must go back to its beginning before continuing.

The clarinet was not "invented." It existed as a folk shawm of inferior rank in a short, cylindrical shape, either with a beating reed cut in the cane itself, or with a separate reed tied on. These instruments, generally known by their French name *chalumeaux*, turned into clarinets when, at the end of the seventeenth century, JOHANN CHRISTIAN DENNER, at Nürnberg, gave them the shapes of oboes, with wooden tubes turned on a lathe and cut into several joints, with a separate bell and two keys—one above the front holes to produce *a′*, and another, opposite in the rear, for *b′*. Denner's son, JOHANN DENNER, working at about 1720, shifted the *b′* hole towards the top in order to facilitate overblowing. At the same time he diminished its size so that it produced *bb′*. Then he pierced an *e* hole into the lengthened lower joint and covered it with a long key to be pressed by the small finger of the left hand. This hole, when overblown, produced *b′* and secured a complete fundamental scale from *e* to *bb′*, and an overblown scale from *b′* on.

Although this instrument was a genuine 'clarinet,' the name itself is not mentioned before 1732 in Johann Gottfried Walther's *Musicalisches Lexicon*. As new names for old things are always hard to establish, the original name *chalumeau* was not only preserved in early Hamburg operas, such as Reinhard Keiser's *Croesus* (1711) and *Serenata* (1716) or Georg Philipp Telemann's *Sieg der Schönheit* (1722), but as late as 1767 in Gluck's *Orfeo*, and it is idle to question whether the instrument intended was an early or an improved chalumeau. The fact that it was prescribed in art works shows that it had become an art instrument.

Clarinets were used in Paris in 1749, where two of them played in Rameau's opera *Zoroastre*, though the score did not indicate them. They were more common after 1760, but played by oboists and therefore never used simultaneously with oboes.

The timbre of these early clarinets was indeed more closely connected with the tone of oboes than the timbre of modern clarinets. The smooth rear surface of the mouthpiece on which the flat reed was placed was shorter and narrower, and the reed consequently was smaller. As a small reed vibrates faster than a large one, the formant (cf. page 354) of the early clarinets must have been higher and the tone lighter and more penetrating. The inverted position of the mouthpiece with the reed on the front, which in some countries was preferred, increased the shrillness. Thus, Johann Gottfried Walther could say in 1732 in his *Lexicon:* "From a distance it sounds rather like a trumpet." This explains the trumpetlike name *clarinet,* or even *clarino,* which is inappropriate for the modern instrument.

The clarinet must have been shrill up to the beginning of the nineteenth century; methods of clarinet playing published before 1850 emphasize the "now fuller, much softer and more agreeable" tone of recent clarinets.

Meanwhile, the mechanical part had also been improved. A fourth key for *f♯* and a fifth one for *g♯* date from the middle of the century.

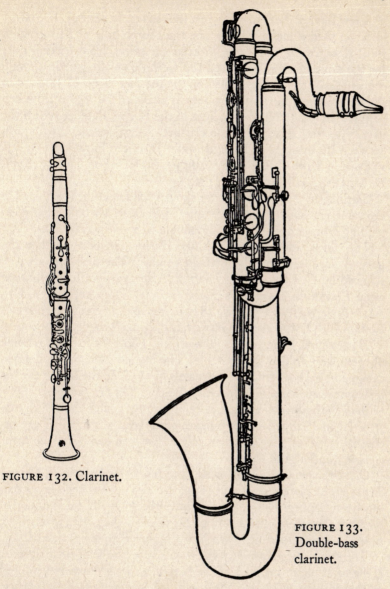

FIGURE 132. Clarinet.

FIGURE 133.
Double-bass
clarinet.

A maker in Braunschweig, Barthold Fritz, is credited with their
introduction. In 1791, Xavier Lefebvre in Paris added a sixth key
for $c\sharp'$. A few years later, Ivan Müller created the modern clarinet
with its thirteen keys for e f $f\sharp$ $g\sharp$ $b\flat$ b $c\sharp'$ $e\flat'$ f' $f\sharp'$ $g\sharp'$ a' $b\flat'$.

A few further dates may interest the reader. In 1808, J.-F. SIMIOT in Lyon used a metal tube to line the thumb hole and protrude a short distance into the bore, to keep the saliva from leaking out; for the same purpose he placed the $b\flat'$ hole on the front although the handle of the key remained on the rear. In 1823, C. JANSSEN in Paris introduced the sliding rollers to facilitate the legato from key to key. After 1839 certain qualities of the Boehm flute, above all the ring-keys, were adapted to the clarinet; specialists may distinguish between the systems of L.-A. BUFFET JEUNE in Paris (1839), LE-FEBVRE in Paris (1846), HYACINTHE E. KLOSÉ in Paris (1843), R. MOLLENHAUER in Fulda (1867).

Clarinets in C, $B\flat$ and A (after about 1808 sometimes combined in the same instrument) were completed to form a whole family extending from octave clarinets to double bass clarinets.

The oldest addition was the *bass clarinet*, an octave below the normal clarinet (generally with an $e\flat$ key). The first one was constructed by G. LOT in Paris in 1772. After his so-called *basse-tube* came HEINRICH GRENSER's *Bassklarinette* (Dresden, 1793), DU-MAS's *basse-guerrière* (Paris, 1810), FRIEDRICH SAUTERMEISTER's *basse-orgue* (Lyon, 1812), GEORG STREITWOLF's model (Göttingen, c. 1833) and C. CATTERINI's *glicibarifono* (Bologna, c. 1835). Some of them were folded like bassoons. The modern straight model was designed by ADOLPHE SAX in Brussels in 1836. In the same year the instrument appeared in Meyerbeer's opera *Les Huguenots*.

Alto clarinets in G existed as early as 1792; later they were constructed in F and $E\flat$. They have never been admitted to the orchestra, but they play a certain role in German bands and, as *tenor clarinets*, in English bands.

Octave clarinets in C, $B\flat$ or $A\flat$, and *fourth clarinets* in F, $E\flat$ and D have made since about 1800. We also possess D clarinets dating from the beginning of the eighteenth century but it is doubtful whether they were intended to be D; possibly they were C clarinets, tuned to some older pitch which was higher than our standard.

The *double bass clarinet*, two octaves beneath the normal clarinet, is the most recent member of the family, although makers ventured on this problem as early as the first decade of the nineteenth century. In 1808, DUMAS in Paris constructed a *contrebasse guerrière*, and in 1839, EDUARD SKORRA in Berlin a *bathyphon*. But the lowest notes in these instruments were weak and dim, and the higher notes could be more easily obtained and were better on a bass clarinet. Consequently they were put aside, until, in 1890, FONTAINE-BESSON in Paris again attempted, and finally succeeded, in making an excellent double bass clarinet. After him, KOHL in New York and EVETTE & SCHAEFFER in Paris, as well as WILHELM HECKEL in Biebrich, constructed good systems. But owing to its high price, this marvelous instrument is very seldom used. (fig. 133)

A separate branch of the clarinet family comprises the basset-horn and the contrabasset-horn. The *basset-horn* is an alto clarinet with a narrower bore, a thinner wall and four semitones beyond the low *e* (which sounds *A* in the usual *F* pitch). The first model, constructed in Germany about 1770, was crescent-shaped. The curved piece of wood was split lengthwise; the two halves then were hollowed, glued together and covered with leather. This was the basset-horn in Mozart's scores. At about 1800 the crescent shape was replaced by a model which was sharply bent at an obtuse or nearly right angle. A few years later HEINRICH GRENSER in Dresden tried to give it the straight form in which it is constructed nowadays. Once more a great composer used it; in 1833, Mendelssohn wrote two concerted pieces for clarinet and basset-horn with piano (op. 113 and 114). It then disappeared totally from the scene, until Richard Strauss assigned a part to it in his opera *Electra* in 1909. (fig. 134)

A *contrabasset-horn*, an octave below the basset-horn in *F*, was constructed in the first half of the nineteenth century by GEORG STREITWOLF in Göttingen; a few new models were introduced from the eighteen eighties on, though the instrument is rare.

Besides the basset-horns, the clarinet family had a second offspring, the *clarinette d'amour*. It was a larger clarinet in *G* or *A♭* with the pear-shaped bell of the oboè d'amore. The first evidence of it is Johann Christian Bach's opera *Temistocle* (1772); but less than thirty years later, in 1801, it was "entirely obsolete." (fig. 135)

THE SAXOPHONE is a wide metal tube of parabolic bore, usually bent to the shape of a tobacco pipe, with the key arrangement of the oboe and a clarinet's mouthpiece. Its sound is incredibly variable. Being intermediate between the timbres of wood and brass instruments, it passes from the softness of the flute over the broad, mellow tone of the cello to the metallic strength of the cornet.

The principal member of the family is the alto, made either in *F* or *E♭*; soprano, alto, tenor and baryton (more correctly, bass) form the usual quartet. Besides, some makers build a sopranino in *F*

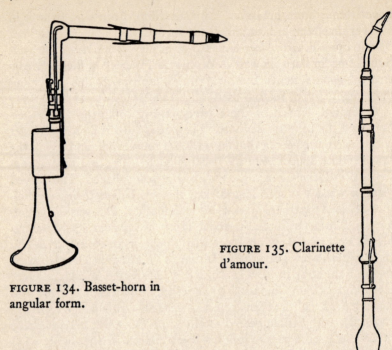

FIGURE 135. Clarinette d'amour.

FIGURE 134. Basset-horn in angular form.

or *E♭* and three big saxophones down to a subcontrabass an octave below the ordinary contrabass. In the United States the tenor in *C* is called *melody saxophone*. Thus, the family comprises:

in *F* or *E♭*	in *C* or *B♭*
Sopranino	Soprano
Alto	Melody (*C*), Tenor (*B♭*)
Baryton (correctly bass)	Bass (correctly contrabass)
Contrabass (correctly subbass)	Subcontrabass

The written range for the entire family is *b♭* to *f³*. (fig. 136)

Predecessors of the saxophone were a clarinet with bent mouthpiece and bell, constructed in 1807 by DESFONTENELLES at Lisieux, and the small octave bassoon, *tenoroon*, built about 1820 by LAZARUS in London with a clarinet's mouthpiece. The saxophone itself was invented about 1840 by the famous ADOLPHE SAX, who then still lived in Brussels. In 1844, Jean-George Kastner introduced it into one of his scores, and it was in continuous use from that time on, above all in France and Italy. Its outstanding role in modern music, however, has been in jazz and swing.

A relative of the saxophone is the wooden *tárogató,* an ancient Hungarian military oboe of wide bore that in 1900 was given a

FIGURE 136.
Saxophone.

clarinet, or rather a saxophone, mouthpiece by W. J. SCHUNDA in Budapest. Its timbre is less brilliant than that of the saxophone.

CHROMATIC HORNS AND TRUMPETS. The usual term *brass instruments* should be avoided in scientific language. All kinds of trumpets and horns can be, and have been, made of other material —horn, tusk, cane, wood, clay, crystal. On the other hand, most saxophones and flutes, and many clarinets, are made of brass in spite of their being called wood-wind instruments.

Another more recent and half-scientific name, *instruments with cup-shaped mouthpieces,* is not recommendable either. Besides being too long, it is not accurate; the funnel mouthpiece of a French horn is not in a proper sense cup-shaped and most primitive horns and trumpets have no mouthpiece at all. Whether cup- or funnel-shaped, the mouthpiece is dispensable. It facilitates and influences tone production by its shape and size, but the essential acoustical factor is the player's lips. This cannot be referred to in terminology as it does not belong to the instrument. (figs. 137, 138)

While the production of sound is due to the lips, the pitch, as in pipes, is determined by the length (and in a very small measure by

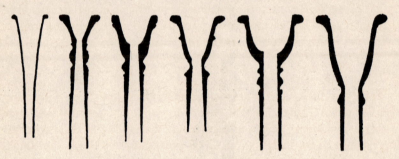

FIGURE 137. Mouthpieces; del. Carmina Manger.

Horn　Soprano　Alto　Tenor　Bass　Double bass

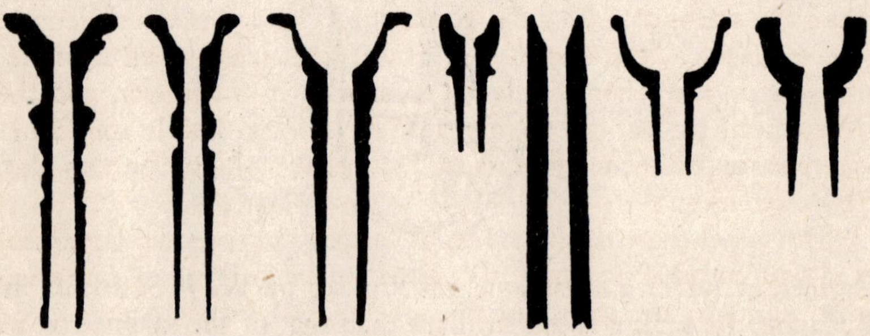

FIGURE 138. Mouthpieces; del. Carmina Manger.

Clarin　modern　principal　curved straight　serpent　bass-horn

trumpet　　　　cornet

the width) of the tube. Again, the lips cause the production of additional notes by the degree of their tension. The lowest tension creates the fundamental. When the player *overblows* by increasing the tension of his lips, the air column is pushed on again, before having had time for a complete vibration. Instead of vibrating in its full length, it then vibrates in its halves, or thirds, or fourths and so on, according to the tension of the lips. Thus, a well-made instrument is able to produce a series of harmonics, formed by the fundamental, its octave, the fifth above, the double octave, the major third above, the fifth above the double octave, etc. If the fundamental is *C*, for instance, this harmonic series is

$$C \quad c \quad g \quad c' \quad e' \quad g' \quad b' \quad c'' \quad d'' \quad e'' \quad f''^+, \text{ etc.}$$

This series is constant in its structure—that is, in the succession of its intervals—but variable in its pitch. A tube three halves as long as the one which produces *C* as the fundamental, produces

$$F_1 \quad F \quad c \quad f \quad a \quad c' \quad e\flat' \quad f' \quad g' \quad a', \text{ etc.}$$

Thus, we distinguish trumpets, cornets, horns 'in' *C* or *B*♭ or any other pitch. This distinction, however, is not sufficient to determine the pitch and size of the instrument, as it does not indicate whether a horn in *C*, for instance, has C_1 or great *C* or small *c* as the fundamental. Therefore, musicians and instrument makers speak of soprano, alto, tenor, bass instruments. This would clearly indicate the pitch and size, if such denominations were consistently applied. Unfortunately, this is not the case. Let us quote two examples only: the large trumpet in *C* or *B*♭, in spite of its having the same length, the same pitch, the same series of harmonics and even a higher range than the tenor trombone, is called a bass trumpet, and the French call the various members of the saxhorn family sometimes soprano, contralto, tenor, bass, sometimes sopranino, soprano alto, tenor and so on.

The use of these names can be preserved, but it should be careful and unmistakable. It ought to be based on the sole reliable criterion that we have: the length of the tube and, in its consequence, the absolute pitch of its harmonics. The following summarizes a consistent application of the terms, in which only *C* and *F* pitches are considered:

Octave (cornet)	c' $c''g''$ . . .
Sopranino (cornet, flügelhorn, trumpet)	f f' c'' . . .
Soprano (cornet, flügelhorn, trumpet)	c c' g' . . .
Alto (cornet, trumpet, trombone)	F f c' . . .
Tenor (trumpet, trombone, horn, euphonium)	C c g . . .
Bass (trombone, horn, tuba)	$F_1 F$ c . . .
Contrabass (trombone, tuba)	$C_1 C$ G . . .
Subbass (tuba)	$F_2 F_1$ C . . .
Subcontrabass (tuba)	$C_2 C_1 G_1$ . . .

We need not list the (theoretically) endless series of its harmonics to locate an instrument. Nor do we designate it by its fundamental, which in the majority of cases cannot even be produced because it demands an unfeasible relaxation of the lips. Instead, we designate an instrument by its *harmonic fifth*, that is, the interval formed by the second and third harmonics. A *C* trumpet and a *C* cornet, for instance, have the harmonic fifth *c′-g′*, a bass trombone and an *F* horn *F-c*.

The available scale is a section out of the theoretical series of harmonics. The place of this section within the series and its range depend on the bore, the mouthpiece, the player's lips and training, and even on the way in which the composer allows the player to approach hazardous notes.

To resume the two main points: the absolute pitch of the series of notes changes with the instrument; but the structure of the series, that is, the proportion between the various notes, is constant. The player's mind is directed towards producing the second or third or fourth harmonic rather than towards hitting *c* or *f* or *a*. The player plays something like an abstract mathematical formula made up of unknown quantities like x, y, z, while the tube itself, according to its length, substitutes definite quantities for them. Taking this into account, trumpeters and horn players use a symbolic notation in *C*, and the instrument they play transposes the fictitious notes into real ones in the required tonality.

Musicians and makers, anxious to have trumpets and horns in the orchestra, which already included trombones, investigated every means of filling the gaps between the harmonics, in order to give these instruments diatonic and even chromatic scales.

SERPENTS AND BASSHORNS. Following this general tendency, makers recalled to life an ancient fingerhole horn—the *serpent*—which, though clumsy, was chromatic. This instrument had been created in the sixteenth century, probably in France, as a double bass of the cornet family. Its serpentine shape was not as elegant as the S shape of the tenor cornet. A wide tube of chestnut covered with black leather was curved in serpentine form to make the six finger-holes reachable; the upper end was provided with a deep mouthpiece of horn or ivory. Serpent players in the seventeenth century must have been great artists; Father Mersenne stresses their versatility in being able to accompany as many as twenty of the most powerful singers and yet play the softest chamber music with the

most delicate grace notes. Later musicians did not share his enthusi-
asm; Berlioz, for instance, referred to it as a barbaric instrument.
The skill had been lost and the serpent was confined to accompanying
the plainsong in Catholic churches. It continued at this task until the
nineteenth century. (fig. 139)

Meanwhile, the large military bands, which sprang into being in
the last quarter of the eighteenth century, used the serpent as a

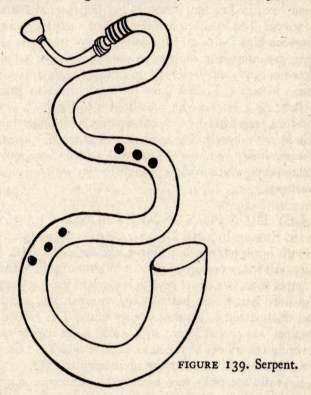

FIGURE 139. Serpent.

foundation, and they did not give it up until the bass tuba and its
relatives were introduced beginning in about 1835. Even the symphonic and opera orchestras kept it; serpents were prescribed, for
example, in Rossini's opera *Le Siège de Corinthe* (1826), Carafa's
Masaniello (1827), Mendelssohn's *Meeresstille und glückliche
Fahrt* (1828), his oratorio *Paulus* (1836), Wagner's opera *Rienzi*
(1842) and Verdi's *Les Vêpres siciliennes* (1855).

This later serpent was improved from the earlier model by a few
keys for chromatic notes and by a more convenient form. An Italian

musician, REGIBO, who lived at Lille in France, was the first, in 1789, to abandon the serpentine tube and to bend it back on itself in the shape of a bassoon. Though this so-called *ophibaryton,* or *Russian bassoon,* was not able to replace the genuine serpent, it was a step in the creation of a new instrument—the *basshorn.* (figs. 140, 141)

Two men invented the basshorn in about 1800, a Frenchman, ALEXANDRE FRICHOT, and an English maker, J. ASTOR. As both of them lived in London, it was called the *English basshorn* on the Continent. The basshorn had the bore of a serpent and the shape of a bassoon plus a wide metallic bell and keys; the cup-shaped mouthpiece was inserted in a crook. In spite of its imperfection, it was accepted in bands and preserved up to about 1830. Increasing the confusion in terms, Frichot gave different names to later improved models. As a *basse-cor* he submitted it to the Paris Conservatoire, and four years later he took out a patent on it under the calamitous title *basse-trompette.* The most improved model was STREITWOLF's *Chromatisches Basshorn* (1820) with a better bore, two open holes and ten keys, which made it possible to play with the same ease in all tonalities.

KEY TRUMPETS AND KEY BUGLES. In 1760, a member of the Russian Imperial Orchestra, KÖLBEL, had given keys to the French horn, but the instrument was not established. Forty years later, in 1801, a certain trumpetist WEIDINGER, in Vienna, gave the trumpet four, five or six keys to bridge the gap between the second and third harmonics; but this *key trumpet,* too, had little success and disappeared in another twenty years. The failure of the key trumpet was probably due to the side holes and to the soft pads covering the insides of the keys, both of which combined to muffle the noble tone of an otherwise uninterrupted tube.

Keys did not make such a noticeable difference in a rude instrument like the *bugle,* which had the relatively largest bore of any horn and, therefore, the broadest tone. Originally a hunter's horn, it became a military instrument when at the end of the eighteenth century battle formation became too large for oral commands to be heard. Its old, semicircular tube had been bent to two right angles. After the Napoleonic wars this form was replaced by the so-called English model, that is, the coiled, trumpetlike form. The pitch of a bugle is generally C or Bb, its harmonic fifth c'/g', its range $c'-g''$. (fig. 142)

In 1810, JOSEPH HALLIDAY at Dublin added, as he said in the

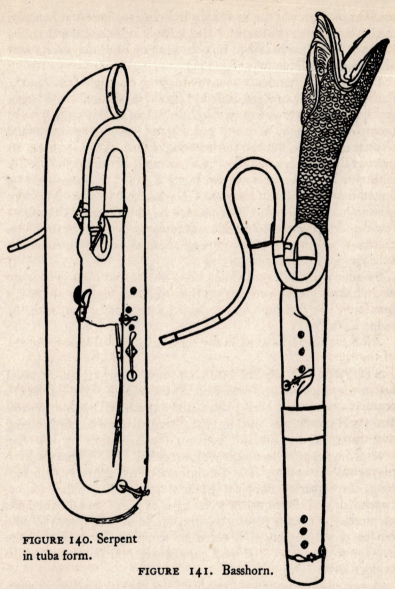

FIGURE 140. Serpent
in tuba form.

FIGURE 141. Basshorn.

specification of his British patent of May 5, 1810, "five keys to be
used by the performer, which, together with its five original notes,
render it capable of producing 25 separate tones in regular progression." Later, the number of keys was increased to seven, the lowest

being open. This was the *key bugle* or *kenthorn,* named in honor of the Duke of Kent; the French called it *bugle à clés,* and the Germans *Klappenhorn.* It was able to hold its position until the second half of the nineteenth century. (fig. 143)

Following the tendency towards forming complete families, the Parisian maker Jean Asté, called Halary, constructed some larger key bugles that he named *ophicléides.* Despite this clumsy term (composed of *ophis,* 'serpent,' and *kleides,* 'keys'), the instrument was not serpentine, but had the bassoonlike form of the basshorn. Its most usual size was a so-called bass (correctly baritone) in *C* or *B♭* with nine to twelve keys and the range B_1 to c''. As early as 1819, Spontini prescribed it in his opera *Olympia,* and, in 1826, Mendelssohn in his overture to *A Midsummer Night's Dream.* Although a few decades later the ophicleide was replaced by the tuba in the orchestra, it was used in Italian, French, Spanish and South American bands up to this century.

Smaller ophicleides with nine keys, in alto and even in soprano pitch, had no greater success than the *ophicléide monstre* of 1821, a bass in *F,* five feet high and provided with eleven keys, with the range E_1 to c'.

All these keyhorns were finally superseded by valve instruments.

STOPPED FRENCH HORNS must, however, be discussed before the valve action is explained. At the middle of the eighteenth century a celebrated horn player at the court of Dresden, Anton Joseph Hampel, who died in 1771, invented a method of bridging over some of the intervals between the harmonics by inserting several fingers held close together into the bell. This is what the horn player calls 'stopping.' He distinguishes three degrees: half-stopping, three-quarter stopping, whole-stopping. The difference between half and three-quarter stopping is so vague that the methods of producing certain notes vary greatly. In certain cases the note can be raised instead of lowered by stopping. Thus, within the average range c to c^3 or f^3 most gaps between the harmonics can be bridged over.

A new playing position of the horn was the essential consequence of this practice. The player was forced to turn his instrument to allow the hand to enter the bell. This was the origin of our modern way of holding it 'pocketwards.'

The soft, almost muffled, tone resulting from this new position is quite different from the brisk sound that the horn had in the first

half of the eighteenth century. Conductors should keep this in mind
when they perform music of the Bach-Handel period.

Hampel's stopping achieved the modern horn timbre which, in
Dayton C. Miller's words, "contains the largest number of partials
yet found in any musical tone. . . . The analysis . . . shows the

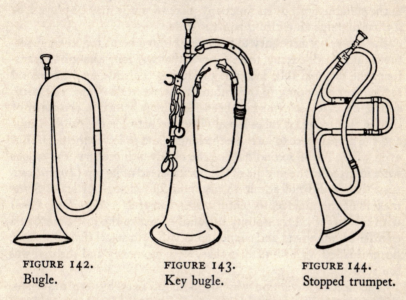

FIGURE 142.   FIGURE 143.   FIGURE 144.
Bugle.   Key bugle.   Stopped trumpet.

presence of the entire series of partials up to thirty, with those from
the second to the sixteenth about equally loud."

A few makers even tried to change the traditional shape of so
inappropriate an instrument as the trumpet was, in order to allow
a stopping hand to enter the bell. (fig. 144)

VALVES. The latest and most effective system of completing the
deficient scales of trumpets and horns is based on the principle of
combining several harmonic scales in one instrument. Scores at the
end of the eighteenth century and at the beginning of the nineteenth
century show many evidences of a preliminary step which consisted
in using two, or four, horns of different tonality to supply the required notes. Four horns, a semitone apart, would provide an uninterrupted chromatic scale from the fourth harmonic on. For obvious reasons, the use of several trumpets or horns in different
tonalities was not satisfactory; the ideal was a chromatic scale controlled by one player with one instrument.

In 1788, an Englishman, CHARLES CLAGGET, obtained a British patent for "uniting two French horns in such a manner that the mouthpiece may be applied to either of them instantaneously as the music may require. One of the trumpets being of the tone D, and the other of the tone E flat, it is evident that by moving the mouthpiece to the suitable horn or trumpet any piece of music may be played, as it then contains an entire chromatic scale."

But it was not necessary to tie several instruments together. A section could be added, say, to an *F* horn, that was long enough to transform the original tube into one producing the scale on *E*, a second section corresponding to the difference between an *F* and a *D* horn, and so on. Such sections had been used long before in the form of *crooks*, that is, coiled tubes loosely inserted between the original tube and the mouthpiece to increase the length and to lower the pitch. But even when, in the second half of the eighteenth century, the crooks were inserted in the middle of the horn instead of its top (*Inventions-horn*), they did not admit an instantaneous change of scale. Some makers of the nineteenth century even constructed *omnitonic horns* with crooks for all transpositions solidly fixed to the instrument in a circular arrangement and connected at will by a small dial. But these horns, loaded with so many crooks, were too heavy and the dial was too slow.

The needed invention was made about 1815 by two musicians, BLÜHMEL in Silesia and HEINRICH STÖLZEL in Berlin. Additional crooks branched off and re-entered the main tube, their inlets and outlets lying close to one another; spring *valves* connected them when pressed down and automatically disconnected them when released. Thus, the action was as fast as that of any keyboard instrument.

Following this first invention countless systems of valves have been devised, and the patent bureaus of all countries are infested with them. Numerous as they are, they can be reduced to two fundamental types—pistons and rotary valves. (fig. 145)

The *piston* has an up-and-down action. When in rest, the piston disconnects the additional crook and allows the wind to pass directly through the main tube. When the piston is pressed down, on the contrary, the direct passage is barred, and the wind is forced to make the detour through the additional crook before re-entering the main tube.

In *rotary valves*, connection and disconnection are effected by a revolving cylinder. The player, however, does not need to make a rotary movement; he presses a key, the vertical motion of which is transformed into rotation.

Rotary valves have always been favored by German players; most other countries have preferred pistons.

The usual number of valves is three:

(1) lowering the original scale by 2 semitones
(2) lowering the original scale by 1 semitone
(3) lowering the original scale by 3 semitones

The combination of any two, or of all three, of these valves can lower the original scale by three, four, five or six semitones. Thus,

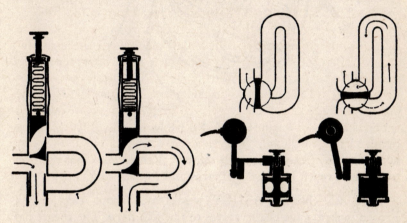

FIGURE 145. Piston and rotary valve, both in rest and action.

even the large gap between the second and third harmonics can be filled, and the range is increased downward six semitones beyond the lowest producible natural note. Some tubas, with a fourth valve lowering the original pitch by a major third or a fourth, can lower the original scale by ten or eleven semitones when all the four valves are functioning.

The accumulation of valves, however, should be avoided, the note made by the use of two valves is a little too high and becomes more inaccurate with each additional valve. This is easy to com·prehend. If valve 3 is supposed to lower the original pitch by a minor third, its additional length must be a fifth of the original tube. But this is not long enough when valves 1 and 2 are already connected. The length, then, is $1 + \frac{1}{8} + \frac{1}{15}$, or $\frac{148}{120}$, instead of the original $\frac{120}{120}$. So the third valve is no longer in correct proportion with the increased tube, and the resulting note is a quarter-tone too high.

The valve action made it possible to construct all sizes and shapes of chromatic brass instruments, thus giving an entirely new timbre

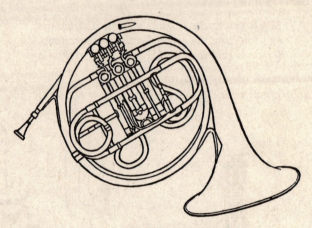

FIGURE 146. French horn.

to the scores of the nineteenth century. Valves were first used on trumpets, French horns, flügelhorns and cornets. (fig. 146)

THE CORNET FAMILY was created about 1825, when French makers gave piston valves to the *post horn*. The cornet has the range and pitch of a $B\flat$ or C trumpet. Its shape, too, is nearly the same, except that it is slightly shorter and wider, and has a relatively longer conical part resulting in a broader and less brilliant tone. Because it is less noble than the trumpet, the Germans have never accepted it in the orchestra. But its greater agility has appealed to Italian and French composers; as early as 1829, Rossini scored cornet parts in his opera *Guillaume Tell*. (fig. 147)

Some cavalry bands include a *cornettino* or sopranino cornet in $E\flat$ with the harmonic fifth $e\flat'$-$b\flat'$ and the range $e\flat'$ to $e\flat^3$; sometimes it is popularly called *piston* or *piccolo*.

The *flügelhorn* is a valve bugle, generally in $B\flat$ and in all respects like the valveless bugle except that it has a chromatic range down to *e*. The original German name (the instrument was first constructed in Austria between 1820 and 1830) is preserved in English-speaking countries; the French call it *bugle*, and the Italians *flicorno soprano*. (fig. 148)

Soon after the construction of the cornet and the flügelhorn, a complete family was built in which some characteristic features of both instruments were combined. Its members are discussed in the following paragraphs.

The *alto horn*, called *Altkornett* in German, *bugle alto* in French and *flicorno alto* in Italian, is coiled either in the shape of a trumpet,

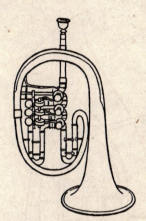

FIGURE 147. Post horn.   FIGURE 148. Cornet.

or upright as a tuba, or circular as a horn. Its usual pitch is *E♭* or *F*, its harmonic fifth *f-c′* and its range *B* to *f″*, or a tone lower. It is played in bands only.

The American *baritone* corresponds to the German *tenor horn*, the French *bugle ténor*, the Italian *flicorno tenore* and the Spanish *baritono*. It is built either in the usual upright form or oval with the bell facing backwards. Its pitch is *C*, its harmonic fifth *c-g*, its range *F♯* to *c″*, or a tone lower.

The American *euphonium* corresponds to the German *baryton*, the French *basse à pistons*, the Spanish *bombardino*, the Italian *eufonio*. Its shape, pitch and range are the same as those of the baritone; but a larger bore gives it a broader, mellower timbre and favors the lower notes. (fig. 149)

The *bass tuba* (called *F* or *E♭ bass* when used in bands) is the Italian *cimbasso* or *tuba* and the French *contrebasse à pistons*. The harmonic fifth being *F-c*, its range is B_1 to *f′* (or a tone lower). An additional major third beneath the lowest note can be obtained on tubas with a fourth valve. The first tuba was suggested by WILHELM WIEPRECHT, musical supervisor of the Prussian Army, and constructed in 1835 by JOHANN G. MORITZ in Berlin; but it was entirely different from ours. (fig. 150)

The *contrabass tuba* (called *BB bass* in bands) is tuned to the lower fourth of the bass tuba. Its pitch is C in orchestras and B in bands; the harmonic fifth is C-G, the range F_1 to c' (or a tone

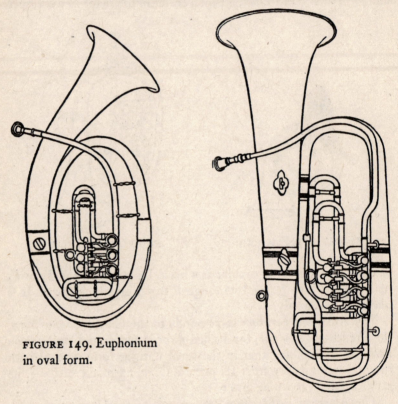

FIGURE 149. Euphonium
in oval form.

FIGURE 150. Bass tuba.

lower); a fourth valve advances the lower limit by a major third. It was invented ten years after the bass tuba (the first model of which had an additional valve that threw the instrument into contrabass C) by V. F. ČERVENÝ, a noted Bohemian maker of brass wind instruments.

Bass and contrabass tubas have been made both in upright form or as *helicons* (from Greek *helikós* 'coiled'). This latter form, apparently invented in Russia, and imitated in 1849 by IGNAZ STOWASSER in Vienna, is a spiral circular form wide enough to allow the player

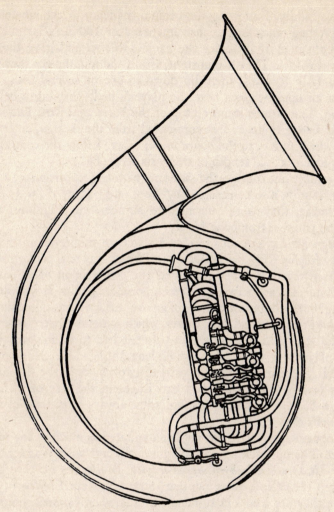

FIGURE 151. Helicon.

to carry the heavy instrument over the shoulder. In the United States the helicon is built with a gigantic movable bell that was suggested by the late bandmaster and composer JOHN PHILIP SOUSA; it is called *sousaphone* in his honor. (fig. 151)

All these cornets, flügelhorns, alto horns, baritones, euphoniums, bass and contrabass tubas were constructed in different countries by different "inventors" between 1825 and 1845 as they were needed in orchestra and band, but with no intention of forming a homogeneous family. Following the general tendency of the nineteenth century, the Franco-Belgian instrument maker ADOLPHE SAX in Paris united them in 1843 under the name *saxhorns* and gave them a uniform model. They are upright. From the mouthpiece they run horizontally forward, then dip down in one or several coils, and end in an upright piece near the player's body forming a bell at the top. The pistons stand on top of the horizontal part. Differing only in size, all pitches are represented from the *suraigu*, an octave above the soprano, to the *bourdon*, an octave below the contrabass, which had an actual length of thirty-six feet. (fig. 152)

One must not confuse the saxhorns with the *saxotrombas*, a forgotten family, also constructed by ADOLPHE SAX in 1845. In type and timbre, they were intermediate between the flügelhorn-tuba and the trumpet-trombone family.

Wagner-tubas. Anxious to obtain a solemn timbre of unfamiliar quality for his *Ring des Nibelungen* (which was first performed in 1876), Richard Wagner suggested the construction of an instrument intermediate between a French horn and a tuba. It was conical throughout, had the outer shape of an oval tuba, a mouthpiece similar to that of the horn and four valves, which sometimes were arranged for the left hand because the instrument had to be fingered by a horn player who was used to having his right hand free for stopping the bell. A 'quartet' was composed of two tenors in the size of Bb horns (range Bb_1 to f'') and two basses in the size of F horns (range B_2 to g'). Their notation is not always consistent, even in Wagner's own scores.

Wagner's innovation has not been imitated as much as one might expect. The outstanding post-Wagnerian scores with Wagner-tubas are Felix Draeseke's *Symphonia tragica*, Bruckner's Seventh Symphony (1884) and, most familiar, Strauss's opera *Electra* (1909) where they are heard in sustained chords when Orestes enters the palace to avenge his father's death.

Inspired by this instrument, FONTAINE-BESSON in Paris (c. 1889) based a complete family of tubas on the same principle, from a soprano down to a double bass, and called them *cornophones*.

VALVE TRUMPETS AND TROMBONES. The trumpet was given valves in about 1820; five years later the Prussian regimental bands owned valve trumpets in Bb (soprano) and Eb (alto). By 1840, valve trumpets were generally accepted in bands and, by 1850, also in orchestras. The orchestral trumpet was tuned to F;

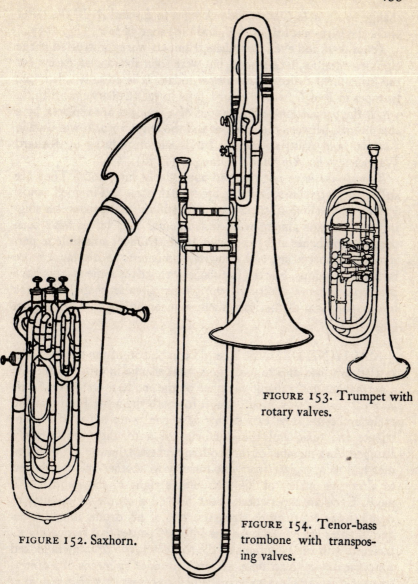

FIGURE 153. Trumpet with rotary valves.

FIGURE 152. Saxhorn.

FIGURE 154. Tenor-bass trombone with transposing valves.

but this instrument disappeared from the orchestra at the end of the nineteenth century in spite of its noble character, because composers used it more and more in its highest register so that the players shifted of their own accord to the soprano trumpet, although its tone was less noble. This trumpet is either tuned to *B♭* with slide change to *A,* or to *C* with slide changes to *B♭* and *A.* In the latter pitch, the harmonic fifth is *c'-g'*, and the range *f♯* to *c³.* (fig. 153)

Tenor, bass and even contrabass trumpets were constructed in the eighteen twenties in Germany, but were soon abandoned, except for the instrument called *bass trumpet* today. It is actually a baritone trumpet in *B* or *C*, with *c-g* (or a tone lower) as harmonic fifth, in which the proportionate dimensions of a trumpet are replaced by a compromise between the trumpet and the tenor horn. It was used in Bavarian and Austrian cavalry bands and introduced by Richard Wagner into his *Ring des Nibelungen* (1876).

Trombones have not changed appreciably since 1600. They are still made with slides, both for use in orchestras and in good bands. Players have clung to their easy adjustability that produces a singing style unique among wind instruments. Yet, valves have been used on trombones and have made the instrument accessible to persons with short arms, and allowed trombonists to display a more brilliant technique. For the trombone with valves some makers have preferred a more functional upright or circular shape, since the traditional form of the instrument is meaningless without a slide. (fig. 154)

MACHINE DRUMS. The old companion of the trumpet, the kettledrum, had also to undergo a vital change in order to become a permanent and reliable member of the modern orchestra. In its classical form it was good enough for both the army band and the early orchestra. The two drums of a pair were expected to contribute the tonic and the dominant of a tonality which rarely changed. As a member of the modern orchestra, however, the drummer had to modulate from one tonality to another and was forced to alter the pitches of his instruments right in the middle of a piece. Even an experienced artist needed a couple of minutes to regulate the fourteen or sixteen screws of his drums until the required notes were found. As this enforced pauses that frequently interfered with the intentions of the composer, the drummers looked for some device to act upon all screws at once by means of a central screw. GERHARD CRAMER was the first to construct such a system at Munich in 1812. J. C. N. STUMPFF in Amsterdam obtained the same result in 1821 by turning the drum itself instead of turning a central screw. The most recent system is the *pedal drum,* in which a pedal acts on the central screw. The more the pedal is pressed the higher

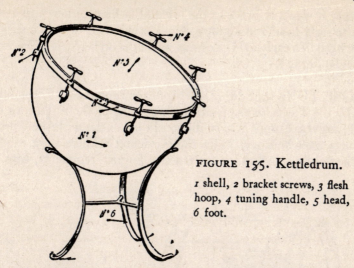

FIGURE 155. Kettledrum.

1 shell, *2* bracket screws, *3* flesh hoop, *4* tuning handle, *5* head, *6* foot.

the tone is raised; in a few seconds the drummer can travel from *F* to *f*. (fig. 155)

DRUMS. Along with the kettledrums, three kinds of cylinder drums entered the regular orchestra—the side drum, the tenor drum and the bass drum.

The *side drum* has a shallow cylinder and two sheepskins, the rims of which are wound over small, circular *flesh hoops* at either end. These concealed flesh hoops are pressed down and kept in place by outer *rope hoops*, which are connected and tightened either by ropes and leather braces or by metal rods and thumbscrews. The upper skin is the *batter head*, the lower the *snare head*, as its resonance is strengthened and sharpened by several gut (or coiled wire) strings stretched across it, which cause the specific rattling timbre of the side drum.

This and its shallowness distinguish it from the deeper and snareless *tenor drum*. (pl. XX b, fig. 156)

The *bass drum* is a big, rather shallow drum, carried so that the heads face sideways, and struck with a heavy, thick-knobbed stick; its tone is low, powerful and indeterminate. Until the beginning of the nineteenth century it was called the *Turkish drum*, and all that is known about it indicates that the name was correctly given. The Italian painter, Vittore Carpaccio, first depicted it in a Turkish band at about 1505, and as late as the first half of the nineteenth century it was still struck in the oriental fashion, either with a stick on the right head and a split rod on the cylinder, or with a stick on each head. An early evidence of its use in the orchestra is in Mozart's *Seraglio* (1782).

THE TURKISH MUSIC. From the conquest of Constantinople by the Turks, in 1453, till the beginning of the eighteenth century, eastern Europe was continuously in contact with the Turkish armies; over and over again the occidental soldiers were exposed to the wild music that intoxicated the Turkish regiments, with the

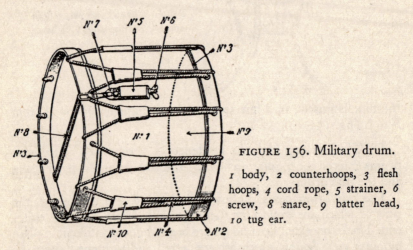

FIGURE 156. Military drum.

1 body, *2* counterhoops, *3* flesh hoops, *4* cord rope, *5* strainer, *6* screw, *8* snare, *9* batter head, *10* tug ear.

shrill tones of oboes and triangles accented by clanging cymbals and rumbling drums. About 1700, after the military power of the Turkish Empire was broken, the victorious European armies began to imitate Ottoman bands. The Poles were the first to adopt *Turkish music,* or *janissaries' music,* a name taken from the sultan's life guards. Following this example, the elector of Saxony, Augustus the Strong, who was king of Poland as well, organized a Saxon band with four cymbalists. The Austrians had their first 'janissaries' in 1741, and the other countries followed. In a narrower sense, the Europeans called Turkish music a combination of bass drum, cymbals and triangle, as, for instance, in Joseph Haydn's Military Symphony (1794). In the bands a jingling crescent was also included.

The introduction of Turkish instruments was accompanied by a predilection for Turkish motifs in the western arts. Examples of this mode can be found in the subjects of numerous comic operas, such as Gluck's *Cadi dupé* (1761) and *La rencontre imprévue* (1764), Mozart's *Seraglio* (1781) and Grétry's *Caravane du Caire* (1783).

THE TRIANGLE is a steel rod bent into an equilateral triangle, suspended on a thread and struck with an iron stick. Many high, dissonant partials drown the fundamental and make the sound tinkling and shrill without a definite pitch.

When the instrument first appeared, in the fifteenth century, it was not always triangular. Italian and English paintings of that epoch show it in a trapezoid form similar to the shape of a medieval stirrup. Accordingly, contemporaneous names indicate sometimes the triangular type, such as French *trepie,* and sometimes the stirrup form, as Italian *staffa* and German *stegereif.* The term *triangle* occurs for the first time in a Württemberg inventory of 1589. Besides these indicative names, triangles are sometimes hidden under the misleading name *cymbal*(*e*), used even by such a careful scholar as Father Mersenne.

Up to the nineteenth century jingling metal rings were usually strung on the horizontal section of the triangle; three was the usual number before 1600, and afterwards five.

For three centuries the triangle was relegated to the so-called *irregular* music. In the eighteenth century it was given a place in the orchestra. In the Hamburg opera it was employed as early as 1710, and seven years later two triangles were bought for the Dresden court orchestra. Further evidences are in Grétry's opera, *La fausse Magie* (1775), Gluck's *Iphigénie en Tauride* (1779), Mozart's *Seraglio* (1781). But in all these scores it was used to give local color. It finally became a permanent member of the orchestra at the beginning of the nineteenth century. An outstanding early example of its use purely as timbre is in the last movement of Beethoven's Ninth Symphony (1823).

THE CRESCENT was an upright pole with a fanciful, half-oriental headpiece of metal, composed of a crescent and several other symbols, from which bells, jingles and, generally, two long horsetails in different colors were suspended. (fig. 157)

The crescent was descended from the Central Asian shaman's staff, which could chase away evil spirits with the tinkling of its jingles. From its home in Central Asia it probably traveled both east to China and west to Turkey. In the time of the Chou dynasty, 1122–255 B.C., Chinese conductors gave the signal to start the music by lifting the dance staff, *hui*, which was ornamented with the sun, stars and two white oxtails. In Turkey these staffs had been given the Turkish crescent as their distinguishing feature, and by the epoch of the Turkish conquest in Europe had become the specific insignia of the highest dignitaries. Like trumpets and kettledrums,

FIGURE 157. Crescent (old form).

they gradually passed from this position until they were mingled with other instruments in the military band. A number of crescents captured from Turkish regiments were brought home and suspended from the walls of European churches and palaces. The crescent did not become a European instrument before 1800. As such it was given various names, among which the French names, *pavillon chinois* and *châpeau chinois,* are the most curious. Possibly some of the fanciful, metal parts of the French crescents were inspired by the eighteenth century French taste for *chinoiserie* rather than by Turkish models. The crescent was short-lived in the Occident, except in Russia and Germany. In the latter country it is still in use.

CYMBALS have rarely been made in the Occident; most of them have been, and still are, imported from China. The best cymbals, however, come from Turkey. These are slightly smaller, flatter, thicker and have more volume; their alloy is said to consist of 78.55% copper, 20.28% tin, 0.54% lead and 0.18% iron.

Cymbals were not always connected exclusively with Turkish music. This book has discussed them again and again since the first mention of them in the chapter on the ancient Near East, and though they were never regular implements of European art music, neither were they entirely absent. The earliest evidence of their introduction into the orchestra is in Nicolaus Adam Strungk's opera *Esther* (Hamburg, 1680). But here and elsewhere during the following century, they were used only to give a specific timbre to exotic subjects. After they were reintroduced with the Turkish music, they lost their atmospheric connotations.

The cymbalist is sometimes omitted from smaller bands and his place taken by the drummer; one of the cymbals is then fastened on the bass drum, while the drummer holds the other in his hand. This is a poor expedient as cymbals should rub each other in one violent sliding movement instead of being clashed together so that their vibration is deadened.

XYLOPHONE. In describing these idiophonic instruments of a relatively recent Asiatic descent, a final section may be given to the xylophone; we have discussed it already in both the primitive and the Southeast Asiatic chapters.

In Europe the xylophone was first mentioned by the organist Arnold Schlick in his book *Spiegel der Orgelmacher und Organisten* (1511) as *hültze glechter*, that is, 'wooden percussion.' From that date it can be traced on woodcuts and in literary sources, but it never became a genuine occidental instrument; wandering peoples only, most of them in eastern Europe and southern Germany, used it in a rather primitive form. It achieved importance when, around 1830, a Russian Jew, J. Gusikov, played it with virtuosity and made it known in the musical centers of the Continent. Felix Mendelssohn, who heard him in 1836, wrote: "With a few sticks, lying on straw and struck with other sticks, he does what is possible only on the most perfect instrument. How from such materials even the small tone produced—more like a Papageno-flute than anything else—

can be obtained, is a mystery to me." Afterwards the xylophone appeared not only in garden concerts and in variety shows, but even
in symphony concerts. Hans Christian Lumbye (1810–1874) employed it in his *Traumbilder*, and Camille Saint-Saëns scored a part
for it in his symphonic poem *Danse Macabre* (1874) to describe the
dry rattling of skeletons.

The modern form of xylophone that such compositions demand
consists of a series of wooden slabs separated by wood or felt iso-
lators resting on cylinders made of bundles of straw (hence the
popular name *straw fiddle*). The slabs, comprising a range of three
chromatic octaves, are arranged in two or more rows indented into
each other.

THE ORGAN, in this period too, summarizes the general musical development of the time. Handel's, Bach's, Couperin's powerful polyphony yields to the poor two-voiced scores of a later
generation; impersonal sublimity was abandoned for personal romanticism. But the organ was by nature polyphonic and impersonal,
and thus, after being in the center of musical life, it became out-
moded. Music moved outside the church although the organ was
still confined there.

Most makers continued in the old routine forms, now unrelated
to musical needs. Others experimented in attempts to adapt it to
the new musical ideals of power and expressiveness and, at least
in the eighteenth century, simplicity. The desire for expression and
simplicity led to the curious *Simplifikationssystem* of Abbé Georg
J. Vogler at Darmstadt, about 1800. It consisted in an appreciable
reduction of stops and pipes. The three manuals were grounded respectively on 32′, 16′ and 8′. But Vogler did not need an actual
32′. He produced it acoustically by the difference frequencies resulting from the simultaneous touch of two higher keys. The notes
c and *g*, for instance, being the second and third partials of *C*,
produce the latter note in the listener's ear as 1 is the difference
between 3 and 2; the same effect results from the combination of *g*
and *c'*, since these notes are the third and fourth partials of *C*
(4 minus 3 equals 1); or from *c* and *e'*, which are its fourth and
fifth partials (5 minus 4). Pulling a fifth with an 8′ stop produced a
16′; pulling a fifth with a 16′ or a third with an 8′ produced a 32′.
Therefore, several ground stops were replaced by thirds and fifths
in Abbé Vogler's system. Mixtures were avoided as confusing. But

expression was increased by a number of crescendo devices. His object was to give "a true picture of a well-organized orchestra."

The simplification system was a failure. Most organists disliked it, saying Vogler's organ was a concert instrument rather than for a church. Not long after Vogler's unsuccessful attempt, the organ in a different form did become a concert instrument. Submitting to the new ideal of a powerful orchestra rich in colors, the organ at the beginning of the nineteenth century entered the concert hall as a part of the orchestra. In this capacity it had to follow all the tendencies of the real orchestra in the nineteenth century, expression, overwhelming power of sound, refined mixing of timbres, swift and continuous transition from shade to shade. The main inventions for the organ made in that time were reflections of orchestral tendencies.

The principals, which in the middle ages had been the only stops, disappeared in a maze of imitations of orchestral solo stops, flutes, oboes, cors anglais, clarinets, trumpets and violins. Such organs were necessarily motley in sound.

Special attention was given to expression, which was provided by two kinds of swells. One was the *Venetian swell*, a box including the pipe work or part of it, with shutters that opened or closed gradually when worked by a pedal; BURKAT SHUDI in London had invented this swell for the harpsichord in about 1760. The second was the German *Rollschweller*, invented in the second half of the nineteenth century. A pedal set a big cylinder into rotation; ledges, arranged on its surface, pushed all the stops one after another, thus causing a rapid crescendo from one weak stop to the full organ.

Overwhelming power of sound was obtained both by increase and by intensification. By 1850 organs with a hundred stops were given to certain large churches; four manuals and two pedals occurred; the wind pressure was considerably increased in all countries; new stops with a particularly heavy wind were introduced, such as *tuba mirabilis*.

Refined mixing of timbres depended partially on the quantity of available stops but even more on a well-organized system of *couplers*, which allowed the player to transfer stops, that is, to play a stop on one keyboard although its position was on another.

Swift and continual transition from shade to shade was due to *combination stops*. The knobs that controlled the stops were duplicated once or twice at the side of the keyboards; before starting his

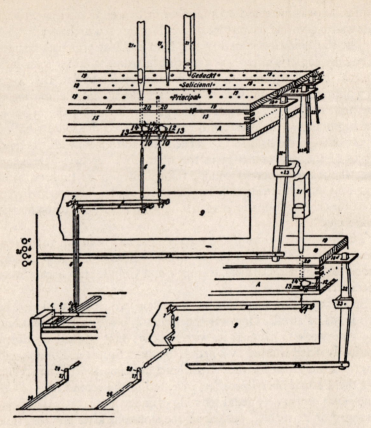

FIGURE 158. Section of a mechanical organ. After H. Schmidt.

1, 2. manual keys, 3. front board, 4. tap wire, 5. adjusting nut, 6. trackers, 7. roller arms, 8. trundle, 9. roller board, 10. hooks, 11. puffers, 12. soundboard spring, 13. pallet guides, 14. pallets, 15. groove, 17. bearers, 18. sliders, 19. rack board, 20. rackboard holes, 21. pipes, 22. backfalls, 23. backfall frames, 24. draw stop rods. 25. stops, 26. pedal keys, 27. squares, 28. adjusting nut, A. windchest.

piece, the organist could prepare a second and a third registration by connecting the knobs desired for later use, and then, by pressing a button, instantaneously replace the first by the second combination.

All these complicated devices required a more reliable action. The action connecting the keys and stops with the pipes was governed by a complicated system of wooden trackers, stickers and

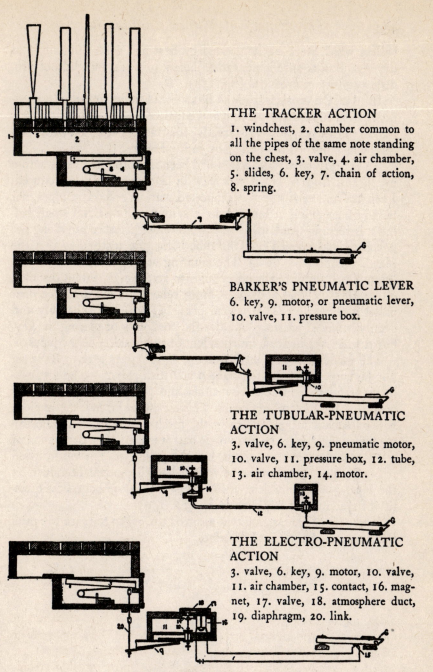

THE TRACKER ACTION

1. windchest, 2. chamber common to all the pipes of the same note standing on the chest, 3. valve, 4. air chamber, 5. slides, 6. key, 7. chain of action, 8. spring.

BARKER'S PNEUMATIC LEVER

6. key, 9. motor, or pneumatic lever, 10. valve, 11. pressure box.

THE TUBULAR-PNEUMATIC ACTION

3. valve, 6. key, 9. pneumatic motor, 10. valve, 11. pressure box, 12. tube, 13. air chamber, 14. motor.

THE ELECTRO-PNEUMATIC ACTION

3. valve, 6. key, 9. motor, 10. valve, 11. air chamber, 15. contact, 16. magnet, 17. valve, 18. atmosphere duct, 19. diaphragm, 20. link.

FIGURE 159. Evolution of the action.

(Reprinted by permission from *The Modern Organ* by Ernest M. Skinner, New York, The H. W. Gray Company, Inc.)

rollers which were easily affected by heat and cold, humidity and dryness. It was unreliable, rather heavy to work and did not produce a consistent pressure. (fig. 158)

In 1832, CHARLES SPACKMAN BARKER in London invented a *pneumatic lever* to facilitate playing and equalize pressure; instead of acting on the valves (*pallets*) directly, the trackers acted on small bellows which opened the pallets by wind pressure.

An entirely *pneumatic action* had been invented five years before by JOSEPH BOOTH, but it was slow in being generally introduced. Each key and each stop was connected with its respective pipes, not by any mechanical action, but by a system of tubes and small bellows. A feeding trunk filled with wind under pressure ran along the keyboard and opened into the tube belonging to the key that the player was pressing down. The entering wind pushed the first bellows, which produced wind enough to act, over a certain distance, on a second bellows and so on, from relay to relay, until the final pallet was reached. This system provided not only reliability and evenly balanced pressure, but also the possibility of placing the keyboard wherever desired, independent of the position of the pipes.

The modern *electro-pneumatic action*, too, goes back to BARKER. On January 22, 1868, he obtained a British patent for an arrangement of "detachable electro-magnet and pneumatic apparatus for operating the pallets" of organs. This meant, in his half-mechanical, half-pneumatic action, replacing the mechanical part by an electromagnetic one, while the pneumatic part was kept. The depression of a key closed an electric circuit, but the pallet was opened by wind pressure. The reader must be referred to the special literature on the history of the modern action for studying the boundless quantity of systems and improvements. (fig. 159)

It was the electric action that allowed the organ to reach the peak that the next chapter is to describe.

Epilogue: The Twentieth Century

AT FIRST sight the orchestra of our epoch seems to be continuing in the same general course on which it started in the nineteenth century. Its outer aspect does not differ from that of Wagner or Beethoven. The instruments, too—violins, flutes, horns, harps, kettledrums, etc.—are the replicas of models made in the eighteenth and nineteenth centuries, and their roles have not changed.

The general tendencies of the nineteenth century have also been preserved and even exaggerated. The orchestras became larger, Schönberg scored some seventy parts in his *Gurrelieder*, and a manager was able in his advertising to boast that Mahler's Eighth Symphony (1910) was *Die Symphonie der Tausend*.

This tendency has been checked by economy as well as by taste. Schönberg and Schreker have written *Kammersymphonien*, Strauss gave his *Ariadne auf Naxos* (1912) a small orchestra, and the score of Stravinski's *L'histoire du soldat* (1918) includes only seven players—six of them play clarinet, bassoon, cornet, trombone, violin and double bass, and a percussionist handles a bass drum, a tenor drum, two side drums, cymbals and a triangle.

This total of four wind and two stringed instruments is an unusual proportion when looked at from the point of view of the nineteenth century. However, *L'histoire du soldat* is not a single case. Confining ourselves to Stravinski's works, we find his *Ragtime* of 1918 written for flute, clarinet, cornet, French horn, trombone, drums, cymbals, cimbalom, violin, viola, double bass; and in several scores, such as the *Symphonies d'instruments à vent* (1920) and the *Octuor pour instruments à vent* (1923), strings are entirely excluded. The same is true in jazz and swing bands.

Though seeming to be a new departure, it is the logical continuation of a nineteenth century tendency. In the seventeenth century the normal orchestra consisted of stringed instruments only. Then wind instruments were added by degrees. At the beginning of the nineteenth century there were usually two members of each wind family in the orchestra, two flutes, two oboes, two trumpets; in the middle of the century three, and at the end four were not infrequent.

There was a similar increase in the importance given to percussion instruments; in *L'histoire du soldat* we saw the unusual proportion of six melodic and six percussion instruments. Alarmists who fear that modern music is receding into a "savage, oriental" stage, because of its interest in percussion, should remember that this is only an advanced stage of a tendency which already manifested itself in the nineteenth century. It differed only by degrees from Haydn's use of 'Turkish Music' in his Military Symphony, from Beethoven's melodic kettledrums in octave tuning in the Scherzo of the Ninth Symphony, from Berlioz's chime of sixteen kettledrums in his Requiem. These classic passages were related to Turkish and Indian practice rather than to European tradition, and the alarmists could have dismissed them, too, as "savage and oriental."

Today, even stringed instruments, such as the piano or the guitar, are often used in ensembles for stressing rhythm rather than for melody and harmony, and the American *banjo* (the body of which is simply a frame drum) has been especially added to bands for this purpose. Just as the seventeenth century constructed its music on the foundation of a 'thoroughbass,' the twentieth century seems to be veering toward a structure of 'thoroughrhythm.'

Percussion, far from being a sympto.n of regression, indicates the revitalizing presence of a motor impulse that for centuries in the evolution of our harmonic style has been repressed and curtailed.

Jazz and Swing, that have glorified rhythm and percussion, have brought with them as companion a cheap sentimentality. New instruments have been created, which in their exaggerated emotionalism caricature true sentiment; the *singing saw* whimpering under the gentle strokes of a hammer or a bow; the metal plate of a *flex-a-tone* whining under the pressure of the player's thumb; *swanee-saxes* and *jazzo-flutes* sliding over the scale; the *Hawaiian guitar* gliding amorously from note to note. All these instruments produce ready-made sentimentality based on excessive vibrato and glissando. The same is true of the new *electric instruments.*

ELECTRIC INSTRUMENTS are a departure from nineteenth century tradition. Because they depend on physical discoveries of this century, they are often considered the most characteristic instruments of our time.

The term 'electric instruments' is loosely applied. It comprises three essentially different kinds of instruments: those with an electric action taking the place of a former mechanical or pneumatic action, such as the electric organ; electromechanical instruments; and radioelectric instruments. Instruments with an electric action instead of a mechanical one will not be discussed in this section.

In *electromechanical instruments,* vibrations are produced in the usual mechanical ways, by hammers striking piano strings in an actual piano, or by a bow acting on the strings of a violin. The electrical piano has no soundboard; other electric stringed instruments retain their soundboards. But all of them are amplified by an electrical device. Their sound vibrations are transformed into electrical vibrations corresponding to the acoustical vibrations amplified by means of vacuum tubes and their associated circuits, and then transformed back again into sound by means of a loud-speaker.

Serious attempts began in 1927 with E. SPIELMANN's *Superpiano;* here the key acts on a lamp, the light of which is transformed into electric vibrations by means of a photocell. Electromagnetic action had already been applied to stringed instruments, such as pianos, violins, cellos and guitars, where it superseded a soundboard and additional strings. On the basis of recent systems of this kind, BIZOS, BOREAU, VIERLING, the physicist W. NERNST and the firm of CARL BECHSTEIN in Berlin constructed the *Neo-Bechstein* in 1931, a piano containing eighteen microphones, making feasible a much longer tone, a crescendo and a great variety of timbres, despite its smaller size.

None of these electromechanical instruments has become important in musical life.

The principle of *radioelectric instruments* is an oscillating electric circuit with a distinct frequency, which can be altered by influencing the capacity of the circuit by any extraneous agent, for instance the player's hand or a wire.

The pioneers in making these instruments were W. DUDDEL (1899) and W. BURSTYN (1911); F. E. MILLER (1915) was the first to introduce the modern electron tube. LEO THEREMIN's *Thereminvox* or *Etherophone* (1924) is a small box containing the apparatus with an antenna on top. The nearer the player's hand comes to the antenna the higher will be the tone. To avoid an eternal legato and glissando, the left hand presses an interruptor after each note; a pedal regulates an interior resistance which controls the volume.

If a wire is used instead of the hand, the player can control the position of the influencing medium more exactly and, in consequence, the exact pitch of each tone. Besides, it is then possible to play more than one note at a time on the same instrument. Consequently, we distinguish between two types of wire electrophones— monophonic instruments and polyphonic instruments.

The most important monophonic instruments are MAURICE MARTENOT's *Ondes musicales* (1928), N. LANGER's and J. HALMAGYI's *Emicon* (c. 1930), and FRIEDRICH TRAUTWEIN's *Trautonium* (1930). The emicon, built in this country, is the only monophonic instrument with real keys. All of them excel in imitating and creating an indefinite number of timbres.

Of polyphonic instruments it will suffice to mention four models: JÖRG MAGER's *Sphärophon* (1926) with keyboards; HELBERGER and LERTES's *Hellertion* (1928) with movable ribbon manuals (similar to those of the trautonium), on which the metric distances correspond to musical distances; P. GIVELET and E. COUPLEUX's *Radio organ* (1932) with seventy-six stops, three manuals and a pedal; LAURENS HAMMOND's *Hammond organ* and *Novachord* (1939), with keys.

A general, though merely technical, distinction between all these systems is whether they use high or low frequencies. High frequencies cannot be made use of in music. But the superposition of two different high frequencies produces a low 'difference frequency' because of interference. The Thereminvox has high frequencies. Low frequency instruments are Hellertion, Trautonium, Emicon; the Sphärophon uses both.

We do not know the destiny of these engineers' inventions, nor can we tell how much they will mean to the future of music. For the time being, they surely owe their existence to the experimentations of electroengineers rather than to any musical need. Most eulogies of electric instruments emphasize their unlimited capacity for dynamic power and varied timbre. This is in line with the trend of the later nineteenth century. But are these the ideals of the future?

Or is this a blind alley from which we must retrace our steps in order to return, not to the path of the nineteenth century, but to a much earlier style, in which our all too personal expression will be replaced by a greater objectivity?

The desire to rediscover the treasures of ancient music began as early as the middle of the nineteenth century. In 1850, a society of conscientious historians and musicians started the gigantic publication of Johann Sebastian Bach's complete works. Many other complete editions were to follow: Handel in 1859, Palestrina in 1862, Mozart in 1876, Schütz in 1885, Purcell in 1889, Lasso in 1894, and besides complete works, selected pieces in the official *Monumenta* and *Denkmäler* of various nations.

The purpose was not so much to be complete as to be correct and to replace those numerous unreliable editions which left out, added and altered according to the personal taste of the "editor" or to the contemporary mode.

Correctness also became more and more the password for the performance of ancient music. Ancient instruments were revived in order to avoid substitutions of inappropriate instruments; *oboi d'amore,* basset-horns and even cornets (*zinken*) came back; *viola d'amore* and *viola da gamba, violino piccolo* and *violoncello piccolo,* harpsichord and clavichord re-entered the orchestra and chamber music; high trumpets were constructed.

It would be wronging the men who were responsible for this attitude to reproach them with sterile literalism. Correctness to them was neither orthodoxy nor pedantry. Their point was to be faithful, not to "history" but to art. They demanded harpsichords, gambas, ancient organs, because they knew that an organ of the nineteenth century killed Bach's severe architecture, that the thick and sensual tone of a violoncello destroyed the delicate line of a gamba composition, that a cross-stringed piano suffocated the unemotional melody of a harpsichord piece. They saw what to a painter would be self-evident, that design and color could not be separated, that an outline drawn by Raphael could not be colored with Cézanne's palette.

It must be admitted, however, that we are far away from coloristic authenticity, even with the resurrection of all these old instruments. Most of our "gambists" play the gamba in the position and in the manner of a violoncello, without frets, the fingerboard being too long and the bridge too high and arched, with a modern bow and modern strings, and there is so little difference in the result that the listener wonders to what purpose the player has taken the trouble to find his way between six or seven strings. Many of our harpsichordists (but they are usually better than the gambists) play on modern reconstructions which, having pedals instead of less convenient hand stops, allow the lady to shift so rapidly from one combination to another that she occasionally indulges in the most astonishing coloristic excesses, to say nothing of her sixteen-foot debauches. Both gambists and harpsichordists believe that they play *the* ancient style. They rarely realize that such a thing does not exist. Style differed with every country, and in every country it changed continuously. A gambist should not play a *recercada* of Diego Ortiz from about 1550 as he plays Handel's sonata and a harpsichordist ought to distinguish between a piece from the *Fitzwilliam Virginal Book* and a concerto of Bach. How extremely seldom is such discrimination found! But it would be unjust to speak of gambists and harpsichordists only; a modern violin, though identical with the violin of 1700 and often the very specimen except for a few millimeters of additional neck length, is not played in the manner of Corelli.

This is said not to discourage eager musicians, but to guide them; difficulties must be seen before they can be conquered.

The reconstruction of ancient instruments as well as critical editions of Complete Works were symbolic of a growing interest in the music of remote epochs. Also originally an outgrowth of the romantic period, the historical movement in music gradually became a leading force in neutralizing the excesses of the later romantic style, such as its decomposition of form, its obliteration of distinct outlines, its harmonic and coloristic superrefinement, its calculated effect on the listener, its exaggerated subjectivity.

In about 1900 this neutralizing tendency found fertile soil in a young generation which came to despise sentimentality, individualism and overrefinement. Opposed to virtuosity and concert display, this generation took refuge in preromantic music, from Bach backwards to the sixteenth and fifteenth centuries. Moreover, the old music and its instruments, such as the recorder, were particularly suited to small musical gatherings where youths and girls played themselves instead of listening to concerts or emulating virtuosi on the piano.

An important group of young composers, too, took their inspiration from the ancient music. They not only wrote fugues, toccatas, concerti grossi, suites, passacaglias and chaconas, but their style emphasized transparence, severity and lack of sentimental features.

The truest mirror of all these contradictory forces, of an exaggerated nineteenth century style as well as of an archaic reaction, is the latest evolution of the organ.

THE ORGAN, in the first third of the twentieth century, continued to overwhelm the listener by its power and size. WALCKER at Ludwigsburg in Württemberg gave five manuals to the organ of St. Michaelis in Hamburg (1912); twelve thousand pipes in 167 stops answered the player's touch. HILL equipped the Cathedral at Liverpool with the same number of stops and manuals in 1921. The Century Hall at Breslau had even fifteen thousand pipes in 187 stops.

These European organs were left behind by The World's Greatest Organ at the World's Fair in St. Louis (1904), which afterwards, in 1917, was brought to Philadelphia and, greatly augmented and increased, was set up in John Wanamaker's store. It has five manuals, 232 stops and eighteen thousand pipes. Running over the booklet issued when the organ was inaugurated, we read:

The organ weighs over 375,000 pounds. More than 120,000 feet of lumber were used in its construction. Total space occupied by organ and blowers, 118,602 feet. The blowers furnish an aggregate column of air at varied pressures of 20,800 cubic feet per minute. The incandescent lights strung along the organ chamber would light the streets of a small town. The largest pipe is of wood, 32 feet long, 27 inches wide, and 32 inches deep in the middle, and weighs 1,735 pounds. It is so large that two men can crawl through it, side by side, on their hands and knees.

The pipe of 1451 at Blois, of which we spoke on page 304, has been forgotten!

The Philadelphia organ kept the blue ribbon for fifteen years only. In 1932 it yielded to EMERSON L. RICHARD's and MIDMER-LOSH's organ in the Convention Hall at Atlantic City, New Jersey. Eighteen thousand pipes? The World's Greatest Organ has 32,882 pipes; it possesses 1,233 stops, including couplers, etc., and seven manuals; the wind pressure is forced up to a hundred inches.

Is this the last word in building organ skyscrapers? We do not know. But we are aware of another fact—that the twentieth century is opposing a very different ideal to the adoration of size.

In the first years of this century, DR. ALBERT SCHWEITZER in Strasbourg and a group of Southwest German organists opened a campaign against the usual organ of their days, with the slogan: Back to Silbermann! The idea was that Bach is still the outstanding composer, even of modern organ playing, and that his compositions should be played in his style, on an organ of his time; the roaring, turbulent and ununified organ of the nineteenth century kills Bach's polyphony and structure. The ideal instrument would be the Franco-German organ of GOTTFRIED SILBERMANN in Freiberg, or ANDREAS SILBERMANN at Strasbourg, the contemporaries of Bach. Back to Silbermann, back to a lower wind pressure to prevent the shrieking of the pipes, to a unity in the palette of timbres starting from Principal 8', to a softer intonation of accessory stops up to 1', and, altogether, to a clear transparency and a silvery radiance.

Just as the complete editions of Bach and Handel were followed by a complete edition of Palestrina, so the Bach organ was followed by an organ in the style of 1600. In 1921, the organ builder OSCAR WALCKER in Württemberg finished the so-called *Praetorius organ* which, at the suggestion of Dr. Wilibald Gurlitt, professor in the University of Freiburg, he had constructed after the specified plan in Michael Praetorius's *Syntagma musicum* of 1618. In the following years both the Silbermann and the Praetorius movement spread over various countries. In Germany and Denmark old SCHNITGER and SILBERMANN organs have been discovered and carefully restored, and a quantity of modern organs has been copied from them. In Paris, the organ at Saint-Gervais, on which Couperin used to play, has attracted the attention of organists and organ builders, and one of the leading firms, GONZALEZ, is substituting archaic scales, pressures and stops for those of the nineteenth century organ.

In the United States, the movement was inaugurated by WALTER HOLTKAMP of the VOTTELER-HOLTKAMP-SPARLING ORGAN Co. in Cleveland, Ohio. From 1932 on, he has built organs with the disposition, scales, and wind pressures of the ancients, at the Cleveland Museum of Art (1933), St. John's Church, Covington, Kentucky (1934), Emmanuel Lutheran Church, Rochester, N.Y. (1936). At first he used the modern stopchamber windchest, in which each chamber of the chest fed all the pipes belonging to the same stop; since 1935, he has adopted the old keychamber chest, in which each chamber feeds all the pipes belonging to the same key, and gives it the mechanical tracker action of the pre-pneumatic epoch.

Despite the cool reception of his first attempts, Holtkamp found a partisan in G. DONALD HARRISON of the AEOLIAN SKINNER ORGAN Co. in Boston, who advocated the same fundamental idea: "The organ has been romanticized and its fundamental character has been lost. It is this character which we have tried to recapture." His program has been realized in five remarkable organs. The first two were modern organs, but influenced by ancient principles. The first one was erected in 1935 at St. John's Church in Groton School, Groton, Massachusetts. From one hundred inches in Atlantic City the pressure is lowered, varying between 2½ and 3¾ inches; its Great Organ, devoid of reeds, is a complete flue-chorus, full and brilliant, the composition, scales, mouths and lips of which are such that it forms one gigantic mixture; many stops can be traced back to Silbermann and Praetorius. As a whole, the tone, though powerful and dignified, has a remarkable homogeneity. The same principles are the basis of a second and a third organ, in the Church of the Advent at Boston, 1936, and in St. Mark's Church, Philadelphia, 1937.

The fourth and fifth organs (1937 and 1939), in the Germanic Museum at Harvard University, Cambridge, Massachusetts, and in the Westminster Choir School at Princeton, New Jersey, are real Praetorius organs, similar to the one erected in the University of Freiburg. Here the wind pressure does not exceed two and a half inches.

Unlike these intentionally archaic instruments, built to play ancient music, Harrison's three first organs are intended for every kind of music, and, in their simplicity, purity and transparency, are perhaps the true expression of the twentieth century.

Terminology

THE rough classification of our modern orchestra does not suffice for scientific purposes. Any classification demands a consistent principle of division, and this is lacking in the common classification. The usual division of the orchestra into stringed, wind and percussion instruments is based on three different principles instead of one: the sonorous material acted upon, in 'strings'; the activating force, in 'wind'; the action itself, in 'percussion.' We might as well divide Americans into Californians, bankers and Catholics.

The common classification is illogical, and is by no means comprehensive even for recent instruments. Friction instruments, the glass harmonica for instance, or instruments with plucked tongues, like the jaws' harp and the musical box, are neither stringed, wind nor percussion instruments; and if the endless world of historic, folk and exotic instruments are included—and no scientific history can exclude them—the disconcerting category, 'Varia,' grows disproportionately.

The cornerstone of a logical as well as universal classification was laid in 1888 by Victor-Charles Mahillon, the memorable founder and first curator of the Brussels *Musée instrumental*. His system, however, had a weakness; it was conceived of not from a general point of view, but by a curator for the purposes of a particular museum, out of the slowly increasing material of his collection. Therefore, a revision became indispensable. Twenty-five years after Mahillon, this rearrangement was undertaken by our late friend, Dr. Erich M. von Hornbostel, and the author of this book; in 1914, they collaborated on a new classification based as far as possible on

454

acoustical principles, which in its essential points has been universally accepted by anthropologists. But a completely logical classification is an impossibility because instruments are the artificial contrivances of man. They do not lend themselves to a consistent system as do plants and animals.

The Hornbostel-Sachs classification has proved useful as a skeleton. In this book, however, the reader will not be bothered with the complications of families, groups and species. Instead he will be given an informal digest of the classification, so that when confronted by an instrument he will be able to recognize its essential features.

Unfortunately, some anthropologists still designate a xylophone as a 'Kaffir piano,' a slit-drum as a 'gong,' a drum as a 'tom-tom.' Museums still label lyres as 'harps,' lutes as 'guitars,' oboes as 'flutes.' We dedicate this chapter to all people concerned with naming and describing instruments, whether in actual use, in the show cases of museums or on paintings and reliefs. Definition and description are reliable only on the basis of a consistent terminology.

IDIOPHONES

The first of the five main classes is called *idiophones;* they are instruments made of naturally sonorous materials not needing any additional tension as do strings or drumskins. In this class it is the player's action that has shaped the instruments, because they have originated from extensions of striking or clapping hands or stamping feet. Accordingly, the basic question is how they are set into vibration.

1. IDIOPHONES STRUCK TOGETHER or *concussion instruments* are pairs of similar instruments. They are either *two-handed,* if each hand holds one part (as with cymbals), or else *one-handed* (or *clappers*), if both parts are held in the same hand (as with castanets). *Cymbals* have *rims* and central *bosses,* or else are *rimless.* It should be indicated, if possible, whether they are violently clashed together or gently brought together in order to cause a tinkling sound (cf. p. 122). *Clappers* must be described according to their materials (metal, wood, bone, ivory), forms (strips, halved tubes, boots, chestnuts) and the number of their striking parts. A combined type is *cymbals on clappers* (p. 103).

2. STRUCK IDIOPHONES consist of one or several pieces made of a sonorous substance and struck with a stick or a similar device with a rotary motion of the arm. Again they are distinguished by their materials (wood, bamboo, stone, glass, metal), forms (slabs, tubes, plates, vessels) and the number of struck parts. If there are sets of struck parts, they are called *xylophones, lithophones, metallophones, crystallophones*. Details on xylophones are on pp. 53, 238, 439, on lithophones on p. 168, on metallophones on p. 239. The struck plate (e. g., the *gong*) differs from the struck vessel (e. g., the *bell*) in that the center is sounding and the rim is dead. The gong is always made of bronze in circular shape; it may be either *flat* or *bulging* or provided with a central *boss;* the bent-down *rim* may be *shallow* or *deep*. Bells may either be *empty* or *clapper bells;* empty bells may be *suspended* or *resting,* clapper bells *suspended* or in the form of *hand bells*. The shapes vary greatly. Sets of bells or gongs, or even stones, are called *chimes*.

3. STAMPED IDIOPHONES are pits, boards, pots, beams, mortars or slit-drums.

4. STAMPING IDIOPHONES, hit on the ground in vertical motion, are sticks, tubes or gourds.

5. SHAKEN IDIOPHONES are *rattles* (not to be confused with clappers). The material is important, but more important is the arrangement of the sounding parts that strike together when the implement is shaken. We distinguish between rattles *strung* on cords (p. 26) or on rods, as in the *sistrum* (p. 89); *sliding* up and down in the hollowed head of a pounding stick, as in some Malayan planters' sticks, or in grooves of a frame (cf. the *angklung* p. 233); contained in a *rattling receptacle* (gourd, basket, box, tube, hollow ring or hollow ball). Instruments of the latter type, consisting of pebbles contained in metal balls or *jingles,* are often incorrectly confused with bells.

6. SCRAPED IDIOPHONES in various forms (cf. p. 43).

7. PLUCKED IDIOPHONES. The most usual is a flexible lamella or tongue attached to a frame, plucked by the finger and resonated by the mouth (*jaws' harp,* p. 58). Sets of tongues, plucked by the thumbs and resonated by a small box, are found in a common African instrument, the *zanza* (in which it is important to indicate whether the tongues are of rattan or iron). In European *musical*

boxes the tongues are cut in a steel comb and plucked by the projecting studs of a revolving cylinder.

8. RUBBED OR FRICTION IDIOPHONES. It is essential to distinguish between rubbing and scraping. The latter results in a series of beats caused by passing a stick over a notched surface; friction is based on adhesion. There are many primitive friction instruments (p. 38). On a higher level we find Chladni's friction rods (p. 403) and the *glass harmonica* (p. 404).

AEROPHONES

Aerophones or 'air instruments' include what are usually called 'wind instruments,' with the addition of a few instruments with a different acoustical principle called 'free aerophones.'

A WIND INSTRUMENT has two essential factors: a tube enclosing a column of air, and a device for setting that air into vibration by interrupting into pulsations the steady breath of the player (or the wind of a bellows). This device may be the compressed lips of the player (*trumpet*), or the to-and-fro movement of a reed (*single reed* in clarinet, *double reed* in the oboe), or the sharp edge of a flute. Both reed pipes and flutes may be included in the general term *pipes*.

Trumpets and horns cannot always be distinguished from one another. Horns generally betray their descendance from curved animal horns by their shape; they are supposed to have a relatively wider and more or less conical bore, and therefore a less brilliant tone. Trumpets, on the contrary, have come from, and are reminiscent of, straight tubes of bamboo or branches of trees. They are supposed to have a relatively narrow and more or less cylindrical bore, and therefore a brighter tone. Though it is easy to distinguish between the extremes of the two types (for instance between the ivory horns and the metal trumpets of Africa, or between the shofar and the hasosra of the ancient Jews), the great number of intermediate forms have been so combined and mingled that there is no clear distinction between them. They can only be grouped together under one large heading, 'horns and trumpets.'

An important detail is the position of the mouth-hole; it is either the upper orifice of the tube (*end-blown*), or it is pierced somewhere in the side as in a transverse flute (*side-blown*). The same distinction occurs in the mouth-holes of trumpets made of conch shells (p. 48).

For the method of designating the pitch of trumpets and horns, see p. 419. Occidental devices for producing a complete scale (slides, keys, valves) are described in the text (pp. 425–428).

PIPES. *Reed pipes* are of three kinds: with a single beating reed (*clarinets*), with a double reed (*oboes*), with a free reed (only in Southeast Asia). The tube is either cylindrical or conical or tapering toward the lower end. The material is usually wood, sometimes metal, sometimes cane; the term 'reed,' referring to material, is confusing and should be avoided. For the variety of double reed pipes see Chapter 15.

In several families of reed pipes the reed is concealed in a *wind cap* preventing the player from grasping the reed directly in his lips (p. 320). The *bagpipe* (p. 281) is an elaboration of the same principle. In describing a bagpipe it does not suffice to enumerate the number of pipes and to indicate their position; it is obligatory to designate the type of reed in both the melody pipe (or *chanter*) and the *drone* pipes, as well as the bore of each.

Flutes are usually tubular; if they are *globular*, they must be designated as such. Flutes are *vertical* if the upper orifice is used as a mouth-hole; they are *transverse* or *cross flutes* if the mouth-hole is cut in the side; they are *whistle flutes* if the player blows from the upper end through a *flue* against the sharp edge of a hole cut in the side. If the sharp edge is formed by cutting a notch in the upper orifice, the instrument is a *notched flute* (p. 179).

At the lower end flutes can be *open*, or they can be *stopped* by a natural node, a plug or a lid. They are the only wind instruments that can be made without an opening at the lower end.

Pan-pipes are sets of flutes, each producing only one note, united either in *raft* or in *bundle* form (p. 177).

In all wind instruments the end near the player's mouth is the *upper end*, the opposite the *lower end*, even if it is tilted upward in playing, as with the bassoon and the tuba. An expanding lower end is called a *bell*. 'Right' and 'left' are seen from the player's point of view; the *front* is away from the player; the *back* is next to the player.

Fingerholes are mostly in front and are counted beginning with the lowest. If all fingerholes are situated in the front, we speak of '6' or '7 fingerholes'; an additional back hole for the thumb should not be included in this figure but added with a plus: 6 + 1 holes. If we know the exact position of the thumb hole, the additional 1 can be replaced by a letter indicating its relative height: *h* (meaning English *high,* French *haut,* German *hoch*) if the hole is above the highest front hole; *e* (meaning English *even,* Latin *equalis,* French *égal*) if the hole is at the height of the highest front hole; *b* (meaning English *below,* Latin *bassus,* French *bas*) if it is below the highest front hole.

FREE AEROPHONES. In 'wind instruments' the sound and pitch are primarily determined by the enclosed column of air. 'Free aerophones,' on the other hand, have no enclosed column of air; they act directly on the outer air. They cause a series of condensations and rarefications by various means. In the primitive *bull-roarer,* for instance, the whirling movement makes eddies directly in the surrounding air.

Another division of Free Aerophones produces sound by a *reed* which divides a wind current into pulsations. Such a reed may or may not have a tube connected with it, but in any case the air column enclosed in the tube is not a factor in determining the pitch. A clarinet and a reed pipe in an organ have both a beating reed and a pipe; in a clarinet the air column in the pipe is acoustically stronger than the reed and therefore determines the pitch; the pipe of an organ reed is so devised that the reed alone determines the pitch, while the enclosed air column acts merely as a resonator to reinforce some partials. *Harmoniums* and *accordions* have reeds without any pipes attached.

Thus, the *organ* belongs in either or both sections of aerophones. Ancient and medieval organs (except for the last part of the middle ages) were composed of flute pipes only. *Regals,* in the later meaning of the word, were exclusively composed of reeds belonging in the category of free aerophones. Large organs of modern time contain both flute pipes and reeds.

MEMBRANOPHONES

The sound is produced by a membrane stretched over an opening. Most, but not all, membranophones are generally called drums. They are classified according to a description of the following features.

1. MATERIAL: wood, coconut, gourd, bamboo, clay, metal.

2. SHAPE: *Tubular drums:* the solid part or *body* is a tube. It is *deep* if the body is longer than the diameter of the skin; it is *shallow* if the body is shorter than the diameter of the skin. We distinguish the following shapes of tubular drums.

> *Cylindrical drums:* the tube is straight
> *Barrel drums:* the tube is bulging
> *Conical drums:* the tube tapers toward one end
> *Hourglass drums:* the tube terminates in cup-shaped ends with a narrower waist between them
> *Footed drums:* generally large and not portable; one end is carved to form a foot or socle
> *Goblet drums:* portable footed drums
> *Handle drums:* with one or more loop handles

Besides tubular drums, there are kettledrums and frame drums.

A kettledrum has a vessel as a body. It is *hemispheric* if the largest diameter is at the top; it is *egg-shaped* if the largest diameter is somewhere below the top. The terms 'deep' and 'shallow' are used as in tubular drums. Extremely shallow kettledrums may be called *bowl drums.*

A frame drum has a frame instead of a body. It is always shallow compared to a tubular drum. It is deep if the frame is deeper than a quarter of the diameter of the skin; it is shallow if the frame is less deep than a quarter of the diameter of the skin.

3. SKINS or *heads.* There are one or two skins. Instead of saying 'drums with one (or two) skins,' it is admissible to speak of 'single-

FIGURE 160. Nailed skin.

headed (or double-headed) drums.' Strings stretched diametrically over one of the heads are called *snares.*

4. FASTENING OF THE SKINS. The skins are *glued* or *nailed* or *buttoned* or *neck-laced* or *braced.* The terms need no explanation, except 'neck-laced,' which means tied with a circular cord near the head. (figs. 160, 161)

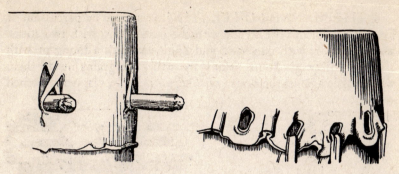

FIGURE 161. Buttoned skin.   FIGURE 162. Braces directly attached.

Braced (or laced) skins exist in numberless varieties, and only a monograph could deal with them exhaustively. Two questions must always be answered: how are the braces attached to the skins, and how are they stretched over the body?

The braces are either *directly* attached, being laced through holes in the edge of the skin; or *indirectly*, the bracing cords being tied to circular *hoops*. A hoop is made either of cord, twisted thongs, rattan ribbons or wood. It is either an *outer hoop* or a *concealed hoop* (rolled up in the edge of the skin). The combination of a concealed and an outer hoop is described on page 435. (figs. 162–166)

The pattern in which the bracing cords or thongs are stretched

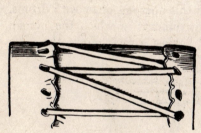

FIGURE 163. Braces in N, directly attached.

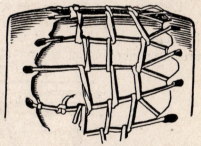

FIGURE 164. Braces in net form, directly attached.

along the body is either in parallel lines, or in the design of N, W, X or Y, or else in the form of a net. (figs. 163, 165, 167)

5. THE PLAYING POSITIONS are *standing* (on the ground or on a stand), *suspended* (from the ceiling, a stand, the player's body); the skins *face sideways* or *up and down*.

6. THE MANNER OF PLAYING is usually by percussion or by friction. Drums are struck with the bare hands, with two sticks, with one stick, with one hand and one stick, with a thong or with a bundle of twigs. Some drums are struck by grains inside them which rattle against the skins (*rattle drums*), or by clappers fastened

FIGURE 165. Braces in Y with a concealed hoop.

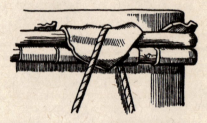

FIGURE 166. Double hoop.

outside and striking the skins when the drum is rapidly twirled to and fro (*clapper drums*). It should be indicated whether, in a double-headed drum, one or two skins are struck.

The various forms of *friction drums* are described on pp. 39–40.

A third way is blowing. Though this does not occur with drums, it is used in *mirlitons*—that is, instruments in which the human breath or vibrating air is directed against a membrane; the same

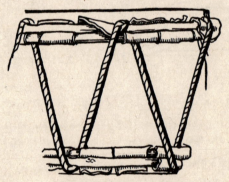

FIGURE 167. Braces in W with double hoops.

principle is used in connection with certain African xylophones (p. 54) and Far Eastern flutes.

Finally, it should be mentioned whether drums are used singly or in pairs or sets.

CHORDOPHONES

Chordophones are instruments with strings. The strings may be struck with sticks, plucked with the bare fingers or a plectron, bowed or (in the Aeolian harp, for instance) sounded by wind. The confusing plenitude of stringed instruments can be reduced to four fundamental types: zithers, lutes, lyres and harps.

A ZITHER has no neck or yoke; the strings are stretched between the two ends of a body, whether this body is in the usual sense a resonator itself, or whether it requires an attached resonator. They are played in many ways. Only a few types will be enumerated.

A *stick-zither* has a stick in place of a resonating body and always needs an additional resonator, generally a gourd, sometimes the mouth of the player. In the *musical bow* (page 56) the stick is flexible. Siamese and Cambodian stick-zithers have only one end flexible. In another group of stick-zithers, of which the Indian *vina* (page 156) is the most intricate member, the stick is entirely rigid. In general the stick is round; but in the Malay Archipelago, Madagascar and Zanzibar, the round stick is replaced by a short lath which the player holds on edge (*lath-zither*).

A *tube-zither* has a tube as a resonating body; the strings are stretched lengthwise. Most tube-zithers are round; some are halved lengthwise (*half-tube zithers*). The strings are usually cut from the surface of the bamboo without being detached (*idiochordic*); rarely the strings are of another material (rattan or wire), in which case we call them *heterochordic*. Several small idiochordic tubes with one string each, tied together in the shape of a raft, form a *raft-zither*.

Board-zithers form the most important category from an occidental point of view because they include our stringed keyboard instruments. The strings are stretched over a board, which is rectangular or trapezoidal or in some other shape, and which is glued onto a shallow box. In the majority of cases the strings are *open*, that is, used in their entire playing length without being stopped by the fingers. In some board-zithers, however, particularly in those used as folk instruments in the Alps and northern and western Europe, one melody string is stretched over a fretted fingerboard (*stopped string*). Most board-zithers are classified either as psalteries or as dulcimers. A *psaltery* is a plucked zither usually with gut strings, while the *dulcimer* has wire strings struck with two light sticks.

Board-zithers are the prototypes of all our stringed keyboard instruments: *clavichords*, in which the strings are gently touched by tangents; *spinets* and *harpsichords*, in which the strings are plucked by jacks; *dulce melos* and *tangentenflügel*, in which the strings are struck by a kind of jack; *pianos*, in which they are struck by hammers. The different forms, upright, grand, square, are fully discussed in the text (Chapter 17).

Long-zithers are intermediate between half-tube and board-zithers. They comprise the Far Eastern instruments of the *shê* and *ch'in* families and are described and classified on pp. 185–188. There are two main types, one with open strings only, and another with one stopped melody string beside the open strings used for accompaniment.

A LUTE is composed of a body, and of a neck which serves both as a handle and as a means of stretching the strings beyond the body. In most cases the strings are stopped. If played with a bow, it is a *bowed lute* or *fiddle*. The body of the lute was originally a fruit shell, and has preserved a bulging shape which was sometimes carved, sometimes composed of thin staves as in our modern lute. Only in a recent stage, shells were made shallow and flat and finally transformed into a box composed of a front, a back and connecting ribs, as in our violins and guitars.

All our lutes, guitars, hurdy-gurdies and the entire families of viols and violins belong in the category of *short lutes*, in which the neck is, morphologically speaking, an elongation of the body (though of course it is added to the body in all recent specimens) and seldom reaches the length of the body. For further terminology see end of the section.

Most primitive and oriental lutes are *long lutes*, in which the neck or stick is longer than the body. We distinguish an older *pierced lute*, with a stick penetrating, or at least entering, the body (p. 102), and a less primitive *long neck lute*, with an attached neck instead of the piercing stick, for instance the Persian sitar-tanbur (p. 255).

A LYRE has a body with a yoke in place of a neck, that is, two arms projecting upward, the upper ends of which are connected by a crossbar. The strings are stretched over the soundboard and are fastened to the crossbar at the top (p. 78). They are either plucked or bowed. There are two main types:

Box lyre, solidly made of a joined box set on its side, with a soundboard of wood (cf. the Greek *kithara* on page 130).

Bowl lyre, loosely made of a shallow bowl set on edge with a soundboard of skin (cf. the Greek *lyra* on page 131).

Lyres are *symmetrical* if the arms are of equal length so that the crossbar is horizontal; they are *asymmetrical* if the arms are of unequal length so that the crossbar is slanting (page 78). For the European lyres see Chapter 14.

THE HARP is the only instrument in which the plane of the strings is vertical, not parallel, to the soundboard; the strings are attached to the soundboard, but run vertically away from it, and not along it. As a rule the strings are numerous and open. All harps are plucked.

In oriental civilizations, both ancient and modern, we distinguish two types:

Arched harps, in which the body is elongated at one end into a curved neck, forming an arch;

Angular harps, in which the body and the stick or neck form an angle.

Description should distinguish between *vertical harps,* which are held with the strings in vertical position and the body held against the player's chest, and *horizontal harps,* which are held with the strings in horizontal position and the body extending away from the player (p. 79).

Occidental harps may be either *diatonic,* with seven strings to the octave, or *chromatic,* with twelve strings to the octave. The diatonic harp sometimes has no device for shortening the strings and raising their pitches, or sometimes has *hooks* and sometimes *pedals* for that purpose. The pedal harp may have a *single* or a *double action* (pp. 399–407).

THE PARTS of a stringed instrument are called by the following names in this book.

The *body* is usually a soundbox or resonator; in rare cases it is only a stick or board. It is always structurally a part of the instrument. Therefore, the term cannot be applied to designate an attached gourd, as in the stick-zither. *Shell* is used by preference when the body is round and reminiscent of the shell, for instance, of a coconut.

Rib is used in two meanings. It designates 1) the side walls, that is, the walls connecting the soundboard and the back of a violin or similar instruments, and 2) the thin flexible staves composing the shell of a lute.

Soundboard is the usually flat front of the body, which receives the vibrations from the strings and reflects them. In practically all cases it is made either of skin or of wood.

Soundholes are, as a rule, cut in the soundboard. Some serve to give the soundboard greater elasticity, some originated as painted or inlaid decorations and only later were perforated and cut out. Their acoustical value is doubtful.

Neck, stick, handle. A *stick* is stuck through the body; a *neck* grows out of it as an organic part of the instrument. Either could be called *handle*.

Fingerboard is the front of the neck in those instruments the strings of which are stopped by being pressed against the wood.

Frets mark off the notes of the scale on the fingerboard. They are either loose and shiftable, consisting of loops of catgut, or stationary, consisting of metal ridges inlaid in the fingerboard.

Pegs, that is, turning pins used to tune the strings, are inserted either from the sides (*lateral pegs*) or from the front (*front pegs*) or from the rear (*rear pegs*). A knob glued fast and unable to be turned should not be called a peg.

The pegs, as a rule, are inserted in a headpiece on top of the neck. This may be 1) a hollow *pegbox* with either the front or the rear left open, 2) a solid *pegblock* or 3) a flat *pegboard* which may be called a *pegdisk* if it is circular or nearly so.

The lower ends of the strings are attached to a *stringholder*. It is either *inferior*, that is, fastened to the lower rib or the lowest point of the body, in which case there must be a bridge on the soundboard; or it is *frontal*, being attached somewhere on the soundboard (as in our lutes and guitars), and then acts as a bridge as well.

The *bridge* is usually a wooden crosspiece wedged on edge between the soundboard and the lower part of the strings, in order to hold the strings away from the soundboard and to transmit the vibrations of the strings to the soundboard. It is an open bridge, if instead of being solid, or nearly solid, it is cut out to form a frame.

Strings are made of various materials (fiber, gut, horsehair, silk, metal) and are arranged either singly, in pairs (as *double strings*) or in threes (*triple strings*), or more. In noting an accordatura, begin with the string corresponding in position to the lowest string of the violin, even if this is the string producing the highest note.

The *general orientation* of stringed instruments is not determined by either the resting or playing position. The *front* is the side along which the strings run; the *back* is opposite; the *top* is the end of the tuning pegs, or of whatever tightening device is used; the opposite is the *lower end*. 'Left' and 'right' should be avoided, or if they must be used, 'left' should designate what in occidental instruments is the treble side, and 'right' for the bass side.

In the harp the terms 'front' and 'back' can be applied only to the body, not to the entire instrument. The front of the body is the soundboard. Notwithstanding this fact, the pillar connecting the foot and the neck of the occidental harp is universally called the *front pillar*.

ELECTROPHONES

ELECTROMECHANICAL INSTRUMENTS are based on vibrations produced in the usual mechanical ways and transformed into electric vibrations.

RADIOELECTRIC INSTRUMENTS are based on oscillating electric circuits. Some have a gliding scale, others have a keyboard. Instruments with a *gliding scale* can be played with or without a manual; *keyboard instruments* are either *monophonic* or *polyphonic*.

A few details are given on pages 447–449.

References

---

1. EARLY INSTRUMENTS

GENERAL: Curt Sachs, *Geist und Werden der Musikinstrumente*, Berlin, 1929; Otto Seewald, *Beiträge zur Kenntnis der steinzeitlichen Musikinstrumente Europas*, Wien, 1934; André Schaeffner, *Originè des instruments de musique*, Paris, 1936—Body movements: Curt Sachs, *World History of the Dance*, New York, 1937, passim—Vedda: Max Wertheimer, *Musik der Wedda*, in *Sammelbände der Internationalem Musikgesellschaft* XI (1910), p. 301.

GOURD RATTLE: Stephen Powers, *Tribes of California*, Washington, 1877, p. 306 f.

STAMPED PIT: C. Sachs, *Geist und Werden der Musikinstrumente*, p. 39—Treasury: Henry B. Guppy, *The Solomon Islands*, London, 1887, p. 143.

STAMPING TUBES: Alfred Métraux, *Le bâton de rythme*, in *Journal de la Société des Américanistes*, 1927, pp. 117–122; Sachs l. c., pp. 73, 74, 75.

STAMPED MORTARS. Rice log: Sachs l. c., p. 206—Siam: *Anthropos* II (1907), p. 627—Taro: W. G. Ivens, *Melanesians of the South-East Solomon Islands*, London, 1927, p. 75—New Guinea: R. Neuhauss, *Deutsch Neu-Guinea*, Berlin, 1911, I 137.

SLIT-DRUM: Sachs l. c., p. 44—Uitoto: Konrad Theodor Preuss, *Religion und Mythologie der Uitoto*, Leipzig, 1921, I 13, 31, 32, 120, 150.

SAND DRUM. New Guinea: Paul Wirz, *Die Marind-anim*, Hamburg, 1922, p. 80—Ethiopia: André Schaeffner, *Origine des instruments de musique*, Paris, 1936, pl. VIII 1.

DRUM: Sachs l. c., p. 53—Schaeffner l. c., pp. 166–176—Africa: Heinz Wieschhof, *Die afrikanischen Trommeln und ihre ausserafrikanischen Beziehungen*, Stuttgart (1933).

DRUM (continued). Chukchee: Bogoras, *The Chukchee religion* in *Jesup Pacific Expedition*, VII—Banyankole: John Roscoe, *The Banyankole*, Cambridge, 1923, p. 44 (condensed)—Wahinda: Richter, *Einige weitere ethnographische Notizen über den Bezirk Bukoba*, in *Mitteilungen aus den deut-*

schen Schutzgebieten 1900, p. 70—Coronation: J. Roscoe, *The Baganda*, London, 1911, p. 25—Koryak: Waldemar Jochelson, *The Koryak*, in *Memoir of the American Museum of Natural History* X (1908), p. 142.

SLIT-DRUM (continued). Creator of the water: Konrad T. Preuss, *Religion und Mythologie der Uitoto*, Leipzig, 1921, I 32—Fidji: Douceré, *Notes sur les populations indigènes des Nouvelles-Hébrides*, in *Revue d'Ethnographie*, 1922, p. 238; Richard Thurnwald, *Im Bismarckarchipel und auf den Salomoinseln*, in *Zeitschrift für Ethnologie* XLII (1910), p. 133—Vulva: R. Thurnwald, *Forschungen auf den Salomo-Inseln und dem Bismarckarchipel*, Berlin, 1912, I 241; R. Parkinson, *Dreissig Jahre in der Südsee*, Stuttgart, 1907, p. 372—Lips: W. G. Ivens, *Melanesians of the South-East Solomon Islands*, London, 1927, p. 169—Language: Henri Labouret, *Langage tambouriné et sifflé*, in *Bulletin du comité d'études historiques et scientifiques de l'A.O.F.*, 1923, pp. 120–158.

RIBBON REED: Sachs l. c., p. 19—Taulipang: Theodor Koch-Grünberg, *Vom Roroima zum Orinoco*, Berlin, 1916, III 276—Madagascar: Curt Sachs, *Les instruments de musique de Madagascar*, Paris, 1938, p. 24.

FRICTION INSTRUMENTS: Sachs, *Geist und Werden*, pp. 48, 90—New Ireland: Augustin Krämer, *Die Malanggane von Tombara*, München, 1925, p. 59—Friction drum: Henry Balfour, *The Friction Drum*, in *Journal of the Anthropological Institute* XXXVII (1907)—Sachs l. c., pp. 136, 232.

BULL-ROARER: I. D. E. Schmeltz, *Das Schwirrholz*, in *Verhandlungen des Vereins für naturwissenschaftliche Unterhaltung zu Hamburg*, vol. IX—Sachs, l. c., p. 10.

SCRAPER: Hawley, *Distribution of the notched rattle*, in *American Anthropologist* XI (1898)—Capitan, *L'omichicahuatzli mexicain et son ancêtre de l'époque du renne en Gaule*, in *XVIe Congrès des Américanistes, Vienne (Autriche)*, 1908 (*Résumé*)—Sachs l. c., p. 16—Mexico: Eduard Seler, *Altmexicanische Knochenrasseln*, in *Zeitschrift für Ethnologie* XLVIII (1916) —Michoacan: Kunike, *Musikinstrumente aus dem alten Michoacan*, in *Baessler-Archiv* II (1911)—Cheyenne: George Bird Grinnell, *The Cheyenne Indians*, Newhaven, 1923, II 58.

FLUTE: Sachs l. c., p. 20—Acoustics: Sir James Jeans, *Science and Music*, Cambridge, 1937—Sentani: Paul Wirz, *Dies und Jenes über die Sentanier*, in *Tijdschrift van het Koninklijk Bataviaasch Genootschap van Kunsten en Wetenschapen* LXIII (1923) 1—Mexico: Hubert Howe Bancroft, *The Native Races of the Pacific States of North America*, London, 1875, II 706—Eduard Seler, *Fray Bernardino de Sahagun*, Stuttgart, 1927, pp. 96, 100—India: Curt Sachs, *Die Musikinstrumente Indiens und Indonesiens*, 2nd edition, Berlin, 1923, p. 144—Cheyenne: George Bird Grinnell, *The Cheyenne Indians*, Newhaven, 1923, I 134—Abruzzi: Ernest Hemingway, *A Farewell to Arms*, ed. New York, 1929, p. 78—Cuna: Narciso Garay, *Tradiciones y cantares de Panama*, s. l. 1930, p. 55—Nose flute: Wilhelm Foy, *Zur Verbreitung der Nasenflöte*, in *Ethnologica* I (1909); Sachs, *Geist und Werden*, p. 116; Schaeffner l. c., p. 246—Ritual: Purbatjareka, in P. de Kat Angelino, *Mudras auf Bali*, Hagen, 1923, p. 68—Astrology: Hellmut Ritter, *Piccatrix*, in *Vorträge der Bibliothek Warburg* 1921–22, Leipzig, 1923, p. 104.

TRUMPET: Sachs l. c., pp. 31, 79, 84, 99, 100, 132; André Schaeffner l. c., p. 261—Babwende: *Zeitschrift für Ethnologie* LXIV (1932), p. 162, fig. 3— Rumania: Béla Bartók, *Die Volksmusik der Rumänen von Maramures*, in *Sammelbände für vergleichende Musikwissenschaft* IV (1923), p. xxvi— Switzerland: Arnold Schering, in *Sammelbände der Internationalen Musikgesellschaft* II (1900), p. 699—Amazon: Theodor Koch-Grünberg, *Zwei Jahre unter den Indianern*, Berlin, 1909, I 189—Brook: ibid. I 314—Holland: *Nieuwe Rotterdamsche Courant*, end of December, 1924—Shell trumpet: Wilfrid Jackson, *Shell-trumpets*, in *Memoirs of the Manchester Literary Society*, LX (1916), p. 8; Sachs l. c., pp. 49, 79, 80, 109; Schaeffner l. c., p. 257 —Kiwai: Gunnar Landtman, *The Kiwai*, London, 1927, p. 402—Formula: Bronislaw Malinowski, *Argonauts of the western Pacific*, London, 1922, pp. 340–342—Madagascar: Curt Sachs, *Les instruments de musique de Madagascar*, Paris, 1938, p. 10—Germany and Bohemia: Elard Hugo Meyer, *Badisches Volksleben*, Strassburg, 1900, pp. 364, 610—New Ireland: Augustin Krämer, *Die Malanggane von Tombara*, München, 1925, p. 53.

POTTERY: Quoted from Alexander A. Goldenweiser, *Early civilization*, New York, 1932, p. 317.

XYLOPHONE: Sachs l. c., p. 279; Siegfried F. Nadel, *Marimba-Musik*, in *Sitzungsberichte der phil. hist. Klasse der Akademie der Wissenschaften in Wien* CCXII, 3, Wien-Leipzig, 1931; Nadel, *Zur Ethnographie des afrikanischen Xylophons*, in *Forschungen und Fortschritte* VIII (1932), pp. 444–445; Schaeffner, l. c., pp. 82–88—Madagascar: Sachs, *Les instruments de musique de Madagascar*, Paris, 1938, pp. 62, 70, 75, 79.

GROUND HARP: Sachs, *Geist und Werden*, p. 60—Portable: Sachs, *Die Musikinstrumente Indiens und Indonesiens*, 2nd edition, Berlin, 1923, p. 77.

GROUND-ZITHER: Curt Sachs, *Geist und Werden der Musikinstrumente*, Berlin, 1929, p. 59—Annam: Gaston Knosp, *Rapport sur une mission officielle d'étude musicale en Indochine*, Leyde, 1911, p. 64—Madoera: J. S. Brandts Buys, *De Toonkunst bij de Madoereezen*, in *Djåwå* VI (1926), p. 61—Java: l. c., p. 62 n—Bube: Günther Tessmann, *Die B.*, Hagen, 1923, p. 206— Makua: Karl Weule, *Wissenschaftliche Ergebnisse*, in *Mitteilungen aus den deutschen Schutzgebieten*, *Ergänzungsheft* I, Berlin, 1908, p. 119.

MUSICAL BOW: Henry Balfour, *The Natural History of the Musical Bow*, Oxford, 1899; Sachs, *Geist und Werden*, p. 281; Percival R. Kirby, *The Musical Instruments of the Native Races of South Africa*, London, 1934, p. 198.

JAWS' HARPS: Curt Sachs, *Die Maultrommel*, in *Zeitschrift für Ethnologie* XLIX (1917); Mme. Alfred Heymann, *La guimbarde*, in *Revue musicale* (1923), pp. 236–246—Austria: Karl Magnus Klier' *Volkstümliche Querflöten und die Maultrommel*, in *Kongressbericht der Beethoven-Zentenarfeier*, Wien, 1927, pp. 375–377; Id., *250 Jahre Maultrommelmacherzunft zu Molln*, in *Tagespost*, Linz a. d. Donau, no. 226, 29. Sept. 1929.

2. THE CHRONOLOGY OF EARLY INSTRUMENTS

Curt Sachs, *Geist und Werden der Musikinstrumente*, Berlin, 1929; Erich M. von Hornbostel, *Ethnology of African Sound-Instruments*, in *Africa* VI

(1933); cf. also C. Sachs, *Towards a prehistory of music,* in *Musical Quarterly* XXIV (1938).

3. SUMER AND BABYLONIA

GENERAL: Carl Frank, *Studien zur babylonischen Religion* I, Strassburg, 1911, pp. 229–235; P. Anton Deimel, *Šumerisches Lexikon,* Rome, 1925; *Šumerisch-akkadisches Glossar,* Rome, 1934; *Akkadisch-šumerisches Glossar,* Rome, 1937; Francis W. Galpin, *The Music of the Sumerians,* Cambridge, 1937 [with care].

IDIOPHONES. American sistra: Karl Gustav Izikowitz, *Musical and Other Sound Instruments of the South American Indians,* Göteborg, 1935, pp. 150–151—Rattles: Ernest Mackay, *Report on the Excavation of the "A" Cemetery at Kish,* II, Chicago, 1929, p. 213, pl. 47.

PIPES. En-lulim: Ira Maurice Price, *The Great Cylinder Inscriptions of Gudea,* Leipzig, 1927, cyl. B 10, 7–10.

HORN AND TRUMPET. *Si:* Price, l. c., cyl. A 28, 18, and B 15, 20—Tushratta: J. A. Knudtzon, *Die El-Amarna-Tafeln,* Leipzig, 1915, I 208 ff.

DRUMS. Gudea inscriptions: Price, l. c., statue E 12, cyl. A 6, 21, A 28, 17—Name-date: François Thureau-Dangin, *Königsinschriften,* Leipzig, 1907, p. 227—"Bull's voice": Price, Cyl. A 28, 17—Lilis: Thureau-Dangin, *Rituels accadiens,* Paris, 1921, p. 12.

LYRE. Pictures: Curt Sachs, *Geist und Werden der Musikinstrumente,* Berlin, 1929, pl. 19; Galpin, l. c., pl. 7.

HARP. Pictures: Galpin, l. c., pl. 5, 6—Classification: Marcelle Duchesne-Guillemin, *La harpe en Asie occidentale ancienne,* in *Revue d'Assyriologie* XXXIV (1937)—Chords: Curt Sachs, *Zweiklänge im Altertum,* in *Festschrift für Johannes Wolf,* Berlin, 1929—Symphona: Jacques Handschin, *Musikalische Miszellen,* in *Philologus* LXXXVI (1930), p. 54.

LUTE. Pictures: Sachs, l. c.; Galpin, l. c., pl. 8—Cappadocia: Julius Lewy, *Kappadokische Tontafeln,* in Max Ebert, *Reallexikon der Vorgeschichte,* Berlin, 1926, VI 216.

DANIEL ORCHESTRA. Sumponiah: E. B. Pusey, *Daniel the Prophet,* Oxford, 1864, p. 29; Phillips Barry, *On Luke XV 25,* in *Journal of Biblical Literature* XXIII ii (1904), pp. 180–190; George F. Moore, *Symphonia not a Bagpipe,* ibidem XXIV ii (1905), pp. 166–175; P. Barry, ibidem XXVII ii (1908), pp. 99–127; Galpin, l. c., p. 67—Symphonia: Athenaeus, *The Deipnosophists,* ed. Charles Burton Gulick, vol. II, London, 1928, pp. 376–377 and 386–387; vol. IV, London, 1930, pp. 488–489 and 490–491 (liber V 193, 195; liber X 439).

4. EGYPT

GENERAL: Curt Sachs, *Die Musikinstrumente des alten Aegyptens,* Berlin, 1921; do not confuse this book with C. Sachs, *Altägyptische Musikinstrumente,* in *Der Alte Orient* XXI (1920) Heft 3/4—Interrelations: Frankfort,

Mesopotamia, Syria and Egypt and Their Earliest Interrelations, in *Anthropological Institute, Occasional Papers* VI (1924).

CLAPPERS: Sachs, *Die Musikinstrumente des alten Aegyptens,* p. 12—Hathor: Sachs, *World History of the Dance,* New York, 1937, p. 85.

SISTRUM: Sachs, *Die Musikinstrumente des alten Aegyptens,* p. 28; B. Bacchinus, *De sistris,* Trajecti ad Rhenum 1696—Thrice: Apuleius, *Metamorphoses,* lib. 11—Turba: Marcus Valerius Martial.

FLUTE. Madagascar: Sachs, *Les instruments de musique de Madagascar,* Paris, 1937, pp. 13, 71, 76, 78.

HARP. Vina: Sachs, *Die Musikinstrumente des alten Aegyptens,* p. 68—Tuning: Sachs, *Zweiklänge im Altertum,* in *Festschrift für Johannes Wolf,* Berlin, 1929, p. 169.

OBOE. Drone: Carnarvon-Carter, *Five Years' Explorations at Thebes,* Oxford, 1912, p. 84, pl. LXIX—Fingerholes: François-Joseph Fétis, *Histoire générale de la musique* I, Paris, 1869, p. 223; T. Lea Southgate, in *Musical Times* (1890) and *Musical News* XXV (1903), p. 103; Victor Loret, in *Journal Asiatique* XIV (1889), p. 111; Victor-Charles Mahillon, *Catalogue du Musée instrumental de Bruxelles,* Gand, 1900, III 292; Charles Kasson Wead, in *Report of the United States National Museum for 1900,* Washington, 1902, p. 427; Sachs, *Die Musikinstrumente des alten Aegyptens,* p. 82.

ANGULAR HARP: Curt Sachs, *Eine ägyptische Winkelharfe,* in *Zeitschrift für ägyptische Sprache* LXIX (1933), p. 68.

LUTE. Gunbrī: Henry George Farmer, *Studies in Oriental Musical Instruments* I, London, 1931, p. 37.

5. ISRAEL

ENGLISH QUOTATIONS from the Bible follow the King James Bible (Authorized Version); from the Mishna: *The Mishna,* translated by Herbert Danby, Oxford, 1933.

GENERAL: Josef Weiss, *Die musikalischen Instrumente des alten Testaments,* Graz, 1895; Sir John Stainer, *Music of the Bible* (new edition by Francis W. Galpin), London, 1914; Heinrich Gressmann, *Musik und Musikinstrumente im alten Testament,* Giessen, 1903; Curt Sachs, *Musik des Altertums,* Breslau, 1924; Sol Baruch Finesinger, *Musical Instruments in the Old Testament,* Baltimore, 1926; Adolphe Lods, *Les idées des anciens Israélites sur la musique,* in *Journal de Psychologie,* 1926; C. Sachs, *Geist und Werden der Musikinstrumente,* Berlin, 1929.

KINNOR: Johann Gabriel Drechssler (d. 1677), *Kinnor ledawid sive De cithara Davidica, Lipsiae*—Coins: Sachs, *Geist und Werden,* pl. 23, fig. 160 —Exile: Ps. 137; Flavius Josephus, *Antiquitates,* lib. VII, cap. 12, 3.

TOF. Wailing women: Mishna, *Kelim* XV 6—Muhammad: Henry G. Farmer, *History of Arabian Music,* London, 1929, p. 28.

PAAMON: *Exodus* 28: 23–25.

SHOFAR: B. Kohlbach, *Das Widderhorn,* in *Zeitschrift des Vereins für Volkskunde* XVI (1916), pp. 113–128; Theodor Reik, *Ritual,* in *The Inter-*

national Psycho-analytical Library, vol. 19, transl. Douglas Bryan, London, 1931, The Shofar, pp. 221–305—Tuyucá: Theodor Koch-Grünberg, *Zwei Jahre unter den Indianern*, Berlin, 1909, I 314—Holland: *Nieuwe Rotter-damsche Courant*, end of December, 1924—Jericho: Book of Joshua, 6: 20. HASOSRA. Commandment: IV *Mos.* 10: 1–10—Elijah: *I Kings*, 18: 27— God awakened by the organ on the island of Rhodos at the beginning of the third century A.D.: *Beilage zur allgemeinen Zeitung*, 1905, p. 45; Flavius Josephus, *Antiquitates*, lib. III c. 12, 6; J. Chr. Büsing, *Dissertatio de tubis Hebraeorum argenteis*, *Bremae* 1745; Curt Sachs, *Die Musikinstrumente des alten Aegyptens*, Berlin, 1921, p. 89.

THE TIME OF THE KINGS. Consecration: II *Chronicles* 5: 12–14.

NEBEL. Phoenicia: Athenaeus, *The Deipnosophists*, lib. IV, cap. 175d; Flavius Josephus, *Antiquitates*, lib. VII, cap. 12, 3.

ASOR. Phoenician ivory: R. D. Barnett, *The Nimrud Ivories*, in *Iraq* II 2 (1935) —St. Jerome: *Hieronymi Opera, Antwerpiae, Plantini* IX, 113.

HALIL. Moses: *Arachin*, cap. II—Jairus: *St. Matthew* IX 23—St. Thomas: *Acta apostolorum apocrypha*, ed. Lipsius-Bonnet II 2, 108—Al-Hijaz: Henry George Farmer, *Studies in Oriental Musical Instruments*, London, 1931, p. 78.

MNAANIM. Rattles: Peter Thomson, in Max Ebert, *Reallexikon der Vorge-schichte*, vol. XII, Berlin, 1928, p. 345; vol. XIII, Berlin, 1929, p. 248; Curt Sachs, *Musik des Altertums*, Breslau, 1924, p. 30.

SELSLIM. Two kinds: Ps. 150, 5—Apocalypsis: fol. 272 v.—Mantovan mscr.: Mantova, Bibl. Civ., ms. C III fol. 2 (facs. in Paolo d'Ancona, *La miniature italienne*, Paris, 1925, pl. 6)—Fresco eleventh century in the cathedral of Kiev, comp. Prohorov, *Materiali po istorii russkih odežd, Sanktpeterburg*, 1881, p. 60—Flavius Josephus, *Antiquitates* lib. VII cap. 12, 3.

PSALMS. "Instruments": Stephen Langdon, *Babylonian Musical Terms*, in *Journal of the Royal Asiatic Society* 1921, p. 169 ff.

6. GREECE, ETRURIA AND ROME

GENERAL: Curt Sachs, *Die Musik des Altertums*, Breslau, 1924; C. Sachs, *Die Musik der Antike*, in Ernst Bücken, *Handbuch der Musikwissenschaft*, Wildpark-Potsdam, 1929; Hermann Abert, *Antike*, in Guido Adler, *Handbuch der Musikgeschichte*, Berlin-Wilmersdorf, 1930, I pp. 35–67 (new edition by Curt Sachs); Louis Harap, *Some Hellenic Ideas on Music and Character*, in *Musical Quarterly* XXIV (1938), pp. 153–168; Otto Johannes Gombosi, *Tonarten und Stimmungen der antiken Musik*, Kopenhagen, 1939; Quotations from Homer after Pope's translation; from Pindar: *Poetae lyrici Graeci*, rec. Theodorus Bergk, Lips. 1853; from Plato, *Laws*: transl. by A. E. Taylor, London, 1934; from Strabo: *The Geography of Strabo*, transl. by Horace Leonard Jones, London, 1928, V, p. 107, 109.

LYRES: Helmut Huchzermeyer, *Aulos und Kithara*, Dissertation Münster, 1931; M. Guillemin and J. Duchesne, *Sur l'origine asiatique de la cithare grecque*, in *L'Antiquité Classique* IV (1935); Gombosi, l. c., Plato: *Laws*

669 C f—Egyptian: Curt Sachs, *Die Musikinstrumente des alten Aegyptens*, Berlin, 1921, p. 49—Four strings: Ludwig Deubner, *Die viersaitige Leier*, in *Mitteilungen des Deutschen Archäologischen Instituts, Athenische Abteilung* LIV (1929), pp. 194–200—Accordatura: Curt Sachs, *Die griechische Instrumentalnotenschrift*, in *Zeitschrift für Musikwissenschaft* VI (1923), p. 289—Ethiopia: M. Mondon-Vidailhet, *La musique éthiopienne*, in Albert Lavignac, *Encyclopédie de la musique*, 1ère partie, vol. V—Playing: Lucius Apulejus, *Floridorum liber* II 15; Camille Saint-Saëns, *Lyres et cithares*, in Lavignac l. c. I, pp. 538–540—Japan: Sir Francis Piggott, *The music and musical instruments of Japan*, 2nd edition, London, 1909, p. 111.—Nete: cf. also Eberhard Hommel, *Untersuchungen zur hebräischen Lautlehre*, Leipzig 1917, p. 39.

HARP: Reinhard Herbig, *Griechische Harfen*, in *Mitteilungen des Deutschen Archäologischen Instituts, Athenische Zweiganstalt (Athenische Mitteilungen)* LIV (1929), pp. 164–193—Magadis: Alkman, *Fragm.* 99 D.—*Odes of Anacreon*, Boston (1903), pp. 15, 19.—Euphorion, in Athenaeus, *The Deipnosophists* XIV 635.

LUTE: Julius Pollux, *Onomastikon* IV 60.

ZITHER. Persian manuscript: Henry George Farmer, *Studies in Oriental Musical Instruments*, London, 1931, frontispiece and p. 15.

PIPES. General: Caspari Bartholini Thom fil. *De tibiis vetervm & earum antiquo vsu libri tres*, Romae 1677, *editio altera* 1679; Albert A. Howard, *The aulos or tibia*, in *Harvard Studies of Philology* IV (1893); Kathleen Schlesinger, *The Greek aulos*, London, 1939 (the author has not yet seen this book)—Java-Madoera: Jaap Kunst & R. T. A. Wiranakoesoema, *Een en ander over Soondaneesche Muziek*, Bandoeng, 1921, fig. 5—Playing: Marcus Terentius Varro, *De re rustica* I 2, 25—*The elegies of Propertius*, ed. Butler & Barber, Oxford, 1933, p. 55 (lib. II, Elegy XXII A 6)—*Plato's Symposium*, transl. by Francis Birrell & Shane Leslie, London, The Fortune Press (1925)—Sakadas: *The Geography of Strabo*, transl. by Horace Leonard Jones, London, 1928, V 109.

BAGPIPES. Nero: Suetonius, *The Lives of the Caesars*, Nero LIV.

CROSS FLUTE: Eugenio Albini, *Instrumenti musicali degli Etruschi e loro origini*, in *L'Illustrazione Vaticana* VIII (1937), pp. 667–671.

PAN-PIPES. Baumeister, *Denkmäler des klassischen Altertums*, s. v. syrinx; Théodore Reinach, in *Pro Alesia*, May, 1907; in *Revue archéologique* I (1907), p. 322; Friedrich Behn, *Eine antike Syrinx aus dem Rheinland*, in *Die Musik* XII (1913).

ORGAN: J. W. Warman, *The Hydraulic Organ of the Ancients*, in *Proceedings of the Musical Association*, 1903–4; Francis W. Galpin, *Notes on a Hydraulis*, in *The Reliquary*, 1904; Hermann Degering, *Die Orgel*, Münster, 1905; Charles Maclean, *The Principle of the Hydraulic Organ*, in *Sammelbände der Internationalen Musikgesellschaft* VI (1905); P. Tannery, *L'invention de l'hydraulis*, in *Revue des Études grecques* XXI (1908); Carra de Vaux, ib; Henry George Farmer, *The Organ of the Ancients from Eastern Sources*, London, 1931; Lajos Nagy, *Az Aquincumi orgona. Die Orgel von Aquincum*, Budapest, 1934—Nero: Suetonius, *The Lives of the Caesars*, Nero XLI.

TRUMPETS. Boston: L. D. Caskey, *Archaeological Notes*, in *American Journal of Archaeology* XLI (1937), pp. 525–527—Rome: Friedrich Behn, *Die Musik im römischen Heere*, in *Mainzer Zeitschrift* VII (1912); Curt Sachs, *Lituus und Karnyx*, in *Festschrift für Rochus von Liliencron*, Leipzig, 1910—Lurer: bibliography in Hubert Schmidt, *Die Luren von Daberkow*, in *Prähistorische Zeitschrift* VII (1915)—Tibet: André Schaeffner, *Origine des instruments de musique*, Paris, 1936, p. 262 n.

IDIOPHONES: Friedrich Adolf Lampe, *De cymbalis veterum libri tres*, 1703—(Sir Richard Ellys), *Fortuita sacra quibus subjicitur commentarius de cymbalis, Rotterodami* 1727.—J. Jüthner, *Die Schelle im Thiasos*, in *Jahreshefte des Oesterreichischen Archäologischen Instituts*, VII (1904), pp. 146 ff.—Hippasos: Hermann Diels, *Die Fragmente der Vorsokratiker*, Berlin 1903, p. 12.

7. INDIA

GENERAL: Curt Sachs, *Die Musikinstrumente Indiens und Indonesiens*, 2nd edition, Berlin, 1923; Claudie Marcel Dubois, *Notes sur les instruments de musique figurés dans l'art plastique de l'Inde ancienne*, in *Revue des arts asiatiques* XI (1937).

INDUS CIVILIZATION. Cymbals: Sir John Marshall, *Mohenjo-Daro*, London, 1931, III pl. CXLII 1, 2, 3, 7, 8—Drum: l. c., pl. XCIV 1, 3, and I, p. 346—Shell trumpet: III, pl. CLV—Lyre: l. c., pl. CIX 206, CXIII 457, 459, 461, 469—Harp: l. c., pl. CV 46; G. R. Hunter, *The Script of Harappa and Mohenjo-Daro*, London, 1934, pl. XXXIII, 146.

VEDIC TIME. *Bakura:* Curt Sachs, *Les instruments de musique de Madagascar*, Paris, 1938, p. 10.

DRAVIDA: Gilbert Slater, *The Dravidian Element in Indian Culture*, London, 1924, p. 80—Tiruchinnam: P. Sambamoorthy, *Catalogue of the Musical Instruments Exhibited in the Government Museum Madras*, in *Bulletin of the Madras Government Museum*, n. s., General Section, vol. II, part 3, Madras, 1931; Jaap Kunst, *Hindoe-Javaansche muziek-instrumenten*, Batavia, 1927, fig. 44—Vina: Curt Sachs, *Die Musikinstrumente des alten Aegyptens*, Berlin, 1921, p. 68.

DRUMS. Twin drums: Colin McPhee, *Children and Music in Bali*, in *Djawa* XVIII (1938), pl. 2 and 3; Andreas Eckardt, *Koreanische Musik*, Tokyo, 1930, pl. XIII, fig. 23.—Drum harmonics: C. V. Raman, Sivakali Kumar, *Musical Drums with Harmonic Overtones*, in *Nature* CIV (1920), p. 500.

SHORT LUTE. Suza: J. de Morgan, *Délégation en Perse*, Paris, 1900, I pl. 8; the same in Kathleen Schlesinger, *The instruments of the modern orchestra*, London, 1910, II pl. 12—Chinese conquest: *The Cambridge Shorter History of India*, New York, 1934, p. 75.

8. THE FAR EAST

GENERAL: Amiot, *Mémoire sur la musique des Chinois*, Paris, 1779; A. C. Moule, *A List of the Musical Instruments of the Chinese*, in *Journal of the*

North-China Branch of the Royal Asiatic Society XXXIX (1908); Francis Piggott, *The Music and Musical Instruments of Japan*, 2nd edition, Yokohama, 1909; Maurice Courant, *Chine et Corée* and *Japon*, in Lavignac, *Encyclopédie de la musique* I 1, Paris, 1913, pp. 77–256; Andreas Eckardt, *Koreanische Musik*, Tokyo, 1930—Six arts: *I-li or Book of Etiquette and Ceremonial*, transl. by John Steele, London, 1917, p. 275—The finish: *The Original Chinese Texts of the Confucian Analecta*, transl. by J. Steele, London, 1861, p. 87—Mencius: ib., p. 489—Good government: ib., p. 210 —Chwang Paou: ib., p. 427—Female musicians: p. 237—Reform: p. 99— Lao-tsze: p. 929—Pa yin: for a different arrangement cp. Otto Kümmel, *Neun chinesische Spiegel*, in *Ostasiatische Zeitschrift*, N. F. VI (1930), p. 175.

SHANG: Herrlee Glessner Creel, *The Birth of China*, New York, 1937— Shih Ching: *The Chinese Classics*, vol. IV, transl. by John Legge, Hong Kong-London, 1871, p. 457.

GLOBULAR FLUTE. Caffres: Henry A. Junod, *The Life of a South-African Tribe*, Neuchatel, 1913, II 249—Bone: H. G. Creel, l. c., p. 99.

STONES. Mencius: *The Original Chinese Texts*, p. 729—Confucius: ib., p. 185 —Venezuela: Karl Gustav Izikowitz, *Musical Instruments of the South American Indians*, Göteborg, 1935, p. 9—Kawa music: Curt Sachs, *Vergleichende Musikwissenschaft*, Leipzig, 1930, p. 71.

BELLS. Primitive: Curt Sachs, *Geist und Werden der Musikinstrumente*, Berlin, 1929, p. 279—Blood: Louis Laloy, *La musique chinoise*, Paris (1910), p. 60—Maiden's blood: E. T. C. Werner, *Myths and Legends of China*, London, 1934, p. 394—Chang Heng: Stefan Balázs, *Die Inschriften der Sammlung Baron v. d. Heydt*, in *Ostasiatische Zeitschrift* N. F., vol. X (1934), p. 28.

DRUMS. Early text: *The Chinese Classics* IV 2, Hong Kong-London, 1871, p. 457—Rattle and clapper drums: C. Sachs, l. c., p. 156, 172—Tso Chuan: H. G. Creel, l. c., p. 153.

PERCUSSION-CLAPPER. Book: Creel, l. c., p. 172.

TROUGH. Poem: *The Chinese Classics*, IV 2, p. 587.

TIGER. Tao: Richard Wilhelm, *Das Wesen der chinesischen Musik*, in *Sinica* II (1927), p. 203 n.

PITCH AND PAN-PIPES. Poem: *The Chinese Classics* IV 2, p. 587—Peru: Raoul et Marguerite d'Harcourt, *La musique des Incas*, Paris, 1925, pp. 35– 53—Cuna: Narciso Garay, *Tradiciones y cantares de Panama*, s. l. (1930), p. 25—Cents: Alexander John Ellis, *Tonometrical Observations on Existing Non-Harmonic Scales*, in *Proceedings of the Royal Society*, 1884, and *Journal of the Society of Arts*, 1885—Karenni: Sachs, *Die Musikinstrumente Birmas und Assams*, pp. 31, 32.—A. H. Fox Strangways, *The Pipes of Pan*, in *Music and Letters* X (1929), pp. 57–64.

FLUTES. 9th century: *The Chinese Classics* IV, iii, i 10.—Hsiao: ib., p. 588. —Yüeh: ib., p. 62, 397.—Measurement: Erich M. von Hornbostel, *Die Massnorm als kulturgeschichtliches Forschungsmittel*, in *Festschrift für P. Wilhelm Schmidt*, Wien 1928.—Madagascar: Curt Sachs, *Les instruments de musique de Madagascar*, Paris, 1938, pp. 66, 77.

MOUTH-ORGAN. Acoustics: Dr. Kwang-chi Wang in a letter to the author, Dec. 1, 1927.—Prototypes: C. Sachs, *Die Musikinstrumente Birmas und Assams*, München, 1917, p. 38.—Sachs, *Die Musikinstrumente Indiens und Indonesiens*, 2nd edition, Berlin, 1923, p. 163.—Laos: Madeleine Humbert-Lavergne, *La musique à travers la vie laotienne*, in *Zeitschrift für vergleichende Musikwissenschaft* II (1934), p. 14–19, with the transcription of four pieces for the khen.—First mention: *The Chinese Classics* IV 245.—Vogler: Hertha Schweiger, *Abbé G. J. Voglers Orgellehre*, Dissertation Freiburg i. B. 1934, Vienna, 1938.

LONG ZITHER. Odes: *The Chinese Classics* IV, p. 4, 252.

9. AMERICA

GENERAL: Raoul et Marguerite d'Harcourt, *La musique des Incas*, Paris, 1925; Eduard Seler, *Mittelamerikanische Musikinstrumente*, in *Globus* LXXVI (1899); Hugo Kunike, *Musikinstrumente aus dem alten Michoacan*, in *Baessler-Archiv* II (1911), pp. 282–284; Charles W. Mead, *The Musical Instruments of the Incas*, in *Anthropological Papers of the American Museum of Natural History* XV, part III, 1924; August Genin, *The Musical Instruments of the Ancient Mexicans*, in *Mexican Magazine* III (1927), pp. 355–362; Karl Gustav Izikowitz, *Musical and Other Sound Instruments of the South American Indians*, Göteborg, 1935.

CENTRAL AMERICAN FLUTES: Diego de Landa, *Relation des choses de Yucatan*, Paris, 1864, p. 127; Hubert Howe Bancroft, *The Native Races of the Pacific States of North America*, London, 1875, II 293, 621, 713; IV 462; Kollmann, *Flöten und Pfeifen aus Alt-Mexico*, in *Bastian-Festschrift* (1896).

SCRAPER: Eduard Seler, *Altmexikanische Knochenrasseln*, in *Globus* LXXIV (1898), pp. 85–93; Capitan, *L'omichicahuatzli mexicain et son ancêtre de l'époque du renne*, Résumé in *XVIᵉ Congrès International des Américanistes*, Vienne (Autriche), 1908.

DRUMS: K. G. Izikowitz, *Le tambour à membrane au Pérou*, in *Journal de la Société des Américanistes*, n. s. XXIII (1931), pp. 163–175; Daniel Castañeda y V. T. Mendoza, *Los percutores precortesianos*, and *Los teponaztlis en las civilizaciones precortesianas*, in *Anales del Museo Nacional de Arqueología* VIII (1933).

PAN-PIPES: Erich M. von Hornbostel, *Ueber ein akustisches Kriterium für Kulturzusammenhänge*, in *Zeitschrift für Ethnologie* XLIII (1911); Mead, l. c., p. 326.

SOUTH AMERICAN FLUTES: Raoul d'Harcourt, *L'ocarina à cinq sons dans l'Amérique préhispanique*, in *Journal de la Société des Américanistes* XXIII (1931), pp. 189–228, pl. XXXV–XL.

10. THE FAR EAST

GENERAL: as in Chapter 8—Mongolia: P. Jos. van Oost, *La musique chez les Mongols des Urdus*, in *Anthropos* X–XI (1915–16)—Turkestan: Arno Huth, *Die Musikinstrumente Ost-Turkistans*, Diss., Berlin, 1928.

CYMBALS. Metal workers: M. A. Czaplicka, *The Turks of Central Asia*, Oxford, 1918, p. 71.

GONG: Heinrich Simbrieger, *Gong und Gongspiele*, in *Internationales Archiv für Ethnographie* XXXVI (1939), 180 pp.

GONG CHIME. Iron workers: Czaplicka, l. c., p. 70.

REED PIPES. Pibcorn: Henry Balfour, '*Pibcorn*' or '*Hornpipe*' in *Journal of the Anthropological Institute of Great Britain* XX (1891)—Biša: Henry George Farmer, *Studies in Oriental Musical Instruments* I, London, 1931, p. 83—Spanish influence: a detailed letter from Mr. Kenzo Sato, formerly my student in Berlin University.

BOWED INSTRUMENTS: Curt Sachs, *Die Streichbogenfrage*, in *Archiv für Musikwissenschaft* I (1918), pp. 3–9.

TRUMPET. Mongolia; Hammer-Purgstall, *Geschichte der Golden Horde*, Pesth, 1840, pp. 214–216—Tibet: David Macdonald, *Mœurs et coutumes des Thibétains*, Paris, 1930, p. 261—South America: K. G. Izikowitz, *Musical Instruments of the South American Indians*, Göteborg, 1935, p. 232.

11. INDIA

GENERAL: C. R. Day, *The Music and Musical Instruments of Southern India and the Deccan*, London, 1891; A. H. Fox Strangways, *The Music of Hindostan*, Oxford, 1914; J. Grosset, *Inde*, in Lavignac, *Encyclopédie de la musique*, first part, vol. I, pp. 257–376; Curt Sachs, *Die Musikinstrumente Indiens und Indonesiens*, 2nd edition, Berlin, 1923; P. Sambamoorthy, *Catalogue of the Musical Instruments Exhibited in the Government Museum Madras*, in *Bulletin of the Madras Government Museum*, N. S. General Section, vol. II, Part III, Madras, 1931.

PRE-ISLAMIC TIMES. Borobudur: Jaap Kunst, *Hindoe-Javaansche Muziek-instrumenten*, Batavia, 1927.

STICK-ZITHER. Early evidence: Ananda K. Coomaraswamy, *Frescoes at Elura*, in *Ostasiatische Zeitschrift*, Neue Folge III (1926), p. 5.

DRUMS: M. Fredelis, *Indian instruments*, in *The Times of India*, Oct. 27, 1920, and Nov. 10, 1920.

12. SOUTHEAST ASIA

GENERAL: Curt Sachs, *Die Musikinstrumente Birmas und Assams*, in *Sitzungsberichte der Kgl. Bayerischen Akademie der Wissenschaften*, Phil.-phil. Kl., Jg. 1917, 2. Abh., München, 1917; Gaston Knosp, *La Birmanie*, in A. Lavignac, *Encyclopédie de la musique*, 1ère partie, vol. V, pp. 3094–3099; Knosp, *Histoire de la musique dans l'Indo-Chine*, ibidem, pp. 3100–3146; C. Sachs, *Die Musikinstrumente Indiens und Indonesiens*, 2nd edition, Berlin, 1923; Daniel de Lange & Joh. F. Snelleman, *La musique et les instruments de musique dans les Indes orientales néerlandaises*, in A. Lavignac, *Encyclopédie de la musique*, 1ère partie, vol. V, pp. 3147–3178; Jaap Kunst en C. J. A. Kunst-v.Wely, *De toonkunst van Bali*, 2 vol., Weltevreden 19–25; The same, *Hindoe-Javaansche muziek-instrumenten*, Batavia, 1927;

J. S. Brandts Buys, *De toonkunst bij de Madoereezen*, in *Djawa* VIII (1928); Jaap Kunst, *De toonkunst van Java*, 's-Gravenhage 1934, 2 vols.; Gaston Knosp, *Rapport sur une mission officielle d'étude musicale en Indochine*, Leyde, 1911; Colin McPhee, *Angkloeng Gamelans in Bali*, in *Djawa* XVII (1937), no. 5–6, 29 pp.; C. McPhee, *Children and Music in Bali*, in *Djawa* XVIII (1938), no. 6, 15 pp.

TUBE ZITHER: Curt Sachs, *Les instruments de musique de Madagascar*, Paris, 1938, pp. 51, 71, 76.

DRUM GONG: Franz Heger, *Alte Metalltrommeln aus Südostasien*, Leipzig, 1902; Victor Goloubew, *Sur l'origine et la diffusion des tambours métalliques*, in *Prehistorica Asiae Orientalis* I (1932), pp. 137–150.

XYLOPHONE. Panataran: ill. in Kunst, *Hindoe-Javaansche muziek-instrumenten*, pl. 50.

GONG: Heinrich Simbriger, *Gong and Gongspiele*, in *Internationales Archiv für Ethnographie*, vol. XXXVI (1939).

13. THE NEAR EAST

GENERAL: Villoteau, *Description historique, technique et littéraire, des instruments de musique des Orientaux*, in *Description de l'Egypte, Etat moderne*, Paris, 1813, 1826; Erich M. von Hornbostel, *Notizen über kirgisische Musikinstrumente*, in R. Karutz, *Unter Kirgisen und Turkmenen*, Leipzig, 1911, pp. 196–218; Jules Rouanet, *La musique arabe*, p. I, vol. V, pp. 2676–2812; *La musique arabe dans le Maghreb*, l. c., pp. 2813–2844; Raouf Yekta, *La musique turque*, l. c., pp. 2945–3064; Cl. Huart, *Musique persane*, l. c., pp. 3065–3083; Curt Sachs, *Geist und Werden der Musikinstrumente*, Berlin, 1929, passim; Henry George Farmer, *A History of Arabian Music to the XIIIth Century*, London, 1929; *Studies in Oriental Musical Instruments*, I, II, London, 1931, 1939; Baron Rodolphe d'Erlanger, *La musique arabe*, 3 vol., Paris, 1930–38; Alfred Berner, *Studien zur arabischen Musik auf Grund der gegenwärtigen Theorie und Praxis in Aegypten*, Leipzig, 1937; C. Sachs, *Les instruments de musique de Madagascar*, Paris, 1938; James Robson, *Ancient Arabian Musical Instruments*, Glasgow, 19??.

HARP. Egypt: Père Belon, *Les observations de plusieurs singularitez & choses memorables*, Paris, 1554.

KETTLEDRUMS. Kus: Farmer, *A History of Arabian Music*, p. 38; Jaap Kunst, *Hindoe-Javaansche muziek-instrumenten*, Batavia, 1927, p. 134, 137, 142—Miniature, Goloubew Collection: George Marteau et Henri Vever, *Miniatures persanes*, Paris, 1913, pl. II; Ph. Walter Schulz, *Die persisch-islamische Miniaturmalerei*, Leipzig, 1914, p. 2.

SHORT LUTE. Eleventh century: Mahmoud el Hefny, *Ibn Sina's Musiklehre*, Diss., Berlin, 1931, pp. 44–50.

LONG LUTE. Al-Farabi: d'Erlanger I, pp. 217–262.

14. EUROPE

GENERAL: Frederick Morgan Padelford, *Old English Musical Terms*, Bonn, 1899; Felipe Pedrell, *Organografía musical antigua española*, Barcelona, 1901; Edward Buhle, *Die musikalischen Instrumente in den Miniaturen des frühen Mittelalters*, vol. I, Leipzig, 1903; Francis W. Galpin, *Old English Instruments of Music*, London, 1910; J. Levy, *Die Signalinstrumente in den altfranzösischen Texten*, Diss., Halle, 1910; Gustav Schad, *Musik und Musikausdrücke in der mittelenglischen Literatur*, Diss., Giessen, 1911; Hortense Panum, *Middelalderens Strengeinstrumenter*, 3 v., København, 1915–1931; Denise Parent, *Les instruments de musique au XIVe siècle*, in *École Nationale des Chartes, Thèses pour le diplôme d'archiviste paléographe*, Paris, 1925 (outline only); Fritz Brücker, *Die Blasinstrumente in der altfranzösischen Literatur*, Giessen, 1926; Curt Sachs, *Handbuch der Musikinstrumentenkunde*, 2nd ed., Leipzig, 1930; Friedrich Dick, *Bezeichnungen für Saiten- und Schlaginstrumente in der altfranzösischen Literatur*, Giessen, 1932; Dorothea Treder, *Die Musikinstrumente in den höfischen Epen der Blütezeit*, Diss., Greifswald, 1933; F. W. Galpin, *A Textbook of European Musical Instruments*, London, 1937; Adam von Ahn Carse, *Musical Wind Instruments*, London, 1939 (the author has not yet seen this book).

HARP. Stone crosses: plate in Galpin, *Old English Instruments*, p. 4; Miniature in St. John's College: plate in Galpin, l. c., p. 218—Planets: K. Bartsch, *Altfranzösische Romanzen und Pastourellen*, Leipzig, 1870, XLIX, p. 58—D'Ingleterre: *La Prise de Cordres et de Sébille* (thirteenth century), verse 29 —Puntos doblados: *Poema de Alfonso Onceno*, str. 410, in W. Giese, *Anthologie der geistigen Kultur auf der Pyrenäenhalbinsel*, Hamburg-Berlin, 1927, p. 163 —Bas et hauls: Erich Hertzmann, *Studien zur Basse danse*, in *Zeitschrift für Musikwissenschaft* XI (1929), pp. 401–405.

LYRE. Vesp. A i: plate in Galpin, l. c., p. 6—Utrecht: E. T. de Wald, *The Illustrations of the Utrecht Psalter*, Princeton (1932)—Voguls and Ostyaks: A. O. Väisänen. *Die Leier der Ob-Ugrischen Völker*, in *Eurasia septentrionalis antiqua*, VI (1930)—Esthonia and Finland: Otto Andersson, *Stråkharpan*, Helsingfors, 1923—Otto Andersson, *The Bowed Harp*, transl. by Kathleen Schlesinger, London, 1930.

MONOCHORD: S. Wantzloeben, *Das Monochord als Instrument und als System*, Halle, 1911—Scotus: Jacques Handschin, *Die Musikanschauung des Johannes Scotus (Erigena)*, in *Deutsche Vierteljahrsschrift für Literaturwissenschaft* V (1927)—Muris: Martin Gerbert, *Scriptores ecclesiastici de musica*, St. Blasien, 1784, III 283b; Berlin, Staatsbibl., Ms. theol. lat. fol. 358.

HURDY-GURDY. Odo: Gerbert, l. c., I 303—Semicircular movement: Percival R. Kirby, *The Musical Instruments of the Native Races of South-Africa*, p. 216.

LUTES. Utrecht Psalter: E. T. De Wald, *The Illustrations of the Utrecht Psalter*, Princeton (1932)—Aureum: J. Rudolf Rahn, *Das Psalterium aureum*, St. Gallen, 1878, pl. VI, XIV—Stuttgart: E. T. De Wald, *The Stuttgart Psalter*, Princeton, 1930—Spanish: the manuscripts themselves in the Biblioteca Nacional in Madrid; cf. also Antonio Blázquez, *Los manuscritos de los comen-*

tarios al Apocalipsis de San Juan, por S. Beato de Liébana, in *Revista de Archivos, Bibliotecas y Museos* XIV (1906), pp. 257–273.

FIDDLE. Etymology: Curt Sachs, *Reallexikon der Musikinstrumente,* Berlin, 1913, p. 139b—Fidlu: T. Hannaas, *Hardingfela,* in *Bergen Museums Aarb.* 1916–17, 3rd series, p. 19—Bowing: Hans-Heinz Dräger, *Die Entwicklung des Streichbogens,* Kassel, 1937; H. Th. Horwitz, *Die Drehbewegung in ihrer Bedeutung für die materielle Kultur,* in *Anthropos* XXIX (1934), p. 123— Geige: Daniel Fryklund, *Etymologische Studien über geige-gigue-jig,* in *Studier i modern Sprakvetenskap* VI (1917), pp. 101–110—Kit: id., *Studien über die Pochette,* Sundsvall, 1917.

CHIMES: Edward Buhle, *Die Glockenspiele in den Miniaturen des frühen Mittelalters,* in *Festschrift für Rochus von Liliencron,* Leipzig, 1910, p. 51 ff.

HORNS AND TRUMPETS: Buhle, l. c., pp. 12–31—Olifant: Ernest Closson, *L'Olifant,* in *Revue belge,* déc. 1926, pp. 446–456.

BAGPIPE. St. Jerome: *Patrologia latina,* v. 30, col. 214–215.

ORGAN: Norbert Dufourq, *Esquisse d'une histoire de l'orgue,* Paris, 1935; Buhle, l. c., pp. 52–101.

PORTATIVE ORGAN: Hans Hickmann, *Das Portativ,* Kassel, 1936—Arnault: *Instruments de musique du XVe siècle. Les traités d'Henri-Arnaut de Zwolle et de divers anonymes,* ed. G. Le Cerf et E.-R. Labande, Paris, 1932, p. XII.

FLUTES: Buhle, l. c., pp. 32–44—Aquamanile: ill. Georg Kinsky, *A History of Music in pictures,* London, 1930, p. 41; M. Klier, *Die volkstümliche Querpfeife,* in *Das deutsche Volkslied* XXV (1923); id., *Volkstümliche Querflöten und die Maultrommel,* in *Kongressbericht der Beethoven-Zentenarfeier,* Wien, 1927, pp. 373–377; id., *Neue Anleitung zum Schwegeln,* Wien, 1931.

REED PIPES: Buhle, l. c., pp. 44–46.

DRUM. Arbeau: German edition, 1878; French edition, 1888; English edition, 1925.

TRUMSCHEIT: F. W. Galpin, *Monsieur Prin and His Trumpet Marine,* in *Music and Letters,* XIV, pp. 18–29.

ZITHERS. Dulcimer tuning: Nicola Podesta, *The National Dulcimer Tutor,* London, 19??.

15. THE RENAISSANCE

GENERAL, as in Chapter 14—Massimo Trojano, *Discorsi,* Monaco, 1568; *Dialoghi,* Venetia, 1569; German translation by Friedrich Würthmann: *Die Vermählungsfeier des Herzogs Wilhelm des Fünften,* München, 1842; Hans Gerle, *Musica Teusch,* Nürnberg, 1532 and 1537; Sylvestro di Ganassi, *Opera intitulata Fontegara,* Venice, 1535; Diego Ortiz, *Tratado de glosas,* Roma, 1553; reprint Berlin, 1913—Virdung: facs. Berlin, 1882—Agricola: reprint Berlin, 1896—Praetorius: reprints Berlin, 1884, and Kassel, 1929—Trasuntinis: Curt Sachs, *Sammlung alter Musikinstrumente zu Berlin, beschreibender Katalog,* Berlin, 1922, p. 69—Fugger: Adolf Sandberger, *Bemerkungen zur Biographie Hans Leo Hasslers,* in *Denkmäler der Tonkunst in Bayern* V 1, Leipzig, 1904, p. L f—Henry VIII: Galpin, *Old English Instruments,* pp. 292–300—Berlin: Curt Sachs, *Musik und Oper am kurbrandenburgischen*

Hofe, Berlin, 1910, pp. 205–207—Vienna: Julius Schlosser, *Alte Musikinstrumente*, Wien, 1920.

ORGAN: Arnold Schlick, *Spiegel der Orgelmacher*, Heidelberg, 1511 (only copy: Library Paul Hirsch, Cambridge); reprints *Monatshefte für Musikgeschichte* Heft 5–6, Leipzig, 1869, and by Paul Smets, 1937, in modern language, by Ernst Flade, Mainz, 1932; Raymond Kendall, *Notes on Arnold Schlick*, in *Acta Musicologica* XI (1939), pp. 136–143; Norbert Dufourq, *Esquisse d'une histoire de l'orgue en France*, Paris, 1935.

REGALS. Henry VIII: Galpin, l. c., p. 293.

RECORDER: Christopher Welch, *Six Lectures on the Recorder*, Oxford, 1911.

ONE-HANDED FLUTE. Lippi: ill. in Curt Sachs, *Reallexikon der Musikinstrumente*, Berlin, 1913, p. 146.

TRANSVERSE FLUTE: Agricola, l. c., f. xiij (p. 25); Sylvestro di Ganassi, *Opera intitulata Fontegara*, Venetia, 1535.

BASSOON: Lyndesay G. Langwill, *Notes on "Three Bassoons" in the National Museum of Antiquities of Scotland*, in *Proceedings of the Society of Antiquaries of Scotland*, v. 67 (1932–33), pp. 335–340; *Some Notes on the Bassoon*, in *The Musical Progress*, 1933, pp. 379–380; *The Curtal* (1550–1750), in *Musical Times*, April, 1937.

RANKETS, etc.: Georg Kinsky, *Doppelrohrblatt-Instrumente mit Windkapsel*, in *Archiv für Musikwissenschaft* VII (1925), pp. 253–296.

RAUSCHPFEIFEN: Curt Sachs, *Sammlung alter Musikinstrumente zu Berlin*, Berlin, 1922, pp. 281–282, pl. 28.

CORNET: Walther, p. 186.

TROMBONE: Francis W. Galpin, *The Sackbut*, in *Proceedings of the Musical Association*, Session 33 (1907), pp. 1–25.

TRUMPET: Werner Menke, *History of the Trumpet of Bach and Handel*, London (1934).

KETTLEDRUMS: Sir James Turner, *Pallas Armata*, 1683.

CLAVICHORD: Fr. A. Goehlinger, *Geschichte des Klavichords*, Diss., Basel, 1910; Cornelia Auerbach, *Die deutsche Clavichordkunst des 18. Jahrhunderts*, Kassel, 1930—Cersne: C. Sachs, *Die Instrumente der Minneregel*, in *Sammelbände der Internationalen Musikgesellschaft* XII (1913), pp. 484–486—Arnault: *Instruments de musique du XVᵉ siècle. Les traités d'Henri-Arnaut de Zwolle et de divers anonymes*, ed. G. Le Cerf et E.-R. Labande, Paris, 1932—Shrewsbury: Galpin, *Old English Instruments*, fig. 20—Ramis: reprint by Johannes Wolf in *Beihefte der Internationalen Musikgesellschaft*, Folge 1, no. 2 (Leipzig, 1901), p. 16—Short octave: G. Kinsky, *Kurze Oktaven*, in *Zeitschrift für Musikwissenschaft* II (1919), pp. 65–82—Bundfrei: Galpin, l. c., p. 115—Caressingly: Karl Philipp Emanuel Bach, *Versuch über die wahre Art das Clavier zu spielen*, Berlin, 1753, Introduction § 15 (reprint, 3rd ed., Leipzig, 1920); Christian Daniel Friedrich Schubart, *Ideen zu einer Aesthetik der Tonkunst*, Wien, 1806, p. 288 f.

SPINETS AND HARPSICHORDS: Eva Ursula Kropp, *Das Zupfklavier*, Diss., Berlin, 1925; Philip James, *Early Keyboard Instruments*, London, 1930—Henry VIII: Galpin, *Old English Instruments*, p. 297—Arabic: Henry George Far-

mer, *Studies in Oriental Musical Instruments* I, London, 1931, pp. 17–24—
Cersne: Curt Sachs, l. c.—Upright: Hans Hickmann, *Das Portativ*, Kassel,
1936, p. 160 f.; Arnault, l. c.; Scaliger, *Poétique*, Lyon, 1561, p. 127—
Single and double: Galpin, l. c., pp. 288–292—Skinner: (Fanny Reed Hammond and Nils J. Ericsson), *The Belle Skinner Collection of Old Musical
Instruments*, 1933, pp. 31–34; Josef Reiss, *Pauli Paulirini de Praga tractatus
de musica*, in *Zeitschrift für Musikwissenschaft* VII (1925), pp. 262–263—
Kefermarkt: Georg Kinsky, *A History of Music in Pictures*, London, 1930,
p. 64.

DULCE MELOS: Arnault, l. c., pp. 19–23.—Tangentenflügel: *Die Regensburger
Klavierbauer Späth und Schmahl*, Diss., Erlangen, 1928.

VIOLS: Sylvestro de Ganassi dal Fontego, *Regola Rubertina*, Venezia, 1542–
1543; reprint Leipzig, 1924; Gerald R. Hayes, *Musical Instruments and
Their Music* II, Oxford, 1930, pp. 1–137.

LUTE: Ernst Gottlieb Baron, *Historisch-theoretische und praktische Unter-
suchung der Lauten*, Nürnberg, 1727; Karl Geiringer, *Vorgeschichte und
Geschichte der europäischen Laute*, in *Zeitschrift für Musikwissenschaft* X
(1928), pp. 560–603.

CITTERN: Curt Sachs, *Sammlung alter Musikinstrumente*, pp. 151–162.

LIRA DA GAMBA: Hayes, l. c., pp. 144–151.

16. THE BAROQUE

GENERAL: as in chapter 15—Berlin: Curt Sachs, *Musik und Oper am kurbrandenburgischen Hofe*, Berlin, 1910, p. 205.

VIOLIN. General: Willibald Leo Freiherr von Lütgendorff, *Die Geigen- und
Lautenmacher*, 3rd edition, Frankfurt a. M., p. 192; Gerald R. Hayes, *Musical
instruments* II, Oxford, 1930, pp. 160–209; Giovanni Maria Lanfranco,
Scintille di musica, Brescia, 1533; Hans Judenkunig, *Utilis et compendiaria
introductio*, Vienna, 1523; Pedro Cerone, *El melopeo y maestro*, Napoles,
1613—Silver strings: Jean Rousseau, *Traité de la viole*, Paris, 1687, p. 24;
Friedrich Zamminer, *Die Musik und die musikalischen Instrumente*, Giessen,
1855, p. 4; Heinrich Welcker von Gontershausen, *Neu-eröffnetes Magazin
musikalischer Tonwerkzeuge*, Frankfurt, 1855, p. 241.

VIOLA D'AMORE: Francis Bacon, *Sylva Sylvarum*, 1648, Century III, no. 280;
Werner Eginhard Köhler, *Beiträge zur Geschichte und Literatur der Viola
d'amore*, Diss., Berlin, 1938.

VIOLA POMPOSA: E. T. Arnold, *Die Viola pomposa*, in *Zeitschrift für Musikwissenschaft* XIII (1930), pp. 141–145; Georg Kinsky, ib., pp. 325–328;
Arnold, ib. XIV (1931), p. 35; F. W. Galpin, ib., pp. 35–38; Hans Engel,
ib., p. 38;—Galpin, *Viola pomposa and violoncello piccolo*, in *Music and
Letters* XII (1931), pp. 354–364.

BARYTON: Daniel Fryklund, *Viola di Bardone*, in *Svensk Tidskrift för Musik-
forskning* IV (1922), pp. 129–152.

BOW: Henry Saint-George, *The Bow*, 3rd edition, London, 1922; Hans-
Heinz Dräger, *Die Entwicklung des Streichbogens*, Kassel, 1937.

ARCHLUTES. Kanz al-Tuhaf: Farmer, *Studies in Oriental Musical Instruments*, London, 1931, I, p. 14 f.

CITTERNS: Galpin, *Old English Instruments*, p. 25 ff.

GUITAR. Espinel: *Revue hispanique* XLI (1917), p. 219; Pablo Minguet y Yrol, *Reglas y advertencias generales para tañer la guitarra, tiple y vandola*, Madrid, 1754.

HARPSICHORD, as in Chapter 15.

CARILLON: William Gorham Rice, *Carillon Music*, New York, 1925; Frank Percival Price, *The Carillon*, London, 1933—Change-ringing: Ernest Morris, *The History and Art of Change-ringing*, London, 1931.

FLUTE: Mauger, *Les Hotteterre*, Paris, 1912.

OBOE D'AMORE. Mahillon: Victor-Charles Mahillon, *Catalogue descriptif*, Gand, 1893, I, 231.

SLIDE TRUMPET: Curt Sachs, *Bach's tromba da tirarsi*, in *Bachjahrbuch*, 1908.

HORNS: Fritz Piersig, *Die Einführung des Hornes in die Kunstmusik*, Halle, 1927; Charles Sanford Terry, *Bach's Orchestra*, London, 1932; Johann Ernst Altenburg, *Versuch einer Anleitung zur heroisch-musikalischen Trompeter- und Pauker-Kunst*, Halle, 1795.

ORGAN: Ernst Flade, *Der Orgelbauer Gottfried Silbermann*, Leipzig, 1926.

PITCH: Alexander John Ellis, *The History of Musical Pitch*, in *Journal of the Society of Arts*, 1877, 1880, 1881, and in his translation of Helmholtz, *On the Sensations of Tone*, 1885.

17. ROMANTICISM

GENERAL: Curt Sachs, *Handbuch der Musikinstrumentenkunde*, 2nd edition, Leipzig, 1930; *Die modernen Musikinstrumente*, Berlin, 1923; Johann Georg Albrechtsberger, *Gründliche Anweisung zur Composition*, Leipzig, 1790—acoustics: Edward Gick Richardson, *The Acoustics of Orchestral Instruments*, London, 1929; Sir James Jeans, *Science and Music*, Cambridge, 1937—England: Francis W. Galpin, *Old English Instruments of Music*, London, 1910—France: Constantin Pierre, *Les facteurs d'instruments de musique*, Paris, 1893.

PIANO: Jacob Adlung, *Musica mechanica organoedi*, Berlin, 1768; *Anleitung zu der musikalischen Gelahrtheit*, Erfurt, 1758 and Dresden-Leipzig, 1783; Curt Sachs, *Das Klavier*, Berlin, 1923; Rosamond E. M. Harding, *The Piano-forte*, Cambridge, 1933; Eva Hertz, *Johann Andreas Stein*, Würzburg, 1937.—Upright: Walter Pfeiffer, *Flügel oder Klavier*, Stuttgart, 1940.

AEOLIAN HARP: J. G. Kastner, *La harpe d'Eole*, Paris, 1856; James Thompson, *Castle of Indolence*, 2nd edition, London, 1748, p. 21.

HARP: Hans Joachim Zingel, *Harfe und Harfenspiel*, Halle, 1932.

FRICTION RODS: Ernst Florens Friedrich Chladni, *Beyträge zur praktischen Akustik*, Leipzig, 1821.

HARMONIUM: Auguste Mustel, *L'orgue expressif*, Paris, 1903.

GLASS HARMONICA: C. F. Pohl, *Zur Geschichte der Glasharmonika*, Wien, 1862; O. G. Sonneck, *Benjamin Franklin's Musical Side*, in *Suum cuique*, New York (1916).

BOEHM FLUTE: Christopher Welch, *History of the Boehm-flute*, London, 1896; H. C. Wysham, *The Evolution of the Boehm Flute*, Elkhart, 1898; Theobald Boehm, *Flutes and Flute-playing*, London, 1910; The same, 2nd English edition by Dayton C. Miller, Cleveland-London, 1922.

CLARINET. Zoroastre: Lionel de la Laurencie, *Rameau et les clarinettes*, in *Revue musicale S.I.M.* IX (1913), p. 2.

SAXOPHONE: Jaap Kool, *Das Saxophon*, Leipzig (1931).

VALVES. Clagget: *Patents for Inventions. Abridgments of Specifications Relating to Music and Musical Instruments. A.D. 1694–1866.* 2nd edition, London, 1871, p. 22.

MACHINE DRUMS: Percival R. Kirby, *The Kettle-drums*, London, 1930.

ORGAN: Ernest M. Skinner, *The Modern Organ*, New York (1917); Hertha Schweiger, *Abbé G. J. Voglers Orgellehre*, Diss., Freiburg, 1934, Wien, 1938; Walter and Thomas Lewis, *Modern Organ Building*, 3rd edition, London, 1939.

EPILOGUE: THE TWENTIETH CENTURY

ELECTRIC INSTRUMENTS. T. Cahill, *Electrical Music as a Vehicle of Expression*, in *Music Teachers National Association Studies*, 2nd series, Annual Meeting 29th in 1907, Hartford, Conn., 1908; Michel Adam, *À propos des instruments de musique radio-électriques et photo-électriques*, in *Revue générale de l'électricité* XXIII (1928), pp. 46–51; Julien, *Applications du courant électrique, des oscillations radio-électriques et des phénomènes photoélectriques à la réalisation d'instruments de musique*, in *Conservatoire National des Arts & Métiers, conférences d'actualités scientifiques et industrielles*, 1929, pp. 141–189; Joseph Schillinger, *Electricity, a Musical Liberator*, in *Modern Music* VIII (1931), pp. 26–31; R. Raven-Hart, *The Development of Electrical Music*, in *Nineteenth Century* CXI (1932), pp. 603–611; Peter Lertes, *Elektrische Musik*, Dresden-Leipzig, 1933; John Mills, *A Fugue in Cycles and Bells*, New York, 1935; Carlos Chávez, *Toward a New Music*, New York, 1937; Arno Huth, *Les instruments radio-électriques*, in *La Nouvelle Encyclopédie française* (1935), 16, 38–1; Mr. John G. MacKenty (*RCA*) had the kindness to look over the electrical section of the book.

ORGAN: W. H. Barnes, *The Contemporary American Organ*, 1933—Atlantic City: T. Scott Buhrman, *The Greatest Organ in the World*, in *The American Organist* XV (1932), p. 467—Philadelphia: *The World's Greatest Organ*, John Wanamaker, Philadelphia (1917)—Harvard: *The American Organist* XX (1937), p. 165—G. Donald Harrison, *The classical organ in the Germanic Museum*, in *Germanic Museum Bulletin* I (1938), p. 36.

TERMINOLOGY

Victor-Charles Mahillon, *Essai de classification méthodique de tous les instruments anciens et modernes*, in his *Catalogue descriptif et analytique du Musée Instrumental du Conservatoire Royal de Musique de Bruxelles*, 2nd edition, Gand, 1893, pp. 1–89—Erich M. von Hornbostel & Curt Sachs,

Systematik der Instrumentenkunde, in *Zeitschrift für Ethnologie*, XLVI (1914) pp. 553–590—George Montandon, *La généalogie des instruments de musique et les cycles de civilization*, Genève, 1919—André Schaeffner, *Projet d'une classification nouvelle des instruments de musique*, in *Bulletin du Musée d'Ethnologie du Trocadéro*, no. 1 (1931), pp. 21–25—A. Schaeffner, *D'une nouvelle classification méthodique des instruments de musique*, in *Revue Musicale* 1932, pp. 215–231—Erich M. von Hornbostel, in his *Ethnology of African Sound-instruments*, in *Africa* VI (1933), pp. 303–311—Schaeffner, *Classification des instruments de musique*, in his *Origine des instruments de musique*, Paris, 1936, pp. 371–377.

Index

Aba (oboe), 248
Abûb, 119
Accordion, 406
Accort, 303
Achilliaca, 261
Aeolian harp, 402-403
Aeoline, aeolodicon, 406
Aerophones, 457
Āghāṭi, 152
Ajabeba, 247
Ala, 293, 342
A-lal, 75, 76
'*Al-'alāmot*, 116-117, 125
ALBISI, 410
Albisifono, 410
'*Al-haśmīnît*, 116-117
Alphorn, 47-48
Al-śaqira, 337
Altkornett, 429
Altobasso, 312
Alto clarinet, 414
Alto flute, 410
Alto horn, 429
Alto oboe, 383
Alû, 76
AMATI, 358
Ambubaiae, 119
"American organ," 406
Amulets, 26, 170
Añafil, 281
Ānanda laharī, 55
Angklung, 233
Annafir, 281
Anthropology and prehistory, 60-62
Archlute, *arciliuto*, 370-372
Ardablîs, 124

Arpicordo, 339, 342
Ascaules, 141
Asor, 117-118
ASTÉ, 424
ASTOR, 422
Aulos, 138-140
Axabeba, 247
Ayacachtli, 194
Ayelit-haśaḥar, 125
Ayon chicuaztli, 194
Ayotl, 195

BABCOCK, 396, 397
Bach trumpet, 329, 449
Bagannâ, 134
Bagpipes
  Babylonia, 84
  Israel, 120
  Rome, 141
  India, 154
  Europe, 281-284, 303, 352
    Types, 283
Bajón, 317
Bakora, bakura, 152
Balag-di, 75
Balag(gu), 75-76
Balag-lul, 73
Balalaika, 273
Bamm, 254
Bāmyā, 223, 230
Bandaïr, 247
Banjo, 134, 190, 446
Barbaṭ, 135, 161, 253
Bárbiton, 135
Baritone, Baryton (tuba), 429
BARKER, 444

489

Baryton (viol), 368
Bassanello, 315
Bass clarinet, 414
Bass drum, 435-436
Basse à pistons, 429
Basse-cor, 422
Basse de viole, 360
Basse guerrière, 414
Basse-orgue, 414
Basset-horn, 415, 449
Basse-trompette, 422
Basse-tube, 414
Bass flute, 410
Basshorn, 422
Bassklarinette, 414
Bassone, 317
Bassoon, 315-319, 352
Bassoon (piano stop), 395
Bass trumpet, 434
Bass tuba, 429-430
Bathyphon, 414
BB bass, 430
Bebung, 334
BECHSTEIN, 447
Bell
    Assyria, 71
    Israel, 109
    Far East, 164, 169-170, 209
    Peru, 200
    India, 222
    Southeast Asia, 235
    Europe, 279, 299, 456
    Magics, 109, 170
    Hand bell, 169, 222, 456
    Wooden bell, 200
    Resting bell, 209
Bell chime
    China, 171-172
    Europe, middle ages, 279-280
    —, Baroque, 378-380
BERGONZI, 359
BERTOLOTTI, 358
Bible-regal, 309
Bin (Egypt), 94
Bin (India), 224
Biia, 212
Bishur, 212
Biwa, 189
BIZOS, 447
Bladder pipe, 283
BLEYER, 397
Blockflöte, 309
BLÜHMEL, 426
Board-zither, 463

Body (stringed instruments), 465
Body, rhythmical movements of the human, 25-26
BOEHM, 408-410
Boehm flute, 407-410
Bombarde, 314
Bombardino, 429
"Bones"
    Sumer, 69
    Europe, 278
Bonnang, 241
BOOTH, 444
BOREAU, 447
Bottesini bow, 363
Bow, 277, 363, 369-370
Bowed instruments, earliest, 216-217
Bowed organ stops, 386
Bowing, 277
Bowl lyre, 465
Bow-lute, 94
Box lyre, 465
"Brass instruments," 417
Bridge, 350, 466
BROADWOOD, 394, 395
Bubbolo, 279
Buccina, 281
BUFFET, 414
Bugaku biwa, 190
Bugle, 48, 420, 428
Buisine, 281
Bull-roarer, 40-43, 53, 61, 63
    Forms, 40-42
    Connotations, 42
    Toy, 43
Bundfrei, 333
Buni, 94
Buri, 210, 228
BURSTYN, 448
BUSCHMANN, 406, 407
Busîne, busûne, 281, 326
Butt, 315

Cai dan bao, 54
Cai dan nguyet, 218
Calandrone, 322
Cälpära, 207
Campanella, 379
Cane flute, 390
Cank, 259
Caño, 258
Capistrum, 138
Caramillo, 288
Carillon, 378-380
    Tower carillons, 378-379

Carillon (*continued*)
  Chamber and orchestra carillons, 379
  Change-ringing, 379-380
  See also Bell chime
Čartār, 257
Cascabeles, 308
Castanets, 103, 455
CATTERINI, 414
Celesta, 379
Celestial music (India), 159
Celestina stop, 403
Cembalo (drum), 289
Cervelas, 319
ČERVENÝ, 430
Cha chiao, 147, 210
Chalemele, 288
Chalumeau, 411
Change-ringing, 379-380
CHANOT, 361
Châpeau chinois, 438
Charamela (*charumela*), 213
Chekker, 336
Chelys, 261
Cheng, 186
Chest, 303, 348
Chicuzen biwa, 190-191
Chifonie, 272
Ch'ih, 178, 213
Children; *see* Toy
Chilitli, 194
Chime, 456
Ch'in, 185, 187-188
Ch'ing, 168, 209
Chirimia, 193
Chitarrone, 370-372
CHLADNI, 403
Chnouē, 100
Choraula, 141
Chordophones, 463
Choristfagott, 317
Chorton, 386
Chorus, 281
Chromatisches basshorn, 422
Chrotta, 261, 262
Chu, 175
Chuk, 175
Chung, 169
Ch'ung tu, 175
Ch'un kuan, 212
Cimball, organ, 308
Cimbalom, 258, 293, 446
Cimbasso, 429
Cinfonia, 272
Cinquiesme, 362

Circumcision, 36, 47, 50, 248
Cithara, 262, 263
Cittern, 345-347, 372-374
Clabiórgano, 342
CLAGGET, 403, 426
Clapper
  Sumer, 69
  Egypt, 88-89, 103
  Greece, 149
  China, 174-175
  Burma, 236
  Europe, 278
  Terminology, 455
Clapper drum, China, 173
Clareta, 328
Clarinet
  Egypt, 91-92
  India, 154
  China, 212
  Europe, 410-415
  Double clarinet, 91-92, 154, 212
  Transpositions, 411
  Organ stop, 441
Clarinette d'amour, 415
Clarino, 412
Clarin trumpet, 328
CLAUSS, 347
Clavecin, 335
Clavicembalo, 335
Clavichord, 303, 330-334, 338, 449
  Wrest plank, 330
  Earliest evidences, 331
  Fingering, 332
  Bundfrei, 333
  Character, 334
  Modern, 449
Clavicylinder, 403-404
Clavicymbalum, 339
Clavicyterium, 342
Claviorgan, 342-343
Clavisimbalum, 338
Clein geigen, 356
Clubs, 69
Çoçoloctli, 192
Cohabitation; *see* Penis
Cohuilotl, 194
Colascione, 257
Color, 48, 50, 164
Combination stops, 441-442
Concussion club, 69
Concussion instruments, 455
Concussion sticks, 88-89
Consort, 303
Contrabasset-horn, 415

Contrabass tuba, 430
Contrebasse à pistons, 429
Contrebasse guerrière, 414
Cor allemand, 384
Cor anglais, 384
Cor anglais (organ stop), 441
Cornet (valve), 419, 428-432
Cornet (Zink), 303, 323-325, 449
Cornet à bouquin, 323
Cornettino (piston), 428
Cornettino (Zink), 324
Corno, 384
Corno da tirarsi, 385
Cornon, 324
Cornophone, 432
Corno torto, 324
Cornu, 147
Cors sarrazinois, 280
Corthol, 317
Cosmology and music, 163-164, 171
Coupler, 441
COUPLEUX, 448
COUSINEAU, 400
CRAMER, 434
Crescendo pedal, 386, 441
Crescent, 437-439
CRISTOFORI, 391-393
Cromorne, 303, 320-322, 352
Crook, 426
Cross flute
    Primitive, 64
    Etruria, 141-142
    India, 159
    Europe, 303, 314, 352, 380-381
    Boehm, 407-410
Cross-stringing, 397
Crot, 262
Cruit, 262
Crwth, 268
Crystallophone, 456
Cuiraxezaqua, 192
Curtal, 315
Cymbal (organ stop), 306
Cymbal (triangle), 437
Cymbals
    Assyria, 71
    Egypt, 103-104
    Israel, 121-123
    Greece, 149
    India, 151, 222-223
    China, 207
    Java, 235
    Burma, 236

Cymbals (*continued*)
    Europe, 436, 439
    Terminology, 455
Cymbals (piano stop), 395
Cymbal-castanets, Egypt, 103
Cymbals on clappers, 103-104, 123
Cymbalum, 279
Cythara, 262, 263, 274

Da daiko, 75, 214
Dāera, 229
Daf, 229
Dā'ira, 246
Dāmāmā, 230, 251
Damaru, 159
Daṣari tappaṭṭai, 149
Dāsatīn, 254
Davaṇḍai, 159
DEBAIN, 406
DENNER, 412
DESFONTENELLES, 416
Dessus de viole, 359
Diapason, 305
Discus, 149
Disk, 149, 223
Dokaku, 210
Dolcian, 317
Dombra, 273
Domed forms, 36
DOMINICUS PISAURIENSIS, 340
"Double" (virginals, etc.), 308
Double bass, 363-364
Double bass clarinet, 414-415
Double escapement, 396
Doucine, 288, 317
Dragonetti bow, 363
Drehleier, 273
Drone
    On reed pipes, 120, 140, 154, 230,
        281-282
    On stringed instruments, 188, 191,
        231, 254, 268, 272, 275, 312, 350
Drum
    Primitive, 31-36, 53, 62, 63
        Forms, 31-33
        Tubular drums, 31
        Cup-handle drum, 32
        Footed drum, 32
        Goblet drum, 32
        Pottery drum, 32
        Frame drum, 33
        Double-headed drum, 33
        Connotations, 34
        Rituals, 35-36

Drum (*continued*)
    Legends, 36
    Sumer, 73-78
        Frame drum, 76
        Goblet drum, 77
    Egypt, 96-97
    Greece, 148-149
    India, 151-152, 154-155, 157-159,
      221, 223-224, 229-230
        Axillary, 151-152, 157
        Frame, 154, 229
        Barrel, 154-155, 157-158
        Cylinder, 157-158
        Pair, 158
        Paste, 158
        Clapper, 158, 159
        Hourglass, 158-159
    Java, 235, 236
    Burma, 236
    Far East, 164, 172-174, 214-216
        Grain filled, 172-173
        Barrel, 173, 214
        Braced, 214
        Hourglass, 215-216
    Mexico, 195-196
    Peru, 200-201
    Near East, 246-247, 249
    Europe, middle ages, 288-290
        Barrel, 289
        Cylinder, 289
        Frame, 289
        Lansquenets', 290
    Europe and America, present, 435-436
Drum chime, 224, 236
Drum-gong, 233-235
Drum sticks, 31, 33, 36, 51, 64, 157
    Hooked, 157, 250
    Piano stop, 395
Dub, 73
DUDDEL, 448
Duff, 246
Dulce melos, 343-344
Dulcian, 352
Dulcimer, 219, 258-259, 292, 343, 391
Dulzaina, 288
Dulzian, 317
DUMAS, 414
Dundubhiḥ, 153
Dung, 210
Dutār, 257

Earth, 31, 36; *see also* Pit
Ebubu, 73
Echo (organ), 386

Ele, 293
Electrophones, 447-449, 467
Electropneumatic action, 444
Elymoi, 139
Emicon, 448
English action, 394
English basshorn, 422
Epigoneion, 137
Épinette, 335
ÉRARD, 396, 400
Êrh hu, 217
Êrús, 109
Escapement, 391
Eschaqueil, 336
Eschequier, 336
ESPINEL, 374
Esrār, 232
ESTEY, 407
Etherophone, 448
Ethics and music, 162-163
Eufonio, 429
Euphone, 403
Euphonium, 419, 429
EVETTE & SCHAEFFER, 415
Exaquier, 336
"Extensions," 28

FABER, 333
Fagotcontra, 317
Fagotto, 317
Fanđir, 274
Fandur, 275
Fang hiang, 208
Farpa, 264
FARRANT, 349
"Father," 53
Féanđir, 274
Feđilo, 275
Feldtrompeter, 328
Fele, 275
Felttrumet, 328
Female connotations, 29, 36, 37, 51, 56,
    112, 169, 172, 176, 198, 214, 241.
    See also Vulva.
Fertility rites, 29, 44, 88, 112, 170.
    See also Rain
Fiddle
    China, 217-218
    India, 226-227, 232
    Java, 242
    Near East, 255
    Europe, 274-278
        Etymology, 274-275

Fiddle (*continued*)
  Earliest evidences, 275
  Tuning, 276
  Bowing, 277
  Rebec, 278
Fiddle, 276
Fidele, 275
Fidlu, 274, 275
Fife, 288, 314
Figuren, 308
Fingerboard, 466
Fingerholes, 99-100, 181-182, 458-459
Fish, 175-176
Flageol, 287
Flageolet, 313-314
Flajolez, 313
Flajos, 287
Flauste, 287
Flauta, 288
Flautino, 313
Flauto, 381
Flauto dolce, 309
Flauto piccolo, 313, 381, 410
Flex-a-tone, 447
Flicorno, 428, 429
Flue, 44, 94
Flügelhorn, 419, 428
Flute
  Primitive, 44-47
  Sumer, 71-72
  Egypt, 90-91
  Israel, 106
  India, 151, 159, 227-228
  China, 164, 166-167, 178-182, 213-214
  C. America, 192-194
  S. America, 198-199
  S. E. Asia, 235
  Near East, 247-248
  Europe, middle ages, 287-288
  — Renaissance, 309-314
  — Baroque, 352, 380-381
  — Present, 407-410
  Beaked flute, 159, 192-194, 248, 309-314
  Cross flute, 44, 142, 179, 213, 227, 235, 287, 314, 352, 380-381, 407-410
  Double flute, 228
  Globular flute, 72, 164, 166-167, 199
  Nose flute, 46-47
  Notched flute, 179, 199, 213
  One-handed, 312
  Triple flute, 228

Flute (*continued*)
  Vertical flute, 44, 71-72, 90-91, 106, 227, 247
  Whistle flute, 44, 72, 159, 192-194, 213, 227, 309-314
Flute (organ stop), 305, 441
Flûte douce, 309
Flûtet, 312
FONTAINE-BESSON, 415, 432
"Foot," 304
Formant, 354-355
Forpex, 338
Forte (piano stop), 394
Frame drum, 33, 76, 96-97, 148-149, 154, 229, 246-247, 289
FRANCO UNGARO, 341
FRANKLIN, 404-405
Free aerophones, 459
Free reed, 183
French horn, 424-425, 426, 384, 420
Fret, 466
FRICHOT, 422
FRICK, 405
Friction idiophones, 457
Friction instruments
  Tortoise shell, 38-39
  Drum, 39-40, 64
  Rubbed wood, 39
Friction rods, 402-404
FRIDERICI, 397
FRITZ, 413
Funeral, 36, 39, 43, 45, 47, 50, 119, 147, 175, 183, 194, 195, 210
Furniture, 304
Fuye, 213

Gaiṭa, 248
Galoubet, 312
Gamakas, 221
Gamba; *see* Viol
Gambang, 238
Gamelan, 236
Ġank, 259
Gargara, 152
Ġawâq, 248
Gekkin, 218
Gemshorn, 306
Gendèr, 239
Genkwan, 218
Geographic method, 62-63
German action, 394
German flute, 287
GEYER, 363

Ghaṇṭā, 222, 235
Ghaṛī, 223
Ghāṭa, 223
Gi-gid, 72
Ginêra, 102
Giraffe piano, 398
Ḡirbāl, 246
Gittit, 125
GIVELET, 448
Glass harmonica, 404-405
Glicibarifono, 414
gLingbu, 228
Glockenspiel, 379
Go kin, 187
Gong, 30, 200, 208, 223, 240-241, 456
Gong chime, 208-209, 236, 241-245
GONZALEZ, 452
Gopī yantra, 49
Gourd bow, 57
Grain measure, 175
Grand, 334
Gravicembalo col pian e forte, 393
Grelle, 288
Grelot, 279
GRENSER, 317, 414, 415
Grosbois, 382
Grosse geigen, 356
Grosszink, 324
Ground-harp, 54-55, 63
Ground-zither, 55-56, 63
GUARNERI, 359
Guitar, 303, 374-375
Gunbrī, 102
Gunibrī, 103
GURLITT, 452
Gusla, 369

Hai lo, 210
HALARY, 424
Halbbass, 363
Half-zither, 292
Ḥalhallatu, 72
Ḥālil, 118-120
HALLIDAY, 422
HALMAGYI, 448
HAMMOND, 448
Hammond organ, 448
HAMPEL, 424
Handle, 466
Hao-tʻung, 210
Hardūlis, 124
Harmonic fifth, 420
Harmonics, 134, 140, 188, 290
Harmonium, 405-407

Harp
  Sumer, 79-82
  Egypt, 92-96
  Israel, 115-117
  Greece, 135-136
  India, 152, 156
  China, 219-220
  Java, 235
  Near East, 259
  Europe, middle ages, 260, 261-264
  — Renaissance, 303
  — Baroque, 352
  — Romanticism, 398-402
  Angular, 79-82, 95-96, 115-117, 135-136, 219-220, 259, 263, Europe
  Arched, 79-82, 92-95, 135-136, 152, 156, 235
  Chromatic, 401
  Double action, 400
  Footed, 94
  Hooks, 398
  Horizontal, 79-82, 152, 156
  Pedal, 399
  Shoulder, 94
  Vertical, 79-82, 92-96, 115-117, 152, 156, 219-220, Europe
Harp (piano stop), 394
Harpa (Swedish), 268
Harpichordum, 339
Harpsichord
  Until 1600: 302, 334-344
  Types and terms, 335
  Earliest evidences, 336
  Echiquier, 336-337
  Scaliger, 338
  Harpsichord in a narrower sense, 337-339, 340
  Single and double strings, 340-341
  Stops, 341
  Combinations, 342
  After 1600: 375-378
  The Antwerp School, 375
  The two keyboards, 376
  The pedals, 377-378
  Modern, 449
HARRISON, 452-453
Ḥaṣoṣra, 112-113
Hautbois, 382
Hautbois d'amour, 383
Hautbois du Poitou, 323
Hautecontre, 362
Hawaiian guitar, 447
HAWKINS, 396, 398
HAYWARD, 377

Healing, 50
HEBENSTREIT, 391
HECKEL, 415
HELBERGER, 448
Helicon, 430-431
Hellertion, 448
Ḥēmât ḥālilim, 121
Hersumper, 290
HESSEL, 405
Heteroglottic, 58
Hichiriki, 212, 323
HIERONYMUS PISAURIENSIS, 341
HILL, 451
Hintersatz, 306
Hirdolis, 124
HOCHRUCKER, 400
Hooked trumpet, 146
HOPKINSON, 405
Hopper, 391
Hora, 210
Horn, 73, 83, 110-112, 228, 280, 303,
    384, 419
Hornpipe, 212
HOTTETERRE, 381
Hsiao, 178
Hsüan, 166
Huancar, 200
Huaȳra-puhura, 197
Hu ch'in, 217
Huehuetl, 195
Hu hu, 217
Hui, 438
Hui hu, 217
Huilacapitztli, 192
Hûltze glechter, 439
Hurdy-gurdy, 271-273
    Oldest type, 271
    Later type, 272
Hydraulis, 143-145

Iba, 89
Ichi-gen-kin, 186
Idiochordic, 56
Idioglottic, 58
Idiophones, 455
Idûtûn, 125
Imbubu, 73
Initiation, 40, 42, 45, 56. See also Cir-
    cumcision
Instromento piano e forte, 341
Instrumento in ottava, 341
Instruments bas et hauts, 264, 382
"Invention" of instruments, 25
Inventionshorn, 426

'Irâqîa, 212
Iron frame, 396

Jack, 334, 338, 343
Jamisen, 219
Janissaries' music, 436
JANSSEN, 414
Jar, 223
Jataga, 186
Jaws' harp, 58-59, 64, 210, 299
Jazzo-flute, 447
Jews' harp; see Jaws' harp
Jhānjha, 223
Jingle, 109, 200, 279, 456
Jingles (organ stop), 308
JORDAN, 386
JUVIGNY, 313

Kāča vīṇā, 232
Kaččhapi vīṇā, 232
Kakko, 214, 215
Kal ko, 215
Kamānga a'ğūz, 255
Kamānga farḥ, 255
Kamānga rūmī, 275
Kamānga soğair, 255
Kammerbass, 363
Kammerton, 386
Kammertrompeter, 328
Kāṃsya, 223
Kanôn, 257
Kao, 75
Kapsel, 393
Karkarī, 153
Karnyx, 147
Kartāl, 71
Katral, 71
Kenthorn, 421
Kerâr, 134
Keren, 110
Kettledrum, 229-230, 249-251, 329-
    330, 434-435
Key (flute), 310, 407, 414
Key (keyboard), 285
Keyboard, 332, 375
Key bugle, 420-421
Keyed guitar, 347
Key trumpet, 420
Khol, 155
Khorāḍhāk, 251
Kin, 187
Kinnarī, 225
Kinnarī vīṇā, 232

Kinnor, 106-108
Kinyra, 107
KIRCKMAN, 395
Kit, 278
Kithara, 130-135
Kitharis, 130
Klappenhorn, 424
Kleine geigen, 356
Kleinzink, 324
KLOSÉ, 414
KLOTZ, 359
K·nn·r, 102
Koboz, kobus, 252
Kobyz, 227
KÖLBEL, 422
Köpfflin-regal, 309
KOHL, 415
Kombu, 148
Komunko, 187
Kortholt, 317
Koto, 133, 187
Krotalon, 149
Kroupalon, 149
Krummhorn, 320
Ku (drum), 172
Ku (lute), 218
Kuan, 176, 178, 179-180, 212
Ku ch'in, 210
Kum, 187
K'ung hu, 219
Kyo pang ko, 75

Labor and music, 88-89
La ch'in, 217
Lamnaṣêaḥ, 125
LANGER, 448
Languages of instruments, 37, 50, 240
La pa (clarinet), 212
La pa (trumpet), 210
Lath-zither, 463
Launedda, 91
LAZARUS, 317, 416
LEFEBVRE, 414
Leier, 272, 276
Leierkasten, 273
LERTES, 448
Lilis, 77
Ling, 169
Lira, 275
Lira da braccio, 350
Lira da gamba, 350
Lirone, 350
Lithophone; see Stone chime
Lituus, 146

Liuto (at)tiorbato, 372
Lo, 208
Long joint, 315
Long octave, 333
LOT, 414
Love, 45
LOVELACE, 361
Lü, 176-177
Lunar; see Moon ceremonials
LUPOT, 359
Lur, 147-148
Lute
  Babylonia, 82-83
  Egypt, 102-103
  Greece, 136-137
  India, 159-161, 231-232
  China, 189-191, 218-219
  Java, 235-236
  Near East, 251-256
  Europe, 273-274, 303, 344-345
Lute-stop, 376
Lyra, 276
Lyraflügel, 398
Lyra viol, 348
Lyra-way, 348
Lyre
  Sumer, 78-79
  Egypt, 100-102
  Israel, 106-108
  Greece, 129-135
  Europe, 260, 264-268
    On Irish crosses, 262
    Area, 264-265
    Types, 266
    Alemannic and Siberian, 267-268
    Survivals, 268
Lyro-viol, 348

M'abuba, 119
Magadis, 136
MAGER, 448
MAGGINI, 358
Magrepha, 124
Magudi, 154
Maḥalat, 125
MAHILLON, 383
Male connotations, 36, 50, 53, 112,
  169, 172, 176, 198, 214, 241.
  See also Penis
Malilu, 72
Mandīrā, 223
Mandola, mandora, 252-253
Man's taboo, 50
Marimba, 54

MARIUS, 391, 397
Marriage, 50
MARTENOT, 448
MARTIN, 406
Mašak, 154
MASON & HAMLIN, 407
Mašroqîtâ, 83
Ma·t, 90, 98
Maṭlaṭ, 254
Maṭnâ, 254
Mayurī, 232
Mazhar, 246
MAZUCCHI, 405
Media ala, 342
Medicinale, 258
Medio caño, 292
Megaphone, 47
Mélophone, 406
Membranophones, 459
Mēn, 107
Meo canno, 258
Meṣi, 73
Metallophone, 149-150, 208, 239, 456
Micanon, 258, 292
MIDMER-LOSH, 451
Milk, 36
MILLER, 448
Minnim, 107
Mirliton, 462
Mixture, 304
Mizhar, 246
Mna'an'îm, 121
Mo kugyo, 175
MOLLENHAUER, 414
MONOCHORD, 268-271
    Test instrument, 268-270
    Musical instrument, 270-271
    Polychordic, 270-271
Moon ceremonials, 30, 36, 37, 50, 51, 56, 110
MORITZ, 430
Mortars, 29
"Mother," 37, 53
Mouth bow, 57
Mouth organ (Asia), 182-184
    Chords, 183
    Prototypes, 183-184
Mouth organ (Europe), 62, 406
Mouthpieces, 418
Mṛdanga, 155, 235
Mṣiltâyîm, 121-122
MÜLLER, I., 413
MÜLLER, M., 398
Muǧnî, mughni, 138, 258

Mu ko, 75
Mundharmonika, 406
Musette (bagpipe), 283
Musette (oboe), 384
Musical bow, 56-57, 63
    Separate resonator, 57
    Gourd bow, 57
    Mouth bow, 57
Musical box, 456-457
Musical glasses, 404
Mūsīqāl, 247
Muštaq sini, 183
MUSTEL, 397
Mute (trumpet), 328
Mute (violin), 354
Mût-lēbên, 125
Mu yü, 175

Nabla, 115
Nacaires, naccheroni, 251
Nachthorn, 386
Nafîr, 281
Nāgarā, 230, 251
Nâgaśuram, 230
Nag's head swell, 386
Nahabat, 229
Nailing, 173
Nail piano, 403
Nail violin, 403
Nakers, 251
Naqqār(y)a, 251
Naqrazān, 251
Naresyuḥ, 268
Nây, 247
Nebel; see Nēvel
Neck, 466
Neo-Bechstein, 447
NERNST, 447
NEUSCHEL, 322
Nēvel, 115-117
Nginâ, 125, 127
Nhīlot, 125
NICHOLSON, 407
NICOLAI, 405
Nicolo, 314
Ni-daiko, 159
Ni-gen-kin, 186
Night, 36
Nīqaṭmón, 109
Nkungu, 57
NOLAN, 407
NORMAN, 359
Nose flute, 46-47, 64
Novachord, 448

Nuzha, 138
Nvālim, 115

Oboe
  Sumer, 72-73
  Babylonia, 83
  Egypt, 98-100
  Israel, 118-120
  Greece, 138-140
  China, 212-213
  India, 230-231
  Burma, 236
  Near East, 248-249
  Europe, 352, 382-384, 449
Oboe (organ stop), 441
Oboè da caccia, 383
Oboè d'amore, 383, 449
Ocarina, 167
Octave (organ stop), 304
Octobasse, 363
O daiko, 75
Oliphant, 280
Olmaitl, 195
Omichicahuaztli, 194
Omnitonic horn, 426
Ondes musicales, 448
Ophicleide, 424
Orchestras, 236-237
Organ
  Israel, 124
  Greece, 143-145
  Europe, middle ages, 284-286
    Until 1000 A. D., 284
    After 1000 A. D., 285
    Keyboard, 286
  Renaissance, 303, 304-308
  Mixture organ, 304
  Solo stops, 395
  Pitch, 306
  English and Italian organs, 307
  "Figuren," 308
  Baroque, 386
    Choir organ
    Great organ
    Pedal
    Praetorius organ
  Romanticism, 440-444
  Twentieth century, 451-453
  "The World's Greatest Organ," 451
  The new ideals: Silbermann and
    Praetorius, 452
Organistrum, 271, 272
Órgano lleno, 305
Orpharion, Orpheoreon, 374

Ottava stesa, 333
Ottu, 230
Overblowing, 418
Overstrung scale, 397

Pa'amon, 109
P'ai hsiao, 177
Pairs, 52-53
Pakhavāja, 230
PAMPHILON, 359
Pañčtār, 257
Pandore, 352, 373-374
Pandur, 274
Pandûra, 137
Panduri, 275
Pandurion, 252
Pang, 209
Pang ku, 149
Pan-pipes
  Primitive, 62
  Greece, 142-143
  China, 164, 177-178
  Peru, 197-198
  Near East, 247-248
  Europe, 288
  Types, 177
Pan-tur, 82
Pavillon chinois, 438
Pedal
  Harpsichord, 377
  Organ, 304
  Piano, 394
Pedal drum, 434-435
Pedal-Klavizimbel, 378
Peg, 466
Pēktis, 136
Pelog, 237-238
Penis, 29, 36, 37, 40, 43, 44, 47, 50,
    51, 56, 175
Penna, 293
Penorcon, 374
PERROT, 336
Pestle, 29
Phallic; see Penis
Phorbeiá, 138
Phorminx, 130
Physharmonica, 406
Pianino, 398
Piano, 391-398
  Invention, 391
  Diagrams, 392
  The German School, 393
  Stops, 394
  The English School, 395

Piano (*continued*)
　The Viennese School, 395
　The French School, 396
　The American School, 397
　The upright, 398
Piano (stop), 394
Piano droit, 398
Pibgorn, 212
Piccolo
　Flute, 410
　Cornet, 428
Pien ch'ing, 169
Pien chung, 172
Piffero, 288
P'in, 224
P'i p'a, 189
Pipes, oriental manner of blowing, 91
Pirouette, 319
Pīsa, 213
PISAURIENSIS, D., 340
PISAURIENSIS, H., 341
Piston
　Cornet, 428
　Valve, 426
Pit, 28, 29, 36, 37, 39, 43, 52, 53, 54,
　56, 63
Pitch, 165, 349, 386-387, 390-391
Pitch-pipes, 176-177
Pizzicato, 357
Planters' sticks, 194
Plectra (spinet), 338
Plectrûn (harp), 263
Plein jeu, 305
Plucked idiophone, 456
Pneumatic action, 444
Pneumatic lever, 444
Po, 207
Pochette, 278
Po fu, 172
Polische geigen, 356
Pommer, 314
Pomposa, 367
Portative organ, 286-287
Posaune, 281, 326
Positive organ, 308
Post horn, 428
Pottery, 51
Praetorius organ, 452-453
Prasārinī vīṇā, 232
Prellmechanik, 393-394
Prestant, 306
Principal, 305
Principal trumpet, 328
Progress and Regression, 60

Psaltêrion, 136
Psalterium, 262. See also *Nēvel*
Psalterium decachordum, 118
Psaltery, 292
Psantrîn, 83, 116
Psilê, 101, 108, 134
Pungacuqua, 194
Pūngī, 154
Pyramid piano, 398

Qānūn, 138, 257
Qarnâ, 83
Qarnu, 73
Qasaʻ, 249
Qaṣaba, 91, 247
Qatros, 83
Qīsab, 247
Qīṭārā, 253
Qithoro, 257
Quinte, 362
Quinton, 361
Quiquiztli, 194
Qūpūz, 252
Quṣṣāba, 91, 247

Rabâb, 242, 253
Rabâb al-moğannī, 255
Rabâb aššāʻir, 255
Rabé, 278
Rabôb, 161
Rack, 334
Racket, 319
Radioelectric instruments, 467
Radio organ, 448
Rain, 38, 42, 50, 170, 175, 194
Raṇa śṛnga, 144, 228
Rang, 208
Ranket, 319-320, 352
Ranket (organ stop), 386
Rapa, 210
Rattle
　Primitive, 26-28, 61, 63, 64
　　Strung, 26-27, 61
　　Bunch, 26-27
　　Gourd, 27-28
　　Basket, 28, 64
　Sumer, 70, 71
　Israel, 121
　India, 151
　Mexico, 194
　Peru, 200
　Terminology, 456
Rauschpfeife, 323, 352

Rauschquinte, 323
Ravalement, 376
Rebab, 242
Rebec, 356
Rebec, 277
Recorder, 287, 303, 309-312, 381, 450
Reed pipes; *see* Clarinet and Oboe
Regal, 308-309
REGIBO, 422
Register (organ), 305
Rejong, 242
Req, 247
"Rheita," 248
Rib, 466
Ribbon reed, 38, 63
Rice ceremonials, 29, 38
RICHARD, 451
Rigol, 308
Ring-key, 407, 414
RÖLLIG, 405
Rollschweller, 441
Rommelpot, 40
Ronker, 40
Rôrphîfe, 288
ROSE, 373
Rota, 262
Rotta, 262
Rotumbes, 289
Round forms, 36
Rubâb, 138
Rubbed idiophone, 38-40, 457
Rubebe, 277
RUCKERS, 375-376

Šabbāba, 247
Sabka, 83
Sackbut, 326
Sacqueboute, 326
Sadiu, 224
Sage-koto, 186
Sahib-nahabat, 229
Salāṣil, 122
Salendro, 237
Šālišīm, 123
SALÒ, 358
Salpinx, 145
Salterio tedesco, 292
Saltirsanch, 262
Sambuca, sambyke, 83, 136
Sānāyī, 230
Sand drum, 31
Ṣang, 259
San-gen-kin, 186

Sangkultap, 268
San hsien, 219
Śankha, 153, 157, 235
Santir, 258
Sanûğ, 123
Sārangī, 226-227
Sārinda, 226
Sarôd, 161
Saron, 239
Sà tai, 242
Satsuma biwa, 190
Śauktikā vīṇā, 232
SAUTERMEISTER, 414
SAVART, 361
SAX, 414, 416, 432
Saxhorn, 432
Saxophone, 415-417
Saxotromba, 432
Scabellum, 149
Scale (organ), 305; (piano), 397
Schachtbret, 337
Schellen, 279
Schlotter, 279
SCHNITGER, 452
SCHNITZER, 315
SCHREIBER, 317, 326
Schreyende pfeiffen, 322
SCHRÖTER, 391
Schryari, 322-323, 352
SCHUNDA, 417
SCHWEITZER, 452
Schweizer pfeiff, 314
Scraper, 43, 61, 63, 176, 194-195, 299
Seḥem, 89
Sei teki, 213
Şelşlīm, 121-122
Šem, Šemšal, 72
Semanterion, 278
Semitones, 332
Serpent, 420-422
Serranae, 139
Sešešet, 89
Setār, 257
Sex connotations, 51-52. *See also* Female, Male, Penis, Vulva
Shaken idiophones, 456
Shaku hachi, 213
Shalishim, 123
Sha lo, 208
Shamanic rites, 27, 33
Shamisen, 219
Shawm, 303, 314-315
Shê, 185-186
Shell, 465

Shell trumpet
  Primitive, 48-50, 53, 62, 63
  Assyria, 73
  India, 151, 152, 156-157
  Mexico, 194
  Peru, 201
  Far East, 210
  Java, 235
Shêng, 182
Shô, 182
Shofar, 110-112
Short octave, 333
Shuang ch'in, 218
SHUDI, 395, 441
Sibs, 248
Side drum, 435
Signals, 37
Si-im, 73
Silbador, 199
SILBERMANN, 386, 387, 393, 452
Sil-sil, 122
Simikion, 137
SIMIOT, 414
Simplifikationssystem, 440-441
Šimpuniâ, 120
Singing saw, 446
"Single," 308
Sistrum, 69-70, 89-90, 121, 456
Sitâr, 231
Sixteen-foot, 377, 450
SKORRA, 414
Šlâṣal, 121
Slendro, 237
Slide (trombone), 325
Slide trumpet, 384-385
Slit-drum, 29-31, 37, 53, 63, 175, 195
  Prototype, 29-30
  Forms, 30
  Connotations, 37
Snare, 289
Šnb, 100
Sobaba, 247
SODI, 375
Sodina, 182
Šofar, 110-112
Solar; *see* Sun
Sona, 213
Sō-no-koto, 186
Sonorous stone; *see* Stone
Sordone, 317-318
Sordun, 319
Šošanim, 125
Soundboard, 466
Soundholes, 350, 466

Sourdine, 319
SOUSA, 431
Sousaphone, 431
Sphärophon, 448
SPIELMANN, 447
Spike fiddle, 242, 255
Spinet, 302, 334-344
  Types and terms, 335
  Earliest evidences, 336
  Echiquier, 336-337
  Scaliger, 338
  Spinet in a narrower sense, 339-340
  Combinations, 342
Spinettino, 340
Square piano, 393, 395, 397
Śr, 97
Śruti, 154, 230
Staffa, 437
STAINER, 359
Stamped idiophones, 29, 456
Stamping idiophones, 28-29, 53, 63, 456
Stegereif, 437
STEIN, 390, 393-394, 395
STEINWAY, 390, 397
Stick (neck), 466
Sticks (concussion), 88-89
Stick-zither, 224-226, 235
Stimmwerk, 304
STODART, 398
STÖLZEL, 426
Stösser, 394
Stone, 164, 168-169, 200
Stone chime, 169
Stop
  Organ, 144-145, 286-287, 305, 440-441
  Harpsichord, 341, 376-377
  Piano, 394
Stopping (French horn and trumpet), 424-425
Stossmechanik, 393, 394
STOWASSER, 430
STRADIVARI, 358-359
Strata of primitive instruments, 63-64
Strawfiddle, 440
STREICHER, 395
STREITWOLF, 414, 422
Stringholder, 466
Strings, 107, 131, 226, 466-467
STUMPFF, 434
Su gu galli, 73, 74
Su hu, 217
Suling, 182

Sumber, 289
Śumponiâ, 121
Sŭmponiāh, 84
Sun, 47
Superpiano, 447
Surle, 249
Surnā, 213, 230
Surnāy, 213
Śŭrnāya, 248
Suru-nai, 213
Sutri-nahabat, 229
Swanee-sax, 447
Swegel, 287
Swell, 394
Sympathetic strings, 227, 255, 272, 366
Symphonei, 341
Symphoneia, 84, 120
Symphonia (hurdy-gurdy), 272
Symphonia (drum), 288
Syrinx, 142

Ṭablā (India), 223, 230
Ṭabl al-ġāwīǧ, 251
Ṭabl al-markab, 250
Ṭabl al-šāwīš, 251
Ṭabl baladī, 248
Ṭabl migrī, 251
Ṭabl šāmī, 251
Ṭabl turkī, 249
Tabor, 289, 312
Tabourin, 329
"Tabrets," 109
Ṭabul (= ṭabl), 249
Ta hu ch'in, 217
Taille, 362
T'ai p'ing hsiao, 213
Tak, 247
Tāl, 71
Tālā, 223, 235
Tambaṭṭam, 154, 229
Tambourin, 289, 312
Tambourin du Béarn, 312
"Tambourine," 33
Tamburi, 232
Ṭanbūr, 255, 256
Tan ch'in, 217
Tangent, 330
Tangentenflügel, 344
T'ao ku, 173
Tār, 256
Tárogató, 417
Tās(ā), 250
TASKIN, 396

Tavil, 215
Tāyuí, 232
Tbn, 97
"Tebuni," 94
Tecciztli, 194
Ṭemmeṭṭama, 154
Temperament, 332
Temple, 289
Tenor clarinet, 414
Tenor drum, 435
Tenor horn, 429
Tenoroon, 317, 416
Tenor violin, 357, 362, 368
Teponaztli, 195
Tepuzquiquiztli, 194
THEEWES, 342
Theorboe, 372
THEREMIN, 448
Thereminvox, 448
Ti, 178
Tibbŭ, 76
Tibia, 138
T'i ch'in, 217
TIELKE, 366
Tiger, 176
Ti-gi, 71
Tīgŭ, 72
Ṭikārā, 230, 251
Timbre(l), 289
Ṭimbūtu, 76
Tiručinnam, 153-154
Ti tse, 213
Tjangkun, 209
Tjapara, 207
Tjing, 208
Tlalpa huehuetl, 196
Tlapitzalli, 192
Ṭof, 108-109
Ṭok, 175
"Tom-tom," 30
Torban, 372
Tournebout, 322
TOURTE, 359, 370
Toy, 28, 38, 43, 71, 151, 166, 167, 173, 212, 299
Transposing instruments, 411
Transverse flute; see Cross flute
Trautonium, 448
TRAUTWEIN, 448
Traversa, 381
Tremulant, 306, 386
Trepie, 437
Triangle, 437
Triangle (piano stop), 395

Trichordon, 137
Trigōnon, 136
Tro khmer, 242
Tromba, 326
Tromba da tirarsi, 385
Trombetta, 281
Trombone, 303, 325-327
    Organ, 306
Trombone, 419, 434
Trompe (organ stop), 306
Trompette marine, 292
Trough, 164, 175
Trumpet
    Primitive, 47-50, 63, 64
    Babylonia, 83
    Egypt, 100
    Israel, 112-113
    Greece, 145-148
    India, 153-154, 156-157, 228
    Mexico, 194
    Peru, 201-202
    China, 210-212
    Java, 235
    Europe, middle ages, 280-281
    Renaissance, 328-329
    Baroque, 384-385
    Present, 419, 432-434
    Transverse trumpet, 48, 64
    See also Shell trumpet
Trumpet (organ stop), 306, 441
Trumpet marine, 292
Trumscheit, 290-292
Tshaing vaing, 224
Tsuri daiko, 214
Tsuzumi, 215
Tuba (Roman), 145
Tuba, 419, 429-430
Tuba mirabilis, 441
Tubecta, 281
Tube-zither, 186
Tui hsiao, 212
Tūnava, 153
Tung hsiao, 180, 213
Tuning forks, 403
Tuning paste (India), 155
Tupim, 108
Turkish drum, 435
Turkish music, 436-437
Turkish music (piano stop), 395
Turya, 228
Tympana, 329
Tympanon, 148
Tympanum, 290

Ub, ub-tubur, ub-zabar, 73
'Ūd, 253
Uḍukkai, 159
'Ugâb, 106
Una corda, 394
Unda maris, 92
UNGARO, FRANCO, 341
Upright harpsichord, 334, 341-342
Upright piano, 397-398
URQUHART, 359
Utricularium, 141

Valves, 425-428
    Invention, 426
    Inaccuracy, 427
Vāṃsī, 159
Vāṇa, 152
Venetian swell, 441
Veṇu, 152
VETTER, 400
Vibrato, 191, 357
Vièle, 275
Vièle à roue, 272
Viennese action, 394
VIERLING, 447
Vihuela, 274, 345
Vīṇā, 94, 153, 156, 224-225, 235
Viol, 303, 347-350, 449
    Families, 347
    Sizes, 348
    Manner of playing, 349
    Soundholes and bridge, 350
Viola, 356, 361-362
Viola, 274
Viola bastarda, 348
Viola da braccio, 347
Viola da gamba; see Viol
Viola da gamba (organ stop), 386
Viola d'amore, 364-367, 449
Viola da spalla, 363
Viola paredon, 368
Viola pomposa, 367-368
Viole d'amour, 366, 367
Violetta, 356, 362
Violin, 302, 352, 353-361 (364)
    Parts, 353-354
    Sound, 354-355
    Origin, 355-357
    Pizzicato and vibrato, 357
    Italian School, 358-359
    French School, 359
    English School, 359
    German School, 359

Violin (*continued*)
  Struggle against the viols, 360
  Innovations, 361
Violin (organ stop), 441
Violino alla francese, 358
Violino ordinario, 358
Violino piccolo, 358, 449
Violino pomposo, 368
Violoncello, 360, 362
Violoncello a cinque corde, 362
Violoncello piccolo, 362, 449
Violone, 362
Virginal, 303, 335
Virginity test, 45-46, 143
VOGLER, 440-441
Vuhudendung, 57
VUILLAUME, 363
Vulva, 29, 36, 37, 50, 51

Wälsche geigen, 356
Wagner-tuba, 432
Wagon, 186
WALCKER, 451, 452
Waldhorn, 375
Waldteufel, 40
Walkingstick flute, 390
Water, 37, 42, 50, 52. *See also* Rain
Water organ, 143-145
WEIDINGER, 422
Whistling pot, 199
WIEPRECHT, 429
WILDE, 402-403
Wind instruments, 457
Wing, 315
With horn, 38
Wol kum, 218
Women as players
  Primitive, 28, 29, 36, 50, 51, 53, 54, 56
  Egypt, 94, 97, 102
  Israel, 108
  Greece, 135, 136, 149
  India, 151, 156, 157
  China, 163

Women as players (*continued*)
  S. E. Asia, 238
  Near East, 246
  Europe, 401, 405
Women's taboo, 36, 38, 42, 48, 111
WOODHAM, 385
Wurubumba, 57

Xylophone, 53-54, 64, 238-239, 439-440, 456
Xylophone (organ stop), 306

Ya chêng, 217
Yak, 181
Yamato fuye, 213
Yamato koto, 186
Yang ch'in, 219, 259
Yo, 178
Yoko fuye, 213
Yonât illêm rḥaqîm, 125
Yü, 176
Yüeh, 178
Yüeh ch'in, 218
Yün lo, 208

Zaḥma, 254
Zanza, 456
Zaqqal, 268
Ziehharmonika, 406
Zîl, 122
Zimbel, 279
Zink, 323-325
Zir, 254
Zither
  Israel, 117-118
  Greece, 137-138
  China, 133, 164, 185-188
  Near East, 247-249, 257-258
  Europe, 292-293
  Terminology, 463
Zummâra, 92
ZUMPE, 395
Zûqra, 248
Zymbelstern, 308